Group Work with Populations at Risk

D1566321

Group Work with Populations at Risk

Fourth Edition

Edited by
Geoffrey L. Greif
Carolyn Knight

OXFORD
UNIVERSITY PRESS

OXFORD
UNIVERSITY PRESS

Oxford University Press is a department of the University of Oxford. It furthers
the University's objective of excellence in research, scholarship, and education
by publishing worldwide. Oxford is a registered trade mark of Oxford University
Press in the UK and certain other countries.

Published in the United States of America by Oxford University Press
198 Madison Avenue, New York, NY 10016, United States of America.

© Oxford University Press 1997, 2005, 2011, 2017

First Edition published in 1996
Second Edition published in 2004
Third Edition published in 2010

A copy of this book's Catalog-in-Publication Data is on file with the Library of Congress

ISBN 978–0–19–021212–4

9 8 7 6 5 4 3 2 1
Printed by Webcom, Inc., Canada

Preface

For this fourth edition, Dr. Carolyn Knight has replaced Dr. Paul Ephross as coeditor. Paul has completely retired after nearly 50 years of social work education and group work practice. He has played a seminal role in so many ways in advancing group work in the profession and, while his direct influence will be missed, his legacy lives on through the contributions of the authors he recruited in earlier iterations of this text. Carolyn was one of those contributors (and a mentee of Paul's) and has also played a leadership role in advancing group work through her teaching, practice, writing, and participation in the International Association of the Advancement of Social Work With Groups.

Carolyn has written two new opening chapters that cover practice skills and what beginning workers need to know to begin practice with groups. These two chapters along with the chapter that follows, which draws on skills that are applicable across a wide range of populations, should broaden the appeal of the book so that it becomes a stand-alone text that educators and practitioners can use to teach and learn about the many facets of group work.

In revising this edition, many issues that are addressed—veterans, child abuse, hate crimes, cancer, immigration, and severe mental illness, to name a few—remain as areas of concern for social workers and other mental health practitioners running groups. All the continuing authors have updated their chapters with relevant interventions, citations, and Web site resources. Sometimes coauthors have been added. In three cases, we asked new authors with fresh perspectives to replace older chapters on topics of importance, for example, interpersonal violence (Shantih Clemans), community trauma (Allison Salloum), and behavioral and emotional problems among children (Jen Clements).

Emerging areas of practice were also identified, as they have been for each revised edition. We added a chapter by Youjung Lee and Paul Gould on immigrants who are caregivers of family members with dementia. As the US population grays and becomes more diverse, this seemed a particularly significant topic. Loretta Hartley Bangs's chapter on group work with substance-abusing clients also pays particular attention to aging substance abusers. Recent headlines have also focused on the plight of victims of sex trafficking in other countries. Two experts, Kristine E. Hickle and Dominique Roe-Sepowitz, have written a chapter on their work with victims of trafficking. New chapters have also been added on working with fathers who have been incarcerated (Geoff) and on parents who experience homelessness (Carolyn), populations that, despite their prevalence, are still underserved. Finally, Loretta Hartley-Bangs, a practitioner with many years of experience, teams up with Carolyn to further our knowledge of working with substance abuse issues, particularly among the aging population.

The chapters in this book follow a similar format that we hope will be helpful to the reader. Each contributor was asked to write a chapter that would answer the following questions:

1. What does the professional literature say about this population?
2. What particular principles should guide a practitioner beginning to work with this population?
3. What common themes have you observed in working with groups composed of members of this population?
4. What are some of the methods that you have found successful and that you recommend for working with this population?
5. What evaluation measures could be used to judge whether members are benefiting from their experiences in these groups?
6. Are there any national resources that can be tapped by practitioners or group members for further information?

We were particularly interested in the common themes that are raised by group members. Practitioners often know how to recruit members for groups, screen them, and start the first session. But once members have introduced themselves, the usual first step, the leader may not know how to proceed. The contributors to this book offer that information by focusing on areas of concern they have most frequently heard identified by group members. The leader is thus prepared to raise, respond to, and reinforce issues related to potential topics or areas of concern that are known to have relevancy for other such groups.

As with the past editions, we hope this volume will help beginning practitioners and students to find their way through the initial sessions with these populations at risk and to gain a sense of the range of interventions available. By knowing in advance what some of the key issues may be for the people and communities being served, the group worker should be well positioned to assist with the difficult transitions that people often face.

G.L.G.
C.K.
Baltimore, Maryland

Contents

Part Five Evaluating Practice and Practice Skills

Contributors

Steven Ball, ACSW, is a private practitioner and adjunct faculty member at Hunter College School of Social Work.

Monica Beltran, MA, BC-DMT, LCSW-C, is a social worker at the Center for Child and Family Traumatic Stress, Baltimore, Maryland.

Joanne M. Boyle, LCSW-C, works for the Veteran's Health Administration and specializes in treating combat-related trauma.

Shantih E. Clemans, PhD, LCSW, is on the faculty of Empire State College Department of Community and Human Services.

Jen Clements, PhD, is associate professor at Shippensburg University and vice-president of the International Association for the Advancement of Social Work With Groups.

Julie Clifton is a social worker in private practice in Melbourne, Florida.

Edna Comer is an associate professor at the University of Connecticut School of Social Work.

Kay Martel Connors, LCSW-C, is a social worker at the University of Maryland School of Medicine, Department of Psychiatry.

Julie A. Ellis, LCSW-C is a social worker for the Department of Veteran Affairs in Memphis, Tennessee.

Paul H. Ephross, PhD, is a professor emeritus at the School of Social Work, University of Maryland.

Charles Garvin, PhD, is a professor emeritus at the School of Social Work, University of Michigan.

George S. Getzel, DSW, is a professor emeritus at Hunter College School of Social Work.

Paul R. Gould, PhD, LCSW, is a visiting assistant professor in the Department of Social Work, Binghamton University.

Geoffrey L. Greif, PhD, LCSW-C, is a professor at the School of Social Work, University of Maryland.

Loretta Hartley-Bangs, LISW-CP, Director of Admissions, Lighthouse Care Center of Conway, Conway, South Carolina.

Juliaty Hermanto, MSW, is a 2015 graduate of the Boston University School of Social Work.

Kristine E. Hickle, MSW, is a lecturer, Course Leader: Master of Childhood and Youth Studies, Department of Social Work, University of Sussex Falmer, Brighton, England.

Megumi Inoue, PhD, is an assistant professor in the Department of Social Work at George Mason University.

Janice A. Iwama, MS, is a doctoral candidate at the School of Criminology and Criminal Justice, Northeastern University.

Carolyn Knight, PhD, is a professor in the School of Social Work, University of Maryland, Baltimore County.

Youjung Lee, PhD, LMSW, is assistant professor, Department of Social Work, and codirector, Institute for Multigenerational Studies, College of Community and Public Affairs, Binghamton University.

Benjamin Lipton, CSW, is a private practitioner and adjunct professor at New York University Ehrenkranz School of Social Work.

Luz M. López, PhD, MPH, LCSW, is an assistant professor at the School of Social Work, Boston University.

Andrew Malekoff, MSW, CAC, is associate director of North Shore Child and Family Guidance Center, Roslyn Heights, New York.

Jack McDevitt, PhD, is associate dean for research and graduate studies and the director of the Institute on Race and Justice in the College of Social Science and the Humanities, Northeastern University.

Andrea Meier, PhD, is an emeritus research associate professor at University of North Carolina at Chapel Hill, School of Social Work.

Darnell Morris-Compton, PhD, is an assistant professor in the Department of Family Studies and Community Development, Towson University.

Elizabeth A. Mulroy, PhD, is a professor emerita at the School of Social Work, University of Maryland.

Betsy Offermann, LCSW-C, is a social worker at the Center for Child and Family Traumatic Stress, Baltimore, Maryland.

Philip Osteen, PhD, is an assistant professor at the School of Social Work, Florida State University.

Susan Rice, DSW, LCSW, is a professor emerita at the Department of Social Work at California State University at Long Beach and teaches courses for seniors through Osher Lifelong Learning Institute in nonviolent conflict resolution.

Dominique Roe-Sepowitz is associate professor, Arizona State University School of Social Work and Director: Office of Sex Trafficking Intervention Research (STIR).

Cynthia Rollo, LCSW-C, is a social worker at the Center for Child and Family Traumatic Stress, Baltimore, Maryland.

Steven R. Rose, PhD, is a professor at the School of Social Work, George Mason University.

Alison Salloum is an associate professor at the School of Social Work, University of South Florida.

Erika M. Vargas, MSW, is a social worker at La Alianza Hispana, Inc. in Roxbury, Massachusetts, Boston University.

Joan C. Weiss, LCSW-C, is the former executive director of the Justice Research and Statistics Association, Washington, DC, and has a private practice in psychotherapy in Rockville, Maryland.

Steve Wilson, PhD, LCSW, is associate professor at the Department of Social Work California State University, Long Beach, where he specializes in social work interventions with older adults with an emphasis on social work practice in end-of-life care.

Group Work Practice Skills

Chapter One

Introduction: The Context of Contemporary Group Work Practice and Education

Carolyn Knight

Group work remains a vital intervention for a wide range of clients facing an array of personal, social, and environmental challenges. From groups for individuals with substance abuse problems or for abused children to advocacy groups for parents of children with developmental disabilities and neighborhood associations that seek to improve the quality of life in the local community, groups are empowering to members at the individual and societal level.

With its emphasis on mutual aid (discussed later in this chapter), members' strengths are revealed and capitalized upon, and their feelings of self-efficacy enhanced. Group participation enhances members' resilience and their ability to grow in the face of adversity (Gitterman & Knight, in press). Group work also can be a vehicle through which social justice and client empowerment are promoted (Dudziak & Profitt, 2012; Staples, 2012).

These benefits reflect the ethical requirements of helping professions such as psychology, counseling, and social work. The respective codes of ethics of these disciplines require professionals to promote client empowerment and social justice (American Counseling Association [ACA], 2014; American Psychological Association [APA], 2003; National Association of Social Workers [NASW], 2008). The social work profession also requires practitioners to adopt a strengths-based orientation when working with clients (NASW, 2008). In this and the chapter that follows, readers will note additional ways in which group work epitomizes the values and ethics of the helping professions.

In many agency-based and private practice settings, the group modality is the preferred option, given its strong evidence base (Blackmore, Tantam, Parry, & Chambers, 2012; Emond & Rasmussen, 2012; Fagan & Catalano, 2013; Rose, 2009; Sloan, Bovin, & Schnurr, 2012). Third-party payers often prefer this intervention because of its cost-effectiveness and demonstrated efficacy (Humphreys, Drummond, Phillips, & Lincoln, 2013; Okumura & Ichikura, 2014). The increased availability and use of manuals—or predetermined curricula—that guide the group worker's actions and structure the sessions are yet another advantage of group intervention, particularly for new or inexperienced group leaders (Galinsky, Terzian, & Fraser, 2006). Manuals provide the leader with suggestions for topics to discuss. This is particularly relevant for psychoeducational groups, discussed later.

Although the demand for skilled group workers remains high, coverage of this modality in social work and other mental health programs has steadily decreased over time (Lorentzen & Ruud, 2014; Simon & Kilbane, 2014). Individual approaches to intervention predominate in the training of future generations of practitioners across all helping professions (Piper, 2007).

This may be the result of the self-reinforcing consequences of the decline in coverage of group work. Many educators have had minimal preparation for and experience with group work. Thus, their ability and willingness to teach about the modality are lessened. Evidence also suggests that what is taught about the modality is often inaccurate and at odds with accepted group work principles, concepts, and practice behaviors (Sweifach, 2014).

Similar problems exist in students' training in the field (Ward & Crosby, 2010). Field supervisors typically lack experience with or adequate preparation for group work (Goodman, Knight, & Khuododov, 2014; Knight, 2009; in press). Thus, they are unable to provide appropriate and knowledgeable supervision regarding the modality or, even more basically, opportunities for students to engage in it.

THE EXPERIENCE OF GROUP MEMBERSHIP: THE POWER OF MUTUAL AID

One of the earliest authors to identify and promote the benefits of group membership was William Schwartz, who observed that the defining characteristic of group work is the multiple helping relationships that are created (1974, 1994). "The group is ... an alliance of individuals who need each other, in varying degrees to work on common problems" (Schwartz, 1974, p. 218). Unlike individual intervention, the source of help is not the clinician, but rather the support and understanding—the mutual aid—that members provide to one another. Members learn and grow from one another with the encouragement of the leader, whose primary task is to "help members use each other, exploit each others' strengths ... and enlist each other in the performance of the common tasks that brought them together" (Schwartz, 1994, p. 579). The concept of mutual aid resonates with mental health professionals' ethical obligations with respect to promoting empowerment and client strengths (ACA, 2014; APA, 2003; NASW, 2008).

When the worker has limited understanding of group work and its essential element, mutual aid, she or he is at risk of engaging in what has been referred to as "casework in the group" (Kurland & Salmon, 2005). Rather than promoting members' relationships with one another and the assistance that is inherent in the process, the leader interacts with members singly, as if they were the only two individuals in the room.

The groups described in this book include individuals with significant challenges and an often powerful sense of urgency for relief. Readers will note that the authors concentrate on members' underlying commonalities and how these, in Schwartz's words, are "exploited" to enhance the functioning and adaptive capacities of one another. Readers can appreciate why the leader may be tempted to respond to an individual member's concerns, to the exclusion of others. Yet, when the worker is mindful of the benefits associated with mutual aid (discussed next), she or he learns to resist the urge to engage individually with any one member, focusing instead on fostering members' interactions with and support of one another.

BENEFITS OF GROUP MEMBERSHIP

Several conceptual frameworks are available that explain the therapeutic benefits of group membership and, particularly, mutual aid (Gitterman, 2004; Northen & Kurland, 2001; Shulman, 2012; Yalom & Leszcz, 2007). Six "curative factors" (Yalom & Lezcz, 2007) are common to each framework, chief among them the experience of universality (Yalom & Leszcz, 2007) or of being all in the same boat (Shulman, 2012). The sense of not being alone and the reassurance that comes with being with others who share similar thoughts, feelings, and experiences is extremely therapeutic. Members' challenges are normalized and validated as they hear others recount similar difficulties. As members are freed up from the feeling of being alone, different, and, often, "crazy," they are able to confront and work on the problems that brought them to the group in the first place.

In individual work, the practitioner can normalize and validate the client's experiences. However, this remains somewhat academic because the worker does not speak from personal experience. Rather, she or he provides general information that indicates that the client is not alone. Take, for example, the case of a bereaved mother who admits to being angry at her son, who died as a result of a drug overdose. In an individual session, the worker might comment, "Your feelings are completely understandable. You are grieving the loss of your son; part of that grieving involves being angry that he left you, and this is particularly true, given how he died." In a group for bereaved individuals, when this mom discloses her anger, others hear their own feelings being voiced, while she is reassured as they acknowledge experiencing similar reactions. In a powerful and direct way, all members' feelings are validated and normalized.

Another factor that is unique to group work is altruism (Northen & Kurland, 2001; Yalom & Lezcz, 2007). Although members clearly benefit from receiving support, advice, and understanding from others in the group, they also benefit from *providing* assistance. This enhances feelings of self-efficacy and reinforces that the individual matters and has something to offer others. There simply is no parallel experience in individual treatment. Clients do not *give* to their worker, at least not in significant ways. It is only in a group context that members can give of themselves to one another, an interaction that benefits both.

Mutual support and demand are two additional factors that help explain the therapeutic benefits of mutual aid (Gitterman, 2004; Northen & Kurland, 2001; Shulman, 2012). Given that members are in the same boat, they have a great deal of credibility with one another. In its most basic form, members convey understanding and offer support to one another, which enhances esteem.

The following brief example illustrates a more subtle version of this dynamic. The group is for latency-age children in foster care. The children present with a range of problematic behaviors that have resulted in frequent moves. The purpose of the group is to provide members with a place to express their feelings and learn to manage them better so that they can achieve greater stability in placement.

> *Dianna:* I don't care what anyone says or does. I ain't going to listen to nobody. I'm going to keep getting in trouble 'til they place me back with my grandmother [*note:* this is not an option as the grandmother is quite elderly].
>
> *Betsy:* Look, I hate living with my foster parents, too. But, man, acting all crazy and stuff ain't going to get you out. You gotta learn to behave yourself if you want to get out, not cause trouble.

An individual worker could make the same sort of comment to Dianna as Betsy did. Yet Betsy's demand for work carries more weight because she has a very personal appreciation for Dianna's feelings and situation. This exchange demonstrates how intertwined mutual support and demand are. As Betsy is urging Dianna to rethink her actions, she is, at the same time, conveying her support, caring, and concern.

Interpersonal learning (Yalom & Lezcz, 2007) is yet another curative factor. Authors have long argued that an individual's sense of self and worth are socially determined. How one feels about oneself influences how one behaves in social relationships, and how one is treated in those relationships reinforces the underlying definition of self. This creates a self-reinforcing cycle that can be very hard to break. Group members often hold negative views of themselves (and others) that are continually reinforced in their social relationships. In a group, this cycle can be broken, as members are accepted, supported, and receive affirmative feedback from each other.

Yalom and Lezcz (2007) refer to the group as a social microcosm, suggesting that members begin to relate to one another as they do with others outside of the group. When maladaptive social behaviors surface in the group, members, with the assistance and encouragement of the leader, can, in a sense, hold a mirror up to one another. Members can begin to see how their behaviors contribute to their difficulties and keep them stuck in self-defeating social interactions.

Instillation of hope is yet another variable that reflects mutual aid (Northen & Kurland, 2001). "Members further along in the resolution of their difficulties are reminded of the gains they have made as they listen to and witness the challenges of others; in turn, members who remain more challenged are buoyed by the progress of others" (Knight, 2014, p. 26).

In addition to these more prominent curative factors, group membership affords clients the opportunity to learn from one another's experiences and benefit from the advice and suggestions they offer to each other (sharing data) (Northen & Kurland, 2001; Shulman, 2012). It also provides members with the opportunity to practice new ways of interacting (behavioral rehearsal) and to learn how to handle and work through conflicts and disagreements (dialectical process) (Shulman, 2012).

Finally, group membership, particularly when participants are with one another over time, affords clients the opportunity to experience intimacy (Yalom & Lezcz, 2007). The advantages of this factor are threefold. First, it can serve as an antidote and "corrective emotional experience" (Yalom & Lezcz, 2007) for members who have little or no exposure to or understanding of connectedness to others. Second, intimacy with others bolsters esteem. Third, it affords members the opportunity to talk openly with others, promoting honest discussion of feelings and learning to work through disagreements and conflicts.

The effectiveness of the group modality typically is assessed utilizing member outcomes such as reduced rates of depression, social isolation, and substance use. Another line of inquiry focuses on the processes that occur *within* the group and sheds light on the impact of the curative factors just discussed. Findings from various practice settings and client populations consistently reveal that group cohesiveness, utilized as an indicator of mutual aid, is associated with member satisfaction and growth, enhanced feelings of self-efficacy, and a reduced risk of dropout (Beed & Hamilton-Giachritsis, 2005; Burlingame, Fuhriman, & Mosier, 2003; Johnson, Burlingame, Olsen & Davies, 2005; Kivlighan, Paquin, & Hsu, 2014; Marmarosh, Holtz, & Schottenbauer, 2005; McWhirter, Nelson, & Waldo, 2014; Norcross & Wampold, 2011).

GROUP TYPES

Not all of these factors will be at work in all groups. Mutual aid will be manifested differently, depending upon the group type, purpose, membership, and structure. In groups with a more educational focus, typically referred to as psychoeducational, socialization, or growth groups (Shulman, 2012), mutual aid is likely to come in the form of members' learning from the leader *and* one another. The reassurance that comes from knowing that they are not alone, that they have a similar need for information, makes such learning easier and more meaningful.

A typical example of this type of group would be a group for parents of newborn babies diagnosed with a developmental disability. Members desire and need information regarding the short- and long-term prospects for their child. They also need to know that their fears, sense of loss, and anger are normal and expected. When these feelings are addressed along with members' need for information, the benefits of the group are maximized. Therefore, the leader has a fourfold purpose: presenting information to members; helping members share information with one another; encouraging members to use one another for support, understanding, and growth; and assisting members in incorporating their learning into their lives.

Support/stabilization groups have less of an educational focus, and, as the term implies, more of an emphasis on members providing reassurance to one another. This type of group maximizes the benefits of the curative factors and is well represented in this book. It is the group type that predominates in clinical practice, though many support groups also have educational elements. The focus is on members' underlying commonalities. The leader has primary responsibility for pointing out these commonalities and encouraging members to use their shared experiences to confront and work through the challenges they face. Typical of this sort of group would be a group for women who are the victims of intimate partner violence. Members may benefit from information provided by the leader, for example, the self-reinforcing cycle of violence. However, the greatest advantage of their participation is the affirmation and resulting courage and sense of empowerment that comes from being with others in the same boat.

Social action groups are quite different in that the focus of change is not primarily on members themselves but rather on a target external to the group. As members develop a "universal perspective" (Shulman, 2012), they appreciate how their broader socio-political-economic environment contributes to the challenges they face. This group type relies upon the fact that there is power in numbers. Members work together to effect change in the wider environment. In so doing, their sense of self-efficacy is enhanced as are feelings of empowerment. Typical of this sort of group is a neighborhood watch group, whereby members take responsibility for safeguarding their community.

A support or psychoeducational group may take on elements of social action. For example, one of the author's students was running a reminiscing group for elders living in an assisted living facility. During the sessions, members consistently complained about the demeanor and attitude of the nursing assistants. The student correctly understood that it was not enough for members to voice their concerns and feel understood and supported by one another. What was needed was action. Therefore, the leader encouraged and helped members to develop and implement a strategy to address their concerns with the agency's administration.

Task and work groups also can take on elements of mutual aid. Group members will work more effectively and successfully with one another if they feel an underlying sense of connectedness and understand they are working toward a common goal and purpose. A supervisory group for student trainees exemplifies this type. In such a group, the supervisor will provide insights and suggestions to members. The group will be more beneficial if the supervisor encourages members to share *their* suggestions and insights with one another. Members also benefit from recognizing they are not alone with the questions and challenges they face as they work with clients.

THE GROUP AS CLIENT

Effective group work practice requires the worker to have an appreciation for the notion of the group as client and the "two client paradigm" (Shulman, 2012). The worker actually has two sets of clients: the group as a whole and each individual member. The group has a life and unique identity of its own, and this is more than just the cumulative impact of each individual member. This is reflected in the group's culture as manifested in norms, roles, and communication patterns, and in its stages of development. "Norms determine how members will work together and participate in the work of the group . . . and define what behaviors are acceptable or unacceptable . . . [R]oles are the expectations that members share the behavior of individual participants" (Knight, 2014, p. 28).

It is important for the worker to appreciate that regardless of the formal, explicit "rules" that are established, as members interact with one another on a regular basis, expectations for collective (norms) and individual (roles) behavior will be formed. Once these expectations are established, they can become very hard to change and have a more powerful impact on the group's functioning than any formal rules that the leader may have enacted. Groups that allow for open and honest communication among members, encourage mutual respect and support, and facilitate shared role behaviors (as opposed to members becoming "stuck" in a particular role) are more effective at fostering mutual aid and therefore more likely to achieve members' collective goals (Chapman, Baker, Porter, Thayer, & Burlingame, 2010; Ogrodniczuk & Piper, 2003).

When the worker understands the concept of group as client, she or he is better able to address problematic role behaviors that may surface. Three of the most frequent— and challenging—roles that surface are the monopolizer, the scapegoat, and the defensive member. Less experienced workers typically assume that the problematic behavior resides solely with the individual member who displays it. From a group-as-a-whole perspective, the worker realizes that the individual's behavior can only exist because it serves some sort of function for the group (Shulman, 2012).

The clearest example of this is the scapegoat. The following brief example illustrates the function and potentially disruptive effects of this dynamic.[1] The setting is an inpatient program for recovering substance abusers. The primary goal of the support group is assisting members in maintaining their sobriety both in the program and as they transition back into the community. A topic that often surfaces in the group is members' histories of trauma such as sexual and physical abuse as children. When this happens, the leader encourages members to support one another, thus normalizing and validating one another's experiences. In the present session, members begin to talk with much regret about behaviors they engaged in when they were using drugs and alcohol.

Don:	When I beat up that cop, I wasn't in my right mind, I hardly remember what happened. I just remember waking up in a jail cell, and they said I put the guy in the hospital. I had a lot of time like that, where I don't know what I did.
Group worker:	That has to be pretty scary, to not really know what you might have done.
Damon:	I trashed my mother's house looking for drugs. I wasn't high, just desperate. I didn't care about no one, not her, not nobody. She tried to stop me and I slapped her, I slapped my momma.
Christopher:	Oh, man, that's rough. Hitting on your own mother. The shit we do for them drugs. I beat up my girlfriend one time when she told me she was going to kick me out if I didn't stop using. I just didn't care about her or no one. I just cared about getting high.
Group worker:	How about you, James? I'm wondering if you can relate to any of this—to feeling guilty and bad about having hurt other people?
James:	I spent some time in jail. I went after my stepfather with a knife one time. I cut him up pretty bad. I don't feel nothing about that though.
Group worker:	So, you hurt your stepfather, but you don't feel anything about that . . .
James (interrupting):	My stepfather messed me up, man.
Group worker:	What do you mean he messed you up?
James:	Well, you know, he, like, messed around with me. You know like sexual stuff and shit. He beat up on me and my sisters. Hurt us real bad. It was real bad *(starts crying)*

    Christopher: Why does he go and talk about that shit for? That's
           some weird shit.
      Damon: *(starts laughing)Several other members also start laughing.*
  Group worker: I'm not sure what's so funny. It sounds like James
           had a pretty rough time of it, and I appreciate, James,
           that you were able to tell the group about this.

This excerpt reflects an all too common phenomenon: The worker fails to understand the group context, and he "sides" with the scapegoat, James. In so doing, he
succeeds only in further alienating James from the group. The other possibility
is the worker sides with the group against the scapegoated individual, assuming
that "if only she or he [the scapegoat] wasn't in this group, it would function
just fine." In either case, the worker errs by not seeing that scapegoating serves a
function for the group. Addressing this dynamic and other problematic ones is
taken up in Chapter 2.

STAGES OF GROUP DEVELOPMENT

A number of authors have proposed conceptual frameworks for understanding
stages of group development. Regardless of the perspective that one adopts, the
underlying principle is the same: As members interact with one another over
time, their collective behavior—the group as a whole—changes. Even in a one-
time-only group, the members' collective behavior changes from the beginning
to the end of the session. These changes are associated with shifting tasks and
roles for the group leader. One of the most useful frameworks is the five-stage
Boston Model (Berman-Rossi, 1993; Garland, Jones, & Kolodny, 1965).

1. *Preaffiliation.* Group culture is nonexistent, and participation may be
   a source of tension for new members. Cohesion is lacking. Members
   are unlikely to see their connections to one another and may experience approach-avoidance reactions. Mistrust of others and the
   leader is likely to exist. This stage represents the preliminary phase
   of work.
2. *Power and control.* At this early stage of the group's existence, members are trying to ascertain whether, where, and how they fit within
   the group. Power struggles exist between members and between the
   members and the leader. Because the group remains threatening to
   members, the risk of dropout is high. Intimacy is lacking, and members
   remain unsure of what is expected of them. This stage occurs in the
   beginning phase of work.
3. *Intimacy.* As members continue to interact with one another and their
   underlying commonalities become more apparent, participation is

experienced as more satisfying. Members are more willing to disclose to one another, increasing cohesion, shared goal orientation, and members' investment in the group. As members become more intimate, the group has moved into the middle or work phase.

4. *Differentiation.* Members' increased comfort with one another encourages them to express themselves more honestly, which reinforces and deepens intimacy. At this stage, conflicts and disagreements are more likely to surface, as members feel safe being themselves. The normative structure is well established and, in fact, hard to modify. This stage also reflects the middle or work phase.

5. *Separation.* Members prepare to end with another, bringing on feelings of loss and sadness. The group may regress to an earlier phase as members attempt to come to terms with having to say goodbye. Earlier dynamics, particularly approach-avoidance, may resurface, increasing the risk that members drop out prematurely. This stage occurs in the ending phase.

It is unrealistic to assume that any group proceeds seamlessly from one stage to the next. Some groups, such as those that have revolving membership or meet only briefly, may have a hard time even getting out of the first stage. In other groups, where individual members leave and new members join, the separation phase may be largely nonexistent, even though the group and the departing individual member will say goodbye to one another. Even in groups that exist over time, there may be progress and then retreat as circumstances change. If a member leaves or a new member joins, it is likely that the group will experience some regression to earlier themes and dynamics, if only for a brief period. In groups where members have experience with one another prior to the start of the group, as in a group in a residential setting, the progression through the stages may proceed more quickly.

The group worker's understanding of these stages provides her or him with guidance as to appropriate roles and tasks. These include interventions that assist the group in deepening its work. In the chapter that follows, the group worker's responsibilities and skills are identified in light of phases of work.

REFERENCES

American Counseling Association (ACA). (2014). *American Counseling Association Code of Ethics.* Washington, DC: ACA.

American Psychological Association (APA). (2003). *Ethical principles of psychology and code of conduct.* Washington, DC: APA.

Beed, A., & Hamilton-Giachritsis, C. (2005). Relationship between therapeutic climate and treatment outcome in group based sexual offender treatment programs. *Sexual Abuse: A Journal of Research and Treatment, 17,* 127–140.

Berman-Rossi, T. (1993). The tasks and skills of the social worker across stages of group development. *Social Work with Groups, 16,* 69–81.

Blackmore, C., Tantam, D., Parry, G., & Chambers, E. (2012). Report on a systematic review of the efficacy and clinical effectiveness of group analysis and analytic/dynamic group psychotherapy. *Group Analysis, 45,* 46–49.

Burlingame, G., Fuhriman, A., & Mosier, J. (2003). The differential effectiveness of group psychotherapy: A meta-analytic perspective. *Group Dynamics: Theory, Research, and Practice, 7,* 3–12.

Chapman, C., Baker, E., Porter, G., Thayer, S., & Burlingame, G. (2010). Rating group therapist interventions: The validation of the group psychotherapy intervention rating scale. *Group Dynamics, 14,* 15–31.

Dudziak, S., & Profitt, N. (2012). Group work and social justice: Designing pedagogy for social change. *Social Work with Groups, 35,* 235–252.

Emond, S., & Rasmussen, B. (2012). The status of psychiatric inpatient group therapy: Past, present, and future. *Social Work with Groups, 35,* 68–91.

Fagan, A., & Catalano, R. (2013). What works in youth violence prevention: A review of the literature. *Research on Social Work Practice, 23,* 141–156.

Galinsky, M., Terzian, M., & Fraser, M. (2006). The art of group work practice with manualized curricula. *Social Work with Groups, 29,* 11–26.

Garland, J., Jones, H. & Kolodny, R. (1965). A model for stages of development in social work with groups. In S. Bernstein (Ed.) *Explorations in group work: Essays in theory and practice* (pp. 12–53). Boston MA: Boston University Press.

Gitterman, A. (2004). The mutual aid model. In C. Garvin, L. Guttierez, & M. Galinsky (Eds.), *Handbook of social work with groups* (pp. 93–110). New York, NY: Guilford Press.

Gitterman, A., & Knight, C. (in press). Resilience and adversarial growth: Promoting client empowerment through group work. *Journal of Social Work Education.*

Goodman, H., Knight, C., & Khuododov, K. (2014). Graduate social work students' involvement in group work in the field and classroom. *Journal of Teaching in Social Work, 34,* 2014.

Humphreys, I., Drummond, A., Phillips, C., & Lincoln, N. (2013). Cost-effectiveness of an adjustment group for people with multiple sclerosis and low mood: A randomized trial. *Clinical Rehabilitation, 27,* 963–971.

Johnson, J., Burlingame, G., Olsen, J., & Davies, R. (2005). Group climate, cohesion, alliance, and empathy in group psychotherapy: Multi-level structural equation models. *Journal of Counseling Psychology, 52,* 310–321.

Kivlighan, D. J., Paquin, J. D., & Hsu, Y. K. (2014). Is it the unexpected experience that keeps them coming back? Group climate and session attendance examined between groups, between members, and between sessions. *Journal of Counseling Psychology, 61,* 325–332.

Knight, C. (2009). The use of a workshop on group work for field instructors to enhance students' experiences with group work in the field practicum. *Social Work with Groups, 32,* 230–242.

Knight, C. (2014). Teaching group work in the BSW generalist social work curriculum: Core content. *Social Work with Groups, 37*, 23–35.

Knight, C. (in press). Social work students' experiences with group work in the field practicum: An updated analysis. *Journal of Teaching in Social Work.*

Kurland, R., & Salmon, R. (2005). Group work versus case work in a group: Principles and implications for teaching and practice. *Social Work with Groups, 28*, 133–148.

Lorentzen, S., & Ruud, T. (2014). Group therapy in public mental health services: Approaches, patients, and group therapists. *Journal of Mental Health Nursing, 21*, 219–225.

Marmarosh, C., Holtz, A., & Schottenbauer, M. (2005). Group cohesiveness, group-derived collective self-esteem, group-derived hope, and the well-being of group therapy members. *Group Dynamics, 9*, 32–44.

McWhirter, P., Nelson, J., & Waldo, M. (2014). Positive psychology and curative community groups: Life satisfaction, depression, and group therapeutic factors. *Journal for Specialists in Group Work, 39*, 366–380.

National Association of Social Workers (NASW). (2008). *Code of Ethics.* Washington, DC: Author.

Norcross, J., & Wampold, B. (2011). Evidence-based therapy relationships: Research conclusions and clinical practices. *Psychotherapy, 48*, 98–102.

Northen, H., & Kurland, R. (2001). *Social work with groups* (3rd ed.). New York, NY: Columbia University Press.

Ogrodniczuk, J., & Piper, W. (2003). The effect of group climate on outcome in two forms of short-term group therapy. *Group Dynamics: Theory, Research, and Practice, 7*, 64–76.

Okumura, Y., & Ichikura, K. (2014). Efficacy and acceptability of group cognitive behavioral therapy for depression: A systematic review and meta-analysis. *Journal of Affective Disorders, 164*, 155–164.

Piper, W. (2007). Underutilization of short-term group therapy: Enigmatic or understandable? *Psychotherapy Research, 18*, 127–138.

Rose, S. (2009). A review of effectiveness of group work with children of divorce. *Social Work with Groups, 32*, 222–229.

Schwartz, W. (1974). The social worker in the group. In R. Klenk & R. Ryan (Eds.), *The practice of social work* (pp. 257–276). Monterey, CA: Wadsworth.

Schwartz, W. (1994). The classroom teaching of social work with groups: Some central problems. In T. Berman-Rossi (Ed.), *The collected writings of William Schwartz* (pp. 574–582). Itasca, IL: F. E. Peacock.

Shulman, L. (2012). *The skills of helping individuals, families groups and communities* (8th ed.). Belmont, CA: Cengage Learning.

Simon, S., & Kilbane, T. (2014). The current state of group work education in U.S. graduate schools of social work. *Social Work with Groups, 37*, 243–256.

Sloan, D., Bovin, M., & Schnurr, P. (2012). Review of group treatment for PTSD. *Journal of Rehabilitation Research and Development, 49*, 689–701.

Staples, L. (2012). Community organizing for social justice: Grassroots groups for power. *Social Work with Groups, 35*, 287–296.

Sweifach, J. (2014). Group work education today: A content analysis of MSW group work course syllabi. *Social Work with Groups, 37*, 8–22.

Ward, D., & Crosby, C. (2010). Using an observation model for training group therapists in a community mental health setting. *Group, 34*, 355–361.

Yalom, I., & Leszcz, M. (2007). *The theory and practice of group psychotherapy*. New York, NY: Basic Books.

NOTE

1 From Knight, C. (2009). *Introduction to working with adult survivors of childhood trauma: Strategies and techniques for helping professionals* (Belmont, CA: Thomson/Brooks-Cole).

Chapter Two

Group Work Practice: Phases of Work and Associated Skills and Tasks

Carolyn Knight

Many of the skills identified in this chapter are discussed in a particular stage of the group's development. In reality, many of these skills will be relevant and utilized throughout the life of the group. However, their greatest impact is likely to be felt in the stage of development in which each is presented. As will be seen, the skills also are interdependent and often used in conjunction with one another.

PRELIMINARY AND BEGINNING PHASES

The success of a group is largely dependent upon the activities the worker engages in prior to its beginning. Groups often founder because the practitioner did not engage in some very basic preparatory activities. First, in agency-based settings, the worker needs to ensure that she or he has staff support. This seems self-evident, but this consideration often is overlooked. Agency staff may be needed to make referrals to the new group. An appropriate space must be made available for the group, one that is private and roomy enough for members to sit in a circle facing one another. In addition, a time frame needs to be found for the group that accommodates other agency-based activities.

To generate agency support and get off on the right foot, the worker should consider developing a proposal that addresses the following considerations. For clinicians in private practice, these same issues will help them create a group work service that is likely to be successful.

1. *Overall goal and purpose.* What will members gain from their participation? In what way will they benefit from being with others in the same boat?

2. *Composition.* Who will the potential members of the group be? What are the commonalities that are needed to promote mutual aid? This consideration is discussed in greater detail later in this chapter.

3. *Type.* What type of group best meets the needs of the members? Group types were identified in the previous chapter.

4. *Structure.* How should the group be structured in terms of number of sessions, number of members, and time frame? This consideration is discussed in greater detail later in this chapter.

5. *Expectations for member participation.* What "rules" should be established so that the group can do its work and mutual aid can be promoted? Should the leader establish these expectations on her or his own or in cooperation with the members?

6. *Leadership.* Will the group be single- or co-led? What will be the primary role of the leader? If the group is co-led, how will the leaders work out their relationship with one another and with the group?

7. *Dealing with sociocultural differences.* What impact will differences between members and between members and the leader have on the group and members' ability to connect with one another? This consideration is discussed in greater detail later in this chapter.

8. *Assessment.* What will be the indicators of the group's effectiveness and its impact on member growth and change? How will these be measured?

9. *The first session.* What are members likely to be feeling and thinking as they come to their first session? What can the leader do to encourage member-to-member interaction and connectedness? This is discussed in greater detail later in this chapter.

Group Composition

Choosing members who are appropriate for group membership is far from a straightforward process. Two basic principles guide the worker's decisions with respect to member selection. The "not the only one" principle (Gitterman, 2005) suggests that "no one member should stand out in a way that separates her or him from others and from the central goal and purpose of the group" (Knight, 2014, p. 30). A complementary principle, "Noah's Ark" (Yalom & Leszcz, 2007) requires that "each member should share with at least one other member core characteristics that are relevant to the group and its purpose" (Knight, 2014, p. 30). Relevant characteristics are both obvious such as race, gender, and ethnicity and subtle such as the nature of the problem that led to the need for the group work service and the individual's interpersonal style.

Using these principles, the worker assesses in what ways the group should be homogeneous and in what ways it can be hetereogeneous. Gitterman observes, "members usually tolerate . . . greater diversity when common interests and concerns are experienced intensely . . . [T]he less the members perceive common interests and concerns, the more homogenous the group composition must be" (2005, p. 81). The following scenario exemplifies Gitterman's observation. In one of the author's groups for adult survivors of sexual abuse, there were six Caucasian women and one African American woman, Helen.

This would appear to violate the "not the only one" principle. The obvious racial difference between Helen and the rest of the group could set her up to feel isolated. Furthermore, assumptions that she might make about others and the assumptions that they might make about her based upon race could impede engagement of all. The author was sensitive to the potential barrier that racial differences might present and was prepared to address this directly. However, members' underlying sense of commonality, coupled with their sense of urgency, outweighed the risk that Helen would feel alone and different. When the group was well underway, Helen did acknowledge, "When I walked through that door for the first time, and saw all these White faces, I wanted to run. I thought, 'No White lady was going to understand what I went through.' But when Marcia [another member] talked about what happened to her, I realized that we were all the same underneath—living with what these perverts did to us."

In another group the author facilitated, the Noah's Ark principle was adhered to with respect to race; there were three African American women and four Caucasian women. Yet one of the members, Susie, had been the victim of horrific, ritualistic sexual abuse at the hands of a satanic cult. Susie's background was different enough from others in the group that the author worried that her feelings of being different and alone would be exacerbated rather than minimized. In fact, Susie was readily embraced by the group, and she quickly felt "at home." Although there were significant differences between her abuse and that of the other members, the underlying feelings that *all* members shared predominated.

Finally, in a group for bereaved individuals led by one of the author's students, members were heterogeneous with respect to gender, race, age, and relationship to the deceased. One member, Hal, had lost his wife to suicide, while the other members were dealing with losses due to natural causes. Even though all members shared many of the same feelings, Hal's unique situation contributed to feelings of isolation. His anger toward his wife was powerful, as was his guilt that he somehow contributed to her death. Every other member experienced these same feelings, but far less intensely. The student emphasized the similarities and commonalities between the members' experiences, a critical group work skill discussed later, but Hal remained isolated. Ultimately he dropped out, in large measure because he felt so different from the others. Had Hal been a different sort of person perhaps he could have overcome his feelings of being alone, with the assistance of the group leader. But this scenario underscores the need for the worker to consider the two principles previously identified.

Research findings consistently reveal that screening of members enhances the development of cohesion and decreases the likelihood of dropout (Capuzzi & Gross, 2002; Coy, Akos, & Moore, 2004; Marmarosh, Markin, & Spiegel, 2013).

Research also suggests that advance preparation, typically in the form of an in-person individual session, in which the potential member provides background information, is introduced to the purpose of the group, and has had a chance to ask questions and express concerns, increases the likelihood that members will engage in and commit to the group experience (Hannah, 2000; Rosenthal, 2005). Preparation of members in advance of the group also is consistent with professional ethics that stress the need for informed consent (ACA, 2014; APA, 2003; NASW, 2008).

In some settings, most notably residential, the worker may not be able to select, screen, or prepare members in advance for group participation. For example, group sessions in an inpatient psychiatric program typically will include all patients on the unit. This does not mean that the group cannot be successful. It does mean the worker must be mindful that she or he may have to work harder to seek and point out underlying commonalities among members. The leader also will need to closely monitor group members' interactions, discussed later, because scapegoating and the development of the isolate role is more likely to occur under these circumstances (Clark, 2002; Coy et al., 2004; Rosenthal, 2005).

Group Structure

Decisions about group structure reflect the well-known expression: Form follows function. Once the worker determines the purpose of the group, she or he must consider what sort of structure will support it. Structural considerations include the following:

1. *Open or closed membership.* Will the group continually remain open to new members? Will members start and finish together? Can a new member join only when an existing member leaves?
2. *Number of sessions.* Will the group be ongoing and open ended? Will it operate for a limited number of sessions? If so, how many?
3. *Length of sessions.* How long will each session be?
4. *Number of members.*
5. *Use of a preexisting curriculum.* Will the leader come prepared with an agenda and topics for discussion whereby one session builds upon the last, or will members engage with one another spontaneously?

Decisions regarding these considerations are often interdependent. Several examples illustrate this interconnection as well as how agency programming and policies can influence structural considerations. In a 30-day inpatient detox program for substance abusers, clients are required to attend daily meetings to promote sobriety, address the challenges associated with this, and explore the underlying factors that led to the substance abuse in the first place. By definition, the group is open ended and ongoing; there is no finite end date. The group also must have an open membership; new members will participate as they enter the program and depart when their 30 days are up.

Given the open-ended and ongoing nature of the group, the use of a preexisting curriculum would be ill advised. The facility serves 60 clients at any one time. The purpose of the group would be significantly undermined if all 60 members attended group together. Therefore, the agency holds multiple sessions throughout the day, limiting the number of members to 10. Each session is 90 minutes long. This group would be best characterized as an ongoing support group. The author describes a group similar to this in her chapter on working with homeless parents living in a shelter.

In contrast, a clinician in private practice is able to create a group from the ground up with no limitations or agency constraints to consider. He would like to facilitate a group for military personnel returning from the Middle East who are struggling with posttraumatic stress symptoms and with transitioning back to civilian life. He envisions a group in which members learn to understand and manage their symptoms and receive validation and support regarding their experiences in and reactions to combat. To increase the potential that the group will achieve its purpose, he has decided upon the following. The group will be limited to 10 members to promote intimacy and honest discussion. It will be a closed member group; members will start and finish together, which also promotes intimacy. There will be no set curriculum from week to week; rather, members will be helped to set their own "agenda" for work and engage openly with one another.

Each session will be 90 minutes in length, and the group will be time limited. Research suggests that time limits promote rapid development of cohesion, reduce the risk of dropout, and enhance member motivation (Jennings, 2007; Piper, Ogrodniczuk, Joyce, & Weideman, 2011). The worker decided upon 16 sessions, believing that this length of time allowed for the development of the intimacy that is central to achieving the group's purpose. This group is a classic support group and is similar in form to the group for survivors of sexual abuse that the author writes about later on in this book.

Finally, a school social worker is asked to provide an anger management group for older elementary school children who are disruptive in the classroom. It will be comprised of third through fifth graders. The worker envisions the group becoming a place where members are helped to better manage *and* understand their feelings. Because members are children who are emotionally and behaviorally challenged, the group will be small, limited to five participants. It also will be highly structured using art and games that the social worker will decide upon in advance and present in each session. The group will run for 30 minutes. Because it is occurring in a school setting, the group will run for an entire semester, making it time limited. To maximize the mutual support and demand that is necessary for the group to achieve its purpose, membership will be closed; the children will start and end together. This group is best viewed as a blend of psychoeducational and support that relies upon activity to accomplish its goals.

The First Sessions

A skill set that is critical to getting the group off to a good start is what Shulman (2012) refers to as intellectual and affective tuning in. Before the worker even starts the first session, he or she anticipates how members might be feeling about their upcoming participation. This skill is comprised of two interdependent tasks. The worker first considers what clients *in general* might be experiencing, based upon knowledge of prospective members' age, gender, status (i.e., mandatory or voluntary), developmental stage, and present-day challenges. This intellectual tuning in is complemented by the worker's consideration of the unique characteristics of each member; based upon this assessment, the worker considers how each member is feeling about embarking upon group membership (affective tuning in).

In the group for elementary school children, the worker would consider both the children's developmental capacities and tasks and the implications these would have, including the types of activities to be used and how the leader would explain the role of the group and the leader (intellectual tuning in). In addition, the worker would consider how each individual member might be feeling about the group, based upon her or his unique circumstances and the mandatory nature of participation. Screening members for the group ahead of time provides the worker with valuable information that assists her or him in tuning in. Even without the benefit of screening, the worker can, at the very least, anticipate that members will have questions about what will be expected of them, will be confused, and perhaps will be frightened about working with others.

Five core skills and tasks surface in the early sessions (Gitterman, 2004; Shulman, 2012). In the first session, the worker provides a clear, nonjargonized explanation of the role and purpose of the group and the leader. These explanations should reflect the purpose of the group that has been established. It also should, in layperson's terms, explain mutual aid and its attendant advantages. Based upon tuning in, the leader should be prepared to address members' questions and concerns directly. Given their unfamiliarity with the worker and one another, members' reactions are likely to be expressed indirectly through nonverbal means such as silence, rolling of the eyes, and nervous behaviors. The skill of directly acknowledging members' concerns from the beginning sends a powerful, instructive message to all that open and honest discussion is encouraged and members' unique perspectives are respected.

In a group with open membership, the worker will need to engage in these same behaviors anytime a new member joins. In this case, the worker can anticipate, for example, that the new member will be particularly anxious about joining others who already know one another. Depending upon the stage of the group's development, the worker could consider asking the members themselves to provide the explanations.

In the children's group just mentioned, the leader's explanation would have to be tailored to members' level of education and cognitive abilities. Their questions about "Why me?" would need to be addressed, as well as assumptions they are likely to hold that the group will be a class and the leader will be a teacher.

A third task that surfaces in the first session is encouraging members to engage in the "problem swap" (Shulman, 2012). The worker asks members to introduce themselves and provide relevant information about themselves. The specific information depends upon the purpose of the group. For example, in the support group for bereaved individuals, the leader could ask members to provide their name as well as the name of their loved one and her or his relationship to the deceased. Other information that could be shared is the cause of death, when it occurred, how the member is doing, and what she or he would like to get out of the group. In contrast, in a group with the same purpose—bereavement support—for *children*, the leader might ask members what grade they are in and what their favorite sport and academic subject is. Eliciting this sort of information reflects the developmental needs of the members and, as discussed later in this chapter, provides the worker with information that allows her or him to point out underlying commonalities.

In a psychoeducational group for parents of babies born with developmental disabilities, members could be asked to share the name and gender of their newborn and feelings and questions they have about their babies' condition. Finally, in the group for veterans struggling with posttraumatic stress disorder and transitioning back to civilian life, the leader could ask members to describe their symptoms and struggles; when, where, and in what capacity they served in the military; and provide information about their families, employment, and the like.

The worker should understand that the *content* of the problem swap is much less important than the way she or he uses it to begin to point out commonalities among members. The leader may choose to go around the room systematically, asking that each member, in turn, introduce herself or himself. However, as one member reveals information, the leader may use this to point out connections to others. The real benefit of the problem swap is that it allows the leader to identify commonalities, another critical group work skill, right from the start. If the worker has engaged in pregroup screening and selection of members, information gleaned from that session can assist with this skill, though individual members' right to privacy will need to be respected. It should be the individual member who discloses new information about herself or himself, not the worker.

This last point is consistent with requirements spelled out in the Codes of Ethics of the American Counseling Association (2014) and the American Psychological Association (2003). Both organizations provide specific guidelines regarding confidentiality in group work. The group worker should not disclose personal information about an individual member to the rest of the group or to others such as the member's individual worker without the member's permission, except in cases of mandatory reporting.

A fourth group work skill, and one that clearly sets it apart from individual casework, is monitoring the group. This should be exhibited from the very beginning of the group's development. As a member is introducing herself or himself to others, the leader is attending to *others* in the group. The leader is able to see members' reactions to the individual who is speaking and can use these reactions to point out commonalities. Monitoring the group also encourages the individual to look to other members, not to the leader. The leader avoids making continuous eye contact with the individual, preferring instead to scan the group as a whole. As group workers become more comfortable engaging in this skill, they are less likely to engage in casework in the group and more likely to encourage member-to-member, rather than member-to-leader, interaction.

The following brief scenario, drawn from a bereavement group for adults dealing with the loss of a loved one, illustrates the use of the problem swap and the skills of monitoring the group and pointing out commonalities. The group worker, who prescreened members for their appropriateness for the group, has asked each member to provide a brief introduction, including who they lost, how they are coping, and with what they are struggling. So far, two members, sitting next to one another, have engaged in the problem swap. As the third member, Miriam, introduces herself, the following exchange occurs:

> *Miriam:* My husband was killed in a car accident. I was driving *(starts to cry)*. A drunken driver crossed the center line . . . there was nothing I could do, that's what the police said. But I feel like if I had just been a bit more attentive, a bit more observant, maybe I could have avoided him. Clint [her husband] died in my arms *(crying uncontrollably)*.
>
> *Group worker:* Obviously, this is very painful for Miriam. I also sense a lot of guilt. I suspect Miriam is not alone in feeling somehow responsible. I noticed, Jim, you were nodding your head when Miriam was talking about her feelings of responsibility. Perhaps you can relate?
>
> *Jim:* *(nods his head)*. My son was only 25. He had a brain tumor. They tried to get it all, but they couldn't. I know it sounds ridiculous, but I feel like he inherited this bad gene from us, from me. I should have known something was wrong with him when he started with the headaches, but I figured it was just stress. If only I'd taken it seriously, paid closer attention . . .

In this group, guilt surfaced as a dominant theme, along with loss, anger, and sadness. It should be noted that of the eight members in attendance, Miriam is the only one who lost a loved one to causes other than natural. This could have set her up to feel different and alone. Yet her underlying feelings were similar to others, and her opening introduction allowed the group worker to point out these similarities from the very beginning. Miriam benefited from discovering— right from the start—that she was not alone. And, by using her disclosures to point out the similarities among members, the worker encouraged members to quickly and readily connect with one another.

A final skill is not unique to group work and is essential to good clinical practice. The group worker should be prepared to directly address the "authority theme" (Shulman, 2014). This skill is most obviously needed when members are mandated clients. The resentment that some or all members may experience as a result of their required participation may impede their ability to connect with one another and with the leader.

This skill also comes into play when differences between the leader and the members call into question the leader's credibility. When this skill is utilized, it reflects the leader's sociocultural sensitivity, consistent with the ethical requirements for mental health professionals (ACA, 2014; APA, 2003; NASW, 2008). Members' assumptions about the leader have the potential to impede engagement. In the group the author facilitates for homeless parents, this is a common and ongoing theme and therefore task. Because membership is continuously changing, the author addresses members' reservations and concerns about her on a regular basis. The author's race and ethnicity, her age, her perceived socioeconomic status, and her lack of personal experience with homelessness and the numerous other challenges members face inevitably lead to questions about her credibility and ability to understand and be helpful.

Group workers, particularly those who are new to the modality, may shy away from engaging in this skill, due to their *own* questions about their ability to be helpful and their reluctance to bring up members' negative feelings. In the author's case, she cannot change who she is and what she has experienced, nor should she have to. What she *can* do is acknowledge openly members' questions and concerns. A typical comment that the author makes is, "I suspect some of you are wondering how someone like me could be helpful to you and understand you and the challenges you face." This simple, direct statement validates members' concerns, giving them permission to express them openly. More important, the author's acknowledgment of the differences begins to diminish their importance and potential to disrupt members' engagement in the group.

In a related vein, the group leader must be sensitive to the assumptions members bring with them about each other, based upon sociocultural differences. As Gitterman (2004) observed earlier, the greater the sense of urgency experienced by members, the less of an issue differences are likely to be. Yet the worker must at least consider that perceived differences can be a hindrance. Similar to the skill of dealing with the authority theme, the worker should be prepared to address members' preconceived notions about one another, including feelings of hostility and suspicion, directly (Chen, Kakkad, & Balzano, 2008; Debak, 2007).

In a mandatory psychoeducational group for adolescents charged with crimes ranging from breaking and entering to assault, the student worker quickly recognized the need to address not only the authority theme but also members' underlying suspicions of one another. The two-session group focused on preparing the members for their court date, identifying possible dispositions of their cases, and making suggestions for how to present themselves in court. Eight members attended, including four African American teens, two Caucasians, and two Latinos. Screening consisted of limiting the group to teens charged with less serious offenses. Although one young woman fit the eligibility requirement, the worker decided that it would not be in her or the group's best interest, because she would be the only female with eight males.

The student was aware in advance that some of the youth had gang affiliations, though none appeared to be "official" members. He also was aware, from his familiarity with the communities from where the members came, that racial and ethnic tensions were high. As a young White man, the worker also assumed the members would be hostile toward him and question his credibility. After introducing himself and his role and the role and purpose of the group, the student worker made the following observation:

> I know you guys come from all over the city, and you don't usually talk to one another, may not even like one another. I also bet that you are wondering what a guy like me can offer you all. You know it all already, right (*smiles*)? Here's the thing ... you all are in the same boat. You're pissed about getting caught, having to come to this group, maybe even a bit afraid of what will happen next. Like it or not, this group is your best shot at getting the judge to go easy on you.

In advance of starting the group, the student expressed misgivings about being so direct, acknowledging that he was worried that he would open up "a can of worms." The author reminded him that *not* addressing members' feelings about one another was not an option. Their hostility and suspicion of one another and the leader wouldn't disappear; it would become an even bigger barrier to the work of the group the longer the worker avoided it. The members readily expressed their hostility toward one another and toward the leader. Rather than trying to squelch this discussion, the worker used members' comments to underscore their underlying commonalities: They might be different and have nothing to do with one another outside the group, but *in* the group, they were the same. Because members were allowed to discuss these issues openly, the barriers created by differences were lessened.

MIDDLE OR WORK PHASE

Some groups may never transition out of the beginning phase such as those with open, revolving membership. Yet in those groups where members are together for some time, the nature of their interactions will begin to shift as a result of their increasing connectedness to and comfort with one another. In a mature group where the group culture is well established and promotes the work of the group, it may appear to the unschooled observer that the group worker is doing very little. In fact, the leader continues to utilize a number of skills, even as members take on increasing responsibility for their work.

A significant skill is a refinement of one introduced in the beginning phase, and that is monitoring the group's normative structure to ensure that it is supporting the group's work. As previously discussed, regardless of any explicit rules that the leader may establish, group members will establish their own "rules" for how they will relate to one another; these expectations grow out of members' ongoing interactions. Ideally, the formal, explicit rules, established by the leader or the leader and members together, are the same as or complement the norms that develop. The work of the group is undermined and mutual aid compromised when the implicit and explicit rules are incongruent. In these instances, members are more likely to adhere to the norms that have evolved over time, rather than the formal rules that have been established. The following is a typical scenario that occurs when the group worker has *not* attended to the group's normative structure.

The setting is an outpatient family service agency that provides a support group for women sexually abused in childhood. The group is ongoing and operates with a closed membership; as one member leaves, a new member enters after being screened. There are eight women. The purpose of the group is to assist members in coming to terms with their past victimization as well as address their current problems in living. The group worker has complained that members are often silent and seem unwilling to talk about their past or present challenges. She also expressed frustration at the frequent absences, despite the rule that members must attend to maximize benefits of their participation.

As the worker and the author talked about the group, it became apparent that when sensitive topics surfaced and explicit details of molestation were revealed, members (*and* the leader) became uncomfortable. The leader acknowledged that it was hard for her to see a group member get upset; she felt "sorry" for her. The worker further recognized that when a member did try to reveal sensitive information, the topic swiftly changed to something less painful or upsetting. Rather than tackling members' abuse head-on, the group norm became one of avoidance, which the leader unwittingly reinforced.

Once the leader began to see what the underlying normative structure of her group was, members' silence and absences made more sense: The formal expectation for members was that they should talk honestly about their experiences and feelings. However, members quickly learned that honest discussion was discouraged; the *actual* expectation was "avoid discussing painful subjects at all costs." Once the worker understood this, she was able to see that members' silence and absences indicated their frustration about and confusion regarding the mixed messages they were receiving. On the one hand, the leader assured them that the group was a safe place where they could talk about the things that mattered to them. On the other hand, the underlying norm dictated the precise opposite. The worker then realized that she needed to engage in a second skill that often comes into play in the work phase: recontracting (Shulman, 2012).

If the leader is closely attending to the normative structure of the group, the need to recontract—to address directly with members how they are interacting and working with one another—often becomes necessary. The worker in the previous example made the following comment as the next session of her group commenced:

> I have noticed that over the last couple of weeks some of you have missed group and that there has been a lot of uncomfortable silence. I think we need to revisit how we are working together. When we started, I suggested that one of the ways that the group would be helpful was for you to talk openly about your experiences and feelings. Yet, I get the feeling that this has been difficult, because it is so painful to hear others' stories and to tell your own. How about if we spend a little bit of time talking about how we can make it easier for you all to be open? I sense that you *want* to do this, but are afraid to because it is so hard, and it hurts so much.

The worker does not beat around the bush about the group's problems. She directly addresses the behaviors she has observed, links them to the underlying problem—the pain and discomfort associated with talking honestly—and suggests members revisit the expectations that guide their working relationships. Members initially were reluctant to respond to the worker's demand for work. The task of examining one's relationships in the immediate present is at best unfamiliar and at worse disconcerting to most individuals. Group members are no exception. The leader may need to persist in asking members to examine their interactions and how these could be modified to enhance the group's work.

Reframing is another skill that group workers will utilize in the work phase, though it will have been introduced in the beginning phase. This cognitive-behavioral technique is not unique to group work, but it is critical to assisting members in seeing their underlying commonalities and enhancing their understanding of themselves and one another, as previous examples have suggested. One question the group worker must constantly ask herself or himself is, "How can this individual's 'story' and reactions resonate with the rest of the group?" The worker attempts to link the individual to the group, and, in turn, the group to the individual. Sometimes the connections are clear, but in other instances, the worker needs to assist members in seeing their underlying bond.

Reframing also may be used to enhance members' understanding of their collective behaviors. In the previous example, the worker reframes members' absences and silence as their reluctance to talk openly about their past. The worker may need to use reframing as a way of addressing problematic dynamics like scapegoating. In a previous example introduced in the last chapter in which scapegoating was illustrated, the worker doesn't recognize the function that this dynamic played for the group: By targeting one member, James, the other members were able to avoid confronting and dealing with their own experiences and feelings. In contrast to what the leader actually said, a more appropriate intervention might look like this:

> I notice a number of you laughing and making fun of James. I am wondering if maybe his disclosure about what happened to him as a child hit just a little too close to home? I suspect that James may not be the only one who was hurt when he was a child. But it can be very hard to talk about this, can't it? It's easier to just laugh it off.

Reframing also will come into play when the leader must address challenging role behaviors themselves. In one of the author's groups for survivors, George was typically silent and withdrawn. He appeared aloof and seemed disinterested. In response, members began to display anger at and resentment of George, conveyed largely through nonverbal behaviors and gestures. The author made the following observation:

> I noticed that George has been very quiet for most of our time together. Some of you may be questioning why he is here. Sometimes it can be really hard for people to disclose their experiences. I suspect that George's silence reflects his discomfort at sharing and maybe his worry that he's all alone, feelings that I suspect everyone can relate to.

The author's comments were met with an uncomfortable silence. Finally, Sally, who was sitting next to George, turned to him and said, "You know, we all think we're different, weird. I know I talk a lot about what happened to me, but it isn't easy. It hurts a lot every time I open my mouth. You're among friends here, George." For one of the first times that he had been attending the group, George looked at the others and offered a "Thanks" to Sally. Although he was never one of the more vocal members, George gradually began to open up. Equally important, members' distrust of George quickly dissipated as they saw themselves in his behavior and actions.

Reframing requires the use of two additional skill sets: elaborating and clarifying. Under the best of circumstances, words are an imprecise way of communicating information between individuals. Therefore, the risk of miscommunication is high. In a group, members are often disclosing sensitive information and experiencing difficult emotions, both of which may not be easily conveyed in words. Furthermore, as with all individuals, members' verbal communication is *always* accompanied by nonverbal behaviors such as facial expressions, bodily gestures, and tone of voice. Difficulties arise when members' (and the worker's) verbal communication is inconsistent with their nonverbal communication. Finally, sociocultural differences between members and between the members and the leader can lead to misunderstanding and miscommunication. Given these challenges, the group worker will need to assist members in communicating more clearly. This includes among other skills:

1. Asking individual members to clarify what they mean
2. Pointing out to individual members when there is an inconsistency between their verbal and nonverbal communication
3. Checking out with the group as a whole their understanding of the disclosures of others and the leader
4. Asking the group as a whole to clarify its reactions to the comments of others and the leader
5. Clarifying the leader's communication and asking for feedback

These skills are used in conjunction with another skill introduced previously in the discussion of the beginning phase, monitoring the group, and with reframing. A major feature of monitoring the group is assessing what individual members are really saying and how other members are reacting to what is being said, or what they *think* is being said. In the case of George, for example, group members interpreted his silence to mean he thought he was better than them. This required that the author reframe his behavior in a way that made sense to members and reinforced underlying similarities.

Empathy skills will surface in the beginning stage of work. They will play a critical role in the middle phase as well. Ideally, as members develop greater comfort with one another, they are able to take on increasing responsibility for providing comfort and support. This is more likely to happen if the worker intentionally models empathy skills in the early phase. The worker must maintain a delicate balance in this regard. As noted in the last chapter, if the worker is not careful, she or he may end up doing casework in the group. The risk is that the worker will jump in and respond empathically to the distress of a member, which denies others the opportunity to do this. As discussed, the individual member benefits from receiving the support of others in the same boat, and the member who provides reassurance benefits through enhanced feelings of self-efficacy.

In the middle phase, members' increasing comfort with one another encourages deeper exploration of thoughts and feelings, particularly in support-type groups. Ironically, as members disclose more sensitive and difficult information, they may have a hard time responding to one another. In these instances, the worker may need to help members support and convey understanding to one another through her or his own displays of empathy as the following scenario illustrates.

In the early phase of a twelve-session, closed membership, psychoeducational group for substance abusers, a number of members had a hard time even accepting they had a problem with drugs and/or alcohol. As the group progressed, members not only accepted responsibility for their addiction, they also began to disclose behaviors they had engaged in to support their addiction. In the eighth session, Paul revealed, with obvious feelings of guilt and remorse, that he had prostituted himself to obtain money for his heroin addiction. His revelations initially were met with silence, a phenomenon all group leaders fear and dread. The group worker astutely refrained from immediately intervening, hoping that another member would respond with concern and compassion. When this did not happen, the group worker made the following comment:

> I really appreciate your honesty, Paul. It took a lot of courage to disclose what you did, and I can tell you have a lot of feelings of shame and guilt about what you did. I couldn't help but notice the silence that followed Paul's comments. I am wondering whether that means that others of you also have done things you regret? Having Paul put into words what he did to support his habit brings it really close to home, doesn't it?

This intervention is noteworthy for three reasons. First, the group leader not only empathizes with the individual, Paul; he also conveys understanding to the group as a whole. Second, the worker's observations reflect his use of the skill of monitoring the group. Finally, his response involves reframing the group response in a way that clarifies what members' silence really meant.

ENDING PHASE

In an ongoing group, this stage of group development may not exist, though members may need to say goodbye to an individual member who is departing, and she or he will need to say goodbye to the group. This stage is most evident in time-limited groups, and the longer the members have been together, the more difficult endings are likely to be. The worker has a twofold responsibility: to assist members to end with another and to end with her or him.

Endings are difficult under the best of circumstances. When members have achieved a level of comfort and intimacy with one another, it can be especially difficult to say farewell. The worker needs to utilize empathy skills to "reach for" members' feelings (Shulman, 2012). These typically include the following:

1. Sadness and loss at having to end meaningful relationships
2. Regret that the individual member did not do more, share more, and so forth
3. Worry that without the group, the individual will backslide
4. Anger at the leader for "making" the group end when the time limit is up
5. Fear of what the future holds
6. Guilt over actions that the individual may have engaged in that may have hurt or upset others

Because members may have great difficulty putting these feelings into words, the leader should look for indications these affective reactions are at play indirectly through collective and individual behaviors. Members may begin to skip sessions, the group as a whole may revert to earlier themes and stages of development, discussion may become superficial, and interactions may become stilted and awkward. When the worker observes these dynamics, she or he can utilize reframing skills to help members to consider their actions in light of their feelings about endings.

In addition to encouraging members to discuss openly their thoughts and feelings about ending, the worker also can help them see the gains they have made, both individually and collectively. Furthermore, the leader should encourage members to examine how they worked together, including what went well and what didn't. Shulman (2012) warns that without the group leader's insistence, members will either avoid endings altogether or will engage in a "farewell party" whereby members focus on the positive, provide empty reassurances to one another that they will "keep in touch," and avoid the difficult work of acknowledging that, at the very least, the group as they know it is ending, and at worst, they are unlikely to see one another again.

Although endings in support-oriented groups tend to be the most difficult, they also can be hard for members of psychoeducational groups. An 8-week group for adolescents dealing with the death of a sibling combined education with support. Members were provided with a place to share their grief; they also were provided with information about grief reactions, ways of coping, and causes of their siblings' death. The intent was to normalize members' feelings, thoughts, and reactions as well as enhance their coping skills, and give them permission to move on with their lives. The leader made it clear from the beginning that the group would meet for eight sessions. She reminded members of this each week by stating how many sessions the group had left. Members were slow to warm up to one another and to the leader, who correctly assumed that this was due to their developmental stage. However, by the fourth session, members were engaged in the group, eager for the information the leader provided, and readily providing support to one another.

In the sixth session, the leader reminded the group that there were three sessions left. Members responded with surprise—most claimed to not remember this. The leader attempted to draw out members' feelings but without success. Members continued on with the session as if they had not heard her. In the seventh session, four of the nine members did not show up. The five members who did come expressed anger—largely directed at the worker—for ending the group "when things were just getting going." Although the worker directly addressed the anger and further suggested that other feelings, such as those noted earlier, may be present and might explain the absences, members avoided altogether any discussion of ending. Prior to the eighth and final session the worker took the unusual but appropriate step of calling all members to request that they attend the last session, telling them that it was important for them to end with one another and with her, so that they could experience closure, rather than a sense that the business of the group was unfinished.

All members did come, and although it took time—the worker described it as like "pulling teeth"—the members were able to engage in an honest discussion of how they felt about ending, what they had learned and gained from the group, and how they would evaluate their working relationship with one another and with the leader. To encourage this discussion, the worker made the following statement:

> I couldn't help but notice that a few of you didn't come last week. I think that this may have had something to do with this being our last session together. Sometimes it seems easier to just walk away than say goodbye to people that matter to us. How about if I get the conversation going by letting you know how it has been for me to work with you all, what I see as your growth as a group and as individuals?

The worker proceeded to share her observations about how the group started off slowly, with members being suspicious of one another and of her, and reluctant to talk to one another, but how it quickly gained momentum. She noted how helpful members were to one another, and how they were able to use the information she provided to them to manage their grief and begin to move on with their lives. She provided specific examples of how members helped one another, took steps to work through their grief, and demonstrated increased strength and resilience. The worker's disclosures ultimately paved the way for members to engage in the same sort of conversation that she had started.

One issue that surfaced was members' guilt that they started out so suspicious of one another and the leader. To achieve closure, it was important that this issue be addressed directly. The worker credited the members for bringing this up, as she herself had missed it. She reassured members that it was normal and under- standable that it would take time for them to warm up to one another and then reminded them how cohesive a group they had become.

CONCLUSION

When group members have the opportunity to deepen their relationships with one another, their collective behaviors change, as do the responsibilities and tasks of the group worker. The tasks and skills identified in this chapter are designed to promote mutual aid by connecting members to one another. For the pur- poses of discussion and clarity, skills and tasks are presented at different stages of the group's development. In some cases—introducing the role and purpose of the group and leader, encouraging members to problem swap and talk about endings—the skills are limited to a particular phase. In most instances the group worker is likely to make use of the skills throughout her or his work. This also will be true in groups that may not progress through the stages due to their struc- ture, for example, open membership and one-session groups.

RESOURCE

International Association for the Advancement of Social Work with Groups Standards for Social Work Practice with Groups http://www.iaswg.org/assets/ docs/Resources/2015_IASWG_STANDARDS_FOR_SOCIAL_WORK_ PRACTICE_WITH_GROUPS.pdf

REFERENCES

American Counseling Association (ACA). (2014). *American Counseling Association code of ethics*. Washington, DC: Author.

American Psychological Association (APA). (2003). *Ethical principles of psychology and code of conduct*. Washington, DC: Author.

Capuzzi, D., & Gross, D. (2002). Group counseling: Elements of effective leadership. In D. Capuzzi & D. Gross (Eds.), *Introduction to group counseling* (3rd ed., pp. 57–88). Denver, CO: Love Publishing.

Chen, E., Kakkad, D., & Balzano, J. (2008). Multicultural competence and evidence- based practice in group therapy. *Journal of Clinical Psychology, 64*, 1261–1278.

Clark, A. (2002). Scapegoating: Dynamics and interventions in group counseling. *Journal of Counseling and Development, 80*, 271–276.

Coy, D., Akos, P., & Moore, J. (2004). Screening of members: "Everyone is welcome." In L. E. Tyson, R. Pérusse, & J. Whitledge (Eds.), *Critical incidents in group counseling* (pp. 9–14). Alexandria, VA: American Counseling Association.

Debak, D. (2007). Attending to diversity in group psychotherapy: An ethical perspective. *International Journal of Group Psychotherapy, 57,* 1–12.

Gitterman, A. (2004). The mutual aid model. In C. Garvin, L. Guttierez, & M. Galinsky (Eds.), *Handbook of social work with groups* (pp. 93–110). New York, NY: Guilford Press.

Gitterman, A. (2005). Group formation: Tasks, methods, and skills. In A. Gitterman & L. Shulman (Eds.), *Mutual aid groups, vulnerable and resilient populations, and the life cycle* (pp. 73–110). New York, NY: Columbia University Press.

Hannah, P. (2000). Preparing members for the expectations of social work with groups: An approach to the preparatory interview. *Social Work with Groups, 22,* 51–66.

Jennings, A. (2007). Time-limited group therapy—Losses and gains. *Psychoanalytic Psychotherapy, 21,* 90–106.

Knight, C. (2014). Teaching group work in the BSW generalist social work curriculum: Core content. *Social Work with Groups, 37,* 23–35.

Marmarosh, C. L., Markin, R. D., & Spiegel, E. B. (2013). Assembling the group: Screening, placing, and preparing group members. In C. L. Marmarosh, R. D. Markin, & E. B. Spiegel, *Attachment in group psychotherapy* (pp. 67–95). Washington, DC: American Psychological Association.

National Association of Social Workers (NASW). (2008). *Code of ethics.* Washington, DC: Author.

Piper, W., Ogrodniczuk, J., Joyce, A., & Weideman, R. (2011). Time-limited short-term supportive group therapy. In American Psychological Association (Ed.), *Short-term group therapies for complicated grief: Two research-based models* (pp. 221–232). Washington, DC: American Psychological Association.

Rosenthal, L. (2005). Castouts and dropouts: Premature termination in group analysis. *Modern Psychoanalysis, 30,* 40–53.

Shulman, L. (2012). *The skills of helping individuals, families groups and communities* (8th ed.). Belmont, CA: Cengage Learning.

Yalom, I., & Leszcz, M. (2007). *The theory and practice of group psychotherapy.* New York, NY: Basic Books.

Chapter Three

A Summary: Skills for Working in Groups Across Populations at Risk

Geoffrey L. Greif, Paul Ephross, and Carolyn Knight

This is a skills book intended to assist practitioners in working with a wide range of populations. Each chapter includes specific recommendations for helping people in pain, people struggling with a significant problem in living, or people who share a common condition or need. Just as there are recurring themes that emerge when working with each of these populations, we believe that common skills are needed for working *across* populations. In essence, each chapter is a look at the trees in the forest. The chapters, taken together, become the forest. In reading across the chapters, skills emerge from the whole forest that can serve practitioners well, both when intervening in the group and when intervening on behalf of the group. Although no particular skill is guaranteed to work with all populations all the time, these skills are sufficiently generic to apply to most situations. We have synthesized and highlighted these skills, borrowed in part from the chapter authors, and present them as guideposts for practice.

The list of skills that follows is not ranked in order of importance. They go from the general to the specific. Some need no explanation.

1. *Understanding the relationship of the worker to the agency (or practice setting) and understanding where both worker and agency fit into the services provided in the community.* Such an understanding, which would include outreach to populations at risk, such as new immigrant groups, sets the context for group work practice, which never occurs in a vacuum. The practice setting is reflected in the group's structure, membership, and purpose.

2. *Understanding how groups flow from beginning to end.* Workers should be familiar with how members begin with a group, continue with a group (the middle stage), and terminate with a group, including where individual members go next if service is still needed. The practice or agency context may preclude group movement through these phases.

For example, in a homeless shelter, clients come and go; the group's membership is in constant flux. In this type of group, members may never move beyond the beginning phase of engagement. The worker must take this into account when determining the group's purpose and goals. Whether a group is able to progress over time or remains in a particular phase, it is essential that the worker understand how individual member behavior *and* the collective behavior of all members are defined by the stage of the group's development. With this knowledge, the worker can maximize member engagement in, and commitment to, the group, foster member growth and change, and deepen the group's work. These phases also guide the worker in determining what skills will assist the group in doing its work. For example, in the beginning phase, members are sizing one another up, unsure about one another's trustworthiness. In response, the worker begins to point out members' underlying commonalties to promote a sense of connectedness and comfort.

3. *Operating with cultural awareness and sensitivity.* The ability to appreciate and convey respect for members' differences, whether they be in the areas of race, class, ethnicity, sexual orientation, age, immigration status, and/or (dis)ability is a central skill that is highlighted throughout this book. This also includes the differences between the members and the leader.

4. *Advocating for and on behalf of the client, the group, and the agency.* Workers should represent client and group interests to the agency, as well as agency interests in the larger social service context. When a worker is employed by the agency, an obligation exists to work on behalf of those served by the agency and to recognize how agency policies impact the clients being served. An obligation also exists to further the cause of the agency in the community in a manner that is consistent with a professional commitment to social justice.

5. *Practicing in an ethical manner.* Workers should abide by standards that are consistent not only with their profession's code of ethics but also with ethical practices mandated by the licensing statutes of the state within which they are practicing. They also should abide by ethical standards propagated by the agency and help their agency to operate in a manner that promotes clients' interests and well-being.

6. *Helping the group establish adaptive norms.* All groups develop norms that define how members work together. These norms may reflect rules specifically established by the leader or the leader and members together. They also will develop naturally as members interact with one another on a sustained basis. The worker has the responsibility to ensure that the normative culture is one that promotes the group's work. Members and the leader need to be able to modify group norms to enhance members'

abilities to achieve their goals. For example, talking about the shame associated with being a victim of domestic violence would be a necessary expectation in a group for survivors of intimate partner violence, yet members may have established a norm in which discussions of painful subjects is avoided.

7. *Self-disclosing in an appropriate manner.* The worker is always sharing something of herself or himself through dress, mannerisms, office décor, and the like. In its simplest form, an appropriate self-disclosure involves telling the group that one is a student or just finished one's master's degree, which is a necessary communication about one's training. Disclosing more personal information (one is married/partnered, has children, has a history of cancer, a parent with dementia, etc.) must be consistent with agency procedures and policies and should be used judiciously to advance the group, rather than meeting the needs of the worker. Members' personal disclosures are much more effective at promoting mutual aid and support than those of the worker. There are times, however, where the worker's disclosures can assist members in sharing with and supporting one another. For example, in a group for survivors of sex trafficking, members may have difficulty confronting their deep feelings of shame and humiliation. The leader may need to first share her or his feelings to pave the way for members to begin to discuss their own.

8. *Engaging group members in setting individual goals for themselves that are consistent with the purpose of the group.*

9. *Seeking feedback from the group.* Workers should inquire about how well members feel the group is working and what else they would like to have occur in the group. This includes feedback about the leader's actions and ideas about the direction the group is taking. While acknowledging their leadership role, workers should also help group members accept ownership for the group and its work.

10. *Demonstrating sensitivity to members' perspectives on change.* The meaning of time varies from one culture and from one individual to the next. "Soon" to one person may mean 30 minutes and to another person a few weeks in the future. Change, then, may be expected more quickly by some members than others. Members' conception of time frames (e.g., how long before I start to feel better?) should be addressed.

11. *Providing information to members that promotes growth and healing.* How one thinks about a problem affects how one feels and what one does about it. Gaining knowledge about the challenges that brought members to the group assists them in resolving these issues and is as important as discussing feelings. Examples include the following: in a group for parents at risk of abusing their children, teaching parents about normal developmental stages in young children; in a cancer

support group, informing cancer patients that depression is common following surgery; in a group that addresses eating disorders, helping young women and men understand societal pressures in relation to body image. The worker is not the only one who provides information to the group. Mutual aid is promoted when members offer insights, information, and suggestions to one another.

12. *Admitting a lack of knowledge or confusion about an issue.* Workers who believe they must be "all knowing" undermine group members' ability to admit that they do not know something and thereby set unrealistically high expectations about what members should know. When the worker does not have an answer to a question, has to do some research to obtain needed information, or must think about an answer before responding, she models for group members that they do not need to have an immediate answer to every question that arises or know everything. In addition, when the worker points out he is confused by something, it allows other members to be confused—a normal state for many clients who are dealing with complex situations where ambiguity is common.

13. *Using activity to promote the group's work and members' goals.* Group work is not always about talking. Activities, like art projects, music, and role playing, allow members to express and manage feelings in alternative, nonverbal ways and are especially helpful for children and adolescents. Adults can also benefit from activities such as mindfulness training and relaxation techniques that can assist members in the group and also can be carried over and utilized outside of the group. A variety of techniques are described throughout the chapters.

14. *Encouraging discussion of feelings and experiences.* Group members should be encouraged to share feelings, thoughts, and experiences that are consistent with the group's purpose and member goals. It is the worker's responsibility to redirect members when discussion detracts from, rather than supports, the work of the group. This often occurs when the group tackles a taboo topic, one that members seek to avoid rather than confront directly.

15. *Showing positive regard for the expression of feelings and thoughts.* The leader should encourage members to disclose relevant personal information and share difficult feelings, crediting them for their courage and willingness to take a risk. However, because the real therapeutic benefit of the group lies in the mutual aid that exists among members, the leader also should urge members to support and respond empathically to one another. This often involves pointing out underlying commonalities among members and reframing an individual member's disclosures so that they resonate with others in the group

16. *Normalizing members' feelings.* Members often assume they are different and alone with the challenges they face. Assuring members that their

experiences and feelings are understandable, normal, and expected reduces the sense of isolation. For example, by conveying to the returning Afghan conflict veteran that what he is feeling is typical given her combat experiences, the worker reassures (and educates) the veteran. Such reassurance helps the veteran feel more connected to and less isolated from others. Feelings and experiences also are normalized in a powerful way when the leader points out commonalities among members and encourages them to connect with and support one another. As members share their experiences, they become acutely aware that they are neither alone nor different. They discover that they are "all in the same boat."

17. *Reaching for members' feelings.* In many groups, the discussion of painful experiences and feelings is necessary to bring about change. The sharing of feelings can lead to catharsis and an opening up of previously taboo subjects. Members' disclosures also provide reassurance as they discover they are not alone, that others share their emotional reactions and experiences. The leader must be cautious when sensitive topics are raised by members or by the leader. Members need to feel safe and have the ability to manage their feelings without being flooded or retraumatized. The worker balances encouraging members to explore taboo topics against ensuring that they are capable of handling the reactions that will ensue. Starting the discussion by saying, "I know this may be painful today, but I think it is important that we talk about what it was like when you were first diagnosed with HIV; became aware you had a substance abuse issue; learned your family member had dementia," and so forth. This acknowledges at the beginning that the discussion to follow may be difficult but also demands necessary work from members.

18. *Partializing presenting problems.* In many instances, members will enter the group with a myriad of challenges and concerns. For example, in a group for individuals with a substance use disorder, members may also struggle with family conflict, problems at work, and mental health issues. A common skill in this case is asking members to examine their problems one at a time and to prioritize which one they would like to focus on first. Partializing concerns helps group members gain some sense of competence and control over the challenges they face.

19. *Demanding work of the group.* Much has been written about this key skill/technique and how the leader might confront members about behaviors and interactions that detract from or undermine the group's work. This can range from individual members who disregard group rules and norms and miss sessions to group-as-a-whole dynamics such as scapegoating and avoidance of work through superficial discussion of irrelevant topics. Although an in-depth discussion is beyond the purpose of this list of skills, the leader must be clear about the reasons for

demanding work and do it in a manner that promotes growth and is nonjudgmental. The leader who avoids this sort of confrontation may send the group a message that they do not have to work on the challenges that brought them to the group.

20. *Using programming effectively.* Programming (such as videos, speakers, role plays, or ice-breaking exercises) must be timed to fit with the group's developmental stage and the developmental stage of the members. Using an exercise that is too revealing too early in the group would be inappropriate just as ending a group with an initial ice-breaking exercise would be ill timed.

21. *Focusing on the here and now.* Although members will need to talk about the challenges they face and what brought them to the group, they often will also need to talk about how they work together in the here and now. For example, in a group for survivors of sexual abuse, members may talk about their mistrust of others as a result of their molestation. As they develop comfort with one another, they are likely to reveal this mistrust in their interactions with one another. Rather than talking about mistrust and hostility in the abstract, the leader can encourage members to examine their interactions with one another as they emerge in the session.

22. *Assisting members to resolve conflicts that emerge in the group.* Workers can assist with conflicts among group members during a meeting by having members process what is going on at the moment. Members can learn that conflict can be resolved in ways that don't involve physical or verbal aggression. To do this, the worker must help members listen and talk to one another in a respectful way. Members may be angry at one another; the challenge to the worker is to help them express and work through this anger in a way that is productive. Members may also learn that they can agree to disagree and that conflict does not have to result in pain, hurt feelings, or rejection. The leader also can assist with conflict resolution between group members and significant others outside of the group. For example, in the group for fathers who are incarcerated, members are taught to recognize when a cycle of negativity is developing over the telephone or during a visit and to take steps to short-circuit it and focus on the positive.

23. *Teaching the importance of "I" messages.* Members are encouraged to take responsibility for their thoughts and feelings. Members also are urged to speak only for themselves and not assume they know what others are thinking, feeling, or saying.

24. *Using national events to teach about human nature and social justice.* The death of Freddie Gray in Baltimore, for example, shootings at movie theaters, the aftermath of Hurricane Katrina, and the untimely deaths of famous people are all events that may be grist for the group's mill

when linked to the purpose of the group. For example, following the death of a well-known person at too young an age, a group could be asked how they wish to be remembered after they die.

25. *Monitoring changes in members.* It is important that the worker develop means through which the impact and effectiveness of the group may be determined. Brief questionnaires can be helpful in getting members to consider their own progress and the impact that the group has had and is having. An awareness of evidence-based practices in approaching the group's presenting problems can guide the worker in deciding which research instruments to use and how to apply them. The authors of each chapter provide suggestions for relevant instruments and useful ways to evaluate the group's impact and members' progress.

26. *Building and reenforcing self-esteem and competence.* A culture of support, acceptance, and understanding—all of which are elements of mutual aid—promotes the self-esteem of members. Furthermore, when members feel more in control of their emotions and achieve an understanding of the challenges they face, feelings of self-efficacy are enhanced.

27. *Remaining comfortable with ambivalence and ambiguity.* Not only are group members sometimes unsure about their desire to change (ambivalence), but easy answers often are not available (ambiguity). Group members and workers need to become comfortable with the fact that most problems and their solutions are not black or white, but rather reflect shades of gray. This lack of certainty is a fact of life that members—and the worker—must accept, remaining flexible in their approaches to themselves and others.

We believe that these skills can be applied across populations and group purposes. Although the emphasis may appear to be on the use of these skills in clinical groups, many of them are appropriate in community organizing and task-oriented groups. Ethical leadership is not confined to any one setting or approach nor is using an ecological perspective on how and why to provide service. Positive regard for others is the sine qua non of social work and other helping professions. As new populations arise with new challenges, we hope the skills learned in this volume can be adapted to meet the needs of future underserved groups of clients.

Part One

Health Issues

Chapter Four

Group Work With People Who Have Cancer

Steven R. Rose and Megumi Inoue

Cancer is a set of diseases that often have major psychological, physiological, and social consequences for patients, as well as for their families and friends. Lifestyle changes, such as increasing the consumption of fruit and vegetables and becoming more physically active, and reducing or avoiding overeating, smoking, alcohol, the sun, and risky sexual behavior, lower the risk of cancer (Spring, King, Pagoto, Van Horn, & Fisher, 2015). The increased prevalence of overweight and obesity among children, adolescents, and adults portends more cases of cancer in the future.

Cancer strikes differentially by demographic factors, including gender, socioeconomic background, race, and age. In the United States, men have a 1:2 lifetime probability of developing cancer, and women have a 1:3 lifetime probability (Groopman, 2007). African Americans are more likely to die of cancer than are Whites, and men are more likely to die of cancer than are women. The American Cancer Society estimated that about 1.6 million new cases of cancer will be diagnosed in the United States in 2015. Furthermore, the American Cancer Society estimated that about 312,150 cancer deaths of men and 277,280 cancer deaths of women would occur in 2015 in the United States, of which lung cancer remains the most common type of fatal cancer for both men and women.

Cancer is a pervasive illness, and the American Cancer Society estimates that three of four families are affected by cancer during the course of a lifetime (Veach, Nicholas, & Barton, 2002). Although the treatment of cancer has become more successful in recent years, the emotional impact on individuals and their families remains great (Edwards & Clarke, 2004). While half of all patients with cancer survived for at least 5 years in 1975–1977, two of three survived for that interval in 2004–2010 (American Cancer Society, 2015a).

A cancer diagnosis is considered to be one of the most feared and serious events of an individual's life. It produces significant stress on all individuals involved (Daste, 1990; Edwards & Clarke, 2004). Before diagnosis, the individual normally experiences illness that progresses to the point where malignancy is suspected. Following this period of illness, the individual is subjected to physiological tests that determine whether cancer is present. The stages that follow diagnosis often include surgery and/or treatment, such as chemotherapy or radiotherapy; evaluation of the patient's prognosis; and medical follow-up. During each of the stages of cancer detection, diagnosis, and treatment, patients face challenging issues, including a sense of threat to their lives, changed self-image, psychological distress, social isolation, and need for social support (Spiegel & Classen, 2000). Patients are often concerned about the implications of the disease for their future quality of life and for their relationships with family members and friends. In addition, they normally experience a wide spectrum of emotions, including anger, fear, sadness, guilt, embarrassment, and shame. Young adults are likely to struggle with anxiety about their self-esteem, physical well-being, sexuality, fertility, and childrearing, which are uniquely associated with their developmental stages (Evan, Kaufman, Cook, & Zeltzer, 2006).

Patients with cancer often express anger at their fate. Anger is frequently directed at the medical staff, who first inform the patient of the disease or treat the patient over the course of the illness, and at family members, who attempt to protect, coddle, or treat the patient differently than they did before the cancer diagnosis. Sadness and depression, which are commonly experienced by patients with cancer, emanate from many sources. The latter include resignation about uncompleted tasks or goals, as well as fear and isolation often resulting from the disease. Physical losses associated with breast, colon, or laryngeal cancer may lead to depression. Often the patient with cancer is unable to discuss fears and emotions with family members, thereby increasing a sense of isolation. Studies have reported that both self-help and therapy groups for patients with cancer allow the expression of fears, as of death, and that such expression has numerous positive effects on the patients' sense of well-being and self-esteem (Omylinska-Thurston & Cooper, 2014; Stang & Mittelmark, 2010).

Patients who undergo radical surgical or treatment procedures that leave visible scars or signs of the disease are susceptible to embarrassment and shame. For example, appliances used by patients with a colostomy often have side effects such as odor, which can cause the patient great embarrassment (Persson & Hellström, 2002). Mastectomy or prostatectomy can cause patients to feel less sexually attractive and desirable to their spouses or lovers (Arrington, 2000; Holmberg, Scott, Alexy, & Fife, 2001).

Changes in bodily function resulting from such procedures also require adjustment by the patient, as well as for family members and friends. These changes can serve as a major inconvenience in planning daily activities, as well as limiting access to activities in which the person previously participated.

Studies have documented the need for social support both as a means of preventing disease and as a factor in recovery from illness (Hurdle, 2001). In dealing with the issues and emotions related to the diagnosis of cancer, family members and friends of the patient can serve as important sources of support (Palmer et al., 2000). However, family members or friends sometimes become overwhelmed with the patient's crisis and withdraw to protect themselves and to deal with their own emotional issues (Daste, 1989). If the supporting person and the patient have had previous relationship difficulties, the former may make attempts to rectify the situation for his or her own benefit without necessarily considering the needs or wishes of the patient. For example, a spouse who is about to leave a failed marriage decides to remain in it ostensibly to protect the patient but in reality to avoid the prospect of facing immense personal guilt. In other situations, family members attempt to support the patient but actually contribute to the patient's emotional distress (Daste, 1990). For example, this occurs when they attempt to treat the patient in the ways they would want to be treated in similar circumstances while ignoring the requests or desires of the patient to be treated as he or she wishes.

Both juvenile and adult patients with cancer often are reluctant to express their fear and sadness with family members because of their desire to protect the family (Daste, 1990; Price, 1992). Siblings of juvenile patients with cancer often experience negative emotions and are unlikely to express these emotions to family members (Evans, Stevens, Cushway, & Houghton, 1992). Kaufman and colleagues (1992) report that cancer diagnoses in children may exacerbate existing problems in dysfunctional families, and the resulting stress can increase the child's illness.

Complementary and alternative methods are increasingly being used in the United States by people with cancer. Support groups are one of the complementary methods frequently used by cancer survivors (Gansler, Kaw, Crammer, & Smith, 2008). Support groups were reported to be used by 9.7% of a sample of 4,139 survivors of 1 of 10 cancers that occur in adults.

Support or self-help groups designed to address the specific needs of patients with cancer and/or their families allow the patient to receive support and express emotions in a nonjudgmental and safe environment. These groups can provide education about the disease and about methods or techniques the patient can use to alleviate stress, anxiety, and depression (Forester, Kornfeld, Fleiss, & Thompson, 1993; Montazeri et al., 2001; Vugia, 1991). Techniques such as visual imagery, self-hypnotic therapy, deep muscle relaxation, and systematic desensitization can also help to counteract the side effects of treatment methods such as chemotherapy (Forester et al., 1993; Harmon, 1991).

To increase the likelihood that patients will attend and participate in cancer support groups, social workers should consider involving the support network of the patient with cancer (Sherman et al., 2008). The social worker should also weigh a wide range of individual and group factors, including the cancer patient identity, practical issues, coping styles, the match between the patient and the group, knowledge of and referral to groups, and solving problems experienced by particular groups (Ussher, Kirsten, Butow, & Sandoval, 2008). Indeed, participation in support groups may be increased by involving the support network of the patient with cancer (Sherman et al., 2008).

Self-help groups are prevalent (Gray & Fitch, 2001). Lieberman (1988) reported that client-led self-help groups appear to have "meaningful roles in helping individuals with psychosocial problems" (p. 168). Empirical studies of professionally led face-to-face cancer support groups for adults indicated that participants tended to be very satisfied with them (Gottlieb & Wachala, 2007). The groups were associated with improvements in morale and quality of life.

Studies attempt to substantiate the effectiveness of one group treatment method over another. Telch and Telch (1986) wrote that supportive group therapy is the most widely used and most intensively studied form of treatment. They concluded that groups that provide intensive coping skills are more effective than traditional supportive group therapy. Helgeson and colleagues (1999) showed the superiority of education groups to peer discussion groups in yielding greater perceptions of vitality, social and physical functioning, fewer role limitations, and marginal effects on general health. In a critical review of the literature, Edelman, Craig, and Kidman (2000) concluded that most of the evidence supports the view that patients who participate in psychoeducational groups receive more benefit than those who participate in groups that are purely supportive. Although a group may be primarily designed to provide education, psychological intervention is typically needed by group members. In a randomized controlled trial, Spiegel and colleagues (1989) showed that a 1-year intervention of supportive group therapy with self-hypnosis for pain was associated with greater longevity for patients with metastatic breast cancer. Fawzy et al. (1993) designed a structured short-term intervention that provided psychological support, disease education, and the development of stress management and coping skills. They showed that men and women with melanoma who took part in the intervention had significantly greater survival and reduced recurrence 5 to 6 years later and increased number and activity of melanoma-fighting natural killer cells.

PRACTICE PRINCIPLES

The practice principles that apply to group work with patients with cancer are similar to those that apply to group work in general. However, the issues that patients with cancer typically face tend to differ from those of other populations and should be kept in mind when composing and facilitating groups. One issue is the treatment status of each group member. Patients who receive chemotherapy or radiation therapy routinely experience side effects such as nausea, pain, or extreme fatigue. During this phase of their cancer treatment, these patients' attendance in groups can be irregular, and they tend to be disoriented and distracted.

Contracting requires much flexibility; contracts should be tailored to each individual member. Given the nature and effects of cancer and its treatment, social workers must strive to understand when members can and cannot attend and participate, and continue to accept them in the group and encourage members to attend and participate.

Termination of these groups often entails flexibility, too. Often, members cannot predict with accuracy when and for how long they can continue to attend. Some groups formed expressly for terminally ill patients with cancer are open groups and continue to function after the deaths of individual members.

Religion can significantly affect the sense of purpose and hope of patients with cancer. Their religious or spiritual orientation may affect their acceptance of various aspects of the disease. In addition, the religion or spirituality of significant others can affect how patients with cancer relate to them. Other factors that are important to group work with patients with cancer include stage of the disease, type of cancer, amount of physical distress, age, level and quality of support from family and friends, the development of mental disorders related to cancer, terminal versus nonterminal status, size of the group, and training of the leaders (Daste, 1990). For example, skilled group leadership has been shown to be an important factor in the success of prostate cancer support groups (Oliffe, Ogrodniczuk, Bottorff, Hislop, & Halpin, 2009).

STAGE OF THE DISEASE

There are many types of cancer that are treatable and curable with early detection. For example, survival rates for skin cancer, breast cancer, and cervical cancer are quite high when they are found at a localized stage (Siegel, Naishadham, & Jemal, 2012). Moreover, some cancers, such as prostate cancer, grow very slowly (American Cancer Society, 2015b), and many patients live with such types of cancer as a chronic condition. However, some types of cancers, such as ovarian cancer and pancreatic cancer, are harder to detect at early stages because their symptoms often do not appear until the advanced stages.

A person's stage of cancer is important to consider when a group is formed because the issues faced by people who are undergoing a curative treatment process or in remission are dramatically different from those of people who are terminally ill. People receiving curative treatment may be suffering from side effects of cancer, dealing with the stigma attached to a cancer-related change in body image, or struggling with maintaining their roles in family and society. The primary concern for people whose cancer is in remission may be the potential recurrence of the disease. On the other hand, people who are approaching the end-of-life stage may be more concerned about their impending death, the process of dying, and the implications of these events for their family and friends. Understandably, patients who are dying may feel envious or resent those whose prognosis is more hopeful. Considering the different issues that patients with a chronic condition experience and those with a terminal condition face, forming a group of patients within a certain stage of cancer would be helpful to maintain greater cohesion in a group (Spiegel & Classen, 2000). Simonton and Sherman (2000) developed a treatment model that addresses patients with various stages of the disease.

DIFFERENCES AMONG AFFECTED GROUPS

Particular types of cancer often have specific implications for group composition. Patients with similar cancers often have similar issues and can relate readily to other patients with the same concerns (Spiegel & Classen, 2000). Patients with breast cancer who have issues related to their sexuality and their perceived loss of femininity tend to feel more comfortable discussing such issues with other patients with breast cancer (Chaves, Haddock, & Rubin, 2014). Persons who have had sarcoma of a limb may have lost an arm or a leg due to amputation or have experienced more limited use of the limb. Issues such as limited mobility may arise among some of these individuals. Patients often appreciate talking with people who know what they are encountering (Spiegel & Classen, 2000).

Cancer, while having similar implications for all patients, strikes a heterogeneous group of individuals. Furthermore, age and stage of life are important considerations that differentiate responses to cancer and have implications for group work. Clearly, pediatric cancer patients require a group setting that is age appropriate and allows them to discuss their unique concerns. Adolescents with cancer are particularly vulnerable. They commonly experience many important losses and changes, including their former selves (prediagnosis person and prediagnosis family); relationships with parents, siblings, and girlfriends/boyfriends; body image; health; school life; independence; certainty about and indications of the future; and hope (Stevens & Dunsmore, 1996). Also, adult patients who are at different stages in life may feel more accepted by those in a similar life stage. They may be better able to deal with issues that suit their particular needs.

These issues and many other related concerns need to be kept in mind by the social worker. All such issues are often discussed with patients before they enter a group in order to offset the possible occurrence of problems at a later date.

LEVELS OF SUPPORT

Support from family and friends affects the morale of the patient with cancer and can be an important factor in group work. Those patients who have less support available to them than do other patients are liable to feel even more depressed and alone in groups where family members and friends are allowed to attend. The social worker should be aware of situations where some patients may not have any supportive family members or friends while other patients seem to have an abundance of such support. One way of preventing the occurrence of this problem is to have separate groups for patients and for family members. As well meaning as family and friends may be, there are issues for which their attendance will inhibit discussion. For example, some patients may feel more comfortable discussing sexual issues among fellow patients without family and friends being in attendance.

There appears to be a relationship between level of support and benefits from group work. One study showed that peer discussion groups were helpful for women with breast cancer who lacked support elsewhere but were not helpful for women who had high levels of outside support (Helgeson, Cohen, Schulz, & Yasko, 2000).

MENTAL DISORDERS

Although in some cases mental disorders are present before the cancer diagnosis, patients often develop such disorders as a result of the disease (Linden, Vodermaier, MacKenzie, & Greig, 2012). Major depressive disorder, associated with significant impairment in functioning, is the most common mental disorder among patients with breast cancer (Hopko et al., 2015). These disorders may be either new mental disorders and/or an exacerbation of previously existing disorders. These factors should be considered by the social worker who composes and facilitates the group. The appropriateness of including patients with major mental disorders should be considered in terms of their ability to interact with other members, engage in the group process, and benefit from it. Furthermore, the locus and type of treatment of mental disorders must be considered.

SIZE OF THE GROUP

Group size can have an impact on the effectiveness and level of intimacy within a group. Spiegel and Yalom (1978), in reporting on their group of patients with metastatic carcinoma, noted that the maximum effective size was seven. When the size of the group reached more than eight, the group was subdivided into two smaller groups (Spiegel & Yalom, 1978). Similarly, in a program designed by Cunningham and colleagues (1991), educational groups ranged in size from 12 to 15 members, but these groups were later subdivided to facilitate discussion (p. 44). Smaller groups are usually more cohesive and develop closer bonds than do larger groups (Daste, 1990).

Group size is often related to other issues, such as the presence of supportive family members and friends. As previously mentioned, the advisability of having family members present during discussions of subjects that the patients want to discuss privately should also be appraised.

WORKER SELF-AWARENESS

Practitioner self-awareness is an important aspect of providing high-quality, professional health care (Epstein, 1999). Among the most important issues in group work with patients with cancer is the social worker's personal orientation to the disease. Often, the person diagnosed with cancer is afraid of death and dying. Because of its importance, it is often necessary for the practitioner to address this issue within the group. Consequently, the practitioner needs to face his or her own feelings regarding death (Firestone & Catlett, 2009). Often the full impact of this issue occurs when one is faced with it personally. This can be a very lonely time, and the issue becomes an existential one as opposed to an interpersonal one. Even in a group setting, members can feel alone and will require a lot of empathic understanding.

The social worker's interaction with the group should be clearly conceptualized and described in the planning phase of the group. The literature is divided on the role of the group facilitator. In a number of groups studied, the role is to educate the group members, whereas in other groups, researchers contend that it is to assist the members in expressing their emotions about their disease. Cunningham et al. (1991) noted that psychological interventions in cancer groups are becoming increasingly common. However, Vugia (1991) considered the role of leaders in self-help support groups as aiding members while allowing the members to maintain some authority (p. 94).

OPEN VERSUS CLOSED GROUPS

Opinions vary among professionals about whether cancer groups should be open or closed. The issue of open versus closed groups depends on the population being served. Both types of groups have advantages and disadvantages. Open groups, for example, allow more utilization, whereas closed groups provide a more intimate atmosphere and allow for more in-depth discussion of sensitive topics.

The literature indicates that cancer groups frequently are open, allowing new members to enter at any time (Daste, 1989). However, other research concludes that groups should be closed to new members after the first few sessions to enhance cohesion of the group and to "allow progressive work and promote good attendance" (Cunningham et al., 1991, p. 44).

Davidson (1985) notes that *burnout* is especially applicable to those working in the field of oncology because death and the threat of death create a large emotional burden. Group work with patients with cancer is challenging and often very trying (Daste, 1990). Persons who conduct group work with patients with cancer should be prepared to discuss such topics as death, dying, disfigurement, pain, and loss of function. Harmon (1991) presents the experience of one group in which a member died and the leaders consequently attempted to prevent the group from acknowledging or discussing it. Yalom and Greaves (1977) found that in their group, the therapists contributed to superficial group interaction because they felt that such topics might be too threatening for patients when, in reality, they were protecting themselves. According to Fobair (1997), open groups, such as drop-in groups, and closed groups, such as supportive-expressive existentialist groups, span a continuum.

COMMON THEMES

Some of the themes that social workers should keep in mind when conducting group work with patients with cancer include the following:

1. Fear of death
2. Fear of disease recurrence
3. Unique problems related to the long- and short-term effects of treatment
4. Changes in personal relationships
5. Economic issues

Other themes in conducting groups with patients with cancer include problems such as changes in sexual function during treatment, partners' reactions to loss of breasts or scarring, and loss of fertility due to some types of chemotherapy. Each of these problems has interpersonal manifestations that become significant in a group setting.

Fear of Death

Although cancer is a more treatable and survivable illness today than in the past, a cancer diagnosis frequently implies the possibility of death. Given cancer mortality rates, the patient's fear of death is often realistic. However, as noted earlier, some cancers are more treatable than others.

As noted, often the patient's family or friends are also frightened by the diagnosis. Sometimes they inhibit the patient from discussing the possibility of death. However, group work can provide the patient with the forum for discussing it. Some authors have reported that patients' anxiety about death was often lessened when they were able to connect on a transcendent or spiritual level (Cunningham et al., 1991). Similarly, Spiegel (1992) found that allowing patients to discuss the possibility of death and its attendant anxieties lessened their fear of death and dying.

Fear of Disease Recurrence

Most patients with cancer experience a fear of recurrence of the disease. This is especially manifested for varying periods of time following initial diagnosis and treatment. Whenever a new pain occurs, an unexplained lump appears, a cough begins, or one of many other conditions arises, the patient with cancer will typically fear the worst. This is perhaps the single most difficult part of coping for those who have had cancer. It is as if a sword hangs over the patient's head from the time of initial diagnosis until the day he or she dies, even though the disease may never reappear. The fear of recurrence becomes a focal point, particularly for patients with cancer who have survived the initial cancer and are in remission.

Long- and Short-Term Effects of Treatment

Other common themes with patients with cancer are the short- and long-term effects of chemotherapy and radiation therapy, such as hair loss. Nausea and vomiting and the inability to maintain earlier eating patterns become recurrent themes.

Interpersonal Relationships

Interpersonal relationships often change when cancer enters the picture. Multiple interpersonal manifestations often provide surprises for group members. Some people with cancer become distanced from friends and family members. Some face constant questioning from others about the cancer, even when they would rather not talk about it. Some people find that their choice of partners becomes more limited, frequently due to fears about the patient's future. This problem may continue long after the person has survived cancer. Some experience either overprotectiveness or distancing from spouses or lovers.

Economic Issues

Often, financial issues have arisen for people with cancer in the US health care system. First, working persons who have taken time off from work associated with their cancer treatment have faced a loss of income if they were unable to make up the missed work in a manner that was acceptable to their employer. Lost wages often created difficulty for many persons with cancer who were faced with covering costs of living. Second, the cost of care frequently exceeded insurance benefits such that even those with insurance tended to be faced with considerable financial hardship. Moreover, insurance companies sometimes attempted to drop clients who were proving very costly to continue to cover. Third, those persons who were fortunate to survive cancer often had great difficulty obtaining or transferring insurance plans due to preexisting condition limitations. Insurance generally became difficult or impossible to obtain following a cancer diagnosis, thereby limiting job mobility (Nessim &

Ellis, 2000). Fourth, patients with cancer and survivors also reported job discrimination in hiring, promotion, and job assignments. Any person who has undergone treatment for cancer is considered legally handicapped and thus has some protection from job discrimination. However, this does not necessarily prevent the occurrence of discrimination.

RECOMMENDED WAYS OF WORKING

The cardinal practice principle is that social workers will be more effective if they compose and structure their groups to best meet the needs of the particular patients with cancer and/or survivors they wish to serve. Rather than placing everyone with a cancer diagnosis into a large group, it is far more beneficial to tailor each group to the specific needs of the prospective members. For example, 8- to 12-year-old children who have undergone chemotherapy or radiotherapy have different concerns than do women dying of breast cancer. People who have been cancer-free for 5 years have a different set of concerns than people who have had a recurrence of the disease in that time span.

To a large extent, the population served in the human service organization (HSO) will determine group composition. For example, a large hospital in a major metropolitan area usually has far more latitude in the numbers and types of groups that it can offer than does a small rural clinic, which may have to offer such groups in concert with other HSOs. The organizational context also determines other group parameters, including size, space considerations, availability of co-leaders, advocacy of services, and the accessibility of ancillary services such as delivery of meals or hospice care.

Group length often has to be tried and tailored to each HSO and the population it serves. Many social workers experience difficulty when they initially specify a certain number of sessions only to discover subsequently that the members, due to difficulties related to their cancer care or other factors related to their illness, find it difficult to work with the preset format. Many HSOs simply offer one large long-term group for all patients and significant others. This approach avoids many selection, time, and member availability issues because the group meets on a regular basis for all who care to attend. However, it also limits the potential that smaller, more carefully planned groups offer.

Group work can be challenging. A case illustrating one of the problems of a large group that is open to all is as follows:

During the weekly meeting of a large support group offered for patients with cancer, friends, and families by a metropolitan treatment center, several newly diagnosed persons attended for the first time. John, a regular member, was suffering from a brain tumor and tended to dominate conversations without allowing others to speak. For this reason, the new members, who were uncomfortable in the group and who were very much in need of support, were denied an opportunity to participate.

The leader must be able to handle difficulties that emerge in such groups. A co-leader pattern is usually preferable to having one leader of the group for patients with cancer. Co-leadership has many advantages over an individual worker pattern, assuming that the co-leaders work well together. For instance, if one worker is absent, the group can still meet. Coworkers can complement and help each other in providing both technical expertise and emotional support. Co-leadership allows more individual attention to be given to distraught members—one worker can attend to the individual while the other attends to the group process.

One key advantage of a coworker pattern with these groups is that it allows the workers to deal with personal crises, which are often severe and require additional attention. If only one worker is present, the group as a whole must wait or must deal with the crises as a whole. In another type of therapy group this might be appropriate, but due to the nature of cancer and the potential for sudden life-or-death issues arising, the fear and panic may be so great that individual intervention is warranted. A case illustrating how co-leadership might be beneficial is as follows:

During one of the sessions of a support group for women survivors of breast cancer, Jackie, who had been doing fine following breast cancer that was diagnosed and treated 2 years earlier, had just learned that her cancer had recurred. She bravely and patiently waited her turn to talk but finally felt overwhelmed by her fear, jumped up, and ran from the room. One of the co-leaders took off after her and spent a lot of time calming her down, as Jackie felt unable to return to the group. The other co-leader was able to continue without her.

EVALUATION MEASURES

Researchers have used many different methods to measure the effectiveness of groups in producing tangible benefits to patients. Instruments are available that measure quality of life, body image, self-esteem, support, and perceived personal control over illness (Helgeson, Cohen, Schulz, & Yasko, 2000). Scales such as those that measure quality of adjustment, stress levels, affect, optimism regarding disease treatment, and overall sensations of pain, discomfort, and anxiety are useful in determining the effectiveness of a cancer group (Goodwin et al., 2001).

In a group organized by Goodwin and colleagues (2001), women with metastatic breast cancer were found to have less tension, depression, anger, confusion, and pain than their control group counterparts a year after randomization. In a postsurgery study of self-perception of women who had a mastectomy, Clarke and colleagues (1982) divided 40 patients into treatment and control groups. Ten weekly group psychotherapy sessions were offered. The authors used Q-sort tests and the Structured and Scaled Interview to Assess Maladjustment. Although both groups showed positive change, the treatment group showed significantly greater improvement.

Other studies, such as one conducted by Kriss and Kraemer (1986), have examined patients periodically over several time periods—for example, three times over 12 months—to determine possible changes following group treatment. Longitudinal studies covering longer periods are also appropriate in determining changes following group treatment.

Many ways exist to conduct research in this area. Both quantitative and qualitative methods are useful in assessing changes. Qualitative research on how cancer is experienced by patients and their families is useful in developing social workers' understanding and empathy, which is necessary for practice (Oktay, 2002). Questionnaires and scales measuring factors such as depression, fear, and coping can be administered. Recording group attendance, degree of participation, and demographic representation by various ethnic/racial and socioeconomic groups will yield data that are useful to the social worker. Research questions should be addressed as early as possible to allow for gathering and analysis of more potential data. Much depends on what the social worker wants to know about the group members and how they cope with cancer.

CONCLUSION

Progress is occurring in the diagnosis and treatment of cancer. Some cancers are like chronic diseases that are not very likely to directly cause a person's death, whereas others are significantly more dangerous. Nevertheless, cancer remains a dreaded disease that places a great deal of emotional and physical stress on patients, their families, and their friends. Many issues involving human relationships emerge when cancer appears. Usually, people with cancer have specific pressing concerns. This further mandates the need for groups designed to meet the specific needs of this population. In some groups, the social worker provides education and/or psychological intervention. Common themes among group members who are patients with cancer provide a basis for group discussion. The social worker must be flexible from the initial conceptualization of the group all the way to termination. Situations that are difficult to handle in a large, open group are often easier for the social worker to manage in a smaller, more carefully selected group.

AUTHOR NOTE

This chapter is dedicated to the memory of Barry M. Daste (1943–2010).

RESOURCES

American Brain Tumor Association
8550 W. Bryn Mawr Ave., Suite 550
Chicago, IL 60631
773-577-8750
800-886-2282
Fax: 773-577-8738
info@abta.org
www.abta.org

American Cancer Society
250 Williams Street NW
Atlanta, GA 30303
Cancer Answer Line: 800-227-2345
www.cancer.org

American Institute for Cancer Research
1759 R Street NW
Washington, DC 20009
202-328-7744
800-843-8114
Fax: 202-328-7226
aicrweb@aicr.org
www.aicr.org

American Childhood Cancer Organization
10400 Connecticut Avenue, Suite 205
Kensington, MD 20895
301-962-3520
800-366-2223
Fax: 301-962-3521
staff@acco.org
www.acco.org

Colorectal Cancer Network
P.O. Box 182
Kensington, MD 20895
301-879-1500
Fax: 301-879-1901
CCNetwork@colorectal-cancer.net
www.colorectal-cancer.net

CureSearch for Children's Cancer
4600 East-West Highway
Suite 600
Bethesda, MD 20814
800-458-6223
Fax: 301-718-0047
info@curesearch.org
www.curesearch.org

Kidney Cancer Association
1234 Sherman Avenue, Suite 203
Evanston, IL 60202
847-332-1051
800-850-9132
Fax: 847-332-2978
office@kidneycancer.org
www.kidneycancer.org

National Breast Cancer Coalition
1010 Vermont Avenue, NW, Suite 900
Washington, DC 20005
202-296-7477
800-622-2838
Fax: 202-265-6854
www.breastcancerdeadline2020.org

National Children's Cancer Society
500 North Broadway, Suite 800
St. Louis, MO 63102
314-241-1600
Fax: 314-241-1996
www.thenccs.org/

National Foundation for Cancer Research
4600 East West Highway, Suite 525
Bethesda, MD 20814
301-654-1250
800-321-CURE
Fax: 301-654-5824
info@nfcr.org
www.nfcr.org

National Ovarian Cancer Coalition, Inc.
2501 Oak Lawn Avenue, Suite 435
Dallas, TX 75219
214-273-4200
888-OVARIAN
Fax: 214-273-4201
NOCC@ovarian.org
www.ovarian.org

Support for People with Oral and Head and Neck Cancer
P.O. Box 53
Locust Valley, NY 11560
800-377-0928
Fax: 516-671-8794
info@spohnc.org
www.spohnc.org

REFERENCES

American Cancer Society. (2015a). *Cancer facts and figures 2015.* Retrieved from http://
www.cancer.org/acs/groups/content/@editorial/documents/document/acspc-
044552.pdf
American Cancer Society. (2015b). *Prostate cancer overview.* Retrieved from http://www.
cancer.org/acs/groups/cid/documents/webcontent/003072-pdf.pdf
Arrington, M. I. (2000). Sexuality, society, and senior citizens: An analysis of sex
talk among prostate cancer support group members. *Sexuality and Culture,*
4(4), 45–74.
Chaves, J., Haddock, C. M., & Rubin, L. R. (2014). Contextualizing African American
and Latina women's postmastectomy social support experiences: Support groups
and beyond. *Women and Therapy, 37,* 242–263.
Clarke, D. L., Kramer, E., Lipiec, K., & Klein, S. (1982). Group psychotherapy with
mastectomy patients. *Psychotherapy: Theory, Research, and Practice, 19*(3), 331–334.

Cunningham, A. J., Edmonds, C., Hampson, A., Hanson, H., Hovanec, M., Jenkins, G., & Tocco, E. (1991). A group psychoeducational program to help cancer patients cope with and combat their disease. *Journal of Mind-Body Health*, *7*(3), 41–56.

Daste, B. (1989). Designing cancer groups for maximum effectiveness. *Groupwork*, *2*(1), 58–69.

Daste, B. (1990). Important considerations in group work with cancer patients. *Social Work with Groups*, *13*(2), 69–81.

Davidson, K. W. (1985). Social work with cancer patients: Stresses and coping patterns. *Social Work in Health Care*, *10*(4), 73–82.

Edelman, S., Craig, A., & Kidman, A. D. (2000). Group interventions with cancer patients: Efficacy of psychoeducational versus supportive groups. *Journal of Psychosocial Oncology*, *18*, 67–85.

Edwards, B., & Clarke, V. (2004). The psychological impact of a cancer diagnosis on families: The influence of family functioning and patients' illness characteristics on depression and anxiety. *Psycho-Oncology*, *13*, 562–576. doi:10.1002/pon.773

Epstein, R. M. (1999). Mindful practice. *Journal of the American Medical Association*, *282*(9), 833–839.

Evan, E. E., Kaufman, M., Cook, A. B., & Zeltzer, L. K. (2006). Sexual health and self-esteem in adolescents and young adults with cancer. *Cancer*, *107*(S7), 1672–1679.

Evans, C. A., Stevens, M., Cushway, D., & Houghton, J. (1992). Sibling response to childhood cancer: A new approach. *Child Care, Health and Development*, *18*, 229–244.

Fawzy, F. I., Fawzy, N. W., Hyun, C., Elashoff, R., Guthrie, D., Fahey, J. L., & Morton, D. L. (1993). Malignant melanoma: Effects of an early structured psychiatric intervention, coping, and affective state on recurrence and survival 6 years later. *Archives of General Psychiatry*, *50*, 681–689.

Firestone, R., & Catlett, J. (2009). *Beyond death anxiety: Achieving life-affirming death awareness*. New York, NY: Springer.

Fobair, P. (1997). Cancer support groups and group therapies: Part I. Historical and theoretical background and research on effectiveness. *Journal of Psychosocial Oncology*, *15*(1), 63–81.

Forester, B., Kornfeld, D. S., Fleiss, J. L., & Thompson, S. (1993). Group psychotherapy during radiotherapy: Effects on emotional and physical distress. *American Journal of Psychiatry*, *150*(11), 1700–1706.

Gansler, T., Kaw, C., Crammer, C., & Smith, T. (2008). A population-based study of prevalence of complementary methods use by cancer survivors: A report from the American Cancer Society's studies of cancer survivors. *Cancer*, *113*(5), 1048–1057.

Gelgeson, V. S., Cohen, S., Schulz, R., & Yasko, J. (2000). Group support interventions for women with breast cancer: Who benefits from what? *Health Psychology*, *19*(2), 107–114.

Goodwin, P. J., Leszcz, M., Ennis, M., Koopmans, J., Vincent, L., Guther, H., . . . Hunter, J. (2001). The effect of group psychosocial support on survival in metastatic breast cancer. *New England Journal of Medicine*, *345*(24), 1719–1726.

Gottlieb, B. H., & Wachala, E. D. (2007). Cancer support groups: A critical review of empirical studies. *Psycho-Oncology*, *16*(5), 379–400.

Gray, R. E., & Fitch, M. (2001). Cancer self-help groups are here to stay: Issues and challenges for health professionals. *Journal of Palliative Care, 17*(1), 53–58.

Groopman, J. G. (2007). *How doctors think.* Boston, MA: Houghton Mifflin.

Harmon, M. (1991). The use of group psychotherapy with cancer patients: A review of recent literature. *Journal for Specialists in Group Work, 16*(1), 56–61.

Helgeson,V. S., Cohen, S., Schulz, R., & Yasko, J. (1999). Education and peer discussion group interventions and adjustment to breast cancer. *Archives of General Psychiatry, 56,* 340–347.

Helgeson, V. S., Cohen, S., Schulz, R., & Yasko, J. (2000). Group support interventions for women with breast cancer: Who benefits from what? *Health Psychology, 19*(2), 107–114.

Holmberg, S., Scott, L., Alexy, W., & Fife, B. (2001). Relationship issues of women with breast cancer. *Cancer Nursing, 24*(1), 53–60.

Hopko, D. R., Cannity, K., McIndoo, C. C., File, A. A., Ryba, M. M., Clark, C G., & Bell, J. L. (2015). Behavior therapy for depressed breast cancer patients: Predictors of treatment outcome. *Journal of Consulting and Clinical Psychology, 83,* 225–231.

Hurdle, D. E. (2001). Social support: A critical factor in women's health and health promotion. *Health and Social Work, 26*(2), 72–79.

Kaufman, K. L., Harbeck, C., Olson, R., & Nitschke, R. (1992). The availability of psychosocial interventions to children with cancer and their families. *Children's Health Care, 21*(1), 21–25.

Kriss, R. T., & Kraemer, H. C. (1986). Efficacy of group therapy for problems with post-mastectomy self-perception, body image, and sexuality. *Journal of Sex Research, 22*(4), 438–451.

Lieberman, M. A. (1988). The role of self-help groups in helping patients and families cope with cancer. *Ca–A Cancer Journal for Clinicians, 38*(3), 162–168.

Linden, W., Vodermaier, A., MacKenzie, R., & Greig, D. (2012). Anxiety and depression after cancer diagnosis: Prevalence rates by cancer type, gender, and age. *Journal of Affective Disorders, 141,* 343–351.

Montazeri, A., Jarvande, S., Haghighat, S., Vadhami, M., Sajadian, A., Elrahimi, M., & Haji-Mahmoodi, M. (2001). Anxiety and depression in breast cancer patients before and after participation in a cancer support group. *Patient Education and Counseling, 45*(3), 195–198.

Nessim, S., & Ellis, J. (2000). *Can survive: Reclaiming your life after cancer.* Boston, MA: Houghton Mifflin.

Oktay, J. S. (2002). Standards for qualitative research with exemplars. In A. R. Roberts & G. J. Greene (Eds.), *Social workers' desk reference* (pp. 781–786). Oxford, UK: Oxford University Press.

Oliffe, J. L., Ogrodniczuk, J., Bottorff, J. L., Hislop, T. G., & Halpin, M. (2009). Connecting humor, health, and masculinities at prostate cancer support groups. *Psycho-Oncology, 18*(9), 916–926.

Omylinska-Thurston, J., & Cooper, M. (2014). Helpful processes in psychological therapy for patients with primary cancers: A qualitative interview study. *Counseling and Psychotherapy Research, 14*(2), 84–92.

Palmer, L., Erickson, S., Shaffer, T., Coopman, C., Amylon, M., & Steiner, H. (2000). Themes arising in group therapy for adolescents with cancer and their parents. *International Journal of Rehabilitation and Health*, *5*(1), 43–54.

Persson, E., & Hellström, A. (2002). Experiences of Swedish men and women 6 to 12 weeks after ostomy surgery. *Journal of Wound, Ostomy, and Continence Nursing*, *29*(2), 103–108.

Price, K. (1992). Quality of life for terminally ill children. *Social Work*, *34*(1), 53–54.

Sherman, A. C., Pennington, J., Simonton, S., Latif, U., Arent, L., & Farley, H. (2008). Determinants of participation in cancer support groups: The role of health beliefs. *International Journal of Behavioral Medicine*, *15*(2), 92–100.

Siegel, R., Naishadham, D., & Jemal, A. (2012). Cancer statistics, 2012. *Ca–A Cancer Journal for Clinicians*, *62*(1), 10–29.

Simonton, S., & Sherman, A. (2000). An integrated model of group treatment for cancer patients. *International Journal of Group Psychotherapy*, *50*(4), 487–506.

Spiegel, D. (1992). Effects of psychosocial support on patients with metastatic breast cancer. *Journal of Psychosocial Oncology*, *10*(2), 113–120.

Spiegel, D., Bloom, J. R., Kraemer, H. C., & Gottheil, E. (1989). Effect of psychosocial treatment on survival of patients with metastatic breast cancer. *Lancet*, *2*(8668), 888–891.

Spiegel, D., & Classen, C. (2000). *Group therapy for cancer patients: A research-based handbook of psychosocial care.* New York, NY: Basic Books.

Spiegel, D., & Yalom, I. D. (1978). A support group for dying patients. *International Journal of Group Psychotherapy*, *28*(2), 233–245.

Spring, B., King, A. C., Pagoto, S. L., Van Horn, L. V., & Fisher, J. D. (2015). Fostering multiple healthy lifestyle behaviors for primary prevention of cancer. *American Psychologist*, *70*, 75–90.

Stang, I., & Mittelmark, M. B. (2010). Intervention to enhance empowerment in breast cancer self-help groups. *Nursing Inquiry*, *17*(1), 47–57.

Stevens, M. M., & Dunsmore, J. C. (1996). Adolescents who are living with a life-threatening illness. In C. A. Corr & D. E. Balk (Eds.), *Handbook of adolescent death and bereavement* (pp. 107–135). New York, NY: Springer.

Telch, E. G., & Telch, M. J. (1986). Group coping skills instruction and supportive group therapy for cancer patients: A comparison of strategies. *Journal of Consulting and Clinical Psychology*, *54*(6), 802–808.

Ussher, J. M., Kirsten, L., Butow, P., & Sandoval, M. (2008). A qualitative analysis of reasons for leaving, or not attending, a cancer support group. *Social Work in Health Care*, *47*(1), 14–29.

Veach, T. A., Nicholas, D. R., & Barton, M. A. (2002). *Cancer and the family life cycle: A practitioner's guide.* New York, NY: Taylor & Francis.

Vugia, H. D. (1991). Support groups in oncology: Building hope through the human bond. *Journal of Psychosocial Oncology*, *9*(3), 89–107.

Yalom, I. D., & Greaves, C. (1977). Group therapy with the terminally ill. *American Journal of Psychiatry*, *134*(4), 396–400.

Chapter Five

Group Work With People Who Suffer From Serious Mental Illness

Charles Garvin

This chapter describes ways of providing group services to people who suffer from serious mental illness. The term sometimes used is *chronic mental illness*, although many practitioners do not use the word *chronic* because of the negative connotation about recovery. Garvin and Tropman (1998, p. 277) use this term to apply to someone with this condition as "an individual who suffers from a major psychiatric disorder such as psychosis, who is so disabled as to have partial or total impairment of social functioning (such as vocational and homemaking activities), and who has had a long or a number of short stays in a mental hospital."

STATISTICS RELEVANT TO THIS POPULATION

According to recent statistics, "One in four adults - approximately 61.5 Americans -experiences mental illness in a given year. One in 17 – about 13.6 million – lives with a serious mental illness such as schizophrenia, major depression or bipolar disorder" (National Institutes of Health, 2013). Until the mid-1950s, many people with these diagnoses were confined in mental hospitals. At that time, however, a movement referred to as *deinstitutionalization* became a major determinant of mental health policy. This movement was propelled by the discovery of psychotropic drugs allowing for amelioration of many of the behaviors of mentally ill people that led to their confinement. These behaviors and symptoms include hallucinations, delusions, and actions seen by others as bizarre, as well as mood swings or severe depression.

Other forces that promoted the declining use of institutional care were humane concerns for the civil liberties of patients and fiscal crises related to the greater costs of institutional compared with the costs of community care. Deinstitutionalization was facilitated by the increasing number of community mental health centers designated to care for mentally disabled individuals in the community.

There have been serious negative effects of the closing of mental hospitals. There are persons with serious mental illness who cannot function in the community because of their behavior and they end up in prisons. Steadman et al. (2009) provided the following statistics:

Prevalence estimates of mental illnesses in US jails have varied widely depending on methodology and setting. Using survey methodology, a 1999 report from the Bureau of Justice Statistics (BJS) estimated that 16.3% of jail inmates reported they had either spent the night in a mntal hospital or had a mental condition (Ditton, 1999). In 2006, BJS reported that 64% of jail inmates had a recent "mental health problem." More recently, Trestman and colleagues (2007) evaluated a cohort of inmates who were not identified at intake as having a mental illness and found that over two thirds met criteria for a lifetime psychiatric disorder, including anxiety disorders and antisocial personality disorder (p. 761).

Statistics, which are unfortunately from the previous decade, indicate that about 150,000 of the seriously mentally ill persons were in institutions, about 750,000 were in nursing homes (including about 400,000 who have behavior changes sometimes found in older adults), and between 800,000 and 1.5 million resided in the community and were likely to receive some form of care through community mental health centers (Garvin & Tropman, 1998, p. 277). Hospital stays are likely to be short, due not only to the use of medications and the provision of community-based services but also to the action of insurance providers who limit the amount of hospital care for which they will pay. Social workers are very likely to be the providers of service, and this service is often in the form of groups. Increased resources have been allocated for research and program development in this field, but much more support is required to realize the aims of the deinstitutionalization movement.

People who suffer from serious mental illness are likely to have other problems as a consequence of their illness. According to Solomon (2008), these people characteristically tend to be unemployed and unmarried and to have difficulty with interpersonal relationships. Given their lack of employment, they tend to be economically disadvantaged and are often financially supported by federal disability benefit programs. In addition, this population is extremely vulnerable to a variety of psychological, medical, and social problems, including cognitive deficits, poor health status, and having relatively high rates of substance abuse, physical and psychological trauma, homelessness, criminal justice involvement, and loss of custody of their children (p. 233).

A recent report from the World Health Organization (2015) states that many mental illnesses are more prevalent among women than men. Among the statistics cited are the following:

- Unipolar depression, predicted to be the second leading cause of global disability burden, is twice as common in women.

- There are no marked gender differences in the rates of severe mental disorders like schizophrenia and bipolar disorders that affect less than 2% of the population.
- The disability associated with mental illness falls most heavily on those with three or more comorbid disorders. Again women predominate.
- Gender-specific risk disorders for common mental disorders that disproportionally affect women include gender-based violence, socio-economic disadvantage, low income and income inequality, low or subordinate social status and rank, and unremitting responsibility for the care of others.

The US Surgeon General (US Department of Health and Human Services, 2009) reported that the US mental health system is "not well equipped to meet the needs of racial and ethnic minority populations" (p. 1). This report indicates that barriers "deter such ethnic and racial minority group members from seeking treatment, and if individual members of groups succeed in accessing services, their treatment may be inappropriate to meet their needs" (p. 1). The aforementioned report links this latter point to differences in coping styles, cultural differences in how individuals experience discomfort, and the likelihood of somatization in many groups, which is the expression of mental distress in terms of physical suffering (p. 5). An additional factor is the use of community and family as resources.

The Surgeon General's report discusses the prevalence of mental disorders among members of different ethnic groups. The incidence among African Americans is higher than that among Whites, but the report attributes this to socioeconomic differences "because when these are taken into account, the prevalence difference disappears" (p. 8). African Americans are also overrepresented in inpatient psychiatric care, being about twice that of Whites.

The Surgeon General's report indicates that it is difficult to provide estimates of mental illness among Asian Americans because of the difficulty of applying standard diagnostic classifications to this population. Asian Americans are, moreover, less likely than other ethnic groups to seek care for mental health problems. According to this report, "One national sample revealed that Asian-Americans were only a quarter as likely as whites, and half as likely as African-Americans and Hispanic Americans, to have sought outpatient treatment" (p. 10). This was attributed by the report to "the stigma and loss of face over mental health problems, limited English proficiency among Asian immigrants, different cultural explanations for the problems, and the inability to find culturally competent services" (p. 10).

The Surgeon General's report further indicates that "several epidemiological studies revealed few differences between Hispanic Americans in lifetime rates of mental illness" (p. 10). There were, however, some differences within these groups with respect to specific mental health problems. The incidence of depressive symptomatology among Hispanic women was greater than that among Hispanic men. Also, both Puerto Rican and Mexican American women are underrepresented in mental health services and overrepresented in general medical services.

With respect to American Indian/Alaskan Native communities, according to the Surgeon General's report, depression is a significant problem. Alcohol abuse is also a major concern, as is the suicide rate. Posttraumatic stress disorder is especially prevalent among American Indian/Alaskan Native veterans compared with White veterans. Members of these groups are also overrepresented in public inpatient care facilities.

CAUSAL FACTORS

Much is unknown about the causes of serious mental illness. Nevertheless, the current consensus is that it is a condition produced by the interaction of biological and social circumstances with the evolving personality of the individual. Thus, it is often referred to as a *biopsychosocial phenomenon*. The basis of the biological input is concluded from the genetic, biochemical changes in the brain, as well as from heredity and twin studies. The social basis is determined from studies of the family, peer group, and other socialization circumstances of the individual. The developmental circumstances are elucidated by examining the life history of the individual in relation to coping patterns (Gerhart, 1990, pp. 17–20).

PRACTICE PRINCIPLES

A number of practice principles are typically applied when working with people with severe mental illness in light of the characteristics of this client group. While individual (Bentley, 2002), family (Sands, 2001, pp. 312–320), and group approaches are all used, the last are especially prominent. One reason is that with respect to the deficits in social skills found among these clients, groups provide an excellent way to learn to relate to others by observing and practicing social behaviors. Groups can also be used to simulate a variety of social circumstances such as those found in job, recreational, and family settings. Groups offer the client an opportunity to learn how others in similar circumstances have coped with a wide range of real-life situations. In addition, groups allow clients to participate at their current level of readiness: Some may be highly active socially, while others are passive participants. This makes a group less stressful for some clients than one-on-one encounters in which they feel a strong expectation to participate actively. On the other hand, some clients may act in ways that other members see as highly inappropriate, express delusions that upset others, or be so stressed by the presence of others that they would be highly disruptive if invited to a group session.

As Revheim and Marcopulos (2006) state, "Psychiatric rehabilitation services are primarily delivered using group modalities. Recent evidence points to the deleterious effects of poor cognitive functioning on group involvement, skill development, and functional outcomes" (p. 38). These authors discuss in their paper why the group offers one of the best modalities for treating these conditions in groups.

A major practice principle for group work with seriously mentally ill clients is to have a good deal of program structure, because an unstructured group may be experienced at best as a waste of time and at worst as highly stressful. Despite this, we have observed many groups led by social workers for these clients in whom the only structure is the opening query, "What would you like to talk about today?" Some members may prefer this experience to the loneliness and boredom of having no social interaction, but this unstructured approach is an invitation to not participate at all, to engage in unfocused complaints about the "system," or to talk in a disorganized manner. A more structured approach involves such actions as presenting information, introducing structured exercises, identifying problems to be solved, and posing useful questions.

Another practice principle is to use a psychosocial rehabilitation approach more than a psychotherapeutic one (Taintor, 2008). According to Sands (2001), psychosocial rehabilitation encourages people who suffer from severe mental illness to develop to their fullest capacities through learning new skills and through acquiring environmental supports. She states that for the social worker, "this means working with the client and community resources to promote the client's physical, psychiatric, and social functioning to the extent possible" (p. 242). She goes on to say that

> Programs of intervention target the individual, family, group, and the social environment. Individual, group, family, or milieu therapy can be utilized to teach individuals skills in activities in daily living (self-care, transportation, laundry), interpersonal behaviors, employment, and problem solving through skills training based on social learning theory. (p. 242)

A traditional psychotherapeutic approach, defined as using psychological interpretations and "depth"-oriented questions to enable the client to examine unconscious mechanisms, is not recommended for use with most seriously mentally ill people, either individually or in groups. As Rapp (1985) states, "Psychotherapy and psychosocial services without drugs may be harmful to the chronically mentally ill, not benign. The most prevalent hypothesis is that they overstimulate the client and lead to tension, anxiety, and exacerbation of symptoms" (p. 36). It is possible that some of these clients might benefit from this type of therapy, individually or in groups, after they have recovered sufficiently from their illness and have developed stronger coping abilities, but these will not be the majority. Some clients, however, who are defined as having borderline personality disorder might benefit from psychotherapy because of their greater ability to reflect on their circumstances.

Earlier social workers who thought of severe mental illness as a psychological manifestation produced by traumatic childhood experiences may have favored forms of psychotherapy for these clients. This, however, is not the view of most social workers today, who understand the biological factors in severe mental illness. A significant consequence of this increased biological understanding is a rejection of approaches that blamed mothers for acting in ways that promoted such illness or that blamed the family for engaging in communication patterns that "drove some family members crazy."

Another practice principle is to find ways to make each group session a rewarding one. This is because these clients are likely to find sessions anxiety provoking; they also have to make a considerable effort to attend, given the lethargy produced in some individuals by their illness. They have to look forward with pleasure to attending, especially when they are living in the community. Even hospitalized clients may resist attending group sessions and, when pressured to do so by hospital personnel, may enter meetings with a feeling of anger.

A major way of rewarding members for attending sessions is to use program activities during at least part of each session. Such activities might include the following:

- A game, especially one designed to teach a useful skill. Some workers have invented board games, for example, that help members to formulate individual goals or identify obstacles to obtaining goals.
- A dramatic activity, such as a role play, in which members practice a social skill
- A musical or craft activity that helps members work together, experience a sense of accomplishment, or express themselves creatively

Another way of rewarding members for coming to meetings is to ensure that they gain a sense of having accomplished something useful at each meeting. This requires the social workers to think in terms of concrete, short-term goals for each session. Examples of such goals are learning a specific social skill, solving an immediate problem, or creating a tangible product such as through a craft activity.

Another type of practice principle is to respond to a psychotic symptom in ways that help the member to cope with it while protecting other members from some of the anxiety produced by the symptom. One way to help individuals cope with psychotic symptoms is by educating them about such symptoms and labeling symptoms as such. Thus, seriously mentally ill members can be taught that hallucinations, for example, can be produced by their illness and that they can use this understanding when experiencing such hallucinations to tell themselves that they are experiencing something unreal. They also can be taught that some people can be told about symptoms (e.g., the social worker), while other people should not be told because they may be upset. The worker can also empathize with the fact that hearing voices or seeing strange images can be frightening. At the same time, the worker can reassure other members that he or she understands and is able to deal with psychotic symptoms, and will help them to understand and respond helpfully when a member is experiencing such symptoms.

Groups for the seriously mentally ill are often time limited and have specific purposes and goals. The length of time varies from one or two sessions while a client is in the hospital to several months for those in the community. However, because recovery from mental illness may be slow and because there may be periods of illness for many years, some groups that members find useful are self-help and support groups in which membership may continue indefinitely, such as Schizophrenics Anonymous and some Alcoholics Anonymous groups attuned to the needs of mentally ill people. Clubhouse-type programs for mentally ill people may sponsor ongoing social activity groups, lunch clubs, and special interest groups.

COMMON THEMES

The earlier discussion of services to people with serious mental illnesses should suggest to social workers that a number of themes frequently arise in such groups. The following are those that we have encountered.[1]

Stigma

These clients are often avoided, persecuted, and denied their rights by others who become aware of their illness. Actions include being fired from jobs, denied housing, refused entry to educational programs, and other serious consequences of having the label "mentally ill." Members of groups will look for help in deciding how and when to explain their illness, how to pursue their rights in an appropriately assertive manner, and how to find advocates to help them obtain things to which they are entitled.

Coping With Symptoms

The terms *positive symptoms* and *negative symptoms* are often used. Positive symptoms are direct consequences of the illness, such as hallucinations, mania, depression, and confused thought processes. Negative symptoms are behavior deficits due to lack of adequate socialization experiences, such as lack of skill in handling social interactions. Group members will ask for help in coping with positive symptoms and in acquiring the skills to eliminate negative ones.

Housing

As indicated earlier, a lack of adequate low-cost housing severely affects this population. Housing is especially a problem to these clients because they may need support to maintain it once they find it, such as learning to care for an apartment, getting along with a landlord, or locating roommates.

Employment

Many of these clients lack employment or employment for which they are adequately compensated. This may be because they have educational deficits, because they cannot tolerate the stresses of jobs for which they were trained, or because of the stigma factor. They may not be aware of vocational rehabilitation services or these may be lacking. They may also require employment in a setting that offers them some form of support or even a so-called sheltered workshop program. Thus, members may ask for help from each other in identifying and utilizing employment resources.

Education

Many of these clients have had their education interrupted by episodes of illness. Despite this, they are as likely to be as capable intellectually of acquiring an education as anyone else. The group is a medium in which they can explore educational opportunities, discover how to cope with school, and learn how to use resources to maintain themselves in an educational program.

Medication Effects

Clients are likely to bring up issues related to the medications they are taking to control their illness. They may not be compliant with their regimen because of a fear of dependence on medication. They may also experience unpleasant side effects of the medication. The medication itself may not be helpful, and the client may be unsure of how to assess this situation and what to do about it. At times, the social workers and other group members may provide useful information. At other times, the social worker will invite medical experts to attend one or more group sessions.

Two family issues are often brought up in these groups. One has to do with parents and siblings with whom the members have conflicts. Some of these conflicts occur because these family members are severely stressed by the client's symptoms. The other issue has to do with the nuclear families that these clients have created and seek to create. They may, for example, have difficulty acting as a spouse and parent. For these reasons, many programs form groups for family members of persons with mental illness and/or refer them to a major self-help organization such as the Alliance for the Mentally Ill (AMI).[2]

Leisure Time

Many of these clients are unemployed and are not attending an educational program; therefore, time hangs heavily on them. Their solution is often to spend a lot of time watching television or "hanging out" in a public place such as the library or park. A major service that can be provided by the group is to help such clients identify interests that can be satisfied, such as engaging in musical activities, attending sports events, or taking courses that further such interests at places such as the local "Y" or adult education program facility. The group can also provide a context for engaging in recreational activities that can then be extended outside of the group.

Problems With the Treatment System

These clients are likely to complain about the way the system reacts to them. Sometimes this is because of the real inadequacies in the system, and sometimes it is because of the challenges these clients provide. An additional factor is that these clients may lack the skill to make their needs known. These complaints may concern difficulty in arranging for appointments with professionals, denial of services, frequent changes in professionals, and various forms of prejudice against them. These issues contribute to low self-confidence and self-esteem. The group can help the members come to terms with situations that cannot be changed while seeking changes that are appropriate and possible. On some occasions, group members can join together to engage in social action to change the system.

RECOMMENDED WAYS OF WORKING

Several different approaches to group work with these clients have emerged in response to the needs of different agency contexts and client themes. We will briefly discuss each of these approaches in terms of these conditions.

Group Work: Mutual Aid

Social workers have used traditional group work methods with the seriously mentally ill and have reported successful outcomes. Poynter-Berg (1994) reports one such group whose members lived in an institution and were identified as schizophrenic. A major theme of this group was coping with issues of intimacy and loss. The members approached the first session hostile to or suspicious of the group experience. The social worker was not as direct as she thought she should have been in establishing a contract with the members in which the purposes of the group and the anticipated activities were clearly enunciated. Nevertheless, the social worker sought to relate to members' feelings as they acted in hostile or disruptive ways. She also sought to introduce activities that were familiar to the women in the group, particularly craft projects. This led to a greater degree of security based on trust of the social worker and each other. A consequence of this was that as a holiday approached, the members talked with each other about painful feelings the holiday evoked, as indicated in the following record excerpt:

> The group members slowly came into the meeting room. Beverly sat with her back to the rest of the group, muttering an occasional "fuckin' mishugana." . . . The women made their instant coffee and drank it, all silently. They were much quieter and still today than usual; they appeared depressed and showed it by their slouched postures and lowered heads. I felt it might have something to do with feelings about Thanksgiving. I said everyone looked quite sad and wondered if they might want to talk about it. Rhoda furrowed her brows and moved her lips. I asked her if she wanted to say something. She shook her head. Another pause. All kept their heads lowered and Arlene, who usually talks to herself, was silent. I said they may all be having thoughts and feelings that the rest of the group might share with them. Silence. I finally said that sometimes it's hard to talk about things that are painful, like being in the hospital on holidays and maybe feeling lonely. Most of the members reacted to this by moving around in their chairs a little. I said I wondered if they did feel sad about tomorrow being a holiday. Rhoda nodded very slightly to herself, but kept her head lowered and didn't speak. Another lengthy pause, with all the ladies looking up at me briefly but not speaking.
>
> When it was time for the group to end, I commented that sometimes it's very hard to talk, like today—and especially when they might be feeling sad. I said I thought next week would be easier. They all looked up at me, and Rhoda smiled, saying, "Have a nice Thanksgiving." (Poynter-Berg, 1994, p. 324)

Task-Centered Group Work

Task-centered group work, like traditional group work, models the process of helping the group to become a mutual aid system in which the members are committed to helping one another. The major difference is that in task-centered work, each member is assisted by other members to define a personal goal, choose activities (tasks) to reach the goal, and carry out these tasks (Tolson, Reid, & Garvin, 2002). While members are helped to express and cope with feelings, this is done in the context of defining and accomplishing tasks. This is accomplished in a limited time, typically about 12 sessions.

Garvin (1992) reported excellent outcomes in using this model in a community mental health setting serving the seriously mentally ill. He tested this approach with four groups composed of members who wished to enhance their use of leisure time. One group was composed of low-functioning clients, another of somewhat higher functioning schizophrenic clients, a third of women who were trapped in highly dysfunctional family situations, and a fourth of clients who were also chemically dependent.

The plan for the 12 sessions was as follows:

Meeting 1	Get-acquainted activities
	Orientation to task-centered work
	Clarification of group purpose
Meetings 2 and 3	Determining members' goals
	Discussion of the idea of tasks
Meetings 4 and 5	Selection of member tasks
Meetings 6–11	Working on tasks
	Learning to overcome barriers to accomplishing tasks
Last meeting	Termination and evaluation

During these meetings, the social workers used a variety of program tools to help the members maintain their interest in the group and sustain their motivation to participate. One example was a series of board games devised by the staff. Each game taught members how to accomplish some aspect of the process, such as formulating goals or tasks. In a goal game, for example, members moved their "pieces" around a board and "landed" on a problem area for which they had to formulate a goal.

Social Skills Training

A great deal of development, as well as research on effectiveness, has been devoted to create models of social skills training for seriously mentally ill clients. According to Burlingame, MacKenzie, and Strauss (2004), the underlying premise of this approach is that deficits in social functioning lead to social isolation, which in turn can exacerbate symptoms and disease management. The modal social skills approach breaks complex interpersonal skills into discrete modules and trains patients in each with behavioral techniques (p. 664).

This approach involves groups, and excellent materials that the social worker can use, such as detailed manuals for practitioners, workbooks for group members, and audiovisual tapes that present models of the skills to be acquired, have been prepared.[3] Liberman et al. (1989) developed separate modules for a variety of social skills, such as recreation for leisure and medication management. Information on teaching friendship and dating skills is also contained in their text *Social Skills Training for Psychiatric Patients* (Liberman, DeRisi, & Mueser,

1989). These authors suggest the following steps for the group facilitator to use in planning a social skills session:

1. Give introduction to social skills training.
2. Introduce new patients.
3. Solicit orientation from experienced patients who can explain social skills training to new patients.
4. Reward patients for their contribution to the orientation.
5. Check homework assignments.
6. Help each patient pinpoint an interpersonal problem, goal, and scene for this session.
7. Target scene and interpersonal situation for dry run role play.
8. "Set up" the scene.
9. Give instructions for the scene.
10. Run the scene as a dry run.
11. Give positive feedback.
12. Assess receiving, processing, and sending skills.
13. Use a model.
14. Ensure that the patient has assimilated the demonstrated skills.
15. Use another model.
16. Give instructions to the patient for next rehearsal or rerun.
17. Rerun scene.
18. Provide summary positive feedback.
19. Give real-life assignment.
20. Choose another patient for the training sequence and return to step 1.

The following is a brief excerpt of a social skills session reported by Liberman et al. (1989):

(Karen, at the invitation of the therapist, has been explaining to a new member, Mark, what the members do in social skills training group. The therapist then turns to Ted, who has been in the group for a week, and asks him to add to what Karen has said.)

> *Therapist:* Great, Karen! Ted, would you add to what Karen said? (Ted has only been in the group for a week. He often gets angry and upset with other people. He decided to seek social skills training because he recently lost his third roommate in 6 months and has begun to realize that he alienates other people, including his coworkers. His boss has told him to improve his relations with workmates or else risk being fired.)
> *Ted:* I don't know, Karen described it.

Therapist: Well, can you think of some of the other things we can focus on?

Ted: You mean like solving our problems by looking at alternatives for communicating? And whether or not we look mad?

Therapist: Right, Ted. We concentrate on facial expression and problem solving, too. When you talk to someone, that person gets a lot of information from seeing the kind of expression on your face. How loud we talk and our tone of voice are really important, too. Ted, how is voice tone different from voice loudness?

Ted: Why don't you pick on someone else?

Therapist: Because you're doing really well. You've only been here a short time, and you've learned a lot. (pp. 84–85)

Inpatient Group Psychotherapy

A major feature of contemporary hospitalization of patients with serious mental illness is that is it likely to be short—perhaps for only a week or two while the patient becomes stabilized after an acute episode. While in the hospital, patients may attend groups on a daily basis. These groups may be very unstructured, and our experience is that they are of limited usefulness. Yalom and Leszcz (2005) have developed and tested an approach they term *inpatient group psychotherapy.* This approach has two variations—one for high-functioning and one for low-functioning patients. The high-functioning patients are able to make a conscious decision to enter the group, can sustain conversations with other patients that focus on interpersonal behaviors, and can remain in the group for approximately 1 hour. The low-functioning patients are unable to sustain that much verbal interaction. The structure of groups for the latter patients, therefore, includes more nonverbal activity such as physical exercise.

In the group for higher functioning patients, the workers ask each member in turn to select a concern (referred to as an *agenda*) that can be worked on in a single session. Examples include telling another group member something about oneself or finding a way of coping with another member's angry response. After social workers have helped each member to choose an agenda for the session, the workers promote group interactions that will allow each member to work on her or his agenda for at least part of the session. Workers must have a good deal of skill in helping members choose a workable agenda and then pursue the agenda as part of the subsequent stage of the group's process.

After the interactional period, workers give feedback to members on how they have worked on their agendas. Yalom and Leszcz (2005) also often invite observers (such as interns) to attend and to comment toward the end of the session on the group's process. Members also are given a brief opportunity to react to this feedback on group processes.

EVALUATION APPROACHES

A great deal of research has been conducted to evaluate services to people with severe mental illness; this had to lead to the development and testing of a variety of instruments to measure client outcomes. The following are some that can readily be used by social workers:

1. Scale for the Assessment of Negative Symptoms; Scale for the Assessment of Positive Symptoms (Fischer & Corcoran, 2007, pp. 650–657). These scales are used by practitioners primarily to assess the symptomatology of schizophrenia.
2. Symptoms Checklist (Fischer & Corcoran, 2007, pp. 823–826). This instrument is designed to measure the frequency of such psychiatric symptoms as tenseness, depressed mood, and difficulty sleeping.
3. Cognitive Slippage Scale (Fischer & Corcoran, 2007, pp. 172–173). This scale is designed to measure the cognitive distortion that is a primary characteristic of schizophrenia.
4. Social Adjustment Scale-Self Report (Fischer & Corcoran, 2007, pp. 752–762). This instrument helps the social worker to assess how adequate the client is in such areas as housework; employment; dealing with salespeople, neighbors, and friends; schooling; and family relations.

CONCLUSION

Group approaches have a great deal to offer to people suffering from serious mental illnesses. These approaches provide experiences in dealing with relationships through group activities, the possibility for mutual aid as members discover the support they can give and receive, and the opportunity for members to learn vicariously when they are not ready to take a more active role. With the large number of investigations currently under way, the future is bright for the creation of even more useful ways of offering group opportunity to these clients.

RESOURCES

Center for Psychiatric Rehabilitation
Boston University
Sargent College of Health and Rehabilitation Sciences
940 Commonwealth Avenue West
Boston, MA 02215
617-353-3549
www.bu.edu/cpr

National Alliance on Mental Illness
2107 Wilson Boulevard, Suite 300
Arlington, VA 22201
800-950-NAMI
www.nami.org

REFERENCES

Bentley, K. J. (Ed.). (2002). *Social work practice in mental health: Contemporary roles, tasks, and techniques*. Pacific Grove, CA: Brooks/Cole.

Burlingame, G. M., MacKenzie, K. R., & Strauss, B. (2004). Small-group treatment: Evidence for effectiveness and mechanisms of change. In M. J. Lambert (Ed.), *Bergin and Garfield's handbook of psychotherapy and behavior change* (5th ed., pp. 647–696). New York, NY: Wiley.

Ditton, P. M. (1999). Mental health and treatment of inmates and probationers. (Pub #NCJ 174463). Washington, DC: US Department of Justice, Office of Justice Programs, Bureau of Justice Assistance.

Fischer, J., & Corcoran, K. (2007). *Measures for clinical practice and research: A sourcebook*. New York, NY: Oxford University Press.

Garvin, C. (1992). A task-centered group approach to work with the chronically mentally ill. In J. A. Garland (Ed.), *Group work reaching out: People, places, and power* (pp. 67–80). New York, NY: Haworth Press.

Garvin, C., & Tropman, J. (1998). *Social work in contemporary society* (2nd ed.) Boston, MA: Allyn & Bacon.

Gerhart, U. C. (1990). *Caring for the chronic mentally ill*. Itasca, IL: Peacock.

Liberman, R. P., DeRisi, W. J., & Mueser, K. T. (1989). *Social skills training for psychiatric patients*. New York, NY: Pergamon Press.

Moxley, D. P., & Finch, J. R. (2003). *Sourcebook of rehabilitation and mental health practice*. New York, NY: Kluwer Academic & Plenum Publishers.

National Institutes of Health, National Institute of Mental Health. (n.d.). Statistics: Any Disorder Among Adults. Retrieved March 5, 2013, from http://www.nimh.nih.gov/statistics/1ANYDIS_ADULT.shtm

Poynter-Berg, D. (1994). Getting connected: Institutionalized schizophrenic women. In A. Gitterman & L. Shulman (Eds.), *Mutual aid groups, vulnerable populations, and the life cycle* (2nd ed., pp. 315–334). New York, NY: Columbia University Press.

Rapp, C. (1985). Research on the chronically mentally ill: Curriculum implications. In J. P. Bowker (Ed.), *Education for practice with the chronically mentally ill: What works?* (pp. 32–49). Washington, DC: Council on Social Work Education.

Revheim, N., & Marcopulos, B. A. (2006). Group treatment approaches to address cognitive defects. *Psychiatric Rehabilitation Journal, 30*, 38–45

Robins, L. N., Locke, B. Z., & Regier, D. A. (1991). An overview of psychiatric disorders in America. In L. N. Robins & D. Regier (Eds.), *Psychiatric disorders in America* (pp. 328–386). New York, NY: Free Press.

Sands, R. G. (2001). *Clinical social work practice in behavioral mental health: A postmodern approach to practice with adults* (2nd ed.). Boston, MA: Allyn & Bacon.

Solomon, P. (2008). Mental health: Practice interventions. In T. Mizrahi & L. E. Davis (Eds.), *Encyclopedia of social work* (Vol. 3, pp. 233–237). New York, NY: Oxford University Press.

Steadman, H. J., Osher, F. C., Robbins, P. C., Case, B., & Samuels, S. (2009). Prevalence of serious mental illness among jail inmates. *Psychiatric Services, 60,* 761–765.

Taintor, Z. C. (2008). Psychosocial and psychiatric rehabilitation. In T. Mizrahi & L. E. Davis (Eds.), *Encyclopedia of social work* (Vol. 3, pp 458–462). New York, NY: Oxford University Press.

Tolson, E. R., Reid, W. J., & Garvin, C. D. (2002). *Generalist practice: A task centered approach* (2nd ed.). New York, NY: Columbia University Press.

Trestman, R. L., Ford, J., Zhang, W., & Wiesbrock, V. (2007). Current and lifetime psychiatric illness among inmates not identified as acutely mentally ill at intake in Connecticut's jails. *Journal of the American Academy of Psychiatry and the Law, 35,* 490–500.

US Department of Health and Human Services, Office of the Surgeon General. (2009). *Mental health: A report of the surgeon general.* Retrieved from http://surgeongeneral. gov/library/mentalhealth/chapter2/sec6.html

World Health Organization. (2015). *Gender and women's health.* Retrieved from http:// www.who.int/mental healthprevention/genderwomen/en

Yalom, I. D., & Leszcz, M. (2005). *The theory and practice of group psychotherapy* (5th ed.). New York, NY: Basic Books.

NOTES

1 Many of these themes as well as helpful approaches for each may be found in an excellent sourcebook on rehabilitation and mental health practice edited by Moxley and Finch (2003).
2 The address of AMI is provided at the end of this chapter.
3 These materials can be obtained from Dissemination Coordinator, Camarillo-UCLA Clinical Research Center, Box A, Camarillo, CA 93011.

Chapter Six

Group Work Services to People Living With HIV/AIDS During a Changing Pandemic

Philip Osteen and George S. Getzel

Beginning in the early 1980s, group work and the acquired immune deficiency syndrome (AIDS) have been closely associated in the first efforts to help people living with the human immunodeficiency virus (HIV)/AIDS (PLWHAs). The model of group work for PLWHAs developed at that time reflected the desperate need to gain social support and to reduce societal isolation.

This chapter reviews the development of group work services to PLWHAs and suggests a reconsideration of the design and implementation of such services in light of the significant changes that have occurred in the treatment of HIV/AIDS and in the sociopolitical and cultural meanings of the disease. An overview of the biopsychosocial factors that surround HIV/AIDS is presented and is related to the core themes that emerge in a support group's interaction and content. The benefits of the group work experience for PLWHAs are identified.

Special attention is given to practice principles for group work with PLWHAs, goals specific to PLWHAs, strategies for group development and planning, the functional characteristics of groups, and the problem-solving process underlying group themes addressed by the group. Guidelines for the social worker's interventions are detailed. Finally, evaluation criteria are suggested.

OVERVIEW

In the more than 30 years since the appearance of AIDS as a major public health problem and the subsequent discovery of HIV, these conditions have significantly impacted the everyday lives of people in far-reaching ways (Cox, 1990; Shilts, 1988; Wright, 2000). In 2010 there were an estimated 47,500 new cases of HIV infection in the United States, with approximately two out of three new cases occurring among men who have sex with men (MSM). Additionally, African American men and women had an incidence rate eight times higher than

Caucasians (Centers for Disease Control and Prevention [CDC], 2012), and Latino/Latinas had incidence rates four times higher than Caucasians (CDC, 2013). As of 2011, more than 1.2 million individuals age 13 or older were estimated to be living with HIV in the United States (CDC, 2013).

The AIDS pandemic has produced creative and humane efforts to prevent the spread of HIV and to care for PLWHAs with serious illness and functional impairments. The use of groups with PLWHAs and with kin, friends, and volunteers caring for them has become an integral aspect of many social service and health care programs (Ball, 1998; Coursaris & Liu, 2009; Edell, 1998; Getzel, 1991a; Hayes, McConnell, Nardozzi, & Mullican, 1998; Lopez & Getzel, 1984, 1987). Beginning with the discovery of the first AIDS cases in New York City, group approaches were quickly picked up by newly developing AIDS community-based organizations in other cities.

Even though MSM represent the highest proportion of new cases of HIV/ AIDS each year (CDC, 2013), HIV/AIDS is no longer limited to this population. Since the 1990s, there have been significant increases worldwide in the proportion of women, children, and men diagnosed with AIDS where infection is attributed directly or indirectly to heterosexual contact (Stine, 2001). The CDC (2013) estimates that 25% of newly reported HIV/AIDS cases in the United States involved high-risk heterosexual contact. In 2010, there were approximately 9,500 newly reported HIV/AIDS cases among women, with the total HIV/AIDS cases among women surpassing 200,000 (CDC, 2013).

HIV infection and AIDS have a profound cultural and economic impact on whole societies (Smith, 2001; Stine, 2001). The HIV disease sequence has a welter of emotional and practical effects on the lives of all involved (Getzel, 1991b; Getzel & Willroth, 2001). The psychosocial consequences of HIV/AIDS in many respects resemble the reactions of other categories of persons to life-threatening disease. For example, the prospect of being infected with HIV or the knowledge of being HIV positive may be met with denial, which is dangerous if a person has unprotected sex.

All major illnesses with disabling and disfiguring consequences can result in depression and agitation; it is very common for sick persons to feel shame and guilt about becoming sick, resulting in bouts of anger, isolation, and self-loathing. Sontag (1978) noted that, historically, serious diseases like cancer and tuberculosis have had complex metaphorical content and values connotations; this has been strongly demonstrated in the case of AIDS. Because the first identified victims of HIV/AIDS were gay men, drug addicts, and poor persons of color in large cities, the stigma attached to persons with the disease has been insidious, resulting in incidents of withdrawal of care by professionals, violation of human rights, and violence against PLWHAs and their families (Altman, 1986; Gant, 2000; Smith, 2001). The societal problems of homophobia, classism, racism, and sexism are exposed and magnified in the presence of HIV/ AIDS.

As we approach the fourth decade of the AIDS pandemic, knowledge about AIDS and HIV has greatly expanded. In 2009, results for the first HIV vaccine study to indicate modest effects were reported following a large-scale, randomized trial in Thailand (Rerks-Ngarm et al., 2009). Although scientists have been unable to create a vaccine to completely prevent the spread of the virus or to find methods to eradicate it in the human body, it is hoped that continued medical research will yield promising solutions (AIDS.gov, 2014). A number of useful medical technologies have been developed to temporarily prevent the replication of HIV in infected persons; these antiviral medications have significantly extended longevity but have not altered the disabling course of disease. Antiviral medications also present significant quality-of-life concerns because of side effects and the uncertain benefits for some individuals (Bartlett & Finkbeiner, 2001).

The extension of life for persons with both HIV and AIDS has increased individuals' overall quality of life and leaves many with a renewed sense of hope; however, it also increases the prevalence of complications from opportunistic infections. The longer persons live with HIV or AIDS, the more apt they are to develop chronic, persistent, disabling, disorienting, and disfiguring conditions (Bartlett & Finkbeiner, 2001). In addition to the physical and medical challenges faced by long-term survivors, increased attention is being given to the unique experiences and psychosocial needs of aging PLWHAs (Nokes, Chew, & Altman, 2003; Robinson, Petty, Patton, & Kang, 2008). According to the most current CDC (2009) surveillance report, 10% of newly reported HIV/AIDS cases occurred in individuals over the age of 50, and more than 150,000 individuals over the age of 50 are currently living with HIV/AIDS.

In contrast, there has also been a marked increase in rates of HIV infection in young adults. Based on the CDC's (2007) most recent surveillance report, 34% of newly reported HIV cases occurred in individuals between the ages of 13 and 29 years. In 2004, it was estimated that nearly 8,000 young people were living with AIDS, a 42% increase since 2000 (CDC, 2006), with the number climbing to approximately 23,000 in 2007.

A reconfiguration of group work services is required to respond more effectively to PLWHAs and the evolution of their biomedical treatment. These changes will be described next.

EVOLUTION OF GROUP WORK WITH PLWHAS

Similar to many vulnerable populations, social support plays a central role in group work with PLWHAs. Support groups have been identified as the single most important and available intervention for PLWHAs (Peterson, Rintamaki, Brashers, Goldsmith, & Neidig, 2012). From the start of the first AIDS service organizations, support groups were recognized as important normalizing experiences for PLWHAs and for kin and friends caring for them (Hayes et al., 1998;

Lopez & Getzel, 1984; Maasen, 1998) and for volunteers in these organizations (Lopez & Getzel, 1984; 1987; Meier, Galinsky, & Rounds, 1995; Moore, 1998; Weiner, 1998). Support groups for professionals working with PLWHAs were recognized as a necessary resource later (Cushman, Evans, & Namerow, 1995; Gladstone & Reynolds, 1997). The use of groups to teach HIV prevention has been extensively reported.

Early in the AIDS pandemic, support groups for PLWHAs focused on issues such as safer sex practices, stigma, death, caregiving, homosexuality, and trust (Peterson, 2009). Groups often consisted of members who had recently become aware of their AIDS diagnosis by becoming seriously ill with *Pneumocystis carinii* pneumonia (PCP), discovering a Kaposi sarcoma (KS) lesion, or developing some other symptom associated with an opportunistic infection. Prior to the development of more effective treatments for these diseases and antiviral medication for HIV, most of the initial cohort joining a group died from complications from AIDS over 1–2 years (Gambe & Getzel, 1989). There was a brief early period "of quiet before the storm," soon followed by multiple hospitalizations, near-death experiences, and the appearance of other opportunistic infections such as taxoplasmosis, cytomegalovirus (CMV) infections, tuberculosis, and so forth. All of these illnesses can result in death but not before causing extreme body wasting, incontinence, mental confusion, blindness, disfigurement, profound neurological impairments, and other dire consequences.

PLWHAs entering a formed group could see themselves in contrast to very sick members and could be in the group as members died in rapid succession. Although this situation was intrinsically frightening, overwhelming, and a basis for dropping out of the group, it also provided an opportunity to understand and prepare for the likely biopsychosocial crises to come. Other group members served as models of forbearance and coping. A member could deal with prospective and current quality-of-life issues while providing help to peers. Group members were seen to be in the same lifeboat "until death do them part."

Although this early model of group support services is still relevant in many respects, it must be adjusted and refined in view of PLWHAs' increased longevity and the highly variegated cohorts of persons now affected by AIDS in many settings. What was once a single model of group work service has become a series of specialized models that reflect with more precision the disease sequence and medical treatment advances.

PRACTICE PRINCIPLES

Work with PLWHAs entails a clear understanding of the functions of a support group. In general, support can be defined in several ways, including structural support, such as size of support network; functional support, such as emotional support; enacted support, such as reassurance and advice; and the subjective sense of support experienced by group members (Hogan, Linden, & Najarian, 2001).

There are several considerations that must be taken into account when developing a group. First, the practice approach to be used in the group should be clearly identified. Will the social worker utilize a specific intervention technique such as cognitive-behavioral group therapy or a more general approach such as supportive-expressive group therapy? The choice of practice approach will determine the role of the social worker as therapist or facilitator and guide decisions about content and practices utilized in the group. Co-leadership of the group is strongly encouraged, and when possible and appropriate, the co-leader should be a peer of the group members.

Decisions about who can be a member of the group are also important. Group homogeneity is thought to be beneficial, and membership in a group could be based on HIV/AIDS status (i.e., only individuals with HIV/AIDS are allowed to participate), gender, sexual orientation, age, or disease stage. Homogeneous group composition allows for more in-depth discussions of members' diagnosis, needed services, and coping strategies. Linguistic barriers may necessitate special groups led in a foreign language or American Sign Language.

The process of creating content for the group should also be decided in advance. More formalized groups may have preset content with each session dedicated to a specific topic, whereas less formal groups might address topics that originate from group members themselves. Regardless of approach, there should be flexibility in the group format to address unexpected topics or issues and to be responsive to group members' needs.

The number of sessions in a group should also be decided in advance. Some groups are time limited consisting of a set number of sessions. These groups often focus on a specific issue such as being newly diagnosed, treatment management, or relationships; they may be more formal in structure. Membership in these types of groups is usually set at the beginning of the group, and the same cohort stays intact for the duration of the group. Other groups may be ongoing with a changing membership over time as new members join and established members leave. The more informal structure allows for a variety of topics and issues to be addressed.

Goals of Support Groups for PLWHAs

Common goals for support groups for PLWHAs (Brashers, Neidig, & Goldsmith, 2009; Ford Foundation, 2012; Maldonado et al., 1996):

1. Building support networks and reducing stigma and isolation
2. Improving social support through family, friends, and peers, including addressing how family, friends, and others respond to them differently

as PLWHAs and how to handle issues of intimacy, receiving help, and gaining acceptance

3. Increasing ability to express emotions such as sadness, anger, guilt, helplessness, and shame associated with the problem of living with HIV/AIDS
4. Integrating changed self, new identity, and body image
5. Normalizing experiences through hearing others' stories
6. Improving coping skills for managing uncertainty about illness, treatment, and relationships
7. Improving relationships with providers and empowering group members to be active participants in their own treatment
8. Detoxifying death and dying by providing opportunities for members to find ways to counter the fright and feeling of powerlessness about death and dying
9. Promoting safer sex practices
10. Helping members examine quality-of-life options (how they want to live and die) prompted by serious illness and potential death from complications from AIDS

Specific Types of Groups for PLWHAs

Orientation Support Group

This group's primary focus is assisting members to cope with the issue of recognizing themselves as persons with HIV/AIDS. This may also mean coming out of the closet as a gay person or a person with a history of drug abuse.

Understanding the practical and emotional consequences of the disease for the person's future orientation and management of different aspects of everyday life becomes important. Parents have to consider custody after they die. All persons must consider how they will manage their income and health care now and if they become unemployed or disabled in the future. Guidance about available health and social services and how to use them is an important aspect of group activities.

Depression, guilt, shame, and powerlessness are reduced as group members gain understanding about the similarity of their reactions and their different coping strategies. The orientation support group is composed of newly diagnosed individuals; it is time limited (six to eight sessions) and focuses on getting on with life after a diagnosis. These groups are most effective when sponsored by community-based organizations.

Relationship Support Group

This group is needed after the initial shock of the diagnosis has been handled. This model of group support focuses on the significant changes in the quantity and quality of interpersonal relationships that ensue for PLWHAs after they and other persons in their lives contemplate the current and prospective consequences of the disease. PLWHAs may see themselves as tainted or, as some PLWHAs have described it, as "soiled goods." The stigma attached to PLWHAs is reinforced when other persons, who were previously close, begin to disengage or abandon them. PLWHAs and others close to them may be troubled by the HIV/AIDS diagnosis and by the disclosure of homosexuality, bisexuality, drug use, or marital infidelity. Just as PLWHAs become preoccupied with recurrent death anxiety, persons close to them must contemplate hospitalizations, new symptoms, and dying. Relatives and others may experience feelings of rage and emotional conflict.

Needless to say, if the PLWHA is presumed to have infected family members, the emotional turmoil and conflict are magnified enormously. Consider the following situation of Mr. A., a 35-year-old man, and his wife of 5 years.

> Mrs. A. has been previously married. While she is pregnant with their second child, she and Mr. A. discover that Mrs. A's first husband died of AIDs (related to a hidden history of drug abuse). HIV tests are given to Mr. and Mrs. A. and their first child; the results for each of them are positive. Mrs. A. has been recently diagnosed with disseminated tuberculosis and AIDS; it will take over a year of testing to determine if the newborn is HIV infected because the mother's and the child's antibody production must be distinguished.

The need for a variety of health and social services for this family now and in the future is apparent. Part of a case plan for Mr. and Mrs. A. can be a relationship support group to address the welter of interpersonal problems they may face. Among the possibilities are a couples support group composed of others in a comparable situation, a women's PLWHA group composed of women infected by spouses, and a caregiver support group of men caring for women with AIDS.

Issues surrounding intimacy and sexual activity are important considerations when addressing interpersonal relationships for PLWHA. Substantial emphasis has been given to the notion of "prevention with positives" in which psychoeducational, biomedical, and social support services are targeted at helping PLWHA reduce the risk of transmitting HIV to current and/or future partners. Depending on agency contexts and funding sources, social workers may be expected, if not required, to incorporate prevention efforts into their group practice. Kalichman, Rompa, and Cage (2005) worked closely with a community advisory group to develop a model for incorporating prevention messages into support groups. HIV-positive community leaders recommended that group leaders approach the issue of prevention within a framework of status disclosure, noting that disclosure of HIV status represents "a nearly universal stressor" for PLWHA (p. 265). Social workers face the daunting challenge of addressing important public health considerations while simultaneously avoiding adding to and compounding feelings of guilt, shame, and anger.

Relationship support groups explore the current stresses in interpersonal relationships arising from being a PLWHA or a caregiver. These groups are time limited, with a focus on providing emotional and practical assistance in working out interpersonal conflicts and finding additional sources of support as the mounting demands of self-care and caregiving create stresses for group members. One objective of these groups is to maximize the autonomy and self-determination of the members as they make choices between the demands originating from the disease and those arising from day-to-day living. A group meeting for 8 to 12 weeks is introduced by the social workers, who state that group members will develop the understanding and skills needed to get on with their lives. Throughout this group experience, the social workers reinforce examples of members' resourcefulness in handling HIV/AIDS-related problems and making life plans. The social workers state that they believe that living with HIV/AIDS means that members get on with their lives, which includes work, friendship, intimacy, and new experiences.

Co-leadership should be considered as a way of modeling roles and providing continuity when a facilitator is absent. The group members may contract for an extension of the group as needed and as resources permit. Emphasis should be placed on enhancing group members' capacity to understand and to manage HIV/AIDS-related problems that typically arise within their kinship and friendship systems. Problems at work may also be discussed.

Relationship support groups require careful intake. The social worker helps the potential group member or couples identify possible interpersonal issues to be addressed in the group. The intake process is expedited when group candidates have first explored interpersonal concerns in an orientation support group. This model of group support can be based in HIV/AIDS community-based organizations, mental health settings, family services agencies, child care agencies, and other settings used by and accessible to PLWHAs, their kin, and others associated with informal caregiving.

Quality-of-Life Support Group

This group is appropriate during periods of serious illness and the end stage of the disease process. It may not address PLWHAs' needs until many years after diagnosis. Life-threatening diseases tend to occur later. PLWHAs frequently experience an asymptomatic period or a period of less dramatic symptomatic display when AIDS and its life-threatening potential need not occupy exclusively PLWHAs' cognitive and emotional lives.

A quality-of-life support group provides PLWHAs with a safe location to discuss their reactions to shortened life. A process of life review, more typically associated with older adults, occurs in the group. It is occasioned by serial losses in the form of disfiguring symptoms, social isolation and abandonment, deaths of others, mental disorganization, and other disabling conditions. The group gives support and guidance as members confront humiliating, severe symptoms. For example, the group allows members to exchange opinions about undergoing experimental treatments that may cause irreversible side effects. Members can openly discuss issues like HIV-related dementia symptoms and even use humor to face the affront of baldness caused by chemotherapy treatments.

Particular symptoms of opportunistic diseases may warrant special efforts to develop homogeneous groups. Groups may be composed of PLWHAs with visual impairments resulting from the activity of a persistent, chronic CMV infection that destroys the retina of the eye, or they may consist of members with rapidly progressing and disfiguring lesions of KS, a form of skin cancer. In such groups, members can provide empathetic support and exchange useful information about resources: how to obtain cosmetics to disguise lesions or community resources for mobility training at home. Quality-of-life support groups are found in HIV/AIDS community-based organizations, hospitals, long-term care programs, hospices, religious organizations, and local health and social service agencies. Parallel groups of this nature for caregivers are also very useful. Co-leadership is strongly recommended to provide continuity of facilitation and emotional support to leaders in these very demanding groups. This support group model is usually open ended in time. Careful consideration and preparation must be given to the introduction of a new member (Gambe & Getzel, 1989).

COMMON THEMES

Recurrent themes emerge in group discussion and interaction that present the social worker and members with rich opportunities to work together. Three common themes are uncertainty, crisis situations, and a changing identity.

Uncertainty

Uncertainty occurs in all support groups during different phases of group development. Group members may experience high levels of uncertainty related to unpredictable disease progression, experimental medications, social relationships, identity, and ambiguous symptoms (Brashers et al. 2009). For example, in the beginning phase of the group, members may express deep ambivalence about being in a group for PLWHAs because they do not understand what HIV/AIDS represents to them. Rather than confront the uncertainty of their life course, they protect themselves against death anxiety through simple denial—maybe they really do not have AIDS or perhaps they are not suited for a group of PLWHAs. Approach-avoidance behaviors appear in the group. Members join subgroups that are in conflict. Some members only want to talk about cures and treatments for HIV/AIDS and castigate others who want to discuss their fear of becoming sick or the recent deaths of friends from complications of AIDS.

Recommended Ways of Working

There is a great temptation to side with one subgroup; this tendency should be avoided. The social worker should make group conflicts a problem for group members to solve. The social worker should assist group members to explore solutions that might simultaneously address the need to accept the uncertainties of disease sequence and treatment while approaching life without a morbid outlook. Group members share thoughts and problem-solve together. The social workers must walk a fine line, carefully accepting different perspectives offered by conflicting subgroups.

If the social worker is not a PLWHA or does not have a background similar to that of the members, he or she may become a target of group members' anger for not having to deal with the same life issues.

The following incident occurred at an early meeting of gay men with AIDS when Robert returns to the group after his lover dies from an opportunistic infection:

> Members are engaged in an intense discussion of the benefits of combining antiviral medications to halt HIV replication when Robert asks, in an offhanded way, if this discussion is boring to the social worker, since he does not have AIDS. Other group members stop and stare at the social worker, who begins to flush. Looking at Robert and the other group members, the social worker says, "The group seems to be reacting to Robert's important question to me."
>
> In defense of the social worker, another member, John, says that you do not need to have AIDS to lead a group of PLWHAs. The social worker indicates that this might be so but wonders if Robert and some other group members might feel differently. An intense group discussion ensues in which Robert talks about his anger about the death of his lover and his distrust of anyone who does not have AIDS and has not suffered. Some group members, while defending the social worker, acknowledge their jealousy in their lives toward people who do not have AIDS. Group members, with the help of the social worker, go on to discuss their concerns about how Robert is managing after the death of his lover. The discussion slowly edges back to new treatments as the session ends.

Crisis Situations

Recurrent biopsychosocial crisis situations arise in the PLWHAs' interpersonal systems that necessitate in-depth attention by the group members. Previous patterns of adaptation and problem solving may no longer be available to PLWHAs in crisis. Acceptance of powerful emotional displays occurs in the support group. Other members can display a sense of mastery by using their learning from undergoing similar crises to help a peer in active crises.

Recommended Ways of Working

The social worker must see the group members as capable of accepting crisis situations that arise among members, avoiding an overprotective stance. To the extent that the social worker encourages members to discuss how they have handled similar situations, mutual aid will be encouraged, in contrast to flight behavior, in which members give facile advice on a one-on-one basis. It is important to point out themes that reflect emotions and ideas shared by the members. The social worker may also help members reach out to each other as crisis situations arise between sessions, assuming that members agree to this type of support during the group's deliberations.

> A crisis situation was revealed in a women's PLWHA group when Mary, in a tearful, agitated manner, told the other members that she had been diagnosed with cervical cancer and would be hospitalized the next day. Mary told the group that she did not care if she lived or died but felt shame for what would happen to her two young children. Shaking convulsively, May wept, saying that she had not planned for guardianship after her husband had died 6 months ago.
>
> Joan held Mary, and the group began telling Mary that they were very worried about her. Tanya said that she used a lawyer from the social work agency when she panicked about going into the hospital. The social worker told the group that it seemed very hard to make a will and guardian provisions. Joan said that you just don't want to think about dying but that you have to be realistic, concluding, "Better late than never." The group then began a discussion about how, after being diagnosed, they had grown more responsible in thinking about their children.

A Changed Identity

A very strong theme that emerges in groups of PLWHAs is participants' change of self-image linked to AIDS. For example, receiving an AIDS diagnosis can be seen as a rite of passage. Normalizing an AIDS identity is a way of coping with an otherwise unacceptable condition that others readily see as a death sentence.

Support groups simultaneously normalize the PLWHA status and provide guidance in understanding this status when representing oneself to outsiders. Strongly associated with a shift of self-definition is a greater capacity to look at the question of mortality and the meaning of a life threatened by AIDS.

Erikson (1964) notes that all stages of the life cycle place demands on the individual to find meaning in life in order to cope with the stresses of existence and reminders of death. Human individuality finds its ultimate challenge when a human being confronts mortality. Identity questions may become exquisitely transparent in the face of death.

Recommended Ways of Working

The group becomes a safe context to discuss concerns and express feelings about the inequity of a life ending too early, unfulfilled goals, unfinished projects, and taking leave of loved ones. With the death of a member, surviving members bear witness to the meaning of the loss and the significance of their own lives. Clearly, the social worker must be prepared to listen and not to quickly reassure. The social worker's guilt and helplessness as a survivor necessitate the presence of supervisory and peer supervision.

> After the group discusses the recent death of a member, Greg says to the social workers, "It is your job to remember us after we all die." The social worker, after some hesitation, replies that the deaths of group members sadden him greatly and he feels the heavy burden of loss, yet he is grateful to be part of the group, where he has met so many wonderful men. He can never forget them.
>
> The social worker asks the group members if they have reactions to his outliving them. Some members joke, saying that he had better enjoy himself when they are gone. Paul says that he is jealous of the social worker. Gradually, the subject is adroitly changed by Paul.

ONLINE SUPPORT GROUPS

As access to the Internet and online resources increases (see also Chapter 14, this volume), there is a growing use of online support groups for PLWHAs and their families, friends, caregivers, and peers. Members of online support groups tend to use this resource primarily for information gathering and sharing, followed by seeking and giving emotional support (Coursaris & Liu, 2009). Numerous benefits have been associated with online support compared to traditional face-to-face support groups (Coursaris & Liu, 2009; Phoenix & Coulson, 2008; Phoenix & Coulson, 2009). Specifically, online support groups (1) provide greater convenience and reduce geographic and time-related barriers; (2) provide greater anonymity; (3) provide access to a larger peer system, which increases access to information, different perspectives, diverse cultures, and a wider array of personal and life experiences; and (4) require fewer resources. Online support groups have been shown to be as effective as face-to-face groups, but there are some limitations to their use. Online groups (1) require access to computers and the Internet; (2) require more time to establish trust and develop relationships; and (3) may delay members' decisions to access professional services. Online support groups often occur in a peer-to-peer framework without the presence of social workers or other professionals, although the inclusion of social workers or other professionals can increase the benefits of the group through facilitation of interactions, management of who may be a part of the group, and guiding discussions to address sensitive but important issues that might be otherwise avoided.

EVALUATION APPROACHES

Although difficult, the evaluation of group support models for different population is very much needed. Consumer feedback about short-term support groups is a good way to begin. Measurements of consumer satisfaction, knowledge gained about resources, and the actual use of services and entitlements should be investigated. More traditional measurements of clinical outcomes such as stress, depression, and psychological functioning should also be used when appropriate and possible.

Quality-of-life support groups present serious concerns, and ethnographic approaches should be considered because of the likelihood of physical fragility and HIV-related dementia among members. Because PLWHAs may feel stigmatized and may have histories of stigma, respect for the integrity of their personal boundaries, confidentiality, and autonomy is critical. PLWHAs should be allowed to tell their stories without prejudice, coercion, or prior interpretation. Telling their stories may represent the human need to be remembered.

RESOURCES

American Foundation for AIDS Research (AmFar)
120 Wall Street (13th Floor)
New York, NY 10005-3902
800-39-amfar
www.amfar.org

Gay Men's Health Crisis
119 West 24th Street
New York, NY 10011
GMHC Hotline: 800-243-7692
hotline@gmhc.org www.gmhc.org
National AIDS Hotline
800-342-2437 (English)
800-344-7432 (Spanish)
800-243-7889 (TSS)
http://www.projectinform.org/hotlines/

San Francisco AIDS Foundation
995 Market Street
San Francisco, CA 94103
California Hotline: (800) 367-AIDS
www.sfaf.org

U.S. Department of Health and Human Services
Rm 443 H
200 Independence Avenue, S.W.
Washington, D.C. 20201
www.aids.gov
https://locator.aids.gov (locate services such as housing, behavioral health treatment)
http://npin.cdc.gov/ (downloadable materials from CDC)
http://cdc.gov/cdc-info/ or 1-800-CDC-INFO (information specialists)
http://aidsinfo.nih.gov (clinical trials)
https://www.aids.gov/federal-resources/policies/health-care-reform/ (healthcare)

REFERENCES

AIDS.gov. (2014). *Vaccines.* Retrieved from https://www.aids.gov/hiv-aids-basics/prevention/prevention-research/vaccines/

Altman, D. (1986). *AIDS in the mind of America.* New York, NY: Anchor Books.

Ball, S. (1998). A time-limited group model for HIV-negative gay men. *Journal of Gay and Lesbian Social Services, 8,* 23–42.

Brashers, D. E., Neidig, J. L., & Goldsmith, D. J. (2009). Social support and the management of uncertainty for people living with HIV or AIDS. *Health Communication, 16*(3), 305–332. doi:10.1207/S15327027HC1603_3

Centers for Disease Control and Prevention. (2012). *Estimated HIV incidence among adults and adolescents in the United States, 2007–2010.* (HIV Supplemental Report 2012). Retrieved from http://www.cdc.gov/hiv/library/slideSets/index.html

Centers for Disease Control and Prevention. (2013). *Monitoring selected national HIV prevention and care objectives by using HIV surveillance data—United States and 6 U.S. dependent areas—2011.* (HIV Surveillance Supplemental Report 2013;18(5)). Retrieved from http://www.cdc.gov/hiv/statistics/basics/

Coursaris, C. K., & Liu, M. (2009). An analysis of social support exchanges in online HIV/AIDS self-help groups. *Computers in Human Behavior, 25,* 911–918.

Cox, E. (1990). *Thanksgiving: An AIDS journal.* New York, NY: Harper & Row.

Cushman, L. F., Evans, P., & Namerow, P. B. (1995). Occupational stress among AIDS social service providers. *Social Work in Health Care, 21,* 115–131.

Edell, M. (1998). Replacing community: Establishing linkages for women living with HIV/AIDS—a group work approach. *Social Work with Groups, 21,* 49–62.

Erikson, E. H. (1964). *Insight and responsibility.* New York, NY: Norton.

Ford Foundation. (2012). *Guidelines for conducting HIV support groups*. Retrieved from http://www.fhi360.org/sites/default/files/media/documents/Guidelines%20in%20Arabic%20and%20English%20for%20conducting%20HIV%20support%20groups_0.pdf

Gambe, R., & Getzel, G. S. (1989). Group work with gay men with AIDS. *Social Casework, 70*, 172–179.

Gant, L. M. (2000). Advocacy and social policy issues. In V. J. Lynch (Ed.), *HIV/AIDS at year 2000: A sourcebook for social workers* (pp. 197–210). Boston, MA: Allyn & Bacon.

Getzel, G. S. (1991a). AIDS. In A. Gitterman (Ed.), *Handbook of social work with vulnerable populations* (pp. 35–64). New York, NY: Columbia University Press.

Getzel, G. S. (1991b). Survival modes of people with AIDS in groups. *Social Work, 36*, 7–11.

Getzel, G. S., & Willroth, S. (2001). Acquired immune deficiency syndrome (AIDS). In A. Gitterman (Ed.), *Handbook of social practice with vulnerable resilient populations* (2nd ed., pp. 39–63). New York, NY: Columbia University Press.

Gladstone, J., & Reynolds, T. (1997). Single session group work intervention in response to employee stress during workforce transition. *Social Work with Groups, 20*(1), 33–49.

Hayes, M. A., McConnell, S. C., Nardozzi, J. A., & Mullican, R. J. (1998). Family and friends of people with HIV/AIDS support group. *Social Work with Groups, 21*, 35–47.

Hogan, B. E., Linden, W., & Najarian, B. (2001). Social support interventions: Do they work? *Clinical Psychology Review, 22*, 381–440.

Kalichman, S. C., Rompa, D., & Cage, M. (2005). Group intervention to reduce HIV transition risk behavior among personal living with HIV/AIDS. *Behavior Modification, 29*(2), 256–285.

Lopez, D. J., & Getzel, G. S. (1984). Helping gay patients in crisis. *Social Casework, 65*, 387–394.

Lopez, D. J., & Getzel, G. S. (1987). Strategies for volunteers caring for persons with AIDS. *Social Casework, 68*, 47–53.

Maasen, T. (1998). Counseling gay men with multiple loss and survival problems: The bereavement group as a transitional object. *AIDS Care, 10*, 57–64.

Maldonado, J., Gore-Felton, C., Durán, R., Diamond, S., Koopman, C., & Spiegel, D. (1996). *Supportive-expressive group therapy for people with HIV infection: A primer.* Palo Alto, CA: Psychosocial Treatment Laboratory, Stanford University School of Medicine. Retrieved from http://www.learningace.com/doc/1507525/1a9835c3afed-0d89bacbb7a82e822a91/groupleaderprimerforhivgrouptherapystudy

Meier, A., Galinsky, M. J., & Rounds, K. A. (1995). Telephone support groups for caregivers of persons with AIDS. *Social Work with Groups, 18*, 99–108.

Moore, P. J. (1998). AIDS bereavement supports in an African American church: A model for facilitator training. *Illness, Crisis and Loss, 7*, 390–401.

Nokes, K. M., Chew, L., & Altman, C. (2003). Using a telephone support group for HIV-positive persons aged 50 + to increase social support and health-related knowledge. *AIDS Patient Care and STDs, 17*(3), 345–351.

Peterson, J. L. (2009). "You have to be positive." Social support process of an online support group for men living with HIV. *Communication Studies, 60*(5), 526–541, doi:10.1080/10510970903260368

Peterson, J. L, Rintamaki, L. S., Brashers, D. E., Goldsmith, D. J., & Neidig, J. L. (2012). Forms and functions of peer social support. *Hournal of the Association of Nurses AIDS Care, 23*(4), 294–305. doi:10.1016/j.jana.2011.08.014

Phoenix, K. H., & Coulson, N. S. (2008). Exploring the communication\ of social support within virtual communities: A content analysis of messages posted to an online HIV/AIDS support group. *CyberPsychology and Behavior, 11*(3), 371–377. doi:10.1089/cpb.2007.0118

Phoenix, K. H., & Coulson, N. S. (2009). Living with HIV/AIDS and use of online support groups. *Journal of Health Psychology, 15*(3), 339–350, doi:0.1177/1359105309348808

Rerks-Ngarm, S., Pitisuttithum, P., Nitayaphan, S., Kaewkungwal, J., Chiu, J., Paris, R., ... MOPH-TAVEG Investigators. (2009). Vaccination with ALVAC and AIDSVAX to prevent HIV-1 infection in Thailand. *New England Journal of Medicine, 361*(23), 2209–2220.

Robinson, W. A., Petty, M. S., Patton, C., & Kang, H. (2008). Aging with HIV: Historical and intra-community difference in experience of aging with HIV. *Journal of Gay and Lesbian Social Services, 20* (1/2), 111–128.

Shilts, R. (1988). *The band played on: Politics, people and AIDS.* New York, NY: St. Martin's Press.

Smith, R. A. (2001). *Encyclopedia of AIDS: A social, political, cultural and scientific record of the HIV epidemic.* New York, NY: Penguin Books.

Sontag, S. (1978). *Illness as metaphor.* New York, NY: Vintage Books.

Stine, G. J. (2001). *AIDS update.* Upper Saddle River, NJ: Prentice Hall.

Wright, E. M. (2000). The psychosocial context. In V. J. Lynch (Ed.), *HIV/AIDS at year 2000: A sourcebook for social workers* (pp. 18–32). Boston, MA: Allyn & Bacon.

Chapter Seven

Group Work to Address Adolescent Alcohol and Other Drug Abuse

Andrew Malekoff

The problematic use of alcohol, drugs, and tobacco is unquestionably the nation's number-one health problem. Although all segments of society are affected, the future of young people is most severely compromised by this epidemic (Hill & Coulson-Brown, 2007). Consistent and extensive surveys identify the United States as having "the highest rate of adolescent drug use of any industrialized nation" (Santrock, 2006, p. 375).

Although there have been cumulative declines of illicit drug use, particularly marijuana and various stimulants, such as methamphetamine and crystal methamphetamine, among teens (grades 8 through 12) between 1997 and 2006, there is a troubling rise in the abuse of prescription painkillers such as OcyContin and Vicodin among adolescents (Zosel, Bartelson, Bailey, Lowenstein, & Dart, 2013). Misconceptions about the safety of these drugs, coupled with ease of access, have contributed to a dramatic increase in teen prescription drug use (Fuller, 2013).

TROUBLING RISE IN THE ABUSE OF PAINKILLERS AND HEROIN

The increase in teenage prescription drug use is, in part, the result of their belief that getting high with these drugs is safe. In addition, they acquire these drugs for free from the medicine cabinets of friends or relatives.

Another disturbing trend is the increase of heroin use among adolescents in the United States. National and statewide surveys suggest that heroin is more readily available, cheaper to purchase, and easier to use than it was a generation ago. The increase in the quality of heroin offers the option of snorting this substance, thereby reducing the stigma associated with needles (Center for

Behavioral Health Statistics and Quality, 2012; Substance Abuse and Mental Health Services Administration [SAMHSA], 2013).

The increase in heroin use among teens is not exclusively an inner-city problem, as some might suspect. For example, in the suburbs of Long Island, New York, just east of New York City, heroin is easy to get and can be bought for as cheap as five dollars a fix, less than the cost of a six-pack of beer (Bolger, 2008). The author, who is the director of a children's mental health and drug treatment agency on Long Island, can attest to the fact that the cost for a fix of heroin has not changed to date.

ALCOHOL AND NICOTINE USE AND ABUSE

Alcohol use among eighth graders has declined by more than one third since its peak level in the mid-1990s. Alcohol use among twelfth graders has also declined by one seventh during the same period of time (Johnston, O'Malley, Bachman, & Schulenberg, 2007). Nevertheless, in 2011 the National Survey on Drug Use and Health (SAMHSA, 2012) reported that 25% of youth aged 12 to 20 years drink alcohol and 16% reported binge drinking.

Despite the promising decline in alcohol use, when teens drink, it is likely to excess. According to a report by Joseph A. Califano (2009), founder of the National Center on Addiction and Substance Abuse at Columbia University, about 20% of 17-year-olds partake in binge drinking in any given month (p. 59). The risk of youth experiencing school, social, legal, and other serious problems is greater for those who binge drink than for those who do not (Miller, Naimi, Brewer, & Jones, 2007).

A national survey (CASA, 2008) on teen and parent substance abuse attitudes found that underage boys and girls prefer sweetened liquor. This is followed in popularity by beer for boys and wine for girls. Naturally, advertisers spend millions of dollars to develop marketing strategies to target teen preferences (Centers for Disease Control and Prevention, 2007) at the same time that public health education campaigns are devised to prevent alcohol and substance abuse.

Although there have been declines in cigarette use for grades 8, 10, and 12, the older adolescent group showed the largest decline among the three grades. The drop in tobacco use among teens offers some evidence of the success of a three-decade-long, and counting, cultural shift that has included increased taxes, bans on smoking in public places, and public health education campaigns (Califano, 2009).

WHEN PARENTS DRINK AND DRUG

There are over 8.3 million children under 18 years of age that grow up in homes with alcohol and other drug-abusing parents (SAMHSA, 2013). These young people are likely to become alcohol or drug abusers themselves without intervention. Parental alcoholism and drug addiction influence the use of alcohol and other drugs in several ways. These include increased stress and decreased parental monitoring. Impaired parental monitoring contributes to adolescents joining peer groups that support drug use. There is a need for an integrated service approach to enhance the lives of these children.

STEROIDS TO IMPROVE ATHLETIC PERFORMANCE AND BODY IMAGE

Any discussion of drug abuse and prevention today must include the use of anabolic steroids by adolescents to improve athletic performance and body image and to increase physical strength, muscle mass, muscle definition, and endurance (National Institute on Drug Abuse [NIDA], 2014, 2006). Well-publicized cases of sports heroes using performance-enhancing drugs have made this a very public and widely debated issue. Prevention requires that pediatricians inquire about anabolic steroid use during routine health maintenance visits given the health risks to the population at risk.

Promising efforts to prevent steroid use include the ATLAS program (The Adolescent Training and Learning to Avoid Steroids) that is geared toward high school football players (NIDA, 2006). In the program coaches and team leaders offer information on the harmful effects of steroids and other substances and teach refusal skills.

ATHENA (Athletes Targeting Healthy Exercise and Nutrition Alternatives) is another program that has proven successful (NIDA, 2006). It is patterned on ATLAS and focused on adolescent girls who are active in athletic competition. Such prevention efforts are typically geared toward adolescents involved in team sports (NIDA, 2006). Good grounding in group work in implementing programs like ATLAS and ATHENA will only serve to strengthen prevention efforts. For more information on ATLAS and ATHENA (2014), please refer to http://www.atlasathena.org/.

SUBSTANCE ABUSE AND SUICIDE RISK

Alcohol and other drug use disorders increase the risk of suicide, especially in older adolescent males when co-occurring with mental health disorders (e.g., mood disorder or disruptive disorders). Younger adolescents, 13 years or under, who participated in heavy episode drinking, were at greater risk of reporting a suicide attempt as compared to those who did not drink heavily. For adolescents 18 years and older, heavy episode drinking increased their suicide attempt risk. Researchers found that feeling "down" significantly increased the risk of self-reported suicide attempts (Cash & Bridge, 2009).

The pervasiveness of the alcohol and other drug abuse and addiction extends well beyond the individual. Alcohol and drug abuse play a major role in tearing apart families, impacting businesses and schools, striking fear in neighborhoods, and clogging the criminal justice and social service systems. As social workers committed to youth, and to the families and communities where they live, we cannot escape the need to address the problems of alcohol and drug abuse, regardless of the setting of our work.

The purpose of this chapter is to highlight group work as a protective factor, a powerful preventive tool for youth who show early signs of alcohol and other drug abuse and who are at risk for alcoholism and drug addiction.

RISK AND PROTECTIVE FACTORS

What differentiates people with negative outcomes from those who grow up in similar circumstances and bounce back from great adversity? This question has stimulated much speculation and a dramatic growth of literature on vulnerability, resiliency and risk, and protective factors (Garmezy, 1991; Glantz, 1995; Landy & Tam, 1998; Rutter, 1979; Sameroff, 1988; Schorr, 1989; Selekman, 2006, 2009; Werner, 1989, 1990; Werner & Smith, 1992, 2001; Werner, Smith, & Garmezy, 1998).

What differentiates youths who become alcohol and drug abusers from their contemporaries from similar backgrounds who do not? This question points to the special concern of those interested in understanding the relationship between risk-reduction strategies and substance abuse prevention (Anthony, Koupernik, & Chiland, 1978; Centers for Disease Control and Prevention, 2009; Griffin, Scheier, Botvin, & Diaz, 2001; Hawkins, Catalano, & Miller, 1992; Vega, Zimmerman, Warheit, Apospori, & Gil, 1993; Werner, 1986).

Risk factors may be driven by constitutional (i.e., physiological) and/or contextual realities (i.e., the physical, cultural, social, political, and economic environment) in the individual's life. Examples of risk factors for youths include having a history of alcohol and drug abuse or addiction in the family; living in a disorganized neighborhood; being a victim of child abuse; having become pregnant; having a chronic history of school failure; being economically disadvantaged; having attempted suicide; and associating with drug-abusing peers.

Protective factors are the individual's constitutional assets (i.e., intelligence, temperament) and family and environmental supports (i.e., a close lifelong bond with an adult relative or mentor) that have the potential to mitigate against risk.

Selekman (2005) offers a summary of some additional resilience protective factors, which include caring and supportive parents, strong social skills, creative problem-solving abilities, pronounced self-sufficiency, healthy management of emotions, and low levels of family conflict (p. 235).

A protective network of supports has the potential to increase the individual's resistance to risk, placing him or her in a better position to avoid and/or overcome alcohol and other drug problems. Group work can be an important part of constructing such a network.

PRACTICE PRINCIPLES AND COMMON THEMES FOR GROUP WORK PRACTICE

The following are practice principles and common themes to use when addressing the issues of alcohol and other drug abuse in groups.

Practice Principles

• *Alliance formation with parents and other involved systems is a prerequisite to establishing an engaged group membership.* The stakes are great during the teenage years. There is a perplexing contradiction between adolescents reaching the peak of physical health, strength, and mental capability and, at the same time, facing greater risks and hazards than ever before. Parents walk a fine line between supporting their children's independence and protecting them from harm. Group workers must be prepared to provide parents with the support necessary to manage this delicate dance (American Academy of Child & Adolescent Psychiatry, 2011). Adolescents cannot be seen in a vacuum. Sanction from parents and cooperation with related systems (e.g., school) are necessary for ongoing work with adolescents. By establishing working alliances with these "significant others," the practitioner models collaboration and establishes the groundwork for mediating with the various systems. Working relationships with parents help to reduce the guilt that children often feel about betraying the family. By establishing working relationships with all involved systems, the possibility of dysfunctional interactions being replicated in the helping system itself is reduced. "Prevention programs seem to work best when they address the total life of the young person and focus on the factors that place him or her at risk" (Dryfoos, 1993, p. 3). In this era of categorical funding for human services, it is not always a simple task to provide comprehensive services. Therefore, collaboration among the various systems that serve youths is essential.

• *An appreciation for paradox and an ability to differentiate the words from the music are essential to working with adolescents in groups* (Malekoff, 1994, 2014). Just beyond the surface of the strident facade or apathetic veneer that many adolescents project are the deeper meanings that not many adults are privileged to discover. Oftentimes the familiar refrain of "Leave me alone!" carefully conceals the cry for help. It's not always easy to hang around to hear the music underneath the static of the words. Yet to work with adolescents one must hang in there. Too many an adult has already bailed out.

- *Cultural awareness and sensitivity are essential for practicing social work with groups in a society of ever-increasing diversity.* Social workers must be aware of racism, sexism, and homophobia, as well as other cultural issues and values, and how they affect group members and how they have affected their own lives. Bilides (1990, pp. 51–56) suggests some guidelines for moving one's multicultural awareness into practice with groups. These include the following: "discuss stereotypes at all levels (personal, familial and societal) . . . point out commonalties . . . explore the meanings of words and language . . . recognize and acknowledge your own discomfort about race, color, ethnicity, and class issues."

- *Use of self and access to childhood memories are important.* Awareness of what the group experience evokes in one is invaluable, especially with a population in motion. These things may include conscious memories of the social worker's earlier years and struggles during adolescence (e.g., personal and/or familial experiences with alcohol and drugs). The worker's feelings that inevitably bubble up in the lively context of the adolescent group must not be ignored. Feelings and experiences can be disclosed at times, however, only with good judgment. For example, the purpose of disclosure should never be to gain the acceptance of the group or to tacitly encourage acting-out behavior for a vicarious thrill. This is where good supervision enters the picture.

- *Be prepared to confront resistance and find ways to motivate involuntary or mandated group members.* Involuntary or mandated group members are a staple for group workers who work with adolescents with problems of drug and alcohol abuse (Malekoff, 2014). Typically, a mandating force is their "motivation" for attending a group. This might include the threat of a court order, legal action, or pressure from parents or other adults in positions of authority.

Resistance may present itself through denial of the problem (i.e., regarding drug use), superficial compliance, testing the limits, silence, externalizing the problem (i.e., blaming others), minimizing, and devaluation of the group worker and or group.

Overcoming resistance among involuntary group members requires worker authenticity and a sense of trust and safety in the group. Clarity of purpose and developing a clear and explicit contract makes a difference, especially when feedback from group members is welcomed and important issues such as confidentiality are discussed openly.

When involuntary group members feel in control of their fate, their motivation increases, as opposed to exhibiting symptoms of the four Rs: reluctance, rebellion, rationalization, and rebellion (Miller & Rollnick, 1991; Shulman, 2009, p. 346). For adolescents with dual diagnoses, more commonly known today as co-occurring disorders, motivational interviewing offers an integrated and nonconfrontational approach (Fields, 2004; Miller, & Rollnick, 1991, 2002; Sciacca, 1996, 2007) that can be helpful in reducing resistance.[1] This combined approach employs acceptance, nonconfrontation, and recognition of the client's readiness levels and assesses change incrementally (Sciacca, 2007).[2]

• *Don't go it alone.* Social workers working with at-risk adolescents in groups need support from colleagues, including consistent and quality supervision. Too many an adult (professional or not) looks awry at the group modality when adolescents are involved. They question the efficacy of the work when confronted with the noise, action, and attitude that seem absent in the adult talking group.

Colleagues with a track record and an inclination to work with youths can be invaluable partners. Such partnership might include good supervision, peer or otherwise, and opportunities for teamwork (e.g., one practitioner works with the adolescent in a group and another sees the parent[s] in some other context). Co-leadership of groups is an approach that must be very carefully considered. Adequate time for planning and reflection must be set aside. Too many human services workers, without adequate group work training, operate under the false assumption that more is better, easier, or less stressful. Maybe. It depends entirely on the match, commitment, and honesty that develop in the partnership. Simply throwing people together to run groups is to be avoided at all costs. As suggested, having a partner or partners outside of the group is some insurance against the pitfalls of going it alone and a viable alternative to coleadership within the group itself. Work with children and adolescents always requires involvement with other helping people and systems.

Common Themes

Groups may be formed specifically for children living in families with a present or past history of alcohol or other drug abuse. Other groups may be composed of youths who evidence a variety of related risk factors. Substance abuse prevalence rates (and practice experience) suggest that in either case the social worker must have knowledge of the impact of alcohol and drug abuse (including alcoholism and addiction) on the individual in the family.

What are the implications of growing up in a dysfunctional family system? How might this affect the individual in the group? How might it affect the group as a whole? (Although the attention here is to substance abuse, these questions may also apply to families in which there is child abuse, domestic violence, or severe mental illness). The following six themes will address these questions.

• *Children who grow up in families with alcohol and drug abuse/addiction learn to distrust to survive.* Attention to the beginning phase of group development is critical in building trust. By using anticipatory empathy to tune in to the group, the practitioner takes an important step in helping to create a safe environment for mutual exchange. The social worker's focus in the beginning is to allow and support distance, search for the common ground, invite trust gently, establish group purpose, facilitate exploration, begin to set norms, and provide program structure (Malekoff, 2014). Beyond a good beginning in the group, the theme of trust–distrust must never be too far from the practitioner's consciousness in working with adolescents from families with a past or present history of alcohol and/or other drug abuse. When unpredictability has dominated an individual's life, he or she is likely to be wary, always sensing disappointment lurking nearby.

• *Children growing up in alcohol or drug-abusing/addicted families become uncomfortably accustomed to living with chaos, uncertainty, unpredictability, and inconsistency.* Children growing up under these conditions have to "guess at what normal is." The group experience must provide a clear structure, with norms and reasonable limits. Issues of membership (Is it an open or closed group? If open, how do new members enter? How do members exit?); space (Is there a consistent meeting place?); and time (Does the group meet at a regular time for a prescribed period?) are all important considerations. Group rituals might be considered to reinforce a sense of order, establish value-based traditions, and promote bonding. For example, in one group a "drug-free pledge" was recited at the beginning and ending of each meeting. Because people tend to learn incrementally, one step at a time, real stability in the group develops gradually and not only as the result of an externally imposed structure, no matter how thoughtfully conceived and humane. The practitioner must be prepared for the unexpected, including the likelihood that group members will reenact aspects of their lives outside of the group in the here and now of the group itself. When the result is unpredictable and chaotic behavior, it creates a live opportunity for exploration and establishing order and consistency in the group. (Redl & Wineman, 1952, referred to this as the "clinical exploitation of life events.")

• *Denial, secrecy, embarrassment, and shame are common experiences of children who live in alcoholic or addicted families.* Joining a group of "outsiders" might in itself be experienced as an act of betrayal, a step toward revealing the "family secret." The worker's awareness of members' pain allows him or her to gently invite trust, paying careful attention to the group members' bruises (emotional and otherwise), and to concerns about trust and confidentiality throughout the life of the group.

• *Growing up with the ever-present threat of violence (verbal and physical) contributes to a pervasive sense of fearfulness, hypervigilance, and despair.* The group must become a place in which differences are safely expressed and conflicts need not be a matter of life and death. Conflicts can be resolved and differences respected in a thoughtful and increasingly mature manner in the group. The group is a place where members can practice putting a reflective pause between impulse and action and in which despair can be transformed into hope.

• *Children who grow up in alcohol- and drug-abusing/addicted family systems become rigidly attached to roles.* Many of those growing up in alcohol- and drug-abusing/addicted systems construct a wall of defenses and repressed feelings by adopting rigid family roles (Wegscheider, 1981). Accompanying these roles are stultifying family rules and unspoken mandates, such as "Don't talk, don't trust, don't feel." A group experience can provide members accustomed to enacting rigid roles with an opportunity for practicing role flexibility, broadening their intrapsychic range and interactive repertoire, and gaining competence in coping with the environment.

• *Growing up in an alcoholic and addicted family system leaves youths with little hope that things will ever change.* The group is a social system that assumes a life of its own, marked by an evolving culture, a history of events, and a developing set of relationships. As in any human relationships, there are decisions to be made, problems to solve, and crises to surmount. If a dysfunctional family system is the only frame of reference for a young person, he or she may have little experience in successfully resolving conflicts or overcoming obstacles. The group can provide members with a growing sense of confidence that difficult and frustrating circumstances can be overcome. The group worker must be tuned in to the sense of hopelessness that such members bring to the group so as not to get easily discouraged himself or herself. It cannot be emphasized enough that group work with this population requires hanging in for the long haul and modeling a sense of hope.

Following is an illustration of a short-term multiple-family group. The setting is an outpatient chemical dependency treatment and prevention program for youths and their families.

PRACTICE ILLUSTRATIONS

Multiple-Family Group Work to Address Alcohol and Other Drug Abuse

The setting for this practice illustration is the Tri-County Chemical Dependency Center for Youth (to be referred to as The Center), which includes an intensive after-school program consisting of a comprehensive blend of group, family, and individually oriented activities. The group program includes services for adults, for children and adolescents, for alcoholics and drug-addicted people, for nonaddicted substance abusers, and for at-risk non-substance-abusing significant other family members (youths and adults).

Some adolescents at The Center are seen as referred clients who are admitted to the program following a formal clinical evaluation. Others are seen in a variety of after-school programs that do not require a formal clinical evaluation. There are also special outreach, advocacy, and group services for Hispanic and Haitian immigrant youths and their families. Many adolescents are participants in both programs, as clients and as community members. Schorr (1989) said it best in noting that "most successful programs find that interventions cannot be routinized or applied uniformly. Staff members and program structures are fundamentally *flexible* and *see the child in the context of family and the family in the context of its surroundings*" (p. 257; emphasis in original).

Groups at The Center vary in composition, length, and purpose. Content may include education, socialization, discussion, counseling, therapy, outings, arts and crafts, cultural awareness activities, and/or community service. Staff members work as partners in teams. This enables program participants to become engaged with the agency, as well as with an individual practitioner. Regularly scheduled team meetings are held for the purposes of case assignment and management, program development, supervision, skill development, and collegial support.

Family involvement is an important value at The Center. All incoming families with adolescents are assigned to an 8-week, multiple-family group program. This program is designed to help families with drug and alcohol problems to decrease isolation, learn from one another, and address the shame that children carry as a secret. The content includes a combination of alcohol and drug education, discussion, role play, and psychodrama. The first two meetings are structured to allow an opportunity for the adults and youths to meet for a brief time in separate groups to identify needs and make connections. The groups are co-led by two or three social workers.

The Multiple-Family Group

The fifth session of one multiple-family group series began with a staff presentation of normal development in the latency and adolescent stages and its relationship to the family life cycle. Psychoeducation on "normal development" is of great value for the family whose members have grown accustomed to uncertainty and to guessing at what "normal" is. In the group, this process serves to provide support, encourage dialogue, and reduce isolation. When the theme of "separation" was presented, one of the group members, a Hispanic mother who understands and speaks English but prefers Spanish, addressed the bilingual worker in her native tongue: "If I may," she began, "I want to respond to something that the other worker said about separation. In my country [Colombia, South America], it is different. The kids are expected to stay with their families until they marry. If they go to college, they stay home. This discussion is a problem for us (*motioning to her husband, a practicing alcoholic*). It is upsetting that the children are encouraged to leave."

Once translated, a lively discussion ensued in this group of four families of various cultural origins (Colombian, African, Yugoslavian, and Italian). They exchanged their beliefs and feelings about separation, which varied from one culture to another. The worker's role was to promote cultural awareness and sensitivity by encouraging group members to share their views. "In rural agrarian societies—the closeness of family members and the individual's sense of being part of a larger whole have always been crucial to the community's survival," for example. In contrast, "In contemporary affluent American society, individualism, achievement, and mobility are generally regarded as the hallmarks of effectively reared offspring" (McConville, 1995, p. 21).

At one point, the Hispanic mother's 17-year-old son, Hector, who was referred to The Center following a single incident of binge drinking, spoke: "I didn't know this." Hector speaks in short, choppy sentences and is encouraged to elaborate. "Well, now that I know [what my mother thinks] I'll think about looking into colleges close to home, but I'm not staying home until I get married." Everyone laughed, including Hector's parents. One of the group workers summed up, turning to Hector, "It sounds like you're willing to negotiate with your parents." He acknowledged her comment with a smile.

In this interchange, the group is warming up to the meeting, testing the waters, and establishing trust. An emotionally charged issue surfaces. Differences along cultural and generational lines are drawn. Four different cultural groups (one bilingual), four sets of parents (and one grandparent), and four sets of adolescents, and no dire consequences occurred. All of the adolescents have abused alcohol or have tried other drugs on at least one occasion. In all four families, the fathers, only one of whom is present, are alcoholic or drug addicted. As is often the case, the adolescents and their presenting problems provide the ticket to getting help. As the session proceeds, separation issues give way to issues of limits, boundaries, and private space. The adolescents and parents begin to draw battle lines as parents reveal their suspicions:

> The group discussion is now heated as the adolescents refer to their parents as "nuts," "stupid," "crazy," and "ridiculous." A 14-year-old girl, Lisa, who verbally assaulted her mother last week, takes the offensive again. When one of the group workers reminds her of the rule of not attacking and allowing others to finish speaking, Lisa smiles and says, "Okay, okay." The group worker then asks what a parent should do if she suspects that her child is using drugs. The parents discuss various strategies, including under what circumstances they would search their children's rooms. Lisa's mother then reveals, somewhat defensively, "People don't know what they would do until it really affects them. I never thought I'd be going through my daughter's room, but I had a feeling and it was right. It was a good thing I followed my instinct because now I can get help." Then for the first time in five meetings, the Hispanic mother spoke in English and directly to Lisa's mother. She exclaimed, "You did right! You did the right thing and I would, too, to help my child." This is a moving moment, in which a mother who is struggling with an aggressive 14-year-old who abuses her in the group setting is supported by others in the presence of her daughter.
> At the same time she is receiving support, her daughter is encouraged to respect the norms of the group by not attacking and by waiting her turn to speak. This provides her with an opportunity to respond differently, to put a reflective pause between impulse and action. Lisa listens intently. Returning to Spanish, the Hispanic mother makes a passionate request of

the worker, "Please tell her if she didn't love her daughter she wouldn't have done this. It is an act of caring, and her daughter is so aggressive. . . ." Once translated, Lisa asks, "What's aggressive mean?" It is described as "hostile."

By this time the group is becoming very intense, as the adolescents are beginning to bond in anger against the parents. Growing up with the ever-present threat of violence (verbal and physical) contributes to a pervasive sense of fearfulness, hypervigilance, and despair. However, the group can become a place in which differences can be safely expressed and conflicts need not lead to disastrous consequences.

> As angry glances are exchanged across the generational dividing line, one of the group workers acknowledges the feelings and suggests an activity to promote empathy. Addressing Lisa, yet speaking to the group, she explains what a role reversal is and that "I find it helpful to try this when parents and children are in conflict." She then asks Lisa, providing an opportunity for her to move out of her rigid role and to empathize, to "put yourself in your mother's shoes. If you thought your child was in danger, that she might have weapons or drugs in her room, would you search it?" She becomes pensive and is clearly thinking deeply about this, as are the others, judging from their facial expressions and body language. She finally responds, "Yes, I think I would." It is with this reflection, as the others soak in her response, that the group moves to an ending. Another group worker, reinforcing the structure, concludes with a brief restating of the rules regarding confidentiality and that there are to be no consequences for what is shared in the group. Lisa seems more relieved than offended by the labeling of her behavior as aggressive and hostile. A limit was being set that, paradoxically, she had been seeking all along. A sense of hope that things can change seemed to have been sparked in the group.

In this illustration, family members of all generations moved closer to the realization that conflicts can be resolved and differences respected in a thoughtful and increasingly mature manner.[3]

Harm Reduction and Reflective Education With Aboriginal Youths in Canada

Harm reduction aims to reduce the harm associated with the use of alcohol and other psychoactive drugs in individuals unable or unwilling to stop. The goal is to prevent harm, rather than the prevention of drug use itself, and the focus on people who continue to use alcohol and other drugs (Harm Reduction International, 2013). *Reflective education* refers to a process that goes beyond simply imparting knowledge, rather to create an "environment of inclusion, mutual aid, constructive conflict and problem solving" (Ghelani, 2011, p. 12).

One method for promoting harm reduction with Aboriginal youths is use of the *talking circle*, an intergenerational approach in which elders—strong role models—using the oral tradition, share stories about a time before alcohol was brought into the community. The stories are used to stimulate conversation about the role of drugs in the Aboriginal community from the perspectives of First Nation, Inuit, and Métis people (Ghelani, 2011).[4] In talking or sharing circles, group members are offered opportunities for culturally relevant collective communication. For example, in one group the issue of healthy choices was discussed.

> In one circle with a handful of teenagers in a First Nations treatment setting, the facilitator showed a film on the consequences of criminal behavior and later asked the group how drugs and alcohol can affect healthy choices. A feather was passed around the circle to signify each member's turn to speak and, one by one, the youths told stories of consuming excessive amounts of alcohol and drugs, blacking out, engaging in unprotected sex, waking up next to strangers, and experiencing feelings of sickness and guilt after partying. Although it was difficult for participants to hold back their comments until the feather made it around the circle, the facilitator was able to redirect cross-talk. When it was the facilitator's turn to speak, he took the opportunity to inquire about the role of drugs in intimate relationships.
>
> During the discussion, the participants learned from each other's experiences while explaining how substances helped them stimulate conversation, overcome nervousness, and live in the moment. One youth shared that it is more difficult to say no while under the influence of alcohol, and a discussion ensued about healthy relationships and sexually transmitted illnesses (STIs). (pp. 15–16)

By using a culturally sensitive approach that combines "talking circles, health education, history lessons, positive role models, traditional teachings, values and ceremonies, and meaningful alternatives to partying . . . minimizing harm may be achieved" (Ghelani, 2011, p. 19).

Thinking Straight and Staying Straight: Cognitive-Behavioral Strategies That Address Social Pressure

Cognitive-behavioral strategies are consistent with the recovery model (Sobell & Sobell, 2011). For example, many catchy slogans or affirmations used in 12-step programs (e.g., "KISS: Keep It Simple, Stupid") support "straight thinking."

Cognitive-behavioral strategies that are effective with individual adolescents with substance abuse problems can be successfully applied to group work with adolescents. Group workers using cognitive-behavioral approaches must first consider the following caveats:

1. Don't dispute the disease model of addictions.
2. Don't avoid or downplay spirituality.
3. Be aware of the phase of recovery and the stage of change.
4. Avoid extensive homework.
5. Be active and challenging.
6. Anticipate several relapses.
7. Address issues of social culture (e.g., peer pressure and choice of friends; Patterson & O'Connell, 2003).

In one adolescent relapse prevention group, the group members addressed social pressure by sharing experiences about how hard it is to go to parties when their peers are smoking pot and drinking. One of the members, Greg, told the others, "It sucks. It's like as soon as I walk in the door they're thinking, 'Here comes Mr. Narcotics Anonymous.' I hate it." "Yeah," Margie added, "I know exactly how you feel. Everyone acts weird, like I have leprosy, like they don't want me there or something." Lots of heads nodded affirmatively. The group worker questioned the validity of their thinking by saying, "I didn't know you all could read minds," challenging them to consider the hold that such automatic thoughts have over them.

After some further exploration to highlight what a powerful grip such thoughts can have, the group worker offered some hope by suggesting that they create a list of "counters to offset irrational automatic thinking." The group members then rolled up their sleeves and together came up with a great working list:

1. These people (peers) care more about getting wasted than where I fit in.
2. They don't know what they are doing to themselves, but now I do.
3. There's no evidence that they think I'm a wimp. Maybe they're just curious.
4. Just because I feel nervous and I have a thought of picking up doesn't mean I have to.
5. Let's say I take a toke and blow my sobriety. Will these people be there for me to help me? (Patterson & O'Connell, 2003, p. 85)

The list becomes a working document, something that the group can come back to after they have tested it out, outside in the "real world." Reframing, examining the evidence and cognitive distortions, and rational countering are used as strategies for coping with social pressure. Offering information about their thinking processes increases their level of awareness, enabling them to better understand their thought processes and take on situations that they might otherwise feel powerless to address (not a bad tool to support recovery, confront social pressure, and prevent relapse).

Connecting, Normalizing, and Motivating
Through a Musical Intervention

Musical intervention in group work with chemically dependent adolescents can foster motivation to achieve and maintain sobriety (Buino & Simon, 2011). You don't need to be young or hip to use music effectively with teenagers. The group worker simply needs to be authentic (McFerran, 2010; McFerran-Skewes, 2004).

Buino and Simon (2011) illustrate the use of a musical intervention in a hospital-based chemical dependency treatment facility for clients 18 years and older. Many of the clients had dual diagnoses with depression and anxiety. The goals of the musical intervention were to strengthen connections and motivate recovery in a nonconfrontational manner.

The three musical interventions are lyric analysis, lyric completion, and song sharing. Songs were either chosen in advance or selected spontaneously in the group. The themes of the songs were about addiction and common challenges of people struggling with chemical dependency.

In the lyric analysis phase, the group worker provides written lyrics and suggests two questions to consider about the lyrics of the chosen song: (1) How is the singer feeling? (2) How are you feeling hearing the song? Reading the lyrics first, then discussing them and then hearing the music ties together layers of thought and emotion in a manner that has the potential to move participants, to dig deeper than conversation alone.

After some discussion the song is played, followed by further discussion intended to elicit greater interaction, deeper interpretation, and eventual return to the group members' collective struggles as they relate to the song. For example, in one song, the theme of ambivalence stood out.

> For some clients, ambivalence is shameful, and shame can be one of the greatest relapse precipitators. Other clients believe that once they are in recovery they are only supposed to have "sober" thoughts, and they should not remember the good feelings . . . In reality, however, alcoholics/addicts experience . . . ambivalence, and normalization of such feelings is essential to minimize the detrimental impact of shame. Therefore, after this kind of musical intervention, discussing the topic openly can promote a more honest and meaningful dialogue and help to prevent relapse. (Buino & Simon, 2011, p. 288)

I tried a similar approach in a school-based mental health program with a group of teenage boys who were experimenting with drugs, but not ready to discuss this openly.

One day I brought in the lyrics and CD of a song from the rock opera *Rent*. *Rent* tells the story of a group of young people who were living an unconventional lifestyle and struggling from day to day in the East Village of New York City. The song "Light My Candle" portrays a conversation between Roger, a former drug user, and Mimi, a current drug user. As they flirt with one another, Roger recognizes the signs of her addiction and says, "I know you—you're shivering!" He tries to reason with her and to counsel her, and she is guarded at first:

> *Roger:* I once was born to be bad, I used to shiver like that.
> *Mimi:* I told you I have no heat.
> *Roger:* I used to sweat.
> *Mimi:* I got a cold.
> *Roger:* Uh huh, I used to be a junkie.
> *Mimi:* But now and then I like to . . . Feel good.

In the group discussion that ensues there is a lot of back-and-forth conversation about drugs and sex. As they become more engrossed in the conversation, they ask to hear the CD. As they listen, you can hear a pin drop. The discussion, combined with the mood and emotion of the song, seem to have a real impact as they move from the more intellectual discussion of the lyrics to the emotion of the song itself. The word that jumps out that best reflects the conversation that ensued after listening to the CD is *empathy*.

In the framework presented by Buino and Simon (2011), the musical interventions that follow lyric analysis are lyric sharing and song completion. Lyric sharing enables members to write their own lyrics, giving voice to their own feelings and experiences. Finally, members have the opportunity to select a song of their own choosing, to share with the group, using whatever technology is most accessible. The group worker asks about the reason for the choice of song and relationship to the group theme. The song is played, written lyrics are shared, and the group worker invites full participation to maximize interaction (and investment) in the musical exploration.

One of the measures of success in using music with this population is when there is a shift from noncompliance to cooperation. Naturally, group workers who wish to use this approach with their adolescent group members must be clear about the group purpose, stage of group development, and capacity of group members to participate in abstract thinking. The activity is *cooperative*, with different choices and points of view adding to the whole, as opposed to *competitive* (e.g., who has the best interpretation, best lyrics, best song choice) and therefore can go a long way to promoting mutual support.

The stigma of addiction can leave chemically dependent persons feeling utterly alone in the world. However, being a part of a group that is engaged in interpreting and writing musical lyrics and choosing songs about addiction, written and sung by accomplished artists, can go a long way toward helping adolescents to normalize their experiences and universalize their feelings, and lessen stigma and feelings of isolation and shame (Buino & Simon, 2011).

EVALUATION

Accountability for efficacy of interventions is becoming increasingly common. Process and outcome evaluation are two approaches that measure effectiveness of the interactive quality of the intervention, for example, and success at meeting goals and objectives (Shulman, 2009, 2011).

A thoughtful evaluation plan can help group workers and members to (1) track the ongoing efficacy of the group purpose and need for adjustments as the group evolves, (2) determine whether the agreed-upon goals have been achieved (e.g., social skill development, symptom reduction, job or school retention, resource acquisition, insight, assertiveness, attenuation of stress, school attendance), and (3) verify whether the group is progressing as planned and according to contract (Corey, 2011).

According to Muraskin (1993), evaluation for drug and alcohol prevention and treatment programs can be conducted for the following purposes:

- To determine the effectiveness of programs for the participants
- To document that program objectives have been met
- To provide information about service delivery that will be useful to program staff and other audiences
- To enable program staff to make changes that improve program effectiveness

Categories of outcome measurement for individuals may include the following variables: use of alcohol and drugs, knowledge of alcohol and drugs, attitudes regarding the use of alcohol and drugs, and ability to refuse using alcohol and drugs in the face of peer pressure, self-esteem, and a sense of hope. Pretests and posttests can be given to determine changes in attitude and habits. Surveys can be developed for this purpose. In the case of drug and alcohol use, many programs (e.g., in treatment-oriented and criminal justice settings) use the Breathalyzer and urine analysis to test for use. Changes in risk and protective status and in level of functioning over time are also variables that can be used to assess change.

Observations of the group members over time, reports from parents and school personnel, and monitoring of academic, social, and extracurricular progress are all important in the process of evaluation. Not to be underestimated is the self-evaluation of the individual, members' evaluations of one another, and the group's evaluation of itself, a standard part of the ending phase of group work.

The DARE (Drug Abuse Resistance Education) program, for example, has been one of the more common school-based programs that target substance use by providing information about drugs. Evaluation studies indicate that DARE has not been effective in reducing drug use. Programs that have been evaluated as effective and that can use group work are those that promote interaction among peers to develop norms and build resistance and other social skills (Silver & Eddy, 2006).

For a comprehensive view of evidence-based programs and practices that include information on evaluation of programs, visit the SAMHSA's National Registry of Evidence Based Programs and Practices (2014) at http://www.nrepp. samhsa.gov/.

CONCLUSION

In multiple-family groups that focus on concerns about alcohol and other drug abuse, attention to building trust over time and in each session is essential. Remember, for many of these families distrust has become the norm. In families in which denial, secrecy, and shame are familiar dynamics, processes of openly communicating feelings must be introduced with great care and sensitivity. One consequence of growing up in such an environment is that individuals have little or no practice with the skills of identifying and labeling feelings. Multiple-family groups can provide family members of all generations with an opportunity to enhance their competence by practicing these skills in a physically and emotionally safe environment.

Culturally relevant practice is essential for reaching youths living in communities with higher risks for early exposure to alcohol and other drug abuse. This was the case for a community of Aboriginal youths in Canada. Harm reduction and reflective education were combined to break through to this entrenched population.

Adolescents in recovery need to develop coping skills for dealing with social pressure. Belonging to a supportive group is a good first step. A cognitive-behavioral approach is a valuable adjunct to any recovery group. Thinking straight and staying straight go together.

The thoughtful use of expressive activities, as the example of a musical intervention illustrates, can address the issues of noncompliance, ambivalence, and motivation for change for adolescents. Engaging adolescents through a carefully structured and well-timed program of lyric interpretation and creation, and song sharing can also help to reduce stigma, shame, and isolation, and elevate the full participation and collaboration of the group. Although not motivational interviewing per se, the use of the arts and other expressive activities should be considered by group workers as they assist adolescents through the stages of change.

Finally, making good connections with caring adults, as well as peers, is essential for adolescents. If a child's job is to explore and a parent's job is to protect, parents and other relevant people in adolescents' lives can help in creating environments that promote positive peer experiences, where teens can safely explore and experiment and avoid behavior that can harm themselves or others.

RESOURCES

Al-Anon Family Group Headquarters, Inc.
1600 Corporate Landing Parkway
Virginia Beach, VA 23454-5617
757-563-1600
757-563-1655
http://www.al-anon.org
http://www.al-anon.alateen.org

Alcoholics Anonymous (AA)
Mailing address
A.A. World Services, Inc.
P.O. Box 459
New York, NY 10163
212-870-3400
http://www.aa.org

Location
A.A. World Services, Inc.
475 Riverside Drive at West 120th Street, 11th Floor
New York, NY 10115
Basic Guide to Program Evaluation by Carter McNamara
http://www.managementhelp.org/evaluatn/fnl_eval.htm

Centers for Disease Control and Prevention
1600 Clifton R.
Atlanta, GA 30333
404-639-3311
http://www.cdc.gov/

Center for Substance Abuse & Prevention (CSAP)
1 Choke Cherry Road
Room 4-1057
Rockville, MD 20857
Beta.samhsa.gov
240-276-2420
http://www.prevention.samhsa.gov

Community Anti-Drug Coalitions of America
625 Slaters Lane, Suite 300
Alexandria, VA 22314
800-54-CADCA
Fax: 703-706-0565
http://www.cadca.org/

Drug Enforcement Administration (DEA)
http://www.usdoj.gov/dea/

Higher Education Center For Alcohol and Drug Prevention
A program from the U.S. Department of Education
43 Foundry Ave.
Waltham, MA 02453
http://www.edc.org/hec/

Join Together Partnership for Drug Free Kids
352 Park Ave. S., 9th Floor
New York, NY 10010
212-922-1560
Fax: 212-922-1570
1-855-DRUGFREE (3784373)
http://www.jointogether.org

MADD (Mothers Against Drunk Drivers)
National Office
511 E. John Carpenter Freeway, Suite 700
Irving, TX 75062
877-ASK-MADD (877-275-6233)
Victim services 24-hour help line:
877-MADD-HELP (877-623-3435)
Fax: 972-869-2206/07
http://www.madd.org/

Nar-Anon Family Group Headquarters, Inc.
22527 Crenshaw Boulevard, No. 200B
Torrance, CA 90505
310-534-8188
800-477-6291
Fax: 310-534-8688
E-mail: WSO@nar-anon.org (English)
E-mail: OSM@nar-anon.org (Spanish)
http://www.nar-anon.org

Narcotics Anonymous (NA)
P.O. Box 9999
Van Nuys, CA 91409
818-773-9999
Fax: 818-700-0700
E-mail: fsmail@na.org
http://www.na.org

National Association for Children
of Alcoholics (NACOA)
10920 Connecticut Ave., Suite 100
Kensington, MD 20895
301-468-0985
888-554COAS
Fax: 301-468-0987
E-mail: nacoa@nacoa.org
http://www.nacoa.org

National Black Alcoholism and Addiction Council, Inc.
1500 Golden Valley Rd.
Minneapolic, MN 55411
407-532-2747
877-622-2674
877-NBAC-ORG (877-622-2674)
Fax: 407-532-2815
E-mail: information@nbacinc.org
http://www.nbacinc.org

National Center on Addiction and Substance Abuse at Columbia University
633 Third Avenue, 19th Floor
New York, NY 10017-6706
212-841-5200
http://www.casacolumbia.org

National Council on Alcoholism and Drug Dependence, Inc.
217 Broadway, Suite 712
New York, NY 10007
212-269-7797
Fax: 212-269-7510
HOPE LINE: 800-NCA-CALL (800-622-2255) 24-Hour Affiliate Referral
http://www.ncadd.org

National Institute on Alcohol Abuse and Alcoholism (NIAAA)
E-mail: Niaaweb-r@exchange.nih.gov
http://www.niaaa.nih.gov

National Institute on Drug Abuse
http://www.drugabuse.gov

Office of National Drug Control Policy (ONDCP)
http://www.whitehouse.gov/ondcp

Parents Helping Parents
Sobrato Center for Nonprofits, San Jose
1400 Parkmoor Avenue, Suite 100
San Jose, CA 95126
408-727-5775
Fax: 408-286-1116
http://www.php.com/

SAMHSA's National Clearinghouse for Alcohol and Drug Information
1 Choke Cherry Rd.
Rockville, MD 20857
877-SAMHSA-7
http://store.samhsa.gov/

SAMHSA Behavioral Health Treatment Services Locator
1-800-662-HELP (4367)
http://www.findtreatment.samhsa.gov/

SAMHSA's National Registry of Evidence Based Programs and Practices
http://www.nrepp.samhsa.gov/

US Department of Education Safe and Drug-Free Schools Program
US Department of Education
400 Maryland Ave., SW
Washington, D.C. 20202
http://www2.ed.gov/osdfs
1-800-USA-LEARN

REFERENCES

American Academy of Child & Adolescent Psychiatry. (2011). *The teen brain: Behavior, problem solving, and decision making.* Retrieved from http://www.aacap.org/cs/root/facts_for_families/the_teen_brain_behavior_problem_solving_and_decision_making

Anthony, E., Koupernik, C., & Chiland, C. (Eds.). (1978). *The child and his family, Vol. 4. Vulnerable children.* New York, NY: Wiley.

Beharie, N., Kalogerogiannis, K., McKay, M. M., Paulino, A., Miranda, A., Rivera-Rodriguez, A., ... Ortiz, A. (2011). The HOPE Family Project: A family-based group intervention to reduce the impact of homelessness on HIV/STI and drug risk behaviors. *Social Work with Groups, 34*(1), 61–78.

Bilides, D. (1990). Race, color, ethnicity and class in school-based adolescent counseling groups. *Social Work with Groups, 13*(4), 43–58.

Bolger, T. (2008, December 18–24). Natalie's law: Long Island press series on heroin use prompts new legislation. *Long Island Press, 6*(50), 8–12.

Buino, S., & Simon, S. R. (2011). Musical interventions in group work with chemically dependent populations. *Social Work with Groups, 34*(3–4), 283–295.

Califano, J. (2009). *How to raise a drug-free kid.* New York, NY: Fireside.

CASA. (2008). *National survey of American attitudes on substance abuse: Teens and parents.* New York, NY: National Center on Addiction and Substance Abuse at Columbia University.

Cash, S. J., & Bridge, J. A. (2009). Epidemiology of youth suicide and suicidal behavior. *Current Opinion in Pediatrics Journal, 21*(5), 613–619.

Center for Behavioral Health Statistics and Quality. (2012). *Results from the 2011 National Survey on Drug Use and Health: Summary of national findings* (HHS Publication No. SMA 12-4713, NSDUH Series H-44). Rockville, MD: Substance Abuse and Mental Health Services Administration.

Centers for Disease Control and Prevention. (2007). Youth exposure to alcohol advertising in magazines—United States, 2001–2005. *Morbidity and Mortality Weekly Report, 56*(30), 763–767.

Centers for Disease Control and Prevention. (2009). *School connectedness: Strategies for increasing protective factors among youth.* Atlanta, GA: US Department of Health and Human Services.

Corey, G. (2011). *Theory and practice of group counseling* (8th ed.). Belmont, CA: Brooks/ Cole.

Dryfoos, J. (1993). Lessons from evaluation of prevention programs. *National Prevention Evaluation Research Collection, 1*(1), 2–4.

Fields, A. (2004). *Curriculum-based motivation group.* Vancouver, WA: Hollifield Associates.

Fuller, D. (2013, 28 May). Increasing problem of prescription drug abuse among youth. *Science Daily.* Retrieved from http://www.sciencedaily.com/releases/2013/05/130528143722.htm

Garmezy, N. (1991). Resiliency and vulnerability to adverse development outcomes associated with poverty. *American Behavioral Scientist, 34*(4), 416–430.

Ghelani, A. (2011). Evaluating Canada's drug prevention strategy and creating a meaningful dialogue with urban Aboriginal youth. *Social Work with Groups, 34*(1), 4–20.

Glantz, M. (1995). *The application of resiliency and risk research to the development of preventive interventions.* Bethesda, MD: National Institute on Drug Abuse.

Griffin, K., Scheier, L., Botvin, G., & Diaz, T. (2001). Protective role of personal competence skills in adolescent substance use: Psychological well being as a mediating factor. *Psychology of additive behaviors, 15*(3), 194–203.

Harm Reduction International. (2013). *What is harm reduction? A position statement from Harm Reduction International.* Retrieved from http://www.ihra.net/what-is-harm-reduction

Hawkins, J., Catalano, R., Jr., & Miller, J. (1992). Risk and protective factors for alcohol and other drug problems in adolescence and early adulthood: Implications for substance abuse prevention. *Psychological Bulletin, 112*(1), 64–105.

Hill, D. C., & Coulson-Brown, D. (2007). Developmental considerations for group therapy with youth. In R. W. Christner, J. L. Stewart, & A. Freeman (Eds.), *Cognitive behavior group therapy with children and adolescents* (pp. 39–63). New York, NY: Routledge.

Johnston, L. D., O'Malley, P. M., Bachman, J. G., & Schulenberg, J. E. (2007). *Monitoring the future, national results on adolescent drug use: Overview of key findings.* Bethesda, MD: National Institute on Drug Abuse.

Landy, S., & Tam, K. K. (1998). *Understanding the contribution of multiple risk factors on child development at various ages.* Quebec City, QB: Hull, Applied Research Branch, Strategic Policy, Human Resources Development.

Malekoff, A. (1994). A guideline for group work with adolescents. *Social Work with Groups, 17*(1/2), 5–19.

Malekoff, A. (2014). *Group work with adolescents: Principles and practice* (3rd ed.). New York, NY: Guilford Press.

Maracle, B. (1993). *Crazywater: Native voices on addiction and recovery.* Toronto, ON: Viking.

McConville, M. (1995). *Adolescence: Psychotherapy and the emergent self.* San Francisco, CA: Jossey-Bass.

McFerran, K. (2010). *Adolescents, music and music therapy: Methods and techniques for clinicians, educators and students.* London, UK: Jessica Kingsley.

McFerran-Skewes, K. (2004). Using songs with groups of teenagers: How does it work. *Social Work with Groups, 27*(2/3), 143–157.

Miller, J. W., Naimi, T. S., Brewer, R. D., & Jones, S. E. (2007). Binge drinking and associated health risk behaviors among high school students. *Pediatrics, 119*, 76–85.

Miller, W., & Rollnick, S. (1991). *Motivational interviewing: Preparing people to change addictive behavior.* New York, NY: Guilford Press.

Miller, W., & Rollnick, S. (2002). *Motivational interviewing: Preparing people to change* (2nd ed). New York, NY: Guilford Press.

Muraskin, L. D. (1993). *Understanding evaluation: The way to better prevention programs.* Washington, DC: US Department of Education.

National Institute on Drug Abuse Research Report Series. (2006). *Anabolic steroid abuse.* Bethesda, MD: US Department of Health and Human Services, National Institutes of Health.

National Institute on Drug Abuse. (2014). *NIDA-funded prevention research helps reduce steroid abuse.* Retrieved from http://www.drugabuse.gov/publications/research-reports/anabolic-steroid-abuse/nida-funded-prevention-research-helps-reduce-steroid-abuse

Patterson, H., & O'Connell, D. (2003). Recovery maintenance and relapse prevention with chemically dependent adolescents. In M. Reinecke, F. Dattilio, & A. Freeman (Eds.), *Cognitive therapy with children and adolescents: A casebook for clinical practice* (pp. 70–94). New York, NY: Guilford Press.

Prochaska, J., DiClemente, C., & Norcross, J. (1992). In search of how people change. *American Psychologist, 47*(9), 1102–1114.

Redl, F., & Wineman, D. (1952). *Controls from within: Techniques for the treatment of the aggressive child.* New York, NY: Free Press.

Rutter, M. (1979). Protective factors in children's responses to stress and disadvantage. In M. W. Kent & J. E. Rolf (Eds.), *Primary prevention psychology: Social competence in children* (Vol. 3, pp. 49–74). Hanover, NH: University Press of New England.

Sameroff, A. (1988, June). *The concept of the environtype: Integrating risk and protective factors in early development.* Keynote address for North Shore Child and Family Guidance Center Conferences, Garden City, NY.

Santrock, J. W. (2006). Life-span development (10th ed.), Boston, MA: McGraw-Hill.

Schorr, L. B. (1989). *Within our reach: Breaking the cycle of disadvantage.* New York, NY: Doubleday.

Sciacca, K. (1996, July 3). On co-occurring addictive and mental disorders: A brief history of the origins of dual diagnosis treatment and program development [published and invited letter to the editor]. *American Journal of Orthopsychiatry, 66*(3). Retrieved from http://users.erols.com/ksciacca/brifhst.htm

Sciacca, K. (2007). Dual diagnosis treatment and motivational interviewing for co-occurring disorders. *National Council Magazine, 2,* 22–23.

Selekman, M. (2005). *Pathways to change: Brief therapy with difficult adolescents.* New York, NY: Guilford Press.

Selekman, M. (2006). *Working with self-harming adolescents: A collaborative strengths-based therapy approach.* New York, NY: Norton.

Selekman, M. (2009). *The adolescent and young adult self-harming treatment manual.* New York, NY: Norton.

Shulman, L. (2009). *The skills of helping: Individuals, families and groups* (6th ed.). Itaska, IL: Peacock.

Shulman, L. (2011). *The skills of helping: Individuals, families, groups, and communities* (7th ed.). Independence, KY: Cengage Learning.

Silver, R., & Eddy, J. (2006). Research-based prevention programs and practice for delivery in schools that decrease the risk of deviant peer influences. In K. Dodge, T. Dishion, & J. Lansford (Eds.), *Deviant peer influences in programs for youth* (pp. 253–277). New York, NY: Guilford Press.

Sobell, L. C., & Sobell, M. B. (2011). *Group therapy for substance abuse disorders: A motivational cognitive-behavioral approach.* New York, NY: Guilford Press.

Substance Abuse and Mental Health Services Administration (SAMHSA). (2012). *Results from the 2011 National Survey on Drug Use and Health: Summary of national findings* (NSDUH Series H-44, HHS Publication No. SMA 12-4713). Rockville, MD: Author.

Substance Abuse and Mental Health Services Administration (SAMHSA). (2013, January 3). *Trends in adolescent substance use and perception of risk from substance use.* Retrieved from http://www.samhsa.gov/data/2k13/nsduh099a/sr099-risk-perception-trends.htm

Substance Abuse and Mental Health Services Administration (SAMHSA). (2014). *National registry of evidence based programs and practices.* Retrieved from http://www.nrepp.samhsa.gov/

Vega, W. A., Zimmerman, R. S., Warheit, G. J., Apospori, E., & Gil, A. C. (1993). Risk factors for early adolescent drug use in four ethnic and racial groups. *American Journal of Public Health, 83*(2), 185–189.

Wegscheider, S. (1981). *Another chance: Hope and health for alcoholic family.* Palo Alto, CA: Science and Behavior Books.

Werner, E. (1986). Resilient offspring of alcoholics: A longitudinal study from birth to age 18. *Journal of Studies on Alcohol, 44*(1), 34–44.

Werner, E. (1989). High-risk children in young adulthood: A longitudinal study from birth to 32 years. *American Journal of Orthopsychiatry, 59*, 72–81.

Werner, E. (1990). Protective factors and individual resilience. In S. Meisels & J. Shonkoff (Eds.), *Handbook of early childhood intervention* (pp. 97–116). New York, NY: Cambridge University Press.

Werner, E., & Smith, R. S. (2001). *Journeys from childhood to midlife: Risk, resiliency and recovery.* Ithaca, NY: Cornell University Press.

Werner, E., Smith, R. S., & Garmezy, N. (1998). *Vulnerable but invincible: A longitudinal study of resilient children and youth.* New York, NY: Adams, Bannaster, Cox.

Zosel, A., Bartelson, B. B., Bailey, E., Lowenstein, S., & Dart, R. (2013). Characterization of adolescent prescription drug abuse and misuse using the Researched Abuse Diversion and Addiction-related Surveillance (RADARS®) System. *Journal of the American Academy of Child and Adolescent Psychiatry, 52*(2), 196–204. doi:10.1016/j.jaac.2012.11.014.

NOTES

1 Prochaska et al., (1992) summarized stages of change as follows: *Precontemplation*: Raise doubt—increase the client's perception of risks and problems with current behavior; *Contemplation*: Evoke reasons to change, risks of not changing, strengthen the client's self-efficacy for change of current behavior; *Determination*: Help the client to determine the best course of action to take in seeking change; *Action*: Help the client to take steps toward change; *Maintenance*: Help the client to identify and use strategies to prevent relapse; *Relapse*: Help the client to review the process of contemplation, determination, and action, without becoming stuck or demoralized because of relapse.

2 Fields (2004) offers a curriculum-based motivational interviewing group that is organized into five sessions and will offer readers a clear approach to using this model in group work.

3 See Beharie et al. (2011) for a description of a family-based intervention—the HOPE Family Project—that offers education and support regarding HIV and alcohol abuse prevention for families of early adolescents, ages 11–14 years, who live in homeless shelters.

4 See Maracle (1993).

Chapter Eight

The Use of Group Work in the Treatment of Substance Use Disorders Among Older Adults

Loretta Hartley-Bangs and Carolyn Knight

Substance use disorders describe a pattern of using a substance that results in impairment in daily living, resulting in a range of adverse consequences. An individual with this disorder will often continue to use the substance despite the negative results. The treatment of substance use disorders has historically relied heavily on group work, both professionally led groups and peer-led groups, such as 12-step programs. This chapter will look at the use of group work in the treatment of adults with substance use disorders, focusing on an often neglected group of individuals: the aging and aged.

REVIEW OF THE LITERATURE

In 1935, one struggling alcoholic, Bill W, met another struggling alcoholic, Dr. Bob. Although the two came from very different backgrounds, they had one thing in common: alcoholism. At that time, very little was known about this disorder, other than it appeared to be chronic and progressive. This lack of understanding led many to believe that it was a moral weakness. There were little to no treatment options available. Those struggling with substance abuse were sent to religious groups to get their "moral house" in order so they could stop drinking. Bill W and Dr. B, two very successful, professional men, realized that they felt better and were able to abstain from alcohol use when they shared their stories with one another without judgment. The two men believed that if this worked for the two of them, it could be helpful to others. This initial coming together of these two men led to what has become an international self-help movement, Alcoholics Anonymous. Thousands of self-help groups continue to function in the service of recovering individuals around the world. This form of group intervention is complemented by the use of professionally facilitated groups, for which there is a solid and ever-expanding evidence base.

Definition of Substance Use Disorders

The *Diagnostic and Statistical Manual of Mental Disorders*, fifth edition (*DSM-5*) (APA, 2013) divides substance use into four groups:

- Impaired control: (1) taking more or for longer than intended, (2) unsuccessful efforts to stop or cut down use, (3) spending a great deal of time obtaining, using, or recovering from use, (4) craving for substance;
- Social impairment: (5) failure to fulfill major obligations due to use, (6) continued use despite problems caused or exacerbated by use, (7) important activities given up or reduced because of substance use;
- Risky use: (8) recurrent use in hazardous situations, (9) continued use despite physical or psychological problems that are caused or exacerbated by substance use; and
- Pharmacologic dependence: (10) tolerance to effects of the substance, (11) withdrawal symptoms when not using or using less.

Substance use disorder is viewed as a chronic condition. As the *DSM* criteria suggest, periods of abstinence are typically followed by active abuse, even in the face of growing negative consequences for the addict (Hussarts, Roozen, Meyers, van de Wetering, & McCrady, 2011).

Etiology and Risk and Protective Factors

In contrast to the perspective on addiction that prevailed at the time of Bill W and Dr. Bob, a perspective that emphasized personal and moral weakness, current views on the causes of substance abuse emphasize a complex interplay of factors, including neurobiological, genetic, behavioral, and cultural (Bennett & Petrash, 2014; Sloboda, Glantz, & Tarter, 2012). Ongoing research suggests that certain individuals may be predisposed to substance use disorders due to genetic factors. Whether addiction to substances develops or not depends upon variables in the individual's environment. These include socioeconomic, cultural, social, and familial influences and exposure to traumatic events (Fothergill & Ensminger, 2006; Ridenour, Maldonado-Molina, Compton, Spitznagel, & Cottler, 2005).

An individual's immediate social environment, particularly her or his relationships with significant others, plays a critical role in determining whether an individual develops a substance use disorder. The influence of social relationships varies and ranges from peer associations that promote (or discourage) substance abuse to family members who support the individual's attempts at recovery or engage in an intervention to encourage the addict to seek treatment (Dopkin,

DeCivita, & Paraherakis, 2011; Hussaarts, Roozen, Meyers, van de Wetering, & McCrady, 2012; Tate et al., 2011).

Much has been written about the existence of mental health problems that often accompany a diagnosis of a substance use disorder. An impressive body of research indicates that individuals diagnosed with substance use disorders are at particular risk of having at least one co-occurring psychiatric condition including anxiety, depression, posttraumatic stress disorder (PTSD), phobias, and bipolar disorder (Bakken, Landheim, & Vaglum, 2007; Brady, Back, & Coffey, 2004; Brady, Haynes, Hartwell, & Killeen, 2013; Carrigan & Randall, 2003). The prevailing view is that the substance misuse serves as a mechanism of self-medication as the individual attempts to manage her or his psychiatric symptoms. However, there is evidence that the substance use disorder may lead to psychiatric problems or, at the very least, precipitate their onset in individuals predisposed to such problems in the first place (Conway, Compton, Stinson, & Grant, 2006: Cosci, Schruers, Abrams, & Griez, 2007; Petrakis, Rosenheck, & Desai, 2011; Santiago et al., 2010; Sbrana et al., 2005).

Evidence indicates that the causes of and trajectory for substance use disorder differ for men and women (Greenfield, Cummings, & Gallop, 2010; Najavits, Rosier, Nolan, & Freeman, 2007; Trucco, Connery, Griffin, & Greenfield, 2007). Women typically have been able to hide their addiction longer than men; thus, their addiction is often more well established and therefore harder to treat. A growing body of evidence suggests that substance use disorders among women are more likely to be the result of prior interpersonal exploitation, particularly sexual abuse in childhood (Ford, Russo, & Mallon, 2007; Maniglio, 2011). Females struggling with substance use disorders also may be at greater risk of co-occurring interpersonal victimization in the form of, for example, prostitution, as a result of their addiction.

Substance Use Disorders Among Older Individuals

According to its most recent research, the United States Department of Health and Human Services Substance Abuse and Mental Health Services Administration (2012) reports that among adults aged 50 to 64 years, the rate of current illicit drug use increased during the past decade. For adults aged 50 to 54, the rate increased from 3.4% in 2002 to 7.2% in 2012. Among those aged 55 to 59, the rate of illicit drug use increased from 1.9% in 2002 to 6.6% in 2012. Among those aged 60 to 64, the rate increased from 1.1% in 2003 to 3.6% in 2012.

These trends reflect the aging of the baby boom cohort (i.e., persons born between 1946 and 1964), among whom the rate of illicit drug use consistently has been higher than that of older cohorts (SAMSHA, 2012). In 2012, only 19.3% of persons aged 65 or older (i.e., born before 1948) reported having ever used illicit drugs in their lifetime, whereas the lifetime rates of use were 47.6% for those aged 60 to 64 (born in 1948 to 1952) and were above 50% for each age group from ages 20 to 59 (born after 1952) (Han, Groerer, Colliver, & Penne, 2009). The problem of aging substance abusers is compounded by the fact that improvements in health care and lifestyle changes have led to an increase in the life expectancy rates for this population (Savage, 2014).

Among older individuals with substance use disorders, the drug of choice is most often alcohol. However, prescription drug misuse has become much more prevalent among this population, resulting from intentional misuse or incidental dependence resulting from medically prescribed use of the drug, typically for pain management. More recently, with the influx of baby boomers into this aging cohort, substance abuse now includes more illicit drugs, including cocaine, marijuana, and opiates (Morse, Watson, MacMaster, & Bride, 2015; Schulte & Yih-Ing, 2014; Wu & Blazer, 2011).

Older individuals who exhibit problematic substance use generally fall into one of two categories: early and late onset (Sacco, Kuerbis, Goge, & Bucholz, 2013). Some individuals manage to use and/or abuse substances throughout most of their lives and survive into old age despite the consequences suffered. The second group began their use and abuse later in life. For each group, aging can exacerbate preexisting risk factors. The first group, often referred to as survivors, present for treatment with a myriad of problems, including, but not limited to, physical/health problems, inconsistent employment, unstable housing, estrangement from family, limited social supports, and mental illness. These issues may be the result of chronic substance use/abuse or may have predated the substance use. The second group, referred to as the reactors, begin to exhibit symptoms of a problem later in life. Some may identify a stressful life event as a precipitant such as death of a spouse/partner, death of a child, retirement, physical infirmity, loss of social contacts, and onset of mental illness.

Group Work With Individuals With Substance Use Disorders

A review of the literature substantiates the effectiveness of group work in the treatment of substance use disorders (Donovan, Ingalsbe, Benbow, & Daley 2013; Orchowski & Johnson, 2012). Groups also can be utilized in conjunction with individual sessions focused on co-occurring challenges with which the individual struggles, as well as medication and psychiatric follow-up.

Research has begun to explain the therapeutic benefits inherent in group work and focuses on the existence of mutual aid (Kelly & Greene 2014). Just as Bill W and Dr. B discovered long ago, when individuals learn they are not alone, that others struggle not only with the addiction and staying clean, but with the accompanying feelings of shame, hopelessness, and guilt, it is easier to take the first steps toward becoming sober. Research also suggests that mutual support and demand (Shulman, 2012), whereby members provide supportive confrontation to one another, are particularly beneficial, since members have credibility with one another.

Those struggling with substance use disorders often seek treatment in response to various pressures, including job jeopardy, legal mandates, family interventions, and medical recommendations. Less frequently, individuals seek treatment due to their own recognition of a problem with addictive substances. Because help-seeking among substance abusers is often mandated and involuntary, engagement strategies to facilitate participation in the group are essential (Dulin, Gonzaleza, Kinga, Girouxa, & Bacona, 2013; Gryczynski et al., 2015; Murphy, Bijur, Rosenbloom, Bernstein, & Gallagher, 2013). The need to identify and intervene earlier in the process of the disease has been emphasized, since this is associated with better outcomes (Tanner-Smith & Lipsey, 2015). The application of motivational interviewing techniques (discussed later), which focus on enhancing client motivation and commitment to change by fostering progress through the stages of change from precontemplation to action, demonstrates strong potential for both engaging and maintaining client commitment to treatment (Shorey et al., 2015).

The treatment of substance use disorders is further complicated by the fact that individuals struggling with addiction also face a myriad of other challenges, including co-occurring mental illness and past and/or present trauma as discussed previously. Thus, groups for individuals with substance use disorders often adopt a dual focus on the abuse of substances and the co-occurring challenges that may have led to and/or resulted from the abuse.

Group Work With Aging Substance Abusers

Despite the growing awareness of the increasing number of aging substance abusers over the past 20 years, services for this population remain limited. The literature on group work with the aging is plentiful. Literature on group work in the treatment of substance abuse abounds. What is lacking is theoretical and evidence-based literature dealing with group work with aging individuals with substance use disorders.

A review of the literature reveals very little beyond the growing prevalence of the problem and the need for age-appropriate assessment tools and skills (Benshoff & Harrawood, 2003; Caputo et al., 2012; Duncan, Nicholson, White, Bradley, & Bonaguro, 2010; Taylor & Grossberg, 2012). For example, screening and diagnostic tools for substance use disorders have not been validated for older persons, leading to inaccurate and improper assessment and treatment. As a result, substance abuse among older adults may go undetected, often for long periods of time, undermining the effectiveness of intervention (Duncan et. al., 2010; Trevisan, 2014).

PRACTICE PRINCIPLES

Self-Awareness

The abuse of substances can lead the addict to engage in behaviors and take risks that practitioners may find difficult to accept and understand. Substance abusers also spend a great deal of time and energy denying they have a problem. Group workers must acknowledge their thoughts and opinions about substance abuse, as well as be aware of their reactions to and feelings about the behaviors and actions members have engaged in to support their addiction. Having a solid understanding of the etiology of substance abuse, as well as associated dynamics such as denial and rationalization, ensures that the practitioner will remain nonjudgmental and maintain appropriate boundaries. Informed supervision, in an environment where honest discussion is promoted, is necessary to assist group leaders in managing their feelings and reactions.

Acceptance of the Client and Understanding the Stages of Change

The group worker must recognize that the client has a right to make her or his own decisions. This includes the decision to accept (or reject) help and commit (or not commit) to abstinence. Many individuals with substance use disorders may not be motivated by a desire to get clean, but rather by a desire to comply with a legal mandate and avoid, for example, prison time or get an employer or family members "off their backs."

The group worker will have to deal directly with members' reluctance to accept they have a problem in a way that respects their perspective but also encourages them to consider the possibility that they may have a problem and that change is possible. If members feel "preached to" or coerced, they are less likely to consider this possibility. In contrast, if they believe the group leader accepts and understands their reluctance, they will be more open to considering change.

Individuals engage in a process of change in stages (DiClemente, 2007; DiClemente, Schlundt, & Gemmell, 2004; Velasquez, Maurer, Crouch, & DiClemente, 2001). These stages include precontemplation; contemplation; preparation; action; and maintenance. Potential group members who present themselves for treatment due to an issue with substance use arrive via many paths, and they may be at different stages of change. Given the denial that often accompanies substance abuse, group workers will need to anticipate that many members will be at the first stage, precontemplation, in which there is a lack of recognition of a problem, or at best, contemplation, whereby the individual considers the possibility that a problem exists.

To help members move through the stages of change, the worker must "start where the client is," recognizing that members may simply not be ready to accept the existence of a problem with substances. The benefit of a group is that members are likely to be at different stages and can, therefore, support but also make demands of one another. This sort of mutual aid assists all in moving forward in accepting they have a problem with substance abuse and taking steps to get and stay clean.

Informed Consent and Confidentiality

All clients, mandated or not, still need to give informed consent for treatment, and group workers must abide by federal and state laws and ethical principles associated with confidentiality. The consequences of substance use disorders often involve others, including family members, employers, and the legal system (Hussaarts et al., 2012). Therefore, the group worker needs to consider the importance and limits associated with confidentiality and balance the members' right to privacy against the interests, needs, and requirements of others with a vested interest in a member's recovery.

COMMON THEMES

The theme that predominates in group work with individuals with substance use disorders is the denial and ambivalence associated with asking for and accepting help and taking the first initial steps toward recovery. Ambivalence about abstention reflects both psychological and physiological factors.

In some instances, individuals with substance use disorders struggle with a physical dependence upon the drug of choice; thus, the prospect of going through withdrawal discourages individuals from attempting sobriety, even with medical intervention that blunts the effects of withdrawal (Ciketic, Hayatbakhsh, Doran, Najman, & McKetin, 2012; Haile, Kosten, & Kosten, 2009). Relatedly, individuals addicted to pain medications may be reluctant to forgo their drug of choice, fearing the return of the pain that led to the dependence in the first place (Minozzi, Amato, & Davoli, 2013). In many instances, the individual has developed a psychological dependence on his or her substance of choice; this can include liking the positive effects the drug produces and/or allowing the individual to escape from painful feelings and experiences (Cheatle, 2014; Hammersley, 2014). In order for group work to be helpful to individuals with substance use disorders, the worker must recognize the very real barriers that these clients face as they consider sobriety.

An often overlooked but common theme in group work with substance abusers is the stigma associated with their disorder as well as behaviors they may have engaged in to maintain their substance abuse (Livingston, Milne, Fang, & Amari, 2012). Although it is true that substance abuse is less likely to be viewed by the general public as a moral weakness or shortcoming as it was in the past, negative stereotypes of substance abusers remain as well as an atmosphere of shaming and blaming. "Substance abuse disorders are often treated as a moral and criminal issue, rather than a health concern. This is especially true of illegal substances which are perceived more negatively than legal substances" (Livingston et. al., 2012, p. 40). In addition, it is still widely assumed that the substance abuser has control over her or his addiction, further contributing to the negative stereotypes associated with the disorder.

A particularly challenging aspect of the social stigma associated with substance use disorder is the extent to which the individual struggling with the disorder internalizes the stereotypes and engages in what has been referred to as self-stigmatizing behavior (Luoma, Kohlenberg, Hayes, Bunting, & Rye, 2008). Individuals with substance use disorders engage in substance abuse and experience feelings of shame, isolation, and self-blame, which, in turn, lead to continued abuse of substances. Furthermore, continued misuse of substances reinforces reduced feelings of self-efficacy and control over the addictive behavior, which contributes to the ambivalence and denial discussed previously (Greenfield, Cummings, & Gallop, 2010).

Research suggests that feelings of shame and self-blame are particularly common among women and the aged (van Olphen, Eliason, Freudenberg, & Barnes, 2009; Wu & Blazer, 2011). In both cases, these heightened reactions appear to be associated with the substance abuser's embarrassment regarding the impact her or his abuse has had on social relationships, particularly familial ones.

An obvious advantage of group participation is that it provides members with the opportunity to experience acceptance and understanding from others "in the same boat." Isolation and self-stigma, as well as feelings of blame and shame, are reduced as members appreciate their commonality as well as learn about the etiology of substance abuse. Group participation is not designed to absolve members of taking responsibility for the actions in which they have engaged and decisions they have made. In fact, members will have an easier time owning up to their mistakes and behaviors if their self-stigmatizing thoughts and actions are reduced.

Because many individuals with substance use disorders deny they have a problem and attend groups involuntarily, the "authority theme" (Shulman, 2012) may be very prominent and one that, if not addressed directly, can undermine the group's effectiveness right from the start. Perhaps more so than with other client populations, individuals with substance use disorders are likely to participate in a group under duress. The mandatory nature of addiction services places the client at risk of dropping out or only superficially participating in treatment, even though many individuals with substance use disorders will only get the needed help if required to do so (Burke & Gregoire, 2007).

If the mandate and the substance abuser's accompanying reactions are ignored, the risk of dropout increases (Bright & Martire, 2013; Rengifo & Stemen, 2013). From the start of the group, the worker will need to acknowledge the reasons for members' attendance and their feelings about this—reactions that are likely to include anger, powerlessness, hostility, and suspicion. The worker cannot alter the circumstances under which members attend the group. What she or he can do is validate the resistance and anger they may experience, lessening the possibility that these reactions will inhibit engagement.

A common theme in groups for aging individuals with substance use disorders is loss and grief. Aging requires ongoing adjustment to changes occurring within the individual and in her or his social environment. This cohort must respond to multiple life losses, including significant relationships with loved ones and friends, careers, and independence. Group participation can provide older individuals with substance use disorders with a safe, supportive environment in which they can discuss the losses they have experienced as well as work on accepting and managing their substance misuse (Kelly, 2005; Kuerbis & Sacco, 2013).

Another theme that emerges in groups for older substance abusers revolves around family issues, most notably resistance to allowing the group member to discuss issues related to death and dying. One member recently echoed a common sentiment, "I cannot discuss this with my children; they won't admit that one day I might die. After all, I'm 90 years old!" In providing members with a place to talk about taboo subjects, like death and dying, the group also assists them in getting and staying sober.

Another theme that predominates in groups for older individuals with substance use disorders is shame and isolation. These reactions are also common among younger abusers but, in the case of older individuals, there is the added pressure to be an appropriate role model for their families and communities. Because many seniors experience these feelings so intensely, their reluctance to participate in a group, which is typical for a substance abuser of any age, is quickly replaced by relief and reassurance as they connect with others dealing with the challenges associated with aging.

RECOMMENDED WAYS OF WORKING

Understanding an individual's motivation is important to engaging her or him in the treatment process (DiClemente, Schlundt, & Gemmell, 2004; Rose & Chang, 2010). Motivational interviewing is based upon five assumptions (Carroll et al., 2006; Miller, 2002). Ambivalence about accepting the need for help is normal and constitutes an important motivational obstacle in recovery. Ambivalence can be resolved by working with the client's intrinsic motivations and values. The alliance between worker and the client is a collaborative partnership to which each brings expertise. An empathic, supportive, yet directive counseling style provides conditions under which change can occur. In contrast, direct argument and aggressive confrontation will tend to increase client defensiveness and reduce the likelihood of behavioral change.

When these assumptions are enacted in a group context, the following strategies and principles increase the likelihood that members will benefit from the intervention. Because moving past denial is a process that takes place over time, a common group goal often focuses on helping members transition from precontemplation and contemplation to preparation and action.

Providing members with factual information about the differences between use, abuse, and addiction helps members move through the stages of change. Encouraging members to identify and acknowledge the progression of their symptoms as well as the consequence of their actions also assists them in moving forward. This must be done, however, using terms that are nonaccusatory and nonstigmatizing. Guilt-inducing language will serve only to keep members stuck, undermining their efforts to move forward. Members will be more receptive to change if they experience empathy and understanding from the leader and one another. This includes expressions of genuine concern for members' physical and emotional safety and well-being.

Members can be encouraged to "experiment" with abstinence or reduce their usage of substances as a way of validating the existence of a problem. This strategy also introduces changes in behavior in a way that is nonthreatening. Individuals with substance use disorders often are "stuck" in the beginning stages because the prospect of getting and staying sober seems so overwhelming.

Motivational interviewing strategies can be easily incorporated into group work with substance-abusing members. Groups with a motivational interviewing orientation are highly interactive, focused on positive change, and harness group members sense of connectedness and being "all in the same boat" to support positive change (Wagner & Ingersoll, 2012). Such groups are conceptualized as operating with four phases: (1) engaging the group; (2) evoking member perspectives; (3) broadening perspectives and building momentum for change; and (4) moving into action.

Although techniques drawn from motivational interviewing can be effective components of any group for substance-abusing individuals, mutual aid remains the foundation of any group approach. The feelings of shame, anger, isolation, and powerlessness that are endemic to addicts are dealt with most effectively in a group setting. As members discover they are not alone, their ability to manage their feelings is enhanced as is their willingness to confront their addiction. Thus, the leader has the responsibility of fostering a group climate that promotes collaborative, trusting relationships between group members. As members come to see their underlying commonalities, they are better able to support *and* demand work from one another.

Incorporating motivational interviewing concepts into mutual aid groups conveys acceptance that members will change at their own pace and validates the reality that many of them are there not by choice but by ultimatum. As discussed earlier, identifying where an individual is with respect to the stages of change is a critical first step in assisting her or him in moving ahead. Members often come to group because they or someone close to them has identified that substance use or misuse is creating a problem in their lives. The individual may or may not agree with this assessment but has agreed to attend because of the negative consequences associated with not attending.

Therefore, an initial goal for members is to determine whether or not there is a problem that needs to be addressed. The process of mutual aid begins quickly when members share their own experiences upon entering the group. They are able to identify with one another as they share feelings of ambivalence, anxiety, anger, and shame. This is a powerful motivator for members in the precontemplation and contemplation stages to take the next step and accept they have a problem.

Participation in a group provides a safe, nonjudgmental venue for individuals to begin to explore their own use as well as all areas of their lives that have been impacted by their addiction. Because of the shame inherently experienced by those struggling with addiction, the ability to talk openly about their problem among people with similar experiences is extremely therapeutic and highly motivating. This venue is a fertile place to share, test out ideas and new behaviors, and gain helpful feedback. For the group facilitator, it allows an assessment of the individual's functioning in an interactive setting. This view is helpful in offering feedback to the individual.

Groups can range from those with more structure and educational focus to those that are more loosely structured and focus more on members sharing information with and supporting one another. For members new to recovery and in the earlier stages of change, psychoeducational groups are an effective starting point. Less structured groups are particularly suitable for individuals who have accepted they have a problem with substances and want to gain or maintain their sobriety.

The group worker may wish to consider whether the group should be single-gender or mixed. As discussed previously, substance use disorder differs in some significant ways for men and women. There is some evidence that women fare better in single-gender groups (Greenfield, Cummings, & Gallop, 2010; Trucco, Connery, Griffin, & Greenfield, 2007). At minimum, the worker should consider whether the underlying similarities between men and women are enough to override the differences.

As discussed, many members will struggle with other problems in living that either result from or led to the substance abuse. Therefore, the group worker should be prepared to address these issues in an appropriate manner. The group may focus primarily on the substance abuse but include validation of members' feelings and experiences and help them see the connection between other problems in living and the substance abuse. In contrast, the group could have a dual focus on the substance use disorder and co-occurring problems such as past trauma, psychiatric conditions, disruptions in interpersonal relationships, grief and loss and the like.

EVALUATION

Evaluation may involve more than just assessing changes in group members' substance use. For reasons discussed previously, a particularly important avenue of assessment is members' degree of motivation for change. In some groups, in fact, enhancing motivation for change may be the primary focus and indication of effectiveness. In groups where members are further along in the stages of change, evaluation is likely to center on substance-using behavior and may range from complete abstinence to reduction in substance usage. Appropriate assessment tools are readily available. Some of the more widely used include the Addiction Severity Index (http://www.sciencedirect.com/science/article/pii/074054729290062S) and assessments based upon the stages of change model (http://www.ncbi.nlm.nih.gov/books/NBK64976/#A62297).

Additional measures can be used to assess whether there are positive changes in other problems in living that members may experience, including employment, relationship issues, and mental and physical health.

RESOURCES

International Association for the Advancement of Social Work with Groups
http://www.iaswg.org

NIDA
http://drugpubs.drugabuse.gov
http://easyread.drugabuse.gov
media@nida.nih.gov

SAMHSA
Substance Abuse and Mental Health Services Administration
1 Choke Cherry Road
Rockville, MD 20857
http://www.samhsa.gov

REFERENCES

American Psychiatric Association. (2013). *Diagnostic and statistical manual of mental disorders* (5th ed.). Washington, DC: APA Press.

Baaken, K., Landheim, A., & Vaglum, P. (2007). Axis I andII disorders as long-term predictors of mental distress: A six-year follow-up of substance dependent patients. *BMC Psychiatry, 7,* 29–38.

Bennett, S., & Petrash, P. (2014). The neurobiology of substance use disorders: Information for assessment and clinical treatment. *Smith College Studies in Social Work, 84*(2–3), 273–291.

Benshoff, J. J., & Harrawood, L. K. (2003). Substance abuse and the elderly: Unique issues and concerns. *Journal of Rehabilitation, 69*(2), 43–48.

Brady, K., Back, S., & Coffey, S. (2003). Substance abuse and posttraumatic stress disorder. *Current Directions in Psychological Science, 13,* 206–209.

Brady, K., Haynes, L., Hartwell, K., & Killeen, T. (2013). Substance use disorders and anxiety: A treatment challenge for social workers. *Social Work in Public Health, 28,* 407–413.

Bright, D. A., & Martire, K. A. (2013). Does coerced treatment of substance-using offenders lead to improvements in substance use and recidivism? A review of the treatment efficacy literature. *Australian Psychologist, 48*(1), 69–81.

Burke, A. C., & Gregoire, T. K. (2007). Substance abuse treatment outcomes for coerced and noncoerced clients. *Health and Social Work, 32*(1), 7–15.

Caputo, F. Vignoli, T., Leggio, L. Addolorato, G., Zoli, G., & Bernardi, M. (2012). Alcohol use disorders in the elderly: A brief overview from epidemiology to treatment options. *Experimental Gerontology, 47,* 411–416.

Carrigan, M., & Randall, C. (2003). Self-medication in social phobia: A review of the alcohol literature. *Addictive Behaviors, 28,* 269–284.

Cheatle, M. D. (2014). Psychological dependence and prescription opioid misuse and abuse. *Pain Medicine, 15*(4), 541–543.

Ciketic, S., Hayatbakhsh, M. R., Doran, C. M., Najman, J. M., & McKetin, R. (2012). A review of psychological and pharmacological treatment options for methamphetamine dependence. *Journal of Substance Use, 17*(4), 363–383.

Conway, K., Compton, W., Stinson, F., & Grant, B. (2006). Lifetime comorbidity of DSM-IV mood and anxiety disorders and specific drug use disorders: Results from the National Epidemiological Survey on Alcohol and Related Conditions. *Journal of Clinical Psychiatry, 67,* 247–257.

Cosci, F., Schruers, K., Abrams, K., & Greiz, E. (2007). Alcohol use disorders and panic disorder: A review of the evidence of a direct relationship. *Journal of Clinical Psychiatry, 68,* 874–880.

DiClemente, C. C. (2007). Mechanisms, determinants and processes of change in the modification of drinking behavior. *Alcoholism: Clinical and Experimental Research, 3,* 13S–20S.

DiClemente, C. C., Schlundt, D., & Gemmell, L. (2004). Readiness and stages of change in addiction treatment. *American Journal of Addictions, 13,* 103–119.

Donovan, D. M., Ingalsbe, M. H., Benbow, J., & Daley, D. C. (2013). 12-step interventions and mutual support programs for substance use disorders: An overview. *Social Work Public Health, 28*(3–4), 313–332.

Dopkin, P., DeCivita, & Paraherakis, A. (2011). The role of functional social support in treatment retention and outcomes among outpatient adult substance abusers. *Addiction, 97,* 347–356.

Dulin, P. L., Gonzaleza, V. M., Kinga, D. K., Girouxa, D., & Bacona, S. (2013). Development of a smartphone-based self-administered intervention for alcohol use disorders. *Alcoholism Treatment Quarterly, 31*, 321–336.

Duncan, D. F., Nicholson, T., White, J. B., Bradley, D. B., & Bonaguro, J. (2010). The baby boomer effect: Changing patterns of substance abuse among adults ages 55 and older. *Journal of Aging and Social Policy, 22*, 237–248.

Ford, J., Russo, E., & Mallon, S. (2007). Integrating treatment of posttraumatic stress disorder and substance use disorder. *Journal of Counseling and Development, 85*, 475–489.

Haile, C. N., Kosten, T. R., & Kosten, T. A. (2009). Pharmacogenetic treatments for drug addiction: Cocaine, amphetamine and methamphetamine. *American Journal of Drug and Alcohol Abuse, 35*(3), 161–177.

Hussaarts, P., Roozen, H., Meyers, R., van de Wetering, B. J., & McCrady, B. (2012). Problem areas reported by substance abusing individuals and their concerned significant others. *American Journal on Addictions, 21*, 38–46.

Fothergill, K. E., & Ensminger, M. E. (2006). Childhood and adolescent antecedents of drug and alcohol problems: A longitudinal study. *Drug and Alcohol Dependence, 82*(1), 61–76.

Greenfield, S., Cummings, A., & Gallop, R. (2010). Self-efficacy and substance use outcomes for women in single-gender and mixed-gender group treatment. *Journal of Groups in Addiction and Recovery, 5*, 4–16.

Gryczynski, J., Mitchell, S. G., Gonzales, A., Moseley, A., Peterson, T. R., Ondersma, S. J., . . . Schwartz, R. P. (2015). A randomized trial of computerized vs. in-person brief intervention for illicit drug use in primary care: Outcomes through 12 months. *Journal of Substance Abuse Treatment, 50*, 3–10.

Hammersley, R. (2014). Constraint theory: A cognitive, motivational theory of dependence. *Addiction Research and Theory, 22*(1), 1–14.

Han, B., Groerer, J. C., Colliver, J. D., & Penne, M. A. (2009). Substance use disorders among older addicts in the United States in 2020. *Addictions, 104*, 88–96.

Kelly, J. F., & Greene, C. M. (2014). Toward an enhanced understanding of the psychological mechanisms by which spirituality aids recovery in Alcoholics Anonymous. *Alcoholism Treatment Quarterly, 32*, 299–318.

Kelly, T. B. (2005). Accumulated risk: Mutual aid groups for elderly persons with a mental illness. In A. Gitterman & L. Shulman (Eds.), *Mutual aid groups, vulnerable and resilient populations, and the life cycle* (3rd ed., pp. 536–572). New York, NY: Columbia University Press.

Kuerbis, A., & Sacco, P. (2013). A review of existing treatments for substance abuse among the elderly and recommendations for future directions. *Substance Abuse: Research and Treatment, 7*, 13–37.

Livingston, J., Milne, T., Fang, M., & Amari, E. (2012). The effectiveness of interventions for reducing stigma related to substance use disorders: A systematic review. *Addiction, 107*, 39–50.

Luoma, J., Kohlenberg, B., Hayes, S., Bunting, K., & Rye, A. (2008). Reducing self-stigma in substance abuse through acceptance and commitment therapy: Model, manual development, andpilot outcomes. *Addiction Research Theory, 16*, 149–165.

Maniglio, R. (2011). The role of child sexual abuse in the etiology of substance-related disorders. *Journal of Addictive Diseases, 30*(3), 216–228.

Miller, P. (1983). *Theories of developmental psychology.* San Francisco, CA: W. H. Freeman.

Minozzi, S., Amato, L., & Davoli, M. (2013). Development of dependence following treatment with opioid analgesics for pain relief: A systematic review. *Addiction, 108*(4), 688–698.

Morse, S., Watson, C., MacMaster, S., & Bride, B. (2015). Differences between older and younger adults in residential treatment for co-occurring disorders. *Journal of Dual Diagnosis, 11,* 75–82.

Najavits, L., Rosier, M., Nolan, A., & Freeman, M. (2007). A new gender-based model for women's recovery from substance abuse: Results of a pilot outcome study. *American Journal of Drug and Alcohol Abuse, 33,* 5–11.

Orchowski, L. M., & Johnson, J. E. (2012). Efficacy of group treatments for alcohol use disorders: A review. *Current Drug Abuse Reviews, 5,* 148–157.

Petrakis, I., Rosenheck, R., & Desai, R. (2011). Substance use comorbidity among veterans with posttraumatic stress disorder and other psychiatric illness. *American Journal on Addictions, 20,* 185–189.

Rengifo, A. F., & Stemen, D. (2013). The impact of drug treatment on recidivism: Do mandatory programs make a difference? Evidence from Kansas's Senate Bill 123. *Crime and Delinquency, 59*(6), 930–950.

Ridenour, T. A., Maldonado-Molina, M., Compton, W. M., Spitznagel, E. L., & Cottler, L. B. (2005). Factors associated with the transition from abuse to dependence among substance abusers: Implications for a measure of addictive liability. *Drug and Alcohol Dependence, 80*(1), 1–14.

Rose, S. D., & Chang, H.. (2010). Motivating clients in treatment groups. *Social Work with Groups, 33,* 260–277.

Sacco, P., Kuerbis, A., Goge, N., & Bucholz, K. (2013). Help seeking for drug and alcohol problems among adults age 50 and older: A comparison of the NLAES and NESARC surveys. *Drug and Alcohol Dependence, 131,* 157–161.

Santiago, P., Wilk, J., Milliken, C., Castro, C., Engel, C., & Hoge, C. (2010). Screening for alcohol misuse and alcohol-related behaviors among combat veterans. *Psychiatric Services, 61,* 575–581.

Savage, C. (2014). The baby boomers and substance use: Are we prepared? *Journal of Addictions Nursing, 25,* 1–3.

Sbrana, A., Bizzarri, J., Rucci, P., Gonnelli, C., Doria, M., Spagnolli, S., & Cassano, G. (2005). The spectrum of substance use in mood and anxiety disorders. *Comprehensive Psychiatry, 46,* 6–13.

Schulte, M., & Yih-Ing, H. (2014). Relation of active, passive, and quitting smoking with incident type 2 diabetes: A systematic review and meta-analysis. *Public Health Reviews, 35,* 1–27.

Shorey, R. C., Martino, S., Lamb, K. E., LaRowe, S. D., & Santa Ana, E. J. (2015). Change talk and relatedness in group motivational interviewing: A pilot study. *Journal of Substance Abuse Treatment, 51,* 75–81.

Shulman, L. (2012). *The skills of helping individuals, families, groups, and communities* (7th ed.). Belmont, CA: Brooks/Cole Cengage Learning.

Sloboda, Z., Glantz, M. D., & Tarter, R. E. (2012). Revisiting the concepts of risk and protective factors for understanding the etiology and development of substance use and substance use disorders: Implications for prevention. *Substance Use and Misuse, 47*(8–9), 944–962.

Substance Abuse and Mental Health Services Administration (SAMSHA). (2013). National Survey on Drug Use and Health: Summary of national findings. Retrieved from http://www.samhsa.gov/data/sites/default/files/NSDUHresultsPDFWHTML2013/Web/NSDUHresults2013.pdf

Tanner-Smith, E. E., & Lipsey, M. W. (2015). Brief alcohol interventions for adolescents and young adults: A systematic review and meta-analysis. *Journal of Substance Abuse Treatment, 51*, 1–18.

Tate, S., Mrnak-Meyer, Shriver, C., Atkinson, J., Robinson, S., & Brown, S. (2011). Predictors of treatment retention for substance-dependent adults with co-occurring depression. *American Journal on Addictions, 20*, 357–365.

Taylor, M. H., & Grossberg, G. T. (2012). The growing problem of illicit substance abuse in the elderly: A review. *Primary Care Companion, 14*, 1–9.

Trevisan, L. A. (2014). Elderly alcohol use disorders: Epidemiology, screening, and assessment issues. *Psychiatric Times, 31*(5), 1–4.

Trucco, E., Connery, H., Griffin, M., & Greenfield, S. (2007). The relationship of self-esteem and self-efficacy to treatment outcomes of alcohol-dependent men and women. *American Journal on Addictions, 16*, 85–92.

Van Olphen, J., Eliason, M., Freudenberg, N., & Barnes, M. (2009). Nowhere to go: How stigma limits the options of female drug users after release from jail. *Substance Abuse Treatment and Prevention Policy, 4*, 10–18.

Velasquez, M., Maurer, G. G., Crouch, C., & DiClemente, C. C. (2001). *Group treatment for substance abuse: A stage-of-change therapy manual.* New York: Guilford Press.

Wagner, C. C., & Ingersoll, K. S. (2012). *Motivational interviewing in groups.* New York: Guilford Press.

Wu, L., & Blazer, D. (2011). Illicit and nonmedical drug use among older adults: A review. *Journal of Aging and Health, 23*, 481–504.

Part Two

Adjusting to Change

Chapter Nine

Social Skills Groups for School-Aged Children and Adolescents

Jen Clements

Social skills are an essential aspect of an individual's growth and have a lasting impact on behavioral, intellectual, and emotional functioning across the life span. Social skills groups are typically offered to children and adolescents and may be facilitated either in a school or outpatient setting. These groups usually focus on building social competence. Gresham, Sugai, and Horner (2001) define social competence as "the degree to which [members] are able to establish and maintain satisfactory interpersonal relationships, gain peer acceptance, establish and maintain friendships, and terminate negative or pernicious interpersonal relationships" (p. 331). An effective social skills group addresses abilities such as communication skills, reading nonverbal cues, making and keeping friendships, and active listening.

REVIEW OF THE LITERATURE

Children spend a majority of their day during the academic year at school. It is in this context that problems in interpersonal relationships with peers and adults may first become apparent. Furthermore, it is in this context that the effects of the child's interpersonal difficulties will be most noticeable. These consequences include poor academic achievement, social maladjustment, and peer rejection (King & Boardman, 2006).

Social skills training is most likely to occur in a group setting (Dennison, 2008). Although social skills groups have been found to benefit the general population of school-aged children, at-risk students (especially those with behavioral and/or emotional problems or developmental disabilities) are the most common beneficiaries of this treatment modality. This section will review a theoretical framework connected to social skills groups in schools, the advantages of using a group setting, and the benefits that social skills groups provide to their participants.

Theoretical Framework

The theory upon which social skills groups are based is social cognitive theory, which is derived from Albert Bandura's social learning theory (Boston University, 2013). This theory emphasizes the impact that cognitive functioning has on behavior as well as on one's definition of self, particularly perspectives on self-efficacy. Self-efficacy refers to the individual's view of her or his ability to achieve mastery over the social environment. The importance of self-efficacy is underscored by research which found that students who had higher levels of self-efficacy were more likely to engage in and persevere through academic and social activities, thus increasing their competence in these areas (Cervantes & Porretta, 2013).

Social cognitive theory focuses on the self-reinforcing nature of social learning: As a child develops positive social skills, her or his feelings of self-efficacy are enhanced, which in turn leads to an increase in prosocial behaviors, enhanced academic achievement, and improved peer interactions. The reverse is also true; when individuals engage in negative behaviors that are met with rejection and sanctions, this reinforces negative definitions of self and diminishes feelings of efficacy and worth. This may reinforce negative definitions of self and diminish feelings of efficacy and worth.

Characteristics of Social Skills Groups

Social skills groups for school-aged children and adolescents share two main elements. Groups provide members with behavioral practice opportunities and rely upon peer interactions and influence.

Practice Opportunities

Participation in a group in an academic setting provides students with the opportunity to practice new behaviors in the presence of others (Lavallee, Bierman, & Nix, 2005; Sommers-Flanagan, Barrett-Hakanson, Clarke, & Sommers-Flanagan, 2000; Whalon, Conroy, Martinez & Werch, 2015). A group format allows for skills practice, peer modeling, and a generalization of skills to other contexts and settings (Lavallee et al., 2005). For example, in a coping and social skills group, students first are helped to see and understand the behaviors that are problematic and necessitated their participation in a group. After identifying a list of healthy, constructive social behaviors, members are able to practice these behaviors with other group members through, for example, role playing (Sommers-Flanagan et al., 2000).

Capitalizing on Peer Influence

In social skills groups, members' relationships with one another are utilized to promote more prosocial interactions (Lavallee et al., 2005). For example, in a study of one approach to social skills training in a group context, the Making

Choices Program, it was found that children who were rated as having a lower risk status for antisocial behavior prior to participation in the group maintained their lower risk status, whereas children who were higher risk moved to lower risk after the intervention (Fraser, Thompson, Day, & Macy, 2014). That is, participants who were more adept at social skills were able to positively influence children whose social skills were more limited.

Benefits of Social Skill Groups

There are a multitude of benefits associated with social skill groups for children and adolescents in academic settings. Research suggests four primary advantages.

Improvement in Peer Interactions

Students who participate in social skills groups develop more positive interactions with peers outside of the group (Dennison, 2008; Garcia, De Pedro, Astor, Lester, & Benbenishty, 2015; Lavallee et al., 2005; Tierney & Dowd, 2000). For example, in a study conducted with children in military families, it was reported that after only three to four group sessions, participants had started making friends with both members and nonmembers of the group (Garcia et al., 2014). Another study found that an increased number of members, at least one fourth, viewed themselves as "having enough friends" after participating in the group intervention, and none of the participants felt that they lost friendships (Tierney & Dowd, 2000).

Improvement in Behaviors

Social skills groups have been found to improve challenging behaviors in children (Brigman, Webb, & Campbell, 2007; Dennison, 2008; Fraser et al., 2014; Lavallee et al., 2005; Tierney & Dowd, 2000). Behavioral improvements may differ between elementary, middle, and high school–aged students. Elementary students who participate in social skills groups demonstrated positive behavioral changes related to an increase in frustration tolerance and an increase in internal locus of control (Dennison, 2008). Middle school students have been shown to have a reduction in anger and an increase in impulse control, whereas high school students were found to have developed higher levels of self-control and demonstrated a decrease in disciplinary issues (Dennison, 2008).

Improvement in Academic Achievement

Participation in social skills groups also was found to improve academic achievement of students of all ages (Brigman et al., 2007; Dennison, 2008). For example, in a study that used the Student Success Skills (SSS) program, which was created from strategies related to both positive social skills and academic achievement, there was a significant improvement in academic performance for participants following the SSS intervention (Brigman et al., 2007).

Improvement in Positive Identity

An individual's interpersonal abilities influence her or his identity and self-worth. A positive self-identity promotes positive social interactions, and positive social interactions reinforce and deepen positive feelings of worth and esteem. Particularly for adolescents, participation in a social skills group can help members develop a positive identity as they learn new ways of relating in a supportive environment (Dennison, 2008; Sommers-Flanagan et al., 2000). For example, it has been found that involvement in a social skills group decreased feelings of loneliness and increased feelings of being accepted by peers (Dennison, 2008). Group members also learned to give and receive positive feedback and incorporate this into their behavioral repertoire. As members identify strengths in others, they are better able to see strengths in themselves, thus enhancing feelings of esteem, worth, and self-efficacy (Sommers-Flanagan et al., 2000).

COMMON THEMES

Diversity and Difference

An important theme when working with children in a social skills group is to be comfortable with diversity and difference within the group. Members are likely to differ in obvious ways such as race, ethnicity, and gender. Differences also will exist in members' backgrounds. Members will only be able to engage with one another and with the leader, who, at minimum, differs from members with respect to age, if differences are acknowledged and underlying commonalities highlighted. The following lengthy excerpt comes from one of my groups and illustrates the importance of addressing diversity and difference between the leaders and the members (Clements, in press). The scenario also exemplifies additional concepts, themes, and ways of working, as discussed later in this chapter.

> I co-facilitate a weekly teen boys group in a primarily urban area 50 miles from the Baltimore metropolitan region. The boys in the group attend the meetings because they recently lost a loved one, and they have been identified by their school counselor as having "behavioral difficulties." These boys are diagnosed with oppositional defiant disorder, attention-deficit disorder, and depression. They come from homes where their parents are in jail, deceased, substance abusers, or otherwise unavailable. The group has been meeting for 3 months.
>
> The boys are leaders, comedians, and poets. They have artistic talents that make our art therapy group very unique. Early in the life of the group, the members decided to name the group the *Difference Makers*. They chose

this name because they would be making something each week. They all also aspired to make a difference in their lives and their communities.

In this particular session, the group began with the usual check-ins. The members were anxious to find out what they were going to make during the session. The boys were unusually quiet, engaging in only limited sharing. When we said that we would be making masks, one of the boys mumbled under his breath, "Masks for kids who are invisible. Great." I heard it but was not sure who else had. I felt a mixture of anxiety and concern. I decided to reach out to him and questioned, "What was that, Sam?" He quickly shut down, and said, "Nah, sorry Ms. Jen. It's nothing." But it was something. I knew it and he knew it, but it just lingered in the air.

It is important to note that this session occurred in April 2015, and a short drive away from our group, Baltimore City was on fire following the death of Freddie Gray while in police custody. I knew these kids on the streets, the ones the media labeled "thugs," and yet I realized I did not really know them at all. I cannot really know them or their story because I am not Black. I am a White social worker of privilege living a life that the boys in my group will likely never know. I have been aware of this in group, but I was especially aware of this difference in this session.

The comment that Sam made under his breath stayed with me. I looked over at my cofacilitator as she handed out materials, unaware of his comment or the unrest in the group that I sensed. For the moment, I decided to store the comment away, hoping that the activity would allow for honest discussion. I also must admit to being afraid of where the discussion might have gone. I was afraid that because of our differences, members would assume I would be unable to help them, understand them, or allow them to be heard and that they would experience me as just one more person who would reject them, the "kids who are invisible," as Sam stated.

We explained to the boys that they would be making masks with images on the front of the mask that showed how they presented themselves to the world and images on the inside of the mask that depicted only what they knew and felt about themselves. This was an intentional risk-taking activity, and we hoped the boys would share their vulnerabilities, as the stage had already been set in previous sessions. After a few minutes all members were at work—painting and creating their masks. Some of the boys talked as they worked, while others worked in silence. When everyone felt they were finished, we began the work of sharing.

James spoke up first, as is typical for the group. He said that the outside of his mask was painted "all black because that is how everyone sees me all the time," and the inside of his mask was his version of the flag for France. He said that he wanted to be a chef, but he had not told anyone except his aunt. The boys were supportive but also teased him a bit, a typical norm in this group.

I asked the group, "Let's compare the inside of the mask with the outside, what do you all think?" One of the boys stated that the masks cannot exist together. He clarified. "You are not ever going to find a Frenchie Chef who's black. Ain't no way that is happening." I asked the rest of the group if they thought that was true. Sam, who made the comment at the beginning of the group, added, "It's not about being Black, it's being invisible. Nobody sees you. That's why you gotta set things on fire, just to be seen." The boys all jumped into the conversation, and began to share stories of both large and micro aggressions that they had experienced. The stories, though hard to hear, were not surprising.

My cofacilitator stated that this was the first time we had ever talked about racism and wondered out loud why that was the case. The members chimed in, in resounding agreement, that they had not wanted to make us feel bad. I had a sickening feeling that we had failed them. For months we had been together, yet we had failed to address the elephant in the room. They felt invisible, and we had not even acknowledged that! The only thing I could think to say was, "Well I want to say to you all that I am sorry. I am sorry that I did not bring this up, and I am sorry that you feel like you need to spare our feelings."

I shared with them how it is hard for me to understand that boys with so much life in them could ever feel invisible but that for the first time today, I began to understand. Another boy said that it was not just being invisible; it was that when people actually saw him, they were afraid. He reported that, "when I walk in town and a lady with her kid sees me and walks the other way 'cause she's scared of me, that hurts and it's not invisible. It's like De-Visible, something less or worse."

The boys agreed with the idea of De-Visible, and we wrote that on a big sheet of paper. I asked them, "How do we work on this and how do we overcome it?" The boys wrote words surrounding the word *de-visible*. The statements were interesting and included expected subjects like "speak up" but also unexpected ones like "sharing a sandwich." We had a good laugh about the sandwich, but all agreed that it was hard to be mad at or afraid of someone when you share a meal.

We wrapped up by having each member give one word describing what he got from the group. *Real*, *truth*, and *honesty* were the words members came up with. We thanked them for taking the risk and told them we hoped they would no longer worry about our feelings. We wanted them to be themselves. The boys agreed, some with smiles on their faces and some with tears in their eyes. The members piled out of the room, and I said goodbye to each of them. Sam left the room last, and I said, "Goodbye, Sam. You know that I *see* you, right?" as tears welled up in my eyes. Sam smiled back at me and said, "I know that you do *now*, Ms. Jen."

The Authority Theme

A second theme is related to the mandatory nature of most members' participation in a social skills group. Typically, a child or adolescent is referred for group intervention by a teacher, parent, school administrator, or therapist. From the prospective member's standpoint, she or he does not have a problem; a common sentiment expressed by group members is, "If only everyone would leave me alone, everything would be fine!"

When members come into the group with this perspective, the worker has no choice but to address it directly. The "authority theme" (Shulman, 2014) refers to the resentment and hostility that members may experience as a result of being forced to attend a group they do not want and do not believe they need. It also reflects members' reservations about the leader, based upon differences, as discussed, and her or his perceived power. In the following case scenario, the group members themselves raised the issue, although in many instances, it will be up to the leader to raise this elephant in the room.

I was facilitating an anger management group that members were required to attend as a condition of their returning to their home school. The members had been placed in the alternative school due to aggressive episodes that resulted in multiple suspensions from their home schools. The members were less than excited to come to the first session. As I started the group with introductions, members quickly shared their frustrations. Jeanette provided her name and then said, "If I don't do this stupid club, I have to stay back at this retard school," referring to the alternative school she was attending. She continued, "I am a prisoner here, just like all of you." She sarcastically asked, "Are we having fun yet?"

I encouraged Jeanette to make the best out of the group, suggesting, "If you have to be here, maybe, just maybe, you can make something out of it." She acerbically replied, "Thanks for that advice, Mrs. Teacher." I assured her that I was not a teacher but, rather, someone who was there to listen to members' concerns, including those related to being at the school and having to attend the group. Initially my comment was met with hostile silence. I then agreed with Jeanette, asking members what it was like to leave their friends, their home school, and have to start all over at the alternative school. Initially I did not have any takers, but I commented that I thought it would be hard to leave what they knew, go to another school with different teachers and new expectations. I also said that they might be just a little bit embarrassed that they were "kicked out" of their home schools, while their friends remained. Initially, members shared somewhat superficial content like complaints about food and being in classes that were boring. As I pressed more, they talked about taking a bus for over an hour each way and dealing with other kids that were more aggressive and "scary." Though they wanted to return to their home schools, they worried that they would be behind academically and would be made fun of. I credited them for being so honest, and suggested that the group could be a place where they could express their feelings and learn to manage them in a way that would facilitate their return to their home schools.

In a social skills group such as the one just described, the worker should expect that members will initially present with angry, hostile feelings, due to their involuntary participation. Workers less familiar with group work and uncomfortable with strong feelings like anger may be tempted to squelch such feelings when they surface, either directly (as they did in my group) or indirectly, through behaviors such as silence, lack of participation, or continuous laughter and sarcastic comments. It is only when the worker addresses members' concerns directly that the group can begin its work. In an anger management group, in fact, as the members begin to talk about their anger at having to attend the group, they *are* beginning the work of the group: They are encouraged to share their feelings, but must do so in a way that is socially acceptable.

Technology and Social Media

Using social media in group work practice is a relatively new approach for the field. Although social media offer opportunities to enhance, improve, and make connections among members of social skills groups, they also present the worker with several challenges. The practice of starting where the client is means that Facebook, Snapchat, or Twitter may be the starting point with children and adolescents. The challenge for workers engaging in group work is to adopt and adapt digital media tools for their group work practice in ways that are purposeful, helpful, and appropriate.

Halabuza (2014) provides several recommendations. The standards around privacy, boundaries, and professional ethics are important to think through in advance of starting the group. I recommend using a professional social media account and maintaining a separate account for personal interactions. In a recent group, members shared that they all had Twitter accounts. We decided to use Twitter as a means through which members could support each other beyond the 50 minutes once a week that they met as a group. An example of something that came out of the group was the following tweet: "@shippen-jen pointing fingers make me want to roll [fight] but im gonna just breathe." Members were able to connect to this member in real time, in the moment that he wanted to act out his aggression, allowing him to make a better, nonviolent, choice.

It is important to talk about safety on the Internet as well as cyberbullying. There are several Internet resources that can be helpful to group members. One

Web page, www.stopbullying.gov, provides several tips that I share with group members. Those taken directly from the Web page include the following:

- Help members be smart about what they post or say. Tell them not to share anything that could hurt or embarrass themselves or others. Once something is posted, it is out of their control.
- Encourage members to think about who they want to see the information and pictures they post online. Should complete strangers see it? Real friends only? Friends of friends? Members should think about how people who aren't friends could use their information.
- Remind members to keep their passwords safe and to not share them with friends. Sharing passwords can compromise their control over their online identities and activities. (See also Chapter 14 of this volume for more on technology and groups.)

Practice Principles

The most important practice principle in working with children in social skills groups is to promote mutual aid. The development of the group as a supportive, safe environment within which new behaviors can be practiced is critical to the group's success. In groups where children and adolescents are working on and practicing new social skills in the group, a sense of trust and connectedness allows them to be able to take risks, engage in "behavioral rehearsal" (Shulman, 2014), and learn from one another and from the mistakes and successes of all members.

Developmentally, children and adolescents look for and need peer support and connection. If the group leader takes over that process and is the primary source of support and understanding, this important curative factor of the group will be denied to members. The group leader's role is to help the members support and challenge each other in the group rather than engage in a round-robin approach where each member takes a turn responding to the leader's questions, suggestions, and insights.

Children and adolescents are in constant movement. For this reason, a traditional talk therapy group session will not be responsive to their developmental needs and ways of working. Purposeful use of activity in the group is a critical aspect of a successful group experience and is a second practice principle. Play in the form of age-appropriate activity *is* the work of children and adolescents (Malekoff, 2014; Middleman & Wood, 1990). I have found that the use of activity can allow the child's or adolescent's eyes to focus on other places, thus decreasing the pressure of intimacy during group discussion. If the eyes and hands are occupied, words are able to flow more easily. Readers will remember in the extended case example presented, it was only when the boys were engaged in making their masks that real, honest discussion began to take place.

In another session of this same group, as the members continued working on their masks, one young man disclosed his deepest fear of becoming a murderer. The members were able to connect with his statement and shared their feelings about the lack of male role models and a sense of a positive future. If this had been presented as a topic of discussion by the leaders, it would likely have been met with awkward silence rather than the robust discussion that ensued while members continued to paint and glue their masks.

A third important practice principle is to facilitate learning through engaging members in everyday activities. When the group simulates real life as much as possible in terms of how members relate to one another, members become aware of their problematic behaviors and also are exposed to more prosocial ones. The group becomes a "social microcosm" (Shulman, 2014). As members develop comfort with one another, they will begin to engage in the very behaviors that necessitated the group intervention in the first place. As these behaviors surface, members can be helped to see the negative consequences as well as substitute new, more adaptive ways of interacting with others.

An example of this occurred in a group for children between the ages of 8 and 11 years old that I led. The goal of the group was to enhance members' ability to manage their anger. One of the members, Tim, was able to share how he could not keep friends and how this made him feel alone. He further shared that other people could not be trusted and that when he tried to be friends with someone, he or she just left him, and he never understood why. He shared that he had "a lot of associates but no friends." This comment was met with another group member's question, "What is an associate?" Tim angrily yelled back, "What are you, an idiot?" which shut down this important conversation.

I asked Tim what he thought had just happened. Initially he shared, "Jose asked a stupid question." I asked, "Then what happened?" Tim responded, "I felt annoyed, and Jose looks funny." I asked Tim what he meant by Jose "looking funny," and Tim shared that he did not know. I asked the other group members what they observed, and they were able to make the observation that Jose felt sad or embarrassed by Tim's "putdown." I then observed that Jose was trying to connect with Tim, and Tim shut him down.

If Tim was going to learn how to make and keep friends, he needed to see the negative impact his impulsive responses had on others. In the session, we talked about the group and how it could be a mini-learning experience for members' lives outside the group. Tim asked the group if he could "re-do" the interaction and explain to Jose what an "associate" was, exposing for the first time his vulnerability and fear of being rejected by others. Like others in the group, Tim was caught in a vicious cycle of fearing rejection by others and then acting in a way that precipitated the very response he anticipated.

A fourth important practice principle is to involve caregivers/parents and teachers in the group process. This does not mean that these individuals participate in the group. Rather, caregivers should be apprised of the behaviors their children are working on so that these can be carried over into and worked on in the home environment. Research reveals that children whose parents are involved in the social skills group demonstrate higher rates of social and emotional development, including enhanced ability to manage stress, heightened feelings of happiness and self-control, improved mental health, supportive peer interactions, and fewer delinquent interactions (Allen & Daly, 2002; Desforges & Abouchaar, 2003). Similarly, teachers can be informed about their student's progress and skills she or he is working on. The process for updating caregivers/parents and teachers should be established at the beginning of the group when the group rules are discussed. In this way, routine updates can be expected by the members and emergency contact can also be made to the adults if necessitated by something the leaders observe in the group.

A simple way that significant others can be included is to have each member carry a journal back and forth between group and home (and the classroom, if relevant). Members write down what they are working on—their successes and areas for improvement—and share this with caregivers/parents and/or teachers. Teachers and parents/caregivers can provide their own observations and words of encouragement. In group, members' journals can be shared with one another and with the leader.

A final principle is making appropriate decisions regarding group composition based upon potential members' developmental stage and age. Although it might be convenient to place children in groups with a wide range of ages or development, too wide a range can be detrimental to the group's development and its goals and purpose. I try to avoid a "one size fits all" approach when working with children. It is important to make sure that the group is age and developmentally appropriate in terms of content and the use of activity. For example, the developmental differences between a 6-year-old child and a 12-year-old child are dramatic. Similarly, a 13-year-old may be different developmentally than a 16-year-old. Although activity might be appropriate to help older youth engage with one another, the group worker will be able to rely upon more traditional talk therapy as cohesion develops. In contrast, when working with younger children, activity will be the central way in which members will engage in mutual aid and work on their interpersonal skills.

RECOMMENDED WAYS OF WORKING

The most important aspect of working with youth of all ages is for the leader to bring as little ego as possible to the group sessions. Early on in my practice, I was asked to facilitate a social skills group with children who had been aggressive in school. The vice-principal referred to them as the bullies of the school. As I began our first group session, one of the boys asked me sharply, "Who the hell are you?" When I shared with him that I was a social worker, and that I had been working with kids for a few years, the energy in the room changed quickly to defensiveness. I quickly read the group, swallowed my need to defend my credentials, and shifted the group back to establishing our purpose together. If I was to judge members on their titles of "bully," and they judged me with my title as "social worker," then we could not get to the connections that needed to develop in our group. Losing the ego means it is okay to be wrong, it is okay to be vulnerable, and it is okay to not have all the answers. In this particular instance, it also meant that I needed to understand members' suspicions about me and address them directly. My ability to be helpful to the members did not lie in my previous experience with children. It depended upon my ability to help them form connections with one another, which started with not shying away from the questions about me.

Readers will remember the powerful effect my apology had on the group described in detail earlier; as I took responsibility for not having previously addressed the elephant in the room—racism—I deepened the connection between myself and the members and also sent a message that it was acceptable to talk about taboo subjects like race and the differences between the members and me.

Another important practice skill is to develop ways to use humor in group work practice. I find that self-deprecating humor is an effective way to connect with both children and, particularly, adolescents. As an adult, each year I find myself further and further away from the current trends or latest ways of speaking among children and adolescents. Before I know it, the children in my groups are LOL'ing (laughing at loud) and ROTFL'ing (rolling on the floor laughing) at me. Expressing my lack of knowledge about what they are saying and admitting I am "OLD" is both an honest response and a way to promote comfort and rapport with one another and with me.

Humor lightens the mood and can make it easier for members to engage with one another in the group's work. However, it is important that it not detract from the group's work. It can be tempting for the worker and members alike to use humor as a defense against the sometimes intense nature of the group. Although the focus of social skills groups is education and behavioral rehearsal, sensitive topics *will* surface. These include traumatic and painful experiences members may have endured and negative feelings about the self, each of which has an influence on and explains the negative behaviors that necessitated the need for the social skills group. Members' feelings must be acknowledged and validated, not ignored through the unproductive use of humor or simple avoidance.

A third critical component of group work with children and adolescents is advance planning. The saying, "When we fail to plan, we plan to fail" is particularly appropos when facilitating social skills groups. Kurland (1978) observes that planning is the most neglected aspect of group work development. Lack of planning in group work with children and adolescents may result in minimal levels of cohesiveness, lack of parent/caregiver and teacher support, and member absences and lateness. These problems undermine the ability of the group to be successful.

Most fundamentally, the goal and purpose of the group need to be clear to the leader, members, caregivers, teachers, *and* the sponsoring institution. As discussed, activities need to be age appropriate and should be decided upon in advance. Having too many activities for the leader to choose from is preferable to having too few. However, the worker should plan to make flexible use of activity, tailoring specific activities to the needs and interests of the members as these surface in the group. A clear timeline also is important, as members are more likely to respond in a positive fashion if they realize that the group has a beginning, a middle, and a finite ending.

It is especially important that the leader decide upon group rules, or expectations for how members will work together. Of particular importance will be expectations regarding confidentiality and its limits; one person talks at a time; members cannot hurt themselves, others, or objects in the group space; members must be respectful of one another; and members must attend all sessions. Some group leaders encourage members to develop their own rules, assuming this leads to ownership of the group. Others assume that this is the leader's responsibility. An approach that combines both allows members to provide their suggestions within a broad framework that the worker already has established. Especially with younger children, it is advisable to have the rules visible and review them at the start of each session.

A challenge that many group workers face when they work with children and adolescents in social skills groups is managing the disruptive behavior of some or all members. Novice group workers tend to use group rules as threats: The member either ceases to engage in the disruptive behavior or she or he will have to leave. This sort of punitive approach is not helpful to the member or to the group as a whole, because members learn that they, too, can be asked to leave if they misbehave by acting out their feelings.

To address disruptive behavior in the group, the leader first must attempt to make sense of what the member is saying through her or his actions. In a previous example, Jeanette presented herself as uncooperative, sarcastic, and somewhat disrespectful toward me. Had I focused on these behaviors, I would have lost her *and* the other members. Instead of reprimanding her for her actions, I attempted to get at what she was really saying. Readers may remember that Jeanette, along with others in the group, were upset at the loss of friends and the familiar surroundings of their home schools, embarrassed at their situation, and worried about what their peers in their home school would say once they returned. As we talked about these feelings, members' interest in the group grew and their mistrust of me was diminished.

The worker also should consider that as members engage in disruptive behaviors, they are demonstrating precisely why they need the group's help. Rather than shutting down a member, the worker can help her or him channel acting-out behaviors into more socially acceptable ones. The worker validates the member's affective reactions, but helps her or him express these in a way that helps keep her or him "out of trouble."

There will be instances where individual members or the group as a whole may act out in a way that is potentially dangerous and/or distracting to the group, undermining its work. In these instances, the worker may need to be more directive. The challenge is to do this in a way that doesn't censor or reprimand members but does reinforce limits of what is and what is not acceptable. Members can first be reminded of the group rules. The leader also can change seating arrangements by separating members who are disruptive from one another or placing a disruptive member next to her or him. The worker also can ask members to engage in a time-out, in which all members take, in my words, "a chill pill."

Because the potential for acting out is high in social skills groups, a simple way of preparing for this is to work with a co-leader. Different models of co-leadership exist in social skills groups, but typically co-leaders divide up the work: One introduces an activity or topic for discussion, while the other monitors members reactions and interactions.

EVALUATION

Using a pre- and postintervention measure at the start and the end of the group can allow the group worker to demonstrate changes in the members. A rapid assessment instrument that can be used pre- and postgroup to accomplish this is the Matson Evaluation of Social Skills with Youngsters (MESSY) (Matson, Rotatori, & Helsel, 1983). The MESSY has been used with children as young as 6 years and as old as 18 years of age. It can be administered both at the pregroup or beginning stage and again at the end of the group.

It is important when working with children that other forms of assessment be utilized. For example, a useful tool that complements the MESSY is The Social Skills Rating System (SSRS), a 52-question parent form and a 51-question teacher form that can assess adolescent cooperation, assertion, responsibility, and self-control (Gresham & Elliott, 1990). Utilizing self-report data from group members and data collected from caregivers/parents and teachers and academic records provides a more comprehensive assessment of a member's progress than either approach alone.

RESOURCES

A number of manuals provide guidelines and suggested activities for social skills training in a group context. A manual can be a valuable tool to assist the worker in planning her or his group, suggesting topics for discussion and related activities. However, a social skills group will be more helpful to members if the worker makes flexible use of the manual. Leaders can come in to each session with an idea of what they would like to present, but they must remain responsive to the immediate needs of members and their sense of urgency about what they wish to discuss.

Some of the more commonly used, evidence-based manuals include the following:

- The ACCEPTS Program: http://www.proedinc.com/customer/productView.aspx?ID=625&SearchWord=ACCEPTS%20PROGRAM
- The EQUIP Program: https://www.researchpress.com/books/528/equip-program
- The PREPARE Curriculum: https://www.researchpress.com/books/818/prepare-curriculum
- Primary Mental Health Project: http://www.promisingpractices.net/program.asp?programid=225
- "Stop and Think" Social Skills Program: http://www.projectachieve.info

REFERENCES

Allen, S. M., & Daly, K. (2002). The effects of father involvement: A summary of the research evidence. *The FII-O News, 1*, 1–11.

Boston University School of Public Health. (2013). *The social cognitive theory.* Retrieved from http://sphweb.bumc.bu.edu/otlt/MPH-Modules/SB/SB721-Models/SB721-Models5.html

Brigman, G. A., Webb, L. D., & Campbell, C. (2007). Building skills for school success: Improving the academic and social competence of students. *Professional School Counseling, 10*(3), 279–288.

Cervantes, C. M., & Porretta, D. L. (2013). Impact of after school programming on physical activity among adolescents with visual impairments. *Adapted Physical Activity Quarterly, 30*(2), 127–146.

Clements, J. (In Press). Invisible people don't need masks. To be published in the 40th Anniversary Double Issue of *Social Work with Groups.* Routledge.

Dennison, S. (2008). Measuring the treatment outcome of short-term school-based social skills groups. *Social Work with Groups, 31*(3-4), 307–328. doi:10.1080/01609510801981219

Desforges, C., & Abouchaar, A. (2003). *The impact of parental involvement, parental support and family education on pupil achievement and adjustment: A literature review.* London, UK: Department for Education and Skills.

Fraser, M. W., Thompson, A. M., Day, S. H., & Macy, R. J. (2014). The making choices program: Impact of social-emotional skills training on the risk status of third graders. *Elementary School Journal, 114*(3), 354–279.

Garcia, E., De Pedro, K. T., Astor, R. A., Lester, P., & Benbenishty, R. (2015). FOCUS school-based skill-building groups: Training and implementation. *Journal of Social Work Education*, *51*(Suppl. 1), S102–S116.

Gresham, F. M., & Elliott, S. (1990). *The social skills rating system*. Minneapolis, MN: American Guidance Service

Gresham, F. M., Sugai, G., & Horner, R. H. (2001). Interpreting outcomes of social skills training for students with high-incidence disabilities. *Exceptional Children*, *67*(3), 331–344.

Halabuza, D. (2014). Guidelines for social work use of social networking. *Journal of Social Work Values and Ethics*, *11*(1), 23–32.

King, P., & Boardman, M. (2006). What personal/social skills are important for young children commencing kindergarten? *Australian Journal of Early Childhood*, *31*(3), 15–21.

Kurland, R. (1978). Planning: The neglected component of group development. *Social Work with Groups*, *1*(2), 248–259.

Lavallee, K. L., Bierman, K. L., & Nix, R. L. (2005). The impact of first-grade "friendship group" experiences on child social outcomes in the fast track program. *Journal Of Abnormal Child Psychology*, *33*(3), 307. doi:10.1007/s10802-005-3567-3

Malekoff, A. (2014). *Group work with adolescents: Principles and practice*. New York, NY: Guilford Press.

Matson, J., Rotatori, A., & Helsel, W. (1983). Development of a rating scale to measure social skills in children: The Matson evaluation of social skills with youngsters (MESSY). *Behaviour Research and Therapy*, *21*(4), 335–340.

Middleman, R. R., & Wood, G.G. (1990). *Skills for direct practice in social work*. New York, NY: Columbia University Press

Shulman, L. (2014). *The skills of helping individuals, families, groups, and communities*. Belmont, CA: Cengage Learning.

Sommers-Flanagan, R., Barrett-Hakanson, T., Clarke, C., & Sommers-Flanagan, J. (2000). A psychoeducational school-based coping and social skills group for depressed students. *Journal for Specialists in Group Work*, *25*(2), 170–190.

Tierney, T., & Dowd, R. (2000). The use of social skills groups to support girls with emotional difficulties in secondary schools. *Support for Learning*, *15*(2), 82–85.

Whalon, K. J., Conroy, M. A., Martinez, J. R., & Werch, B. L. (2015). School-based peer-related social competence interventions for children with autism spectrum disorder: A meta-analysis and descriptive review of single case research design studies. *Journal of Autism and Developmental Disorders*, *45*(6), 1513–1531. doi:10.1007/s10803-0152373-1

Zastrow, C. H., & Kirst-Ashman, K. K. (2010). *Understanding human behavior and the social environment*. Belmont, CA: Brooks/Cole, Cengage Learning.

Chapter Ten

Group Work With Older Adults

Steve Wilson and Susan Rice

The purpose of this chapter is to provide the beginning group worker with an understanding of conducting social group work with older adult clients. The demographics of the older adult population in this country and others dramatically demonstrate that the aging population is growing and will potentially need not only more gerontological social workers but also improved service programming by group workers. Therefore, a compelling need exists to provide effective, user-friendly group work services to older adults to enhance both the quality and the span of their lives.

There is a second important need for social workers to provide effective group work for the older adult population: One of the primary problems of older adults is social isolation. Distinct from feelings of loneliness that can stem from a sense of loss of companionship, social isolation has been identified as a lack of social engagement and meaningful relationships with others (Dury, 2014). This isolation can also be a chronically stressful condition to which individuals who are undergoing multiple transitions in older adulthood are particularly vulnerable. Furthermore, interventions that enhance the level of social involvement may buffer the effects of stressful events experienced among older adults (Wethington, Moen, Glasgow, & Pillemer, 2000). It has been well documented that group work with older adults can improve psychological, physiological, and social well-being because groups can work to reduce isolation through the collective sharing of feelings, successes, and life stressors experienced in later adulthood (Goelitz, 2001, 2003; Gore-Felton & Spiegel, 1999). Thus, what better method is there than working with older adults in group settings to help them address their daily dilemmas?

REVIEW OF THE LITERATURE

What defines an "older adult" population? A variety of definitions have been used, focusing on the difference between the "young-old" and the "old-old"

(Neugarten, 1975). Age 65 has been identified with older adulthood since that has been a traditional retirement age and when Medicare coverage is activated. However, adults between ages 55 and 74 are considered "young-old," adults between 75 and 84 are deemed "middle-old," and those over the age of 85 are classified as the "oldest-old" (Harrigan & Farmer, 2000; McInnis-Dittrich, 2014). All groups are different, yet they all face the same unrelenting biology of aging.

The aging process apparently involves failure of the surveillance, repair, and replacement process typical of a young body (McInnis-Dittrich, 2014). The body loses the ability to replace cells that compose most of its tissues. The immune system often loses the ability to eliminate cancerous cells. Tissues that are damaged in daily life can no longer be repaired. When all of these processes occur, the organism begins to deteriorate and eventually dies. This accounts for the physical and mental deterioration that occurs in old age, although for many people it does not happen fast enough to cause severe functional problems before some disease or occurrence causes immediate death.

The terminology used to define age-related memory changes have changed over the past few years. The term "senility" was, at one time, identified as a term to describe the changes occurring through the process of aging causing a progressive decline in functioning and cognitive abilities (Beers & Berkow, 2000). However, a more commonly used description of memory changes is "mild cognitive impairment" in older adults. This condition typically refers to a slight, but noticeable, decline in memory function in the person, but not necessarily in other cognitive functions that would impede activities of daily life or independent living (Petersen et al., 2014). It is important to remember that common forgetfulness is considered normal aging and not necessarily dementia related. Poor short-term memory can happen at any age as a part of the normal aging process. In fact, one recent study concluded that aspects of age-related cognitive decline can even begin in healthy educated adults when they are in their 20s and 30s (Salthouse, 2009).

However, all adults age very differently. Some older adults acquire diseases and impairments in their young-old age, whereas others seem to live disease-free and later are identified as having died of "old age." *Successful* or *healthy aging* refers to a process by which harmful effects of aging are minimized as much as possible, preserving function until a natural process of age-related deterioration occurs. Adults who age successfully typically avoid experiencing many of the undesirable features of aging and strive to remain both physically and mentally active throughout their later years.

It is important for new group workers to reflect on their personal beliefs and attitudes about aging and older adulthood. Later life can be associated with positive connotations such as increased wisdom or valued expertise. However, just as often there can be many negative connotations such as physical and mental health impairment, disease, and the end of life. These stereotypes have been con-tradicted in countless books and scholarly journals, but distorted media repre-sentations of stereotypes associated with later life can influence the public about perceptions of senility, crankiness, and slowness of movement and thought as we enter old age. Just as significant as the real changes that take place in an older adult are the perceived changes, those largely due to the ageism that permeates our society.

Ageism refers to the negative stereotyping of older adults based upon their age (Salzman, 2006). This term was initially coined by Robert Butler in 1969, who thereafter became the founding director of the National Institute on Aging (Achenbaum, 2015). Ageism has the potential to lead to ageist discrimination practices. Although ageism is the negative *attitude* toward older adults, ageist discrimination is the negative *behavior* directed to them. Stereotypes of older adults are usually derogatory and convey an attitude that older adults are less valuable as human beings, thus justifying inferior or unequal treatment of them. For example, the typically negative ways in which older adults are portrayed in the media that can reach millions of people on a daily basis reinforce stereotypi-cal ageist attitudes. That message is even reinforced by the medical profession as biases against older adults in treatment, and condescending attitudes have been reported to be prevalent among health care professionals (Kane & Kane, 2005). Typically, this is seen in extremely brief medical office visits and a disregard for the physical complaints presented by an older patient.

Many older adults can begin to believe that they are not capable of rehabilita-tion as their body is something that he or she no longer controls. For instance, when a person forgets the house keys and says, "I must be getting senile" and the reply is, "It happens to everyone over 60 (or 70 or 80)," the individual be-lieves that her memory is failing and that there is nothing she can do about it. Consequently, the stereotype becomes self-fulfilling with the individual be-lieving her own time of life is a period of mental and physical frailty. It is ap-parent how easily older adults, and often families around them, can slip into a mindset that allows deterioration to occur without being concerned that unusual biological changes contribute to a delay in seeking the necessary professional care. Thus, as health symptoms or concerns among older adults are dismissed as typical "aging," conditions can go undiagnosed and, consequently, undertreated (Salzman, 2006).

GROUP WORK INTERVENTIONS

One method of assisting older adults is to provide social support opportuni-ties, which have been documented repeatedly in the literature as benefiting both mental and physical health (Eng, Rimm, Fitzmaurice, & Kawachi, 2002; Jacobs,

Masson, & Harvil, 2002; McInnis-Dittrich, 2014; Seeman, Lusignolo, & Albert, 2001). Moreover, findings from the gerontological literature show that merely having knowledge that support from others is available if necessary (such as perceived or anticipated support) may be even more beneficial to an older adult's well-being than receiving the support itself or having a large social support network group (Krause, 1997). These findings suggest that pertinent to well-being and overall successful aging are perceptions among older adults of the strength of their own "social safety net" and not merely increasing the size or contact frequency of their social network (Fiori, Antonucci, & Cortina, 2006; Haber, 2013; Krause, 2001). Such a "social safety net," in which the individual is aware that others are available to help, provides encouragement for the individual to solve problems autonomously, which in turn allows for healthy feelings of personal control, self-worth, and independence (Fiori, Antonucci, & Cortina, 2006; Krause, 2001).

Social support groups are an effective way of providing this support. Berkman and Glass (2000), in their extensive literature review, detailed several benefits of social support that reduce the consequences of stress—namely, access to useful information, instrumental help, and emotional support. Furthermore, social support groups can "normalize" the concerns of the members, which is central to mutual aid. Community-based senior centers, in which older adults often find a network of peers with whom they can share common ground, are a frequent source of and resource for these groups, which provide a great range of social support. Senior centers are a resource that provides an array of services that includes social, nutritional, health, and educational services, as well as recreational activities that promote social interaction (Gelfand, 2006). Senior centers have offered essential services to older adults since 1947, such as health, social, and educational services. There are currently approximately 15,000 senior centers that serve 10 million older Americans annually (National Council on Aging, 2006). Studies have indicated that program participants among senior centers have reported greater psychological well-being (Mehta & Ching Ee, 2008), as well as perceived physical and emotional well-being, suggesting that senior centers can serve as a protector and buffer of the negative consequences of stress in older adulthood (Fitzpatrick, Gitelson, Andereck, & Mesur, 2005). This chapter uses a mutual aid model to explore the practice principles, themes, and ways of working with older adults to help improve their quality of life.

PRACTICE PRINCIPLES

Group work practice has been defined in a number of ways. In working with older adults, the majority of support groups function most effectively using the mutual aid model of practice, first described by Schwartz (1961) and developed and elaborated on by Gitterman and Shulman (1994). The mutual aid model states that clients have difficulties that arise from three interrelated problems of living: life transitions, environmental pressures, and maladaptive interpersonal processes. Using the mutual aid process to address these problems gives each member of a group the ability to help every other member through a naturally occurring process. Self-help mutual aid groups are typically peer led, address a common problem or condition, and are voluntary in their enrollment. The purpose and role of a professional or leader in such a group is to be a mediator, facilitating the engagement of individual members within the group as a whole. Through the mutual aid process, group cohesion is developed (Goelitz, 2004). The mutual aid model allows older adults to function in a way that draws on their strengths and allows them maximum freedom in determining the scope and course of the group.

How do these general practice principles coincide with group work with older clients? Most social work practitioners envision a model of social work practice (individual or group) that includes a focus on assessment, planning, contracting, building rapport, direct action, indirect action, evaluation, and then termination (Toseland & Rivas, 2008). Each phase needs to be modified to accommodate the needs of groups composed of older clients. In all phases of practice, the level of the social worker's activity with older adults in a group setting is high, perhaps higher than in working with younger clients. The reasons for this are numerous. Many older clients have had minimal exposure to the world of social work. They have, more or less, adequately resolved their problems throughout their lives, counting on informal support systems to help them through hard times. As adults reach later life, such as in their 80s and 90s, those informal systems often disappear. The individual is left to struggle on his or her own and often seeks social work services perhaps for the first time, without really knowing what to expect. The worker's job is then to model what a group member may do by being active in the group from the very beginning. For example, in assessment, the social worker is often trying to understand the degree to which group members are willing to provide mutual aid and to share their solutions to a problem. The worker needs to demonstrate actively how the mutual aid process takes place. The worker does this by drawing on his or her knowledge of each member's experience and encouraging that member to share that experience with others in the group. The worker also encourages all members to see the similarities among them and tries to help each client understand the source of his or her discomfort.

Contracting is often done on an informal basis in support groups for older adults because the themes of groups are so amorphous. In general, when a younger client or a client with a concrete need contracts for services (or a worker offers services), there is a fairly clear understanding of what the agency is prepared to offer and what the client wants to receive. Groups with clear contracts include those where clients want to learn to be better parents or where older people are learning to deal with insulin-dependent diabetes to manage their illness effectively. However, social support groups for older adults are often seen as a forum for members to adjust to losses or changing life situations. That rubric could fit almost everyone, and so, in practice, the contract becomes a statement of allowing members to decide, as they participate in the group, what the benefits might be and what they might want to focus on. Thus, treatment goals can be established by the group, for the group. Some goals will be universal for all group members, whereas others will be individual. Such informality also provides a safety net that allows fearful, timid clients to "try out" the group without being committed to one specific goal for change in their lives. Informality does not necessarily mean lack of clarity. Shulman (1999) describes contracting as clarifying the worker's purpose and role. He stresses the importance of eliminating jargon in contracting and urges workers to state clearly what they can offer. For example, in a group that has been formed to help frail older clients to continue living independently in the community, a leader might say, "This group will be a place where you can explore the feelings you have about living alone or feeling isolated some of the time." Each client is then free to pick up on that theme in whatever way seems appropriate.

There is a general belief that older adults need support and encouragement more than they need confrontation (Corey & Corey, 2002). The goal of group work with older adults is less oriented toward radical personality change than it is toward making quality of life in the present more meaningful and enjoyable, such as by alleviating some of the negative aspects of the older adults' life through addressing their struggles with increased dependency (Kivnick & Murray, 2001) and facilitating the need for vital involvement with ideas, materials, activities, people, and institutions (Erikson, Erikson, & Kivnick, 1986). The social worker, for example, is more likely to be an advocate for the group that needs help with transportation (indirect intervention) than he or she is to empower the members to either work out the transportation problem with one another as a way of building strength or advocate for themselves (direct intervention) (Kivnick & Stoffel, 2005). Often, however, workers try to make it easier to attend the group as part of the goal of offering a service that will enhance the quality of members' lives.

The theme of learning to resolve conflict is related to this goal. Many theorists agree that conflict is an integral part of group development, and it allows members to become intimate and work together more beneficially (e.g., Kottler, 2001; Wallach, 2004). For older adults, however, conflict is often seen as threatening to the relationships they are taking significant risks to build (Bergstrom & Nussbaum, 1996). Still, learning skills of conflict resolution can allow true intimacy to develop in groups, facilitating the mutual aid process.

Termination is another area that needs to be planned carefully in groups with older people. Termination is important both in the here and now, and because of the memories the experience evokes for clients in relation to past terminations in their lives (Shulman, 1999). For people who are seeing friends, family members, and acquaintances die on a regular basis, all endings take on an especially poignant meaning. In fact, many older adult clients will bluntly say that they do not want to become close to other group members "because they're only going to die anyway." However, group endings can serve as a vehicle for the discussion of end-of-life talk and for relating group termination to the many losses experienced by older adults at the end-of-life stage (Goelitz, 2004; Toseland & Rizzo, 2004). Thus, many group workers, and those who attend groups, believe that the benefits of forming close relationships with others in mutual support to improve their quality of life outweigh the pain associated with separations and endings.

To use the termination stage effectively as a tool for assisting older adults with end-of-life issues, social workers need to make group endings positive and honest, allowing the expression of a wide range of feelings. This may require the discussion of termination early in the group process and continuously readdressing the topic despite potential resistance from members (Goelitz, 2004). Or, similarly, when a group ends, the members need to be helped to express the importance that it has had in their lives, as well as frustrations about what was not accomplished in the group. Toseland and Rizzo (2004) have suggested ending groups gradually, even extending the time between meetings and encouraging follow-up meetings with participants to ease the separation.

Finally, social workers need to facilitate an open and comfortable environment during any incidences of early termination of individuals who leave the group. For example, when a person drops out of a group because he or she is too ill to attend, it is useful to encourage the others in the group to write to the member or pay a visit to the member's home or the hospital to provide closure. This is not only helpful to the individual who has left but also provides a reassuring message to the older adult participants in the group: *My absence is important, and people care about what happens to me.* Overall, it is imperative that social workers be aware of their own feelings about endings and the termination process so as to effectively implement the discussed strategies and allow for open expression and exploration among group members. That said, it is also important to suggest that open-ended groups that *do not* terminate can be valuable in a mutual aid context as well. Recognizing the need for an ongoing group social support for older adults with common life problems may be a treatment goal in and of itself.

COMMON THEMES

The most common themes encountered in groups for older adults are loneliness, social isolation, loss, poverty, the feeling of rejection, the struggle to find meaning in life, dependency, feelings of uselessness, hopelessness, and despair, fears of death and dying, grief over losses, sadness over physical and mental deterioration, depression, and regrets over past events (Corey & Corey, 2002). If this seems like a list of negative, depressing concerns, one can turn to an emphasis on the wellness model of aging (Crowther, Parker, Achenbaum, Larimore, & Koenig, 2002; Rowe & Kahn, 1998; Sheehy, 1995), which says that the norm is very different from that of people who are struggling. However, as discussed, it is difficult to age without struggling. By definition, *older adulthood* includes multiple and sequential losses.

We need to keep the wellness model of aging in mind so that we do not stereotype all older adults as invalids with persistent mental and physical health problems. However, we also need to recognize and appreciate the degree to which physical changes affect mental status and emotional involvement in different situations. A balance needs to be achieved between focusing on positive and negative themes.

Some groups can be used to promote activities that emphasize the positive, whereas others can use activities that allow for the safe expression of negative feelings. For example, music can be used to enhance the psychological, emotional, and physical well-being of older participants (Blank, 2009; Bright, 1997; Grobman, 2009), as studies have shown that it can facilitate in the engagement of social activities; allows people to feel accepted, valued, and needed (Hays, 2006); assists people in the understanding of the society in which they live (DeNora, 2000); and can serve as a vehicle for self-expression, mood enhancement, and spiritual awareness (Sloboda & O'Neill, 2001). More specifically, when used with older adults, music has even been shown to foster communication among people with Alzheimer's disease and other dementias by serving as a link between the past and present (Koger, Chapin, & Brotons, 1999) and has been found to stimulate frail older adults in residential care into participating in physical movement and exercise (Johnson, Otto, & Clair, 2001). Moreover, a recent study examined the importance of music in enhancing well-being among older adults and found that it served to assist in feelings of competence, feeling less isolated, connecting with others, and encouraging the maintenance of good health (Hays, 2006).

Nonetheless, the efficiency of the human body does decline gradually with age, as older adulthood can be marked by a variety of physical and cognitive changes (Nelson-Becker, 2004), such as depression (National Institutes of Health, 2007), and a variety of chronic health conditions and comorbidities (Fillenbaum, Pieper, Cohen, Cornoni-Huntley, & Guralnik, 2000). Ironically, what people are most aware of first are the cosmetic changes associated with aging, such as whiter hair, more wrinkles, and musculoskeletal changes such as loss of bone density and a widening pelvis. These are the changes that cause many people to *feel* that they are getting old, although these conditions do not relate to physical functioning at all.

Mental health functioning is perhaps the essence of who we are and, when one sees one's functioning deteriorating, or sees it in others, the effects are devastating. Alzheimer's disease causes cruel changes in a person's personality and cognitive abilities that effectively isolate the person from everyone. It is currently estimated that 5.1 million people aged 65 and older suffer from Alzheimer's disease, a number that is expected to nearly triple by 2050 (Hebert, Weuve, Scherr & Evans, 2013). Group work services to such clients can have a number of beneficial effects (Clare, 2002; Goldsilver & Gruneir, 2001), including a chance to foster peer experiences and emotional support, stimulating and encouraging the functioning of all remaining intellectual and social capacities, affirming a sense of individual identity, eliminating frustrating expectations, and replacing them with supportive social and group controls. Although this chapter focuses on older adults as clients, it is important to note that groups for family caregivers can also help relieve the tension and strain that tear families apart as they watch a loved one, previously capable, competent, and intelligent, deteriorate. A national study of caregivers to persons over the age of 50 revealed that support groups were ranked among the top-six outside services used by caregivers (National Alliance for Caregiving and AARP, 2004).

Loneliness and Social Isolation

Loneliness, social isolation, and poverty are familiar themes in groups composed of older clients. As the population enters older adulthood, the male-to-female ratio also changes dramatically. In 2008, men in the 55- to 64-year-old age group totaled 11% of the population and, comparatively, women in the 55- to 64-year-old age group totaled 11.3%. However, in the 80 + age group, men totaled only 2.4%, while women accounted for 4.1%, nearly twice the number of men (US Census Bureau, 2009a).

Among people who were older than 75 years, only 38% of women were married; for women aged 85 and over, just 18% were married (Federal Interagency Forum on Aging-Related Statistics, 2012). Ethnic differences also exist. In 2012, non-Hispanic Whites accounted for 80% of the population aged 65 and older, while African Americans accounted for 9%, Hispanics totaled 7%, and Asians accounted for 3% (Federal Interagency Forum on Aging-Related Statistics, 2012).

Income also changes with gender, age, and living arrangements. In 2007, 8.8% of older adults aged 65 to 74 years were below the poverty line. This number increases to 9.8% of those aged 75 to 84 years, and it increased yet again to 13% of those 85 years and older (US Census Bureau, 2009b). Older women, in general, have a higher poverty rate than older men; 12% of women aged 65 and older were under the poverty line in 2007, while only 6.6% of men were at that level (US Census Bureau, 2009b). African American and Hispanic women may be at particular risk for poverty (Stanford & Usita, 2002; US Census Bureau, 2006).

Social isolation is also known to contribute to higher rates of substance abuse and suicide (DeSpelder & Strickland, 2009). Moreover, rates of substance abuse are high among older adults, with reports of alcohol abuse being as high as 15% (Blow, Oslin, & Barry, 2002), as well as reports of the intentional or accidental misuse and abuse of prescription drugs by older adults (Sadock & Sadock, 2003). In addition, suicide has been reported as a problem among older adults, particularly among older men (Bartels & Smyer, 2002). Group work interventions can directly address this phenomenon and impact the populations involved (McInnis-Dittrich, 2014). More specifically, group interventions have been found to be effective in reducing social isolation among older adults (Cattan, White, Bond, & Learmouth, 2005). Feelings of uselessness, hopelessness, despair, and regrets over past events are also the foci of many discussions in social support groups. Moreover, retirement represents a significant milestone for older adults. Research has identified a variety of experiences and consequential issues among those transitioning into retirement (Kim & Moen, 2002; Marshall, Clarke & Ballantyne, 2001; Szinovacs & Davey, 2005). Particularly for men in our society, there can be a loss of meaningful job roles, income, productivity, and even their identity, because these work relationships have been central throughout adult life (Carter & McGoldrick, 1999).

One way to conceptualize these feelings is through the work of Erik Erikson. Erikson (1963) describes the last two developmental stages of life—generativity versus stagnation and ego integrity versus despair—as two sides of a coin. *Generativity* refers to the concern about establishing and guiding the next generation. When one feels that one has not been instrumental in this process, either through one's own children or by giving to society in a larger way, a pervasive sense of stagnation occurs. *Ego integrity* is the sense that one has accepted "one's one and only life cycle as something that had to be and that, by necessity, permitted of no substitutions" (Erikson, 1963, p. 268). If one cannot feel that way about one's life, despair is the result. If one looks back at one's life and blames oneself for the paths not taken, the overall feeling is one of making wrong choices. Older adults often struggle with issues of regret in groups.

Death, Dying, and Grief

Death and dying remain taboo subjects in our society. Many people of all ages cannot (or will not) openly discuss these significant issues, although they secretly harbor strong feelings about them. Elizabeth Kubler-Ross (1975) has described America as a "death denying society," as we typically evade issues surrounding death and our own finiteness out of fear. It has been postulated that this is due to the anxiety that death and dying elicit, causing discomfort among people otherwise surrounded by a pleasure-driven and narcissistic American culture (Johnson & McGee, 2004). However, talking about death is emotionally laden because it activates our own sense of mortality and fears of loss and separation.

In a youth-oriented society, the impact of multiple losses in later life, including the loss of meaningful employment, loss of financial income, loss of friends and support systems to death, family transitions, and loss of physical functioning in the case of chronic illnesses, coupled with ageist societal attitudes toward older adults, can cause many older adults to feel depressed and depreciate their own sense of worth. Unfortunately, this can also lead to a medicalization of their bereavement-related feelings (Garavaglia, 2006). In an attempt to find a quick remedy to pervasive sadness often associated with personal losses, many older adults turn to pharmacological interventions to relieve these feelings of grief-related sadness. Medications can temporarily ease the symptoms of grief; however, a psychosocial grief group intervention might be the best treatment for this type of condition. Allowing the open expression of grief, inviting the support of others in similar situations, and experiencing the universality of feelings can produce profound results for those facing life losses.

Meanwhile, the controversy continues about how death should occur and how much control we should have over it. Hospice care allows a terminally ill person to die with palliative interventions. Essentially, hospice care provides continuous pain and symptom management for the patient until such time as death occurs. However, end-of-life care has also led to bioethical decisions regarding the moral distinction between "ordinary" versus "extraordinary" care (DeSpelder & Strickland, 2009). When is artificial nutrition, artificial hydration, or breathing equipment considered "ordinary" care with conventional and proved outcomes, as opposed to "extraordinary" care that has life-sustaining interventions with an uncertain outcome and may even be considered intrusive to the patient? The withdrawal of these interventions can cause even more moral ambiguity for patients and families. These circumstances can lead to discussions in groups beyond hospice and palliative care to end-of-life issues involving physician-assisted suicide or euthanasia. The theme of death, dying, and loss recurs in groups, although it is rarely brought up unless the group worker is willing to facilitate the sharing of painful and risky feelings related to the topic.

RECOMMENDED WAYS OF WORKING

First, to work with clients, we need to reach them. A sobering fact is that for most types of social work services, including group work, minorities are served less often—not because there are fewer potential clients for a given service but because of perceived and actual barriers to receiving that service (Palinkas et al., 2007). For example, many concrete services specifically developed for older adults (e.g., homemaker services, home health care, congregate meals) are used primarily by older white adults, despite the fact that older persons of color have been reported to have greater needs, as studies have found that older minority groups have an increased risk for disease and dysfunction in activities of daily living (Hayward & Heron, 1999; Williams & Wilson, 2001), have a higher amount of functional disabilities, and have greater prevalence of disease (Wallace & Villa, 2003) than their White counterparts. Older adults belonging to minority groups have been repeatedly reported in the literature to delay use of professional assistance or abstain from accessing formal support (Hinton, 2002; Ho, Weitzman, Cui, & Levkoff, 2000; Markides, Eschbach, Ray, & Peek, 2007). Successful attempts to increase minority representation in client groups include efforts to increase the cultural competence of the workers. This is seen in speaking in the client's own language or having workers with cultural similarity interact with the client, which makes the act of accepting help much easier (Min, 2005; Valle, 1998). Because in our country ethnic minority status is often tied to lower income, accessibility issues need to be addressed, too, including transportation, cost of services, and flexibility of hours.

Second, in developing groups of clients, it is important to pay attention to issues of homogeneity and heterogeneity (Corey & Corey, 2002). In general, groups need to have maximum homogeneity in terms of degree of vulnerability and capacity to tolerate anxiety. In other words, the ego strength of all members needs to be at similar levels. On the other hand, maximum heterogeneity in participants' conflict areas and patterns of coping allows input of new ideas and perspectives on the situations that clients face. Regardless of the themes discussed, this balancing rule between difference and similarity will allow participants to use the mutual aid model to share with each other. These themes can be incorporated in most groups that allow clients to determine the focus of the discussion.

An example of this is that for 5 years, one of the authors directed a weekly support group for members of a retirement community. Pairs of undergraduate students facilitated weekly support groups that lasted for a full academic year and combined small-group discussions and programs with occasional large-group workshops and potluck dinners (Black, Kelly, & Rice, 2005). These groups were ongoing, in the sense that many members stayed with the groups from year to year, but the student workers changed every September. As people grew older and frailer, there was a fairly high degree of turnover among the group members, and ways of working with them needed to change while maintaining the initial purposes of the group.

An example of this was the use of group members bringing some favorite food dishes to share with others, specifically for potluck dinners. These dinners were initially a wonderful opportunity for members to demonstrate their culinary skills and to "give," in a concrete way, to their friends and to the student workers. Over time, the participants' cooking abilities faltered as their vision, hearing, and health deteriorated. It was decided to cater the main dish for the potluck dinners, and the members brought desserts to share. Even with dessert, however, we saw a gradual change from the "famous homemade recipe for brownies" to boxes of cookies that were store bought. This change saddened those staff who had been with the group from the beginning. However, it was a richly expressive example of changing the parameters of the situation so that the members could still enjoy the essence of the program. Most recently, the potluck dinners were changed to potluck luncheons because more members were having trouble getting out at night even within their gated community. Workers must be sensitive to the environmental changes that need to be made to allow the substantive work of the group to continue. The purpose of the potluck dinners has remained constant: They combat the social isolation and loneliness of the senior community members (about 70% of whom live alone) and allow them to feel part of a community and a family.

In addition, workshops held twice each semester gave members specific skills to improve their ability to function within the group. For example, one of the authors held a 3-hour workshop on conflict resolution skills, including teaching "I-messages," discussing innate styles of conflict ("turtles" or "sharks"), and demonstrating skills of negotiation and mediation. A presentation of these skills coupled with an opportunity to discuss the feelings attached to them primed members to use them outside of the group.

In addition to retirement communities, groups for older adults can be located in institutions. In contrast to retirement communities, where residents live independently in whatever manner they choose, institutions provide the assistance needed for their residents to perform the tasks of daily living at the cost of lessened freedom. In an examination of institutions, Schmidt (1990) begins by describing people's feelings about them. "Most elderly persons entering a home for the aged view this move as their last one. But, whatever sense of loss they may feel, they are concerned also with the life they can make there. Thus, homes for the aged become laboratories of human behavior as residents deal with change on a scale for which their previous lives have not prepared them" (p. 1).

Reminiscence Therapy in Groups

Reminiscence storytelling is another form of group work therapy that focuses on increasing social interaction to decrease depressive symptoms, such as feelings of loneliness and sadness (Bohlmeijer, Smit, & Cuijpers, 2003). Reminiscence work has also been shown to strengthen confidence and enhance social contacts of older adults with depressive symptoms and certain forms of dementia (Van Puyenbroeck & Maes, 2008). The literature identifies several forms of reminiscence therapy. Two key forms are instrumental reminiscence and integrative reminiscence (Watt & Cappeliez, 2000). Instrumental reminiscence uses memories to recall past positive coping strategies, which can possibly be used during stressful life events in the present. The other form, integrative reminiscence, uses a cognitive-behavioral model whereby the participant uses constructive reappraisal of emotions and interpretations of his or her central life events. Both forms of reminiscence work well with older adults who are experiencing depressive symptoms or life challenges (Watt & Cappeliez, 2000).

Reminiscence can stimulate memories that can be used as part of a participant's narrative and autobiography. This can be done through use of all the senses. It can be done visually through use of historical photographs or video clips from past events (such as USO shows or celebrities from earlier generations).

Reminiscence can also be auditory through music, such as using familiar radio shows or early television shows, CDs of historically famous performers, or even making their own music with various musical instruments. It can include olfactory senses such as using smell kits of spices and scents such as cinnamon, cedar, or different foods. It can be tactile though the touching of objects, feeling fabric textures, painting, and even pottery work.

For younger group workers, reminiscence can be a way to learn about the past and gain a deeper understanding of the group members as they hear about the experiences that brought their clients to the present. Group members feel an increased sense of understanding and support for each other as they witness the commonality of their experiences.

Grief Support Groups

Grief counseling is a form of group work with older adults that focuses on the participants' intense feelings of loss, most often after a death. Grief counseling works well in group settings because peer support and relationships with others who can empathize with one's loss can help reduce feelings of isolation caused by grief. In some cases a grief counselor may facilitate the grief group, but it can be a mutual aid format as well. The facilitator or counselor is not the expert; instead, "the grief counselor acts as a fellow traveler rather than consultant, sharing the uncertainties of the journey, and walking alongside, rather than leading the grieving individual along the unpredictable road toward a new adaptation" (Neimeyer, 1998, p. 200). Essentially, the role of the facilitator is to be "present" for the bereaved, helping the group best by simply actively listening and demonstrating empathy.

Although much has been written about stage and task models of grief therapy (Kübler-Ross, 1969; Rando, 1993; Worden, 2002), contemporary grief work models follow a more integrative method similar to reminiscence by allowing the person to recollect and reexperience her life with the deceased in order to cherish old attachments. This allows the bereaved to make sense of her loss with the aim of adapting to life without that person.

Peer Support Groups for Health Promotion

Many older adults also see a benefit in joining a mutual aid peer support group that may not be professionally led by a health or mental health social worker. These groups can supplement the services of mental health professionals by allowing peers with similar conditions to share mutual concerns and exchange practical information for mutual benefit (Haber, 2013). Member-led peer groups unite aging adults in an organized manner often central to health-related themes such as weight management, heart disease, diabetes, smoking cessation, family caregiving, or coping with widowhood (Haber, 2013). These types of peer support groups are not antiprofessional; some groups develop a hybrid model whereby a professional worker is available ("on stand-by") should the members require guidance or group problem-solving suggestions, thus allowing professional group work interventions when needed. Peer support can also be valuable for older persons with chronic illness conditions, such as breast or prostate cancer, or depression for support and mutual education on treatment approaches (Davison, Pennebaker, & Dickerson, 2000). Often these illness-specific, peer-led groups provide a safe environment in which members can share their experiences, exchange practical information, and find emotional support from others who have some understanding of what they are going through.

Group Work Activities

Programming (using an activity to further a treatment goal for the group) can also be used in beneficial ways to build group cohesion or to simply facilitate discussion. In one group session of the support group program described earlier, the worker brought in the game "Trivial Pursuit" (immensely popular at the time). The game consists of a board, dice, and cards with questions on them, asking for answers about different topics, including science, nature, history, entertainment, arts and leisure, and sports. The usual game rules were modified for this group by abandoning the board, the dice, and the competitive aspect of the game. Instead, the worker read a question and all group members tried to answer it, often asking each other questions about their personal circumstances during the event in question. For example, to the question of when a baseball player broke a major league record, the answer came via a path that included deciding if it was before or after World War II, where each group member had been during those years, and what they were doing. Again, this became a form of reminiscence therapy. There was no score keeping and no winner or loser. The group spent as much time as they wanted on one question, and it ended when the right answer was given or the group as a whole gave up. The entire session used only four or five cards from the game, but the group emerged with a sense of closeness and cohesiveness that had not been present previously.

Some groups use a psychoeducational model to help older adults acquire new skills and behaviors to overcome life-challenging problems such as loneliness, grief and loss issues, and even health promotion concerns such as weight management or other behavior changes. Group counseling may not be as valuable for some older adults given their need for both concrete educational information as well as emotional support in a group context. Schneider and Cook (2005) stress that the planning of a psychoeducational group should be systematic and well thought out with each session to include objectives, information to be imparted, life-skill experiential activities, and process questions to reinforce the connection between the information and the experience. Fundamental to planning a psychoeducational group is selecting an appropriate topic and developing a curriculum of instruction and activities. Without a curriculum to guide the session, leaders may concentrate on only one aspect of the group experience, such as the education component, while missing the mutual support and discussion aspect relating to how the information affects individual's lives.

Evaluating Success

How does one know when a group is successful? Or if the treatment goals have been met? Much has been written about single-subject design and about the importance of every practitioner's evaluation of his or her own practice (Bloom, Fischer, & Orme, 2003; Nugent, Sieppert, & Hudson, 2001). This emphasis exists because we need to know if the money spent on a resource is effective and if the interventions we are using are helpful. To evaluate social support groups for older adults, one of the most effective ways is to go to the source: the consumer.

In many groups, sessions end with a 1-minute evaluation. This evaluation consists of three questions: (1) What was the most helpful thing that happened for you here today? (2) What was the least helpful thing that happened for you here today? (3) What would you suggest that we do differently next time? If the clients are able to write, this can be done on a sheet that is handed to each member. If writing is too burdensome, the clients can answer these questions quickly in a round-robin format.

More formal evaluations can be done at the midpoint and/or endpoint of a time-limited group. Clients can be asked about their overall satisfaction, about the effectiveness of specific techniques or sessions, and about how the enjoyment of their group is related to the goals they wanted to reach. This can be done via mail to increase the objectivity or verbally by a colleague (e.g., a worker at an agency or center) who the participants may recognize but is not affiliated with the group.

As with all evaluations, the introduction of the evaluation is crucial to its success. If the worker asks for feedback with leading questions that imply that only positive feedback is welcome, then that may be what he or she will get. If the members think that the continuation of the program is riding on their feedback, the responses may be greatly distorted. Allowing time for objective and subjective critique sends a welcome message to participants. It puts them in control of their group and enables them to make it the best it can be through their feedback. With groups of older adults, as with other groups, evaluation should be an ongoing part of group work that contributes to the group's overall effectiveness.

CONCLUSION

The primary reason that group work with older adults is so effective is that human beings are programmed to connect with others. Older age becomes a time when natural, informal connections falter due to illness, deaths, difficulties in mobility, and exhaustion. Providing ways to bolster human connection, through use of mutual aid groups, is one of the most valuable services that group workers can offer at this important time in an adult's life.

RESOURCES

Administration on Aging
Center for Communication and
Consumer Services
330 Independence Avenue SW, Room 4656
Washington, DC 20201
202-619-7501
http://www.aoa.gov/NAIC/

Administration for Community Living (ACL)
One Massachusetts Avenue NW
Washington, DC 20001
Public Inquiries: 202-619-0724
http://www.acl.gov/

Alzheimer's Association
225 N. Michigan Avenue, Floor 17
Chicago, IL 60601
800-272-3900
http://www.alz.org

American Association for Retired Persons
601 E Street NW
Washington, DC 20049
800-424-3410
http://www.aarp.org

The Association for Specialists in Group Work
(an affiliate organization of the American
Counseling Association)
5999 Stevenson Avenue
Alexandria, VA 22304
800-347-6647
http://www.asgw.org

GriefShare
P.O. Box 1739
Wake Forest, NC 27588
800-395-5755
http://www.griefshare.org

IASWG (formerly AASWG)
101 West 23rd Street, Suite 108
New York, NY, 10011
855-775-7045
http://iaswg.org/

National Adult Protective Services Association (NAPSA)
1900 13th Street Suite 303
Boulder, CO 80302
720-565-0906
http://www.napsa-now.org

National Institute on Aging
31 Center Drive, MSC 2292
Bethesda, MD 20892
800-222-2225
http://www.nia.nih.gov/

National PACE Association™
801 North Fairfax Street Suite 309
Alexandria, VA 22314
703-535-1565
http://www.npaonline.org/

REFERENCES

Achenbaum, W. A. (2015). A history of ageism since 1969. *Generations*, *39*(3), 10–16.
Bartels, S. J., & Smyer, M. A. (2002). Mental disorders of aging: An emerging public health crisis? *Generations*, *26*, 14–20.
Beers, M. H., & Berkow, R. (Eds.). (2000). *The Merck manual of geriatrics* (3rd ed.). Rahway, NJ: MERCK Publishing.
Bergstrom, M. J., & Nussbaum, J. F. (1996). Cohort differences in interpersonal conflict: Implications for the older patient-younger care provider interaction. *Health Communication*, *8*, 233–248.

Berkman, L. F., & Glass, T. (2000). Social integration, social networks, social support, and health. In L. F. Berkman & I. Kawachi (Eds.), *Social epidemiology* (137–173). New York, NY: Oxford University Press.

Black, J., Kelly, J., & Rice, S. (2005). A model of group work in retirement communities. In B. Haight & F. Gibson (Eds.), *Burnside's working with older adults: Group processes and techniques* (4th ed., pp. 273–285). Boston, MA: Jones & Bartlett.

Blank, B. T. (2009). David's harp: Bringing healing through music. *The New Social Worker, 16*(1). Retrieved from http://www.socialworker.com/home/component/remository/showdown/14/

Bloom, M., Fischer, J., & Orme, J. (2003). *Evaluating practice: Guidelines for the accountable professional.* Boston, MA: Allyn and Bacon.

Blow, F. C., Oslin, D. W., & Barry, K. L. (2002). Use and abuse of alcohol, illicit drugs, and psychoactive medication among older people. *Generations, 25*, 50–54.

Bohlmeijer, E., Smit, F., & Cuijpers, P. (2003). Effects of reminiscence and life review on late-life depression: A meta-analysis. *International Journal of Geriatric Psychiatry, 18*, 1088–1094.

Bright R. (1997). *Wholeness in later life.* London, UK: Jessica Kingsley.

Carter, B., & McGoldrick, M. (1999). *The expanded family life cycle: Individual, family, and social perspectives* (3rd ed.). Boston, MA: Allyn and Bacon.

Cattan, M., White, M., Bond, J., & Learmouth, A. (2005). Preventing social isolation and loneliness among older people: A systematic review of health promotion interventions. *Ageing and Society, 25*, 41–67.

Clare, L. (2002). We'll fight it as long as we can: Coping with the onset of Alzheimer's disease. *Aging and Mental Health, 6*, 139–148.

Corey, G., & Corey, M. (2002). *Groups: Process and practice* (6th ed.) Monterey, CA: Brooks/Cole.

Crowther, M. R., Parker, M. W., Achenbaum, W. A., Larimore, W. L., & Koenig, H. G., (2002). Rowe and Kahn's model of successful aging revisited: Positive spirituality: The forgotten factor. *Gerontologist, 42*, 613–620.

Denora, T. (2000). *Music in everyday life.* Cambridge, UK: Cambridge University Press.

DeSpelder, L. A., & Strickland, A. L. (2009). *The last dance: Encountering death and dying* (8th ed). New York, NY: McGraw-Hill.

Dury, R. (2014). Social isolation and loneliness in the elderly: An exploration of some of the issues. *British journal of community nursing, 19*(3), 125–128.

Eng, P. M., Rimm, E. B., Fitzmaurice, G., & Kawachi, I. (2002). Social ties and change in social ties in relation to subsequent total and cause-specific mortality and coronary heart disease incidence in men. *American Journal of Epidemiology, 155*, 700–709.

Erikson, E. (1963). *Childhood and society.* New York, NY: W. W. Norton.

Erikson, E. H., Erikson, J. M., & Kivnick, H. Q. (1986). *Vital involvement in old age.* New York, NY: W. W. Norton & Company, Inc.

Federal Interagency Forum on Aging-Related Statistics. (2012). *Older Americans 2012: Key indicators of well-being. Federal Interagency Forum on Aging-Related Statistics.* Washington, DC: US Government Printing Office.

Fillenbaum, G. G., Pieper, C. F., Cohen, H. J., Cornoni-Huntley, J. C., & Guralnik, J. M. (2000). Comorbidity of five chronic health conditions in elderly community residents: Determinants and impact on mortality. *Journal of Gerontology: Medical Sciences, 55*A, 84–89.

Fiori, K. L., Antonucci, T. C., & Cortina, K. S. (2006). Social network typologies and mental health among older adults. *Journals of Gerontology Series B: Psychological Sciences and Social Sciences, 61*(1), P25–P32.

Fitzpatrick, T. R., Gitelson, R., Andereck, K. L., & Mesbur, F. S. (2005). Social support factors and health among a senior center population in Southern Ontario, Canada. *Social Work in Health Care, 40*(3), 15–37.

Garavaglia, B. (2006). Avoiding the tendency to medicalize the grieving process: Reconciliation rather than resolution. *The New Social Worker Online.* Retrieved from http://www.socialworker.com/home/component/magazine/edition/Summer-2006-Edition/

Gelfand, D. (2006). *The aging network: Programs and services* (6th ed.). New York, NY: Springer.

Gitterman, A., & Shulman, L. (Eds.). (1994). *Mutual aid groups and the life cycle* (2nd ed). New York, NY: Columbia University Press.

Goelitz, A. (2001). Dreaming their way into life: A group experience with oncology patients. *Social Work with Groups, 24*, 53–67.

Goelitz, A. (2003). When accessibility is an issue: Telephone support groups for caregivers. *Smith College Studies in Social Work, 73*, 385–394.

Goelitz, A. (2004). Using the end of groups as an intervention at the end-of-life. *Journal of Gerontological Social Work, 44*(1/2), 211–221.

Goldsilver, P. M., & Gruneir, M. R. (2001). Early stage dementia group: An innovative model of support for individuals in the early stages of dementia. *American Journal of Alzheimer's Disease, 16*, 109–114.

Gore-Felton, C., & Spiegel, D. (1999). Enhancing women's lives: The role of support groups among breast cancer patients. *Journal for Specialists in Group Work, 24*, 274–287.

Haber, D. (2013). *Health promotion and aging: Practical applications for health professionals.* New York, NY: Springer.

Harrigan, M. P., & Farmer, R. L. (2000). The myths and facts of aging. In R. L. Schneider, N. P. Kropf, & A. J. Kisor (Eds.), *Gerontological social work: Knowledge, service settings and special populations* (2nd ed., pp. 26–64). Belmont, CA: Brooks/Cole.

Hays, T. (2006). Facilitating well-being through music for older people with special needs. *Home Healthcare Services Quarterly, 25*(3/4), 55–73.

Hayward, M., & Heron, M. (1999). Racial inequality in active life among adult Americans. *Demography, 36*, 77–92.

Hebert, L. E., Weuve, J., Scherr, P. A., & Evans, D. A. (2013). Alzheimer disease in the United States (2010–2050) estimated using the 2010 census. *Neurology, 80*(19), 1778-1783.

Hinton, L. (2002). Improving care for ethnic minority elderly and their family caregivers across the spectrum of dementia severity. *Alzheimer's Disease and Associated Disorders, 16*(2), 50–55.

Ho, C., Weitzman, P. F., Cui, X., & Levkoff, S. E. (2000). Stress and service use among minority caregivers to elders with dementia. *Journal of Gerontological Social Work, 33*, 67–88.

Jacobs, E., Masson, R., & Harvil, R. (2002). *Group counseling: Strategies and skills* (4th ed.). Monterey, CA: Brooks/Cole/Thomson Learning.

Johnson, C. J., & McGee, M. (2004). Psychosocial aspects of death and dying, *Gerontologist, 44*(5), 719–722.

Johnson, G., Otto, D., & Clair, A. (2001). The effect of instrumental and vocal music on adherence to a physical rehabilitation exercise program with persons who are elderly. *Journal of Music Therapy, 38*(2), 82–96.

Kane, R. L., & Kane, R. A. (2005). Ageism in healthcare and long-term care. *Generations, 29*(3), 49–54.

Kim, J., & Moen, P. (2002). Retirement transitions, gender and psychological well-being: A life-course, ecological model. *Journals of Gerontology Series B: Psychological Sciences and Social Sciences, 57*, 212–222.

Kivnick, H. Q., & Murray, S. V. (2001). Life strengths interview guide: Assessing elder clients' strengths. *Journal of Gerontological Social Work, 34*(4), 7–32.

Kivnick, H. Q., & Stoffel, S. A. (2005). Vital involvement practice: Strengths as more than tools for solving problems. *Journal of Gerontological Social Work, 46*, 85–116.

Koger, S., Chapin, K., & Brotons, M. (1999). Is music therapy an effective intervention for dementia? A meta-analytic review of literature. *Journal of Music Therapy, 26*, 2–15.

Kottler, J. (2001). *Learning group leadership: An experiential approach.* Boston, MA: Allyn and Bacon.

Krause, N. (1997). Anticipated support, received support, and economic stress among older adults. *Journal of Gerontology: Psychological Sciences, 52*, 284–293.

Krause, N. (2001). Social support. In R. H. Binstock & L. K. George (Eds.), *Handbook of aging and the social sciences* (pp. 272–294). San Diego, CA: Academic Press.

Kübler-Ross, E. (1969). *On death and dying.* New York, NY: Macmillan.

Kubler-Ross, E. (1975). *Death: The final stage of growth.* New York, NY: Simon and Schuster.

Markides K. S., Eschbach K., Ray, L. A., & Peek, M. K. (2007). Census disability rates among older people by race/ethnicity and type of Hispanic origin. In J. L. Angel & K. E. Whitfield (Eds.), *The health of aging Hispanics: The Mexican-origin population* (pp. 26–39). New York, NY: Springer.

Marshall, V. W., Clarke, P. J., & Ballantyne, P. J. (2001). Instability in the retirement transition: Effects on health and well-being in a Canadian Study. *Research on Aging, 23*, 379–409.

Mehta, K. K., & Ching Ee, J. C. (2008). Effects of good life program on Singaporean older adults' psychological well-being. *Activities, Adaptation and Aging, 32*(3/4), 214–237.

McInnis-Dittrich, K. (2014). *Social work with older adults: A biopsychosocial approach to assessment and intervention* (4th ed.). Boston, MA: Allyn and Bacon.

Min, J. W. (2005). Cultural competency: A key to effective future social work with racially and ethnically diverse elders. *Families in Society, 86*, 347–358.

National Alliance for Caregiving & AARP. (2004). *Caregiving in the US* Bethesda, MD: Author.

National Council on Aging. (2006). *Fact sheet: Senior centers*. Retrieved from http://www.ncoa.org/content.cfm?sectionID=103&detail=2741

National Institutes of Mental Health. (2007). *Older adults: Depression and suicide facts (fact sheet)*. Retrieved from http://www.nimh.nih.gov/health/publications/older-adults-depression-and-suicide-facts-fact-sheet/index.shtml

Neimeyer, R. A. (1998). *Lessons of loss: A guide to coping*. New York, NY: McGraw-Hill.

Nelson-Becker, H. B. (2004). Meeting life challenges: A hierarchy of coping styles in African American and Jewish American older adults. *Journal of Human Behavior in the Social Environment, 10*(1), 155–174.

Neugarten, B. (1975). The future and the young-old. *Gerontologist, 15*, 4–9.

Nugent, W., Sieppert, J., & Hudson, W. (2001). *Practice evaluation for the 21st century*. Monterey, CA: Brooks/Cole (Wadsworth Press).

Palinkas, L. A., Criado, V., Fuentes, D., Shepherd, S., Milian, H., Folsom, D., & Jeste, D. (2007). Unmet needs for services for older adults with mental illness: Comparison of views of different stakeholder groups. *American Journal of Geriatric Psychiatry, 15*, 530–540.

Petersen, R. C., Caracciolo, B., Brayne, C., Gauthier, S., Jelic, V., & Fratiglioni, L. (2014). Mild cognitive impairment: a concept in evolution. *Journal of Internal Medicine, 275*(3), 214–228.

Rando, T. (1993). *Treatment of complicated mourning*. Champaign, IL: Research Press.

Rowe, J., & Kahn, R. (1998). *Successful aging*. New York, NY: Pantheon Books.

Sadock, B. J., & Sadock, V. A. (2003). *Kaplan & Sadock's synopsis of psychiatry* (9th ed.). Philadelphia, PA: Lippincott Williams & Wilkins.

Salthouse, T. A. (2009). When does age-related cognitive decline begin? *Neurobiology of Aging, 30*(4), 507–514.

Salzman, B. (2006). Myths and realities of aging. *Care Management Journal, 7*(3), 141–150.

Schmidt, M. G. (1990). *Negotiating a good old age: Challenges of residential living in late life*. San Francisco, CA: Jossey-Bass.

Schneider, J. K., & Cook, J. H., Jr. (2005) Planning psychoeducational groups for older adults. *Journal of Gerontological Nursing, 31*(8), 33–38.

Schwartz, W. (1961). The social worker in the group. In *The Social Welfare Forum* (pp. 146–177) New York, NY: Columbia University Press.

Seeman, T. E., Lusignolo, T. M., & Albert, M. (2001). Social relationships, social support, and patterns of cognitive aging in healthy, high-functioning older adults: MacArthur studies of successful aging. *Health Psychology, 20*, 243–255.

Sheehy, G. (1995). *New passages: Mapping your life across time*. New York, NY: Random House.

Shulman, L. (1999). *The skills of helping individuals, families and groups* (4th ed.). Itasca, IL: F. E. Peacock.

Sloboda, J., & O'Neill, S. (2001). *Music and emotion: Theory and research*. Oxford, UK: Oxford University Press.

Stanford, E. P., & Usita, P. M. (2002). Retirement: Who is at risk? *Generations, 26*(11), 45–48.

Szinovacs, M. E., & Davey, A. (2005). Predictors of perceptions of involuntary retirement. *Gerontologist, 45*, 36–47.

Toseland, R., & Rivas, R. (2008). *An introduction to group work practice* (6th ed.). Boston, MA: Allyn and Bacon.

Toseland, R. W., & Rizzo, V. M. (2004). What's different about working with older people in groups? *Journal of Gerontological Social Work, 44,* 5–23.

US Census Bureau. (2006). *Income, poverty and health insurance coverage in the US, 2005.* Retrieved from http://www.census.gov/prod/2006pubs/p60-231.pdf

US Census Bureau. (2009b). *Poverty status of the population 55 years and over by sex and age: 2007. Current population, annual social and economic supplement, 2008.* Retrieved from http://www.census.gov/population/www/socdemo/age/older_2008.html

US Census Bureau, Population Division. (2009a). *Current population survey, annual social and economic supplement, 2008.* Retrieved from http://www.census.gov/population/www/socdemo/age/age_sex_2008.html

Valle, R. (1998). *Caregiving across cultures: Working with dementing illness and ethnically diverse populations.* Washington, DC: Taylor & Francis.

Van Puyenbroeck, J., & Maes, B. (2008). A review of critical, person-centered and clinical approaches to reminiscence work for people with intellectual disabilities. *International Journal of Disability, Development and Education, 55,* 43–60.

Wallace, S., & Villa, V. (2003). Equitable health systems: Cultural and structural issues for Latino elders. *American Journal of Law and Medicine, 29,* 247–267.

Wallach, T. (2004). Transforming conflict: A group relations perspective. *Peace and Conflict Studies, 11,* 76–95.

Watt, L., & Cappeliez, P. (2000). Integrative and instrumental reminiscence therapies for depression in older adults: Intervention strategies and treatment effectiveness. *Aging and Mental Health, 4,* 166–177.

Wethington, E., Moen, P., Glasgow, N., & Pillemer, K. (2000). Multiple roles, social integration, and health. In K. Pillemer, P. Moen, E. Wethington, & N. Glasgow (Eds.), *Social integration in the second half of life* (pp. 48–74). Baltimore, MD: Johns Hopkins University Press.

Williams, D., & Wilson, C. (2001). Race, ethnicity, and aging. In R. H. Binstock & L. K. George (Eds.), *Handbook of aging and the social sciences* (4th ed., pp. 160–178). San Diego, CA: Academic Press.

Worden, J. W. (2002). *Grief counseling and grief therapy: A handbook for the mental health practitioner* (3rd ed.) New York, NY: Springer.

Chapter Eleven

Culturally Responsive Group Work With Immigrant Family Caregivers

Youjung Lee and Paul R. Gould

Extensive research has been conducted to identify the typical concerns and needs of family caregivers in the United States. Programs designed to respond to the unique needs of individual caregivers have been shown to reduce incidents of caregiver burnout and depression (Belle et al., 2006). However, caregivers (for the purposes of this chapter, we are referring to spouses, children, and other relatives except where specifically highlighted) are not always able to recognize or articulate their needs. This observation is especially valid with immigrant families facing cultural differences and language barriers (Sue, Cheng, Saad, & Chu, 2012). This chapter discusses the needs of immigrant family caregivers and describes a culturally responsive psychoeducational support group conducted with Asian immigrant family caregivers in collaboration with the Korean American Alzheimer's Coalition (KAAC). The group work model was evaluated with Korean American dementia family caregivers in Queens, New York, from July 2009 through January 2010 (Lee & Yim, 2013). Although Asian populations differ from one another substantially, the experiences of many immigrant groups in the United States are similar. Here, we hope to provide a guide for issues to consider when working with immigrant family caregivers with the recognition that any group work intervention needs to be culturally responsive.

The older adult population in the United States is growing rapidly and becoming more racially and ethnically diverse. Between 2012 and 2050, the population of White adults who are 65 years old and over is expected to decrease by 18%, whereas all other older adult racial groups (i.e., Hispanic, African, Asian, and others) are expected to increase (US Census Bureau, 2014). The number of Asian older adults is predicted to increase from 3.8% in 2012 to 7.1% by 2050 (US Census Bureau, 2014). Subsequently, the number of family members serving as caregivers will also increase.

PRACTICE PRINCIPLES

The term *immigrant* encompasses an extensive and highly diverse array of ethno-cultural factors that influence how individuals and families function in the community. Family caregivers have played a significant role as a social resource in the aging immigrant community; however, despite a need for resources and information among this growing caregiver population, the services available to them are limited (Chu & Sue, 2011). This unmet need is particularly evident in terms of immigrant caregivers, whose experience can be expected to be unlike those of White dementia caregivers due to differences in norms, practices, and expectations regarding their role. For example, many Asian older adults who came to the United States in their later years tend to have limited English-speaking abilities. The lack of skilled nursing facilities and adult daycare programs equipped with bilingual services or adequate multicultural competencies (regarding food, spiritual practices, and family roles) poses immense difficulties and places extra burdens on the patients and their caregivers. Most first-generation elders are hesitant to step outside their own family boundaries due to language barriers and challenges (Lee & Smith, 2012). Due to a lack of culturally sensitive services, immigrant families experience social isolation and marginalization, preventing them from receiving appropriate medical support and community-based education. In many cases, the caregivers fail to provide adequate care for the patients due to overwhelming mental, economic, and/or social burdens.

Understanding the Needs of Family Caregivers

Family caregivers are often negotiating multiple responsibilities and roles, including parenting, career, and personal health, in addition to providing care to their older family member. Caregivers experience their own responses to their family member's disease and needs, others' activities related to caregiving, and to the caregiving process itself. Furthermore, there exists a wide range of disparities among caregivers' experiences and the negative consequences caregiving has on their personal lives (Lahaie, Earle, & Heymann, 2013). These may include depression, high levels of stress, a sense of burden, and a variety of physical and other mental health concerns (Cassie & Sanders, 2008). Group work practitioners should keep in mind they are working with two sets of interrelated client needs simultaneously—the needs of the caregiver, as well as the needs of the person receiving care. The practitioner strives to assist caregivers in identifying and maintaining their personal needs while still providing care to their family member. This requires a high degree of cultural sensitivity and responsiveness on the part of practitioners.

Information Regarding the Disease and Treatment

Caregiving is required when an individual's ability to perform activities of daily living is compromised, typically as a result of injury or disease. In the case of aging adults, individuals often experience a variety of progressive physiological and cognitive changes that inhibit their ability to remain independent. In this context, family caregivers seek information regarding how the disease may progress, effective treatments to either cure or manage the condition, rates of decline, medications, and services available to assist their ailing family member. Medical information can be complex and difficult to understand. This may be exacerbated by differences in language and a limited understanding of Western medicine.

Understanding Cultural Context of Disease and Treatment

Cultural belief systems influence how immigrant families view disease, mental health concerns, treatment recommendations, and caregiving roles. Cultural perspectives regarding the meaning of disease vary greatly. For example, Eastern cultures often incorporate a mind-body-spirit context as part of their understanding of disease and healing (Feltham, 2008; McCabe, 2008). Applying such a perspective, disease may be perceived as the result of spiritual deficits or misaligned energy flow in the body. The family's view of healing may favor spiritual or energy-based interventions, such as Reiki, to resolve the health issues. In addition, many East Asian cultures somaticize emotional distress and mental illness, identifying physical manifestations instead of psychological symptoms (Kim & Lopez, 2014; Mak & Zane, 2004). These culturally rooted perspectives influence how families choose to proceed with treatment and care. Among Western practitioners, particularly those in medicine, these actions are often misinterpreted as "resistance" or "noncompliance" with a treatment regimen. Clinicians should elicit caregivers' unique perspectives and incorporate these themes during group work. Furthermore, advocacy on the part of the family may be necessary to educate other health professionals regarding the need to incorporate cultural preferences into treatment planning.

Family Systems and Cultural Roles

Family structures and cultural roles are influenced by ethnocultural factors and belief systems. These structures guide decision-making practices, living arrangements, assignment of caregiving responsibilities, educational priorities, and sharing of financial resources. For example, hierarchical family structures are often observed among Asian American immigrants (Yee, Su, Kim, & Yancura, 2009). This influences who family members may turn to for advice, direction, and assignment of tasks. Among Latin American immigrant populations, practitioners may encounter the concept of familism, which means "the perceived strength of family bonds and sense of loyalty to family" (Luna et al., 1996, p. 267). In immigrant families with high familism, the needs of the family system may outweigh those of any single family member. The concept of familism is also often observed among Asian immigrant families. In addition, in the Asian American community, the Confucian principle of filial piety requires that children and younger adults provide care for the elderly members of the family. Filial piety is a social value that deeply influences the parent–child relationship in East Asian populations (Sung, 1997). The concept of filial piety in Confucianism involves ideas about children's responsibility to their parents, and it essentially guides offspring to recognize the care they received and reciprocate for their aging parents (Yeh & Bedford, 2003). In the Asian immigrant culture, this concept may explain a family's decisions and expected roles of adult children in a caregiving context.

The diverse and unique family structures shared among immigrant populations provide an important context for group work. Practitioners must explore and take into account the culturally rooted family structures and modify intervention strategies to align with the clients' prescribed responsibilities and priorities. It is equally important for practitioners to examine their own biases and reactions to these cultural differences and avoid projecting their own family structures and expectations upon immigrant caregiving families.

Psychoeducation and Emotional Support

Psychoeducational group interventions offer components of both education and support that are based on learning theory and utilize behavioral procedures (Corey, 2008). Time-limited intervention focuses on fostering group participants' social support and providing education regarding necessary skills. The effectiveness of psychoeducational group interventions with dementia caregivers has been well established (Tompkins & Bell, 2010). Psychoeducational groups have demonstrated effectiveness in decreasing caregivers' burden and increasing their well-being (Martin-Carrasco et al., 2009). A meta-analysis conducted by Sorenson, Pinquart, and Duberstein (2002) found that psychoeducational interventions and psychotherapy present the most consistent short-term benefits among various interventions for family caregivers.

The psychoeducational model is similarly effective with Asian caregivers. Au and colleagues (2010) found that Chinese dementia caregivers who participated in a psychoeducational group demonstrated improved self-efficacy for dealing with disruptive dementia-related behaviors and managing upsetting thoughts in the caregiving situation compared with the caregivers who did not participate in the group. The group members also tended to adopt healthier coping strategies, including the use of rational problem solving and distancing. Furthermore, the researchers found that self-efficacy had the effect of mediating between social support and depression among caregivers. The findings highlight the significant role of enhanced self-confidence experienced by caregivers through the psychoeducational group work model.

Case Example: A Psychoeducational Support Group for Asian American Dementia Caregivers

Considering the significant needs of and cultural barriers experienced by Asian immigrant dementia caregivers, the following psychoeducational support group model was developed specifically for this typically marginalized population. This model adopted original ideas from Aranda and Knight's (1997) sociocultural stress and coping model. Their model recognizes ethnicity as a structural status variable and a factor that impacts each step of the stress and coping process. According to Aranda and Knight (1997), "Ethnicity and culture play a significant role in the stress and coping process of caregivers to the elderly as a result of a) a differential risk for specific health disorders and disabilities, b) variation in the appraisal of potential stressors, and c) the effect on stress-mediating variables such as social support and coping" (p. 343). The authors emphasize that their minority ethnic culture explains caregivers' appraisal of the caregiving process and its associated responsibilities. Cultural expectations influence caregivers' roles, coping strategies, and perceptions; these may act in contradictory directions simultaneously, perpetuating both support and burden. For example, immigrant family caregivers may experience less emotional distress within the cultural context due to the support from extended families or positive appraisal based on familism. However, cultural influence can work in negative ways if family caregivers adopt nonproductive or avoidant coping styles.

In developing the group work model, special attention was paid to the translation of materials. Language as a carrier of culture (Bernal, Bonilla, & Bellido, 1995) contains subtle nuances of specific content, so mechanical translations of intervention or educational materials do not guarantee caregivers' satisfaction with social services. To provide quality social support and satisfactory social services for immigrant caregivers, the interventions and social services were infused with specific cultural content, such as *Hwa-byung*, meaning "anger disease" in Korean culture (American Psychiatric Association, 2000), familism (Luna et al., 1996), and filial piety (Yeh & Bedford, 2003) in the group materials. Additionally, honorifics, expressions with connotations of respect when referring to older or social superiors, were consistently utilized in the material designed for Asian family caregivers.

Practitioners working with Asian immigrants need to provide opportunities for dementia patients and their families to receive information that improves their understanding of the illness, the importance of proper diagnosis of the disease, and related social services available in the community. As part of this process, it is crucial to have mental health practitioners who understand the significance of the family's culture and shape a productive relationship with the clients (Sue et al., 2012). Utilizing service providers who understand the client's culture can increase the family's receptivity to the service. In Scharlach and colleague's (2006) study, racially and ethnically diverse family caregivers shared their experience with the attitudinal and structural barriers to their utilization of services. One Korean caregiver expressed, "I want to take [care] of my mother and mother-in-law myself, particularly if they become ill, because I couldn't trust them in other people's hands. Nurse's aides don't even understand Korean and don't really care" (p. 145). Chinese caregivers shared the lack of culturally sensitive services and the difficulty with finding services in Cantonese, which decreased their utilization of social services. Another Asian caregiver reported that "Service would be more useful if they were more tailored to care [about] recipients' cultural traditions, such as having an option of getting Chinese food with Meals-on-Wheels instead of the typical American dishes usually provided by the program" (Scharlach et al., 2006, p. 146).

Based on a literature review of the cultural implications relevant to the Asian immigrants and the effectiveness of psychoeducational groups (Au et al., 2010; Tompkins & Bell, 2010), the following culturally responsive psychoeducational support group model was developed and evaluated with Korean American dementia caregivers (Lee & Yim, 2013). The aims of the group were to (a) help the immigrant dementia caregivers develop active coping skills through learning and to practice cognitive and behavioral techniques in culturally competent ways; (b) increase the use of social support; and (c) increase the quality of mental health by reducing caregiving stress.

The Korean American Alzheimer's Coalition (KAAC) announced this project to dementia caregivers in the community, and the participants were selected based on their cognitive functioning skills and caregiving situation. The service was limited only to Korean-speaking family caregivers to provide culturally responsive group work to the immigrant family caregivers. Once the participants were selected, details about the group were provided before the first meeting. The monthly group took place at a Korean church in a metropolitan area with a high Korean immigrant population, and each session lasted approximately 60–90 minutes. The group was a closed group with membership limited to nine members. The group participants were heterogeneous with respect to gender, age, and relation to care receivers (i.e., spousal caregivers and adult child caregivers who provide care for their parent with dementia).

The sessions combined education with support. In every session except the last, a presentation was made and then the group participants engaged in the mutual aid process by sharing experiences and suggestions with one another. The mutual aid process was facilitated with the assistance of a social worker. In this group work model, the education component included information about dementia and dementia caregiving skills, culturally responsive anger management and coping skills, and community resources. The support component consisted of discussions regarding the caregivers' expected roles and the meaning of caregiving in their respective cultures, and developing active coping skills (Lee & Yim, 2013).

In the model, we emphasized the positive aspect of caregiving using cultural "calibration" (Jones, Zhang, Jaceldo-Siegl, & Meleis, 2002). Jones and colleagues describe the experience of 41 Asian American caregivers and the skills the caregivers used to manage caregiving challenges. Most of the caregivers in the Jones et al. study used a family-connected approach in a caregiving situation. The caregivers indicated that they live with two sets of standards, one deriving from their original culture and the other from American culture. In this potentially conflicted process, the caregivers experience a positive adjustment of both values and cultures. The attempt to resolve cultural conflicts often requires careful interactions with family members. The researchers described the process as a "calibration" or a negation of the expected level of care in each culture. The immigrant caregivers adopt the "calibration" to achieve a healthy balance between two culturally different roles and ultimately to create a new identity in the family caregiving context (Jones et al., 2002).

Based upon our success with this model, we offer it as a guide for work with other immigrant groups, particularly Asian immigrant populations.

Session Guide

Session One: Group members are asked to introduce themselves to the other group members and group facilitators. The goals and objectives of this group are identified by the group facilitators. Contracting skills to establish a structure for the work (Shulman, 2011) are used in this session. The group facilitators focus on clarifying the role of the group facilitators, soliciting group members' feedback, and identifying the group rules (e.g., keeping confidentiality and being respectful of other group members). As an introduction to the educational component, relaxation techniques that can be used in a daily caregiving situation are demonstrated. Relaxation techniques are introduced and periodically revisited during subsequent sessions.

Session Two: A presentation is given in which the definition, types, etiology, and available treatments for dementia are introduced. Relevant resources and reading materials regarding dementia are provided as part of the presentation. Shulman (2011) cautions facilitators that the presentation of too much information can lead group members to "tune out" or disengage from the presentation due to an overwhelming amount of content. Therefore, the facilitators structure the session to allow the group members to interact with the information regarding dementia and strategies to manage the disease; this approach personalizes the information which makes the discussion more meaningful to participants.

Session Three: Dementia caregiving skills are discussed (e.g., issues relating to patients' diet, bathing, and nutrition) as well as the importance of and skills for maintaining the mental and physical health of caregivers. The group participants are encouraged to share their caregiving experiences and difficulties, after which the group facilitators responded to additional questions regarding caregiving issues. Group members are encouraged to provide suggestions to other caregivers based on their own experiences. In this session, participants may begin to demonstrate group cohesion and mutual support after sharing their experience and knowledge related to dementia caregiving in the community. Written materials regarding dementia caregiving skills and tips for maintaining mental health are provided at this session and revisited during the remaining sessions.

Session Four: Based on the development of mutual support and group co-hesion in the prior sessions, the group facilitators provide behavioral modifica-tion skills training and explain the importance of maintaining mental health during caregiving. Effective skills for managing dementia-related behaviors (e.g., memory loss, declines in self-care, aggression, wandering, refusal of care support) are discussed. The facilitator also leads a discussion on *Hwa-byung* or anger dis-ease (American Psychiatric Association, 2000). Family caregivers often struggle with *Hwa-byung* in relationship to dementia caregiving or other family-relates stressors, and fulfillment of the culturally dictated expectations of spouses and children in traditional Korean culture. In past groups, group members have ac-tively participated in the discussion regarding *Hwa-byung* and shared their per-sonal struggles with the anger syndrome in relationship to their caregiving role. Several group members shared that their feelings were validated by learning that *Hwa-byung* is an officially defined disease in mental health.

In this session, the adequate use of language metaphors reduces intervention anxiety and supports the cultural context of immigrant caregivers (Bernal et al., 1995). The benefits to family caregivers (i.e., education on anger management and discussion of the development of active coping skills) will be limited if the group facilitators do not address *Hwa-byung* and the underlying reasons that familial caregivers struggle with the disease. The discussion of the culture-bound syndrome with other caregivers who share a similar cultural background can become a critical step in the process of immigrant family members expressing their needs and finding their voice in the caregiving context.

A similar phenomenon was observed in a study by Chan and O'Conner (2008) with Chinese family caregivers, where the concept of "speaking out" was dis-cussed as a critical component of a culturally competent practice model for Asian family caregivers. In their study with Chinese Family Support Group members, the researchers addressed the concept of "speaking out" in Asian culture, facili-tating opportunities for the caregivers to (a) challenge the negative connotation of "speaking out" in the caregiving context, (b) reframe and acknowledge the im-portance of "speaking out," and (c) reenvision a new perspective for family care-giving consistent with their cultural context (Chan & O'Conner, 2008). Sharing such a cultural concept with other group members from a similar cultural back-ground not only validated members' feelings and experiences; it also helped them to understand their needs for the eventual utilization of social services.

Session Five: Cognitive-behavioral techniques (Corey, 2008) are utilized to address methods of stress management. During the session, the family caregivers review their preconceived beliefs and receive support to modify the dysfunctional notions generated by caregiving into adaptive/healthy consequences. The group facilitators revisit the cultural syndrome *Hwa-byung* and common unhealthy coping skills (i.e., avoidance) that Asian family caregivers usually adopt in a care-giving situation. Following the discussion, the group learns about healthy coping strategies (i.e., active coping). The group members review common coping skills that they use during the daily caregiving situation, and the leaders reinforce the importance of utilizing active and healthy coping strategies.

As part of the utilization of active coping styles, effective communication skills are introduced, and the group members are asked to participate in role playing with other group members. Role playing enables the group members to identify their communication styles. It also helps caregivers to assert themselves and express their needs and concerns to other family members and health care professionals. Because cultural and attitudinal barriers hinder immigrant caregivers' utilization of mental health services (Sue et al., 2012), learning the skills of active coping and effective communication could help their positive interaction with health service providers.

Session Six: The role of social support in dementia caregiving is presented. Because caregiving is considered a family responsibility among Asian family caregivers (Scharlach et al., 2006), caregivers often do not seek social support or professional services in caring for their spouse or parent with dementia. Therefore, the concept of dementia, including dementia as a disease (see Session Two), and the importance of the utilization of professional services are revisited. As group members accept the importance of seeking professional service and support, they are encouraged to review their social support and ways to enhance the quality of that support. They also revisit their definition of social support and have a chance to positively reframe their perspective on using this to enhance their ability to cope with family caregiving responsibilities. For example, formal and informal support from a local Korean church is identified as a primary social resource. More important, caregivers are asked to share their concerns regarding the adequacy of Korean-language health care materials and services.

Session Seven: A presentation is given regarding community resources for family caregivers in the area. The resource package includes information about adult day care centers and nursing homes for Korean-speaking dementia patients, and it provides information on legal and financial issues relating to dementia caregiving. This session reinforces the importance of utilizing health care services as a resource in dementia care.

Session Eight: This concluding session provides group members with opportunities to identify and share the positive aspects of dementia caregiving, as well as find meaning in the care they provide. Group members are also asked to talk about resilience and their management skills as a caregiver and a member of society in a foreign country. The group facilitators help the caregivers identify personal growth and find meaning in the caregiving experience, which serve as significant reinforcements for them to continue to care for their loved ones. Jones et al.'s (2002) concept of "calibration" is used in this session to achieve a healthy balance between two culturally different roles and ultimately to create a new identity in the family caregiving context. The group session concludes with closing remarks by the members and the leaders.

COMMON THEMES

After the conclusion of the group sessions with Korean American dementia care-givers, a focus group was conducted to explore the effectiveness of the model we just described and implications for culturally responsive group work practice. The immigrant family caregivers experienced feelings similar to those of their Western counterparts. These include feelings of being inadequately prepared to provide care, frustration with their family member, and being burdened by the caregiving process. However, cultural factors produce additional and unique needs among the immigrant caregivers. Several cultural themes and practice implications emerged from the focus group and discussions among service provid-ers. These themes and practice implications center on knowledge of the disease, inadequacy and isolation, depression, burden and cultural expectations, a closed culture, mental health stigma, familism and filial piety, and heterogeneity among immigrant family caregivers.

Knowledge of the Disease

Dementia is a complex set of symptoms that arise as a result of physiologi-cal changes in the brain. There are multiple diseases that result in dementia, including Alzheimer's disease, vascular (multi-infarction) dementia, dementia with Lewy body, and dementia with Parkinson's disease. The presentation of symptoms may be subtly different within each subtype. Families often do not understand the etiology or progression of the specific disease subtype. In addi-tion to understanding the mechanisms and symptoms of the disease, caregivers seek information about treatment, particularly medications and health services.

One spouse caregiver from the group shared that "I had limited knowledge even though I have been taking care of my husband for a while. However, I learned a lot from the professionals in this group. This education group was really help-ful. I got confused when he was diagnosed with dementia since we didn't have in-formation and support related to disease" (Lee & Yim, 2013, p. 20). If the group addresses a broader range of dementia diagnoses, it is important to highlight different disease trajectories, symptoms, and treatments among group members. This permits group members to share the commonalities of their experiences and suggestions with one another but also recognizes that their experiences may be unique based upon the disease subtype. One caregiver said the following:

> I learned a lot from here. I didn't know about the [Alzheimer's] disease. I only knew about dementia. I learned that there are many types of dementia, such as Parkinson's disease, and different symptoms of dementia from the lecture and other group members' experiences. Previously, I didn't understand my husband behavior's, but now I know that he does do that because of the disease. It makes me understand and protect him. (Lee & Yim, 2013, p. 20)

Inadequacy and Isolation

Lack of knowledge of the disease typically results in caregiver frustration with the loved one. With little support or training, caregivers struggle to respond to increasingly difficult and illogical behaviors. As the disease progresses, the person with dementia has greater difficulty performing instrumental and basic activities of daily living (IADLs and ADLs). This progressive decline in independent functioning necessitates increasing levels of supervision and assistance to execute functions ranging from maintaining finances, shopping, preparing meals, and managing transportation to dressing, grooming, eating, and toileting. Caregivers feel less competent to meet their family member's needs and respond to erratic or illogical behaviors. In particular, they may feel less competent to manage medications, make appropriate health care decisions, and maintain their loved one's safety and dignity in the home. Due to a lack of culturally responsive and bilingual services for Asian immigrant families, caregivers are often unable to communicate effectively with health care providers, identify services that may be integrated with the family's cultural practices, and understand their unique psychosocial experiences.

Depression

Depression is a common occurrence among all caregivers, although Asian immigrant families may present their experiences differently than do their White counterparts. In contrast to Western medicine, which typically treats physical and mental health separately, Eastern cultures maintain an integrated perspective regarding mind and body. Asian family caregivers are less likely to express feelings of sadness, grief, or regret. Instead, they are more likely to recognize the physical consequences of these experiences, such as changes in sleep patterns, appetite, and fatigue. Although Western health systems have historically labeled this as *somatization*, this terminology may mislead practitioners to harbor the belief that Asian family caregivers do not experience psychological distress. Instead, group facilitators should address how caregivers' feelings are related to the physical manifestation of depression.

Burden and Cultural Expectations

Cultural factors may impact Asian immigrant family caregivers in both positive and detrimental ways. For example, Korean family caregivers may experience less emotional distress within their cultural context, whereas this same cultural context may inhibit effective coping by promoting avoidance. This phenomenon can be found among male caregivers as well. Due to the expected image originating from traditional Asian society, Asian males tend to underutilize support groups or local resources. Therefore, culture can simultaneously support caregivers and increase the burden placed on family caregivers.

Furthermore, Korean American adult child caregivers who take care of their parents generally experience greater difficulties in caregiving than spouse caregivers (Lee & Smith, 2012). The adult child caregivers suffer from their position between Korean and American cultures when they attempt to play the expected cultural role appropriately with limited cultural knowledge and support. Thus, while implementing family support education in the work with the group, there needs to be a stronger emphasis on cultural education in addition to education about the illness itself.

Caregivers want to have professional mental health services from practitioners who have information specific to their cultural backgrounds and understand the caregiving dynamics and the decisions that the caregivers make within the cultural context. The Korean immigrant caregivers reported feeling validated when their mental health service provider understood the caregiver's decision not to participate in the dementia family caregivers' support group to avoid hurting their family's reputation (Lee & Yim, 2013).

Closed Culture

Asian immigrants' culture tends to be relatively closed. Many Asian Americans reside in metropolitan areas, where they create and live in their own cultural enclaves. The Asian immigrants reside in a homogeneous and protected environment, where the level of acculturation does not vary greatly within the population. For example, Harwood, Ownby, Burnett, Barker, and Duara (2000) also found a similar phenomenon among Cuban immigrants. The immigrants tend to live in a homogeneous environment where they have generated their own cultural community and replicated their cultural origins and behaviors. They create and benefit from their own social support system. The immigrant families and their caregivers generally participate in local churches and senior centers. Maintaining a trusting and continuing connection with the community is central to the recruitment and retention of Asian family caregivers. Asian immigrants encountering language and cultural barriers have suffered negative experiences in the United States. The only way to decrease their anxiety and retain them in social work services is to establish a trusting connection between practitioners and Asian American family caregivers.

Additionally, to find and recruit "gatekeepers" in each immigrant community can increase the rate of successful inclusion of Asian immigrant caregivers. The gatekeepers can also be central sources of information for immigrant families. The gatekeeper who has authority in each immigrant community can open the door for the mental health practitioner and also provide resources to the caregiver. Moreover, when mental health practitioners receive access to the community, they should have an understanding of the definition of and perspective toward mental health services in Asian culture. In many Asian cultures, caregiving is viewed as a source of fulfillment and treated as a family concern (Scharlach et al., 2006). Therefore, receiving social services or participating in mental health services related to family caregiving can suggest the family members' failure to provide adequately for their loved one, a deviant behavior in the culture. The service provider should address the cultural context and support the caregivers' adaptive values (i.e., receiving professional services to improve family caregiving).

This phenomenon was also identified by one of the group participants. A spouse caregiver shared that utilization of home care is a new concept in her culture because dementia caregiving is typically handled within a family network. She said, "When my husband was discharged from a hospital, they sent us a home care aide for three weeks. They sent us a Korean one, because we are Koreans I guess . . . when the home care aide came to our house, she was just another guest . . . my husband treated the home care worker as a guest since she is a Korean. He argued that we cannot treat her as our maid since she is Korean" (Lee & Yim, 2012, p. 22).

Mental Health Stigma

Research shows Asian Americans tend to utilize mental health services less due to the stigma associated with mental health. Abe-Kim et al.'s (2007) analysis of data from the National Latino and Asian American Study (NLAAS) found that only 8.6% of Asian Americans seek any mental health services, whereas 17.9% of the general population seeks assistance from a mental health or health care professional. Moreover, Asian Americans are less likely to use mental health services when they are in need of these services. Only 34.1% of Asian Americans who received a *DSM-IV* diagnosis sought mental health services. The corresponding percentage for the general population was 41.1%.

Among Asian Americans, the shame of losing family face and the stigma related to mental health issues significantly influence the low level of utilization of mental health services. Chu and Sue (2011) explained, "Asian Americans tend to avoid the juvenile justice or legal systems, mental health agencies, health services, and welfare agencies" (p. 4). For them, the utilization of these services can represent a tacit acceptance that they have these problems, which carries a social stigma, and their use of the services can, therefore, result in stigmatization in public (Chu & Sue, 2011). The negative attitude toward mental health services is more prevalent among Asian older adults. Compared to younger Korean American adults, Korean American older adults aged 60 or older viewed a mental health issue as personal weakness, and having a family member with a mental health issue conveys shame to the whole family (Jang, Chiriboga, & Okazaki, 2009). Discussing mental health issues with outsiders may be tantamount to tarnishing the image of older individuals and their whole families in the community.

In addition to the stigma attached to mental health issues in Asian culture, dementia-related diseases are regarded to a certain extent as part of normal aging in Korean culture (Watari & Gatz, 2004), and many Asian families share similar perceptions of dementia (Hinton, Guo, & Hillygus, 2000). Therefore, Asian American families find no reason to seek assistance with their aging members' memory loss, which is thought to be part of normal aging. This is also a common phenomenon in other Asian cultures. Hinton et al. (2000) found that one of the barriers to the recruitment of Chinese American caregivers for research is that dementia is construed as a normal part of the aging process rather than as a disease.

Familism and Filial Piety

Research has demonstrated that immigrant caregivers prefer extended family networks to formal services in the caregiving process (Dilworth-Anderson, Williams, & Gibson, 2002) and familism can be one of the explanations for this preference. China, along with other East Asian countries, including Korea, have been strongly influenced by Confucianism, in which family cohesion and continuity are the most important components that sustain the community and the state (Sung, 2001; Yao, 2000). To immigrant families, familism buffers the effects of risk and enhances adaptation to culture (Bullock, Crawford, & Tennstedt, 2003). Additionally, to immigrant families, familism often means that families do not wish to discuss sensitive issues and seek help. Most likely, this attitude means that families are the first and, possibly, the only source from which help is sought (Hicks & Lam, 1999). Familism sometimes makes Asian immigrant family caregivers keep their loved ones at home, and they try to retain caregiving within their family network for multiple reasons until the patient and family require professional assistance (Watari & Gatz, 2004). Along with cultural barriers to health care systems, cultural expectation and social reward play a role in the choice of the immigrant caregivers not to replace informal care with outside services (Bullock et al., 2003).

In addition to familism, filial piety is one of the core ideas of Confucian ethics (Yeh & Bedford, 2003) that influences Asian family caregivers. In Asian culture, the idea of filial piety implies the teaching that children should respect their parents and take care of their old parents (Lee & Sung, 1998). This cultural phenomenon explains the acceptance of the role of the caregiver for one's parent. The high level of filial piety, along with extended family support in the collectivistic culture, influences the lower burden experienced by Korean American family caregivers compared with White family caregivers (Lee & Sung, 1998).

Heterogeneity Among Immigrant Caregivers

From our experience leading groups, we found that the needs of spouse caregivers and the needs of child caregivers differ. Spouse caregivers want more formal support, such as respite care and education regarding dementia and dementia caregiving, and they preferred to receive this information in Korean. In contrast, child caregivers need culturally responsive group work that focuses on anger management and coping skills. Child caregivers say that they benefit from participating in the group when they learn coping skills and disclose information about caregiving difficulties without worrying about the expectations from their traditional Asian family or immigrant community. One son said, "It is so great to hear someone say it is ok to be mad at my mother" (Lee & Yim, 2013, p. 22). He expressed that the acceptance and approval given by other Korean caregivers regarding his reactions to his mother's problem behaviors were validating.

Additionally, we observed the heterogeneity between the two caregiving groups in terms of their perception of family caregiving. Spouse caregivers perceived the caregiving as part of their life work. For spouses, taking care of their partner was similar to the caregiving role they expected when taking care of their own children. In contrast, adult child caregivers viewed the parent caregiving as additional work. To build culturally responsive and respectful rapport with family caregivers from diverse backgrounds, mental health practitioners need to research and understand the clients' beliefs, traditions, and expected roles in their cultural context.

Additionally, we have learned from our experience that many of the caregivers with limited English proficiency cannot adequately respond to government agencies on time due to the language barrier and lack of translators available to them. These limitations eventually lead to immigrant elders' loss of opportunity to benefit from public services. The shortage of diverse and trained professionals can limit the quality of services that Asian seniors and their family caregivers receive.

CONCLUSIONS

This group work approach illustrates that providing psychoeducational and supportive family services based on the sociocultural stress and coping model (Aranda & Knight, 1997) is beneficial for Korean American families. The importance of providing culturally responsive individualized services based on the needs and context of the caregivers (i.e., the severity of the disease and the relationship of the caregiver to the care recipient) cannot be overemphasized. Social services, their delivery systems, and associated developments can produce more effective results if they are supplemented by culturally and linguistically responsive services.

Finally, our experience demonstrates the significant role of cultural responsiveness for social work providers. Sometimes practitioners and policymakers assume that a single intervention or policy can meet the needs of the subgroups or populations belonging to a broad ethnic group. However, historical and political considerations are important for understanding the differences within ethnic groups of Asian immigrants. Moreover, maintaining an awareness of acculturation levels, migration stress, and immigrant status of clients from different cultures is important to consider because these areas can result in barriers to the receipt of services.

RESOURCES

Alzheimer's Association (information on dementia and family caregiving):
http://www.alz.org/

Asian Pacific Islander Dementia Care Network
https://www.caregiver.org/asian-pacific-islander-dementia-care-network

Family Caregiver Alliance: National Center on Caregiving
https://www.caregiver.org/

REFERENCES

Abe-Kim, J., Takeuchi, D. T., Hong, S., Zane, N., Sue, S., Spencer, M. S., . . . Alegría, M. (2007). Use of mental health-related services among immigrant and US-born Asian Americans: Results from the National Latino and Asian American Study. *American Journal of Public Health, 97*, 91–98.

American Psychiatric Association. (2000). *Diagnostic and statistical manual of mental disorders* (4th ed., text rev.). Washington, DC: Author.

Aranda, M., & Knight, B. (1997). The influence of ethnicity and culture on the caregiver stress and coping process: A socio-cultural review and analysis. *Gerontologist, 37*, 342–354.

Au, A., Li, S., Lee, K., Leung, P., Pan, P-C., Tompson, L., & Gallagher-Tompson, D. (2010). The coping with caregiving group program for Chinese caregivers of patients with Alzheimer's disease in Hong Kong. *Patient Education and Counseling, 78*, 256–260.

Belle, S. H., Burgio, L., Burns, R., Coon, D., Czaja, S. J., Gallagher-Thompson, D., . . . Zhang, S. (2006). Enhancing the quality of life of dementia caregivers from different ethnic or racial groups: A randomized, controlled trial. *Annals of Internal Medicine, 145*, 727–738.

Bernal, G., Bonilla, J., & Bellido, C. (1995). Ecological validity and cultural sensitivity for outcome research: Issues for cultural adaptation and development of psychosocial treatments with Hispanics. *Journal of Abnormal Child Psychology, 23*, 67–71.

Bullock, K., Crawford, S., & Tennstedt, S. (2003). Employment and caregiving: Exploration of African American caregivers. *Social Work, 48*, 150–162.

Cassie, K. M., & Sanders, S. (2008). Familial caregivers of older adults. *Journal of Gerontological Social Work, 50*(Supp. 1), 293–320.

Chan, S. M., & O'Conner, D. L. (2008). Finding a voice: The experience of Chinese family members of participating in family support groups. *Social Work with Groups*, *31*, 117–135.

Chu, J. P., & Sue, S. (2011). Asian American mental health: What we know and what we don't know. *Online Readings in Psychology and Culture*, *3*, 4.

Corey, G. (2008). *Theory and practice of group counseling* (7th ed.). Belmont, CA: Thompson Brooks/Cole.

Dilworth-Anderson, P., Williams, I., & Gibson, B. (2002). Issues of race, ethnicity, and culture in caregiving research: A 20-year review (1980–2000). *Gerontologist*, *42*, 237–272.

Feltham, C. (2008). Here comes everybody: Multicultural perspectives on the body in counseling, psychotherapy and mysticism. *Counselling Psychology Quarterly*, *21*(2), 133–142.

Harwood, D., Ownby, R., Burnett, K., Barker, W., & Duara, R. (2000). Predictors of appraisal and psychological well-being in Alzheimer's disease family caregiver, *Journal of Clinical Geropsychology*, *6*, 279–297.

Hicks, M., & Lam, M. (1999). Decision-making within the social course of dementia: Accounts by Chinese-American caregivers. *Culture, Medicine and Psychiatry*, *23*, 415–452.

Hinton, L., Guo, Z., & Hillygus, J. (2000). Working with culture: A qualitative analysis of barriers to the recruitment of Chinese-American family caregivers for dementia research. *Journal of Cross-Cultural Gerontology*, *15*, 119–137.

Jang, Y., Chiriboga, D. A., & Okazaki, S. (2009). Attitudes toward mental health services: Age-group differences in Korean American adults. *Aging and Mental Health*, *13*, 127–134.

Jones, P. S., Zhang, X. E., Jaceldo-Siegl, K., & Meleis, A. I. (2002). Caregiving between two cultures: An integrative experience. *Journal of Transcultural Nursing*, *13*, 202–209.

Kim, J. M., & Lopez, S. R. (2014). The expression of depression in Asian Americans and European Americans. *Journal of Abnormal Psychology*, *123*(4), 754–763. doi:10.1037.a0038114

Lahaie, C., Earle, A., & Heymann, J. (2013). An uneven burden: Social disparities in adult caregiving responsibilities, working conditions, and caregiver outcomes. *Research on Aging*, *35*(3), 243–274.

Lee, Y., & Smith, L. (2012). Qualitative research on Korean American dementia caregivers' perception of caregiving: Heterogeneity between spouse caregivers and child caregivers. *Journal Human Behavior in the Social Environment*, *22*, 115–129.

Lee, Y., & Sung, K. (1998). Cultural influences on caregiving burden: Cases of Koreans and Americans. *International Journal of Aging and Human Development*, *46*, 125–141.

Lee, Y., & Yim, N-Y. (2013). Korean American dementia caregivers' experience of a psychoeducational support group: Investigation of role of culture. *Social Work with Groups*, *36*, 13–26.

Luna, I., Ardon, E., Lim, Y., Cromwell, S., Phillips, L., & Russell, C. (1996). The relevance of familism in cross-cultural studies of family caregiving. *Western Journal of Nursing Research*, *18*, 267–274.

Mak, W. W. S. & Zane, N. W. S. (2004). The phenomenon of somatization among community Chinese Americans. *Social Psychiatry and Psychiatric Epidemiology, 39,* 967–974. doi:10.1007/s00127-004-0827-4

Martin-Carrasco, M., Martin, M., Valero, C., Millan, P., Garcia, I., Montalban, S., . . . Vilanova, M. (2009). Effectiveness of a psychoeducational intervention program in the reduction of caregiver burden in Alzheimer's disease patients' caregivers. *International Journal of Geriatric Psychiatry, 24,* 48–499.

McCabe, G. (2008). Mind, body, emotions and spirit: Reaching to the ancestors for healing. *Counselling Psychology Quarterly, 21*(2), 143–152.

Scharlach, A. E., Kellam, R., Ong, N., Baskin, A., Goldstein, C., & Fox, P. J. (2006). Cultural attitudes and caregiver service use: Lessons from focus groups with racially and ethnically diverse family caregivers. *Journal of Gerontological Social Work, 47,* 133–156.

Shulman, L. (2011). *The skills of helping individuals, families, groups, and communities* (7th ed.). Belmont, CA: Brooks/Cole.

Sorenson, S., Pinquart, M., & Duberstein, P. (2002). How effective are interventions with caregivers? An updated meta-analysis. *Gerontologist, 42,* 356–327.

Sue, S., Cheng, J. K. Y., Saad, C. S., & Chu, J. P. (2012). Asian American mental health: A call to action. *American Psychologist, 67,* 532–544.

Sung, K. (1997). Filial piety in modern times: Timely adaptation and practice patterns. *Australasian Journal on Ageing, 17*(1, Suppl.), 88–92.

Sung, K. (2001). Elder respect: Exploration of ideals and forms in East Asia. *Journal of Aging Studies, 15,* 13–26.

Tompkins, S., & Bell, P. (2010). Examination of a psychoeducational intervention and a respite grant in relieving psychosocial stressors associated with being an Alzheimer's caregiver. *Journal of Gerontological Social Work, 52,* 89–104.

US Census Bureau. (2014). *An aging nation: The older population in the United States,* Retrieved from http://www.census.gov/prod/2014pubs/p25-1140.pdf

Watari, K., & Gatz, M. (2004). Pathways to care for Alzheimer's disease among Korean Americans. *Cultural Diversity and Ethnic Minority Psychology, 10,* 23–38.

Yao, X. (2000). *An introduction to Confucianism.* Cambridge, UK: Cambridge University Press.

Yee, B., Su, J., Kim, S., & Yancura, L. (2009). Asian American and Pacific Islander families. *Asian American psychology: Current perspectives,* 295-316.

Yeh, K., & Bedford, O. (2003). A test of the dual filial piety model. *Asian Journal of Social Psychology, 6,* 215–228.

Chapter Twelve

Group Work With Immigrants and Refugees

Luz M. López, Erika M. Vargas, and Juliaty Hermanto

In 2012, the US Census Bureau estimated that the US population would gain a total of 41.2 million net new international migrants by the year 2050 (Cohn, 2012). Members of immigrant and refugee groups demonstrate considerable strengths in the face of the many obstacles that they face. A strengths-based approach to work with immigrants is essential in social work and especially in group work. This approach focuses on how members of these groups have been able to adapt and transition to the United States, identifies the supports available to immigrants, and how different groups ascribe meaning to the purpose of their migration (Garcia, 2008). In addition, many immigrant families come to the United States with high aspirations in regard to work and education and often develop cohesive networks of fellow immigrants from their countries of origin (Shields & Behrman, 2004).

Immigrants and refugees also face many challenges when arriving in a new country, ranging from understanding the immigration system, legal challenges, lack of access to resources, discrimination, and upheavals in family structures (Sue & Sue, 2012). It must be noted that migrants to the United States come from various political, cultural, and socioeconomic backgrounds and do not comprise a homogenous group. Even though Latinos/Hispanics and Asians comprise the fastest growing subset of the immigrant population (Cohn, 2012), many different ethnicities exist within these two categories. For instance, Mexican immigrants may face greater legal scrutiny than migrants from other countries in the Latino/Hispanic diaspora due to national concerns over undocumented migrants from Mexico (Sue & Sue, 2012). Many immigrants from Cambodia have arrived in the United States as refugees and often demonstrate symptoms of posttraumatic stress disorder (PTSD) (Valencia, Lee, & DeLeon, 2012). Additionally, immigrants from Haiti and Africa may encounter barriers due to fears and misconceptions of HIV/AIDS or due to prevalent racial prejudice in the United States.

The experience of being a member of an immigrant group in the United States and participating in a support group can mirror or reflect the experience of adapting to a new culture and a new environment. It may be helpful for group leaders to think of these as a parallel process. Just as leaving one's homeland in search of work or a "better life" can simultaneously be an exciting and frightening experience, joining a group can stimulate such mixed feelings. When most immigrants arrive in the United States, they adapt to a different culture and set of values. Similarly, a group member's ethnic identity and culture of origin impact the development of group dynamics, the level of cohesiveness, and the group members' interactions and relationship building with one another.

This chapter will focus on the experiences particular to immigrants and refugees. An understanding of the immigration process, including the process of acculturation, can contribute to a practitioner's cultural competence (Bacallao & Smokowski, 2005). This chapter will expand group workers' awareness of acculturation, biculturalism, and concepts related to ethnic and racial cultural values. It will also familiarize the readers with transnational family communications and further explore the differences between working with immigrants and those who are refugees. In addition, the chapter will provide case examples with Cambodians, Somali and Bhutanese youth groups, Latinos/Hispanics, and others. The chapter will also highlight limitations in finding evidence-based group work curricula for immigrant groups and proposes further identification and application of resiliency building in group modalities with this diverse population.

The first section will offer a review of the literature; the next section will provide an overview of the acculturation process and other immigration concerns, followed by guidelines for group leaders and case study illustrations. The chapter ends with a section on evaluation and resources available for immigrants and refugee groups.

REVIEW OF THE LITERATURE

Cultural traditions and values are defined and maintained through interactions between people in society. Chau, Yu, and Tran (2011) point to the fluidity of culture and argue that culture is often "created and recreated" through the interactions between individuals, dominant structures, and other institutions and is mitigated by factors such as gender, race, age, and class. Therefore, acculturation and biculturalism must be seen as dynamic and didactic processes.

Breton (1999) posits that a "structural approach"—one that considers the structures of opportunities available to immigrants and refugees in a new country—to working with immigrants is integral, as it does not assume that a lack of integration with the dominant culture is a problem rooted within individuals or their families. That is, culturally competent practice among group workers must consider the larger societal structure within which immigrants seek inclusion and understand the barriers that prevent acculturation. Breton also argues that social workers must seek to "establish credibility" in immigrant communities because there are many reasons for migrants to distrust formal institutions and they may choose to rely more heavily on informal networks of support.

Group workers must also be aware of the "normative shock" that many immigrants, especially women, may experience when interacting with agencies that operate within the dominant structure. Many immigrant women are used to matriarchal models, where they are the leaders, "doers and movers" in their family. Others may have followed more traditional gender norms in their home countries, which may have prevented them from being able to speak freely in formalized settings and, therefore, adjusting to a group where they are expected to "speak their minds" might be a challenge (Breton, 1999).

Every ethnic population has its own set of characteristics that influence a practitioner's approach to social work with that particular group. Working in groups with immigrants and refugees means understanding what it is like for members to be in two cultures; sometimes in two cultures with opposing values, (i.e., individualism vs. collectivism), but adapting to a new culture, language, and lifestyle in the United States. Cultural competency in social work practice is defined by Lu, Lum, and Chen (2001) as a "clinician's acceptance and respect for cultural differences, self analysis of one's own cultural identity and biases, awareness of the dynamics of differences in ethnic diverse groups and the need for additional knowledge research" (p. 3). The dynamics of culture are constantly changing based on the introduction of new technologies, methods of communication, and influences from outside forces; thus, creating a need for new knowledge and research.

Celia Falicov (2007) emphasized having an awareness of current trends in multiculturalism as pivotal for clinicians establishing a relationship with Latinos/ Hispanics and other immigrant groups. Falicov (2007, 2015) also suggests that the future trend of multiculturalism competency is something that is never mastered, but something that one strives for and constantly reevaluates.

DIFFERENCES IN WORKING WITH IMMIGRANTS VERSUS REFUGEES

Immigrants refer to those individuals or families who come into the United States and stay. Emigrants refer to people who leave their homeland. The term *migration* is often used to refer to one of these types of travel from one country to the next. Refugees are those who flee in search of refuge from war, political oppression, religious persecution, and/or violence. For refugees coming to the United States, the process of moving to another country is often not by choice. Sometimes they are forced to be in exile or have to flee their homeland due to fear for their lives and are unable to have contact with family members in their country of origin.

Refugees have a particular set of experiences (i.e., escaping from political turmoil, violence, or war and applying for political asylum) that are unique to their country and which may influence group dynamics. In addition to leaving their homeland under these difficult circumstances and having to adapt to a new culture and new language, refugees may also be dealing with significant trauma histories, which may not be the presenting problem or the focus of a particular support group. A group discussion may trigger past memories and reveal diverse reactions from the group participants, underscoring the hardships they may have encountered as refugees.

The facilitator of a group with immigrants and refugees should not be afraid to acknowledge previous experiences of oppression, trauma histories, and other topics that may be taboo. This is shown in the following excerpt from a mixed group of immigrant and refugee parents who are working on bridging cultural generational gaps with their teenage children:

> Facilitator: As immigrants or refugees from diverse countries, some group members may have experienced violence, political persecution, or trauma. In this group we're going to build a community environment with trust, so that we can talk about these challenges and eventually look at the strengths you have in coping and surviving these difficult situations. We may also find some commonalities between your experiences as parents and the different expectations you may have for your teenage children.

This scenario was part of a parenting group, not a trauma-focused group, yet it was important to examine how the members' immigration history may have affected their current relationships with their teenage children. Opening such a discussion by acknowledging their past history (without soliciting all the details of the experience) can lead to group cohesion and mutuality among group members. The group then becomes a vehicle for an appropriate intervention that assists immigrants and refugees during their transition to this new country, and as they initiate the acculturation process.

ACCULTURATION VERSUS ASSIMILATION

An understanding of the immigration process, including the process of acculturation, can contribute and make a difference in the development of group work (Bacallao & Smokowski, 2005).

Culture, according to Lu, Lum, and Chen (2001), represents the language, religious ideals, habits of thinking, patterns of social and interpersonal relationships, prescribed ways of behaving, and norms of conduct that are passed on from generation to generation. The process of acculturation involves adjusting to a new environment, which holds different cultural norms, behaviors, and values from one's own. Research indicates that how an individual resolves the point of conflict, or differences between two cultures is indicative of his or her emotional, mental, physical, and social well-being (Bacallao & Smokowski, 2005; Feliciano, 2001; Furman et al., 2009; Gil, Vega, & Dimas, 1994). There are two ways of resolving the conflict: (1) assimilation and (2) acculturation/biculturalism.

When the exchange between the two cultures results in an individual giving up his or her way of life and taking on the customs and beliefs of the dominant culture, this is assimilation. Assimilation has been identified as a risk factor for increased negative health behaviors and mental health problems (Bacallao & Smokowski, 2005). Immigrants who are highly assimilated struggle with identity. They drop their cultural identity and adopt the identity of the host culture in order to gain a sense of belonging within the dominant culture. High levels of assimilation are also associated with an increase in risky behavior (drinking, marijuana use, dropping out of high school). Therefore, assimilation is the least desired form of acculturation.

On the other hand, acculturation and biculturalism, being able to navigate both cultures comfortably without losing the culture of origin (Robbins, Chatterjee, & Canda, 2006), has been found to be a protective factor against the stress of immigration (Bacallao & Smokowski, 2005). Recent waves of immigrants are living in two cultures, maintaining ties to their homeland while also adapting to different values, beliefs, language, and behaviors of the US American culture.

Feliciano (2001) uses alternation theory, that is, fluid movement between two cultures while retaining the primary cultural identity, to explain this recent phenomenon. The author (Feliciano, 2001) further points out that there are many benefits to retaining one's primary cultural identity by becoming bicultural. For instance, bicultural Latinos/Hispanics suffer less stress, report stronger family pride, experience fewer occurrences of depression, and have stronger bilingual abilities (Feliciano, 2001). In addition, bicultural Latinos/Hispanics, in comparison to highly assimilated Latinos/Hispanics, reach higher levels of quality of life and better psychological adjustment (Lang, Muñoz, Bernal, & Sorenson, 1982). Therefore, by these measures, biculturalism is the optimal achievement of the acculturation process.

The immigration and acculturation process is accompanied by changes and stressors as one adapts to the mainstream culture of the United States. It is important for group facilitators to explore the different catalysts behind the reasons for immigration. Immigrants and refugees are not a homogeneous group. Each country has diverse cultures, ethnic backgrounds, and sociopolitical climates.

EVIDENCE-BASED PRACTICE

In recent years, the emphasis has shifted more to the implementation of evidence-based group interventions. Evidence-based practice (EBP) is concerned with promoting effective practice through integrating the best available research with clinical expertise in the context of client characteristics (i.e., values, religious beliefs, worldviews, goals, and treatment preferences) and sociocultural factors (American Psychological Association, 2006). However, there are some limitations of EBP that every group worker should be aware of when working with immigrants and refugees.

One consideration posed by Chen, Kakkad, and Balzano (2008) is how to develop and maintain multicultural practice, on the one hand, and incorporate EBP, on the other. Chen et al. (2008) also emphasize that multicultural competence is not static, but rather varies according to the specific composition of the group as well as the attributes of the group facilitator. Any discussion of developing evidenced-based interventions with multicultural competence should take into account the visible or invisible diversity in the group membership, as well as the cultural background of the group facilitator. Race and ethnicity matter and having multicultural competency will make a difference in group dynamics.

In the case of Latino/Hispanic immigrants, they may present for social work services and group work in relatively small numbers as compared with other ethnically diverse groups in the United States. Therefore, the issue of identifying best practices for Latinos/Hispanics has not been a pressing matter for researchers or practitioners, at least at the national level (Ortiz & Aranda, 2009). Often, when using scales or instruments, substantial psychometric work is needed before the study is undertaken (Bernal & Rodriguez, 2009) in order to ensure linguistic and cultural accuracy. Competence to lead research efforts with ethnic minority samples requires the usual set of scientific and scholarly skills as well as added multicultural competencies. The latter may also include translations and cultural adaptations and the development of bilingual instruments or measures to test the effectiveness of these interventions (Bernal, Rodriguez & Domenech, 2009). As the numbers of Latinos/Hispanics continue to increase, more research in this area will be needed that combines multicultural competence and evidence-based practice.

GROUP STRATEGIES WITH IMMIGRANTS AND REFUGEES

It is essential for the group facilitator to conduct a cultural assessment of each individual group member and of the group as a whole. The clinician should ask about each individual's country of origin, length of time in the United States, and reasons for immigration (was it voluntary or did the person arrive as a refugee?). The clinician will also want to inquire about the generation status of each group member (i.e., first- or second-generation immigrant), first language learned, and dominant language spoken at home.

For group leaders interviewing prospective clients for participation in group treatment, there are a number of appropriate questions that could be asked related to country of origin, conditions of migration, level of acculturation, and cultural identity. Therefore, the typical question, "What brings you here today" should go beyond the reasons for coming to that particular group and further explore the reasons for coming to the United States. The following go-around exercise could be useful when starting a group, "Before we start, let's go around, say your name, which country you are from, and how long you've been in the United States." These questions provide the context for future discussion on acculturation, conditions of migration, and cultural identity.

Another important aspect to explore within the group is long-distance relationships with family members who remained in the country of origin. With increased access to transnational communications, the cultural and socioeconomic level in the homeland affects the psychological adjustment of Latino/Hispanic and other immigrant groups (Falicov, 2015). For instance, the separation of various family members from one another is common in the immigration experience. One or both parents may emigrate first, leaving the children behind with a grandmother or other family members. In other situations, it is parents, siblings, aunts, and uncles who are left behind. The group leader should highlight the resources, strengths, and values in each group member to reshape behaviors, roles, relational patterns, and attitudes within their family and as the group members adjust to being in the United States.

The family ties and long-distance communication tools may be an important topic of discussion in groups with immigrants and refugees. Falicov (2015) identified relational stress as being at the center of a new immigrant's experience. Alternatively, the widespread use of technology (i.e., phone cards, email, cell phones, and video conferencing) enables families to maintain emotional and economic connections across continents. These connections make it possible for immigrants to continue to feel connected and share developmental milestones with the family (Falicov, 2015).

Participants' diverse experiences and family histories can be shared among group members while promoting an environment of respect and acceptance of multiple worldviews; this would affirm and promote culturally competent and responsive group cohesion.

Two group models that illustrate these strategies are from the Boston Children's Hospital Refugee Trauma and Resilience Center, which is dedicated to understanding and promoting the healthy adjustment of refugee children and adolescents who have resettled in the United States. In partnership with refugee communities and agencies in Massachusetts, they developed two culturally specific youth support groups.

The Somali Youth Group, developed by Saida Abdi and Amanda Nisewaner, is intended to offer a safe and structured environment to learn about the differences between US and Somali culture, and to provide a space in which participants can explore their differences and learn valuable social, self-regulation, and school readiness skills. Most important, it is a space where refugee youth can find a sense of belonging and competence, and practice skills to thrive in their new home in a safe and supportive environment. Integration of the participants' own values and their shared ownership in the group are essential to the group's success.

For example, one of the most common cultural differences is making eye contact. In Somali culture to look an elder or an authority figure in the eye is taboo, whereas in American culture, not making eye contact can be viewed as disrespectful. This is the same in the Latino and Asian cultures. Children are instructed not to look directly in the eyes of their elders or persons of authority.

In this Somali refugee youth group there are two facilitators, one from a similar cultural group and one from the American culture. The group leaders serve as cultural brokers, explaining the cultural differences or cultural expectations in the United States and always respecting and celebrating the traditions and beliefs of the youth's culture.

An adaptation of this group manual was created for Bhutanese youth. The Bhutanese adaptation was developed by Dr. Molly Benson and Radha Adhikari at Boston Children's Hospital Refugee Trauma and Resilience Center. This group work model focuses attention on cultural differences. For example, the manual includes cultural information for group leaders, including the awareness of the fact that large numbers of Bhutanese are Hindu, a religion that includes a hierarchical caste system. The caste system in the United States affects marriages, childbirth, funeral rites, and other religious activities. It is often more appropriate for cultural brokers to answer questions dealing with these caste systems, religious beliefs, or ethnic differences within communities. However, it is also important for cultural brokers to stress that differences are accepted and that mutual respect is productive.

For these and other immigrant and refugee youth who moved to the United States at a young age, the challenge may not be in adapting to a new environment, but in meeting family expectations, which may be different from the cultural norm in the United States.

For instance, in the United States, it is typical for an 18-year-old to leave home for college or work, and this is viewed as part of the process of individuation and independence for these young adults. However, for Latino/Hispanic parents and their children, leaving home can become a point of contention. The expectation in traditional Latino/Hispanic culture is to uphold *colectivismo* and *familismo* by maintaining close contact (i.e., attending family events and celebrating holidays together) and fulfilling responsibilities to assist other family members (Falicov, 2007). The young adult may feel torn between fulfilling his or her own desires (i.e., going on a ski trip with friends over the holidays) and upholding *colectivismo* (i.e., going home for the holidays to spend time with the family).

Another challenge later generation Latinos/Hispanics may encounter is that various family members have differing levels of linguistic ability in Spanish and English. Children or youth who stop speaking Spanish may have difficulty communicating with their grandparents. They may also be unable to read history books or sing *poesías* and songs in Spanish, which keeps their countries' written and oral history alive. The significance of detaching from cultural traditions and losing the ability to read in Spanish is that it may result in a loss of understanding and identification with one's ethnic roots and cultural history.

Additional challenges for immigrants and refugees may include having family members with different levels of acculturation and exposure to institutional racism, oppression, and economic disparities. Many immigrants and refugees experience the stress of poverty, a different pace of life, and social isolation (Gurman & Becker, 2008; Sorensen, López, & Andersen, 2001). Often, there are expectations on the individual in the United States to provide financial support for family members who remain in the homeland. Furthermore, such individuals have to learn to navigate through the immigration process to obtain a visa or permanent residency in the United States.

GROUP WORK WITH LATINO/HISPANICS

It is important to keep in mind the diversity of Latino/Hispanic immigrants, who come from 20 different Spanish-speaking countries (Bernal et al., 2009).

Latinos/Hispanics are also the fastest growing minority group. By the year 2050, it is estimated that there will be a population of 132.8 million Latino/Hispanics, spread out across the nation. Sixteen states have at least a half-million Hispanic residents, with clusters in large metropolitan areas like Metro-Dade County in Florida, New York City, Los Angeles County, and in areas along the Mexican border (US Census, 2009b). The rapid increase and spread of Latinos/Hispanics across the nation indicate a growing need for culturally sensitive and bilingual social workers in all 50 states who are proficient in culturally specific group interventions.

Latinos/Hispanics represent a multicultural and a multiracial group with diverse Spanish language usage and expressions, migration patterns, social and economic conditions, and educational backgrounds (Padilla & Pérez, 2003). Yet Latinos/Hispanics are also a single unit, in the sense that many have a common legacy evident in a shared language and cultural values. The sense of oneness is, of course, defined by context (Falicov, 2015). For example, belonging to a Latino/Hispanic social group can create the sense of oneness because everyone in the room values the central role of family in the same way; however, there may be differences in communication styles and belief systems within each family or among group members.

The Latino/Hispanic experience of immigration, adaptations, motives, challenges, and resiliency is important to understand with particular attention to how cultural changes among Latinos/Hispanics bring a unique perceptive to social work practice and group work. Each Latin American country, with its unique sociopolitical history, develops its own way of responding to situations that influences the way inhabitants behave within that social framework. For instance, every country has unique phrases used to express joy or concern that may be particular to a specific region and may not carry the same meaning in another Spanish-speaking country. Therefore, when transnational Latinos/Hispanics share their ideas in a group setting in the United States, the facilitators have an additional task of encouraging openness and understanding of these unique cultural identities. Thus, knowledge of the social context, meanings, and consequences of immigration patterns is essential if the group facilitator is to provide culturally competent services and support.

Dominican Republican immigrants and migrating US Americans who live in Puerto Rico have added to Puerto Rican culture. The sociopolitical climate also varies from one Latino/Hispanic country to another. For example, Costa Rica does not have an army, whereas in Mexico it is common to see the military individuals armed with automatic rifles standing among civilians on street corners.

Puerto Ricans have a distinctive pattern of circular migration. They also may have an assortment of reasons for leaving the Island and moving to the US mainland; however, they are in a unique situation because they are US citizens and passport holders. Their travel to and from Puerto Rico is done with relative ease in comparison to other immigrants groups who are restricted by immigration laws limiting international movement to the United States due to visa requirements, national quotas, and financial obstacles (Deren et al., 2003). For Puerto Ricans, "circular migration" is a common pattern of movement that paints a picture of the "revolving door" relationship that often exists for many between the Island and the mainland United States (Duany, 2002; López, Zerden, Fitzgerald, & Lundgren, 2008). When considering this group, it is necessary to distinguish between:

> The "one way migrants" who move permanently to the U.S. mainland; the "return migrants" who migrate to the U.S. mainland but after many years return to the Island and reestablish residence; and the "circular migrants" who migrate back and forth between the Island and the United States mainland spending substantial periods of residence in both places. (Acevedo, 2004, p. 69)

An increasing number of recent immigrants maintain intense connections with their home countries and extended families who live there. The complexity of relationships that arise from transnational connections calls into question dominant discourses about family bonds and requires that we adopt new theory and social work treatment considerations. Falicov (2015) proposes new approaches in family therapy by focusing on three crucial contexts for work with immigrants: the relational, the community, and the cultural-sociopolitical. A relational context looks at the family system and reframes relationships and roles of family members. A community context examines the relationship between immigrants, their homelands, and the new environment, and finds ways to rebuild their social capital. In a cultural-sociopolitical context, the focus is on approaches to social justice and overcoming the racism and discrimination experienced by immigrants. The group facilitator can highlight the intersection of the three contexts as members relay their stories.

In the group work service delivery arena, many strategies can be implemented to facilitate a Latino/Hispanic program's cultural sensitivity. Ensuring that recruiting materials and group curricula are translated into Spanish, having bilingual staff available, and addressing convenient group meeting times are some measures that increase a program's cultural sensitivity. It is essential to also include cultural adaptations. The term *cultural adaptation* (Whaley & Davis, 2007) refers to changes in the approach to providing services, in the nature or expression of the therapeutic relationship, or in components of the treatment itself to accommodate the cultural beliefs, attitudes, and behaviors of the target group member.

In a culturally diverse group, assessment of acculturation level, conceptualizations of health and mental health, and the experience of physical or emotional symptoms within different contexts (i.e., school, family, and work) should be considered for each individual member and for the group as a whole. Groups are most successful when both the facilitator and individual members agree on the treatment goals and form a strong therapeutic alliance (Chen et al., 2008); consequently, cultural differences, roles, and alliances will need to be examined.

Specific Techniques for Latinos/Hispanics

- Story circles/storytelling in groups creates a space for members to listen and share personal migration experiences, relationship building across cultural lines, collective problem solving, and social action.
- Group work enhances opportunities for learning about one's ethnic heritage through creative artistic expressions, special formats such as theatre groups, video making, artwork, and/or paintings. This is also effective when English is not the first language of the group members.
- Integrating culturally specific and/or culturally adapted curricula for structured, time-limited psychoeducational groups also strengthens and increases the effectiveness of group work with Latino/Hispanics.

THEMES AND CONCEPTS IN WORKING WITH LATINOS/HISPANICS

1. *Collectivism and Individualism*: often focusing on family traditions and rituals, it emphasizes "close nurturing and supportive interpersonal relationships"; it is valued in most Latino/Hispanic cultures over *individualism*, which is a more prominent value in mainstream US culture (Acevedo, 2008; Mason, Marks, Simoni, Ruiz, & Richardson 1995, p. 7). *Collectivism* points to Latinos/Hispanics' tendency to think of collective well-being (that is, that of the family) over one's individual needs.

2. *Familismo/Familism*: a deeply ingrained sense of being rooted in the family. The term refers to attitudes, behaviors, and family structures within an extended family system (Acevedo, 2008). The family is the primary unit within Latino/Hispanic culture. Sometimes it also involves a sense of responsibility or obligation to support the family emotionally and materially (Mason et al., 1995, p. 7).

3. *Personalismo*: a cultural concept that guides interpersonal relationships, highlighting Latino/Hispanics' desire for intimate, personal relationships and individualized attention (Galanti, 2003).

4. *Simpatía*: refers to the desire for Latinos/Hispanics to maintain harmony, politeness, and respect in relationships (Mason et al., 1995). Members of a group may focus on interpersonal relationships and emphasize the need for promoting behaviors that result in pleasant social interactions and harmony between members (Varela, Sanchez-Sosa, Biggs, & Luis, 2008).

5. *Respeto*: Respect for individuals, especially for figures of authority or elders. Participants may not raise questions or express different point of views to a social worker, group leader, or a person in authority to avoid being disrespectful (Gurman & Becker, 2008).

These concepts are part of a Latino/Hispanic's cultural identity, but they vary according to acculturation level, age, gender, national origin, sexual orientation, geographic region and rural-urban-focus, and other related factors (Delgado, 2001, 2007). Research on help-seeking behaviors has shown that Latinos/Hispanics most often turn to community members, and particularly indigenous leaders, before contacting formal helping networks (Delgado, 2007). Group recruitment strategies may incorporate community leaders in a participatory process. As trusted members of the community, the community leader accompanies the group facilitator in his or her outreach and recruitment efforts. They can help identify potential members and promote the group.

Case Scenarios

The following two scenarios illustrate the application of the aforementioned cultural concepts and multicultural competencies.

Scenario 1

This includes a Latino/Hispanic facilitator and a seemingly homogenous group. However, is any group truly homogenous? Each member brought his or her own past and present experiences into the group such as different age of entry into the United States, length of residence in the state or region, exposure to racism, and perception of acceptance into a new community. In this group there were also differing socioeconomic levels and retention of cultural traditions in the home. About five members retained cultural traditions, three kept very few traditions, and two did not celebrate any cultural traditions. The members' relationship with family members who stayed in the home country also followed diverse patterns of long-distance communication. How is the topic of diversity and openness to different points of view encouraged in this group? How do these differences impact group dynamics?

The first task for the group leader is to foster a safe environment by establishing guidelines for expressing different ideas and beliefs without making assumptions. For instance, he or she may start by stating that members may have different levels of comfort speaking Spanish or English. The group facilitator may initiate a discussion about the preferred language to be used in the group. Would only Spanish be spoken or both Spanish and English? There may be different levels of fluency among group members, which can affect group dynamics. What if the group agrees to speak in Spanish, yet there are a few second-generation Latinos/Hispanics who have a lower level of fluency? On the other hand, some people may be more comfortable expressing feelings in Spanish, and they may not be able to express themselves as easily in English. Group facilitators and/or group members should offer to translate in these situations.

Scenario 2

The group members are all Latinos/Hispanics, and the facilitator is Caucasian but speaks Spanish fluently. What kind of dynamics could occur in this type of group? There can be a certain level of acceptance of the facilitator as "one of us." She or he has learned the language and is open to the Latino/Hispanic culture. Although, at the same time, some members may feel the facilitator can't understand everyone's perspective because she or he did not grow up in a Latino/Hispanic family. The facilitator may be open but may also miss a cultural reference mentioned in the group. In this case it would be important for the group leader to encourage the members to be open about this. It is not the sole responsibility of the facilitator to bring attention to something that was missed in the group. All the members can participate and assist in this process. Relationship building is important in all groups, but especially in Latino/Hispanic groups because of their collective-oriented culture. Emphasis on developing trust and openness in the group would encourage the sharing of each member's individual ideas.

In addition, the use of self is a key element for the group facilitator. The facilitator may share personal experiences more openly, if they are related to the purpose and goals of respect toward the group's values and goals (Camacho, 2001). A Latino/Hispanic facilitator may share more openly about his or her own migratory experience, while a member of a different ethnic group may share his or her experiences as a non-Latino/Hispanic who is open to learning more about each group member's culture.

Recommendations for Group Practice With Immigrants and Refugees

To work effectively with immigrant and refugees, social workers must be able to acknowledge and value their diversity (Camacho, 2001). A goal of conducting culturally diverse groups is that the facilitator will embrace differences among members because groups will rarely be culturally or ethnically homogeneous. Furthermore, members can learn different ways of relating to each other and develop effective problem-solving strategies—the diversity of membership can be used as a group strength if the leader highlights this in an effective way.

Groups are microcosms of communities. Understanding why the members came to a particular group and what expectations they hold is part of assessing the appropriateness of the member for group participation and possible differences among group members. Some members join groups with individuals from the same cultural or ethnic background because they feel they will find support and understanding from individuals who have had similar experiences.

Members in diverse groups worry about their sense of belonging and their capacity to influence the group's purpose. According to Schiller (2007), groups are characterized by the members' need for inclusion during the beginning phase and by the development of a relational model, where there is intimacy, interdependence, and separation among members, during later stages. Members who identify strongly with a subgroup(s) may feel in the minority despite being a part of the group's majority. For example, "a member whose country of origin is Japan may feel that he or she does not have the same degree of influence in a group of mostly Mexican members" (Camacho, 2001, p. 137). Helping the group develop trust and acceptance of each member's cultural assets could make a significant difference in the success of the group.

Another example of a culturally responsive group intervention is the *Kaffa* ceremony for refugee women from East Africa. In a small-scale study conducted by Loewy, Williams, and Keleta (2002), it was found that a coffee ceremony held in home that would be a familiar environment to Ethiopian and Eritrean women led to greater group solidarity and fostered mutual trust among group members. In the *Kaffa* intervention, group members participated in a ritual of roasting coffee beans, making, and serving each other coffee while several topics surrounding their immigration were broached. Throughout multiple sessions, these women, all of whom were survivors of significant trauma in their home countries, began to share their stories of survival and resilience as well as their concerns about acculturation. Loewy, Williams, and Keleta make the point that modern psychotherapy is bounded within Euro-centric, individualistic, middle-class values that often do not allow for interventions to be tailored to the needs of non-Western cultures. For instance, it may feel safer for many East African women to meet in a home or a familiar setting where they have many of the tools to complete the ritual of roasting and making *Kaffa*. This goes against practices in many different agencies that require clients to come to an office for meetings. According to this model, culturally responsive group workers must bridge the gap between the structure provided through modern psychotherapy and the traditions embraced by the populations they serve.

Benefits of Group Work and Resiliency Building

- Group work provides a source of social networking and social support and decreases isolation for immigrants and refugees.
- Groups are mechanisms for addressing intergenerational gaps within immigrant and refugee families.
- Support groups highlight the member's inner strengths in the process of leaving his or her country of origin and adapting to a new culture and new environments.
- Group work offers a medium for interpersonal learning where experienced immigrants share their knowledge with those with less time residing in the United States.
- Participation in groups increases knowledge of and access to local health services, education, job training programs, housing, and employment opportunities.

Evaluation

A very limited number of evaluation tools have been developed and tested specifically for immigrants and refugees. Often, validated English tools are translated into other languages. However, these translations have to take into account the linguistic level of the group members. Such tools may also have to incorporate specific cultural terminology or less academic language; some words may also be added that are from a particular country or region. Example: In a psychoeducational group, when asked about level of knowledge of HIV transmission, a Spanish translation may use the words *propagar, transmitir,* or *pasar. Pasar* is a more common or familiar term than *propagar.* All these terms could be included in a questionnaire. For recent immigrants, the use of symbols or drawings may be another mechanism that could be helpful in an evaluation tool. For example, on a questionnaire assessing the level of satisfaction with the group process, draw-ings that represent being happy, satisfied, sad, or frustrated could be included to ensure that the respondent understands the concept. Members may need to be reassured that the tools are only going to be used for the group leader's benefit in understanding the success of the group and that their responses will not affect the service they receive from the agency in any way.

RESOURCES

Asian American & Pacific Islander Outreach Resource Manual National Alliance on Mental Illness (NAMI)
http://www2.nami.org/Content/ContentGroups/Multicultural_Support1/AAPIManual.pdf

Center for Disease Control (CDC) Fact Sheets on HIV/AIDS Across Racial/Ethnic Groups
http://www.cdc.gov/hiv/risk/racialethnic/index.html

¡Cuídate! is a six-session psychoeducation group aimed at increasing Latino/Hispanic youth's HIV/AIDS knowledge. Topics (i.e., condom negotiation, re-fusal of sex, and correct condom use skills) are introduced through the use of interactive games, group discussion, role plays, video, music, and mini-lectures.
https://effectiveinterventions.cdc.gov/en/HighImpactPrevention/Interventions/Cuidate.aspx

Cultural Pride is a teaching unit comprised of 11 lessons that can be easily adapted to develop a psychoeducation group. It emphasizes a strengths-based approach to developing self-esteem in youths, grades 5–8.
http://www.eric.ed.gov/ERICWebPortal/custom/portlets/recordDetails/detailm-ini.jsp?_nfpb=true&_&ERICExtSearch_SearchValue_0=ED303541&ERICExt Search_SearchType _0=no&accno=ED303541

Dichos is a therapy group that provided therapeutic use of the Spanish language. *Dichos* or sayings are used to engage participants in discussing a wide range of issues. It utilizes cultural and familial relevance, vivid imagery, and flexibility to build rapport and decrease defensiveness.
http://www.ncbi.nlm.nih.gov/sites/entrez?Db=pubmed&Cmd=Search&Term=%22Aviera %20A%22%5BAuthor%5D&itool=EntrezSystem2.PEntrez.Pubmed.Pubmed_ResultsPanel.Pubmed_DiscoveryPanel.Pubmed_RVAbstractPlus

En Busca de la Seguridad (Seeking Safety, by Lisa Najavitz, PhD) is a trauma/PTSD and substance abuse cognitive-behavioral group that has been translated to

Spanish. It covers 25 topics on how to seek safety in your life. The group can be used with female, male, and mixed-gender groups. http://www.seekingsafety.org/3-03-06/aboutSS.html

Facts About Stigma and Mental Illness in Diverse Communities (NAMI)
http://www2.nami.org/Template.cfm?Section=Multicultural_Support1&Template=/ContentManagement/ContentDisplay.cfm&ContentID=113595

The Kaffa Ceremony is an intervention designed for group counseling with East African female refugees. The ceremony is designed to "bridge the gap" between normative standards of Western counseling and East African culture to allow for the processing of trauma for many of the group members. http://www.unevoc.unesco.org/e-forum/EbscohostTVET.pdf

Latino Outreach Resource Manual (NAMI)
http://www2.nami.org/Content/ContentGroups/Multicultural_Support1/Latino_Manual.pdf

Parenting Fundamentals (formerly called the Parenting Education Program) is a group-based education and skills training program for parents who speak English or Spanish. These parents often come from lower socioeconomic backgrounds, have immigrant families, and/or are involved with the court or social service system. The program is designed to improve parenting strategies to help parents improve their children's social skills, behavior, emotional regulation, and cognitive abilities.
http://nrepp.samhsa.gov/ViewIntervention.aspx?id=286

Project AWARE is a study that aims to improve mental health among Chinese American, Vietnamese American, and Korean American women through group therapy sessions, which are sensitive to the particular cultural experiences and challenges facing these populations.
http://www.bu.edu/awship/be-aware-of-aware/what-is-aware-asian-womens-action-for-resilience-and-empowerment/

Refugee, Trauma and Resiliency Center, Boston Children's Hospital, Massachusetts
http://www.childrenshospital.org/centers-and-services/programs/o-_-z/refugee-trauma-and-resilience-center-program/research-and-innovation

TAFES (Tea and Families Education and Support) is an intervention designed to promote mental health among recently resettled Kosovar refugee families. The initiative consisted of a multifamily group intervention for six sessions over 8 weeks in conjunction with home-based services, which emulated Kosovar values of family solidarity and cohesiveness while also maintaining sensitivity toward unfamiliarity and distrust of mental health systems prevalent in the Kosovar community.
https://www.ncbi.nlm.nih.gov/pubmed/12586963

Voices/Voces is a single-session group curriculum that targets African American and Latino/Hispanic men and women. The purpose of the group is to increase condom usage. The video is available in English and Spanish. http://www.effectiveinterventions.org/go/interventions/voices-/-voces

REFERENCES

Acevedo, G. (2004). Neither here nor there: Puerto Rican circular migration. In D. Drachman & A. Paulino (Eds.), *Immigrants and social work: Thinking beyond the borders of the United States* (pp. 69–85). New York, NY: The Haworth Social Work Practice Press.

Acevedo, V. (2008). Cultural competence in a group intervention designed for Latino/Hispanic patients living with HIV/AIDS. *Health and Social Work*, *33*(2), 111–120.

American Psychological Association Presidential Task Force on Evidence-Based Practice. (2006). Evidence-based practice in psychology. *American Psychologist*, *61*, 271–285.

Bacallao, M. L., & Smokowski, P. R. (2005). "Entre dos mundos" (between two worlds): Bicultural skills training with Latino/Hispanic immigrant families. *Journal of Primary Prevention*, *26*(6), 485–509.

Bernal, G., & Rodriguez, M. (2009). Advances in Latino/Hispanic family research: Cultural adaptations of evidence-based interventions. *Family Process*, *48*(2), 169–178.

Bernal, G., Rodriguez, M., & Domenech, M. (2009). Advances in Latino/Hispanic family research: Cultural adaptations of evidence-based interventions. *Family Process*, *48*, 169–178.

Breton, M. (1999). The relevance of the structural approach to group work with immigrant and refugee women. *Social Work with Groups*, *22*(2/3), 11–27.

Camacho, S. (2001). Addressing conflict rooted in diversity: The role of the facilitator. *Social Work with Groups*, *24*(3/4) 135–152.

Chau, R. C. M., Yu, S. W. K., & Tran, C. T. L. (2011). The diversity based approach to culturally sensitive practices. *International Social Work*, *54*(1), 21–33.

Chen, E., Kakkad, D., & Balzano, J. (2008). Multicultural competence and evidence-based practice in group therapy. *Journal of Clinical Psychology*, *64*(11), 1261–1278.

Cohn, D. (2012). Census bureau lowers US growth forecast mainly due to reduced immigration and birth. *Pew Research Center*. Retrieved from http://www.pewsocialtrends.org/2012/12/14/census-bureau-lowers-u-s-growth-forecast-mainly-due-to-reduced-immigration-and-births/

Delgado, M. (2001). *Where are all the young men and women of color? Capacity enhancement practice and the criminal justice system.* New York, NY: Columbia University Press.

Delgado, M. (2007). *Social work with Latino/Hispanics: A cultural assets paradigm.* New York, NY: Oxford University Press.

Deren, S., Oliver-Vélez, D., Finlinson, A., Robles, R., Andia, J., Colón, H., . . . Shedlin, M. (2003). Integrating qualitative and quantitative methods: Comparing

HIV-related risk behaviors among Puerto Rican drug users in Puerto Rico and New York. *Substance Use and Misuse, 38*(1), 1–24.

Duany, J. (2002). *Puerto Rican nation on the move: Indentities on the Island and in the United States.* Chapel Hill: University of North Carolina Press.

Falicov, C. (2007). Working with transnational immigrants: Expanding meanings of family, community, and culture. *Family Process, 46,* 157–171.

Falicov, C. (2015). *Latino families in therapy: A guide to multicultural practice.* (2nd ed.). New York, NY: Guilford Press.

Feliciano, C. (2001). The benefits of biculturalism: Exposure to immigrant culture and dropping out of school among Asian and Latino/Hispanic youths. *Social Science Quarterly, 82*(4), 865–879.

Furman, R., Negi, N. J., Iwamoto, D. K., Rowan, D., Shukraft, A., & Graff, J. (2009). Social work practice with Latino/Hispanics: Key issues for social workers. *Journal of Social Work, 54*(2), 167–174.

Galanti, G. (2003). The Hispanic family and male-female relationships: An overview. *Journal of Transcultural Nursing, 14*(3), 180–185.

Garcia, B. (2008). Theory and social work practice with immigrant populations. In E.P. Congress & F. Chang-Muy (Eds.), *Social work with immigrants and refugees: Legal issues, clinical skills, and advocacy* (pp.79–102). New York, NY: Springer.

Gil, A. G., Vega, W. A., & Dimas, J. M. (1994). Acculturative stress and personal adjustment among Hispanic adolescent boys. *Journal of Community Psychology, 22*(1), 43–54.

Gurman, T., & Becker, D. (2008). Factors affecting Latina immigrants' perceptions of maternal health care: Findings from a qualitative study. *Health Care for Women International, 29,* 507–526.

Lang, J. G., Muñoz, R., Bernal, G., & Sorensen, J. (1982). Quality of life and psychological well-being in a bicultural Latino/Hispanic community. *Hispanic Journal of Behavioral Sciences, 4,* 433–450.

Loewy, M. I., Williams, D. T., & Keleta, A. (2002). Group counseling with traumatized East African Refugee Women in the United States: Using the Kaffa ceremony intervention. *Journal for Specialists in Group Work, 27*(2), 173–191.

López, L., Zerden, L. Fitzgerald, T., Lundgren, L. (2008). Capacity enhancement prevention model for Puerto Rican injection drug users in Massachusetts and Puerto Rico. *Evaluation and Program and Planning Journal, 31,* 64–73.

Lu, Y. E., Lum, D., & Chen, S. (2001). Cultural competency and achieving styles in clinical social work practice: A conceptual and empirical exploration. *Journal of Ethnic and Cultural Diversity in Social Work, 9*(3/4), 1–32.

Mason, H. R. C., Marks, G., Simoni, J. M., Ruiz, M. S., & Richardson, J. L. (1995). Culturally sanctioned secrets? Latino/Hispanic men's nondisclosure of HIV infection to family, friends, and lovers. *Health Psychology, 14*(1), 6–12.

Ortiz, L., & Aranda, M. (2009). Guest editorial for special issue on "Intervention outcome research with Latino/Hispanics: Social work's contributions." *Research on Social Work Practice, 19*(2), 149–151.

Padilla, A., & Perez, W. (2003). Acculturation, social identity and social cognition: A new perspective. *Hispanic Journal of Behavioral Sciences, 25*(1), 35–55.

Robbins, S. P., Chatterjee, P., & Canda, E. R. (2006). *Contemporary human behavior theory: A clinical perspective for social work.* Boston, MA: Pearson.

Schiller, L. Y. (2007). Not for women only: Applying the relational model of group development with vulnerable populations. *Social Work with Groups, 30*(2), 11–26.

Shields, M. K., & Behrman, R. E. (2004). Children of immigrant families: Analysis and recommendations. *Children of Immigrant Families, 14*(2), 4–15.

Sorensen W., Lopez, L., & Anderson, P. (2001). Latino/Hispanic AIDS immigrants in the Western Gulf States: A different population and the need for innovative prevention strategies. *Journal of Health and Social Policy, 13*(1), 1–19.

Sue, D. W., & Sue, D. (2012). Counseling immigrants and refugees. In *Counseling the culturally diverse: Theory and practice* (6th ed., Chapter 21, pp. 457–469) John Wiley & Sons, Inc., Hoboken: New Jersey

US Census Bureau. (2009a). *Census Bureau estimates nearly half of children under age 5 are minorities: Estimates find nation's population growing older, more diverse.* [Press Release]. Retrieved from https://www.census.gov/newsroom/releases/archives/population/cb09-75.html

US Census Bureau. (2009b). *Census Bureau releases state and county data depicting nation's population ahead of 2010 census: Orange, Fla., joins the growing list of "majority-minority" counties.* [Press Release]. Retrieved from https://www.census.gov/newsroom/releases/archives/population/cb09-76.html

Whaley, A. L., & Davis, K. E. (2007). Cultural competence and evidence-based practice in mental health services: A complementary perspective. *American Psychologist, 62*, 563–574.

Chapter Thirteen

Group Work With Combat Veterans: Vietnam Through the Persian Gulf Era

Julie A. Ellis and Joanne M. Boyle

"There are an estimated 23.4 million veterans in the United States, and 2.2 million service members including National Guard and Reservists" (Substance Abuse and Mental Health Services Administration, 2011, p. 40). Of these, approximately 2.7 million service members have been deployed in the Operation Enduring Freedom, Operation Iraqi Freedom, and Operation New Dawn (OEF/OIF/OND) conflicts since 2001. With the close of the Iraq War in 2010, and drawdown of troops in Afghanistan beginning in 2014, large numbers of service members have returned home to their families and their communities. Additionally, some of them have separated from or been discharged from the military. These service members are attempting to reintegrate into their families, communities, and work environments. "Many veterans return from deployment relatively unscathed by their experience, but others return from deployment with a multitude of complex health outcomes that present life-long challenges and hinder readjustment" (Institute of Medicine, 2014, p. 3). Many men and women have been exposed to prolonged periods of combat, leading to combat stress and multiple exposures to traumatic events (Rand Corporation, 2008).

"The hallmark injuries of the recent conflicts in Iraq (2003–2011) and Afghanistan (2001–present) are blast injuries and the psychiatric consequences of combat particularly posttraumatic stress disorder" (Institute of Medicine, 2012, p. 1). Mental health symptoms can manifest in a variety of ways and may emerge immediately or several years after deployment. Intervention through the use of groups can help reduce the impact of these potentially chronic symptoms in new veterans (Hoge et al., 2004). We first discuss some of the issues returning veterans experience and then describe a group designed to assist veterans with these issues.

WHO ARE VETERANS OF 20TH-CENTURY
WARS, AND WHAT DO THEY EXPERIENCE?

Veterans can be categorized into three main groups: Active Duty (AD), United States National Guard (USNG), and Individual Ready Reserves (IRR). During peacetime, the AD component secures our land and our seas by working in their respective roles in the military. During peacetime, those in the USNG and IRR serve on active duty status one weekend a month and 2 weeks a year, while the rest of their time is spent as civilians. The wars in Afghanistan and Iraq have relied heavily on USNG and IRR personnel to maintain appropriate combat power in the overseas operations. Many of these troops experienced multiple deployments—some participating in their fourth or fifth combat tours. The experience of the USNG/IRR veterans varies from the AD service member. The USNG/IRR individuals have to leave their home, civilian employment, and family to fulfill their commitment and duty to the country for a specified period of time. These individuals are brought together from different geographic locations. After their tour of active duty, they return to their life and often have difficulty reacculturating. They can feel isolated because they are not surrounded by the men and women with whom they spent the past several months and who understand what they have experienced.

The AD component has a somewhat different experience, whereby the military member returns from war still surrounded by his or her battle buddies. The people the AD service member served with during deployment are the same men and women with whom they work on a day-to-day basis. They all have had similar experiences and have a clearer understanding of the adversities that have been faced while at war. The AD component faces the difficulties of readjustment together when returning home. All combat veterans are returning to their home communities typically with a sense of "meaning and gratification in their helper roles in Iraq and Afghanistan" (Litz, 2009, p. 2) but often to an environment that is no longer familiar. Repeat deployments increase stress and strain on the service member and family exponentially (Rand Corporation, 2008). These individuals typically have changed views of themselves, others, and their world.

This changed worldview is not a surprise. These men and women have survived in a war zone from 6 to 18 months at a time with little or no break or relief. "There is no safe place and no safe role. Soldiers are required to maintain an unprecedented degree of vigilance and to respond cautiously to threats" (Litz, 2009, p. 1). While at war, these men and women develop "battle mind." Battle mind consists of combat skills and a battle mindset that sustains survival in the combat zone (Walter Reed Army Institute of Research, 2006). War/combat skills are necessary to remain safe and to accomplish the mission. These war skills must be transitioned into skills for home once the service member returns from battle to avoid their taking a toll on social and behavioral health (Walter Reed Army Institute of Research, 2006). Once the service member returns home, the battle mind mentality typically remains for a period of time while the war skills are transitioned into productive home skills. For example, battle mind keeps the service member alert, surveying the area for threats such as sniper fire or mortar attacks. He or she is trained to be unpredictable and to avoid open exposure unless necessary. This skill once returning home may make the service member feel anxious in large groups or situations where he or she may feel confined. The service member may find himself or herself continually scanning the surroundings (e.g., home, mall, etc.) for possible threats. The act of continual scanning and alertness is known as tactical awareness. Should this skill remain highly intact after returning from the battlefield, it may result in hypervigilance at home. Battle mind can be controlled over time by learning to identify and manage "personal trauma triggers," that is, learning how to relax, monitoring tendencies toward escalation, identifying patterns leading to isolation, and evaluating the reactions to minor events.

A trauma trigger is a symptomatic reaction from one of the senses (touch, taste, smell, sight, or sound) or a familiar feeling directly connected to an actual traumatic event that was experienced. Trauma triggers are the brain's way of protecting or alerting of possible danger, but the use of context processing to help differentiate danger versus safety is not used. Personal trauma triggers are "cues" to alert/ready the body to danger and are linked to fearful events. The fearful events are brought to consciousness via pathways. Research has focused on the changes in gene expression in the limbic brain regions (hippocampus and amygdala) for those who have been involved in stressful events:

> Neurobiological studies have shown that the noradrenergic stress-system is involved in enhanced encoding of emotional memories, sensitization, and fear conditioning, by way of its effects on the amygdala. Chronic stress also affects the hippocampus, a brain area involved in declarative memories, suggesting that hippocampal dysfunction may partly account for the deficits in declarative memory in posttraumatic stress disorder (PTSD) patients. Deficits in the medial prefrontal cortex, a structure that normally inhibits the amygdala, may further enhance the effects of the amygdala, thereby increasing the frequency and intensity of the traumatic memories. (Elzinga, 2002, p. 1)

Research has shown that there "are critical differences between the ways people experience traumatic memories versus other significant personal events" (Van der Kolk & Fisler, 1995, p. 518). Immediately after a fearful/traumatic event, fear conditioning takes place in our prefrontal cortex (part of the amygdala portion of our brain.) But after some time passes, the retrieval of that information shifts from the amygdala to the prefrontal cortex of the thalamus, and communicates with a different part of the amygdala which orchestrates fear learning and expression. This movement is believed to "integrate fear with other adaptive responses, such as stress, thereby strengthening the fear memory" (National Institute of Mental Health, 2015). The postulate that the brain has the ability to heal, change, and "rewire itself" after emotional and physical traumas was introduced by psychologist D. O. Hebb in his 1949 book, *The Organization of Behavior*. This process has become known as neuroplasticity, and it is being widely studied regarding its use in trauma-related care. The body of research suggests that new neuropathways can be formed with therapeutic work and practice. That being said, neuroplasticity and experience-based interventions can have significant implications for PTSD recovery and treatment.

In *Courage After Fire: Coping Strategies for Troops Returning From Iraq and Afghanistan and Their Families*, Armstrong, Best, and Domenici (2006) review the positive and negative effects of war and outline common reactions when transitioning from combat to home. These issues may include anxiety, hyperarousal, anger, and isolation. During deployment, adrenalin levels are much higher than normal to keep the service member battle ready. These increased adrenalin levels may partly speak to why many returning veterans partake in thrill-seeking and risk-taking behaviors. Clinicians and family members may notice that the veteran has an increased desire for immediate gratification, perhaps stemming from anxiety and hypervigilance. These symptoms have implications for treatment regimens, as the veteran may not stick with traditional treatment programs or the services that he or she sought. We must be aware of the clear unmet need for treatment among OEF/OIF/OND veterans. The Rand study notes only about half of those who met criteria for PTSD or depression had sought help from a provider in the past year, and of these, fewer than half received minimally adequate treatment consisting of "(defined as [1] taking a prescribed medication for as long as the doctor wanted and having at least four visits with a doctor or therapist in the past 12 months or [2] having had at least eight visits with a mental health professional in the past 12 months, with visits averaging at least 30 minutes" (Rand Corporation, 2008, p. 482). "It is important to note that poor engagement in mental health treatment is not unique to veterans" (Seal et al., 2012, p. 451). Social workers have the opportunity to support these men and women in their reintegration by allowing them time to process their experiences, exploring their battle mind skills, and assisting them in finding equilibrium in their "new normal." It is important to assist these service members in making sense of their experiences, providing validation and education, and normalizing some of the symptoms they are experiencing. Consideration must be made regarding the support system for these returning veterans and inclusion of them in their treatment. Their recovery and reintegration to "normal" must encompass not only their trauma issues but also their relationship and work issues.

"Problems with family relationships, relationships with other people or day-to-day life should not be overlooked" (National Center for Posttraumatic Stress Disorder, 2006, p. 4). With the family being the primary source of support for the returning soldier, there is risk of disengagement from the family at time of return from a war zone. Roles and responsibilities within the family have changed. Children have grown and developed new social skills. The spouse has taken on more responsibilities and control of the family while the veteran is/was deployed. The service member has changed as well. A challenge for everyone in the family is learning how to reconnect and establish a new "normal." When the veteran returns home, the spouse might be eager to return many responsibilities to the veteran, and the veteran may not be ready to accept them. Conversely, the veteran may desire to take over his or her previous roles/responsibilities, and the home spouse may want change the way tasks were done prior to the veteran's deployment. Children become used to the "home" parent disciplining and caring for them; when the returning veteran attempts to discipline them, it may be met with resistance. The returning veteran may feel very isolated when at home and may wish to spend time with battle buddies rather than with family and friends. Everyone in the family needs to acclimate to a new family pattern that works for all involved (National Center for Posttraumatic Stress Disorder, 2006). Problems with acute stress disorder and PTSD can cause difficulty with the competency and comfort the returning solder experiences as a parent and partner (Ruzek et al., 2004). Returning service members need to relearn how to feel safe and trusting, and family members need to feel they can connect with and are important to the service member. Screening for problematic behaviors when working with these men and women and their families is important (Hankin, Spiro, Miller, & Kazis, 1999). Consider extending treatment to spouses, children, parents, or whoever is included in their immediate support system. "Support for the veteran and family can increase the potential for the veteran's smooth immediate or eventual reintegration back into family life, and reduce the likelihood of future more damaging problems" (Ruzek et al., 2004, p. 8).

As the Iraq and Afghanistan conflicts are sustained in new ways, returning service members seeking care will benefit from a holistic and integrated system of services. OEF/OIF service members have sustained traditional battle injuries and have been exposed to new challenges and conditions due to intense blast exposures, urban warfare, and multiple and prolonged deployments. "Current battlefields produce a wide variety of injuries ranging from dermatological irritants to penetrating wounds, burns, complex fractures, and severe musculoskeletal strains" (Brown, 2008, p. 344.) In addition to these physical wounds, psychological and traumatic brain injuries are to be considered. The physical injuries of war such as amputations, burns, and fractures are easily seen and treated. The others are not. Some data suggest that the psychological toll of the deployments may be significantly higher than the toll of physical injuries (Rand Corporation, 2008). Although research suggests that most trauma survivors experience some PTSD symptoms soon after a traumatic event, these symptoms abate after a few months at home (Blanchard, Jones-Alexander, Buckley, & Forneris, 1996; Riggs, Rothbaum, & Foa, 1995).

Approximately one in five veterans of the wars in Iraq and Afghanistan has major depression or PTSD (Rand, 2008). "Many people will never have all the symptoms or the right combination of them to meet the criteria for a full diagnosis of PTSD but may suffer with many symptoms nonetheless. Increased exposure to combat-related trauma is associated with an increased risk for PTSD" (Institute of Medicine, 2014, p. 3). Although the rate of co-occurring substance use disorders among veterans of Iraq and Afghanistan is unknown, research suggests veterans with current PTSD or depression symptoms were approximately four times more likely to self-report alcohol misuse (Heltemes, Clouser, MacGregor, Norman, & Galarneau, 2014, p. 395).

There is increasing concern about the incidence of suicide attempts and suicide (Kang & Bullman, 2008). The Department of Veterans Affairs estimates 22 veterans commit suicide daily. Data from the Department of Defense and the Department of Veterans Affairs suggests rates over the past 10 years for the US military have increased. "Two recent studies demonstrate that veterans, both males and females, were more likely to die of suicide than their nonveteran counterparts" (Kang et al., 2015, p. 99). However, contrary to initial beliefs, "deployment to the war zone itself did not contribute to the excess suicides in veterans" (p. 96). In fact, research suggests the deployed veterans had a lower risk of suicide compared with nondeployed veterans (Kang et al., 2015; LeardMann et al., 2013). If those not deployed to the combat zone are more at risk, then who might be? Reger and colleagues report:

> Those who separated from military service were at increased risk of suicide compared with those who had not separated. Among those who had separated from service, both those who deployed and those who had not deployed showed similarly elevated risks for suicide. Risk for suicide was highest among those who separated after shorter periods of military service. Compared with those with 4 or more years of military service, individuals with less than 4 years of service had an increased rate of suicide. (Reger et al., 2015, p. 567)

The military branches have instituted suicide-prevention programs in the hope of educating service members about the warning signs and broadening the discussion regarding resources available to assist them or their battle buddy. Additionally, the VA has expanded their mental health services and outreach to all veterans. The VA has developed a program specifically for the returning combat veteran. Staff members provide screening, treatment, and education for veterans and their families. Outreach is provided through multiple contacts by the VA staff as the service member is leaving active duty. Additionally, VA staff offer workshops and classes in the community, partner with local organizations and groups, and participate in local events in the hope of reaching the returning veterans where they live and work and easing their transition.

Encouragingly, "a common upward trend in utilization of Mental Health services and downward trend in stigma over the course of the Iraq and Afghanistan wars" has occurred (Quantana et al., 2014. p. 1676). That being said, many service members still do not seek mental health services or remain in treatment because of stigmatic barriers and the impact that diagnosis may have on their career. Service members believe that mental health care or a diagnosis may affect their future security clearance, which is essential in remaining in the service. They may also worry that peers will question their reliability in future combat situations and that family members will see mental health issues as a weakness rather than an injury. The Department of Defense recognizes these issues and the resistance many service members have toward mental health services. Although stigma deters many soldiers from accessing mental health care, studies show that spouses are often more willing to seek care for themselves or their soldier-partner, making them important in early intervention strategies (Miliken, Auchterlonie, & Hoge, 2007). There is growing research evaluating the effects of deployment on familial relationships and the effects that social supports can have in mitigating negative consequences of war. The Department of Defense and the Department of Veterans Affairs (VA) have partnered to develop a program for returning veterans, where they and their fellow service members, as well as their family members, participate in reintegration and reunion workshops. These reintegration seminars provide a great deal of education to the service member and family, to raise awareness, provide information and resources, and to initiate discussions regarding historically difficult issues such as PTSD, financial difficulties, and others. The Department of Defense is committed to transforming its culture by emphasizing that seeking treatment is an act of courage and strength. The Marines, for example, have begun embedding a mental health professional in combat units before, during, and after service in Iraq and Afghanistan. The goal is to build trust and rapport of the clinician among the Marines, by providing continuity and familiarity.

OEF/OIF/OND veterans have some unique characteristics in comparison to veterans from prior wars: OEF/OIF/OND service members are generally younger, more likely to be female, less likely to be married or divorced, and more often are working (Fontana & Rosenheck, 2008). Fontana and Rosenheck also describe this new group of veterans as being more socially integrated than their veteran predecessors, and they also report higher levels of violence, alcohol abuse, and drug abuse. Identification of all these characteristics becomes important in identifying new treatment strategies for work with this group.

Returning veterans present with a myriad of issues that typically encompass relationship and familial issues; difficulties returning to and maintaining gainful employment; questions regarding their identity and self-view; and struggles with anger, rage, and the legal consequences that sometimes stem from these struggles. These and countless other issues provide opportunities in group work to focus on their strengths and challenges. Returning veterans do not want the symptoms or the diagnosis to define them. They may recognize that their rage, anger, or inability to connect with others is problematic but are often unable to commit to consistent treatment, a hallmark symptom of PTSD. It is not unusual for a clinician to hear, "I wish there was just a pill to make all of this better." The goals of treatment should be aimed at helping veterans gain meaning and an understanding of what has occurred, aiding them in learning new coping strategies. Additionally, treatment should help to foster strengths and a focus on the positive aspects of life, while also helping them to accept limitations and minimize destructive behaviors. To help connect veterans and their families to services, treatments may need to be available during nonconventional hours.

Deployments are difficult at best; veterans' families are faced with adjusting to the deployment of a loved one, as well as with the readjustment of that person returning home and attempting to again find his or her place in the relationship. Often readjustment groups are a meaningful and productive way to assist these returning veterans while also providing them an opportunity to come together in a space where others speak their common language, hear their common themes and issues, learn from others who have gone before them, and understand the code and honor of the military.

PRACTICE PRINCIPLES

The group discussed in the following pages takes place at the Baltimore Vet Center. The "Veteran Survivor's Group" is open to most OEF/OIF/OND veterans, as well as veterans from other conflicts, who are enrolled in the Vet Center Program, otherwise known as Readjustment Counseling Services. This organization falls under The Veteran's Health Administration (VHA). Group participants are most often referred after a thorough psychosocial intake assessment by a trained clinician (sometimes the second author, to be referred to as the leader). If the veteran did not receive his or her intake from the leader, then the intake notes are reviewed for each referral by the leader, after consultation with the assessing clinician, to ensure that the referral is appropriate. Veterans with active substance abuse disorders are encouraged to address their substance abuse before attending the group or to come after some considerable progress in treatment. Those with a serious mental illness, such as schizophrenia, may not be a good fit for the group. Considerations, though, are made on a case-by-case basis.

The Veteran Survivor's Group is a multiwar integrated group. It was established this way because of the potential for in-group mentoring and a way for the Vietnam Veterans to find new meaning in their 40-plus-year struggle for validation and acceptance, while simultaneously serving the newer combat veteran population. The Veteran Survivor's Group was initially started in the late 1990s for Vietnam veterans. It was an ongoing support group for Vietnam veterans to discuss their war histories, personal struggles with PTSD symptoms, get support, and find new and improved ways to cope with their symptoms. It has always been an open group so members may enter at any time. This works well because the sessions do not necessarily build on each other. The group provides both psychoeducation and mutual support. Although the weekly individual "check-in" frames the discussion, other topics may be raised.

There is no formalized contracting, as with closed groups, just a brief recap of the rules when a new member starts. Clear instructions and information are given to the veteran at the intake and prior to attendance at the first group. In this manner, the veteran has a sense of what the group may be able to offer and what topics will be discussed. Common anxieties about being in a support group are discussed prior to the veteran starting group. Potential referrals are typically given flyers on the group, or the intake clinician may see if the leader is available for a brief screening with the veteran to prepare the veteran for the group. The leader's contact information is also on the flyer and potential members are free to call with any questions or concerns. Educating staff is a critical element in the process, so they are able to refer and educate potential members appropriately. The leader of the group is not a veteran. This is disclosed at the outset of the group, while also highlighting 11 years of experience working with the combat veterans and the OEF/OIF/OND population. The purpose of this is to communicate some degree of familiarity with the population, while pointing out that only the members can really "know" what it is like to be deployed to a war zone. Just as with any population at risk, a good group leader does not need to be part of the population receiving services as long as the leader acknowledges this and comes from a place of wanting to help and to understand. Those leaders without substantial experience working with the population must become familiar with military culture and the specifics of current military engagements. This can be done by observing other veteran groups facilitated by other clinicians, clinical supervision and consultation, talking with nonclient veterans, and using good sources on the Internet or in professional journals. The point is to demonstrate a working knowledge that reflects a stance of caring about the issues faced by the population, while not mistaking researched knowledge with experience. Even within the group, experiences vary. Some members may have been exposed to heavy combat during an invasion campaign, while others may have served their time in base camps, onboard a ship off of the Vietnam Coast, or on a ship near Kuwait. Still others may have been treating injured service members on the battlefield or in a nearby medical facility. The variety of experiences and differences adds value to the group.

Although many assume that the group would be composed mainly of men in their 60s (Vietnam) or 20s (OIF/OEF/OND), the group members on a given day are an accurate snapshot of the population based on several demographics. Usually there are one or two officers, whereas the rest served as enlisted personnel. Group members range in age from the early 30s to the late 70s, and the veterans may have been on one deployment or several. Some members appear to be affluent, whereas others are barely working class and would be considered impoverished, by today's standard of living. Women clients in the Vet Center typically prefer their women's group. The women in that group are survivors of military sexual trauma or have experienced significant combat. The common bond among all group members is that each individual is currently experiencing, or has significantly experienced, some sort of difficulty readjusting to civilian life. For the Vietnam veterans, this group is often their only source of social interaction and support.

The leader and other clinicians at the Vet Center noted that it was increasingly difficult to keep members of the OIF/OEF/OND population engaged in mental or behavioral health treatment for extended periods of time. Yet the demand for services within the population is increasing, perhaps due to greater societal awareness of common readjustment issues and reduced stigma about seeking mental health services.

The group meets for 1.5 hours once a week from 4:30 to 6:00 PM each Thursday. This time was chosen after carefully considering data collected through client surveys, needs assessments, and anecdotal evidence that suggested evening appointment times were most likely to be kept due to work and childcare obligations. The group leader begins with group rules and confidentiality requirements. The leader explains that he or she must breach confidentiality for certain client reports, such as threatening harm to self or others. Members are encouraged to be respectful of other group members' feelings and views. When a new group member attends, the group members take turns introducing themselves and sharing a little information about where they served during their deployment as well as what brought them to the group. It may be easier to ask one of the "senior" members of the group, who has previously presented and appeared to benefit from the group, so that he or she can perhaps serve as a model to newer members. In this sense, the group rules are enforced only to ensure safety, comfort, and some degree of order. The members are all familiar with the expectations of proper deportment from their military days, so making excessive rules for group behavior may serve to limit a member's willingness to enter more taboo areas, where he or she may need the most support or constructive feedback from a peer. By setting a respectful tone as the group leader and generally being warm and open, the members will tend to follow this lead. A mutual respect exists among the members that crosses racial, gender, age, and service branch differences to allow for less formalized rule setting. The members often report that civilians cannot "understand" what it is like to have served in a combat zone. The leader can use this point to direct questions back to the group and reinforce the group's importance, because the experts on their situation are in the room. At the beginning of the group, if no new members are present, members are asked to check in and share anything that they struggled with the previous week as well as any gains or improvements in behavior that they exercised to make progress in their recovery from PTSD. This leader has noted that members will typically mingle for several minutes after the group in the group room or office building lobby. This time of engaging is neither discouraged nor encouraged and has occurred naturally from the inception of the group. Typically, lighter subjects are discussed, or a more experienced group member will assist a newer client in navigating the VA system or by offering support in another way. Some members request time individually with the leader to discuss a certain aspect of their care. If the leader has the time, the issue can be addressed then, or another appointment time is scheduled. Some members attend every week, whereas others may come once or twice a month. Additional services, such as an appointment with a medication provider or referral to another treatment program, are offered on an as-needed basis.

COMMON THEMES

Feeling Alone

For the OIF/OEF/OND veterans, the most common theme reported at intake, and initially in the group, is a sense of feeling alone or that nobody understands them. The group offers a place for the veteran to gain a sense of being understood and of belonging. The Vietnam veterans offer insight to the OIF/OEF/OND veterans based on their own history of readjustment problems. The leader attempts to foster openness in the group and encourages personal stories of struggle, barriers to seeking help, and interventions that worked. Often members will report that the group is the only place they feel they can open up about their issues and frustrations. Once an issue is disclosed in group discussion, many members can relate on some level, through either their own experiences or the experiences of a fellow veteran. By stating this common theme of "aloneness" upfront, the leader is attempting to quickly connect with the group and reassure members that others have similar feelings, thoughts, or experiences.

Renegotiating Roles in Families and Relationships

Deployment and time apart present many challenges for OIF/OEF/OND soldiers and their family systems left behind. Some veterans may have been able to keep in constant contact with their families, especially when the Internet is available. Other veterans may not have been as fortunate, with some unable to make firm commitments as to when they could talk, based on the availability of communication devices and time. Each veteran presents a unique situation. Family members may have taken on new roles or duties, and the veteran may have missed important family milestones due to deployment. Often a veteran reports some degree of tension renegotiating a place in the family system, which has functioned without him or her for some time. The veteran may feel that he or she is not as needed as believed, or, conversely, that his or her absence may have been a major contributor to family disruption during deployment. The veteran may feel guilty and be the focus of some resentment because of problems that occurred during deployment. Family tension is not unusual and, when discussed in group, can make this issue more universal and less of an issue about the veteran. Often the older veterans can offer valuable feedback based on their own experiences. The leader can point out that it is not unusual to experience difficulty during any adjustment and transition period, such as entering a new grade in school, moving to a new area, or finding a civilian job. This can shift thinking from an emotionally loaded area (family disruption) to a more pragmatic area, where the veteran has succeeded in the past with similar skills. Members are often asked to think of times they have gone through changes before and reflect on strengths they have used during previous adjustment periods in their life. Members have reported complicating factors such as new illnesses, loss of financial stability (many Reserve and Guard members take significant pay cuts or do not have time to devote to finances while deployed), a death or loss in the family, behavioral problems with children, and partners who have left the relationship or engaged in extramarital affairs during a deployment. The group facilitator can assist the members with identifying their resiliency and adjustment skills, allowing new perceptions of problem solving. This helps to identify rigid and inflexible patterns of thinking. The older Vietnam veterans also assist the younger veterans by sharing problems and barriers they experienced trying to reintegrate with their families years ago. They are able to share years' worth of insight and experience. Again, the leader should be allowing space for members to safely discuss their frustrations or issues with their family, to gain support and a sense that they are not unique in having a difficult time readjusting to a support system or lamenting the loss of one. Once the issues are discussed, the leader can attempt to guide members into exploring their feelings and thoughts they may have difficulty expressing in a meaningful way to their support system. Personal vignettes are used to illustrate common readjustment issues the older veterans experienced upon their return home from deployment. These are often helpful with the younger veterans, in broaching the topic in a constructive way, as they can normalize a family issue and lower defenses.

"Crazy" Veterans

Some members will state that their families, friends, peers, and colleagues are convinced, or will assume, that their time away at war has made them "crazy." The Vietnam veterans can often relay stories of their return home that illustrate this stigma. Depending on knowledge about their service time, those whom the veterans leave behind may develop preconceived notions of how the returning veteran may behave post deployment. They may even attempt to fit the veteran into their expectations. Often members report a polarized reaction upon return, where the member is either praised as a hero or condemned as a "crazy" veteran.

Both reactions can elicit strong emotions. Getting members to discuss ways they have been received is helpful, as well as ways they have found helpful for dealing with this adjustment. Sometimes this may take the form of shared experiences from the Vietnam veteran group members, as previously stated. The group facilitator may also offer the members educational materials to take home or reliable literature on Web sites, so the family can receive more realistic and less sensationalized news about the readjustment process.

Often members discuss how some civilians ask questions, such as "Did you kill anyone?" or "Did you see anyone get blown up by an IED?" These types of questions can, and often do, provoke an angry response. When this topic is brought up, most members will have stories to share. The veteran cannot control the well-meaning civilian who asks a stupid question but can exercise control in his or her response. Recognizing that the civilian does not understand can often deescalate a situation, as does having stock answers to insensitive questions that the veteran can offer without much thought. The goal is to avoid acting out of anger (after being triggered) and reliving a painful situation. Sometimes humor can be interjected into this often stressful component of the readjustment process. One veteran reported that a "preppy kid" attending the same introductory-level college class asked the veteran: "What's it like over there?" Not wanting to go into details with a person he just met, the veteran responded with humor, telling the civilian that if he really wanted to know what it was like, "Go home. Stick your head in the oven at 200 degrees and have someone nearby continually throw sand all over your body." Here, the veteran used humor to deescalate and move forward, rather than discussing his difficult times in combat or becoming angry and combative. As a side note, the veteran and "preppy kid" got along well during the class from that point on and found they had some common interests. Consider how different this member's college experience would have been if he had acted on his initial impulse to verbally or physically lash out.

Arousal and Alertness

The veteran may be transitioning from a war zone where trash/debris along the side of the road (a typical way to hide improvised explosive devices, or IEDs) is a threat. Enemies in the combat zone are typically unknown to the veteran, so, for protection, the veteran may have developed a constant state of alertness. Although this type of alertness is part of the normal human response to promote survival, always being on guard and treating others as potential threats can pose problems in a civilian context. Group members often report having difficulty tolerating large crowds, traffic, or unfamiliar areas. Sometimes members report acting on their feelings and engaging in defensive measures when they felt threatened. Several OIF/OEF/OND group members have shared experiences driving in which they became overly anxious after spotting trash or an animal carcass along the side of the road. The leader continually reassures members that remaining vigilant and on guard was helpful during the deployment and must be hard to let down. Here, the goal of the leader is to shift focus away from the members' feelings of guilt or dysfunction, to a more normalized approach, suggesting that their reactions are part of human nature. Working from this perspective, the members may be allowed to share experiences where they have acted on their feelings of being threatened and develop ways to check in the next time they have those feelings. Some veterans have experienced a decrease in arousal after exposing themselves to the triggering stimulus, like driving past a dead animal carcass multiple times. Mindfulness and relaxation, as well as breathing exercises, are introduced in the group to give veterans tools to ground their thinking, reduce anxiety and tension, and prevent escalation into a panic attack. Introducing the exercises in the group serves two distinct functions. For starters, the members are taught ways to self-soothe in a safe environment, and they can use and practice the exercises they have found to be helpful. Second, by modeling these exercises where the veteran is asked to pay attention to sensory awareness, the leader can use him and the power of the group to help veterans engage in these activities and build skills, where they may otherwise have been resistant. When angered or threatened, veterans can engage in grounding exercises to offer them some time to decide about the appropriateness of the array of choices available in a given context. Being supportive and understanding the member's situation destigmatizes a common response style adopted during the uncommon conditions of a war zone.

Isolation

Often veterans of both war eras struggle with irritability and discomfort in sharing their feelings. As a result, veterans establish a pattern of isolative behavior. Vietnam veterans often refer to this pattern as "going to their bunker." The pattern is very similar for the OIF/OEF/OND veterans as well. One of the OIF/OEF/OND veterans talks openly about "hating stupid people." He feels uncomfortable around his civilian coworkers because he does not feel as though they "get it." The veteran explained that, as a result of war, he has a "life or death" mentality. The veteran shared that he feels as though most conversations are petty and meaningless. Because of this, he chooses to isolate himself at work instead of socializing with his coworkers over lunch or break times.

In addition, tension often exists between veterans wanting to reengage in previously enjoyable activities and concern that they may "get triggered" by an environmental stimulus, display anxiety, or act out inappropriately. This worry can also lead to isolation. Normalizing these reactions by talking about them serves an important function for the group.

Isolation may also be a sign of intense sadness or guilt and, in this case, the veteran may need to feel very comfortable to discuss particulars. Many veterans who have lost a battle buddy to suicide or an attack suffer from survivor's guilt and have difficulty connecting with new people. Veterans also report having difficulty giving up the controlled environment of their apartment, house, "man cave," and so on for an unpredictable environment outside. Isolation may also be employed to avoid embarrassment. Many members have recalled how they have "hit the deck" after hearing a car backfire, for instance. One member, who was also a Gulf War veteran, indicated that after the "hundredth time," he started to laugh at this survival behavior and his friends and wife would even tease him a bit. Previously, out of regard for the member's sensitivity to this matter, his friends and wife pretended they had not seen him, or ignored it, although the member knew they saw him and surely thought he was "nuts." The new and humorous response, the member admitted, had taken him many years to develop, and choosing to view his response with some humor has made ducking less embarrassing. Here the member took the approach that he would probably respond to loud and sudden noises for the rest of his life in some way, due to being injured by an explosion. After many years fighting against it, he had accepted his response and chose to laugh at himself and be open to it, rather than becoming angry, embarrassed, or sad. He offered hope to other members and espoused greater flexibility and less self-criticism. He also encouraged the other member not to be embarrassed and to go after his love interest, with a new sense that his response was not unusual given his experiences.

Anger and Irritability

Irritability and episodes of anger are common symptoms with veterans who are having readjustment difficulty or have been diagnosed with PTSD. The group members often share times when they have experienced irritability or an angry episode. The group members provide support, often mixed with some humor, and ask thought-provoking questions about how things could be handled more effectively in the future. The group facilitator often asks probing questions about their experiences to help the veterans uncover what triggered the escalated emotional response. The group members build on those questions to promote self-awareness and explore a variety of more appropriate responses, if faced with similar conflict in the future. One group member shared an experience he had while rushing to get ready to go to an event. The veteran shared that he was frantically looking for his wallet and could not find it anywhere. He stated that he became extremely agitated and began yelling at his wife and accusing her of moving his things. He was already running late to leave and decided to leave the house without his wallet. He explained to the group that when he came home that evening, he found his wallet on the kitchen chair, where he had been sitting earlier that day. The group laughed with the veteran after telling his story. They also discussed the additional conflict that was caused with his wife due to jumping to a conclusion and his irritability. The group members played out several different ways that situation could have been handled using grounding and coping skills.

EVALUATION

Evaluation in the group has focused on decreasing symptoms and improving social functioning. During the initial intake, the veteran receives a thorough psychosocial assessment, which includes screenings for depression, PTSD, substance abuse, and a suicide risk assessment. This particular group is designed to target returning veterans and the smaller population of older veterans entering treatment for the first time. The group is designed as a mentoring group for veterans who are having adjustment issues and is a part of adjunctive treatment. Evaluation tools have included a needs assessment where veterans identify what has been helpful about the group as well as what might be added or changed to improve the group once a veteran has completed treatment at the Vet Center. From the needs assessments, overall, veterans who have attended this group found it to be beneficial. This group has had consistent attendance and continues to grow. The group is viewed as a success as veterans continue to return and refer their other veteran friends. This group usually receives two new referrals per week.

Research evaluating the effectiveness of group and individual treatment for the OEF/OIF/OND population is scarce at this time. It is unclear whether the OEF/OIF/OND population is similar enough to combat veterans from other wars to adapt or use existing treatments with good efficacy. Current research projects are under way evaluating the use of trauma-focused cognitive-behavioral therapies with exposure therapy, cognitive processing therapy, and early interventions and screening, as well as the impact of psychopharmacology, physical injuries, women veterans, and dual diagnosis. Efforts are under way to find the most effective treatment options and care.

CONCLUSION

"Veterans surviving combat deployments possess a tremendous number of strengths and the intensity of caring for them are [sic] balanced by the value of working with someone to transform his or her life following the trauma of combat" (Batten & Pollack, 2008, p. 938). Returning veterans may present themselves for care through a number of avenues. It is important that clinicians be prepared to meet them in a way that is engaging, focused, and respectful. These men and women have taken a risk by entering treatment given the perceived and sometimes real cost to their promotion potential in the military and loss of esteem from some of their battle buddies who stigmatize mental health services.

Each of these men and women has strengths that need to be emphasized. Their treatment needs to be succinct and meaningful to them as individuals and allow them to serve others as this is part of their military training. Clinicians must be aware of the myriad issues that this population brings and be prepared to provide referrals and services as needed. Additionally, clinicians should be mindful that these men and women have access to multiple health care systems, which creates a unique situation in which veterans can, and often do, seek care from providers who may not communicate to coordinate their care (Shen, Hendricks, Zhang, & Kazis, 2003). Although access to care and options are important, these veterans may be receiving care through multiple systems where the providers do not communicate or know that the veteran receives care elsewhere. Such issues may need to be addressed during the course of clinical work. It is essential that the clinician's skill set is expanded and updated to manage the complex needs of the returning veteran population. Additional research is needed to identify the most appropriate and effective treatment strategies for the various groups within the OEF/OIF/OND population. Group work, with all it has to offer this population, should be included in these strategies.

DEDICATION

We dedicate this chapter to our colleague, Lt. Col. Juanita Warman, who was killed at Fort Hood in November 2009.

RESOURCES

American Psychiatric Association
http://www.psych.org
100 Wilson Boulevard, Suite 1825
Arlington, VA 22209

American Psychological Association
http://www.apa.org
750 First Street NE
Washington, DC 20002

Anxiety Disorders Association of America
http://www.adaa.org
8730 Georgia Avenue, Suite 200
Silver Spring, MD 20910

Association for Behavioral and Cognitive Therapies
http://www.aabt.org
305 Seventh Ave, 16th Floor
New York, NY
212-647-1890

The Center for Study of Traumatic Stress
University Health Services
http://www.usuhs.mil
4301 Jones Bridge Road
Bethesda, MD 20814

VA National Suicide Hotline: (800) 273-TALK (8255)
Department of Veterans Affairs
http://www.va.gov

Institute of Medicine: Veterans
http://www.veterans.iom.edu
500 Fifth Street NW
Washington, DC 20001
202-334-2352

International Society for Traumatic Stress Studies
http://www.istss.org
111 Deer Lake Road, Suite 100
Deerfield, IL 60015
847-480-9028

National Center for PTSD
http://www.ncptsd.va.gov

PTSD Info Line: 802-296-6300
National Institute of Mental Health
http://www.nimhinfo@nih.gov
6001 Executive Boulevard
Bethesda, MD 20892
866-615-6464 (toll-free)

National Mental Health Organization
http://www.nmha.org

National VA Caregiver Support Program
http://www.caregiver.gov
1-855-260-3274

SAMHSA's National Mental Health Information Center
http://www.mentalhealth.samhsa.gov
P.O. Box 2345
Rockville, MD 20847

REFERENCES

Armstrong, K., Best, S., & Domenici, P. (2006). *Courage after fire: Coping strategies for troops returning from Iraq, Afghanistan and their families.* Berkeley, CA: Ulysses Press.

Batten, S. V. & Pollack, S. J. (2008). Integrative outpatient treatment for returning service members. *Journal of Clinical Psychology, 64,* 928–939.

Blanchard, E. B., Jones-Alexander, J., Buckley, T. C., & Forneris, C. A. (1996). Psychometric properties of PTSD Checklist (PCL). *Behavior Research Therapy, 34,* 669–673.

Brown, N. D. (2008). Transition from the Afghanistan and Iraqi battlefields to home: An overview of selected war wounds and the federal agencies assisting soldiers regain their health. *Journal of American Association of Occupational Health Nurses, 56,* 343–346.

Elzinga, B. M. (2002). Are neural substrates of memory the final common pathway in posttraumatic stress disorder (PTSD)? *Journal of Affective Disorders, 70*(1), 1–17.

Fontana, A. M., & Rosenheck, R. (2008). Treatment-seeking veterans of Iraq and Afghanistan: Comparison with veterans of pervious wars. *Journal of Nervous and Mental Disease, 196,* 513–521.

Hankin, C. S., Spiro, A., Miller, D., & Kazis, L. (1999). Mental disorders and mental health treatment among U.S. Department of Veterans Affairs outpatients: The Veterans Health Study. *American Journal of Psychiatry, 156,* 1924–1930.

Hebb, D. O. (1949). *The organization of behavior.* New York, NY: Wiley.

Heltemes, K. J., Clouser, M. C., MacGregor, A. J., Norman, S. B., & Galarneau, M. R. (2014). Co-occurring disorders in veterans and military service members. *Addictive Behaviors, 39*(2), 392–398.

Hoge, C. W., Castro, C. A., Messer, S. C., McGurk, D., Cotting, D., & Koffman, R. L. (2004). Combat duty in Iraq and Afghanistan, mental health problems, and barriers to care. *New England Journal of Medicine, 351,* 13–22.

Institute of Medicine. (2012). *Treatment for posttraumatic stress disorder in military and veteran populations: Initial assessment.* Washington, DC: National Academies Press.

Institute of Medicine. (2014). *Treatment for posttraumatic stress disorder in military and veteran populations: Final assessment.* Washington, DC: National Academies Press.

Kang, H. K., & Bullman, T. A. (2008). Risk of suicide among US veterans after returning from the Iraq or Afghanistan war zones. *Journal of American Medical Association, 300,* 652–653.

Kang, H. K., Bullman, T. A., Smolenski, D. J., Skopp, N. A., Gahm, G. A., & Reger, M. A. (2015). Suicide risk among 1.3 million veterans who were on active duty during the Iraq and Afghanistan wars. *Annals of Epidemiology, 25*(2), 96–100.

LeardMann, C. A., Powell, T. M., Smith, T. C., Bell, M. R., Smith, B., Boyko, E. J., . . . Hoge, C. W. (2013). Risk factors associated with suicide in current and former US military personnel. *Journal of the American Medical Association, 310*(5), 496–506.

Litz, B. (2009). *A brief primer on the mental health impact of the wars in Afghanistan and Iraq.* Washington, DC: National Center for Post-Traumatic Stress Disorder.

Miliken, C. S., Auchterlonie, J. L., & Hoge, C. W. (2007). Longitudinal assessment of mental health problems among active and reserve component soldiers returning from the Iraq War. *Journal of American Medical Association, 298,* 2141–2148.

National Center for Posttraumatic Stress Disorder. (2006). *Returning from the war zone: A guide for families of military members.* Washington, DC: National Center for Posttraumatic Stress Disorder.

National Institute of Mental Health. (2015). *Serving in Iraq, Afghanistan not behind rising suicide rates in military: Study.* Retrieved from http:www.nim.nih.gov/medlineplus/news/fullstory_151789

Quantana, P. J., Wilk, J. E., Thoamas, J. L., Bray, R. M., Rae Olmstead, K. L., Brown, J. M., ... Hoge, C. W. (2014). Trends in mental health services utilization and stigma in US soldiers from 2002–2011. *American Journal of Public Health, 104*(9), 1671–1679.

Rand Corporation. (2008). *Invisible wounds of war: Psychological and cognitive injuries, their consequences, and services to assist recovery.* Retrieved from http://www.rand.org/pubs/monographs/MG720

Reger, M. A., Smolenski, D. J., Skopp, N. A., Metger-Abamukang, J. J., Kang, H. K., ... Gahm, G. A. (2015). Risk of suicide among US military service members following Operation Enduring Freedom or Operation Iraqi Freedom deployment and separation from the US military. *JAMA Psychiatry, 72*(6), 561–569.

Riggs, D., Rothbaum, B. O., & Foa, E. B. (1995). A prospective examination of symptoms of post-traumatic stress disorder in victims of nonsexual assault. *Journal of Interpersonal Violence, 10,* 201–214.

Ruzek, J. I., Curran, E., Friedman, M. J., Gusman, F. D., Southwick, S. M., Swales, P., ... Whealin, J. (2004). *Treatment of the returning Iraq War veteran.* Washington, DC: National Center for Posttraumatic Stress Disorder.

Seal, K. H., Abadjian, L., McCamish, N., Shi, Y., Tarasovsky, B. A., & Weingardt, K. (2012). A randomized controlled trial of telephone motivational interviewing to enhance mental health treatment engagement in Iraq and Afghanistan veterans. *General Hospital Psychiatry, 34*(4), 450–459.

Shen, Y., Hendricks, A., Zhang, S. I., & Kazis, L. E. (2003). VHA enrollees' health care coverage and use of care. *Medical Research and Review, 60,* 253–267.

Substance Abuse and Mental Health Services Administration. (2011). *Leading change: A plan for SAMHSA's roles and actions 2011–2014.* (HHS Publication No. [SMA] 11-4629). Rockville, MD: Substance Abuse and Mental Health Services Administration.

Van der Kolk, B. A., & Fisler, R. (1995). Dissociation and the fragmentary nature of traumatic memories: Overview and exploratory study. *Journal of Traumatic Stress, 8*(4), 505–525.

Walter Reed Army Institute of Research (WRAIR). (2006). *Battle mind training: Transitioning from combat to home.* Washington, DC: Walter Reed Army Institute of Research.

Chapter Fourteen

Group Work With Supercomputers in Our Pockets: Integrating Smartphones Into In-Person Group Interventions

Andrea Meier, Edna Comer, and Julie Clifton

The worldwide adoption of smartphones and other wireless mobile devices (WMDs) has transformed our lives.[1] The technology contained in the smartphone in my pocket gives me more computing power than that in all of the computers available to NASA in 1969, when it placed two astronauts on the moon (PhoneArena.com, 2014). The array of WMDs now at our disposal has profoundly impacted how we communicate and interact within and across all system levels.

The benefits of smartphones are clear. They enable us to communicate by voice and text, participate in our online social networks, document our lives and events with shareable photos and videos, engage in commerce, and access resources using the Internet at almost any time and anywhere. Used appropriately and competently, these communication channels and media can serve as the means for "e-empowerment" for individuals, their families, and communities.

Technological innovations often give rise to consequences that far outrun their inventors' original visions (Naimi & French, 2010). Once *adopted*, users find ways to *adapt* their new tools to unanticipated purposes. WMDs, and specifically smartphones, are stellar examples of this phenomenon. Smartphones are the physical "objects of desire" situated in the midst of all the systemic factors and forces that simultaneously open opportunities while also creating risks when overused or abused. To some degree, the conditions are ripe for all of us smartphone users to be members of a "population at risk." Unfortunately, smartphones also increase the types of risks and costs for smartphone users who are already vulnerable for other reasons. The concatenation of the sophisticated designs of smartphones that reinforce frequent use coupled with unstable personality types, and psychological and social stressors can contribute to maladaptive coping and technology addictions. Furthermore, ubiquitous smartphone-mediated access to Internet social networks and social media can create ongoing distractions and opportunities for abusive communications. At the extreme, smartphones are being used for crimes, such as murder threats (Burness, 2015), bomb threats (Trump, 2014), cyberstalking (Office of Attorney General of Massachusetts, 2015), "sextortion" (Navy Criminal Investigative Service Public Affairs, 2015), and recruitment into cults (del Rio, 2008) and radical groups (Homeland Security Institute, 2009).

The effective use of WMDs has come to be called "digital/media literacy"—the 21st-century skills now needed for living and working in media- and information-rich societies (Amichai-Hamburger, 2013). In 2015, the Association of Social Work Boards published its *Model Regulatory Standards for Technology and Social Work Practice* (ASWB International Technology Task Force, 2015). This document advocates that conditions of rapid technological change should be driving social workers to embrace an expanded professional mission that includes helping their clients learn how to function safely and competently in both "real-world" and virtual, digital environments. Social workers now need to assess protective factors, such as their clients' access to technology, their levels of technology-related skills, and how smartphone use might help them acquire or enhance those skills . They must also take the risks associated with WMD use into account when designing and implementing interventions.

This chapter will address the social and psychological impacts of WMDs, focusing particularly on smartphones, from three vantage points. First, it will review sociodemographic trends in smartphone use and our emerging understanding of the contributing factors and impacts of maladaptive use. Second, it will describe some of the systemic implications of clients with smartphones in clinical settings, from agency policies for client recruitment, assessment, and confidentiality. Finally, it will describe a generic intervention design for groups aimed at treating a range of different problems, but which now also must address the needs of members whose smartphone use exacerbates their other health and emotional problems.

TRENDS IN SMARTPHONE USAGE

Since introduction of smartphones in 2007 (McCarty, 2011), smartphone ownership has become ubiquitous across all sociodemographic groups. However, ownership rates vary somewhat by gender, age, race/ethnicity, educational attainment and income levels, and urban or rural residency. This suggests that many clients whom social workers see—including a substantial number of children and youth—are likely to have their own smartphones. These adoption patterns change rapidly. Social workers who want to understand how these trends may be playing out in lives of their clients should obtain the current, reliable information from reliable sources, such as the Pew Research Center, which has been systematically tracking Internet-related technology adoption and social impacts since 1994 (Pew Research Center, 2015).

Pew researchers discovered another trend that will affect the ways social workers communicate with their clients. Consumers, particularly young adults between the ages of 18–34 years, are increasingly giving up their landline phones in favor of mobile phones. Over 40% of adults and over 47% of children are "wireless dependent." They live in homes have with only wireless phones. Of particular significance for social workers, a 2015 Pew survey found that people who are likely to seek services, those with relatively low incomes and educational attainment levels, younger adults, and non-Whites, are especially likely to be "smartphone dependent" (Smith & Page, 2015).

The ways that smartphones are used are also evolving. According to a 2014 Pew survey, voice and video calling, and email remain popular, but text messaging is the most popular and widely used smartphone feature, especially among younger users (Smith & Page, 2015). In 2014, there was a major tipping point in user behaviors. The use of smartphones for information seeking, commerce, social networking, and entertainment (video, music, and podcasts) overtook their use for communication (Smith & Page, 2015).

SMARTPHONES: A NEW DIGITAL DIVIDE?

"Digital divide" is the term used to describe the socioeconomic differences in access to opportunities to access information and communication technologies and the use of the Internet for a wide variety of activities (Pick, Sarkar, & Johnson, 2015). WMDs have created new digital divides. Because they become so much a part of our lives, it is easy to lose track of the types of connectivity users have, and resources they can access vary with the kind of devices they own. These differences are related to the costs of the devices, connectivity services, and user skills. As such, they represent an invisible digital divide that has implications for group workers when they try to incorporate smartphone-based activities in their groups. For example, users who have computers and smartphones with greater speed and functionality can access information and resources more easily than those with older, slower devices. Older or disabled users may find it difficult to see the small screens of their smartphone or make accurate gestures to use their apps. Thus, if social workers address access to digital resources issues in their work with clients, they can empower clients by helping them find smartphones and other WMDs that are adapted to their capabilities.

I$train: Smartphone Impacts on Family Finances

Social workers also need to be aware of the impacts of smartphone ownership on household budgets. The rapidly increasing sophistication of smartphone technology and phone manufacturers' intensive marketing campaigns make it difficult to resist the temptation to own the latest versions that offer greater convenience, capability—and status. If a household decides to purchase phones for each family member, this multiplies the cost. By contrast, landline phones and cable cordless phones are site-specific and can be used by everyone in a household. They are also a predictable monthly cost and do not involve any other kind of technology.

In addition to the cost of the device itself, smartphones require WiFi access. The cost of phones will vary according to the type of phone and number of phones in a household, *and* the type and length of the Internet provider service contract. Rates for cell phone use depend on when and how long the smartphone is used and the type of data accessed (e.g., text, Web, video, etc.)—all of which are difficult to monitor and control. As a result of these factors, smartphone use is increasingly eating into family budgets. Families are now making decisions about basic expenditures—food, clothing, and entertainment—based on what it will cost to pay for their collective technology use (Troianovsky, 2012).

As families shift from home-based landline phones to arrangements where each member has his or her own cell phone, knowing how to contact clients in their households has become much more complicated. Where a message to a specific person using a landline phone could be conveyed by other family members, now callers must assume that only the owner of the phone will receive the message. Adding to the possibility of missed connections is the greater likelihood of theft, breakage, or loss because phones are carried around instead of left in a stationary location at home.

TECHNOSTRESS: VARIETIES OF MALADAPTIVE SMARTPHONE USE

In 2014, Americans spent, on average, 3 hours a day on their smartphones, communicating and using their apps, and accessing the Web (Brustein, 2014). This astounding investment of our personal time to these kinds of activities has major implications for our quality of life—in our interpersonal and family relationships, education, work productivity, spiritual pursuits, creative endeavors, and other kinds of leisure activity. The intense interest in WMDs and the increasing number of ways we use them has also given rise to a growing awareness of the potential risks associated with "technostress," the inability to cope with information and communication overload (Ragu-Nathan, Tarafdar, Ragu-Nathan, & Tu, 2008).

The number of smartphone apps is skyrocketing. And the number of ways that apps can be used in sequence and combination is increasing by the day. These circumstances force us to reexamine our assumptions about what is "normal" smartphone use and what is maladaptive. Many users rely on their smartphones to avoid boredom and numb themselves emotionally—a syndrome now referred to as "soft addictions" (Smith & Page, 2015; Wright, 2006). When the preoccupation with and intensive use of smartphones and other WMDs begins to interfere with a user's health, relationships, and/or productivity at school or work, it indicates a progression toward problematic mobile device use (PMDU). When PMDU becomes compulsive and results in significant life losses, it is classified as a "technology addiction," a behavioral addiction similar to gambling (Griffiths, 2000).

A subtype of technology addiction is a type of impulse control disorder, sometimes called "screen addiction." This kind of addictive behavior is attributed to the psychological regression caused by intensive exposure to WMD screens in combination with all the ways the users can be in contact with each other (Young, 2015). Here, perpetrators use smartphones and Internet maliciously to target other users, traumatizing them through sexual harassment, cyberbullying, cyberinfidelity, cyberstalking, and a range of other criminal behaviors.

CAUSES AND IMPACTS OF MALADAPTIVE SMARTPHONE USE

In this chapter, we assume that clients' experiences with their smartphones are likely to emerge as issues in the context of other emotional problems that social workers treat. Researchers have identified a variety of negative impacts of excessive device use. This section provides a summary of these emerging issues. The final section on group intervention will suggest ways that these issues can be raised in the context of members' discussions of their other problems and give examples of activities that can encourage healthier, more constructive smartphone use.

Physical Health Concerns

PMDU has been associated with a variety of health problems that may come up in groups. Excessive WMD screen exposure, especially with smartphones, reduces the brain's melatonin production, resulting in difficulties falling asleep (Harvard Health Letter, 2012; Thomee, Harenstam, & Hagberg, 2011). Poor-quality sleep in both men and women is associated with lifestyle-related stress, depression, anxiety, and a variety of chronic disorders (Polo-Kantola et al., 2014). PMDU has also been found to be related to reduced physical activity, increased snacking, and rates of obesity (Lajunen et al., 2007), which, in turn, increases long-term risks for diabetes, metabolic syndrome, cardiovascular diseases, and many other chronic conditions (National Heart Lung and Blood Institute, 2012). Paradoxically, a category of smartphone apps, mHealth apps, is being developed and intensively researched to determine their effectiveness for helping people monitor and control these same conditions (Xu & Liu, 2015).

Emotional Distress

In this context, emotional distress includes both mood and impulse control disorders. Inappropriate technology use can precipitate anxiety, low self-esteem, and depression (Cheever, Rosen, Carrier, & Chavez, 2014; Roberts, Pullig, & Manolis, 2015). It can also exacerbate impulsivity, attention-deficit/hyperactivity disorder (ADHD) symptoms, and narcissism (Bian & Leung, 2014). Emotionally unstable individuals may show symptoms of "soft addiction" when they compulsively check their e-mails, send texts, tweet, and surf the Web to alleviate boredom and to distract themselves from and sooth their negative emotions.

Psychologist Judith Wright coined the term "soft addictions" to describe behaviors that are pleasurable, harmless activities (e.g., eating, sleeping, eating, shopping, texting, and surfing the Web) but which become addictive when they are done for more than their intended purpose (Wright, 2006). Often these activities involve a series of "small time wasters" done compulsively in a "zoned-out" state in which the person cannot remember what he or she has done, seen, or felt and which do not result in a sense of satisfaction.

Soft addiction behaviors are misguided attempts at self-care, motivated by the desire to relax, to distract or amuse ourselves, or to cope with strong emotions. Often these behaviors are driven by longstanding feelings of unworthiness, inadequacy, or being unlovable, or other unmet needs. As with hard addictions (e.g., behavioral or drug addictions), people with soft addictions often minimize or deny the extent of their compulsive behaviors. They become anxious, defensive, or angry when a behavior is restricted or they are confronted about it (Cheever et al., 2014).

Communication Overload

The Internet exposes us to complex communication inputs from diverse sources and multiple channels, which often demand rapid responses. Smartphone users can experience "communication overload" when they are expected to filter, assimilate, and respond appropriately to these heavy flows of informational and emotional messages (Chen & Lee, 2013). Because smartphones are now considered essential for personal and professional communication, obsessive smartphone checking can be a coping strategy for alleviating stress and anxiety while managing role responsibilities (Reeves, Reynolds, Coker, & Wilson, 2010). Over time, the demands caused by communication overload can result in poor decision making, loss of motivation, anxiety, depression, and physical and emotional fatigue.

Fear of Missing Out

Fear of missing out (FoMO) is a variant of communication overload. It is defined as "the uneasy and sometimes all-consuming feeling that you're missing out, that your peers are doing something, are in the know about, or in possession of more of something better than you" (JWT Intelligence.com, 2012). Such anxieties arise because smartphone users can know what others in their online social networks are discussing and doing all the time. But because there is no way they can participate in all the potentially rewarding experiences they know about, they must also miss out on some of these pleasures.

Hypertexting and Hypernetworking

These two compulsive uses of smartphones, most often seen in youth, increase users' risks for other problems (Frank, Dahaler, Santurri, & Knight, 2010). PMDU levels of hypertexting for teens was originally defined in Frank's 2010 study as exchanging over 3,000 texts per month. However, texting frequencies appear to be increasing rapidly. In PMDU, hypernetworking is defined as spending more than 3 hours per day using social media (Frank et al., 2010). These behaviors occur across demographic groups, but they are more often found among teens. Teens who engage in hypertexting are also much more likely to engage in other high-risk behaviors, including drinking, sexting, and premarital sex (Frank et al., 2010).

Youth and adults who are intensely preoccupied with their social network sites are at risk for communication overload because they increase the volume, sources, and complexity of their exposure to all of this communication. Excessive involvement with social media can also threaten users' self-esteem through negative social comparisons (Fardouly, Diedrichs, Vartanian, & Halliwell, 2015). Social network users often put a positive spin on their online personas, only reporting their most positive experiences.

Depression

PMDU can be a symptom of depression *and* can itself be a cause of depression (Billieux, 2012). For example, intensive smartphone multitasking has been found to be associated with higher depression and social anxiety (Becker, Alzahabi, & Hopwood, 2013). The behavioral addictions model suggests that smartphone users may become depressed and anxious if their compulsive multitasking causes them to become distracted and interferes with their family life, work, and other activities, contributing to interpersonal conflicts and other losses.

These attentional shift difficulties may also explain how compulsive texting can result in feelings of depression and anxiety. Compulsive texters devote an excessive amount of their attention to waiting for replies rather than pursuing more rewarding activities (Lu et al., 2011; Rosen, Cheever, & Carrier, 2012). When those responses are delayed, these users often believe, usually incorrectly, that their correspondents are rejecting them.

Impulsivity

Impulsive people have a strong need for arousal and social interactions (Roberts et al., 2015). They have problems staying focused on the task at hand and in persevering to attain their goals (Billieux, Van der Linden, & Rochat, 2008). Whenever they are bored or frustrated, impulsive smartphone users are likely to distract themselves by surfing the Web and networking with contacts on their devices. People who are low in perseverance and suffer from low self-esteem from not achieving their goals may be plagued with irrelevant thoughts, distressing feelings, and memories, which then increase their cravings to use their smartphones as distractions (Billieux et al., 2008).

Narcissism

Addictive smartphone use has been found to be associated with narcissistic personality traits, including self-promotion, vanity, grandiosity, power fantasies, and superficial relationships (Pearson & Hussain, 2015). Recent research suggests that using smartphones compulsively to "snap" self-portrait photographs ("selfies") and share them on social networking sites is an expression of narcissistic needs because they enable senders to attract attention and admiration, and demonstrate dominance (Weiser, 2015). Excessive WMD use can contribute to narcissistic behaviors even in people who would otherwise not meet the diagnostic criteria (Pearson & Hussain, 2015). As with other aspects of PMDU, determining what is excessive and/or compulsive is problematic, because snapping selfies and other photos is so prolific across all social media sites.

Interpersonal Tensions

Because smartphone use pervades all aspects of our social lives, it impacts the entire cycle of social relationships: casual friendships, dating and mating, marital relations, infant attachment, and parenting. It is important that social workers recognize the difficulties PMDU can create in different kinds of relationships. When smartphone users are in the presence of other people, they can become mesmerized by the smartphone screens, making it difficult for them to engage in the behaviors that communicate interest and empathy: sustained eye contact, listening attentively, and monitoring others' emotions and behavior (Przybylski, Murayama, DeHaan, & Gladwell, 2013).

Smartphones as "Instruments of Trauma"

On balance, smartphones are having positive and empowering impacts. However, email, texting, and social networking via smartphones can also be done deliberately for harassment and other malicious purposes. Such posts can be anxiety producing and traumatizing to targeted recipients and, potentially, should be viewed as criminal acts on the part of perpetrators. Social workers need to be aware that some clients (or members of their families) could be targets of this kind of destructive behavior—or, conceivably, that a client could be actively engaging in one or another form of malicious use. The three most common types of malicious smartphone use are sexting as sexual harassment (see, e.g., Wolack & Finkelhor, 2011), cyberbullying (see, e.g., Hinduja & Patchin, 2014), and cyberinfidelity. For adults who are married or in committed relationships, relationship dissatisfaction and impulsivity can lead to infidelity using smartphones (see, e.g., Cappetta, 2011).

ASSESSING MALADAPTIVE MOBILE DEVICE USE

Given the widespread and intensive use of smartphones in our lives, distinguishing between "heavy, normal use," soft addiction, problematic use, and addictive behavior is not easy. Researchers often use the two descriptors, "problematic" and "addictive" smartphone use, interchangeably (Cheever et al., 2014). Technological addictions are defined as "nonchemical (behavioral) addictions, which involve human-machine interaction. They can either be passive (e.g., TV) or active (e.g., computer games), and usually contain inducing and reinforcing features which may contribute to the promotion of addictive tendencies" (Griffiths, 2000, p. 211).

In the case of maladaptive smartphone use, this specific kind of technology addiction can be recognized by six categories of technology addiction behaviors. (See Table 14.1 for a summary of these six categories of PMDU/addictive smartphone use.) The ways these behaviors play out across life domains will be discussed in more detail later in the chapter.

The differences between PMDU and technology addiction are matters of degree. The two syndromes vary in the intensity and destructiveness of the smartphone-based activities and the severity of their consequences. Instruments for measuring for technology addiction have been based on other kinds of behavioral addictions, such as compulsive gambling (Smetaniuk, 2014). One example, Smetaniuk's *The Adapted Cell Phone Addiction Test (ACPAT)*, is an inventory developed for research use that has been standardized on both college students and adults in the general population. This instrument has 20 items based on Griffiths behavior categories, which are rated on a 5-point scale (1 = rarely; 5 = always) with a maximum possible score of 100. Scores between 20 and 49 indicate a low to moderate degree of PMDU, whereas scores between 80 and 100 are diagnostic of severe addictions.

From a clinical perspective, the validity of this instrument is somewhat limited because it does not include an exploration of possible issues in the broader ecosystem of clients' smartphone use, such as overall WMD screen exposure, household financial strain caused by smartphone use, or smartphone-mediated

Table 14.1 Categories of Smartphone Problematic Use/Addictive Behaviors

Categories	Behaviors
Salience, or preoccupation with smartphones	When an individual is not engaged in smartphone use, he or she will have intrusive thoughts or cravings about the next opportunity to use their phone.
Mood modification	When a user has an emotional response as a consequence of smartphone use, this is an indication that the smartphone is being used as coping strategy, which produces a rewarding "high," or a sense of relief at being able to escape negative feelings or situations.
Tolerance	The user finds that he or she must use the smartphone longer and in more ways in order to experience prior levels of satisfaction. Often smartphones users will start with a planned activity (e.g., calling or texting a friend) but then, without taking other commitments and responsibilities into account, begin off-task multitasking (reading emails, answering texts, surfing the Web, etc.). Smartphone users may feel driven to own the newest model of their device or the newest version of their apps, or purchase more apps than they can ever use.
Withdrawal	When a user is unable to use his or her smartphone, he or she experiences distress, anger, anxiety, or intrusive thoughts related to the phones. Such situations include forgetting or losing the device; settings with no WiFi service; settings where smartphone use is banned; or the person they wanted to contact did not have a phone available.
Increased conflicts and losses	The user ignores environmental and social cues about when it is appropriate to use a smartphone, resulting in interpersonal conflicts that result in significant losses (e.g., jobs or relationships) due to uncontrolled smartphone use.
Relapse	After temporary improvements, the user fails in his or her efforts to moderate smartphone use in response to criticism and losses.

Source: Definitions adapted from Griffiths (2000).

traumas. The first author has developed and expanded version of the ACPAT, the *Mobile Device Use Assessment* (MDUA) (see Appendix 14.1) that includes the 20 original ACPAT items but also questions covering the other missing issues. The use of the MDUA as an assessment tool for group members is discussed later in this chapter.

PRACTICE GUIDELINES

The first part of this chapter presented an overview of the ways that WMDs, and specifically smartphones, are affecting our lives, as empowering resources and stressors. This section will explore some of the emerging practice implications of smartphone use within broader social services systems. Here we examine macrolevel issues at the program planning stage and how clients' adoption of smartphones may influence agency policies, including information access, professional boundary issues, and client recruitment, screening, and assessment procedures (Shulman, 2012).

ORGANIZATION-LEVEL IMPACTS

Access to Information About Services

Because many consumers now surf the Web to find out about community services, provider organizations now face challenges of fitting in the costs of Web site development and maintenance into their already-tight budgets. Program planners now need to consider accessibility issues (Nash, 2013), including whether their Web sites are optimized for smartphones (Foss, 2012). Many social services organizations do not yet have smartphone-optimized Web sites. Going forward, these deficiencies are increasingly likely to deter clients who rely on their smartphones to access community resources. In the context of agency services, they are also likely to affect who will be seeking programs that offer group support.

Collecting Client Contact Information

Client reliance on smartphones will also affect agency intake procedures. All client intake forms are designed to capture names, addresses, phone numbers, and—more recently—email addresses. All of this information is important for maintaining contact, but it does not account for the ways clients may be using their mobile devices. Many smartphone users now prefer to be texted rather than called or emailed. Others only monitor contacts from their personal social networks through their favorite social media sites. Many will ignore calls and allow their inboxes to fill, forcing callers to text them. As part of crisis management planning, clients should be asked to specify the best way to contact them.

In addition, because smartphone users carry their devices with them all the time, there is a much greater risk that they will be damaged, lost, stolen, or hacked than if they relied on landline phones. If clients who lose access to their smartphones do not have a landline backup and/or cannot afford to replace their devices immediately, social workers will have no way of reestablishing contact. This means that client intake procedures must now collect information for emergency contacts in case the smartphone-based connection no longer works.

Consent forms will need to specify that the group leader (or authorized designee) may make contact and under what circumstances (Zur, 2012).

Professional Boundaries and Informed Consent

Social work ethics mandate that workers respect their clients' autonomy and privacy. That said, smartphones make online personal information easily available and tempting to use. These circumstances are affecting professional practice across system levels, putting social services agencies under pressure to develop social media policies to protect clients.

Social workers may be tempted to use their smartphones to search the Web to see what they can discover about their clients' backgrounds (Harbeck & Wesala, 2015). However, such searches risk violating professional boundaries if done without clients' expressed consents. One organizational response would be to have practitioners address this concern directly by including a provision in their informed consent forms that states that social workers may conduct Web searches on their clients before the beginning of therapy or during therapy as part of crisis outreach (Zur, 2012). A second aspect of informed consent, the risks to confidentiality between clients when clients have smartphones in groups, is discussed in the section on "Agency Responses to Client Violations of Confidentiality Rules."

Screening and Assessment

There is little research evidence available to help group leaders resolve the question of whether to allow members to keep their smartphones with them during group sessions. There are some settings, such as inpatient psychiatric and drug treatment facilities and jails, where the need to limit access to the outside world makes such restrictions reasonable and possible. Other examples of groups where access to smartphones should be prohibited during sessions could include therapeutic groups for highly vulnerable people who are asked to share deeply personal information, which, if disclosed beyond the group, could result in physical, emotional, or reputational harms.

As we have seen earlier in the chapter, most smartphone users now view their devices as necessary for functioning in the modern world. Leaders have to decide on the trade-offs between two kinds of risks. Allowing members access to their smartphones during sessions may increase their distractibility. On the other hand, restricting phone access may raise members' anxiety and precipitate power struggles that have the unintended consequence of making members less able to accept the social learning and support that groups can provide.

Social service agencies and mental health providers' intake forms typically do not collect data on clients' technology use. The rapidly changing technology environment poses challenges for how to gather this information. Using Mobile Device Use Assessment (see Appendix 14.1) in the intake process lets the leader know what kind of phone each member has and each member's overall screen exposure. This, in turn, can be helpful for understanding the extent to which the associated benefits and risks of smartphones are shared experiences within the group. The results of the smartphone assessment can be used to orient the client's expectations about smartphone use during group sessions. The goal is to make it easier for clients to overcome their natural ambivalence to being vulnerable in the presence of others, and commit to being in the group.

Informed Consent

The widespread use of smartphones in the era of social media has increased the range of risks, and it has complicated the informed consent process for group leaders and members. Clients' informed consents now need to address risks and benefits of members' technology access over the life of the group and beyond. As licensed professionals, social worker group leaders are mandated to maintain client confidentiality. There is, however, no guarantee that other group members will keep that information private. In most states, other group members are considered "third parties," invalidating the principle of confidentiality.

Groups vary in their opportunities to work through informed consents with members. For single-session or open-membership groups, there may be little pre-screening. Members may not receive an informed consent form until they arrive at the session. This means that all publicity about the group should include information regarding whether or not members will be allowed to bring their smartphones to sessions. During the first session, whether smartphones are allowed in the group or not, the leader should lead a discussion about the implications of members' ability to communicate about the group or other members to their online social networks and beyond.

Group leaders will need to help members develop their own group norms around social media use to help them feel safe and ask them to commit explicitly to adhere to them. The Center for Ethical Practice suggests three kinds of situations when rules and expectations regarding smartphones and confidentiality should be reviewed and reinforced: (1) when a new member joins the group; (2) when a group member raises concerns about smartphones and confidentiality; and (3) whenever group dynamics create the need to remind members about confidentiality rules (Center for Ethical Practice, 2015).

Agency Responses to Client Violations of Confidentiality Rules
Organizations that sponsor groups will need to develop their own social media policies to specify the consequences if group members are caught violating confidentiality norms online. When such violations are discovered (e.g., a comment about another client is found on a social media site), agency policy can allow the group as a whole to decide whether a member can remain in the group. However, if the group decides that a member should be expelled, there are still risks for the group. An angry and impulsive member may seek revenge and exacerbate the

situation by posting inflammatory comments about what went on using social media. Agencies need to have policies and procedures in place to ensure that a staff member will meet the terminated client immediately after he or she leaves the session to help the client understand the reason for the expulsion, to help him or her regain composure, and to come up with other constructive ways to get the client's needs met. If a client has a history of extreme impulsivity or problems with anger, follow-up contacts should be scheduled to ensure that the client gets the support he or she needs.

GROUP WORK FOR MALADAPTIVE SMARTPHONE USE

The intervention group program design outlined here is based on a time-limited (e.g., 8–10 weeks), closed-membership model that is appropriate for working on specific problems and skill development (Brandell, 2011). This format allows for the development of trust and mutual aid between members, time to learn about how mindfulness practice can enhance emotional resilience, and for collaborating in creative activities that promote noncompulsive use of mobile devices.

Leader Professional Development

The intervention model described here includes frequent use of mindfulness practices. There is now an extensive body of research evidence attesting to the efficacy of mindfulness-based therapies for reducing stress and improving clinical outcomes across diverse psychological conditions, including depression, anxiety, relationship problems, addictions, and chronic pain (Garland, 2013). An in-depth discussion of mindfulness and its applications in groups is beyond the scope of this chapter, but a brief description of the three interdependent elements of mindfulness provides a foundation for the description for the ways that mindfulness practice is used in the intervention described here.

Mindfulness (Garland, 2013) is:

- a naturalistic mindset that is a basic and inherent capacity of the human mind and a state of mind characterized by an attentive and nonjudgmental metacognitive monitoring of moment-by-moment cognition, emotion, perception, and sensation without fixation on thoughts of past;
- a set of practices taught and trained in mindfulness-based interventions that are designed to evoke and foster the state of mindfulness involving the repeated placement of attention onto an object (e.g, breathing or other body sensations) while alternately acknowledging and letting go of distracting thoughts and emotions; and

- a trait or disposition that can be developed over time through the repeated practice of engaging in the state of mindfulness leading to a consistent, nonjudgmental, nonreactive awareness of one's thoughts, emotions, experiences, and actions in everyday life. (p. 440)

Mindfulness training is included in this intervention because anxiety and depression are common problems addressed in group interventions—and because smartphones can contribute to these kinds of emotional distress. In the group, members are offered instruction in mindfulness and encouragement to practice mindfulness during sessions. The goal is to help them develop skills in regulating negative emotions that may arise during group discussions around the program's focal issues, as well as those evoked elsewhere by their life circumstances or their smartphones.

To be effective in leading this proposed kind of group, leaders will need to invest in their own professional development and to familiarize themselves with what mindfulness is and how to help members acquire mindfulness skills. Formal training programs in mindfulness for clinicians are now widely available.

Preparing for the First Session

Leaders should review the intake information they have on each member to identify potential causes of anxiety, depression, or impulsivity and be prepared to educate members about problematic smartphone use within the context of the group's focal concerns. Specifically, leaders need to reinforce the message to clients, first heard during intake, that the urge to use their phones in the group might be caused by anxiety over what is being discussed in the group. They need to be able to empathize with members' desire to have access to their phones and map out in advance activities that would provide experiences of mindfulness about their emotional states and constructive smartphone use. (See examples in the section on "Middle-Stage Group Activities.")

Initial Sessions

As in all group interventions, the leader begins by reviewing the purpose of the group and invites members to introduce themselves and share what they hope to get out of being in the group. Because the leader will know how many members own or share smartphones, she might use an ice-breaker exercise in which members describe their favorite ways for using their own smartphones or those devices they share with others. This may result in disclosures about how much time members spend looking at mobile device screens and the ways that their screen exposure affects them.

Norm setting is a key part of the first-session contracting process. In addition to reviewing expectations for attendance and respectful interactions, this is the time to introduce information about the role that smartphones will play in the group. The discussion of norms should be buttressed with an overview about the social and psychological impacts of smartphones and the phenomena of soft addictions, problematic phone use, and "screens addiction." This information will provide the context for negotiating whether and how members will use their smartphones in sessions.

The overarching purpose of the norm-setting negotiations is to help members to understand how protecting confidentiality can help them feel safe. If members have shared how they use social media, the discussion should include a review of the sponsoring organization's rules about confidentiality and a request for members' commitment not to post content about the group online. This discussion may also lead to initial disclosures about members' experiences (positive and negative) in their online social networks and how they are related to other aspects of their lives.

The initial session continues the contracting and education processes around the group's focal concerns. Specifically, it also presents information on the use of mindfulness as a way of coping with negative emotions. Using a round-robin activity, members can be asked to share what prompted them to join the group. If appropriate, the group leader can probe with inquiries about how his or her smartphone use contributes to or helps in coping with challenges.

In this phase, the leader can follow up on the information provided in the intake interview about mindfulness with a brief mindfulness exercise. (See Appendix 14.2 for a sample meditation script.) After completing the meditation, the discussion can address members' questions about what mindfulness is. Members are invited to share their thoughts and feelings that arose during the meditation—possibly including urges to use their smartphones.

At the end of the first session, members are offered a chance to comment on how well the group is going and what was the most important thing they learned. They can be encouraged to think aloud about how they could apply their learning between sessions, including brainstorming about how they could use their smartphones to work on issues (Shulman, 2012).

Although the social work profession is still debating the value and risks of member contacts between sessions, the ethical principle of client autonomy leads to the conclusion that members "own their own lives" and can do what they want to outside of the group (Shulman, 2012). Smartphones make it easy for group members to be in touch between sessions. However, members may differ in their willingness for such contacts, making this a subject for negotiation. The leader must ensure that members not feel forced to share their contact information.

If most members are willing to disclose contact information and begin planning how they will be in touch, the "nondisclosers" may become fearful that they will be missing out on an important aspect of the group. (For more detailed discussion about the "fear of missing out" in smartphone use, see the earlier discussion of FoMO.) The leader should inquire to see whether any members have this concern. If so, their disclosures can stimulate discussions on the ways these anxieties can impel members' hypertexting and hypernetworking outside the group. Finally, those who do share contact information need to set reasonable expectations for how quickly other members respond. Members' reactions (e.g., fear of rejection) to their peers who are slow to—or never do—respond can become part of ongoing discussions about ways to develop and sustain satisfying in-person and online relationships.

The description of the first session is presented here as an example of how the issues related to screen exposure and use can be incorporated into the discussion. Subsequent sessions can use similar semistructured discussions and activities that explore the group's focal issues and provide opportunities for mindfulness practice. In each session, the group leader decides whether it is appropriate to ask members to reflect on ways that their smartphones are a cause or response to intense emotions, and to explore how their devices can be used to increase their resourcefulness.

MIDDLE-STAGE GROUP ACTIVITIES

In the group's middle stage, therapeutic work of the group goes on at the intrapsychic, interpersonal, and collective levels. Intrapsychically, members continue to work on their ability to tolerate ambivalence and difficult emotions. At the interpersonal level, they explore how much they can trust each other, and learn about and accept individual differences. (In this context, group leaders will need to explore whether conflicts regarding smartphone use in the group are about the actual behavior or are used to divert attention from other tensions.) At the group level, members may elect to enter roles that fit the group's need for different kinds of leadership and their own needs for acceptance and approval. Group discussions and activities are aimed at helping members develop a shared view of the group's purpose, offering each other mutual aid in accomplishing their personal goals (possibly including teaching each other—and the leader—how to do new things on their smartphones). Ideally, they also experience the synergistic convergence of individual and collective purpose.

Group activities can have obvious psychoeducational purposes, but they can also be paired with therapeutic goals. Group activities involve the constructive uses of smartphones that group members can do to promote their physical well-being, positivity, and empowerment. The activity categories are aligned with the categories of concerns described in the literature review. With each topic, a psychoeducational objective is specified along with a suggested activity designed to help members achieve it. Some activities offer members opportunities to learn to be more mindful—especially in their use of their smartphones. Other activities aim to extend members' understanding about how they can use their smartphones to be more personally resourceful and empowered in their communities.

Enhancing Physical Well-Being

Objective: Members learn how to find online health information and apps that they can use to understand health problems and support healthy active lifestyles.

Suggested Activities

Members use their smartphones to research the Web for ideas to help increase their levels of physical activities. They search for information about stretching and pleasant places to walk, jog, or ride bikes. They can use their phones to find opportunities to exercise in groups (e.g., charity walk/runs and bike rides) and to find community health promotion events, such as health fairs and farmers' markets. In discussions, they compare their experience of doing these activities with and without their smartphones.

Emotional Self-Regulation and Mindfulness Activities

Objective: The use of mindfulness practice in this context is to help members improve their attentional control and emotional self-regulation to counter negative moods, interrupt dysfunctional cognitions contributing to soft addictions or PMDU, and to promote positivity. The mindfulness exercises may also be used to help members be calmer and self-compassionate during the group and beyond. Mindfulness apps developed both for iPhone and Android smartphones can be used to reinforce and deepen members' practice. (For example, see Buddhify [Broida, 2014] and the Living Well app [LivingWell. org, 2015]).

Suggested Activities

Members use their smartphones to search online for information about mindfulness practices and mindfulness apps they can use between sessions. Members each find a mindfulness meditation he or she likes and leads the group through it in one of the sessions. Members discuss their reactions (positive or negative) to the meditation.[2] They discuss what happens as they try to initiate their mindfulness practice and use mindfulness in their daily lives.

Interrupting Soft Addictions and "Getting More out of Life"

Soft addiction behaviors, including excessive smartphone use, are conditioned, automatic responses to stress. Increasing mindfulness enhances the capacity to acknowledge and be present to strong emotions, opening opportunities to consider alternative, more rewarding behaviors that are aligned with personal values and life visions. Wright's book, *The Soft Addiction Solution*, offers a variety of exercises to help members (and leaders) identify their soft addiction behaviors and their emotional roots.

Suggested Activities

Members identify times in the previous week when their smartphone use was the initial activity that led to a series of other soft addiction behaviors. They explore the "zoning out" experience, identifying what was happening and their feelings immediately before they started using their phones and how they felt afterward. They explore what needs their soft addiction behaviors were intended to satisfy and the limiting beliefs that prevent them from desiring and pursuing more out of life. Members track choices that they made (e.g., eating, buying, smartphone and media use, etc.) over the course of 2 days. They rate how satisfying the activity was, and identify one potentially more satisfying activity they could have chosen at the time. In the group, members explore what they learned by tracking their life choices and the extent to which those choices were driven by emotional cravings or guided by a commitment to a higher value. Between sessions, they develop their own descriptions of "a life well-lived" and share them with the group.

Strengthening Family and Other Close Relationships

Objective: Members increase their understanding of the ways that smartphones can help families stay connected and their activities coordinated but also be distracting and emotionally distancing. Activities listed here are designed to help members understand how smartphone use can stress or strengthen their relationships with families and friends. Some activities aim to help members use their phones to find pleasurable things to do with friends and family that do not encourage phone use.

Suggested Activities

Members describe how they use smartphones to keep in touch with distant family members and organize family events. They discuss times when they use their phones to avoid interacting with family members and reflect on what motivates this behavior. They do role plays about conflicts over smartphone use in their families and friendships. In their roles as partners and children, they share their feelings about being ignored or family events where smartphone use disrupts activities.

Trauma Recovery

Objective: Members who experienced traumas of any kind can use their phones to find support services. (These examples all have smartphone optimized Web sites: The Returning Veterans Project, https://www.returningveterans.org/; Charlotte NC Refugee Support Services, http://www.refugeesupportservices. org/; Indiana and Kentucky Services for Victims of Intimate Partner Violence, http://www.thecenteronline.org). They learn how to use their smartphones to call for emergency services, to access support services after traumatic events, and to mobilize resources to speed recovery.

Suggested Activities

Members use their smartphones to compile information about victim support and advocacy groups in their community. They use their smartphones to participate in advocacy projects related to their traumatic experiences such as online community fundraising campaigns or community service projects, and discuss their reactions to being involved in these activities. Are their feelings about these activities (e.g., empowering or anxiety provoking) changing how they use their smartphones?

Strengthening Communities

Objective: Group members explore the extent to which the problems that spurred them to seek group interventions have structural and systemic causes. In some groups, it may be appropriate for members to engage in critical analyses about how macro-level conditions are affecting them personally and explore how to become better advocates (Finn, Jacobson, & Campana, 2004). They can learn how smartphones can be used to find advocacy resources beyond the group—including local and state politicians and lobbyists. Members can surf the Web to learn about groups that are engaged in documenting and protesting community issues.

Suggested Activities

Members can use their smartphones between sessions to contact experts and authorities to learn more about problems and possible solutions. They can improve their communication skills by crafting scripts for talking with community leaders and politicians over the phone. They can use their smartphones to find community groups that are studying some aspect of their focal concerns, discuss how they will recognize an effective advocacy group, and the implications of becoming a member.

GROUP ENDINGS

In the final sessions, members are offered opportunities to consider the ways they have grown by being in the group. They discuss what they have given to and received from each other, the skills they have acquired, and what they have accomplished as a group (Zastrow, 2001). Because concerns with soft addictions and PMDU are emergent within the group context, members should be encouraged to offer their feedback about the relevance of these issues in their lives. Members should also be asked about their reactions to the mindfulness training and to reflect on the difference—if any—those practices made in helping them to use their smartphones in healthy and resourceful ways.

When a multisession group ends, members may want to stay in contact with each other going forward. Smartphone connectivity allows members many choices. In most cases, those members who became close during the program will naturally continue to stay in touch. The group leader can offer to collect and distribute the names and contact information for all the members who are willing to share it. Because some members may wish to stay connected through social media, the leader should remind those members that they should protect each other's confidences and apply the values of mutual respect and support in all future contacts.

EVALUATION

The intervention model described here was inspired by the expectation that social workers will soon need to address issues related to soft addictions, PMDU, and screen addictions in their groups. However, this model is untested in terms of its relevance to clients and its feasibility and effectiveness. Assuming that resources are available for evaluation, leaders are encouraged to conduct two kinds of evaluations on it (Toseland & Rivas, 2012). Formative evaluations assess acceptability and feasibility. In this case, formative evaluations will help determine whether it is possible and reasonable to expect group leaders to address both focal psychosocial issues and PMDU, *and* encourage smartphone-based activities within a single group.

This intervention model only assumes that group leaders will apply their practice wisdom to decide whether and how to bring up smartphone-related issues—*not that they will be required to do so.* Therefore, in an evaluation, it will be important to track the extent to which these issues are discussed over the life of the group. For this purpose, the organization may choose to develop tailored, online process note forms for the leader that include opportunities to document the frequency with which leaders raise these themes, their comments on what prompted their decisions to do so, and members' reactions.

In the early development stage of a group intervention, data should be collected to assess process outcomes (Comer & Meier, 2011) such as member retention and members' satisfaction with their individual and group accomplishments. Questionnaires should address generic group characteristics: what members liked or disliked about the group; format and activities; the group's effectiveness on the extent to which the group accomplishes its objectives; and the leader's effectiveness as a facilitator—behaviors and activities used to help the group achieve its purpose.

Because the group design includes members' experiences with their smartphones and activities to promote constructive smartphone use, postgroup surveys should also include questions about members' assessment of the value of the information they received about maladaptive and constructive smartphone use, and whether and how their smartphone habits changed over the course of the group. Finally, since the intervention promotes mindfulness practice, items should also cover whether and how mindfulness practice helped enhance their emotional positivity.

Smartphone-Based Data-Collection Strategies

In a typical group, paper-and-pencil forms may be preferred to ensure that all members complete them before the end of the last session. However, when members are all smartphone users, agency data-collection options are expanded. An organization may decide to use online surveys using SurveyMonkey or other applications that provide links that can be distributed by email or text (Beard, 2013). These procedures can save on costs for distribution, data collection, and analysis, but they often result in poor completion rates (Extension.org, 2013). Group leaders can improve response rates by reminding members to watch for the messages.

An alternative strategy would be to use smartphone surveys to spark members' reflections about the group. Members can be asked to complete the online survey on their smartphones during the second-to-last session and then return for the final session to celebrate the group's accomplishments and discuss the results of the evaluation.

FUTURE PROSPECTS

Echoing Star Trek's tag line, this chapter has "boldly gone where no group workers have been before." It links the dazzling promise of smartphone-based innovations with our emerging understanding of the psychosocial pathologies caused by maladaptive smartphone use and excessive screen exposure. Social workers should plan to assess their clients for how their lives are being impacted by WMDS and to help them come up with strategies for constructive coping. The group intervention envisioned here, while untested, shows promise because the generic design integrates established group work techniques with evidence-based mindfulness practices that are applicable to the needs of members across a wide range of at-risk populations.

REFERENCES

Amichai-Hamburger, Y. (2013). *The social net: Understanding our online behavior* (2nd ed.). Oxford, UK: Oxford University Press.

ASWB International Technology Task Force. (2015). *Model regulatory standards for technology and social work practice*. Retrieved from https://http://www.aswb.org/wp-content/uploads/2015/03/ASWB-Model-Regulatory-Standards-for-Technology-and-Social-Work-Practice.pdf

Beard, R. (2013, October 2). *8 customer satisfaction software tools (Comparison and review)*. Retrieved from http://blog.clientheartbeat.com/customer-satisfaction-software/

Becker, M. W., Alzahabi, R., & Hopwood, C. J. (2013). Media multitasking is associated with symptoms of depression and social anxiety. *Cyberpsychology, Behavior, and Social Networking, 16*(2), 132–135. doi:10.1089/cyber.2012.0291.

Bian, M., & Leung, L. (2014). Smartphone addiction: Linking loneliness, shyness, symptoms and patterns of use to social capital. *Media Asia, 41*(2), 159–176.

Billieux, J. (2012). Problematic use of the mobile phone: A literature review and a pathways model. *Current Psychiatry Review, 8*(4), 200–307. doi:10.2174/157340012803520522#sthash.nnqmmnFM.dpuf

Billieux, J., Van der Linden, M., & Rochat, L. (2008). The role of impulsivity in actual and problematic use of the mobile phone. *Applied Cognitive Psychology, 22*, 1195–1210. doi:10.1002/acp.1429

Botto, A. A., Mariewicz, M., & Malekoff, A. (2015). *How adolescents use mindfulness to help themselves and one another: Sharing their strategies.* Paper presented at the The XXXVII Annual Symposium of the INternational Association for Social Work with Groups, Chapel Hill, NC. June 4–7, 2015.

Brandell, J. R. (2011). *Theory and practice in clinical socialwork* (3rd ed.). Thousand Oaks, CA: Sage.

Broida, R. (2014). *Buddhify 2 brings mindfulness meditation to iOS.* Retrieved from http://www.cnet.com/news/buddhify-2-brings-mindfulness-meditation-to-ios/

Brustein, J. (2014). *We now spend more time staring at phones than TVs.* Retrieved from http://www.bloomberg.com/bw/articles/2014-11-19/we-now-spend-more-time-staring-at-phones-than-tvs

Burness, A. (2015, March 21). Sheriff: Girl tried to kill mother. *Boulder Daily Camera*, pp. 1A, 5A.

Cappetta, A. (2011). *Emotional health: The truth about online cheating.* Retrieved from http://www.everydayhealth.com/emotional-health/0608/the-truth-about-online-cheating

Center for Ethical Practice. (2015). *Ethical information: Informed consent discussions in group therapy.* Retrieved from http://www.centerforethicalpractice.org/ethical-legal-resources/ethical-information/ethical-obligations-informed-consent/informed-consent-discussions-in-group-therapy/

Cheever, N. A., Rosen, L. D., Carrier, L. M., & Chavez, A. (2014). Out of sight is not out of mind: The impact of restricting wireless mobile device use on anxiety levels among low, moderate and high users. *Computers in Human Behavior, 37*(August), 290–297. doi:10.1016/j.chb.2014.05.002

Chen, W., & Lee, K. H. (2013). Sharing, liking, commenting, and distressed? The pathway between Facebook interaction and psychological distress. *Cyberpsychology, Behavior and Social Networking, 16*(10), 728–734. doi:10.1089/cyber.2012.0272

Comer, E., & Meier, A. (2011). Using evidence-based practice and intervention research with treatment groups for populations at risk. In P. Ephross & G. Greif (Eds.), *Group work with vulnerable populations* (3rd ed., pp. 459–488). New York, NY: Oxford University Press.

del Rio, L. S. (2008). The internet as a new place for sects. *Cultic Studies Review, 7*(1), 20–41.

Extension.org. (2013). *When is it a good idea to use an online survey for evaluting extension program?* Retrieved from http://www.extension.org/pages/69133/when-is-it-a-good-idea-to-use-an-online-survey-for-evaluating-extension-programs-.VZAvmxNVikp

Fardouly, J., Diedrichs, P. C., Vartanian, L. R., & Halliwell, E. (2015). Social comparisons on social media: The impact of Facebook on young women's body image concerns and mood. *Body Image, 13*, 38–45. doi:10.1016/j.bodyim.2014.12.002

Finn, J., Jacobson, M., & Campana, J. (2004). Participatory research, popular education, and popular theater. In C. Garvin, L. Gutierrez, & M. Galinsky (Eds.), *Handbook of social work with groups* (pp. 326–343). New York, NY: Guilford Press.

Foss, E. (2012). *How-to: Quickly optimize your website for mobile devices.* Retrieved from http://www.nten.org/articles/2012/how-to-quickly-optimize-your-website-for-mobile-devices

Frank, S., Dahaler, L., Santurri, L. E., & Knight, K. (2010). *Hyper-texting and hyper-networking: A new health risk category for teens?* Paper presented at the American Public Health Association, 138th Annual Meeting, Denver, CO, November 6–10, 2010.

Garland, E. L. (2013). Mindfulness research in social work: Conceptual and methodological recommendations. *Social Work Research, 37*(4), 439–448. doi:10.1093/swr/svt038

Griffiths, M. (2000). Does internet and computer "addiction" exist? Some case study evidence. *Cyberpsychology, Behavior and Social Networks, 3*(2), 211–218.

Harbeck, E. H., & Wesala, A. (2015). Social media & social work ethics: Determining best practices in an ambiguous reality. *Journal of Social Work Values and Ethics, 12*(1), 67–76.

Harvard Health Letter. (2012). Blue light has a dark side. *Mind & Mood.* Retrieved from http://www.health.harvard.edu/staying-healthy/blue-light-has-a-dark-side

Hinduja, S., & Patchin, J. W. (2014). *Cyberbullying identification, prevention, and response.* Retrieved from http://cyberbullying.org/Cyberbullying-Identification-Prevention-Response.pdf

Homeland Security Institute. (2009). *White paper: The Internet as a tool for recruitment and radicalization of youth.* Washington, DC: US Department of Homeland Security, Science and Technology Directorate.

JWT Intelligence.com. (2012). *JWT: Fear of missing out (FOMO).* Retrieved from https://www.jwt.com/en/worldwide/thinking/fearofmissingoutupdate/

Lajunen, H. R., Keski-Rahkonen, A., Pulkkinen, L., Rose, R. J., Rissanen, A., & Kaprio, J. (2007). Are computer and cell phone use associated with body mass index and overweight? A population study among twin adolescents. *BMC Public Health, 7,* 24. doi:10.1186/1471-2458-7-24

LivingWell.org. (2015). *The LivingWell app.* Retrieved from http://www.livingwell.org.au/get-support/living-well-app/

Lu, X., Watanabe, J., Liu, Q., Uji, M., Shono, M., & Kitamura, T. (2011). Internet and mobile phone text-messaging dependency: Factor structure and correlation with dysphoric mood among Japanese adults. *Computers in Human Behavior, 27*(5), 1702–1709. doi:10.1016/j.chb.2011.02.009

McCarty, B. (2011). The history of the smartphone *The Next Web.* Retrieved from http://thenextweb.com/mobile/2011/12/06/the-history-of-the-smartphone/

Naimi, L. L., & French, R. M. (2010). The unintended consequences of technological innovation: Bluetooth technology and cultural change. *IPSI BgD Transactions on Internet Research, 6*(2), 3–13.

Nash, N. B. (2013). *Creating an ADA-compliant website.* Retrieved from http://www.techrepublic.com/blog/web-designer/creating-an-ada-compliant-website/?

National Heart Lung and Blood Institute. (2012). What are the health risks of overweight and obesity? *Health Information for the Public: Health Topics.* Retrieved from http://www.nhlbi.nih.gov/health/health-topics/topics/obe/risks

Navy Criminal Investigative Service Public Affairs. (2015). *Online "sextortion" scheme targets service members.* Retrieved from http://www.navy.mil/ah_online/ftrStory. asp?id=85723

Office of Attorney General of Massachusetts. (2015). Cyber stalking. *Cyber Crimes.* Retrieved from http://www.mass.gov/ago/about-the-attorney-generals-office/community-programs/cyber-crime-and-internet-safety/cyber-crimes/cyber-stalking.html

Pearson, C., & Hussain, Z. (2015). Smartphone use, addiction, narcissism, and personality:A mixed methods investigation. *International Journal of Cyber Behavior, Psychology and Learning, 5*(1), 17–32. doi:10.4018/ijcbpl.2015010102

Pew Research Center. (2015). *Internet use over time.* Retrieved from http://www.pewinternet.org/data-trend/internet-use/internet-use-over-time/

PhoneArena.com. (2014). *A modern smartphone or a vintage supercomputer: Which is more powerful?* Retrieved from http://www.phonearena.com/news/A-modern-smartphone-or-a-vintage-supercomputer-which-is-more-powerful_id57149

Pick, J. B., Sarkar, A., & Johnson, J. (2015). United States digital divide: State level analysis of spatial clustering and multivariate determinants of ICT utilization. *Socio-Economic Planning Sciences, 49,* 16–32. doi:10.1016/j.seps.2014.09.001

Polo-Kantola, P., Laine, A., Aromaa, M., Rautava, P., Markkula, J., Vahlberg, T., & Sillanpaa, M. (2014). A population-based survey of sleep disturbances in middle-aged women—Associations with health, health related quality of life and health behavior. *Maturitas, 77*(3), 255–262. doi:10.1016/j.maturitas.2013.11.008

Przybylski, A. K., Murayama, K., DeHaan, C. R., & Gladwell, V. (2013). Motivational, emotional, and behavioral correlates of fear of missing out. *Computers in Human Behavior, 29*(4), 1841–1848. doi:10.1016/j.chb.2013.02.014

Ragu-Nathan, T. S., Tarafdar, M., Ragu-Nathan, B. S., & Tu, Q. (2008). The consequences of technostress for end users in organizations: Conceptual development and empirical validation. *Information Systems Research, 200819*(4), 417–433.

Reeves, J., Reynolds, S., Coker, S., & Wilson, C. (2010). An experimental manipulation of responsibility in children: A test of the inflated responsibility model of obsessive-compulsive disorder. *Journal of Behavior Therapy and Experimental Psychiatry, 41*(3), 228–233.

Roberts, J. A., Pullig, C., & Manolis, C. (2015). I need my smartphone: A hierarchical model of personality and cell-phone addiction. *Personality and Individual Differences, 79,* 13–19. doi:10.1016/j.paid.2015.01.049

Rosen, L. D., Cheever, N. A., & Carrier, L. M. (2012). *IDisorder: Understandng our obsession with technology and overcoming its hold on us.* New York, NY: Palgrave-Macmillan.

Shulman, L. (2012). *The skills of helping individuals, groups, and communities* (7th ed.). Belmont, CA: Brooks/Cole.

Smetaniuk, P. (2014). A preliminary investigation into the prevalence and prediction of problematic cell phone use. *Journal of Behavioral Addictions, 3*(1), 41–53. doi:10.1556/JBA.3.2014.004

Smith, A., & Page, D. (2015, April 1). *U.S. Smartphone use in 2015.* Retrieved from http://www.pewinternet.org/files/2015/03/PI_Smartphones_0401151.pdf

Thomee, S., Harenstam, A., & Hagberg, M. (2011). Mobile phone use and stress, sleep disturbances, and symptoms of depression among young adults—a prospective cohort study. *BMC Public Health, 11*(66). http://www.biomedcentral.com/1471-2458/11/66 doi:10.1186/1471-2458-11-66

Toseland, R. W., & Rivas, R. F. (2012). *An introduction to group work practice* (7th ed.). Boston, MA: Allyn & Bacon.

Troianovsky, A. (2012). Cellphones are eating the family budget. *Wall Street Journal.* Retrieved from http://www.wsj.com/articles/SB10000872396390444408330457801 8731890309450

Trump, K. (2014, February 25). *Schools face new wave of violent threats sent by social media and other electronic means, study says.* Retrieved from http://www.schoolsecurity. org/2014/02/schools-face-new-wave-of-violent-threats-sent-social-media-electronic-means-study-says/

Weiser, E. B. (2015). #Me: Narcissism and its facets as predictors of selfie-posting frequency. *Personality and Individual Differences, 86,* 477–481. doi:10.1016/ j.paid.2015.07.007

Wolack, J., & Finkelhor, D. (2011, March). *Sexting: A typology.* Retrieved from http:// www.unh.edu/ccrc/pdf/CV231_Sexting Typology Bulletin_4-6-11_revised.pdf

Wright, J. (2006). *Soft addiction solutions.* New York, NY: Jeremy Tarcher.

Xu, W., & Liu, Y. (2015). mHealthapps: A repository and database of mobile health apps. *JMIR mHealth and uHealth, 3*(1), e-28. http://mhealth.jmir.org/2015/1/e28/ doi:doi:10.2196/mhealth.4026

Young, K. S. (2015). *Screen addiction.* Retrieved from http://netaddiction.com/ compulsive-surfing/

Zastrow, C. (2001). *Social work with groups: Using the class as a group leadership laboratory* (5th ed.). Pacific Grove, CA: Brooks/Cole.

Zur, O. (2012). Therapeutic ethics in the digital age: When the whole world is watching. *Psychotherapy Networker, July/August,* 1–10. http://www.psychotherapynetworker. org/magazine/currentissue/item/1740-therapeutic-ethics-in-the-digital-age

APPENDIX 14.1: MOBILE DEVICE USE ASSESSMENT

In the box on the right, please write the number (between 0 and 5) which describes how often your mobile phone affects your thoughts and behavior. *Not Applicable = 0, Rarely = 1, Occasionally = 2, Frequently = 3, Often = 4, Always = 5*	Frequency Rating
1. How often do you find that you stay on your cell phone longer than you intended?	
2. How often do you neglect household chores to spend more time on your cell phone?	
3. How often do you prefer the excitement of your cell phone use more than intimacy with your spouse or partner?	
4. How often do you form new relationships with people who call or text you on your cell phone?	
5. How often do other people in your life complain to you about the amount of time you spend on your cell phone?	
6. How often do your grades or school work suffer because of the amount of time you spend on your cell phone?	

7. How often do you check your incoming messages before something else that you need to do?

8. How often does your job performance suffer because of the amount of time you spend on your cell phone?

9. How often do you become defensive or secretive when someone asks you what you are doing on your cell phone?

10. How often do you block out disturbing thoughts about your life with soothing thoughts about using your cell phone?

11. How often do you find yourself anticipating the next time when you can use your cell phone?

12. How often do you fear that life without your cell phone would be boring and joyless?

13. How often do you snap, yell, or get annoyed if someone bothers you while you are using your cell phone?

14. How often do you oversleep due to late-night cell phone use?

15. How often do you feel preoccupied with your cell phone even when it's off, or fantasize being connected with someone?

16. How often do you find yourself saying "Just a few more minutes" when on your cell phone?

17. How often do you try to cut down on the amount of time you spend on your cell phone—and fail?

18. How often do you try to hide or invent excuses about how long you've been on your cell phone?

19. How often do you choose to spend more time on your cell phone instead of going out and spending time with other people?

20. How often do you feel depressed, moody, or nervous when you are not using your cell phone, but then feel better when you are able to use it again?

Total

A. In the past 12 months, have you ever felt coerced to send or accept explicitly sexual texts or photographic/video images through your mobile phone or device? Yes ☐ No ☐

B. In the past 12 months, Has anyone ever tried to recruit you into a gang, cult, or extremist group through your mobile phone or social networks? Yes ☐   No ☐

C. In the past 12 months, have you ever been the victim of any crimes (identity theft, aggravated sexting, stalking, extortion, or threats of bodily injury) perpetrated through your mobile phone? Yes ☐   No ☐

APPENDIX 14.2: EXAMPLE OF A MINDFULNESS MEDITATION SCRIPT

Leader's Introduction. We often treat our thoughts as if they are facts. For example: "I am no good at this," "He's is a jerk," "Nobody understands me," "I am brilliant," etc. When we have a thought, many times it can condense into a belief. A belief is just a thought or thoughts that I have a lot of the time. Beliefs can then be taken as facts. For example: "The world is flat"—enough people had that thought often enough for it to be assumed to be a fact for centuries! When we start to pay attention to our thoughts, with a gentle curiosity, then we start to think about thinking and we move away from believing that the thought is a fact.

Let's start this experience by paying attention to your breath. Allow yourself to notice any thoughts that come into your head as you are aware of your breathing. Notice, pay attention to, and accept these thoughts without judgment. Thoughts are not bad or good, positive or negative; they just are what they are—the thought that you happen to be having at this particular moment.

You may become aware that you are having difficulty thinking about your thoughts—so think about that. You may be thinking: "I can't do this very well." That's a thought, too. Allow yourself to think about that.

Some people like the metaphor of allowing the thoughts to just float like leaves on a stream, or clouds in a sky, noticing each passing thought and then the one that comes after it, and then the one that comes after that. A Buddhist idea is to think of thoughts as pages written on water. Let's breathe together in silence for one minute. You may notice that just at the moment you become aware of a thought, it passes and is replaced by another thought. That's what happens—thoughts come, and they go.

Finally, bring yourself back to awareness of the breath.

NOTES

1 WMDs include mobile phones without Internet connectivity, tablets, electronic games, laptop computers, and Internet-ready television.
2 Some members may find it uncomfortable to sit quietly with their eyes closed in the presence of others (Botto, Mariewicz, & Malekoff, 2015). Their reactions can lead to discussions about other methods of mindfulness practice (e.g., walking, savoring a glass of water, etc.).

Part Three

Violence: Victims and Perpetrators

Chapter Fifteen

Group Work With Adult Survivors of Childhood Sexual Abuse

Carolyn Knight

S exual abuse is defined as sexual contact between a child or adolescent and a person in a position of power and authority. It includes, but is not limited to, vaginal and anal penetration, oral sex, masturbation, and exposure to or participation in pornography. The prevalence of sexual abuse in the general population is difficult to determine due to a lack of a uniform definition and victims'— particularly male victims'—unwillingness or inability to disclose (Valerio, 2011). But conservative estimates suggest that one third of adult women and one quarter of adult men have experienced some form of sexual abuse prior to reaching age 18 (Brown, Reyes, Brown, & Gonzenbach, 2013; Finkelhor, Ormrod, Turner, & Hamby, 2005). Research also indicates that a majority of individuals seeking or required to seek treatment for current problems in living in a range of settings, such as child welfare, addictions, forensics, and mental health, are likely to be survivors (Arata & Lindman, 2002; Breslau, 2002).

REVIEW OF THE LITERATURE

Long-Term Consequences of Sexual Abuse

Survivors of sexual abuse experience a range of emotional problems, including low self-esteem, guilt, shame, fear, social isolation, and depression. Substance abuse, self-injury, sexual dysfunction, eating disorders, symptoms of posttraumatic stress disorder (PTSD), such as flashbacks and hypervigilance, and sexual revictimization as an adult also are common long-term effects (Brown, Schrag, & Trimble, 2005; Filipas & Ullman, 2006; Kamen, Bergstrom, Koopman, Lee, & Gore-Felton, 2102; Solomon & Heide, 2005; Walker, Hernandez, & Davey, 2012; Wiechelt, Lutz, Smyth, & Syms, 2005). Variables such as age of onset, relationship of the perpetrator to the victim, and length and type of sexual violation have been found to influence the severity and nature of the long-term challenges survivors face (Kristensen & Lau, 2011; Yancy & Hansen, 2010). Mitigating factors include the child or adolescent victim telling someone and being believed and supported and the prevention of any further abuse.

Survivors are likely to develop core beliefs about themselves and their social world that are characterized by mistrust, powerlessness, and a lack of safety, security, and control (Karakurt & Silver, 2014; Valerio & Lepper, 2009). Survivors also tend to lack "self-capacities" (McCann & Pearlman, 1990), which include, among others, the ability to self-soothe, regulate affect, and handle disagreements and conflict. More fundamentally, sexual abuse can rob the individual of a stable sense of self (Saha, Chung, & Thorne, 2011).

Differences in how men and women respond to sexual abuse have been observed and can be attributed to the nature of the victimization and sociocultural context (Alaggia & Millington, 2008). Men typically have been sexually abused by men and struggle with what they perceive to be the homosexual nature of their abuse (Alaggia & Mishna, 2014). A common sentiment the author has heard from male group members is, "I *must* be gay if I 'had sex' with another guy." This sentiment tends to be especially strong in those instances where the victim was sexually aroused. Sexual arousal is especially likely to occur among boys, thus intensifying feelings of shame and confusion (Easton, 2013).

Self-blame, although common for both men and women, tends to be more problematic for men. Male survivors must reconcile their victimization with what they perceive to be expected of them as men (Kia-Keating, Sorsoli, & Grossman, 2010). A group member, Nick, stated, "I'm the man. I'm supposed to be the one who comes in and protects others from harm. I'm not supposed to be the helpless victim." Nick was 8 years old when he was sodomized and forced to perform oral sex on his camp counselor during a weekend camping trip. Nick tried to escape, but the counselor threatened to leave him in the woods and to harm him and his family if he told anyone.

Male survivors also may experience more extreme feelings of isolation and inadequacy than women as well as greater difficulty managing anger (O'Leary & Barber, 2008). Most males who were sexually abused in childhood do *not* go on to molest children, yet there is evidence that male survivors are at greater risk for sexually abusing others, perhaps as a way of managing feelings of inadequacy and anger (Connolly & Woollons, 2008).

Memory loss and dissociation can provide all victims with ways of coping, when few other resources are available. There is debate about the validity of "recovered memories" (Malmo & Laidlaw, 2010), but there is ample evidence that male and female survivors of sexual abuse often have limited or incomplete memories of their victimization and may recall aspects of it years later, especially when they are in counseling (Alison, Kebbell, & Lewis, 2006; Crowley, 2008; McNally, 2003; Nemeroff, 2004).

Almost all survivors exhibit the mildest form of dissociation, in which feelings are split off from experiences. For example, the survivor can recount her or his "story" devoid of any affect. With dissociative identity disorder (DID), the most extreme manifestation of dissociation, feelings, memories, and experiences may be housed in separate parts of the self. There may be little awareness among these parts of one another. Debate centers on the legitimacy of DID (Piper & Merskey, 2004), though evidence suggests that when survivors have experienced ritualistic sexual abuse, they are particularly likely to develop separate and distinct parts of the self (Bottoms, Najdowski, Epstein, & Badanek, 2012; Ross & Ness, 2010). Women are more likely to be diagnosed with DID, but it is not clear whether this reflects differences between men's and women's responses to sexual abuse, the nature of their victimization, or how they are assessed.

Advantages of Group Membership for Adult Survivors

A fundamental advantage of group membership for survivors is that the experience of being with others with a similar history normalizes experiences and current challenges (Huss, Elhozayel, & Marcus, 2012). Second, as a result of discovering they are "all in the same boat" (Shulman, 2012), survivors' feelings of being alone and different are lessened. Third, group membership affords survivors the opportunity to develop connections to one another, which is inherently therapeutic, since it provides them with a corrective emotional experience (Yalom & Leszcz, 2007). Members' relationships with one another enhance their worth and esteem and challenge directly their distortions in thinking about self and others (Fritch & Lynch, 2008). Finally, participation in a group provides members with the opportunity to develop self-capacities as they learn from and provide support to one another.

Research supports the efficacy of groups for survivors of childhood sexual abuse who present with a range of current problems in living (Brown, Reyes, Brown, & Gonzenbach, 2013; Lundquist, Svedin, Hansson, & Broman, 2006; Wright, Woo, Muller, Fernandes, & Kraftcheck, 2003). Results of numerous studies reinforce the benefits unique to group membership and reflect the considerations noted earlier (Hebert & Bergeron, 2007; Martsolf & Draucker, 2005; Ryan, Nitsun, Gilbert, & Mason, 2005; Sayin, Candansayar, & Welkin, 2013).

A more structured group that has a psychoeducational component and focuses on present-day challenges and normalization of members' experiences often is a necessary starting point for survivors (Cole, Sarlund-Heinrich, & Brown, 2007; Gerrity & Mathews, 2006; Klein & Schermer, 2000; Kreidler, 2005). A group with a focus on members' relationships in the here and now and in which they are encouraged to disclose their victimization and confront their feelings often is more appropriate for individuals who are more stable in functioning and have achieved some basic insight into their difficulties (Classen et. al., 2011; Elkjaer,

Kristensen, Mortensen, Poulsen, & Lau, 2014; Spiegel, Classen, Thurston, & Butler, 2004; Valerio & Lepper, 2010).

Groups for survivors of sexual abuse typically are small, six to eight members, to encourage intimacy and honest discussion. Groups can be open ended or time limited. Time-limited groups, in which members start and finish together, have the advantage of promoting intimacy and have been found to enhance client motivation and attendance (Classen et. al., 2011; Valerio & Lepper, 2010).

Given survivors' tendency toward isolation and feeling different, the worker must attend to composition issues, selecting and screening members for their appropriateness for the group. The "not the only one" principle (Gitterman, 2005) is helpful in this regard. No one member should stand out in a way that isolates her or him from others in the group. A complementary principle is "Noah's Ark," which suggests that each member should share with at least one other member characteristics that are central to or relevant for the group's focus (Yalom & Leszcz, 2007). Survivors' sense of urgency tends to mitigate the potentially disruptive effects of racial and cultural differences. Yet, in a group that includes men and women, only one man or one woman in the group would be ill advised, because she or he would stand out in a way that is significant to the group's purpose.

PRACTICE PRINCIPLES

The first practice principle lays the foundation for five others and is that group intervention should enhance members' self-capacities, promoting more successful coping with present-day challenges. If survivors are empowered to better manage the difficulties they experience currently, this begins to correct long-held, self-defeating beliefs about the self. This principle reflects an important reality associated with working with adult survivors of sexual abuse; most do *not* come into clinical settings specifically to work on their past trauma. Rather, they seek out or are required to seek treatment for current problems in living that stem from and reflect their past (Knight, 2009).

A second principle is the need to foster *mutual* aid in the group. Survivors of sexual abuse struggle with multiple problems in living, and their sense of urgency may lead the group worker to engage in "casework in the group" (Kurland & Salmon, 2005) rather than group work. When the worker devotes too much attention to individual members, she or he denies them the support and acceptance of other members and denies members the satisfaction and sense of esteem that comes from helping others, known as altruism (Yalom & Lezcz, 2007).

A third principle is that the group should adopt an appropriate treatment focus. There is nothing inherently therapeutic about encouraging survivors to talk about their past victimization (Classen et. al., 2011; Wright et al., 2003). A trauma-focused orientation—in which members are encouraged to explore their past and its associated feelings and experiences—can be retraumatizing and undermine the development of self-capacities. For most clients, present focused treatment—in which the past abuse is acknowledged and validated but not explored in depth—must precede trauma-focused work.

A fourth practice principle is closely related and is the need for the worker to maintain a trauma-sensitive orientation in her or his work. This means understanding the ways in which members' current problems in living, as well as their relationships with one another and with the group leader, reflect their experiences as victims of sexual abuse. Transference reactions are common and reflect survivors' core beliefs about others, beliefs characterized by fear, hostility, and mistrust. When these surface in the group, the worker can assist members in seeing how their past abuse gets in the way of their ability to engage successfully with others. Furthermore, survivors' feelings of powerlessness are likely to impede their ability to successfully confront the problems in living that brought them into treatment in the first place. As survivors see the connection between the past and the present, they are better able to negotiate their current challenges.

A fifth principle is that the group worker must remain mindful of boundaries, given survivors' lack of self-capacities and an integrated sense of self. Individual members may need assistance in distinguishing their feelings and experiences from others in the group. One of the benefits of group membership is that hearing the stories and experiences of others is validating. Yet the worker must look for signs of what is referred to as group contagion, whereby members' feelings become enmeshed and interchangeable (Alonso & Rutan, 1996). The group leader also must check her or his reactions to the group and its members. It is all too easy for the worker to get caught up in members' pain and distress. To some extent, the leader's reactions may reflect countertransference; however, the reality is we are human, and we will be touched—often deeply—by group members, their stories, and witnessing their affective reactions.

A final principle addresses the impact that working with survivors of sexual abuse has on the helping professional. When working with survivors of sexual abuse, the group worker will be indirectly traumatized (Knight, 2009). Therefore, she or he needs to be proactive in engaging in self-care strategies and develop ways of minimizing the impact of the work (Clemans, 2004; Cunningham, 2004). This includes giving voice to personal feelings and reactions about the work, seeking out supervisory support, and maintaining and deepening personal relationships.

Survivors can be difficult to engage in a working relationship. The range and depth of problems in living they experience can be overwhelming, and their stories of exploitation can be painful to hear. Group workers can experience intrusive symptoms analogous to those associated with PTSD, known as secondary traumatic stress (Figley & Kleber, 1995), and distortions in thinking about self and others, known as vicarious traumatization (Pearlman & Saakvitne, 1995).

Indirect trauma also can be manifested in a diminished capacity to empathize, known as compassion fatigue (Figley & Kleber, 1995).

Indirect trauma is not countertransference, which involves reactions to particular clients, often in response to the worker's personal issues (Pearlman & Saakvitne, 1995). However, the professional's efforts to protect herself or himself from being indirectly traumatized can lead to countertransference reactions like denial, avoidance, and overidentification (Cramer, 2002; Pearlman & Saakvitne, 1995).

COMMON THEMES

Themes in the Beginning Phase

In any group, new members want to know, "Who are these people?" and "How can this group help me?" (Shulman, 2012). These questions can be especially pressing for survivors of sexual abuse, given their mistrust of self and others. Survivors of sexual abuse often have had numerous experiences with helping professionals that were not helpful; therefore, they may be particularly likely to question the value of group membership (Palmer, Brown, Rae-Grant, & Loughlin, 2001).

Survivors' feelings of being alone and different tend to dominate early sessions. Members are likely to assume that they were somehow to blame for their sexual abuse and adhere to the "everyone but me" perspective, convinced that everyone but them is a victim who did not deserve the abuse (Knight, 2009). This belief is often manifested through members' reluctance to disclose sensitive information out of fear that they will be rejected or judged.

The following excerpt comes from a session of the group for homeless parents that the author facilitates (described in Chapter 24). Many of the clients in the homeless shelter at which the author volunteers are also survivors of childhood sexual abuse. Although this is not the focus of the group, it surfaces regularly, and inevitably, when a member discloses the abuse, she or he does so with great hesitancy and shame. In the exchange that follows, the disclosure of one member, whose sense of urgency to share was great, resulted in others acknowledging their own histories. As members discover they are not alone, this is liberating and reassuring.

> *Monique:* This is only my second day at the shelter (*crying*). I am so scared. I am 6 months pregnant and I have no one. NO ONE!
>
> *Author:* So you are all alone. That's a scary place to be.
>
> *Monique:* The father of my baby . . . he . . . he . . . stabbed me and beat me up (*continues crying*). He be like all the rest—just use me, use my body. My father, my stepfather, my foster parents.

Author: It sounds like Monique had some terrible things happen to her. One of the things that comes up a lot in this group is past abuse and trauma members have experienced, and how alone and different folks feel.

Angela: I feel you, Monique. I was raped by my grandfather when I was 6, and by my cousin when I was 10. I feel so ashamed and dirty (*starts to cry*).*Several other members start to cry.*

Author: It seems like Monique has hit a raw nerve . . .

Monique: (*interrupts*) I always felt so different, so alone. Like I couldn't relate.

Tanya: Believe me, honey, you ain't the only one. I know it feels like it, but we ain't. My daddy started messing with me when I was just 5 years old, and I never talked about it. It feels good to know others been messed with.

Finally, survivors' distortions in thinking about self and others may cause them to approach others in the group as well as the worker with a mixture of hostility and skepticism. In groups that include men and women, this hostility is likely to be particularly strong, because sexual abuse distorts survivors' views of gender, sex, and sexuality. Therefore, the group leader should anticipate that transference reactions will surface early and powerfully (Ziegler & McAvoy, 2000). This is discussed in more detail later.

Themes in the Middle Phase

Members' sense of urgency may lead to the rapid development of intimacy, which in turn fosters the dynamics discussed next. Yet the group worker should anticipate that the themes that surface in the beginning phase may continue and be maintained, when the group is relatively short term and involves changing membership. Such groups are less likely to develop a sufficient level of mutual trust; thus, disclosures may remain somewhat limited and superficial. In such groups, the leader may need to continue to maintain a more present-focused perspective, normalizing and validating members' feelings.

The worker should anticipate that when members have the opportunity to connect on a deeper level and develop greater comfort with one another, they will be able to talk more openly about their abuse, which can lead to strong emotional reactions. Members may experience some relief and sense of validation, but this is likely to be tempered by fears about being overwhelmed and flooded.

As members hear the stories and witness the distress of others, they may adopt the "that's not me!" perspective (Knight, 2009). They seek to distance themselves from others as a way of protecting themselves from the feelings being expressed. The following example comes from a long-term, trauma-focused group for female survivors with eating disorders. In the previous sessions, members talked more openly and graphically about their sexual abuse as children. One member, Paula, struggles with the group's focus on such painful content, questioning the need for this.

> *Becky:* The more we talk about what happened when we were kids, the more I feel ashamed of myself and dirty. And when I feel like that I want to purge. It's like I just want to get that shit out of me.
>
> *Andrea:* When I was 9, my Sunday school teacher took a bunch of us on a picnic. I remember he took me into the bathroom and started touching me. He told me I was beautiful—that I could be a model. I was so scared, and I knew that what he was doing was wrong, but I just felt like I was frozen in place. He would be like "I can't help myself. You're just so beautiful. I can't help myself." That really messed me up. I just felt like it had to be my fault. Somehow, when I don't eat, I feel more in control and more powerful. I know it sounds weird, but that's how it feels to me.
>
> *Pam (co-leader):* It seems like you all are now really seeing the connection between what happened to you as children and the eating problems you have now. Sometimes it's about punishing yourself, sometimes it's about feeling more in control, sometimes it's about covering up your femininity, and sometimes it's all those things. What I sense is that all of you are becoming aware of feeling shame and humiliation.
>
> *Paula:* I am not sure why we have to talk about this. When I joined this group, I thought it was going to be a place where I could learn how to eat healthier and manage my eating disorder. What's the point of dredging up the past? How's that going to help us now?
>
> *Marcus (co-leader):* It is hard to talk about this, isn't it, Paula? When you hear others talking about what happened to them as children, it is painful—especially since there's not much you can do about it now.
>
> *Paula:* My brother raped me for years, and his friends paid him so they could rape me, too. There's not a day goes by that I don't think about what happened to me. What good does it do to talk about this now? They [*referring to other members of the group*] just need to get on with their lives.

Pam: It would be nice, wouldn't it, if you all could just forget about it and move on? It just isn't that easy, I'm afraid. This group can help each of you put the past behind you so that it doesn't control you. It can also help you gain control of your eating disorder so that it doesn't control you either.

Cautious optimism about the group can give way in the middle phase to a second theme, which is disillusionment with the group. This may be manifested by members desiring to quit or who are missing sessions. Dissociation, either by individual members or by the group as a whole, also may occur. Absences and dissociation reflect additional ways that members distance themselves from the work of the group. The group worker should be prepared to discuss both of these dynamics directly with members and, in the case of dissociation, help members understand the protective role that it serves.

A third theme in the middle phase reflects members' growing realization that they were, in fact, victims as children, which results in anger at perpetrators and at those who did not protect them. A related theme is anger at the unfairness of the victimization, which can lead to the question, "Why me?" This may take the form of anger at God and anger at the group worker, because she or he is not "in the same boat" as the members.

The following excerpt comes from a group for male and female survivors that the author facilitated. Members had been meeting for about 16 weeks, and the exchange occurred in response to Paul's disclosure that his mother had recently died. A number of members expressed anger at Paul's mother.

Author: So it seems like some of you believe that the passing of Paul's mother is a good thing. That he is better off without her, since she wasn't much of a mother to him anyway.

Peter: Right! Like he told her what happened when she was a kid, and all she does is say, "That happened years ago, get over it!?" What kind of shit is that?!

Lucy: My parents are still alive, but I stay as far away from them as possible. They continue to treat me like I'm the black sheep. Ain't that a bitch? My grandfather and my uncle molest me, and it's my fault—I'm the one with the problem!

Melinda: My father died several years ago. I was glad to see him go. He was a son of a bitch until the day that he died. (*Starts to cry.*) *Silence. Paul is teary-eyed as are several other members.*

Author: I see some of you crying. I am wondering what's going on for you all. There was all this anger, and now, it seems to be something else. *Silence.*

Melinda: Why did this have to happen? Why?! What did I do to deserve what happened?

Lucy: I'm angry at my parents, sure. But somehow it's not enough to be angry at them. It's like I get angry at the world! At everyone and everything for what happened to me.

Susan: Right! What was so wrong with us that we could be hurt like this? Why didn't it happen to you (*pointing at me*)? Oops . . . I'm sorry, I shouldn't have said that.

Author: No need to apologize. That is the question, isn't it? Why you and not me? I wish I could give you an answer that would satisfy you all. But I really can't. Bottom line is that it wasn't fair, and you didn't deserve it.

Paul: Right now, I am not even angry, I'm not even asking myself "Why me?" I have, I guess, but not now. Now, all I feel is lost and alone. My mother—my mom—is dead.
Members are silent and crying.

Author: It seems like you all go back and forth in your feelings. It's the anger at the abusers and at others who didn't care or protect you, the sense of unfairness and injustice. But, beneath that, it seems, there's the loss. And for Paul, there's the realization that with his mom dead, he'll never have the relationship with her that he wanted. It's like the dream of having a mom—a real mom—dies when his mom died.
Members are silent and continue to cry.

Unlike this scenario, group leaders should anticipate that members are often not able to express negative feelings openly, particularly if these involve the leader. In this example, members were able to handle their emotional responses, but group workers also should be prepared to assist members in managing their feelings as a way to enhance self-capacities, as well as process members' reactions to the pain and distress of others.

Another theme, regret, reflects members' attempts to reconcile behaviors and choices they made as adults. Although members may come to accept that they were, in fact, victims as children, they have difficulty reconciling behaviors they have engaged in as adults such as addiction and prostitution. Feelings of guilt, embarrassment, and shame can surface. Regret also can reflect members' realization of all that they have lost as a result of their victimization.

Finally, members' increasing comfort with one another will allow them to interact more genuinely. Manifestations of transference may be quite powerful, because members' comfort with one another will encourage honest expression of feelings. Mutual acceptance also will lead to feelings of affection, which can be both affirming and disconcerting, since they are in such contrast to members' previous relationships and their resulting views of others.

In the following case example, transference is evident, as are members' under-lying feelings of connectedness. This example comes from a 12-session group for substance-abusing women who are survivors of sexual abuse. One of the members, Dawn, has missed two sessions without explanation.

Laura (leader): Dawn, we've noticed that you have missed and I'm won-dering if everything is okay?

Dawn: Yeah, everything's fine. I'm not using or nothing. I just have had a lot on my plate. I am sorry, y'all (*to the group*). I'll be here from now on.

Sarah: It's fine by me, I know how that is. Shit happens, right? (*Smiles.*)

Laura: Shit does happen (*smiles*). But, I have to wonder whether some of you might be just a little bit pissed that Dawn missed? Even just a little bit?

Mona: Well, I have to admit, I was, like, if I have to be here, why doesn't she (*pointing to Dawn*). (*Turning to Dawn*) I mean, I really am not angry, but I did miss you, and I did sort of think you were ditching us. And that sort of bothered me.

Dawn: I am sorry. I didn't mean anything by it. It's not you guys, I love you guys. You are there for me, and I really mean that. It's just life, you know? It's gets too overwhelming sometimes. *Silence.*

Laura: I am thinking that some of you might be feeling a bit guilty for being upset with Dawn? Life does get overwhelming for all of you.

Debra: Speaking for me, I am used to this shit. People say they're going to be there for you and they aren't. It ain't no big deal to me.

Sarah: Right, I got enough problems of my own, I don't need to be worrying about Dawn and her shit.

Laura: I sense some real anger here. At Dawn? Maybe at others who have let you all down and not been there when you needed them?

Dawn: I really am sorry! You all are like my family—more than like family. I didn't mean to let you down.

Mona: I feel the same way, Dawn. But I was worried about you. I really thought maybe you were using again or something.

Laura: What I am sensing is that you all have come to care about one another a lot.
Members nodded their heads.

Sarah: I'm sorry, Dawn. I shouldn't have gotten pissed. You all are like my sisters. My family. I just got pissed, thinking you were like everybody else.

> *Laura:* So, even though you care about one another, sometimes you get angry, which is part of any relationship. And sometimes that anger is really about other people in your lives.

Themes in the Ending Phase

Endings can be difficult for survivors of sexual abuse, especially in a group with a high level of intimacy (Knight, 2009). In such groups, members will have developed a level of comfort with one another that provides affirmation and validation. Therefore, denial of the group's ending can be a prominent theme. A related theme is members' concern that any positive changes that have occurred in themselves or their lives are due to the group. They worry that they will "fall apart" or "go backwards" once the group ends. This reflects members' underlying and longstanding beliefs about themselves as worthless.

The group worker will need to assist members in talking about their work together and their fears about going on without the support of the group. The group worker also should help members identify the gains they have made. In cases where a member leaves an ongoing group, the worker will need to help the member end with the group and the group to end with her or him, thus minimizing feelings of abandonment, guilt, and anger.

RECOMMENDED WAYS OF WORKING

A strategy that is critical to reducing survivors' sense of isolation is the worker's ability to connect the individual to the group and the group to the individual. This requires that the group leader reframe individual members' experiences and reactions so that they resonate with others. Cognitive-behavioral techniques are especially helpful (McDonagh et al., 2005; Messman-Moore & Resick, 2002). The uniqueness of members' experiences is not ignored, but it is the underlying commonality of their experience that is emphasized.

Working in the here and now is a second strategy that can be especially useful and, at times, necessary. The group leader may need to assist members in examining directly how their beliefs about others get in the way of their relationships. The worker can help individual members see the impact that their actions and reactions have on others. In the following excerpt from one of the author's groups, it actually is another group member who suggests that Bob's anger at Denise was really a reflection of his anger at his mother.

In the twelfth session, Denise was again saying that she was never going to get hurt again: "I'm going to live my life as I see fit, fuck everybody else." Bob refused to look at Denise, and played nervously with his hands. One of the other women said, "Come on Bob, you look upset. What's up? Is it Denise?" Bob acknowledged, "As soon as she opens her mouth, I get pissed off at her. I'm sick of her bullshit. This 'I don't care' shit gets on my nerves big time." Such an outburst from Bob was very uncharacteristic. However, he openly struggled with his feelings about his mother, whom he described as uncaring and as never having hugged or touched him. In a previous session, he had tearfully exclaimed, "I am 55 years old. In my whole entire life, I never remember—ever—my mother kissing me or touching me. I don't really remember her ever even really looking at me. Even now, when she talks to me, she doesn't really look at me." In response to Bob's anger at Denise, another member of the group observed, "Denise really stirred up something for you, didn't she? Who does she remind you of? Isn't that how you think of your mother, like she's cold and hard?"

Working in the here and now also is necessary, given members' tendency to dissociate. The group worker needs to look for signs of dissociation among individual members and the group as a whole and be prepared to process this directly. The group leader cannot compel survivors to explore their feelings, but she or he can alert them when they have "taken off" and assist them in identifying what triggered this reaction. As survivors do this, they are learning to be more affectively present.

A third strategy is that group leaders must be prepared to use their feelings and reactions as a way to validate and normalize members' feelings. There will be times when the worker will need to put into words his or her reactions to members' disclosures, because members themselves may be unable to do so. Sharing one's feelings and reactions is an example of what is more widely known as use of self and therapist "transparency" (Shulman, 2012). The following example comes from a 20-session group that the author led that included four women and three men, all of whom were survivors of sexual abuse. This excerpt occurred in the twelfth session.

> *Norm:* I've been thinking a lot more about what happened to me. It just keeps coming up, even though I don't want it to.
> *Author:* So, maybe it's time to talk about it? Let the group know? Just get it out?
> *Norm:* So, in middle school, I was a walker. Had about a half mile or so walk home from school. These guys—they were like in high school, I think. They and this older man would all hang out at the man's house, and I'd have to walk by on my way home. One day they grabbed me and hauled me into the

garage. They each took turns with me. Raped me. Sodomized me. Made me suck on them. This happened a lot all through middle school. They'd just wait for me to come by, laugh and make fun of me, and then grab me.

Silence. Some members are teary-eyed.

Author: Wow, Bill. How awful for you . . .

Norm (interrupting): I'd go home and my clothes would be all messed up. I'd have semen on me, and I'd be limping and stuff. What they did to me, when they sodomized me, it would be so painful. I could hardly walk.

Peter: Oh man, Bill. That's fucking awful. That is sick stuff.

Lucy (crying): I'm so sorry for you, Bill. What about your parents? Did you tell your parents?

Norm: I never said anything. To anyone. For two fucking years, these assholes did this shit to me. And I didn't say anything. I tried to once, but it wasn't any use. I remember coming home and my mother telling me, "You stink." Making me go take a shower, telling me that I was too old to go around smelling like a "cesspool." She'd say this a lot, but she'd never ask me what happened or act like anything was wrong.

Silence.

Author: So, what's going on with you all? Bill's disclosures seem to have hit people really hard.

Silence. Some members are teary-eyed; others are rocking back and forth or clenching their fists.

Author: What Bill has shared with us is incredibly painful. Very powerful. I am finding myself going between feeling sick to my stomach and totally disgusted with what these guys did to him to feeling such hurt for what Bill had to endure to being enraged—ENRAGED—at his mother for not seeing what was right in front of her face.

Silence.

Author: I am thinking that others of you are feeling the same sorts of things I am feeling, and these feelings are incredibly powerful, and scary. And that you all would like to just run from them. Shut down and just run.

Denise: These fucking people! It's bad enough that we had these weirdos molesting us, but then we had parents who just didn't give a shit. No one gave a shit about us! No one!

In previous sessions, Norm had characterized his parents as cold and distant and had described incidents that suggested he experienced a great deal of emotional and physical neglect. Other group members described similar experiences, but prior to this session, members had avoided the intense pain that was associated with their abuse. Norm's honesty signaled his—and the group's—readiness to confront their feelings. Yet his disclosures initially were met with silence and little, if any, affect. Members resorted to the ways of coping with feelings that had allowed them to survive their abuse—they dissociated. Thus, it was necessary for the author to share her own feelings of anger—rage, really—and sadness.

A fourth practice approach requires that the group worker be prepared to balance the expression of feelings with containment, so that members' self-capacities are not undermined. Guided imagery, journaling, art, and other nonverbal techniques have been found to be helpful for adult survivors and can be used for expression or containment (Avrahami, 2005; Naparstek, 2004; Nelson & Loomis, 2005; Park & Blumberg, 2002; Pizarro, 2004). The author often asks members to bring in photographs of themselves as children. Showing the photographs in group inevitably leads to the expression of strong feelings of sadness, loss, and anger. However, members' feelings can become so intense that they need help in containing them. When this happens, the author suggests that she keep the photographs and the feelings they generate. Turning the photographs and the feelings over to the author enhances members' self-capacities and promotes containment.

A final way of working reflects the controversy that surrounds recovered memories and DID. It is important to maintain a position of neutrality and work *with* members' memories and fragmented sense of self rather than engaging in "memory work" or "self-work" (Geraerts et. al., 2009). Critics of memory recall and the DID diagnosis correctly note that if the professional assumes that the survivor has repressed memories of sexual abuse, she or he may very well recall such memories. If the clinician assumes members have different parts of the self, these are likely to surface (Colangelo, 2009; Geraerts, Raymaekers, & Merckelbach, 2008). In the course of group treatment, members may dissociate, and they may spontaneously recall aspects of their abuse. If these phenomena occur, the group work can normalize and reframe them as ways survivors have coped with their traumatic experience. However, the leader should avoid seeking them out, assuming they are there, or creating a group specifically for this purpose.

EVALUATION

Ironically, an indicator of a successful group experience can be members' difficulties ending with one another, given their struggles with intimacy. More objective measures of the group's success will reflect the group's purpose. At minimum, however, it can be helpful to ascertain whether group participation has altered members' views of themselves and others. A rapid assessment instrument that can be used pre- and post-group to accomplish this is the Beliefs Associated with Childhood Sexual Abuse (BACSA) (Jehu, Klassen, & Gazan, 1986).

Generally, survivors of sexual abuse will participate in groups at least in part because of problems in living they are experiencing in the present. Therefore, it would be important for the group worker to assess whether participation in the group had any effect on the difficulties that necessitated the group in the first place. Members can provide a self-anchored rating of their progress or can be asked to complete one of the many rapid assessment instruments available to measure behavioral and emotional problems such as depression, substance abuse, eating disorders, and low self-esteem.

AUTHOR NOTE

Some of the case examples in this chapter first appeared in Knight, C. *Introduction to working with adult survivors of childhood trauma: Techniques and strategies.* Belmont, CA: Thomson Brooks/Cole, 2009.

RESOURCES

National Institutes of Health
MEDLINE Plus
http://www.nlm.nih.gov/medlineplus/childsexualabuse.html

Rape, Abuse, and Incest National Network
https://www.rainn.org/get-info/effects-of-sexual-assault/adult-survivors-of-childhood-sexual-abuse

Sidran Institute
200 East Joppa Road, Suite 207
Baltimore, MD 21286-3107
http://www.sidran.org/

REFERENCES

Alaggia, R., & Millington, G. (2008). Male child sexual abuse: A phenomenology or betrayal. *Clinical Social Work Journal, 36*, 265–275.
Alaggia, R., & Mishna, F. (2014). Self psychology and male child sexual abuse: Healing relational betrayal. *Clinical Social Work Journal, 42*, 41–48.

Alison, L., Kebbell, M., & Lewis, P. (2006). Considerations for experts in assessing the credibility of recovered memories of child sexual abuse: The importance of maintaining a case-specific focus. *Psychology, Public Policy, and Law, 12*, 419–441.

Alonso, A., & Rutan, S. (1996). Separation and individuation in the group leader. *International Journal of Group Psychotherapy, 46*, 149–162.

Arata, C., & Lindman, L. (2002). Marriage, child abuse, and sexual revictimization. *Journal of Interpersonal Violence, 17*, 953–971.

Avrahami, D. (2005). Visual art therapy's unique contribution in the treatment of posttraumatic stress disorders. *Journal of Trauma and Dissociation, 6*, 5–38.

Bottoms, B. L., Najdowski, C. J., Epstein, M. A., & Badanek, M. J. (2012). Trauma severity and defensive emotion-regulation reactions as predictors of forgetting childhood trauma. *Journal of Trauma and Dissociation, 13*, 291–310.

Breslau, N. (2002). Epidemiological studies of trauma, posttraumatic stress disorder, and other psychiatric disorders. *Canadian Journal of Psychiatry, 47*, 923–929.

Brown, D., Reyes, S., Brown, B., & Gonzenbach, M. (2013). The effectiveness of group treatment for female adult incest survivors. *Journal of Child Sexual Abuse, 22*, 143–152.

Brown, R., Schrag, A., & Trimble, M. (2005). Dissociation, childhood interpersonal trauma, and family functioning in patients with somatization disorder. *American Journal of Psychiatry, 162*, 899–905.

Classen, C., Cavanaugh, C., Kaupp, J., Aggarwal, R., Palesh, O., Koopman, C., ... Spiegel, D. (2011). A comparison of trauma-focused and present-focused group therapy for survivors of childhood sexual abuse: A randomized controlled trial. *Psychological Trauma: Theory, Research, Practice, and Policy, 3*, 84–93.

Clemans, S. (2004). Recognizing vicarious traumatization: A single session group model for trauma workers. *Social Work with Groups, 27*, 55–74.

Colangelo, J. (2009). The recovered memory controversy: A representative case study. *Journal of Child Sexual Abuse, 18*, 103–121.

Cole, K., Sarlund-Heinrich, P., & Brown, L. (2007). Developing and assessing effectiveness of a time-limited therapy group for incarcerated women survivors of childhood sexual abuse. *Journal of Trauma and Dissociation, 8*, 97–121.

Connolly, M., & Woollons, R. (2008). Childhood sexual experience and adult offending: An exploratory comparison of three criminal groups. *Child Abuse Review, 17*, 119–132.

Cramer, M. (2002). Under the influence of unconscious process: Countertransference in the treatment of PTSD and substance abuse in women. *American Journal of Psychotherapy, 56*, 194–210.

Crowley, M. (2008). Three types of memory for childhood sexual abuse: Relationships to characteristics of abuse and psychological symptoms. *Journal of Child Sexual Abuse, 17*, 71–88.

Cunningham, M. (2004). Avoiding vicarious traumatization: Support, spirituality, and self-care. In N. Boyd Webb (Ed.), *Mass trauma and violence: Helping families and children cope* (pp. 327–346). New York, NY: Guilford Press.

Easton, S. D. (2013). Disclosure of child sexual abuse among adult male survivors. *Clinical Social Work Journal, 41*, 344–355.

Elkjaer, H., Kristensen, E., Mortensen, E., Poulsen, S., & Lau, M. (2104). Analytic versus systemic group therapy for women with a history of child sexual abuse: 1-year follow-up of a randomized controlled trial. *Psychology and Psychotherapy: Theory, Research, and Practice, 87*, 191–208.

Figley, C., & Kleber, R. (1995). Beyond "victim": Secondary traumatic stress. In R. Kleber, C. Figley, & B. Gersons (Eds.), *Beyond trauma: Cultural and societal dynamics* (pp. 75–98). New York, NY: Plenum.

Filipas, H., & Ullman, S. (2006). Child sexual abuse, coping responses, self-blame, post-traumatic stress disorder, and adult sexual revictimization. *Journal of Interpersonal Violence, 21*, 652–672.

Finkelhor, D., Ormrod, R., Turner, H., & Hamby, S. (2005). The victimization of children and youth: A comprehensive national survey. *Child Maltreatment, 10*, 5–25.

Fritch, A., & Lynch, S. (2008). Group treatment for adult survivors of interpersonal trauma. *Journal of Psychological Trauma, 7*, 145–169.

Geraerts, E., Lindsay, D., Merckelbach, Jelicic, M., Raymaekers, L., Arnold, M., & Schooler, J. (2009). Cognitive mechanisms underlying recovered memory experiences of childhood sexual abuse. *Psychological Science, 20*, 92–98.

Geraerts, E., Raymaekers, L., & Merckelbach, H. (2008). Recovered memories of childhood sexual abuse: Current findings and their legal implications. *Legal and Criminological Psychology, 13*, 165–176.

Gerrity, D., & Mathews, L. (2006). Leader training and practices in groups for survivors of childhood sexual abuse. *Group Dynamics: Theory, Research, and Practice, 10*, 100–115.

Gitterman, A. (2005). Group formation: Tasks, methods, and skills. In A. Gitterman & L. Shulman (Eds.), *Mutual aid groups, vulnerable and resilient populations, and the life cycle* (3rd ed., pp. 73–110). New York, NY: Columbia University Press.

Hebert, M., & Bergeron, M. (2007). Efficacy of a group intervention for adult women survivors of sexual abuse. *Journal of Child Sexual Abuse, 16*, 37–61.

Huss, E., Elhozayel, E., & Marcus, E. (2012). Art in group work as an anchor for integrating the micro and macro levels of intervention with incest survivors. *Clinical Social Work Journal, 40*, 401–411.

Jehu, D., Klassen, C., & Gazan, M. (1986). Cognitive restructuring of distorted beliefs associated with childhood sexual abuse. *Journal of Social Work and Human Sexuality, 4*, 49–69.

Kamen, C., Bergstrom, J., Lee, S., & Gore-Felton, C. (2012). Relationships among childhood trauma, posttraumatic stress disorder, and dissociation in men living with HIV/AIDS. *Journal of Trauma and Dissociation, 13*, 102–114.

Karakurt, G., & Silver, K. (2014). Therapy for childhood sexual abuse survivors using attachment and family systems theory orientations. *American Journal of Family Therapy, 42*, 79–91.

Kia-Keating, M., Sorsoli, L., & Grossman, F. K. (2010). Relational challenges and recovery processes in male survivors of childhood sexual abuse. *Journal of Interpersonal Violence, 25*, 666–683

Klein, R., & Schermer, V. (2000). Introduction and overview: Creating a healing matrix. In R. Klein & V. Schermer (Eds.), *Group psychotherapy for psychological trauma* (pp. 3–46). New York, NY: Guilford Press.

Knight, C. (2009). *Introduction to working with adult survivors of childhood trauma: Techniques and strategies*. Belmont, CA: Thomson Brooks/Cole.

Kreidler, M. (2005). Group therapy for survivors of childhood sexual abuse who have chronic mental illness. *Archives of Psychiatric Nursing, 19*, 176–183.

Kristensen, E., & Lau, M. (2011). Sexual function in women with a history of intrafamilial childhood sexual abuse. *Sexual and Relationship Therapy, 26*, 229–241.

Kurland, R., & Salmon, R. (2005). Group work versus casework in a group: Principles and implications for teaching and practice. *Social Work with Groups, 28*(3/4), 121–132.

Lundquist, G., Svedin, C., Hansson, K., & Broman, I. (2006). Group therapy for women sexually abused as children: Mental health before and after group therapy. *Journal of Interpersonal Violence, 21*, 1665–1677.

Malmo, C., & Laidlaw, T. (2010). Symptoms of trauma and traumatic memory retrieval in adult survivors of childhood sexual abuse. *Journal of Trauma and Dissociation, 11*, 22–43.

Martsolf, D., & Draucker, C. (2005). Psychotherapy approaches for adult survivors of childhood sexual abuse: An integrative review of outcomes research. *Issues in Mental Health Nursing, 26*, 801–825.

McCann, I., & Pearlman, L. (1990). *Psychological trauma and the adult survivor.* New York, NY: Brunner/Mazel.

McDonagh, A., Friedman, M., McHugo, G., Ford, J., Sengupta, A., Mueser, K., … Descamps, M. (2005). Randomized trial of cognitive-behavioral therapy for chronic posttraumatic stress disorder in adult female survivors of childhood sexual abuse. *Journal of Consulting and Clinical Psychology, 73*, 515–524.

McNally, R. (2003). Recovering memories of trauma: A view from the laboratory. *Current Directions in Psychological Science, 12*, 32–35.

Messman-Moore, T., & Resick, P. (2002). Brief treatment of complicated PTSD and peritraumatic response in a client with repeated sexual victimization. *Cognitive and Behavioral Practice, 9*, 89–95.

Naparstek, B. (2004). *Invisible heroes: Survivors of trauma and how they heal.* New York, NY: Bantam Dell.

Nelson, G., & Loomis, C. (2005). Review: Self-help interventions improve anxiety and mood disorders. *Evidence-Based Mental Health, 8*, 44.

Nemeroff, C. (2004). Neurobiological consequences of childhood trauma. *Clinical Psychiatry, 65*, 18–28.

O'Leary, P., & Barber, J. (2008). Gender differences in silencing following childhood sexual abuse. *Journal of Child Sexual Abuse, 17*, 133–143.

Palmer, S., Brown, R., Rae-Grant, N., & Loughlin, M. (2001). Survivors of childhood abuse: Their reported experiences with professional help. *Social Work, 46*, 136–145.

Park, C., & Blumberg, C. (2002). Disclosing trauma through writing: Testing the meaning-making hypothesis. *Cognitive Therapy and Research, 26*, 597–616.

Pearlman, L., & Saakvitne, K. (1995). *Trauma and the therapist: Countertransference and vicarious traumatization in psychotherapy with incest survivors.* New York, NY: W. W. Norton.

Piper, A., & Merskey, H. (2004). The persistence of folly: A critical examination of dissociative identity disorder. Part I. The excesses of an improbable concept. *Canadian Journal of Psychiatry, 49*, 592–600.

Pizarro, J. (2004). The efficacy of art and writing therapy: Increasing positive mental health outcomes and participant retention after exposure to traumatic experience. *Art Therapy, 21*, 5–12.

Ross, C., & Ness, L. (2010). Symptom patterns in dissociative identity disorder patients and the general population. *Journal of Trauma and Dissociation, 11*, 458–468.

Ryan, M., Nitsun, M., Gilbert, L., & Mason, H. (2005). A prospective study of the effectiveness of group and individual psychotherapy for women CSA survivors. *Psychology and Psychotherapy: Theory Research and Practice, 78,* 465–479.

Saha, S., Chung, M., & Thorne, L. (2011). A narrative exploration of the sense of self of women recovering from childhood sexual abuse. *Counselling Psychology Quarterly, 24,* 101–113.

Sayin, A., Candansayar, S., & Welkin, L. (2013). Group psychotherapy in women with a history of sexual abuse: What did they find helpful? *Journal of Clinical Nursing, 22,* 3249–3258.

Shulman, L. (2012). *The skills of helping individuals, families, groups, and communities* (7th ed.) Belmont, CA: Thomson Brooks/Cole.

Smolar, A. (2003). When we give more: Reflections on intangible gifts from therapist to patient. *American Journal of Psychotherapy, 57,* 300–323.

Solomon, E., & Heide, K. (2005). The biology of trauma. *Journal of Interpersonal Violence, 20,* 51–60.

Spiegel, D., Classen, C., Thurston, E., & Butler, L., (2004). Trauma-focused versus present-focused models for women sexually abused in childhood. In L. Koenig & L. Doll (Eds.), *From child sexual abuse to adult sexual risk: Trauma, revictimization, and intervention* (pp. 251–268). Washington, DC: American Psychological Association.

Valerio, P. (2011). Who let the boys in? Discussion of an NHS mixed gender group for victims of childhood sexual abuse. *British Journal of Psychotherapy, 27,* 79–92.

Valerio, P., & Lepper, G. (2009). Sorrow, shame, and self-esteem: Perceptions of self and others in groups for women survivors of child sexual abuse. *Psychoanalytic Psychotherapy, 23,* 136–153.

Valerio, P., & Lepper, G. (2010). Change and process in short and long-term groups or survivors of sexual abuse. *Group Analysis, 43,* 31–49.

Walker, M., Hernandez, A., & Davey, M. (2012). Childhood sexual abuse and adult sexual identity formation: Intersection of gender, race, and sexual orientation. *American Journal of Family Therapy, 40,* 385–398.

Wiechelt, S., Lutz, W., Smyth, N., & Syms, C. (2005). Integrating research and practice: A collaborative model for addressing trauma and addiction. *Stress, Trauma, and Crisis, 8,* 179–193.

Wright, D., Woo, W., Muller, R., Fernandes, C., & Kraftcheck, E. (2003). An investigation of trauma-centered inpatient treatment for adult survivors of abuse. *Child Abuse and Neglect, 27,* 393–411.

Yalom, I., & Leszcz, M. (2007). *The theory and practice of group psychotherapy* (5th ed.). New York, NY: Basic Books.

Yancy, C., & Hansen, D. (2010). Relationship of personal, familial, and abuse-specific factors with outcome following childhood sexual abuse. *Aggression and Violent Behavior, 15,* 410–421.

Ziegler, M., & McAvoy, M. (2000). Hazardous terrain: Countertransference reactions in trauma groups. In R. Klein & V. Schermer (Eds.), *Group psychotherapy for psychological trauma* (pp. 116–137). New York, NY: Guilford Press.

Chapter Sixteen

Group Work With Victims of Hate Crimes

Joan C. Weiss, Jack McDevitt, and Janice A. Iwama

Incidents of harassment, intimidation, assault, or vandalism can be particularly traumatic and have long-lasting effects when directed against people because of their race, ethnicity, religion, sexual orientation, or disability.[1] The terms *hate crime, bias crime,* and *ethnoviolence* are used interchangeably to describe such incidents. This chapter will provide social workers with an understanding of the nature of such incidents, their effects on victims, and issues to consider when working with hate crime victims.

Knowledge of the character and impact of hate crimes is critical for all group work because any group may include members who are victims of hate crimes. These experiences may affect their reactions and behaviors to a wide range of issues and actions, as well as to other people both in and out of the group who may be similarly affected. In communities dealing with intergroup tensions and incidents, there may be a clear need for a group for victims of hate crimes. Hate crimes can occur anywhere—in neighborhoods, workplaces, schools or colleges, or commercial settings. Such incidents may occur when a member of a minority group is the first to appear on a neighborhood block or in an office; in houses of worship, schools, or other public places; or while just walking down a street. Often these incidents are not reported to officials because victims do not trust the police or fear retaliation from the offender or the offender's friends. Increasingly, these incidents are publicized in the social media, which can increase the impact on victims and also have an indirect effect on other members of the victim's group.

A group format is well suited to this population for several reasons. All members of a family are affected when one member has been victimized, so group work with one or more families may be indicated. Also, when one person in a community has been targeted, based upon race or religion, for example, there are frequently others who share similar experiences or fears in becoming the next victim, and victims often experience numerous incidents over time rather than one isolated event. Because being a victim of a hate crime stigmatizes and isolates individuals, sharing the experiences and ways of coping in a group format can be cathartic and healing and can provide a support network for the future. In addition, being able to air grievances with others, such as anger toward police or public officials, can serve to both validate the feelings and help dissipate the impact for the victim.

REVIEW OF THE LITERATURE

Although victimization based on someone's race, ethnicity, religion, or sexual orientation is not a new phenomenon, it is only during the past 35 years or so that social workers have worked with groups whose primary characteristic is their members' experiences of hate crimes. Prior to that, people who were victimized because of their group identity, rather than for any act they committed, turned to institutions representative of these groups for support. African Americans could count on support from the NAACP or local churches; Jews turned to the Anti-Defamation League or the American Jewish Committee, and so on. Informal support often came from family members and neighbors but seldom did discussions of these incidents occur outside of the affected groups. Victims of hate crimes have started to receive more attention in recent years because of publicity about specific incidents, information reported by advocacy organizations, changes to federal and state legislation, and a better understanding of the extent of hate crimes reported by agencies and victims across the country.

Among the first police agencies to begin collecting data on hate crime, in 1979, were the Baltimore County Police Department, the Boston Police Department, and the New York City Police Department. In these early attempts to collect hate crime data, the decision generally followed the establishment of a hate crime investigative unit in the agency to address particular events in order to document the activities of these hate crime units as well as identify the scope and trends of hate crimes in the community. In Boston, for example, the Boston Police Department created the Community Disorders Unit in April of 1978 after a series of racially motivated attacks in the city following court-ordered busing of school children to achieve racial balance. Local events similarly led to data collection efforts in Baltimore County and New York City.

A number of national advocacy groups began to collect information on hate incidents involving their constituents starting in the 1980s. The Anti-Defamation League (ADL) began to collect data on hate incidents that came to their attention in their annual Audit of Anti-Semitic Incidents in 1979. In 1981, the Southern Poverty Law Center (SPLC) began to publish its Intelligence Report, which documented hate crimes committed by members of extremist organizations. The National Gay and Lesbian Task Force, now called the National LGBTQ Task Force, published its first annual report on homophobic violence and intimidation in 1984 following a national survey to capture information on this type of discrimination. At the same time, a number of human relations commissions around the county, such as in Los Angeles, California, and Montgomery County, Maryland, began to collect and publish data on hate crimes.

This decentralized and uncoordinated approach made it difficult to understand the prevalence of hate crime in the United States. Furthermore, the definition of what qualified as a hate crime and what groups were covered, varied based on the source—for example, police department reports versus hotlines run by advocacy groups—and the particular state statute.

National Legislation

With a rising level of interest in understanding the nature and prevalence of hate crimes across the United States during the 1980s, the Hate Crime Statistics Act (HCSA) of 1990 (28 U.S.C. § 534) ordered that a system be created to collect data on hate crimes, that is:

> ... crimes that manifest evidence of prejudice based on race, religion, disability, sexual orientation, or ethnicity, including where appropriate the crimes of murder, non-negligent manslaughter; forcible rape; aggravated assault, simple assault, intimidation; arson; and destruction, damage or vandalism of property.

In 1994, the Violent Crime Control and Law Enforcement Act (28 U.S.C. § 994) expanded the scope of the HCSA of 1990 to include crimes based on disability and increased penalties for federal crimes committed on the basis of the actual or perceived race, color, religion, national origin, ethnicity, or gender of any person. And in 2009, the federal government expanded federal hate crime law through the Matthew Shepard and James Byrd, Jr. Hate Crimes Prevention Act (HCPA), which expands the authority of federal officials to investigate and prosecute hate crime cases where local authorities are unwilling or unable to act, and includes data collection on crimes directed against individuals because of their gender or gender identity and hate crimes committed by or against juveniles.

Breadth of the Problem

Several sources of national data show the prevalence of hate crimes; each has advantages and drawbacks. The FBI began collecting data after the passage of the HCSA through the Uniform Crime Reporting (UCR) Hate Crime Statistics Program. The UCR Program collects data from over 18,000 police agencies around the country. Since 1996, the number of hate crime incidents reported to the FBI has declined steadily except for an anomalous peak in 2001 and a slight increase in 2006–2008. The total number of reported hate crimes dramatically dropped from 9,730 in 2001, when hate crimes reported were at their highest, to 5,479 hate crime incidents in 2014 (Federal Bureau of Investigation, 2015).

While the distribution of hate crimes by type of bias motivation (race, religion, etc.) has followed a consistent pattern over time, current events, new legislation, and changes in law enforcement policies and practices have had a significant impact on the reporting of hate crime (e.g., Disha, Cavendish, & King, 2011; Gan, Williams, & Wiseman, 2011; Grattet & Jenness, 2008; King & Sutton, 2013; Legewie, 2013; McDevitt et al., 2003; McVeigh, Welch, & Bjarnason, 2003; Rubenstein, 2003). For example, according to the FBI hate crime statistics, 481 anti-Arab and anti-Muslim hate crimes were reported in 2001, of which 58% were perpetrated right after the 9/11 terrorist attacks. Added protections that were introduced in 2009 for crimes motivated against individuals based on their gender or gender identity have been connected to an increase in the reporting of hate crimes motivated by sexual orientation. Since 1996, the percentage of the total number of hate crime incidents motivated by sexual orientation grew from little over one tenth in 1996 to nearly one fifth in 2012.

In 2012, nearly half of the hate crime incidents reported were motivated by race (48.3%) and a smaller percentage were motivated by religion (19.0%), sexual orientation (19.6%), ethnicity/national origin (11.5%), and disability (1.6%). Of the 2,797 racially motivated hate crimes, about two thirds were anti-Black (65%) and nearly a quarter was anti-White (23%).

As with many large-scale data collection systems, the UCR Program has known limitations, such as underreporting and misclassification. Because the data are based on the number of crimes that are reported to police officials and how the crimes are classified by police officials, if a victim does not report a crime to police, regardless of the reason, the crime will not be included in the UCR numbers. And a racially motivated assault might be reported as an aggravated assault and not a bias-motivated assault because of a lack of training or bias on the part of the officers, or because the police agency might fear that reports of bias crimes might label the community as racist or homophobic (Cronin, McDevitt, Farrell, & Nolan, 2007; McDevitt, Cronin, Balboni, Farrell, Nolan, & Weiss, 2003). In addition, a large number of communities either do not report at all or they report zero hate crimes. Although many small jurisdictions may not experience a hate crime during a particular year, some of the jurisdictions that report zero crimes raise questions about data accuracy; for example, Miami reported zero hate crimes in 2012, whereas Boston reported more than 200.

Over the last two decades, a growing number of law enforcement agencies have started participating in the FBI's National Incident-Based Reporting System (NIBRS), which is a more comprehensive and detailed crime reporting system than the UCR and provides a better understanding of what occurred during an incident rather than simply the number of events. However, as of June, 2013, only about one third of the population (30%) was included in the NIBRS reporting based on the jurisdictions covered by law enforcement agencies that currently report incident-level information to NIBRS. Also, as with the UCR data, misclassification still occurs (Haas, Nolan, Turley, & Stump, 2011). Nonetheless,

NIBRS is valuable because of the level of detail it provides about each incident and the fact that it holds promise for more accurate and robust national data on hate crimes in the future. In 2008, NIBRS reported 3,017 bias-motivated incidents, making up less than 1% of the total number of reported incidents.

In addition to the data collected from law enforcement agencies, the Bureau of Justice Statistics (BJS) has collected data on hate crimes since 2003 through its National Crime Victimization Survey (NCVS), which measures crimes perceived by victims or households. According to the most recent report, the number of hate crime victimizations increased between 2004 and 2012, from 281,670 to 293,790, but the change was not found to be statistically significant (Wilson, 2014). In contrast to the FBI's programs, which collect data on hate crimes reported to the police, the NCVS allows the victim to define whether a hate crime occurred and asks whether it was reported to the police. Therefore, it measures the number of hate crimes both reported and not reported to the police (see Figure 16.1). In 2012, only about one third, 34%, of the hate crime victimizations were reported to police, whereas 60% were not reported.

However, hate crime data from NCVS are limited because NCVS only collects information from household members over the age of 12, and it excludes those living in military barracks or institutions such as nursing homes and prisons as well as the crew of vessels. Also, NCVS did not originally track repeated incidents of victimization, also known as "series victimizations," that occurred to

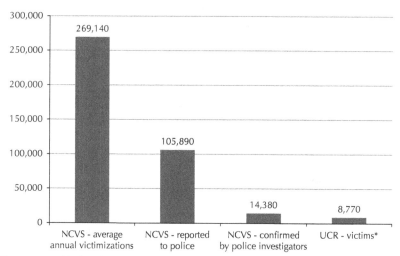

Figure 16.1 National Crime Victimization Survey (NCVS) and Uniform Crime Reporting (UCR) annual average hate crime victimizations, 2004–2012.

Source: Wilson, M.M., (2014). Hate Crime Victimization, 2004–2012—Statistical Tables. Based on data collected from the UCR Hate Crime Statistics Program 2003–2012 and NCVS 2003–2012.

a victim within a short time frame and were similar in quality. Starting in 2010, BJS modified its approach so that up to a maximum of 10 incidents experienced by the victim can be counted. In addition, the passage of the Matthew Shepherd and James Byrd, Jr. Act of 2009 added crimes motivated by bias based on gender or gender identity to the list of protected categories under the federal hate crime statute (Langton & Planty, 2011).

Therefore, there are significant differences between the two principal sources of annual information on hate crime data in the United States. The NCVS collects information on incidents and victimizations whether or not they were reported to law enforcement agencies. Hate-motivated incidents in NCVS are defined by the victim and the presence of crime scene evidence and, therefore, include incidents that may not be founded or recorded by police investigations as hate motivated. The UCR captures hate crimes against all individuals, regardless of age, as well as hate crimes against organizations, institutions, schools, churches, and businesses, whereas NCVS excludes individuals under the age of 12 and those living in institutions. Finally, the UCR includes hate crime homicides, which are excluded from the NCVS.

Given the differences between the UCR and NCVS programs, there are a number of points to note when comparing the trends in hate crimes between the two sources. First, hate crime victimizations reported to police from 2008 to 2012 declined steadily according to UCR, whereas NCVS found no statistically significant change during this time period. Second, UCR reported lower hate crime victimizations in 2012 than in 2004 and NCVS found no statistically significant different in the number of hate crime victimizations reported to police in 2004 (127,390) and 2012 (98,460). Finally, NCVS reported an annual average of 269,140 hate crime victimizations from 2004 to 2012, of which 105,890 were reported to police. However, of the 14,380 hate crime victimizations that were confirmed by police investigators from 2004 to 2012, FBI's UCR data reported an annual average number of 8,770 hate crime victims during the same period (Figure 16.1). Given the gaps in data collection, it is clear that improvement is needed in both sources of annual data collection on hate crimes.

RESEARCH ON VICTIMS

Little research has been conducted on victims of hate crimes—their responses to incidents and the impact of victimization on their lives. Nor is there a body of research on the best modes of treatment for hate crime victims, or the extent to which their needs differ from those of other types of crime. What is evident from both anecdotes and the quantitative research is that reactions to being the targets of hate crimes are both similar to and different from those of victims of random acts of violence. On the one hand, the feelings of victims of hate crimes are common to victims of crime in general: anger, fear, and vulnerability. Many crime victims experience psychosocial adjustment problems, including disorientation, fear, helplessness, anger, and depression (Davis, 1987; Office for Victims of Crime, 1994; Resick, 1987). Furthermore, being victimized by crime sparks fear of further victimization, often resulting in changes in behavior (Skogan, 1987).

As with other crime victims, the seriousness of the crime does not necessarily determine the extent of reactions of a victim of a hate crime or ethnoviolence (Ehrlich, Larcom, & Purvis, 1994). That is, someone who is the victim of repeated harassment where there is no physical injury may take longer to recover emotionally and return to a normal pattern of activities than would someone who is the victim of a serious physical assault. The duration of reactions and level of life disruption depend on a host of factors, including the social context of the incident, the meaning of the incident to the victim, the availability of a network of support, and the individual's coping mechanisms.

On the other hand, being targeted for who one is rather than for something one has done creates fears and feelings that separate victims of hate crimes from victims of random violence. Research findings indicate that victims of hate crimes do suffer more in response to incidents of comparable violence than do victims of random crimes (Dunbar, 2006; Ehrlich et al., 1994; Iganski, 2001; McDevitt et al., 2000). If one is convinced that being a victim was a coincidence of time and place, at least one can try to avoid those circumstances. But correctly believing that one is being attacked for how one looks, or for one's identity in a given group, can create an ongoing level of fear that one is forever at risk.

Another characteristic of hate crimes is that they are often committed by strangers (Harlow, 2005; Levin & McDevitt, 2003). Recent research in England concludes that even in crimes where the victim and offender know each other, the relationship is very casual, often a neighbor or coworker (Mason, 2005). Attacks by strangers tend to raise the anxiety of the victim and, in the case of hate crimes, all those who share characteristics with the victim. When victims believe that any stranger may attack them, their level of concern and anxiousness can be further heightened.

In 1986, the National Institute Against Prejudice and Violence conducted a pilot study of the effects of hate crimes on minority group members.[2] Ten focus groups were convened around the country, and victims, identified through police departments, human rights organizations, and community leaders, were interviewed using open-ended questions. Crimes the victims had experienced included physical assault; harassment and threats by mail, telephone, and in person; vandalism of their homes; and symbols or slogans of hate on their property. The costs to victims can be emotional, physical, and financial, and the effects can be long lasting. The most prevalent reaction was one of anger toward the perpetrator (68%), followed by fear for the safety of their families (51%). Over one third indicated feelings of sadness. Behavioral changes were also reported by one third of the victims. Actions taken by the victims included moving, reducing social interactions, taking security measures, and purchasing guns, both for increased safety and in preparation for retaliation if attacked again. Almost one third of the victims never reported their experiences to the police (Barnes & Ephross, 1994; Ephross, 1994; Ephross, Barnes, Ehrlich, Sandnes, & Weiss, 1986; Weiss, 1990).

The first national study designed to assess the prevalence and impact of ethnoviolence and other forms of victimization was also conducted by the National Institute Against Prejudice and Violence in 1989. Telephone interviews, using a stratified random sample, were completed with 2,078 respondents. To determine how the experience of being victimized in general compared with being victimized because of prejudice, interviewers asked subjects about symptoms they experienced that are associated with stress. A comparison of four groups of respondents—nonvictims, victims of group defamation, victims of random crimes, and victims of hate crimes—revealed that victims of ethnoviolence experienced the greatest number of negative psychophysiological symptoms as well as the most social and behavioral changes of any group. (Examples of psychological and psychophysiological symptoms included feeling depressed or sad, feeling more nervous than usual, having trouble sleeping, and feeling very angry. Social and behavioral changes included items such as "moved to another neighborhood"; "tried to be less visible"; "bought or started carrying a gun"; "took a self-defense class.") The study concluded that victims of ethnoviolence exhibited more symptoms with greater frequency than did victims of random violence (Ehrlich et al., 1994).

Another study, which was conducted in Boston from 1992 to 1997, compared the impact of aggravated assault in bias-motivated cases and non-bias-motivated cases. The researchers found that bias crime victims were more likely to be attacked by a group of attackers than nonbias victims, and bias crime victims were significantly less likely to have a prior relationship with the offender. Nearly all bias assaults were committed by strangers, and most of those victims reported that the assault was an unprovoked attack. Whereas the victims of nonbias assaults could foresee how they could prevent such crimes in the future by changing their behavior, bias crime victims expressed feelings of frustration and felt powerless to protect themselves in the future. On measures of postevent stress, bias victims had a higher incidence of adverse psychological sequelae than the nonbias control group on all 19 of the items measured. Bias victims also felt less safe after the crime and suffered more health problems (McDevitt et al., 2001).

PRACTICE PRINCIPLES

One challenge in establishing a group for victims is that hate crimes that are reported to criminal justice authorities are relatively rare in any given community. Although formally recognized hate crimes might be rare, many more individuals experience incidents motivated by bias or bigotry that may not rise to the level of a hate crime under current state or federal statutes. These victims also experience many of the same reactions, including feelings of fear, vulnerability, and anger. A group can be more easily established, and more bias crime victims serviced, if agencies and workers use a broad definition of who is a hate crime victim.

Maintain Objectivity and Balance

In working with victims of hate crimes in groups, it is critical that social workers be in touch with (1) their own personal experiences with hate crimes that might affect the way they view others' experiences and (2) prejudices that might interfere with working with such victims. As NASW's 2007 cultural competency guidelines state,[3] workers not only must demonstrate respect for those who are different from the worker but also are required to examine their own cultural backgrounds and experiences, and to acknowledge how fears, ignorance, and the "isms" (racism, sexism, ethnocentrism, heterosexism, ageism, classism) have influenced their attitudes, beliefs, and feelings. Although this principle applies under all circumstances, working with victims of hate crimes calls for a particular combination of skills:

> A worker must be empathic and sensitive to the pain, yet maintain sufficient detachment to be effective. . . . Maintaining this delicate balance can cause a worker considerable stress. Additional strain often derives from the inherent limits of the situation: legal remedies are often infeasible or unenforceable. The perpetrator is nameless and faceless, official response sometimes denigrates the experience, and the ultimate enemy—the conditions and institutions that breed the isms in society—seem undefeatable. (Weiss & Ephross, 1986, p. 134)

Understand Intergroup Relations

It is important that the social worker not only have a general understanding of the history of minority groups and their interactions with each other but also to have a clear sense of the intergroup factors that exist in the community in which one is working. This is true in general, but particularly so for those dealing with hate crimes. Isolated incidents can lead to widespread intergroup conflict, and lower levels of harassment can escalate into more violent acts (Iganski, 2001; Levin & Rabrenovic, 2001; McDevitt et al., 2001; Wessler & Moss, 2001). The stereotypes minority groups have about each other, and the possibility of competition between victim groups, can interfere with the goals of the group. The social worker must understand the history and current state of Black–Jewish relations in a community, for example, or the feelings of other minority groups regarding the apparent success of Asian American immigrants.

Current events that have an impact are critical to consider. Events like the terrorist acts of September 11, 2001, created thousands of victims and also had a ripple effect, resulting in crimes directed at those perceived as Muslim and Arab American and, hence, connected somehow to the terrorism. Other factors that exist in the group, often as silent contributors to tension, are race/ethnicity and social class, the interplay of which influences reactions such as resentment and lack of empathy and must be understood.

Group workers must also keep abreast of legislative and political events and changing social mores that affect members of the group and attitudes of others. For example, recent and rapid changes in laws pertaining to the gay and lesbian community can have a dramatic impact. As of early 2015, 37 states had legalized same-sex marriage, and a decision by the Supreme Court on whether state bans on same-sex marriage are unconstitutional is pending. Such changes in community norms, while offering greater acceptance to long ostracized minority group members, can also inflame preexisting prejudices and can lead to an increase in hate crimes against the subject group. Although not new, violence directed against transgender individuals has increasingly received media coverage. As some groups, such as gay couples, become more mainstream, formerly more hidden minorities sometimes emerge from the shadows, with their greater visibility resulting in more, and more widely reported, victimization.

Focus on the Present and on the Individual

The issues surrounding intergroup relations and the historical factors affecting victims' feelings demand that the social worker acknowledge the impact of the past. Racial/ethnic group histories can become a major force to be contended with in victim groups and can be used by group members to avoid dealing with the current victimization issues. Victims may want to talk about historical events that affected their families and are recalled by the current incidents. Without minimizing the impact of history, the social worker must help the individual and the group stay focused on the effects of recent events and how they affected the victim. It is important that group members be helped to see the costs and benefits of identifying themselves as victims, and the positive results that could result from their gaining a feeling of empowerment.

COMMON THEMES

Fear

The fear connected with hate crimes often affects not only the individual victim but the victim's family and community as well. An underestimated aspect of hate crimes is the ripple effect on the community. One case one of the authors dealt with involved a Black family who had a cross burned on their lawn. They had a young daughter and, after the incident, were very fearful that the unknown perpetrator would attack again. Overly cautious behavior began to govern their lives. They would no longer allow their daughter to walk alone to her friends' houses on the same block, for fear that she might be in danger. Worse, families in the neighborhood—well-meaning and supportive on the surface—would not let their children visit the home of the victim family, for fear that their children might be in danger if another, more serious, incident occurred while they were visiting.

Herek (2009) discusses violence against individuals because of their presumed sexual orientation as a manifestation of "sexual stigma"—that is, society's negative regard for any nonheterosexual behavior, identity, relationship, or community. He notes that sexual minority victims of hate crimes not only have the same psychological sequelae as other victims but also may be motivated to engage in self-protective behaviors such as concealing their sexual orientation. Such reactions would restrict their opportunities for normal social interaction and receiving support.

Fear associated with having been targeted for attack can manifest itself in the group. Individuals may be highly suspicious of others and be reluctant to trust the social worker, or, if it was a racial incident, any members of another race, for example. A primary focus of initial stages of the group should be to help members feel safe in the group so acute symptoms can be addressed.

Anger

Many victims of hate crimes are angry. The anger is directed not just toward the perpetrator, whether known or unknown. Frequently, there is a great deal of anger toward the police. The rate of arrest for crime is low to begin with, and it is extremely low in cases of property crime where the perpetrator acted under cover of darkness, without witnesses. Victims often feel frustrated by the lack of resolution and afraid of the nameless, faceless enemy, about whom they can do nothing. That frustration is often directed at the police and other aspects of the criminal justice system, and it can extend to others in the school or other site of attack, because victims often are not sure who sympathizes with them and who sympathizes with the enemy. Anger and frustration may also be directed at the social worker and other members of the group.

Members must be given an opportunity to vent their feelings and have them validated by others in the group, lest they turn the anger toward themselves. A major goal of the group is to help the victims move beyond their anger so that they can deal with the aftermath of incidents constructively and have their daily routines return to normalcy.

Physical and Psychological Symptoms and Behaviors

Like other types of victimization, hate crimes can result in a wide range of physical and psychological symptoms. Examples of physical symptoms are changes in sleep patterns (difficulty falling asleep, waking frequently during the night), weight loss or gain, onset or exacerbation of back pain or other ailments, and development of nervous tics. Psychological symptoms may include fear of all strangers who look like the perpetrator (or imagined perpetrator); being particularly jumpy in response to unexpected noise; acting suspicious of everyone, including friends and acquaintances, if the act was committed by a stranger ("How do I know whom I can trust?"); or having intrusive thoughts about the incident. Changes in behaviors include resuming or increasing smoking or drinking, changing routes walked or driven to work, changing jobs, moving, staying home, or becoming particularly protective of children. Some symptoms may manifest themselves in ways victims may be unaware of. Conversely, victims can blame their victimization for things that occur in their lives that may or may not be connected to the victimization.

A critical role for the social worker in working with groups of victims of hate crimes is to facilitate discussions of symptoms and behaviors that are problematic for the group members and to help them separate the ones related to the victimization from the ones that need other types of attention. Because of the wide-ranging nature of symptoms that need to be addressed in the wake of hate crime experiences, effective treatment often requires the integration of behavioral, cognitive, and multicultural counseling modalities (Dunbar, 2001). Furthermore, when working with members of a minority group, workers should be sensitive to the possibility of unexpressed victimization as an underlying issue in cases of depression and/or anxiety.

Literature on working with trauma victims can be useful. When mutual aid is provided in a group setting, it can be beneficial for members working through the effects of trauma such as posttraumatic stress disorder. Although group members may be frightened by, and attempt to avoid, powerful displays of emotion, talking about the feelings, not just about the trauma itself, is critical to healing (Knight, 2006). As stated earlier, self-awareness on the part of the worker is critical. The importance of an understanding by the worker of the impact of having had similar life experiences to the clients or, conversely, of attitudes and feelings that might interfere with the work cannot be overstated. Social workers who are uncomfortable with painful experiences in their own lives may find it difficult to encourage painful disclosures by others (Brown, 1991).

Dealing With Legal Issues and the Criminal Justice System

It is important that the social worker be able to serve as an advocate for the victim and make appropriate referrals to legal resources while maintaining clear boundaries. Hate-motivated incidents may not always be crimes by legal definition but can affect the victim in significant ways nonetheless. Some victims, for example, may be suffering because of repeated verbal harassment where there is no legal recourse because the incidents did not rise to the level of criminal behavior. In some cases, the victim may be working with the police to identify perpetrators; in others, there may be no leads to the perpetrators. In still other cases, the victims may be loath to report the victimization to police either because of fear (as in the case of undocumented individuals who are victims) or because of past experience of unresponsiveness of the police (Doerner & Lab, 1995). Issues and concerns frequently arise that are related to working with the criminal justice system. Victims worry, "Will I be in danger if I identify the perpetrator or testify at a trial? Will my family? Can the police protect me? What will happen during the trial? Who will pay for the damage to my property?"

As with all groups, members can benefit a great deal from each other's experiences. Social workers should be knowledgeable about the laws and criminal justice practices that apply both in the state and the local jurisdiction in which they work, and be able to answer basic questions. To do so, workers should familiarize themselves with the reporting structures and their implications in the jurisdictions in which they practice. Although it is appropriate for social workers to be advocates, and identify appropriate resources and information within the criminal justice system that might be helpful to clients, they should not give advice on whether to press charges or take particular actions that the police or others might recommend; instead, they should facilitate group members' own decision-making processes.

Continued Interaction With an Offender/Perpetrator

When the incidents have occurred in the workplace or when the perpetrator is someone the victim comes into contact with regularly, such as a next-door neighbor, victims need guidance on how to handle unavoidable interactions and how to avoid confrontations. These incidents often take the form of persistent harassment, sometimes in subtle ways over a long period, and are designed to force the victim to react. The offender may be trying to force the victim to quit her job or move out of the community. Victims need help in assessing the possible ramifications of taking formal actions to stop the perpetrators. Discussion of the pros and cons of such actions, and of how best to handle interactions with the perpetrators, often forms a significant part of a group's content and consciousness.

RECOMMENDED WAYS OF WORKING

Agency Context

Workers need to understand and consider the auspices under which the group will meet. Organizational issues that are critical include goals and objectives, history, traditions, funding (including fees), records, authority, communication, and psychosocial climate (Wickham, 2003). One type of agency particularly well suited for convening groups of hate crime victims is a local human rights (or human relations) agency that traditionally deals with cases of discrimination in housing, employment, and public accommodations. Some human relations commissions have a community relations component that specializes in intergroup conflict in the community. Certain school systems, those used to dealing with intergroup tension, can also provide the official context for such groups, particularly when juveniles are involved, either as victims or perpetrators. Mental health associations or interfaith organizations also often have programs designed to promote positive intergroup relations and can provide a setting for groups of hate crime victims.

For groups of hate crime victims, the *meaning* of the setting to the members is important to consider. The members should feel safe. For example, if a school was the site of the incident, it might not be a good place to meet, although an exception to this situation might be a group whose purpose is to bring together victims and offenders.

Time Frame

Hate crime victims need immediate crisis counseling and help in dealing with the initial aftermath of the incident. It is important to provide assistance within a few days so that the immediate fear of danger can be addressed. Although there is no reason that groups of victims should not meet for a long period (12 months or more), and the group members could certainly provide support for each other through the often grueling aspects of arrest and trial, if they occur, the most critical time is often the first few weeks following an incident when the victim is feeling particularly vulnerable and angry. A short-term group (8 to 10 weeks) can frequently address the most critical issues.

Open Versus Closed Groups

Although either type can be used, there are several advantages to an open group when working with victims. One never knows when support for victims will be needed, and it is better for a victim to have immediate access to an ongoing group, and deal with problems of acceptance and entry, than to have to wait until a new group starts. Incidents, with or without physical harm, should be treated as crises initially. It is important to note that victims at different stages can help each other, not only with emotional support but also with practical advice (such as dealing with the police and other aspects of the justice system).

Co-Leadership Team With Different Races, Ethnicities, or Orientations

Victims of hate crimes are often more wary of other groups after an incident. Although a co-leadership team can represent only a few categories, it is frequently advantageous for such a team to work with a victim group. Co-leaders can diffuse the fear and distrust that might exist toward a particular person who might look like the perpetrator. Co-leaders can model openness about racial or other sensitive issues. In addition, co-leadership can provide mutual support for workers when group interactions are especially charged or volatile. Although White social workers may feel less successful when working with minority group members than do minority social workers (Davis & Gelsomino, 1994), a co-leadership team may contribute to the success of the group.

WORKING WITH THE ENTIRE FAMILY WHEN THE VICTIM IS A CHILD

Sometimes the group consists simply of the family. An important issue when a child is targeted, either in the neighborhood or in school, is that of parents becoming overprotective. In some cases, the child may want to return to normal routines, which may make parents uneasy. Parents sometimes want the child to change schools or stop walking to school, when the child is worried more about the stigma attached to those behaviors than to any danger. In other cases a child who has been harassed or intimidated is too ashamed to tell parents and is worried about their reaction, particularly if the parents have shared stories of their own experiences. This is a particular problem for youth who are harassed because they are perceived to be members of the LBGTQ community and have not spoken about sexual identity with their parents. The social worker can help family members separate the realities from the fears and help the parents and child sort out what is relevant from the past and what needs to be addressed now.

DEALING WITH LANGUAGE BARRIERS

An inadequate command of the English language coupled with cultural differences may prevent some victims of hate crimes from reporting incidents or participating in programs of support. Studies by service providers have pointed to the language barrier as one factor that makes access to services difficult for some minority groups (Browne & Broderick, 1994). Provision of service may be complicated by relationships within a family where children are fluent in English and serve as interpreters for parents. In such cases, the children may be more comfortable dealing with the authorities and the justice system, whereas the parents are distrustful and anxious. There are several ways to address the language barriers. One is for materials providing helpful information and resources to be printed in as many languages as possible for a given community. Another is to limit some groups to a particular victim population and arrange for an interpreter to work with the social worker if a social worker who speaks the language of the victims is not available or trained to work with groups. In addition, social workers can train bilingual members of the victim community to serve as facilitators in self-help groups. Of course, attempts by the worker to gain even minimal command of other languages are helpful and appreciated by group members.

MEDIATION BETWEEN THE VICTIM AND THE OFFENDER

Ad hoc short-term groups can be an important tool of social workers dealing with hate crimes. Mediating the conflict between the victim and the offender can be the purpose of such group, particularly when there is continued interaction between the victim and the offender through work, school, or neighborhood contact. Critical group work skills are required for effective mediation. Following is a case study of a successful use of mediation:

> A 16-year-old White youth assaulted a Black youth the same age on a bas-
> ketball court during an informal after-school game, calling him names such
> as "dirty nigger." The fight was stopped by a school official. Police were not
> called because there were no serious injuries and no weapon was involved.
> Because a racial epithet had been used, however, and officials learned that
> the White youth had been harassing the Black youth for some time, they
> contacted the local human-relations commission and asked for assistance.
> There was fear that the tension between the youths would spill over to other
> students and become more violent. The community relations specialist, a
> White female social worker, had the school arrange a meeting with both
> youths at the school one evening. Each student was required to bring one
> parent. The social worker brought a Black male police officer experienced
> in community relations work. No school official was permitted to partici-
> pate. Over the course of two sessions of 2 hours each, the Black student
> had a chance to talk about his feelings about being called racist names and
> being attacked. The White student expressed no remorse at first, only anger
> toward the Black student, who had teased him for months because he was
> very small in stature. When the Black student realized how painful the
> White youth's experience of being small was for him, and had been for
> years, he was able to forgive the assault. The mediation was followed up by
> periodic contacts for the rest of the school year; the intervention was suc-
> cessful in averting what could have been an explosive situation.

EVALUATION APPROACHES

There have been no rigorous evaluations of work with groups of hate crime victims. It would not be too difficult to evaluate the impact of such groups, however,

if a social worker wanted to do so. The primary purpose of such groups is to help victims express and work through the psychological and psychophysiological symptoms they experience, and empower them to make critical decisions relevant to the criminal justice system if that is relevant, and about choices they need to make (such as whether to report to the police, interact with the offender, move, change jobs, etc.).

One way to evaluate the effectiveness of the group experience is to have members fill out questionnaires at the inception and conclusion of their group experience. The questionnaire would ask for information regarding the nature of the incident, symptoms they are experiencing, concerns they have, and decisions they would like to make. They could then complete a similar questionnaire at the termination of their time in the group, and possibly also at a point in the future, to measure changes in attitudes and experiences and to determine how much they felt they had accomplished. A somewhat stronger research design might compare these responses to other groups of hate crime victims who did not engage in postincident group therapy.

With juveniles, both they and their parents could fill out relevant questionnaires. Follow-up could be done with them as well as with their teachers, if the victimization was affecting classroom performance and/or behavior.

CONCLUSION

Groups offer particular advantages for work with victims of hate crimes. Working with such groups calls for sophisticated knowledge both of the issues involved and of group work skills. Social workers must have a clear understanding of the manifestations of victimization based on race, religion, ethnicity, sexual orientation, gender identity, or disability in order to determine whether crises in the group are related to group process, the stage of development, or to individuals' experiences of trauma.

An issue that cannot be avoided is the proliferation of modes of technology and their potential for victimization (see also Chapter 14, this volume). Cyberbullying is getting considerable attention; there are not only regular reports in the media, but efforts by schools to address the effects on students. *Hate Crimes in Cyberspace* (Citron, 2014) focuses primarily on attacks against women, but it highlights the insidiousness and profound impact on victims of Internet harassment and threats of violence. Such attacks call for innovative modes of treatment. Social workers, who are in the forefront of working with groups, need to think creatively about ways to work with victims of cyberattacks, perhaps exploring the role of online groups for this purpose.

Knowledge about hate crimes is also valuable for social workers called on to work with other types of groups. Interorganizational task groups or committees created to address the issue of violence in schools, workplaces, or communities would benefit from social workers' knowledge of hate crimes and the ways they affect both individuals and the groups to which they belong. Additional information about hate crimes could be obtained from a local police department or human rights agency or from the resources listed at the end of this chapter.

RESOURCES

American-Arab Anti-Discrimination Committee
1732 Wisconsin Avenue, NW
Washington, DC 20007
202-244-2990
http://www.adc.org

Anti-Defamation League
823 United Nations Plaza
New York, NY 10017
202-885-7700
http://www.adl.org

Asian American Legal Defense and Education Fund
99 Hudson Street, 12th Floor
New York, NY 10013
212-966-5932
http://www.aaldef.org

Leadership Conference on Civil Rights
1629 K Street NW, 10th Floor
Washington, DC 20006
202-466-3311
http://www.civilrights.org

NAACP National Headquarters
4805 Mt. Hope Drive
Baltimore, MD 21215
877-NCCAP-98
http://www.naacp.org

National Center for Transgender Equality
1327 Massachusetts Avenue, N.W., #700
Washington, DC 20005
http://www.transequaliy.org

National Coalition of Anti-Violence Programs
and The Anti-Violence Project
240 West 35th Street, Suite 200
New York, NY 10001
212-714-1184
http://www.ncavp.org

Southern Poverty Law Center
400 Washington Avenue
Montgomery, AL 36104
334-956-8200
http://www.splcenter.org

US Department of Justice Community Relations Service
600 E Street, NW, Suite 6000
Washington, DC 20530
202-305-2935
http://www.usdoj.gov/crs

REFERENCES

Barnes, A. J., & Ephross, P. H. (1994). The impact of hate violence on victims: Emotional and behavioral responses to attacks. *Social Work*, *39*(3), 247–251.

Berk, R. A., Boyd, E. A., & Hammer, K. M. (1992). Thinking more clearly about hate motivated crimes. In G. Herek & K. Berrill (Eds.), *Hate crimes: Confronting violence against lesbians and gay men* (pp. 137–143). Thousand Oaks, CA: Sage.

Brown, L. (1991). *Groups for growth and change*. New York, NY: Longman.

Browne, C., & Broderick, A. (1994). Asian and Pacific Island elders: Issues for social work practice and education. *Social Work*, *39*(3), 252–259.

Citron, D. K. (2014). *Hate crimes in cyberspace*. Cambridge, MA: Harvard University Press.

Cronin, S. W., McDevitt, J., Farrell, A., & Nolan, J. J. (2007). Bias-crime reporting: Organizational responses to ambiguity, uncertainty, and infrequency in eight police departments. *American Behavioral Scientist*, *51*, 213–231.

Davis, L. E., & Gelsomino, J. (1994). An assessment of practitioner cross-racial treatment experiences. *Social Work*, *39*(1), 116–123.

Davis, R. C. (1987). Studying the effects of services for victims in crisis. *Crime and Delinquency*, *33*(4), 520–531.

Disha, I., Cavendish, J. C., & King, R. D. (2011). Historical events and spaces of hate: Hate crimes against Arabs and Muslims in post-9/11 America. *Social Problems*, *58*(1), 21–46.

Doerner, W. G., & Lab, S. P. (1995). *Victimology*. Cincinnati, OH: Anderson.

Dunbar, E. (2001). Counseling practices to ameliorate the effects of discrimination and hate events. *Counseling Psychologist, 29*(2), 279–307.

Dunbar, E. (2006). The importance of race and gender membership in sexual orientation hate crime victimization and reportage: Identity politics or identity risk? *Violence and Victims, 21*(3), 323–337.

Ehrlich, H. J., Larcom, B. E. K., & Purvis, R. D. (1994). *The traumatic effects of ethnoviolence*. Baltimore, MD: The Prejudice Institute.

Ephross, P. H., Barnes, A. J., Ehrlich, H. J., Sandnes, K. R., & Weiss, J. C. (1986). *The Ethnoviolence Project Pilot Study*. Baltimore, MD: National Institute Against Prejudice and Violence.

Federal Bureau of Investigation, U.S. Department of Justice. Uniform Crime Reports. (2015). Hate crime reports. Retrieved November 2, 2015 from: https://www.fbi.gov/about-us/cjis/ucr/hate-crime/2014

Gan, L., Williams, R. C., & Wiseman, T. (2011). A simple model of optimal hate crime legislation. *Economic Inquiry, 49*(3), 674–684.

Grattet, R., & Jenness, V. (2008). Transforming symbolic law into organizational action: Hate crime policy and law enforcement practice. *Social Forces, 87*(1), 1–28.

Haas, S. M., Nolan, J. J., Turley, E., & Stump, J. (2011). *Assessing the validity of hate crime reporting: An analysis of NIBRS data*. Charleston, WV: Criminal Justice Statistical Analysis Center.

Herek, G. M. (2009). Hate crimes and stigma-related expeiences among sexual minority adults in the United States. *Journal of Interpersonal Violence, 24*(1), 54–72.

Iganski, P. (2001). Hate crimes hurt more. *American Behavioral Scientist, 45*(4), 626–638.

King, R. D., & Sutton, G. M. (2013). High times for hate crimes: Explaining the temporal clustering of hate-motivated offending. *Criminology, 51*(4), 871–894.

Knight, C. (2006). Groups for individuals with traumatic histories: Practice considerations for social workers. *Social Work*, 24(1), 20–30.

Langton, L., & Planty, M. (2011). *Hate crimes, 2003–2009*. Washington, DC: Bureau of Justice Statistics, US Department of Justice. Retrieved from, http://www.bjs.gov/content/pub/ascii/hc0309.txt

Legewie, J. (2013). Terrorist events and attitudes toward immigrants: A natural experiment. *American Journal of Sociology, 118*(5), 1199–1245.

Levin, J., & Rabrenovic, G. (2001). Hate crimes and ethnic conflict. *American Behavioral Scientist, 45*(4), 574–587.

Mason, G. (2005). Hate crime and the image of the stranger. *British Journal of Criminology, 45*, 837–859.

McDevitt, J., Balboni, J., & Bennett, S. (2000). *Improving the quality and accuracy of bias crime statistics nationally*. Washington, DC: Bureau of Justice Statistics, US Department of Justice.

McDevitt, J., Cronin, S., Balboni, J., Farrell, A., Nolan, J., & Weiss, J. (2003). *Bridging the information disconnect in bias crime reporting*. Washington, DC: Bureau of Justice Statistics, US Department of Justice.

McVeigh, R., Welch, M. R., & Bjarnason, T. (2003). Hate crime reporting as a successful social movement outcome. *American Sociological Review, 68*, 843–867.

Rubenstein, W. B. (2003). The real story of U.S. hate crime statistics: An empirical analysis. *Tulane Law Review, 78*, 1213–1246.

Weiss, J. C. (1990) Violence motivated by bigotry: "Ethnoviolence." In *Encyclopedia of social work* (18th ed., 1990 supplement, pp. 307–319). L. Ginsberg, Ed. Silver Spring, MD: National Association of Social Workers.

Weiss, J. C., & Ephross, P. H. (1986). Group work approaches to hate/violence incidents. *Social Work, 31*(2), 132–136.

Wessler, S., & Moss, M. (2001). *Hate crimes on campus: The problem and efforts to confront it.* Washington, DC: Bureau of Justice Assistance, US Department of Justice.

Wickham, E. (2003). *Group treatment in social work* (2nd ed.). Toronto, ON: Thompson Educational.

Wilson, M. M. (2014). *Hate crime victimization, 2004–2012.* Washington, DC: Bureau of Justice Statistics. Retrieved from http://www.bjs.gov/index.cfm?ty=pbdetail&iid=4905

NOTES

1 Legislation in some jurisdictions has expanded the reach of protected classes. For example, in May 2009, Maryland became the first state to extend hate crime protection to homeless people, and a number of state statutes and the federal statute include gender and gender identity. Although the information contained in this chapter is relevant to persons victimized because of any group affiliation, the focus is on race, religion, ethnicity, and sexual orientation, only because far less information is available about working with other populations in a hate crimes context.

2 The National Institute Against Prejudice and Violence closed in 1995; some of its work was continued by The Prejudice Institute.

3 "Indicators for the Achievement of the NASW Standards for Cultural Competence in Social Work Practice" is posted on the National Association of Social Workers Web site (www.socialworkers.org) under NASW Standards, 2007.

Chapter Seventeen

Group Work With Survivors of Sex Trafficking

Kristine E. Hickle and Dominique Roe-Sepowitz

According to the Victims of Trafficking and Violence Protection Act (TVPA, 2000), sex trafficking involves the "recruitment, harbouring, transportation, provision, or obtaining of a person for the purpose of a commercial sex act" (22 U.S.C. § 7102). The TVPA further clarifies that sex trafficking occurs when there is evidence that a commercial sex act is induced by force, fraud, or coercion unless the victim is under the age of 18, in which case no evidence or proof is required. The prevalence of sex trafficking in the United States is currently unknown, as no uniform data collection system exists to track identified victims and the nature of sex trafficking victimization is often covert (Macy & Graham, 2012). Since the TVPA was enacted in the United States, and the United Nations adopted the Palermo Protocols (2000) using similar language to define sex trafficking, global awareness and understanding regarding sex trafficking victimization continues to grow.

This includes an increased awareness of related forms of sexual exploitation. This form of violence occurs in the context of a relationship between a vulnerable person and an individual or group who uses a position of power to profit socially, politically, or financially (herein a specific overlap in the definition of sex trafficking) from the vulnerable person's sexual exploitation (Gerassi, 2015). In this chapter, we will use the term "sex trafficking" throughout, as it is consistent with the TVPA definition and encompasses the sexual exploitation of children and youth, including both commercial sex exchanges and other forms of exploitation.

REVIEW OF THE LITERATURE

Negative Consequences of Experiencing Sex Trafficking

Survivors of sex trafficking often report experiences of coercive and violent relationships, substance abuse, economic instability, and exposure to trauma that can result in physical and mental health issues, and feelings of having lost control over their lives. Relationships with traffickers are often further complicated by an emotional connection or bond that is established by a trafficker who initially pursues a romantic relationship with a potential victim, builds trust by providing for basic needs or giving gifts, and/or then isolates the victim from positive social support (Reid, 2014; Williamson & Prior, 2009). Women and girls working for a trafficker (i.e., pimp or facilitator) often are taught to abide by strict rules that are enforced with physical violence (Raphael, Reichert, & Powers, 2010).

Trafficked individuals may also experience violence perpetrated by customers who purchase sexual services from them in both indoor and outdoor settings (Church, Henderson, Barnard, & Hart, 2001; Dalla, 2003; Raphael & Shapiro, 2004). Male and transgender sex workers report being robbed by clients (Weinberg, Shaver, & Williams, 1999), and, among homeless young people who engage in survival sex to meet basic needs, a recent report found that initial sex trading "frequently turned into coercive and violent trafficking experiences" (Covenant House, 2013, p. 6). Survivors of sex trafficking may also suffer from drug or alcohol addiction (Potterat, Rothenberg, Muth, Darrow, & Phillips-Plummer, 1998; Reid & Piquero, 2013). Young et al. (2000) found that some sex industry workers (who may or may not have been trafficked/exploited) reported using drugs to help cope with internal (i.e., trauma and psychological distress) and external (i.e., violence) stressors. The abuse of substances, in turn, renders victims more susceptible to further trauma and violence, thus perpetuating the cycle that keeps individuals vulnerable to sexually exploitative relationships and drug addiction.

These experiences contribute to psychological distress, the development of trauma symptoms, and other mental health concerns (Burnette et al., 2008; Vanwesenbeeck, 2005). In a study of 204 trafficked women and girls across seven European countries, a majority reported mental health symptoms, including depression (54.9%), anxiety (48%), and posttraumatic stress disorder (77%) (Hossain, Zimmerman, Abas, Light, & Watts, 2010). These findings highlight the importance of recognizing and addressing the mental health consequences of sex trafficking victimization in services for trafficking survivors.

Benefits of Group Work With Survivors of Sex Trafficking

Group work offers an efficient and effective means to address traumatic experiences (Foy, Eriksson, & Trice, 2001). To date, the research on group work with adults or young people who have experienced sex trafficking is limited. However, group work has long been used to address traumatic experiences among victims of related experiences, including childhood sexual abuse (Avinger & Jones, 2007) and domestic violence (Straka & Montminy, 2006) and, as such, represents the kind of good practice upon which interventions for sex-trafficked individuals should be built (Dodsworth, 2014). Group work can be helpful in promoting self-disclosure and reducing isolation among members (Olson-McBride & Page, 2012). This is particularly important for sex trafficking survivors who often feel isolated, ashamed, or fearful about the consequences of disclosing what has happened (Hickle, 2014; Raphael et al., 2010). In a recent study of a group for sex-trafficked adolescent girls, Thomson et al. (2011) found that the group treatment format was specifically effective in helping participants acknowledge sex trafficking experiences in their lives and committing to a comprehensive treatment plan.

Group work also provides the opportunity to bring taboo subjects out into the open (Drumm, 2006). For sex trafficking survivors, these taboo subjects may include involvement in pornography, sex trading for drugs, or being trafficked by family members. The group format allows members to talk about these taboo subjects without requiring high levels of self-disclosure (Avinger & Jones, 2007). In our own work creating a group intervention for sex-trafficked girls, this became a key component of the group's success, as group members began to engage with strong emotions and connections to the group leaders and other group members while remaining safe and stable throughout the group experience (Hickle & Roe-Sepowitz, 2014).

Groups for sex trafficking survivors may vary in size and composition, depending on the setting in which a group takes place. However, group leaders should be intentional about identifying inclusion criteria prior to beginning the group, communicating a clear definition of sex trafficking to potential group members and/or those responsible for referring members to the group. Many people are still likely to hold misconceptions about the nature of sex trafficking.

Groups can be provided in an open or closed format depending on the setting and the group leadership's preference. Developing a curriculum around an open group format with 10 or 12 weeks of topics can be successful in settings where the nature of service provision is voluntary (e.g., drop-in centers for homeless youth) or the length of involvement in services is unpredictable (e.g., residential treatment, detention centers). In addition, the emerging research on intervention services for sex trafficking victims indicates that these services must be flexible (Gibbs, Hardison Walters, Lutnick, Miller, & Kluckman, 2015). A more open group format allows for flexibility as members may need several interactions with service providers before they fully engage with intervention services. A closed group may be preferable in court-ordered and prison settings with the requirement that the participant must commit to completing the group series in sequence or in those situations where an increased level of intimacy is needed to assist members in connecting with and disclosing information to one another.

Groups for survivors of sex trafficking are often conceptualized as gender-specific (i.e., girls only), though we have run both gender-specific (women or girls only) and mixed-gender groups. In each case, the organizational context has determined if the group was heterogeneous or homogeneous with respect to gender. For example, in a girls' residential treatment program or a women's prison, gender specific was the only choice. In settings like a drop-in center for homeless and runaway youth, having the group available to all possible attendees of any gender was most appropriate. It is important to consider that sex trafficking victims of any gender can also transition into being sex traffickers. These victims/traffickers can participate in recruitment activities and training and managing other sex trafficking victims in the role of a "bottom bitch" or to simply survive the experience by obeying their trafficker. This issue of victim/trafficker can be discussed in a sex-trafficking-specific group, but the group leaders should be alert for recruitment behaviors and actions of dominance and control between group members.

COMMON THEMES

Past and Present Trauma

Sex trafficking victimization occurs within the wider context of survivors' lives. For many, difficult experiences early in life such as child maltreatment, parental substance abuse, and domestic violence within the home result in posttraumatic symptoms that emerge before being trafficked (Dalla, 2003; Nadon, Koverola, & Schludermann, 1998). When survivors leave sex trafficking situations and begin to feel safe, the abusive experiences that occurred outside sex trafficking relationships may become important to address.

In the group intervention we created, topics including familial abuse, domestic violence, and understanding posttraumatic stress disorder (PTSD) are presented alongside discussions about sex trafficking (Hickle & Roe-Sepowitz, 2014). This approach aims to give group members ownership of their experiences, without presuming that one traumatic experience can be prioritized over others. Group leaders should consider ways to offer flexible sessions wherein members feel safe to explore a range of experiences and should not assume that members view their own sex trafficking experiences as the most difficult form of victimization they have endured. In fact, members may minimize their trafficking experiences as they hear the disclosures of others (Hackney, 2015).

Group leaders should also be mindful of the potential for diverse experiences to isolate members or create divisions within the group (Gitterman, 2005). It is particularly important that group members are not revictimized within the group by other members who further stigmatize their experience. For example, in a group I (first author) facilitated, an adolescent girl told the group about feeling betrayed by a boyfriend who convinced her to sell sex and hand over the money she made directly to him. Another group member said that she would never hand over the money she earned, implying that she would never be so easily deceived. This response had the potential to further stigmatize the first girl who shared her experience and to create an unsafe atmosphere for all within the group. It was important for us, as group leaders, to address the interaction by reminding the group of the rules (including "no judging"), communicating our commitment to keeping group members safe, and generalizing the experience of betrayal so that other group members could connect to (and affirm) the young woman's experience.

Anger and Aggression

Sex trafficking survivors often are characterized as helpless victims in media, popular culture, criminal justice, and immigration systems (Hua & Nigorizawa, 2010). This can limit the available narratives with which survivors are able to identify, along with the range of emotions and behaviors they are "allowed" to exhibit. Expressing and managing anger and aggression have not been discussed at great length in terms of the treatment needs of sex trafficking survivors. It has been our experience, however, that group leaders should be prepared to address these reactions when they emerge in a group setting. Aggressive behavior has been associated with PTSD in other populations, including combat veterans (Begic, 2001), so group leaders should be prepared to address both anger and aggression as themes that may emerge within a group of sex trafficking survivors who are likely to also be experiencing posttraumatic stress symptoms (Roe-Sepowitz, Hickle, & Cimino, 2012).

Group members will need to develop skills for how to express anger in healthy and safe ways, and be given opportunities to increase emotional literacy so that they can identify the feelings and emotions that often underlie or accompany anger. Group members may also need opportunities to explore alternatives to aggressive behavior. One particularly effective group activity we use involves brainstorming the differences between aggressive and assertive behaviors. Group members are led to explore scenarios in which they may typically use aggressive actions to feel safe or in control of a situation. They are then encouraged to explore how these scenarios could be approached using assertive behaviors, including openly expressing feelings, listening to others, accepting responsibility, maintaining self-control, and setting boundaries.

Grief and Loss

Dealing with grief and loss is also an important part of recovering from the trauma associated with sex trafficking victimization (Pierce, 2012). Prior research indicates that group work is an effective means to address traumatic grief and loss among adolescents (Saltzman, Pynoos, Layne, Steinberg, & Aisenberg, 2001) and adults (Sikkema et al., 2006). Group leaders can prepare to address grief and loss by first determining the degree to which group members have achieved a sense of safety and stability (Herman, 1992), as the approach may vary depending on the stability of group members. Group leaders should aim to maintain a level of safety throughout the group that protects members from becoming triggered or retraumatized. Group leaders should seek to empathize with and affirm members' experiences of grief and loss, educate members on the varied symptoms and experiences that accompany grief, and explore coping skills useful for managing grief and loss.

Trafficked individuals often need to mourn the loss of relationships, inno-cence, trust in self and others, identity, and feelings of self-worth (Williamson & Folaron, 2003). It is particularly important for group leaders to be aware of grief and loss issues related to children that may arise when working with adult women. In a qualitative study of 19 women who had left the sex trade industry, Hickle (2014) found that a majority (n = 13) had children and their relationships with children were a source of guilt, stress, and heartache. For many women, the sadness and guilt that accompanied losing custody of children as a result of in-volvement in sex work and/or drug addiction was a primary factor that kept them from attempting to leave a sexually exploitative situation. For some women, re-gaining custody may not be a goal that is feasible (Arnold, Steward, & McNeece, 2000), so group leaders should be mindful that any group of adult female survi-vors of sex trafficking may include mothers with varied and complex experiences associated with parenthood. This includes women who are working to regain custody and make up for lost time, along with others who need space to process the grief accompanying the loss of parental rights.

Regardless of age and gender, survivors of sex trafficking may also need space to grieve the loss of close friends or companions who died under circumstances related to trafficking, including violence from customers (Salfati, James, & Ferguson, 2008), gang or drug-related deaths, and suicide. The difficult circum-stances under which significant others died can cause survivors to experience disenfranchised grief (Doka, 1989), which occurs when the context of the loss is socially undesirable, leaving the bereaved individual to grieve alone. Group work provides a unique space to legitimate feelings of loss while helping survivors gain coping skills that prevent these feelings from becoming overwhelming and chronic.

Another area of loss that may arise during the life of the group is the loss of op-portunity, particularly once members have become stable and are able to process the things that have happened in their lives and the choices they have made. Loss has long been understood as an important theme in the psychosocial treatment of alcohol and drug addiction, as people in recovery come to terms with the losses they have suffered: the loss of a coping mechanism (alcohol or drugs), loss of physi-cal health, loss of employment, self-esteem, confidence, and "the loss of unrealized expectations" (Goldberg, 1985, p. 40). Groups for trafficked individuals can pro-vided the space to openly discuss these losses, find necessary support from peers experiencing similar losses, gain confidence, and explore identity in new ways.

Trust and Intimacy

Navigating intimate relationships, including family, friends, and romantic part-ners, is another theme that may arise during group work with sex trafficking survivors. Past experiences of coercion, exploitation, competition, and mistrust can make basic socialization and relationship building quite challenging in a group setting, as individual members are reluctant to trust both facilitators and other group members. Group members also are likely to need the opportunity to explore how to reestablish both personal and sexual boundaries, as these are essential to exiting sexually exploitative situations (Roe-Sepowitz et al., 2013).

One participant in Hickle's (2014) study explained the difficulty in developing new norms associated with sexual relationships, saying, "It took me a long time to be sexual again at all . . . I didn't want to be touched. It was almost as if I had the fear in the back of my mind that if anybody touched me at all that everything was gonna break and I was gonna go back" (pp. 68–69). This individual went on to talk honestly about her current relationship, reporting that while she felt that she had developed a healthy understanding of her sexuality, "there are certain things sexually that I'll never be able to do again ever. I can't wear lingerie. I can't do it. I cannot bring myself to even remotely go there. So there's little things like that just stick with you." These relationship difficulties as well as the negative definitions of self can inhibit sex trafficking survivors from moving forward and successfully engaging with positive support networks and romantic relationships. Thus, group facilitators should acknowledge these difficulties, including those related to sexual consent and intimacy, as normative challenges that can be addressed in the group setting and explored through learning about healthy relationships and interpersonal behaviors, beginning with those that develop in the group.

PRACTICE PRINCIPLES

To address these themes, along with others that may arise, we have conceptualized some key principles that can be helpful in developing group content to meet the needs of many diverse experiences associated with sex trafficking victimization. These principles are based upon several years of group work practice, including creating and piloting a group now called Sex Trafficking Awareness and Recovery (STAR). The group was adapted to meet the needs of adults and young people in a variety of settings, and these principles include education, mutual aid, addressing shame and stigma, and managing strong emotions (Hickle & Roe-Sepowitz, 2014).

Importance of Education

Group leaders must begin by educating members about the definitions and scope of sex trafficking, as members often do not identify as sex trafficking victims. Engaging group members in a discussion about how they might define sex trafficking and related terms, including exploitation, trafficker, boss/manager, prostitution, force, and coercion, can be a useful starting point for allowing members to feel a sense of belonging in the group and begin to recognize that no one can impose a label on them (i.e., "sex trafficking victim"). An educational approach also can be empowering because it provides survivors with the language to describe their experiences and prepares them to identify exploitative relationships in the future.

Promoting Mutual Aid

To help group members establish trust and begin practicing healthy relationship behaviors, group leaders should introduce activities that promote mutual aid between members. This may simply mean prompting others' feedback when a group member shares her or his experiences, eliciting opinions and advice from group members, and providing encouragement when group members are supportive of one another. In a group of adolescents, this may also mean creating activities that allow group members to team up and work together. Although these are common elements of almost any group, it is important that leaders prioritize opportunities to build trust among members and help them practice helping one another, as these abilities often have been damaged through the trafficking experience. Once members begin to feel connected to the group and one another, they can become invaluable resources for helping one another feel less isolated and less ashamed of their experiences.

Reducing Shame

As part of their control techniques, sex traffickers often isolate victims and seek to normalize the sexual abuse victims endure (Reid, 2014). They may have been warned or threatened not to tell anyone about the exploitative relationship, and have experienced further isolation from family, friends, or service providers who saw their behaviors as "promiscuous." As a result, group work with sex trafficking survivors must provide opportunities to reduce the shame associated with the victimization. A primary task for group leaders is engaging in self-reflection to ensure they do not hold any negative views that might reinforce what victims have already been told about themselves and their past and/or present sexual behaviors. Group leaders should be comfortable talking about a range of experiences employing the language members are likely to use to describe sexual acts and body parts. We have found that group members often do not disclose what happened until we, as the group leaders, have made it acceptable by raising taboo topics directly.

For example, in a group that I (first author) cofacilitated, we planned an activity where we brainstormed types of exploitation. I gave several examples throughout the discussion and intentionally brought up ones I believed group members would find uncomfortable to reveal on their own. I asked how pornography might be related to sexual exploitation and gave an example of girls who have been forced to watch pornography or willingly posed for sexual pictures and videos only to be blackmailed with them later. I then mentioned parents who trafficked their own children.

One member responded by saying that both of my examples were relevant to her, sharing that she had been trafficked by her mother, who was a sex worker and forced her to watch pornography with customers while they waited to see her mother. In this scenario, my examples opened the way for her—and then others—to disclose sensitive information. By raising these sources of exploitation directly, I paved the way for her to reveal her own experiences, which in turn, encouraged others to do the same. It was equally important that group time be devoted to helping members respond with support, understanding, and affirmation to one another's disclosures.

Creating a Culture of Safety

Finally, group leaders should aim at all times to help group members maintain a sense of safety within the group and learn new ways of managing strong emotions both in the group and in their daily lives. In the section that follows, we will provide practical recommendations, beginning with a discussion on how to prioritize safety within groups of sex trafficking survivors.

RECOMMENDED WAYS OF WORKING

A primary recommendation for group work with sex trafficking survivors is to emphasize individual and group safety, as this is critical to the therapeutic benefits of this modality. Individual safety may involve symptom stability, including sleeping well, limited intrusive thoughts while awake or asleep, having healthy eating habits, avoiding drugs or alcohol and self-harming behaviors, and avoiding or minimizing suicidal or homicidal thoughts. Individual safety also includes gaining control of anger, dissociation, and depression symptoms so the group material will not constantly trigger group members (Najavits, 2008). Individual safety also can include ending or avoiding involvement in complex relationships that include violence, substance use, or abusive interactions. Group safety requires a complex balancing act by the group leaders wherein group members are encouraged to discuss their experiences and feelings in a climate of support and understanding as well as to maintain stability and manage their feelings.

Utilize a Trauma-Informed Perspective

A trauma-informed perspective is a necessary foundation for establishing safety within the group. The traumatic events that survivors experience prior to—and during—sex trafficking victimization can change how survivors develop emotionally and may contribute to the difficulties forming relationships and engaging in the problematic and high-risk behaviors discussed throughout this chapter (Ko et al., 2008). Awareness of the impact of traumatic events on group participants, including a trauma screening, and having more intensive or individual trauma-focused treatment available to the group participants are elements of applying trauma-informed care to groups with sex trafficking victims (Ko et al., 2008).

Group leaders should have a solid foundation in treating trauma, and they must understand how complex trauma symptoms manifest in the group, including dissociation, avoidance, and hypervigilance. Group workers also must be sensitive to the risk of members being triggered by their own disclosures as well as those of others. Group leaders should have an agreed-upon plan of action to use if a group participant leaves the room or appears to be overwhelmed, uncontrollably dissociating, or dangerous to herself or others.

Another component to establishing safety is emphasizing a strong commitment to confidentiality, along with explaining the reasons why and the circumstances under which the group leader must break confidentiality. These should be discussed or reviewed at the beginning of each group. A group expectation of "no judging others" also promotes safety and is essential because being the victim of trafficking is, in and of itself, stigmatizing.

Survivors have engaged in actions that bring about strong feelings of guilt, shame, and embarrassment. Thus, nonblaming and nonshaming statements must be encouraged. Group leaders must be sure to adopt an attitude of nonjudgmentalism and recognize how trafficking debases and demoralizes its victims.

Address Ambivalence About Change

Many of the clients who have attended the sex trafficking victim groups we have facilitated have not explored their sex trafficking experiences prior to attending the groups. Some have lived in very high-stress situations where discussing experiences and feelings was discouraged and even risky. Like other types of victimization where secrecy is a part of the experience, group members may be resistant to or fearful of talking about their lives. Therefore, they should become engaged in group discussions at a pace that feels safe to them. Initially, group leaders may need to intentionally limit disclosure to prevent individual members and the group as a whole from becoming emotionally flooded.

Survivors of sex trafficking may experience ambivalence about the prospect of change, due to their limited exposure to a life or lifestyle that is different from the one in which they have been immersed for so long. Survivors' lowered expectations for themselves also may prevent them from believing change is even possible. Motivational interviewing and cognitive-behavioral techniques can be utilized in the group to challenge members' expectations for themselves, as well as encourage them to believe that change is possible by encouraging small, incremental steps (Sobell, Sobell, & Agrawal, 2009).

Maintain Flexibility

Groups with highly traumatized participants require flexibility. Group participants may need a few seconds to tell their story but at other times may need much more time. Following a structured curriculum with highly traumatized, sex-trafficked group participants has been successful because it provides members with a sense of security and safety. However, even in such structured groups with an agenda of topics, the leader should recognize that the disclosures of a member can take the group in an unanticipated direction. In both structured and unstructured groups, the group worker needs to encourage the group to be responsive to an individual's sense of urgency. Both the group and the leaders must be prepared for members to react at times with intense affect and/or dissociative symptoms. Members can be helped to tolerate these emotional displays and, in the case of dissociation, understand the protective function this behavior serves.

Survivor as a Cofacilitator

In some instances, a survivor of trafficking can be considered as a cofacilitator (Hickle & Roe-Sepowitz, 2014; Hotaling, Burris, Johnson, Bird, & Melbye, 2004; Thomson, et al., 2011). A survivor cofacilitator can assist the group development in a number of ways, including giving credibility to the group; using her or his recovery and change process as an indication that change is possible; and validating problems in living that she or he and members of the group have in common such as substance use and a history of sexual abuse or domestic violence (Hickle & Roe-Sepowitz, 2014). The survivor cofacilitator can also lead the group into topics and territory that may be difficult for other members to confront. Given the commonality of experience, it may be less threatening for the survivor cofacilitator to raise taboo topics than for the group worker who does not share the same history.

In such cases where a survivor assumes co-leadership responsibilities, her or his role and responsibilities must be clearly articulated and understood by members and leaders. Boundaries must be well defined, and it must be understood that the survivor is functioning as a *leader*, not as a member. Her or his shared experiences with members serve to encourage open discussion, particularly of sensitive subjects, and inspire hope among members. The survivor *facilitates* mutual aid owing to her or his unique position, but does not directly benefit from it.

EVALUATION

Measuring the success of a group intervention for survivors of sex trafficking can be difficult, considering the varied and complex needs of the individual members. Evaluation measures for members should be identified prior to starting the group, and the degree to which their goals are achieved can then be assessed at the group's conclusion.

In a group of adolescents who have been referred by others and/or are required to attend, it may be useful for group leaders to assess members' willingness to self-identify as having been trafficked or sexually exploited by the end of the group. This approach to evaluation emphasizes participants' readiness to change and is an important part of helping sex trafficking survivors participate more fully in all aspects of the services available to them (Hickle & Roe-Sepowitz, 2014; Thomson et al., 2012).

The transtheoretical—or stages of change—model is a useful framework for assessing readiness to change and has been used among trafficked adolescent girls (Thomson et al., 2012). Because many trafficked individuals may be reluctant to change, for reasons discussed previously, progress through the changes of stage, from precontemplation and contemplation through action and maintenance, can be a useful and practical measure of the group's impact. Considering the high proportion of sex trafficking survivors who meet criteria for PTSD (Hossain et al., 2010), group leaders may want to utilize a pre- and postmeasurement of trauma symptom reduction. For example, the Trauma Symptom Inventory (Briere, 1996a) and Trauma Symptom Checklist for Children (Briere, 1996b) are two instruments that have been established as valid and reliable measures of trauma symptomology. Finally, group leaders may want to assess other aspects of emotional, behavioral, or relational health, including reduction in substance abuse and self-harming behaviors, and an increase in self-esteem and self-worth. Self-rating questionnaires or focus group sessions may be useful in capturing change in these areas.

RESOURCES

National Human Trafficking Resource Center
Hotline: 1-888-373-7888 (for referrals or help-seeking)
or text "BeFree" (233733)
Website: http://traffickingresourcecenter.org/
Report a tip: http://traffickingresourcecenter.org/report-trafficking
E-mail: nhtrc@polarisproject.org
Polaris
P.O. Box 65323
Washington, DC 20035
Tel: 202-745-1001 Fax: 202-745-1119
Website: http://www.polarisproject.org/about-us/contact-us

REFERENCES

Avinger, K. A., & Jones, R. A. (2007). Group treatment of sexually abused adolescent girls: A review of outcome studies. *American Journal of Family Therapy, 35*(4), 315–326. doi:10.1080/01926180600969702

Arnold, E. M., Stewart, J. C., & McNeece, C. A. (2000). The psychosocial treatment needs of street-walking prostitutes: Perspectives from a case management program. *Journal of Offender Rehabilitation, 30*(3/4), 117–132.

Begic, D. (2001). Aggressive behavior in combat veterans with post-traumatic stress disorder. *Military Medicine, 166*(8), 671.

Briere, J. (1996a). *Trauma symptom checklist for children.* Odessa, FL: Psychological Assessment Resources.

Briere, J. (1996b). *Trauma symptom inventory.* Odessa, FL: Psychological Assessment. Resources.

Burnette, M. A., Lucas, L., Ilgen, M., Frayne, S. M., Mayo, J., & Weitlauf, J. C. (2008). Prevalence and health correlates of prostitution among patients entering treatment for substance use disorders. *Archives of General Psychiatry, 65*(3), 337–344.

Church, S., Henderson, M., Barnard, M., & Hart, G. (2001). Violence by clients towards female prostitutes in different work settings: Questionnaire survey. *British Medical Journal, 322*(7285), 524–525.

Covenant House New York. (2013). *Homelessness, survival sex, and human trafficking: As experienced by the youth of Covenant House New York.* Retrieved from http://www.covenanthouse.org/sites/default/files/attachments/Covenant-House-trafficking-study.pdf

Dalla, R. L. (2003). When the bough breaks: Examining intergenerational parent-child relational patterns among street-level sex workers and their parents and children. *Applied Developmental Science, 7*(4), 216–228.

Dodsworth, J. (2014). Sexual exploitation, selling and swapping sex: Victimhood and agency. *Child Abuse Review, 23*(3), 185–199. doi:10.1002/car.2282

Doka, K. J. (1989). Disenfranchised grief. In K. J. Doka (Ed.), *Disenfranchised grief: Recognizing hidden sorrow* (pp. 3–11). Lexington, MA: Lexington Books.

Drumm, K. (2006). The essential power of group work. *Social Work with Groups, 29*(2/3), 17–31.

Foy, D. W., Eriksson, C. B., & Trice, G. A. (2001). Introduction to group interventions for trauma survivors. *Group dynamics: Theory, Research, and Practice, 5*(4), 246–251.

Gerassi, L. (2015). From exploitation to industry: Definitions, risks, and consequences of domestic sexual exploitation and sex work among women and girls. *Journal of Human Behavior in the Social Environment, 25*(6), 591–605. doi:10.1080/10911359.2014.991055

Gibbs, D. A., Walters, J. L. H., Lutnick, A., Miller, S., & Kluckman, M. (2015). Services to domestic minor victims of sex trafficking: Opportunities for engagement and support. *Children and Youth Services Review, 54*, 1–7. doi:10.1016/j.childyouth.2015.04.003

Gitterman, A. (2005). Group formation: Tasks, methods, and skills. In A. Gitterman & L. Shulman (Eds.), *Mutual aid groups, vulnerable and resilient populations, and the life cycle* (3rd ed., pp. 73–110) New York, NY: Columbia University Press.

Goldberg, M. (1985). Loss and grief: Major dynamics in the treatment of alcoholism. *Alcoholism Treatment Quarterly, 2*(1), 37–46.

Hackney, L. K. (2015). Re-evaluating Palermo: The case of Burmese women as Chinese brides. *Anti-Trafficking Review, 4*, 98–119. doi:10.14197/atr.20121546.

Herman, J. (1992). *Trauma and recovery: The aftermath of violence.* New York, NY: Basic Books.

Hickle, K. (2014). *Getting out: A qualitative exploration of the exiting experience among former sex workers and adult sex trafficking victims.* Unpublished doctoral dissertation, Arizona State University, Tempe, AZ.

Hickle, K. E., & Roe-Sepowitz, D. E. (2014). Putting the pieces back together: A group intervention for sexually exploited adolescent girls. *Social Work with Groups, 37*(2), 99–113. doi:10.1080/01609513.2013.823838

Hossain, M., Zimmerman, C., Abas, M., Light, M., & Watts, C. (2010). The relationship of trauma to mental disorders among trafficked and sexually exploited girls and women. *American Journal of Public Health, 100*(12), 2442–2449.

Hotaling, N., Burris, A., Johnson, B. J., Bird, Y. M., & Melbye, K. A. (2004). Been there done that: SAGE, a peer leadership model among prostitution survivors. *Journal of Trauma Practice, 2*(3–4), 255–265. doi:10.1300/J189v02n03_15

Hua, J., & Nigorizawa, H. (2010). US sex trafficking, women's human rights and the politics of representation. *International Feminist Journal of Politics, 12*(3–4), 401–423.

Ko, S. J., Ford, J. D., Kassam-Adams, N., Berkowitz, S. J., Wilson, C., & Layne, C. M. (2008). Creating trauma-informed systems: Child welfare, education, first responders, healthcare, juvenile justice. *Professional Psychology: Research and Practice, 39*, 396–404.

Macy, R. J., & Graham, L. M. (2012). Identifying domestic and international sex-trafficking victims during human service provision. *Trauma, Violence, & Abuse, 13*(2), 59–76. doi:10.1177/1524838012440340

Nadon, S. M., Koverola, C., & Schludermann, E. H. (1998). Antecedents to prostitution: Childhood victimization. *Journal of Interpersonal Violence, 13*(2), 206–221.

Najavits, L. (2008). Treatment of posttraumatic stress disorder and substance abuse. *Alcoholism Treatment Quarterly, 22*, 43–62.

Olson-McBride, L., & Page, T. F. (2012). Song to self: Promoting a therapeutic dialogue with high-risk youths through poetry and popular music. *Social Work with Groups, 35*(2), 124–137. doi:10.1080/01609513.2011.603117

Pierce, A. (2012). American Indian adolescent girls: Vulnerability to sex trafficking, intervention strategies. *American Indian and Alaska Native Mental Health Research, 19*(1), 37–56.

Potterat, J. J., Rothenberg, R. B., Muth, S. Q., Darrow, W. W., & Phillips-Plummer, L. (1998). Pathways to prostitution: The chronology of sexual and drug abuse milestones. *Journal of Sex Research, 35*(4), 333–340.

Raphael, J., Reichert, J. A., & Powers, M. (2010). Pimp control and violence: Domestic sex trafficking of Chicago women and girls. *Women and Criminal Justice, 20*(1–2), 89–104. doi:10.1080/08974451003641065

Raphael, J., & Shapiro, D. L. (2004). Violence in indoor and outdoor prostitution venues. *Violence Against Women, 10*(2), 126–139. doi:10.1177/1077801203260529.

Reid, J. (2014). Entrapment and enmeshment schemes used by sex traffickers. *Sex Abuse: A Journal of Research and Treatment*, 1–12. doi:10.1177/1079063214544334

Reid, J. A., & Piquero, A. R. (2013). Age-graded risks for commercial sexual exploitation of male and female youth. *Journal of Interpersonal Violence, 29*, 1747–1777. doi:10.1177/0886260513511535

Roe-Sepowitz, D. E., Hickle, K. E., & Cimino, A. (2012). The impact of abuse history and trauma symptoms on successful completion of a prostitution-exiting program. *Journal of Human Behavior in the Social Environment, 22*(1), 65–77. doi:10.1080/10911359.2011.598830

Salfati, C. G., James, A. R., & Ferguson, L. (2008). Prostitute homicides: A descriptive study. *Journal of Interpersonal Violence, 23*(4), 505–543. doi:10.1177/0886260507312946

Saltzman, W. R., Pynoos, R. S., Layne, C. M., Steinberg, A. M., & Aisenberg, E. (2001). Trauma-and grief-focused intervention for adolescents exposed to community violence: Results of a school-based screening and group treatment protocol. *Group Dynamics: Theory, Research, and Practice, 5*(4), 291.

Sikkema, K. J., Hansen, N. B., Ghebremichael, M., Kochman, A., Tarakeshwar, N., Meade, C. S., & Zhang, H. (2006). A randomized controlled trial of a coping group intervention for adults with HIV who are AIDS bereaved: Longitudinal effects on grief. *Health Psychology, 25*(5), 563. doi.org/10.1037/0278-6133.25.5.563

Sobell, L., Sobell, M., & Agrawal, S. (2009). Randomized controlled trial of a cognitive-behavioral motivational intervention in a group versus individual format for substance abuse disorders. *Psychology of Addictive Behaviors, 23*, 672–683.

Straka, S. M., & Montminy, L. (2006). Responding to the needs of older women experiencing domestic violence. *Violence against Women, 12*(3), 251–267. doi:10.1177/1077801206286221

Thomson, S., Hirshberg, D., Corbett, A., Valila, N., & Howley, D. (2011). Residential treatment for sexually exploited adolescent girls: Acknowledge, commit, transform (ACT). *Children and Youth Services Review, 33*, 2290–2296. doi:10.1016/jchildyouth.2011.07.017

Trafficking Victims Protection Act. (2000). Pub. L. No. 106-368, Division A, 103(8), 114 Stat 1464 (signed into law on October 29, 2000).

Vanwesenbeeck, I. (2005). Burnout among female indoor sex workers. *Archives of Sexual Behavior, 34*(6), 627–639. doi:10.1007/s10508-005-7912-y

Weinberg, M. S., Shaver, F. M., & Williams, C. J. (1999). Gendered sex work in the San Francisco Tenderloin. *Archives of Sexual Behavior, 28*(6), 503–521.

Williamson, C., & Prior, M. (2009). Domestic minor sex trafficking: A network of underground players in the Midwest. *Journal of Child and Adolescent Trauma, 2*(1), 1–16. doi:10.1080/19361520802702191

Young, A. M., Boyd, C., & Hubbell, A. (2000). Prostitution, drug use, and coping with psychological distress. *Journal of Drug Issues, 30*(4), 789–800.

Chapter Eighteen

Group Work With Survivors of Intimate Partner Violence

Shantih E. Clemans

Intimate partner violence (IPV), also known as domestic violence, refers to "an ongoing pattern of coercive control maintained through physical, psychological, sexual, and/or economic abuse that varies in severity and chronicity" (Warshaw, Sullivan, & Rivera, 2013, p. 1). IPV can include physical violence, emotional abuse, financial abuse, stalking, and rape (Breiding et al., 2014; Howard, Riger, Campbell, & Wasco, 2003). Researchers have found that IPV is hard to categorize; however, it is commonly understood as a pattern of abuse that begins slowly and intensifies over time (National Coalition Against Domestic Violence, n.d.b.; Pyles & Postmus, 2004). Often the intimate partner relationship is an established one, and there is some aspect of trust between partners. This trust is important because victims sometimes are caught off guard when the abuse begins. However, survivors are also torn by a complicated array of feelings about their relationships, including love, loyalty, fear, and self-blame. These emotional consequences make domestic violence a particularly challenging problem to understand and to stop.

Although the dynamics of IPV vary and no two domestic violence situations are exactly the same, IPV often is cyclical in nature. The violence may be almost imperceptible in its early stages. Then, relatively calm periods are followed by episodes of violence or abuse, which result in conciliatory behavior on the part of the abuser, such as promises that the abuse will not happen again and pleas to be forgiven. Inevitably, the abuse reoccurs when the abuser becomes angry and/or feels a need to maintain control over the relationship. The cycle repeats itself and continues. Over time, the abuse tends to escalate in severity and frequency.

Quite often, emotional abuse is part of the dynamic, resulting in the victim being blamed and internalizing the blaming messages from the abuser. Only when the abuser accepts responsibility for the violence and abuse can the cycle actually be broken. Survivors often are loyal to their abusers, and some see speaking out and seeking help as a form of betrayal. IPV does not end when and if the survivor is able to successfully leave the relationship. Control, coercion, stalking, and even murder remain pernicious ways for the abuser and the abusive relationship to continue to maintain a tight grip on the victim's life (Breiding et al., 2014; Pyles & Postmus, 2004; Warshaw et al., 2013).

SURVIVORS OF INTIMATE PARTNER VIOLENCE

A complex, pervasive phenomenon rooted in socially sanctioned male power and privilege, IPV primarily counts women as victims. Almost 2 million women in the United States are abused each year by their intimate partners (National Coalition against Domestic Violence, n.d.a.). Over the past 30 years, researchers have examined the dynamics of IPV and the populations of people affected by violence in intimate relationships (Breiding et al., 2014; Pyles & Postmus, 2004) as well as help-seeking behavior among survivors (Liang, Goodman, Tummala-Narra, & Weintraub, 2005).

Abuse of power occurs in all types of relationships, including same-sex couples (Calton, Cattaneo, & Gebhard, 2015; Edwards & Sylaska, 2013), among people with disabilities (Berwald & Houtstra, 2002; Pyles & Postmus, 2004), and men (Brieding et al., 2014; Tsui, 2014). Although it is difficult to know exactly the number of LGBT individuals who have experienced IPV, research has shown that within the LGBT population, IPV occurs at a rate equal to or even higher than the heterosexual community. Women with disabilities have a 40% greater risk of IPV, especially severe violence, than women without disabilities. One in seven men has been a victim of severe IPV (Breiding et al., 2014; National Coalition against Domestic Violence, n.d.a.).

Consequences of Intimate Partner Violence for Survivors

Although those who have experienced IPV and abuse are diverse in their experiences and circumstances, there are common social, psychological, and emotional consequences, as well as signs of strength and resilience. Survivors frequently experience severe emotional distress. Depression and anxiety are common, specifically symptoms of posttraumatic stress disorder (PTSD), such as fear, anxiety, hypervigilance, nightmares, and panic attacks. Fear, including a realistic fear of being killed by the abuser, is one of the most pronounced consequences. Survivors who have experienced multiple victimizations, specifically childhood sexual abuse or other childhood traumas, often experience a more complicated picture; for example, they may have difficulty understanding and managing their emotions, which can present challenges for their ability to care for themselves (Knight, 2006; Warshaw et al., 2013). Personal relationships are also affected. For example, survivors may struggle to establish and maintain healthy relationships based on trust and equality.

Survivors who represent "minority" victim populations experience specific consequences that merit attention and sensitivity from service providers. For example, male victims may struggle to report the abuse for fear that they will not be believed, will be belittled, or that their masculinity will be questioned (Tsui, 2014). LGBT survivors are less likely than their heterosexual peers to come forward and ask for help. Among many reasons, they may fear "airing their problems" in public, may be threatened by their partner to be "outed," and/or fear anti-LGBT bias among service providers (Calton, Cattaneo, & Gebhard, 2015).

GROUP WORK WITH INTIMATE PARTNER VIOLENCE SURVIVORS

As the field of IPV has developed over time, the benefit of group participation for victims has been demonstrated. Groups are a significant and ubiquitous service component of shelters and community-based programs serving survivors of IPV (O'Brien, 2009). Groups have continued to be important for survivors of IPV for several reasons:

1. They provide support and understanding to survivors who typically feel alone and isolated.
2. They offer opportunities for members to learn about the dynamics of abuse, decreasing their sense of self-blame.
3. They can teach members self-care strategies and boost self-esteem.

Connecting with others who share similar feelings and experiences is one important way to begin the healing process. Groups offer survivors of IPV important, life-affirming opportunities to meet others in "the same boat" and to connect through sharing stories, feelings, and experiences. Groups offer a safe space for members to come to receive support and guidance and to talk openly with others on a life circumstance that is embarrassing, shameful, and painful. Groups also provide members with opportunities to talk about "taboo" topics in a supportive and nonjudgmental environment. This is especially important for a population who often feels the burden of self-blame and may have internalized the powerful messages from the abuser that "this is all your fault." Herman notes, "Traumatic events [such as IPV] call into question basic human relationships; they breach the attachments of family, friendship, love and community" (Herman, 1997, p. 49). As members share their experiences and develop connections to one another, they are simultaneously relearning—or learning for the first time—what it means to be in a relationship that is nonexploitive and safe.

The professional literature includes a wide range of models and practice approaches for group work in the field of IPV. Groups vary in purpose. Some groups exist to address the emotional and psychological consequences of IPV, as well as to provide practical support and guidance on concrete realities such as orders of protection, child care, and legal processes. Other group approaches help communities learn about violence, empower vulnerable populations to find a voice to take action and speak out, and promote social change. Many groups that address IPV include some aspects of education about power dynamics and an emphasis on teaching victims that the abuse is the abuser's responsibility and is connected to larger social issues, such as male privilege (Anderson, 2010). Groups for abusers/batterers are an essential treatment component in the IPV field with some similarities to groups for survivors. Because of differences in practice principles and other dynamics, the focus of this chapter is on group work with survivors, not on perpetrators or offenders of IPV.

The major group models reflected in this chapter include feminist, mutual aid, and cognitive-behavioral. Within each model there are specific approaches geared toward various populations of members. There is overlap among these categories, and efforts are made in this chapter to be as specific as possible in highlighting relevant theoretical and practice issues.

Groups Informed by Feminist Principles

Feminist self-help groups in the battered women's movement of the 1970s were instrumental in bringing public awareness of the realities of domestic violence. Groups were also crucial as forums to support victims and mobilize community responses. "Before shelters, national hotlines, and formalized and funded programs existed, self-help support groups met in church basements, hospital waiting rooms, and late night eateries" (O'Brien, 2009, p. 195).

Early in the battered women's movement, groups emphasized a consciousness- raising process: small groups of women telling their stories of abuse at home, often for the first time. "Consciousness raising groups provided forums for women to openly criticize sexist views toward women, and the impact of patriarchal forces on women's development and experiences" (Israeli & Santor, 2000, p. 234; Wood & Roche, 2001). The purpose of these groups was not to improve the emotional and psychological aspects of victim's lives, but to bring to light the reality of abuse that had been kept hidden and secret. Similar groups also existed as part of the antirape movement (Clemans, 2005). In their study of feminist therapy effectiveness, Gorey, Daly, Richter, and colleagues (2002) found that the most common feminist intervention reflected in the literature was group work with the emphasis on women's lives and experiences as its focal point.

Groups Informed by Mutual Aid Principles

Mutual aid, a major group work model, is essentially the dynamic and interactive process where members come together to receive help and support and become stronger through giving and receiving of such help. The dynamics of mutual aid have been widely reported and described in social work: (1) sharing data; (2) dialectic process: sharing different points of view; (3) discussing taboos openly; (4) all-in-the-same-boat phenomenon; (5) mutual demand; and (6) mutual support. Mutual aid groups are especially relevant to survivor groups as they encourage group members to participate with one another in a democratic and empowering manner (Shulman, 2012). Moreover, mutual aid groups "provide the impetus for members to act and gain greater control and mastery over their environments" (Gitterman, 2004, p. 99).

Steinberg (2002) explains that one particularly important mutual aid process is the sharing of different voices and perspectives:

> When peers exchange ideas, feelings, attitudes and personal stories, in an attempt to help one another think things through, not only do they provide opportunities to identify those voices that have served them well in the past but they create new opportunities to learn new voices as well. (p. 35)

Groups Informed by Cognitive-Behavioral Principles

The cognitive-behavioral model is another major group work model that has relevance in the field of IPV. Cognitive therapy is connected to the idea that what we think directly informs how we act and how we feel. Cognitive-behavioral group work incorporates "behavioral, cognitive, and small group strategies" (Rose, 2004, p. 110). Cognitive-behavioral therapy (CBT) groups are among the dominant group models in social work and have a strong evidence base (Easton, 2007; Rose, 2004). CBT groups focus on helping members change their thinking and then their specific behaviors, such as improving social skills or managing anxiety in new situations (Rose, 2004).

In this example, group members are asked to pay attention to their thinking about the abuse in their relationship.

> *Group worker:* Let's go around the room and think about this question: What causes domestic violence?
>
> *Lisa:* The abuse was my fault. My husband always said so.
>
> *Beth:* Yeah. I know that if I did something different, he would not have hit me.
>
> *Group worker:* So, you both think that you are to blame for the abuse?

In the continuation of this session, the group worker first helps members identify their thoughts about the abuse, for example, who is responsible. The thoughts are then challenged and ultimately replaced with new thoughts that are based on learning about the dynamics of IPV.

PRACTICE PRINCIPLES

Not every group model meets the needs of every survivor of IPV. Although the models, practice approaches, and populations described here are unique in their own ways, they share common principles for the group worker.

The first is the importance of "starting where the client is" and the recognition that not all members want the same thing or are at the same stage in healing. A second common principle is the focus on the emotional, physical, and psychological safety of members, including the careful respect of member and group confidentiality. Coming forward to seek help is a courageous but frightening process. Therefore, group workers need to maintain clear boundaries of confidentiality. Education as power is another principle. Participation in an IPV group helps members learn, understand, and internalize the dynamics of IPV in a supportive atmosphere. Last is the principle of valuing group membership and contributions, where the group worker and members recognize the inherent benefit of members coming together to learn, share, and grow. Specifically among populations of people who are vulnerable and may struggle to experience autonomy in their everyday lives, this group work principle is especially needed.

Group and Member Developmental Stages

Groups have life cycles: planning, beginnings, middles, and endings. The role of the group worker and the participation of the members evolve over time. There are specific dynamics that occur in the beginning phase, and the worker needs to be mindful, always, of the developmental phase of the group (Berman-Rossi, 1992; Kurland & Salmon, 1998). There is a sequence to group work with survivors of IPV, meaning "first things first." Not only are survivors of IPV vulnerable to continued abuse, they are also ready for different things at different times. Moreover, a group worker needs to recognize the importance of first establishing safety. Other work needs to wait until a group member feels safe, and the therapeutic relationship has been established. This takes time. Group workers who are educated and attuned to the dynamics of IPV incorporate into their group practice a version of Herman's three stages of healing: (1) safety; (2) remembering and mourning; and (3) reconnection (Herman, 1997). Herman's model has widely influenced other models and approaches and is relevant to a wide range of survivors of violence.

Despite differences in purpose, groups for IPV survivors emphasize and reinforce the importance of safety. For many survivors, there is fear that revictimization will occur. It is not uncommon for survivors to return to their abuser many times before they leave permanently. Regardless of circumstance, groups need to be created from the beginning as nonjudgmental and open to the various stages of a survivor's recovery process. Ultimately, the group must start where the survivor is, build upon members' strengths and courage, and consciously empower members by presenting them with accurate information regarding the cycle of violence.

Compassion and Empathy

In my work with students, I often describe the field of IPV as at once emotionally demanding and rewarding, meaningful, and life affirming. The trauma field forces a worker to confront human cruelty. Group members vary in their goals and reasons for seeking help. Not everyone successfully escapes abuse; it is often a long process, which can be difficult for group workers who are eager to see change happening quickly.

As an undergraduate social work student, one of my first field placement assignments was to cofacilitate a group for women in a domestic violence shelter. The group met in a little back room, with folding chairs, a smattering of children's toys, a dusty maroon couch, and the all-important coffee pot. I was scared, maybe even more than some of the women. I was unsure of myself, and I questioned whether I had anything at all to offer the group members. I was unsure of the group's purpose, even though it had been explained to me many times in supervision and by the group members themselves. I did not know then of the potential that was present in a group of eight or nine abused women, trying to find a path free of violence. I did not know then that the simple, powerful process of coming together to share life experiences and everyday feelings could actually be transformative for each woman, for the group as a whole, and even for me, the then-inexperienced social work student.

Making a commitment to work with this population, especially in a group, takes courage, patience, sensitivity, and caring. Regardless of the type of group, communicating compassion and empathy is critically important, especially in the beginning phase of work with survivors. Recognizing the strength of members to come to a group is also essential. Though they may not view themselves as such, victims of IPV are in fact survivors.

Probably more than other trauma areas, the IPV field attracts and encourages former victims to train to become shelter volunteers, staff counselors, or administrators. Survivors have the ability to "walk in another person's shoes" and offer insight and personal experience on the painful and damaging realities of IPV. However, with or without an acknowledged history of IPV, group workers need to be especially cognizant and well practiced in maintaining boundaries between themselves and the survivors they are helping. For example, the group worker's disclosures can convey to members understanding and empathy, but they must reflect the needs of the members, not the worker.

Strength and Resilience

The group worker needs to be sensitive to group members' risk and protective factors. Risk factors make healing more complex and group participation more difficult. These include multiple victimizations, mental illness, and substance abuse. Protective factors are those variables that contribute to the strength and resiliency of the survivor. A group worker needs to recognize the strength of group members who come forward to participate in a group that addresses issues that are private, painful, potentially embarrassing, and shameful. Survivors of IPV are strong and resilient (Anderson, 2010). Resilience refers to the ability to bounce back from traumatic or damaging life events to be stronger than before. There is a growing literature on resilience, and it is an especially important concept for beginning group workers to understand. In a group, some members might appear more resilient than others. Moreover, members can bring out and acknowledge the strength they see in each other. "Sharing one's story of adversity" can be, in and of itself, a source of strength and bravery for the member and inspiring for the group as a whole (Anderson, 2010).

Understanding Dynamics of Interpersonal Violence and Complex Consequences

Skillful work with survivors of IPV and abuse requires professional knowledge about the dynamics of IPV, as outlined earlier. Learning about the dynamics of IPV in supportive, comprehensive staff/volunteer training is an essential first step. Most domestic violence shelters rely heavily on volunteers and are mandated to provide education on dynamics, crisis intervention, resources, and referring processes.

Self-Care

Direct practice in the trauma field, especially group work, is emotionally challenging, and there are significant risks to a worker's emotional and psychological well-being (Clemans, 2004a; Cunningham, 2003; Dane, 2000; Figley, 2002; Harr & Moore, 2011; Pearlman & Saakvitne, 1995). It is absolutely essential for practitioners working in the IPV field to learn, early on, about the dangers of secondary traumatic stress, vicarious traumatization, and burnout. Clinicians workers who work with clients affected by traumatic life events such as IPV, sexual assault, and child abuse are vulnerable to experiencing vicarious traumatization (VT). VT is a way of framing the emotional, physical, and spiritual changes experienced by those who provide counseling and other direct services to survivors. For example, like the clients they work with, clinicians are at risk of viewing their social world as unsafe and unpredictable. Secondary traumatic stress refers to symptoms that mirror PTSD in clients, such as anxiety, nightmares, and feeling numb. Workers may experience parallel symptoms as survivors. Burnout refers to the effect on the worker of concrete aspects of one's job, such as long hours, low pay, limited time off, or unsafe working conditions. Knowing about these potential consequences will help bolster workers, especially group workers, to embark on the emotionally complex work with an open mind and practiced tools for worker self-care.

A related professional development strategy is the availability of regular supportive supervision with a person skilled in both group work dynamics and trauma work. Supervision needs to encourage honest conversation about the group and the workers' feelings and experiences, in a safe, supportive space without judgment (Campbell, 2002; Clemans, 2004a, 2004b).

The desire of the group worker to be the "rescuer"—to save the survivor from her or his abusive situation is understandable and may be a reflection of the secondary effects of trauma work. Group workers must also recognize and accept that individuals attempting to recover from IPV are not all the same—some may return to the abusive patterns, while others may find the group the impetus they need to escape. In every case, the practitioner must respect individual members' decisions regarding leaving (or staying) with their partner. Supervision is critical to assisting workers in establishing and maintaining appropriate boundaries.

Because IPV is an abuse of power, it is vital that group workers make conscious efforts to empower members to take ownership of their personal recovery. At the same time, workers need to achieve a balance between encouraging members to own their recovery process and maintaining an ethical approach to practice guided by the agency and the social work profession. Workers also need to be aware of not replicating abusive power dynamics in the group, although there are inevitably power/authority issues. The group should be prepared to talk openly about authority issues as they emerge in groups. This serves as a powerful model of nonexploitive relationships based upon mutual respect and reciprocity.

Remaining mindful of not replicating feelings such as shame, isolation, fear, and unworthiness, workers need to help members see their underlying commonalities of experience, despite apparent differences in race, ethnicity, or sexual orientation. For example, members of color or lesbians or members who speak primarily another language should not feel they are the "only ones" in the group. As members grasp their similarities, feelings of isolation dissipate quickly.

Recognizing Clients' Complex Histories

Group workers need to develop a trauma-informed approach to practice. This includes a sensitivity to the multiple traumas in many survivors' lives, the importance of focusing on physical and emotional safety needs first, the need to recognize and validate the strength of coming forward to seek help, and the difficulty associated with revealing secrets, often of a taboo nature, in a group (Knight, 2015).

Survivors of IPV often have complex histories related to other forms of trauma—such as childhood victimization, sexual violence, and physical assault. Survivors may have co-occurring disorders, such as mental illness or substance abuse, as well as social barriers and circumstances that make the process of coming forward for help particularly daunting. These barriers also may interfere with the momentum and motivation needed to continue in ongoing therapy, if this is indicated (Knight, 2009). Some survivors are also offenders and some offenders have histories of victimization. Workers need to know when to refer members to other agencies or when to consult with sister organizations to learn the best practice approaches. At the same time, workers benefit from applying both the ecological and strength perspectives when learning about and planning for helping survivors in a broad and inclusive way.

COMMON THEMES IN GROUP WORK WITH SURVIVORS OF INTIMATE PARTNER VIOLENCE

In work with survivors of IPV, several pronounced themes emerge and will be discussed in more detail: (1) shame and blame; (2) secrecy and isolation; and (3) respecting differences.

Shame and Blame: "I always blamed myself"

Shame and blame are two related themes in group work with IPV. Part of the dynamic of IPV is for victims to assume responsibility for the violence. Women and girls are especially vulnerable for being blamed for gender-based violence and abuse and internalizing this view.

In a group, members may express feeling at fault for what happened in their intimate relationship. Before jumping in to correct a member's self-blame, the worker can help the group explore the reasons why abuse and violence occur. The process of members talking openly over time, and hearing that others also blame themselves, can assist the group in moving forward. Related to this is the survivor's loyalty to the abuser, and her or his wish to protect the abuser. The assumption of blame underscores the need for survivors to be provided with accurate information about IPV and the cycle of violence.

Secrecy and Isolation

IPV is a crime of silence. Telling their story, for some survivors, may occur for the first time during a group session. Breaking taboos in a supportive group atmosphere is an important aspect of group work. IPV is in itself taboo. Although many survivors who join a group specifically for IPV have acknowledged, to some degree, the violence in their relationship, members are likely to still be in some denial about the abuse and the impact it has had on their social, emotional, physical, and psychological functioning.

Respecting Differences

Survivors in groups come together to share common life experiences and similar feelings. However, there needs to be room in the group to acknowledge and respect differences among the group members. For example, members may be at different points in their healing. Some members may have reported the abuse to the police, while others, more commonly, have not and express reluctance about doing so. Although most women do not report their crimes to the police (Campbell, 2002; Herman, 1997), in one particular group most of the members did. When one woman disclosed her decision not to inform the authorities, she was initially met with judgment. The following vignette illustrates this theme (Clemans, 2005):

> *Sandy:* I went to the ER after the last abuse and the doctor put a lot of pressure on me because I did not want to involve the police.
>
> *Jada:* You didn't report it? Why not? What about all the other women who could be the next victims? What about your kids?
>
> *Marie:* Yeah! Don't you think it's our responsibility to speak up and stop the cycle of abuse?
>
> *Group worker:* It's important to remember that each of you in this group has made different choices and decisions. You did not choose to be abused [or to be in a violent relationship] but you can choose and decide what happens now. I hope as a group those choices can be respected.
>
> *Sandy:* I know your hearts are in the right places, but you have to understand that I need to do things in my own way. I feel a little like I am being judged when the people who truly deserve judgment are the men who hurt us.
>
> *Jada:* I am sorry, Sandy, for coming across like that. I feel bad now. I wish someone had prevented the abuse from happening to me. I am so sad about it.
>
> *Group worker:* I wonder how you all feel about what Jada just said. Even though you are all different, I wonder if there are common feelings of sadness among you? (pp. 71–72)

WAYS OF WORKING IN GROUPS WITH SURVIVORS OF INTIMATE PARTNER VIOLENCE

Groups that are well thought out and allow for flexibility in purpose, structure, and content tend to be the most successful. The purpose of the group needs to be clear, even if it will change over the life of the group (Kurland & Salmon, 2006). One example of a purpose in a group for survivors in a shelter might be: To learn to live in a relationship free of violence. Another example might be: To learn about the cycle of violence to better protect members from future violence. Another group, for example for lesbian and gay young people, might use different language appropriate to the members and their unique needs and might have as its purpose: To acknowledge the isolation and shame and to find ways to be in a relationship free of violence.

Consciously using the group's developmental stages of beginnings, middles, and endings/transitions helps keep the group moving forward and also is responsive to the evolving needs of the members. The purpose can change over time, depending on the needs and goals of the members. Purpose also evolves as members become more comfortable with one another (Kurland & Salmon, 2006). As the group develops, members need to be encouraged to articulate the purpose of the group in their own words, fostering ownership of and commitment to the group.

Active and Engaged Leadership

I have found that a group leader needs to be organized and active (keeping focused on the "flow" of the group's work) and willing to confront situations directly. I also create "group communities" where I ask members to identify what is important to them in their participation in the group. Especially with survivors of IPV, group leadership needs to be simultaneously direct and supportive. This example shows the possible tone a group worker might take in a first session:

> *Group worker:* Welcome to the survivors' group. I know for some of you, this is a scary thing—not just the violence you have experienced but also coming to a group to talk about it. I want to stress that this group is about you. What *you* want to get out of group is most important. I will guide the discussions and encourage active participation. Let's go around the room and I ask you to say your name and something specific you would like to get out of this group.

Carefully Attending to Confidentiality

Speaking out does not happen automatically and members first need safety, trust, and a clear sense of the group's purpose. It is important to speak openly and regularly about confidentiality to support and reassure members. This, in turn, encourages them to open up and disclose personal experiences within a context of support and understanding.

Ever mindful of the dynamics of IPV and the fear survivors come to group with, a group worker needs to be both direct and compassionate when addressing issues of confidentiality. How a group worker addresses and maintains confidentiality in the group changes over the phases of the group. For example, in the beginning (first session), a worker might address confidentiality in the following way:

> *Group worker:* Welcome to the survivors' group. I am glad to see all of you here. I can appreciate how difficult, even scary, it is for some of you to come here today and to speak openly about painful issues, issues that maybe you have tried to keep to yourself. Everything that is discussed here in this group is confidential, meaning that it is not OK to share anything from this group outside with others who are not in this group. There are a few exceptions, for example, if you are in danger of harming yourself or another person, we (group workers) are obligated to tell someone to keep you safe. Can anyone share why confidentiality is so important?

Sensitivity to Power Dynamics

Group membership can bring with it ambivalent feelings about asking for and needing help and feeling powerless. Members are coming from experiences where there is an abuse of power. Therefore, as a group worker, one needs to be conscious of articulating the role of authority in a group. Although a group worker is the "authority" in the room, it is important to be skillful in acknowledging the complex roles authority has played in the lives of survivors of IPV. Here is an example of a group worker navigating this issue:

> *Group worker:* If you remember from our last session, we agreed that today we would discuss the topic of children. Does anyone have any thoughts on that topic?
>
> *Helen:* Whatever you say goes, you are the leader, so we listen to you.
>
> *Martha:* Yeah, I agree—it's not up to us. You are the professional here, not us.
>
> *Group worker:* I appreciate everyone's comments. It is true that I am the group worker, but your voices and opinions are extremely important to the group. I recognize, as survivors of domestic violence, that most of you have always felt powerless in your lives, so being asked to decide on things, such as what we will discuss as a group, might feel uncomfortable to you.

Consciousness-Raising and Member Empowerment

The more information members have on power dynamics and reasons why abuse happens, the more meaningful the group will be. Having an understanding of why abuse happens and the dynamics of IPV can help reduce the self-blame survivors often experience. Depending on the purpose of the group, a group worker can incorporate specific information about dynamics and causes of IPV, as seen in the following example of a support group where a more seasoned member takes on the role of educating newer members about IPV:

> *Group worker:* Hi everyone. Welcome back to the domestic violence support group. We have some new members here. Kelly, do you mind starting off the discussion about domestic violence and why we blame ourselves?
>
> *Kelly:* Hi everyone. Some of you are probably feeling the way I did when I first came here. You feel like what happened is your fault. But it's not. Domestic violence is the abuser's fault. He decided to hit you, right?
>
> *Jan:* He didn't actually hit me.
>
> *Kelly:* It does not matter; abuse is the abuser's fault. Not ours.
>
> *Group worker:* That's right, Kelly. Intimate partner violence is an abuse of power where survivors like yourselves are made to feel responsible, as if you did something to cause the abuse, but that is not true.

Use of Activity

For many survivors, coming forward to disclose abuse is a painful and frightening experience. "Telling the story" is important but not always necessary for every member. Part of this depends on the purpose of the group and the needs of members. This speaks to the importance of careful planning before the group begins and clarity about what group members are attempting to achieve together. Many survivors of traumatic life events, including IPV, find it challenging, if not impossible, to share personal feelings associated with the violence. Others have not "tuned in" to their emotions and need another, less threatening way to access their feelings. Stories and experiences of abuse are taboo for many survivors, so discussing experiences and feelings out loud can be scary.

Creative arts offer members opportunities to express themselves in an imaginative way that is helpful and, for some, less threatening than speaking verbally. Members can be encouraged to draw out feelings and experiences or work with clay to create representations of what happened to them or to express feelings (i.e., through punching the clay). Journaling also can be a powerful means through which members can express their thoughts and feelings. Members may be asked to read their thoughts aloud, if they are comfortable doing so, or they can use writing as a vehicle for getting out painful stories and feelings.

EVALUATION OF GROUPS FOR SURVIVORS OF INTIMATE PARTNER VIOLENCE

Group work practice with survivors of IPV can be evaluated at various points in the life of the group. For example, in the beginning phase, members' ability to articulate their personal goals for group attendance and their commitment to these goals can be assessed. In the middle phase, members can be asked to evaluate how the group is going and what changes they see occurring in themselves and their situations. As the group winds down, the impact of the group on members can be ascertained using the same criteria as in the middle phase.

There are specific factors that make it hard to assess the effectiveness of groups for survivors of IPV. Multiple victimizations of members, such as trauma in childhood, history of rape and sexual victimization, sexual harassment, and fear of speaking out, can make it very difficult for many survivors to come forward. When selecting an effective evaluation measure for this population, Sullivan (2001) stresses that it is important to understand and specifically articulate how survivors will benefit. Group members need to first articulate their goals, as not all members will have the same aspirations. When deciding on evaluation measures, considerations associated with safety, confidentiality, and self-determination must be kept in mind.

Appropriate evaluation measures for group interventions with survivors of IPV may include the following:

- Enhanced understanding of the causes and consequences of IPV and available resources
- Improved ability to stay safe/implement a safety plan, if needed
- Increased ability to understand complex feelings
- Heightened feelings of empowerment and self-efficacy

In groups for IPV survivors, there are ways to generate feedback from members to achieve a sense of whether they are benefiting from group membership and to make any changes in the purpose or the content. These can be completed verbally or in writing and include the following:

- Check-in at the beginning of each session to see what members' immediate concerns are and to take the pulse of the group
- Halfway-point check-in to allow specific time halfway through a group cycle to see how things are progressing from the members' perspectives

- Asking for feedback—regularly assess how members are experiencing the group
- Final check-in to allow members to reflect on their group experience and their thoughts, feelings, and questions going forward

RESOURCES

INCITE! Women of Color Against Violence: http://www.incite-national.org/

National Coalition Against Domestic Violence: http://www.ncadv.org/

National Online Resource Center on Violence Against Women: http://www.vawnet.org/

Office on Violence Against Women: http://www.justice.gov/ovw

REFERENCES

Anderson, K. A. (2010). *Enhancing resilience in survivors of family violence*. New York, NY: Springer.

Berman-Rossi, T. (1992). Empowering groups through stages of group development. *Social Work with Groups, 15*(2/3), 239–256.

Breiding, M. J., Smith, S. G., Basile, K. C., Walters, M. L., Jieru, C., & Merrick, M. T. (2014). Prevalence and characteristics of sexual violence, stalking, and intimate partner violence victimization—National Intimate Partner and Sexual Violence Survey, United States, 2011. *MMWR Surveillance Summaries, 63*(8), 1–18.

Calton, J. M., Cattaneo, L. B., & Gebhard, K. T. (2015). Barriers to help seeking for lesbian, gay, bisexual, transgender, and queer survivors of intimate partner violence. *Trauma, Violence & Abuse*. doi:1524838015585318.

Clemans, S. E. (2004a). Recognizing vicarious traumatization: A single session group model for trauma workers. *Social Work with Groups, 27*(2/3), 55–74.

Clemans, S. E. (2004b). Life changing: The experience of rape crisis work. *Affilia, 19*(2), 146–159.

Clemans, S. E. (2005). A feminist group for women rape survivors. *Social Work with Groups, 28*(2), 59–75.

Cunningham, M. (2003). The impact of trauma work on social work clinicians: Empirical findings. *Social Work, 48*, 451–459.

Dane, B. (2000). Child welfare workers: An innovative approach to interacting with secondary trauma. *Journal of Social Work Education, 36*(1), 27–38.

Easton, C. M. (2007). A cognitive behavioral therapy for alcohol dependent domestic violence offenders: An integrated substance-abuse violence treatment approach (SADV). *American Journal on Addictions, 16*(1), 24–31.

Edwards, K., & Sylaska, K. (2013). The perpetration of intimate partner violence among LGBTQ College youth: The role of minority stress. *Journal of Youth and Adolescence, 42*(11), 1721–1731.

Figley, C. R. (2002). *Treating compassion fatigue.* New York, NY: Routledge.

Gitterman, A. (2004). The mutual aid model. In C. D. Garvin, L. M. Gutierrez, & M. Galinsky (Eds.), *Handbook of social work with groups* (pp. 93–110). New York, NY: Guilford Press.

Gorey, K. M., Daly, C., Richter, N. L., Gleason, D. R., & McCallum, M. A. (2002). The effectiveness of feminist social work methods: An integrative review. *Journal of Social Service Research, 29*(1), 37–55.

Harr, C., & Moore, B. (2011). Compassion fatigue among social work students in field placements. *Journal of Teaching in Social Work, 32,* 350–363.

Herman, J. (1997). *Trauma and recovery.* New York, NY: Basic Books.

Israeli, A. L., & Santor, D. A. (2000). Reviewing effective components of feminist therapy. *Counselling Psychology Quarterly, 13*(3), 233–247.

Howard, A., Riger, S., Campbell, R., & Wasco, S. (2003). Counseling services for battered women: A comparison of outcomes for physical and sexual assault survivors. *Journal of Interpersonal Violence, 18*(7), 717–734.

Knight, C. (2006). Groups for individuals with traumatic histories: Practice implications for social, workers. *Social Work, 51,* 20–30.

Knight, C. (2009). *Introduction to working with adult survivors of childhood trauma: Techniques and strategies.* Belmont, CA: Thompson Brooks/Cole.

Knight, C. (2015). Trauma-informed social work practice: Practice considerations and challenges. *Clinical Social Work Journal, 43*(1), 25–37.

Kurland, R., & Salmon, R. (1998). *Teaching a methods course in social work with groups.* Alexandria, VA: Council on Social Work Education.

Kurland, R., & Salmon, R. (2006). Purpose: A misunderstood and misused keystone of group work practice. *Social Work with Groups, 29*(2–3), 105–120.

Liang, B., Goodman, L., Tummala-Narra, P., & Weintraub, S. (2005). A theoretical framework for understanding help-seeking processes among survivors of intimate partner violence. *American Journal of Community Psychology, 36*(1-2), 71–84.

National Coalition against Domestic Violence. (n.d.a.). *National statistics.* Retrieved from http://www.ncadv.org/learn/statistics

National Coalition against Domestic Violence. (n.d.b.) *What is domestic violence?* Retrieved from http://www.ncadv.org/need-support/what-is-domestic-violence

Pearlman, L. A., & Saakvitne, K. W. (1995). *Trauma and the therapist: Countertransference and vicarious traumatization in psychotherapy with incest survivors.* New York, NY: W. W. Norton.

Pyles, L., & Postmus, J. L. (2004). Addressing the problem of domestic violence: How far have we come? *Affilia, 19*(4), 376–388.

Rose, S. D. (2004). Cognitive-behavioral group work. In C. D. Garvin, L. M. Gutierrez, & M. Galinsky (Eds.), *Handbook of social work with groups* (pp. 110–135). New York, NY: Guilford Press.

Shulman, L. (2012). *The skills of helping individuals, families, groups, and communities* (7th ed.). Belmont, CA: Brooks/Cole.

Steinberg, D. M. (2002). The magic of mutual aid. *Social Work with Groups, 25*(1/2), 31–38.

Sullivan, C. (2001). Evaluating the outcomes of domestic violence service programs: Some practical considerations and strategies. *VAWnet.org, National Resource Center on Domestic Violence.* Retrieved from http://www.vawnet.org/applied-research-papers/print-document.php?doc_id=380

Tsui, V. (2014). Male victims of intimate partner abuse: Use and helpfulness of services. *Social Work, 59*(2), 121–130.

Warshaw, C., Sullivan, C., & Rivera, E. A. (2013). A systematic review of trauma-focused interventions for domestic violence survivors. *National Center on Domestic Violence, Trauma, and Mental Health.* Retrieved from http://www.nationalcenterdvtraumamh.org/wp-content/uploads/2013/03/NCDVTMH_EBPLitReview2013.pdf

Wood, G. G., & Roche, S. E. (2001). Representing selves, reconstructing lives: Feminist group work with women survivors of male violence. *Social Work with Groups, 23*(4), 5–23.

Chapter Nineteen

Group Work With Children Impacted by Sexual Abuse

Betsy Offermann, Monica Beltran, Cynthia Rollo,
and Kay Martel Connors

Research indicates that child maltreatment such as child sexual abuse (CSA) causes changes in the developing brain and its functioning and alters a child's developmental trajectory, including the ability to be resilient and adjust later in life (De Bellis, Spratt, & Hooper, 2011). Social workers can strengthen children's and their families' efforts to recover and cope with the aftermath of CSA and work to reduce future victimization through psychoeducation, social support, and trauma-focused group work.

Although not all children and adults who were sexually abused develop behavioral or mental health disorders, most would benefit from treatment that focuses on managing posttraumatic stress reactions as well as the familial, psychological, and social aftermath of this widespread childhood trauma. Group work has been widely used for treating children affected by CSA. However, studies indicate mixed efficacy for some group approaches largely due to the lack of specificity in group format, recruitment criteria, and availability of control groups (England & Connors, 2005; Knight, 2006; Smith & Kelly, 2008). In this chapter, the authors report on the current research on CSA and highlight evidence-based treatments, core components, and practice approaches associated with effective group therapy for sexually traumatized children and their families.

DEFINING CHILD SEXUAL ABUSE AND ITS PREVALENCE

In 2012, approximately 63,000 cases of child sexual abuse were reported, according to the National Child Abuse and Neglect Data (NDCAN) (US Department of Health and Human Services, Administration for Children and

Families, Administration on Children, Youth, and Families, & Children's Bureau, 2012). These numbers are based on investigated reports of CSA, data from other sources, such as lifetime prevalence reports, and indicate that CSA occurs at a higher rate than is reported to child protection agencies (Finkelhor, Ormrod, Turner, & Hamby, 2005). Emerging high-risk populations for CSA are unaccompanied minors and domestic minor sex trafficking (DMST) victims. In recent years there has been a significant increase in unaccompanied minors from Central America entering the United States fleeing from gang activity, violence, abuse, poverty, and political unrest (Kennedy, 2014). These youth are at risk for and are being sexually assaulted while migrating or upon their arrival in the United States. Other children enter as sex-trafficked youth (National Immigrant Justice Center, 2014). It was estimated that between 60,000 and 90,000 unaccompanied minors may have attempted to enter the United States in 2014 (Fernandez, Chavez-Duenas, & Consoli, 2015; Kennedy, 2014). There are an estimated 100,000 to 300,000 children are at risk of commercial sexual exploitation in the United States at any given time (Smith, Vardaman, & Snow, 2009). Individual risk factors for sex trafficking include poverty, homelessness, unemployment, a history of sexual abuse, and history of mental health issues (Clawson, Dutch, Solomon, & Grace, 2009). Rejection by biological or foster families can increase vulnerability to sex trafficking (Clawson, Dorais, & Feldstein, 2005). It is estimated that familial and societal pressures that may increase risk of trafficking include family or relatives involved in commercial sex, a prevalent local gang culture (Dorais, Corriveau, & Feldstein, 2009), and socioeconomic disadvantages associated with race (Kramer & Berg, 2003).

CSA is the sexual victimization of a child by an adult or older child (most often a male acquaintance or member of the family), and it is frequently accompanied by coercion, threats, and force. The National Child Abuse and Neglect Data System defines CSA as a range of sexual acts that may include oral, genital, or anal penetration, as well as sexual touching, exposure, exploitation, and voyeurism. Legal definitions vary by state.

According to the US Department of Health and Human Services Child Maltreatment Report for 2012, substantiated reports of CSA were highest among children younger than 9 (at 34%), followed by children between the ages of 12 and 15 (at 26%). After the age of 6, girls are sexually abused at a higher rate than boys (Finkelhor et al., 2005). Although CSA, as a single event or a pattern of abuse, occurs in all communities and regardless of racial background, ethnicity, or socioeconomic status, children living in poverty and exposed to multiple traumatic events, such as community and domestic violence, are at a higher risk of sexual victimization (Finkelhor et al., 2005).

Due to the secrecy surrounding CSA and children's understandable reluctance to report it, social workers need to be aware and educate parents, teachers, and community organizations about the signs of CSA. Signs include children exhibiting increased nightmares, high levels of distress and fearfulness, withdrawn behaviors, anger or aggressive outbursts, problematic sexualized behaviors, and knowledge of sexual information not consistent with what is age appropriate. Victims of DMST often do not self-identify as victims. The result is a denial of the victimization due to fear of the physical and psychological abuse inflicted by the trafficker and/or due to the trauma bonds developed through the victimization process. The bond between a victim and her trafficker/pimp is referred to as a "trauma bond." Trauma bonds are a major hurdle to the identification, rescue, and restoration of the DMST victim as the symptoms include failure to self-identify, returning to the trafficker/pimp, and other discouraging reactions. Dr. Patrick Carnes, an expert on trauma bonds, explains, "This [traumatic bonding] means that the victims have a certain dysfunctional attachment that occurs in the presence of danger, shame, or exploitation. There is often seduction, deception, or betrayal" (Carnes, 1997, p. 29).

Social workers should also be alert to signs in adults who, when interacting with children, display or have a history of inappropriate behaviors. These behaviors can include making sexually provocative or degrading comments or jokes, patting others on the buttocks, initiating intimate/romantic/sexual contact, using corporal punishment on children they are supervising, allowing or encouraging youth to go to Internet sites with sexual content, using electronic communication to send youth sexually oriented photographs or messages, showing pornography, involving youth in pornographic activities, and/or having a known history of sexual perpetration.

Equally as important is the process of grooming. Grooming is a process in which a predator actively works to gain the trust of the child and the parent. A predator may pretend to be interested in dating the parent but is really interested in the child. Or a predator may offer to babysit for free or do other favors for the family in order to gain access to the child. The grooming typically takes places over a period of months in order to break down the child's defenses and increase the child's acceptance of physical touch. Social media platforms such as Facebook, Twitter, and Instagram are a breeding ground for perpetrators to entice new victims by creating a false sense of connection. Sexting is more prominent in these arenas as well, and teens will often not realize how far reaching and cruel social media can be or how it can contribute to potential victimization.

Social workers can help others better understand why children are reluctant to disclose CSA or recant their disclosures, so that they can help stop the abuse and the healing process can begin. Parents, teachers, and providers need to understand that children who have been sexually abused often feel shame and guilt. They fear the perpetrator will hurt them or their family. Children also fear that they will not be believed if they disclose the abuse and that they may be removed from their homes.

REVIEW OF THE CHILD SEXUAL ABUSE LITERATURE

Effective treatments are essential tools in reducing the long-term negative effects of CSA. Multiple studies indicate that children who have been sexually abused are at high risk of serious mental and behavioral health disorders and poor social and emotional outcomes (Kendall-Tackett, Williams, & Finkelhor, 1993; Trickett & Putnam, 1993). CSA can result in posttraumatic stress disorder (PTSD), ranging from acute to chronic in nature. Symptoms of PTSD include reexperiencing the abuse, intrusion, numbing, avoidance, negative alterations in cognitions and mood, hyperarousal, and reactivity (American Psychiatric Association, 2013). Victims of CSA report four times as many self-harm or suicide attempts and twice as many episodes of revictimization, including sexual abuse, rape or assault, domestic violence, and physical affronts (Noll, Horowitz, Bonanno, Tricket, & Putnam, 2003). A hallmark longitudinal study on CSA provided evidence of the biopsychosocial impact of CSA on 82 females across developmental stages (Putnam, 2003). Although the findings identify the resilience of these young women, they also highlight the toll CSA has had on their physical and psychological health and social development. When compared with their peers, these women had lower social competence; lower academic performance; higher school avoidance; more depression; increased self-harm and suicidal behaviors; more dissociation; more sexual acting-out behaviors; more behavior problems and delinquency; lower self-esteem; higher rates of teen sexual activity and pregnancy; higher rates of substance abuse; poorer physical health, including obesity, hormonal disruption, and gastrointestinal complaints; lower rates of health care utilization; and more sleep disturbances (Noll, Horowitz, et al., 2003; Noll, Trickett, & Putnam, 2003).

In attempting to explain the complexities of CSA and its sequelae, researchers have investigated risk and protective factors, such as abuse (e.g., duration, severity), family (e.g., maternal mental illness and substance abuse; parental history of victimization; family communication, functioning, and ability to protect its members), socioeconomic risk factors (e.g., poverty, homelessness, access to services), and child characteristics (e.g., age, gender, intelligence, temperament). The Adverse Childhood Experiences (ACE) Study is one of the largest investigations ever conducted to assess associations between childhood maltreatment and later-life health and well-being. The ACE Study findings suggest that certain experiences are major risk factors for the leading causes of illness and death as well as poor quality of life in the United States. Realizing these connections is likely to improve efforts toward prevention and recovery (Felitti et al., 1998). Child outcomes are mediated by parent and family responses to their sexual trauma. To support child adjustment, family members need to nurture and protect their child as they learn about the impact of CSA and to apply consistent parenting practices that help children stay on their developmental trajectory (Cohen & Mannarino, 2000). Another major factor influencing adjustment is children's cognitions, including attributions associated with the abuse and use of coping strategies (Valle & Silovsky, 2002). Children may attribute sexual abuse to internal or external factors; for instance, they may blame themselves or the dangerousness of the world. Children who recognize that the abuser is responsible for his or her actions fare better later in life than do children who assume some blame (Lev-Wiesel, 2000).

In an effort to negate long-term mental health and adjustment problems, group therapy can have a positive impact on these cognitive factors by setting forth treatment goals to correct cognitive misattributions, increase self-esteem, reduce isolation, strengthen coping skills, and promote prosocial behaviors (Hetzel-Riggins, Brausch, & Montgomery, 2007; Silverman et al., 2008). Increasing access to resources and strengthening the child and family's capacity for resiliency are essential protective factors in the recovery process (Wilcox, Richards, & O'Keefe, 2004).

PRACTICE PRINCIPLES AND GUIDELINES

Social workers in the mental health and child welfare fields are challenged to apply research findings effectively to their complex daily work with children and families affected by CSA. Social work group practice focusing on mutual aid, strengths, and empowerment is well suited for children and families affected by trauma, including CSA (Knight, 2006). Therapeutic groups offer opportunities to reduce the isolation that often accompanies CSA as well as support coping and resilience through educating clients on the impact of CSA and teaching effective psychological and prosocial skills (Knight, 2006). The following sections detail the practice guidelines for social workers conducting groups aimed at reducing risks and supporting growth and recovery among children and families impacted by CSA. The sections include information on the impact of culture on CSA, screening/assessment, core components, and available group treatments for CSA. Tips for successful implementation and common themes observed in groups are included.

Cultural Considerations

Respect for clients' cultural, geographical, religious, spiritual, and ethnic identities is a core social work value, and effective practitioners seek to understand and mobilize cultural resources to help the child and family recover from CSA. Mental health professionals must increase their knowledge and skills in delivering culturally competent child sexual abuse treatment and at the same time be aware of and reflect on their own assumptions, biases, and countertransference

(Fontes & Plummer, 2010). Cultural perceptions about healing, and receptivity to and perceived helpfulness of mental health services, impact the treatment process and vary based on experience with mental health care and the child welfare system, racial/ethnic discrimination, degree of acculturation, and the family's cultural and spiritual beliefs and traditions (US Department of Health and Human Services, 2007). African American families who have had negative encounters with the police and feel that they have been treated unfairly in the criminal justice system through discriminatory or racist practices may be less apt to rely on child welfare systems to respond to sexual abuse allegations (Lowe, Pavkov, Casanova, & Wetchler, 2005). The following example illustrates how spiritual and cultural values can affect the course of CSA treatment:

> A mother brought her 11-year-old daughter for treatment after she had disclosed that her father had sexually abused her on multiple occasions. The mother reported that she was reluctant to have her daughter participate in therapy that encouraged her daughter to talk about what happened, and she did not want to testify against the father in court. She reported that she had talked with her family and pastor about her doubts and they advised her to focus on forgiving the father (a central theme in Christian religions) rather than prosecuting him for the crime of CSA. During this time, a family had been murdered in the community for informing the police of neighborhood drug-dealing activities and citizens were being threatened to "Stop Snitching." The mother and daughter felt frightened and conflicted by their cultural context and spiritual beliefs. The therapist asked the mother to invite her family to treatment and provided information on CSA to the pastor. Eventually, the mother and daughter participated in trauma-focused cognitive-behavioral therapy and completed the trauma narrative. They testified in court and the father pled guilty; he was charged and incarcerated.

Cultural norms, religion, and beliefs often determine the family's views on sexuality, nudity, discipline practices, family boundaries, respect for elders, personal and familial privacy, gender and family roles, and acceptance of strangers (Haboush & Alyan, 2013; Saunders, Berliner, & Hanson, 2004). Haboush and Alyan (2013) state that "Arab culture emphasizes the central role of family and importance of preserving family honor, including female virginity, and the essential role of religion; as a result, sexual issues are generally not openly discussed" (p. 501). Kenny and Wurtele (2008) conducted a study with Latino preschoolers about their knowledge of the proper names for breasts, penis, and vulva. Results showed that none of the children could accurately name them. Traditional Latino cultural norms may inhibit discussions about sexuality between children and their caregivers which can inhibit sexual abuse disclosure (Fontes & Plummer, 2010; Kenny & Wurtele, 2013).

Although more research is needed to understand how sociocultural factors affect CSA, it is clear families' and caregivers' responses to CSA and the cultural context have a powerful effect on outcomes for children (Cohen & Mannarino, 2000; Kiser & Black, 2005; Saunders et al., 2004; Zajac, Ralston, & Smith, 2015). Culturally relevant, trauma-informed engagement strategies that research indicates are effective in groups include addressing stigma associated with CSA and use of mental health services; understanding the acceptable range of emotional expressions and attitudes regarding the "telling of family business"; attending to concrete barriers to services (e.g. lack of insurance, language barriers, transportation, and child care); conducting structured intakes and follow-up telephone calls; offering social support and multifamily groups; partnering with families to develop a treatment plan that best fits their preference; supporting parents' and caregivers' efforts to understand the impact of CSA on their child's development and in advocating for needed services; and offering groups in settings that are more accessible to families (e.g., pediatricians' offices, schools, and faith-based or community organizations) (Cohen et al., 2001; McKay, Hibbert, Hoagwood, et al., 2004; Snell-Johns, Mendez, & Smith, 2004). Building on the inherent strengths of the family and their community, combined with identifying group interventions that are effective and congruent with the families' cultural values and norms, increases the likelihood that children will receive the care they need. Finally, much more research is needed to increase the knowledge base of how effective CSA treatment adaptations are to different cultural groups (Murray, Nguyen, & Cohen, 2014).

Screening and Assessment

Social workers preparing to start group therapy with this population should conduct comprehensive biopsychosocial assessments to better understand the impact of each child's symptoms on the child and his or her family. The National Child Traumatic Stress Network defines *trauma-informed care* as including trauma-specific, developmentally relevant screening, assessment, and treatment (www. nctsn.org). Standardized measures should assess for posttraumatic stress, depression, anxiety, and behavioral symptoms. Higher avoidance symptoms have been associated with lower treatment completion rates (Murphy et al., 2014). Assessing the level of avoidance symptoms can prepare group leaders for potential participation barriers and the engagement strategies that may be needed. Although the tools for forensic assessment have improved, standardized CSA clinical assessments are rare (Lev-Wiesel, 2008). Social workers must be cautious to avoid misdiagnosing children who have been sexually abused. For example, many behavioral symptoms are indicators of more than one mental health diagnosis; children with trauma symptoms can be misdiagnosed as having attention-deficit/hyperactivity disorder (ADHD) (Cohen & Mannarino, 2000).

In addition to assessing a child's individual strengths and needs, effective assessment practices emphasize focusing on family relationships, as well as environmental and cultural contexts. Structured interviews and standardized measures guide the process of gathering information to design a treatment plan that fits the families' needs and allows the family and social worker to monitor change over time. The overall goal of treatment is to reduce symptoms and increase child and family safety, health, and well-being (de Arellano & Danielson, 2008).

A trauma-informed initial assessment provides psychoeducation to the child and caregiver about the focus, goals, and expectations of the group to determine client readiness to participate. Some clients benefit from joining a group after they have started sexual abuse–focused individual or family therapy. This may provide the opportunity for the child to increase his or her comfort addressing sexual abuse in a safe therapeutic environment. Another consideration is the client's willingness to be in a group. It is recommended that clients not be mandated to attend a group related to sexual abuse.

> A 16-year-old African American female was attending family therapy to address her trauma and depressive symptoms following the sexual abuse by her older cousin. She had started to make progress addressing the sexual abuse but still presented with significant depressive symptoms and social isolation. Her therapist and mother thought that a group would help decrease her isolation and allow her to connect with others who have had a similar experience. The client did not want to attend the group and, although the therapist believed she was ready, the therapist knew she would need to wait until the client recognized this and was willing to give it a try.

An assessment of the client's basic self-regulation skills and high-risk symptoms that could negatively impact the ability of the client to benefit from the group or could impact the overall group functioning is also recommended.

Group Treatments

Group work is frequently used in the treatment of CSA. Clinical research is advancing the field's efforts to identify the most effective group treatment for victims of CSA (Harvey & Taylor, 2010; Hetzel-Riggin et al., 2007; Tourigny & Hebert, 2007). The Institute of Medicine and California Evidence-based Clearinghouse for Child Welfare define "evidence-based practice" (EBP) as interventions that are theoretically sound; consistent with practice principles and values; acceptable and applicable to clients; effective and have no or low risks associated with them; and manualized and supported by at least two randomized controlled treatment outcome studies that indicate the treatment is superior to the comparison treatment (Institute of Medicine, 2001).

Several evidence-based and evidenced-informed trauma-specific therapies (beyond the scope of this chapter to describe in depth) have been developed through collaborations between researchers and clinicians and have been used successfully with CSA. These include trauma-focused cognitive-behavioral therapy (TF-CBT) (Cohen, Mannarino, & Deblinger, 2006); cognitive-behavioral interventions for trauma in schools (CBITS) (Jaycox, 2004); structured psychotherapy for adolescents responding to chronic stress (SPARCS) (Habib, Labruna, & Newman, 2013).); safety, mentoring, advocacy, recovery, and treatment (SMART) (Offermann, Belcher, Johnson, & Johnson-Brooks, 2008); and trauma adaptive recovery group education and therapy (TARGET) for adolescents and preadolescents (Avinger & Jones, 2007; Hetzel-Riggin et al., 2007). Group-based TF-CBT with war-affected, sexually exploited girls in the Democratic Republic of Congo was evaluated in a randomized controlled trial in which those that received TF-CBT demonstrated significantly greater reductions in symptoms compared with the wait-list condition (O'Callaghan, McMullen, Shannon, Rafferty, & Black, 2013).

Multiple studies and systematic reviews indicate that cognitive-behavioral therapy (CBT) is highly effective for the treatment of PTSD symptoms, including CSA (Avinger & Jones, 2007; Harvey & Taylor, 2010; Hetzel-Riggin et al., 2007; MacDonald, Higgins, & Ramchandani, 2009; Silverman et al., 2008; Tourigny & Hebert, 2007). A Cochrane review found that cognitive-behavioral therapy (CBT) had the greatest efficacy of the reduction of PTSD symptoms as well as a significant decrease in depressive symptoms (Gillies, Taylor, Gray, O'Brien, & D'Abrew, 2012).

Common treatment elements found in cognitive-behavioral approaches for PTSD include psychoeducation, relaxation, affective modulation, exposure, and cognitive restructuring (Dorsey, Briggs, & Woods, 2011). Project SAFE is an example that utilizes a standardized cognitive-behavioral group treatment for families who have experienced CSA. It focuses on "(a) the individual/self (e.g. self-esteem, self-blame, internalizing difficulties), (b) interpersonal relationships (e.g. social skills, externalizing problems with peers and family), and (c) sexual development and behaviors (e.g., sexual knowledge, sexual abuse-specific psychoeducation, sexual behavior problems" (Hubel et al., 2014, p. 307).

Group work with children who have experienced sexual abuse is effective for early latency-aged children through adolescence. For example, group CBT has been found to decrease future sexual acting out and offenses in children who have experienced sexual abuse (Carpentier, Silovsky, & Chaffin, 2006). There is also evidence that treatment of young sexual abuse victims helps reduce symptoms, as well as prevent potential negative outcomes (Deblinger, Stauffer, & Steer, 2001). School-aged children who are familiar with classroom formats and enjoy peer interaction feel comfortable in groups. They can benefit from the interactive format focusing on action-oriented planning and coping. Group therapies are also highly effective for adolescents as peer identification and interactions are a developmental priority. Tourigny, Hébert, Daigneault, and Simoneau (2005) found that adolescent girls who had been sexually abused and participated in group therapy had an increased sense of empowerment, better relationships with their mothers, and a decrease in symptoms of PTSD after group therapy. Another study with adolescent girls found group participation helped decrease depressive and PTSD symptoms (Smith & Kelly, 2008). Connecting with peers facing similar problems reduces the shame and isolation surrounding CSA for all age groups (Avinger & Jones, 2007). Parallel caregiver and child sexual abuse groups, where the child and caregiver participate in separate groups at the same time, also have positive outcomes (Hubel et al., 2014). Parental involvement in treatment has been shown to decrease parental abuse-related distress and depressive symptoms and increase parenting and safety skills (Cohen, Deblinger, Mannarino, & Steer, 2004; Hubel et al., 2014; Tavkar & Hansen, 2011). Children and adults can benefit from the unique experience groups offer to give and receive help from others (Knight, 2006).

Therapeutic Stance

Beginning group leaders need training and supervision to conduct groups or any other type of treatment with children who have been sexually abused. Social workers planning to conduct such groups must be creative and consistent in setting limits and managing challenging behaviors in the group. Empathy and acceptance are key elements in creating a safe space for children in group to discuss their thoughts, feelings, and memories. Social workers are challenged to develop the capacity to feel deeply for what the children are feeling without losing their own perspective (Compton & Galaway, 1989). The following are best practice guidelines for group leaders in conducting sexual abuse groups: provide a safe, structured, and consistent therapeutic environment; avoid aligning with the victim and rejecting the perpetrator; express warmth and positive regard for group members; communicate in a clear, calm, and direct manner; establish and model clear boundaries and roles; and eliminate secrecy (Deblinger, 1996).

Implementation Guidelines

Getting Started
Group treatment is a cost-effective modality, allowing multiple children with varying symptoms to be treated simultaneously (Hubel et al., 2014). However, it requires adequate space, supplies, and support for successful implementation. In addition to receiving training and adhering to evidence-based or promising group therapy models, organizational support is critical to successful implementation (Fixsen, Naoom, Blasé, & Friedman, 2005). The availability of a confidential, child-friendly group room equipped with both art and play supplies helps to build group cohesion and trust. Unfortunately, such resources and supplies

are often difficult to obtain in agencies with budget and space limitations. Social workers' initiative and ingenuity are essential to overcoming these obstacles.

> In one urban agency, group leaders effectively advocated for the conversion of a staff room into a child's play room. They negotiated for the exclusive use of the room for evening group sessions, while agency social workers were given daily access to conduct child interviews. Another group leader got several donations from community toy and art stores. The result: an exceptionally well-stocked playroom well beyond the agency's limited budget.

Group Structure

The group's structure is largely determined by the model, but here are some general considerations:

1. *Open- vs. closed-ended group:* Research indicates that participants can benefit from both types of groups, and participants have demonstrated increased use of problem-solving and coping skills as well as social support-seeking behaviors (Tourginey & Hebert, 2007). However, the lack of fluid membership in an open-ended group can be a challenge for the leader who has to prepare the space and supplies each week and it is often contraindicated for CSA abuse victims who flourish from the structure, predictability, trauma containment, safety, and cohesion present in a close-ended group.

2. *Group composition:* Age, development, and gender are important factors in composing a CSA group. Younger children's groups should be smaller, with four to six children. Adolescent groups can be larger, with 10 members being the upper limit. Leaders must carefully distinguish between children's chronological age and developmental age.

Brianna is a small-in-stature and emotionally immature 12-year-old, who had been sexually abused by her step-father and a boy in the neighborhood for over a year. Her placement in a preadolescent group was fraught with difficulties. Brianna was overwhelmed with the other members' desire to talk about how their abusive experiences have influenced their interest in boys and issues more directly related to sexuality. Brianna often shut down and isolated herself in the corner. Group leaders transferred Briana to the latency age group where her emotional/developmental needs were better met.

3. *Co-leaders:* There are many advantages to co-leadership in CSA groups. Co-leaders can provide each other support and encouragement and an opportunity to discuss the group process with another colleague. Continuity problems are reduced when one leader is absent. Also, having two observers reduces the likelihood of missing important interchanges among the members. A major challenge to co-leadership is the organizational cost, which, at times, is prohibitive. Another challenge could be interleader conflict. Group leaders need to be aware

of possible conflicts and be willing to examine them constructively so that group effectiveness is not impaired. Co-leadership can also provide excellent opportunities to model conflict resolution behavior for the group members.

During a group activity, group leaders intentionally disagreed on the best approach to splitting the members into smaller groups to model the problem-solving process. The group leaders enlisted the children to offer suggestions for the best way to resolve the issue, and the group members were able to offer practical strategies for random assignment into smaller groups. Group leaders were able to praise and reinforce group members' use of coping and problem-solving skills toward positive outcomes.

Developmental Considerations

In preparing for group work with sexually abused children, a developmental approach that includes cognitive-behavioral interventions that focus on the impact of the traumatic experience(s) (understanding the trauma story, correcting misattributions and cognitive distortions) is recommended. This approach can also help to decrease isolation, increase support and sense of safety, normalize responses to trauma, increase understanding of sexual abuse, support emotional regulation (e.g., coping with traumatic memories and reminders, stress inoculation techniques), and support adjustment to secondary adversities (e.g., removal from home, court testimony, unsupportive maternal response, etc.) (McFarlane, 1996; Tavkar & Hansen, 2011). Groups enable children to form bonds with peers in a structured environment that enables them to discuss feelings and ideas openly, with reduced risk of inappropriate negative interactions (e.g., teasing, ridicule) and discussion of individual differences that often hinder relationships among them in unstructured interactions. Through the use of developmentally appropriate structured activities, children and adolescents are often able to articulate personal feelings and provide interpersonal feedback to their peers that they would have difficulty verbalizing to adults (Trotzer, 2006). It is recommended that groups be designed to capitalize on the skills they have attained and to adjust for the skills they have yet to attain.

Emotional Regulation

Children experience a range of feelings related to CSA, including, fear, anger, pleasure, shame, guilt, and sadness (Berliner, 1991; Browne & Finkelhor, 1986). Putman (2009) points out that the effects of CSA "can leave the child survivor feeling that he or she has little to no control over his or her actions, emotions, thoughts, and behaviors" (p. 88). It is not uncommon for CSA survivors to experience emotional dysregulation, which may place teens at risk for engaging in sexual behaviors to self-soothe (Messman-Moore, Walsh, & DiLillo, 2010; Walsh, DiLillo, & Scalora, 2011). Children experience emotional reactivity, emotional numbing or constriction, and decreased ability for empathic responses (Kim & Cicchetti, 2010). These effects lead to difficulties in peer relationships. Effective groups address these symptoms by providing psychoeducation and building coping and prosocial skills through group activities. Children often express anger toward the caretaker who did not protect them from the abuse or who did not respond protectively after the abuse was revealed. Guilt or shame often accompanies perceptions that they are responsible for the sexual abuse, its disclosure, and the resulting family disruption. The following example illustrates the complexity of these emotional responses:

> Vicki's father forced her to adopt her deceased mother's parental and marital role. Disclosure occurred when neighborhood children saw Vicki's father raping her through the bedroom window. Thirteen-year-old Vicki believed herself to be an "unfit parent" who caused her five siblings to be placed in three different foster homes.

Depression and Self-Harm

Depression, suicide, and self-mutilation have been observed in both sexually abused children and adults (Noll et al., 2003; Pisaruk, Shawchuck, & Hoier, 1992). Young (1992) hypothesizes that self-abuse may occur when survivors believe they cannot trust their own bodies because they feel vulnerable or ashamed or because they felt some pleasure while the abuse was occurring. Social workers should evaluate all children in CSA treatment for possible depression and suicidal ideation and listen during group for overt or covert references to self-harm.

> Twelve-year-old Michah, who was sexually abused by her mother's three boyfriends, reported in group that "it would be easier if I were dead so I would not have to deal with all of this." Group leaders validated the difficult experiences Michah and other group members have faced, normalized having a range of thoughts and emotions, and addressed how to access supports for help managing these emotions. One group leader then met individually with Michah to assess if she had any current intent to harm herself and to develop a safety plan. Michah was able to contract for safety and planned to follow up with her mother after group.

Creating Boundaries and Setting Limits

Offenders often used and abused their position of authority to gain control over and sexually exploit children (Kloess, Beech, & Harkins, 2014). Children may generalize this misuse of authority to their social workers and expect them, too, to abuse their authority. This can result in avoidant or oppositional behaviors. Social workers can use this testing of authority as an opportunity for children to experience authority in a more appropriate manner. It is the group leaders' responsibility to set and adhere to clear, consistent rules, routines, and structure to model clear communication and healthy relationships. Group rules teach children that they will not be permitted to hurt themselves or another group member, nor will they be permitted to break or destroy any of the toys or equipment in the playroom. Group members require a high degree of trust and comfort to discuss their sexual abuse experiences. Limits and clear expectations set by the group leaders help reduce anxiety and build a foundation of trust so that the members can feel safe engaging in treatment (Mathews & Gerrity, 2002). Group leaders must address when boundaries are crossed in order to help maintain appropriate boundaries to help the child learn the skills to prevent future revictimization (Mathews & Gerrity, 2002). These authors suggest that therapists who have their own child sexual abuse history access supervision and be conscientious about countertransference and maintaining healthy boundaries with clients.

Confidentiality

It is important for children to clearly understand the principles of confidentiality and all exceptions that result in information being shared with other professionals or their caregivers. Group leaders should tell participants that if they say anything indicating that they may be or have been abused or hurt again, either by themselves or by others, their group leaders will take action to protect them. This statement should be made in the initial interview and reiterated throughout the life of the group. In the authors' experience, this message does not inhibit children's discussion or revelations. Children will continue to reveal important information, counting on social workers to act responsibly and to take protective action on their behalf. When social workers give unrealistic assurances of confidentiality or fail to take protective action, children can be harmed and their trust irrevocably broken. If a child's statement must be revealed, group leaders should inform the child of the decision and the reasons (Koverola, Murtaugh, Connors, Reeves, & Papas, 2007).

Managing the Therapist's Reaction to Traumatic Stories

Group work with children affected by CSA is very intense. Social workers have to manage their own reactions to the stories of trauma, as well as their own stress and feelings related to this challenging work. Social workers are uniquely vulnerable to symptoms of burnout, secondary traumatic stress, and vicarious trauma. Research suggests that the greatest benefits are most effectively addressed through a combination of self-care strategies and top-down, organizational interventions. However, much work is needed in this area (Many & Osofsky, 2011). Debriefing, reflective supervision, peer-to-peer support, and/or group supervision are all effective strategies to support social workers to manage their reactions to vicarious trauma (Osofsky, Putnam, & Lederman, 2008). Currently, researchers are ex-amining the concept of vicarious resilience. Hernandez et al. (2007) contend that therapists may become resilient as readily as they may become wounded by empathically engaging with a client's trauma material.

Group Techniques

The agenda and activities are determined by the model and its session goals or structure. In general, activities are designed to be safe, relevant, and fun. Group members are likely to present with a range of sexual abuse experiences and symptoms, and group techniques are successful when they are able to address this variability (Hubel et al., 2014). Establishing rules, boundaries, limits of confidentiality, and group rituals at the start of group can help provide containment and predictability, which is particularly important for children who have experienced sexual abuse. This may include providing guidelines or limits for the level of detail group members share about their sexual abuse. This will help prevent members from being burdened by other members' traumatic experiences (Wanlass, Moreno, & Thomson, 2006). Topics that are commonly addressed within the group include safety and boundaries; secrecy; guilt; shame and responsibility; self-esteem; body image; assertiveness; and healthy relationships. A variety of approaches (e.g., process oriented, expressive, practice based) can be used to address these topics. Following are some general groups techniques that help build rapport, trust, and cohesion and have relevance in many settings.

Icebreakers

Icebreakers help build rapport in the first group and can be used at the start of sessions to help build group cohesion. Young children especially enjoy name games that make the chore of learning new names fun. Older children respond well to activities designed to ease their anxiety about the group in more sophisticated and direct ways. Using "getting to know you" activities that promote discussion about favorite movies, music, or video games, as well as things they do not like, eases anxiety and helps them find common ground. Some topics commonly incorporated in icebreakers may be potential triggers related to a child's sexual abuse (e.g., family, siblings, and living situations).

> Thirteen-year-old Jen, who was sexually abused by her brother, expressed that she was always anxious that peers would ask why her brother was not currently living at her home. She tried to avoid answering questions that related to her family.

It is important that the theme of sexual abuse be directly described by the group leaders at the start of the group. It can be helpful to utilize an activity designed to increase members' comfort with this topic. The Safety Boat is an activity that can be introduced at the start of group to establish the common experience of sexual abuse among group members. Group leaders introduce the concept "We are all in the same boat" and members are encouraged to draw a picture of themselves and something or someone that helps them feel safe in a section of a boat. All the pictures are connected and the concept of safety and building group cohesion is discussed (Offermann, 1998).

> During one group, after all group members' pictures were connected, 7-year-old Davon suggested that a gold line be drawn around the entire boat to be a "safety shield" to represent the safety within the group.

Encouraging members to contribute their own creative ideas will help them develop ownership in the group, which will enhance the group process and individual client gains.

Creative Activities

There is a long tradition of using expressive therapies or techniques to promote emotional expression (Caholic, Lougheed, & Cadell, 2009; Hetzel-Riggin et al., 2007). Making collages, drawing, writing poetry, and writing songs are excellent ways for children to express feelings, develop self-esteem, tell their story, and build relationships in a nonthreatening manner. Emerging research supporting the use of creative approaches includes a Holistic Arts-Based Group Program (HAP), which teaches mindfulness through arts-based methods. A study of HAP with children in need found decreased self-reported emotional reactivity following treatment (Coholic, Eys, & Lougheed, 2012). Coholic (2011) suggests that utilizing arts-based methods to build mindfulness skills is particularly well suited for children who have experienced trauma due to the safe and engaging format. Additionally, Shechtman and Mor (2010) found a reduction in PTSD symptoms and anxiety in children and adolescents that participated in an expressive-supportive therapeutic group.

Meaning making has been identified as an important yet challenging element of recovery following sexual abuse (Cohen, Mannarino, & Deblinger, 2006; Simon, Feiring, & McElroy, 2010). Expressive techniques that help a child make meaning of his or her trauma can be a powerful part of the group therapy experience. The Monument Quilt, a community-based art project, was created by survivors of sexual trauma and their supporters to transform the current culture of public shame into one of public support. In collaboration with this project, an expressive arts group was developed to create individual fabric quilts that visually represented the story of members' experience as CSA survivors. The Monument Quilt will culminate with an historic display in Washington, DC, where thousands of fabric squares from survivors of sexual trauma will blanket the National Mall, spelling out "Not Alone" (https://themonumentquilt.org/). Group leaders facilitated a discussion of the way monuments serve to honor the heroes of our history, to grieve the losses of violence, and to remember and reflect. Group members acknowledged the impact of shame and silence related to sexual abuse and expressed the importance of helping survivors find their voice.

Role Playing

Techniques that are well suited for cognitive-behavioral interventions can help children of all ages to practice coping and problem-solving skills. Participants role-play interpersonal dilemmas with which they are struggling and can practice talking with someone about a difficult topic or personal feelings (Beidel, Turner, & Morris, 2000). Group members can role-play scenarios related to personal safety and assertiveness that can help build and strengthen these skills while decreasing feelings of shame (Deblinger & Runyon, 2005).

Bibliotherapy

Bibliotherapy is often used to address many of the common themes in CSA groups. These include books that provide psychoeducation about CSA (normalize responses to the abuse), decrease isolation, demonstrate resiliency and strength, promote emotion identification and expression, support disclosure and narration, and teach safety skills. It is particularly helpful to utilize stories that incorporate similar situations to group members. These would include books that include a perpetrator who is known to the child, a child who has a change of placement following the abuse, and children from various cultural backgrounds (Ginns-Gruenberg & Zacks, 2011). Books or stories that utilize metaphors for abuse or use fictional characters can allow a child to connect the experiences of those in the book to their own experiences in a less threatening manner (Betzalel & Shechtman, 2010; Ginns-Gruenberg & Zacks, 2011). Books should be selected purposefully and address specific goals of the group. A short bibliography is provided at the end of this chapter.

Skill in Group Termination

Saying goodbye is an opportunity to celebrate accomplishments and practice coping with difficult feelings, such as sadness, anger, and anxiety. Group leaders must not only pay attention to the structured activities planned for the end of group, but to the process as well (Heiman & Ettin, 2001). Sexually abused children often have experienced many abrupt and traumatic endings in their lives. Their own separation or family member's removal leaves little or no opportunity to say goodbye to family members or neighborhood friends. The reality of these traumatic, abrupt endings in these children's lives should be considered in determining guidelines for group termination. Thoughtful and planned termination can provide an opportunity for members to have a positive and rewarding ending.

During the last session of the Monument Quilt group, members had the opportunity to share about their work and what they gained from the group experience. As each individual shared, other group members offered support and encouraging feedback. Fourteen-year-old Sofia exhibited a high level of avoidance and previously had not narrated much of her CSA, even though she had participated in sexual abuse–focused family therapy. During the final group session, Sofia was able to appropriately talk about the impact of her CSA and indicated that she shared with the group in greater detail than she had ever shared with anyone before. The group offered her support, and she identified that the group had been helpful in making her realize that she is not alone as a survivor of sexual abuse. All members expressed feeling reluctant to end, but they were proud about the work they had accomplished.

Social workers conducting groups with sexually abused children should provide a well-defined termination process when members enter the group. By making group termination an expected and positive outcome, social workers can help children plan more thoroughly for endings.

EVALUATION

A review of the literature reveals that many researchers evaluate groups' effectiveness by investigating the amelioration of or reduction in posttraumatic stress symptoms (Deblinger, 2001; Trowell et al., 2002). The following assessment tools measure changes in PTSD symptoms and can be administered at the beginning and end of treatment: UCLA PTSD Index for DSM-5 (Pynoos & Steinberg, 2013), the Child PTSD Symptom Scale (CPSS) (Foa, Johnson, Feeny, & Treadwell, 2001), and the Trauma Symptom Checklist for Children (TSCC) (Briere, 1996). These measures are considered standard in evaluating the posttraumatic symptoms of avoidance, arousal, and reexperiencing.

CONCLUSION

Therapeutic groups offer opportunities to reduce PTSD symptoms and isolation often associated with CSA. Effective group treatments support the development of new coping skills, increase emotional regulation, foster resilience through educating clients on the impact of CSA, and teach effective psychological and prosocial skills (Knight, 2006). The authors have found conducting groups with sexually abused children to be a professionally rewarding experience. Group work using trauma-focused cognitive-behavioral interventions is highly effective in reducing posttraumatic stress symptoms and addressing the psychosocial needs of this vulnerable population. In our experience, some children who refuse to speak about their abuse and are quiet and reticent in individual therapy disclose their victimization more readily within groups and experience relief on meeting and hearing from other children with similar experiences. The experienced therapist uses the relationships within the group to support and enhance the treatment experience. Whenever the opportunity arises, the group leader should help connect members to members. When shared histories are acknowledged, the sense of belonging is increased, greater cohesion takes place, and prosocial skills and support are promoted. Group therapy is most effective in combination with individual and family therapy in the treatment of CSA.

RESOURCES

Resources on Defining Child Sexual Abuse

Centers for Disease Control and Prevention link for preventing child sexual
http://www.cdc.gov/ncipc/dvp/PreventingChildSexualAbuse.pdf.

Child Welfare Gateway Information
http://www.childwelfare.gov:80/index.cfm

National Child Traumatic Stress Network Fact Sheets on CSA
http://www.nctsn.org/trauma-types/sexual-abuse

Resources for Preparing to Work With Children Impacted by Child Sexual Abuse

The Promise of Trauma-Focused Therapy for Childhood Sexual Abuse This DVD was developed to provide information on the impact of CSA and highlight critical elements for successful treatment. http://www.nctsnet.org/resources/audiences/parents-caregivers/treatments-that-work

READING LIST FOR CHILDREN

Bean, B., & Bennett, S. (1997). *A guide for teen survivors: The me nobody knows.* San Francisco, CA: Jossey-Bass.

Bell, R. (1998). *Changing bodies, changing lives: Expanded 3rd edition: A book for teens on sex and relationships.* New York, NY: Times Books.

Carter, W. L. (2002). *It happened to me: A teen's guide to overcoming sexual abuse.* Oakland, CA: New Harbinger.

Cook, J. (2007). *Personal space camp.* Chattanooga, TN: National Center for Youth Issues.

Crisci, G., Lay, M., & Lowenstein, L. (1998). *Paper dolls, paper airplanes: Therapeutic exercises for sexually traumatized children.* Indianapolis, IN: Kidsrights.

Farber Straus, S. (2013). *Healing days: A guide for kids who have experienced trauma.* Washington, DC: Magination Press.

Hansen, D. (2007). *Those are MY private parts.* Redondo Beach, CA: Empowerment Productions.

Hindman, J. (1985). *A very touching book . . . for little people and big people.* Baker City, OR: Alexandria Associates.

Holmes, M. M. (2000). *A terrible thing happened.* Washington, DC: Magination Press.

Jessie. (1991). *Please tell! A child's story about sexual abuse.* Center City, MN: Hazelden Foundation.

Sheppard, C. H. (1998). *Brave Bart: A story for traumatized and grieving children.* Grosse Pointe Woods, MI: Institute for Trauma and Loss in Children.

Saltz, G. S., & Cravath, L. (2005). *Amazing you! Getting smart about your private parts.* New York, NY: Penguin Group.

Stauffer, L., & Deblinger, E. (2004). *Let's talk about coping and safety skills: A workbook about taking care of me!* Hatfield, PA: Hope for Families.

REFERENCES

American Psychiatric Association. (2013). *Diagnostic and statistical manual of mental disorders* (5th ed.). Arlington, VA: American Psychiatric Association.

Avinger, K. A., & Jones, R. A. G. (2007). Group treatment of sexually abused adolescent girls: A review of outcome studies. *American Journal of Family Therapy, 35,* 315–326.

Beidel, D. C., Turner, S. M., & Morris, T. (2000). Behavioral treatment of childhood social phobia. *Journal of Counseling and Clinical Psychology, 63,* 1072–1080.

Berliner, L. (1991). Cognitive therapy with a young victim of sexual assault. In W. N. Friedrich (Ed.), *Casebook of sexual abuse treatment* (pp. 93–111). New York, NY: W. W. Norton.

Betzalel, N., & Shechtman, Z. (2010). Biblotherapy treatment for children with adjustment difficulties: A comparison of affective and cognitive bibliotherapy. *Journal of Creativity in Mental Health, 5,* 426–439.

Briere, J. (1996). *Manual for the Trauma Symptom Checklist for Children (TSCC).* Lutz, FL: Psychological Assessment Resources.

Browne, A., & Finkelhor, D. (1986). Impact of child sexual abuse: A review of the research. *Psychological Bulletin, 99*(1), 66–77.

Carnes, P. J. (1997). *The betrayal bond: Breaking free of exploitive relationships.* Deerfield Beach, FL: HCI Publisher.

Carpentier, M. Y., Silovsky, J. F., & Chaffin, M. (2006). Randomized trial of treatment for children with sexual behavior problems: Ten year follow-up. *Journal of Consulting and Clinical Psychology, 74,* 482–488.

Clawson, J., Dutch, N., Solomon, A., & Grace, L. (2009). *Human trafficking into and within the United States: A review of the literature.* Washington, DC: US Department of Health & Human Services.

Clawson, J., Dorais, M., & Feldstein, P. (2005). *Rent boys: The world of male sex workers* Montréal, QB: McGill-Queen's University Press.

Cohen, J. A., Deblinger, E., Mannarino, A. P., & De Arellano, M. A. (2001). The importance of culture in treating abused and neglected children: An empirical review. *Child Maltreatment, 6,* 148–157.

Cohen, J. A., Deblinger, E., Mannarino, A. P., & Steer, R. A. (2004). A multi-site, randomized controlled trial for sexually abused children with PTSD symptoms. *Journal of the American Academy of Child and Adolescent Psychiatry, 43,* 393–402.

Cohen, J. A., & Mannarino, A. P. (2000). Predictors of treatment outcome in sexually abused children. *Child Abuse and Neglect, 24,* 983–994.

Cohen, J., Mannarino, A. P., & Deblinger, E. (2006). *Treating trauma and traumatic grief in children and adolescents.* New York, NY: Guilford Press.

Coholic, D. A. (2011). Exploring the feasibility and benefits of arts-based mindfulness-based practices with young people in need: Aiming to improve aspects of self-awareness and resilience. *Child Youth Care Forum, 40,* 303–317.

Coholic, D., Eys, M., & Lougheed, S. (2012). Investigating the effectiveness of an arts-based and mindfulness-based group program for the improvement of resilience in children in need. *Journal of Child and Family Studies, 21,* 833–844.

Coholic, D., Lougheed, S., & Cadell, S. (2009). Exploring the helpfulness of arts-based methods with children living in foster care. *Traumatology, 15*(3), 64–71.

Compton, B. R., & Galaway, B. (1989). *Social work processes.* Pacific Cove, CA: Brooks/Cole.

de Arellano, M. A., & Danielson, C. K. (2008). Assessment of trauma history and trauma-related problems in ethnic minority child populations: An informed approach. *Cognitive and Behavioral Practice, 15,* 53–67.

De Bellis, M., Spratt, E., & Hooper, S. (2011). Neurodevelopmental biology associated with childhood sexual abuse. *Journal of Child Sexual Abuse, 20*(5), 548–587.

Deblinger, E. (1996). *Treating sexually abused children and their nonoffending parents A cognitive behavioral approach.* Thousand Oaks, CA: Sage.

Deblinger, E., & Runyon, M. (2005). Understanding and treating feelings of shame in children who have experienced maltreatment. *Child Maltreatment, 10,* 364–376.

Deblinger, E., Stauffer, L. B., & Steer, R. A. (2001). Comparative efficacies of supportive and cognitive behavioral group therapies for young children who have been sexually abused and their nonoffending mothers. *Child Maltreatment, 6,* 332–343.

Dorais, M., Corriveau, P., & Feldstein, P. (2009). *Gangs and girls: Understanding juvenile prostitution.* Montréal, QB: McGill-Queen's University Press.

Dorsey, S., Briggs, E. C., & Woods, B. A. (2011). Cognitive behavioral treatment for posttraumatic stress disorder in children and adolescents. *Child and Adolescent Psychiatric Clinics of North America, 20*(2), 255–269.

England, S., & Connors, K. M. (2005). Group work with sexually abused children. In G. L. Greif & P. H. Ephross (Eds.), *Group work with populations at risk* (2nd ed., pp. 267–286). New York, NY: Oxford University Press.

Felitti, V. J., Anda, R. F., Nordenberg, D., Williamson, D. F., Spitz, A. M., Edwards, V., . . . Marks, J. S. (1998). Relationship of childhood abuse and household dysfunction to many of the leading causes of death in adults. The Adverse Childhood Experiences (ACE) Study. *American Journal of Preventative Medicine 14*(4), 245–58.

Fernandez, I. T., Chavez-Duenas, N., & Consoli, A. I. (2015, January). *Guidelines for mental health professionals working with unaccompanied asylum-seeking minors.* National Latina/o Psychological Association. New Mexico State University, Milwaukee, WI

Finkelhor, D., Ormrod, R. K., Turner, H. A., & Hamby, S. L. (2005). The victimization of children and youth: A comprehensive, national survey. *Child Maltreatment, 10*(1), 5–25.

Fixsen, D. L., Naoom, S. F., Blasé, K. A., & Friedman, R. M. (2005). *Implementation research: A synthesis of the literature.* Tampa: University of South Florida, Louis de la Parte Florida Mental Health Institute, National Implementation Research Network.

Foa, E. B., Johnson, K. M., Feeny, N. C., & Treadwell, K. R. H. (2001). The Child PTSD Symptom Scale: A preliminary examination of its psychometric properties. *Journal of Clinical Child Psychology, 30*(3), 376–384.

Fontes, L. A., & Plummer, C. (2010). Cultural and disclosure issues. *Journal of Child Sexual Abuse, 19*, 491–518.

Gillies, D., Taylor, F., Gray, C., O'Brien, L. D., & D'Abrew, N. (2012). Psychological therapies for the treatment of post-traumatic stress disorder in children and adolescents. *Cochrane Database of Systematic Reviews, 12*, CD006726. DOI: 10.1002/14651858.CD006726.pub2

Ginns-Gruenberg, D., & Zacks, A. (2011). Effectively incorporating bibliotherapy into treatment for child sexual abuse. In P. Goodyear-Brown (Ed.), *Handbook of child sexual abuse: Identification, assessment, and treatment* (pp. 377–398). Hoboken, NJ: Wiley.

Habib, M., Labruna, V., & Newman, J. (2013). Complex Histories and Complex Presentations: Implementation of a Manually-Guided Group Treatment for Traumatized Adolescents. *Journal of Family Violence, 28*, 717–728.

Haboush, K. L., & Alyan, H. (2013). "Who can I tell?" Features of Arab culture that influence conceptualization and treatment of child sexual abuse. *Journal of Child Sexual Abuse, 22*, 499–518.

Harvey, S. T., & Taylor, J. E. (2010). A meta-analysis of the effects of psychotherapy with sexually abused children and adolescents. *Clinical Psychology Review, 30*, 517–535.

Heiman, M. L., & Ettin, M. F. (2001). Harnessing the power of the group for latency aged sexual abuse victims. *International Journal of Group Psychotherapy, 51*, 265–280.

Hernandez, P., Gangsei, D., & Engstrom, D. (2007). Vicarious resilience: A new concept in work with those who survive trauma. *Family Process, 46*, 229–241.

Hetzel-Riggin, M. D., Brausch, A. M., & Montgomery, B. S. (2007). A meta-analytic investigation of therapy modality outcomes for sexually abuse children and adolescents: An exploratory study. *Child Abuse and Neglect, 31*, 125–141.

Hubel, G., Campbell, C., West, T., Friedenberg, S., Schreier, A., Flood, M. F., & Hansen, D. J. (2014). Child advocacy center based group treatment for child sexual abuse. *Journal of Child Sexual Abuse, 23*, 304–325.

Institute of Medicine. (2001). *Crossing the quality chasm: A new health system for the 21st century.* Washington, DC: National Academies Press.

Jaycox, L. (2004). *Cognitive-behavioral intervention for trauma in schools.* Longmont, CO: Sopris West.

Kendall-Tackett, K. A., Williams, L. M., & Finkelhor, D. (1993). The impact of sexual abuse on children: A review and synthesis of recent empirical studies. *Psychological Bulletin, 113*, 164–180.

Kennedy, E. (2014). No children here: Why Central American children are fleeing their homes. *American Immigration Council (AIC)*. Retrieved from http://www.immigrationpolicy.org/perspectives/no-childhood-here-why-central-american-children-are-fleeing-their-homes

Kenny, M. C., & Wurtele, S. K. (2008). Preschoolers' knowledge of genital terminology: A comparison of English and Spanish speakers. *American Journal of Sexuality Education, 3*, 345–354.

Kenny, M. C., & Wurtele, S. K. (2013). Latino parents' plans to communicate about sexuality with their children. *Journal of Health Communication, 18*, 931–942.

Kim, J., & Cicchetti, D. (2010). Longitudinal pathways linking child maltreatment, emotion regulation, peer relations, and psychopathology. *Journal of Child Psychology and Psychiatry, 51*, 706–716.

Kiser, L. J., & Black, M. A. (2005). Family processes in the midst of urban poverty. *Aggression and Violent Behavior, 10*, 715–750.

Kloess, J. A., Beech, A. R., & Harkins, L. (2014). Online child sexual exploitation: Prevalence, process and offender characteristics. *Trauma, Violence and Abuse, 15*(2), 126–139.

Knight, C. (2006). Groups for individuals with traumatic histories: Practice considerations for social worker. *Social Work, 51*, 20–30.

Koverola, C., Murtaugh, C., Connors, K., Reeves, G., & Papas, M. A. (2007). Children exposed to intra-familial violence: Predictors of attrition and retention in treatment. *Journal of Aggression, Maltreatment and Trauma, 14*, 19–42.

Kramer, L., & Berg, B. (2003). A survival analysis of timing of entry into prostitution: The differential impact of race, educational level, and childhood/adolescent risk factors. *Sociological Inquiry, 73*, 511–528.

Lev-Wiesel, R. (2000). Quality of life in adult survivors of childhood sexual abuse who have undergone therapy. *Journal of Child Sexual Abuse, 9*, 1–13.

Lev-Wiesel, R. (2008). Child sexual abuse: A critical review of intervention and treatment modalities. *Children and Youth Services Review, 30*, 665–673.

Lowe, W.Jr., Pavkov, T. W., Casanova, G. M., & Wetchler, J. (2005). Do American ethnic cultures differ in their definitions of child sexual abuse? *American Journal of Family Therapy, 33*, 147–166.

MacDonald, G., Higgins, J. P. T., & Ramchandani, P. (2009). Cognitive-behavioral interventions for children who have been sexually abused. *Cochrane Database of Systematic Reviews, 4*, CD001930.

Many, M., & Osofsky, J. (2011). Working with survivors of child sexual abuse: Secondary trauma and vicarious traumatization In P. Goodyear-Brown (Ed.), *Handbook of child sexual abuse: Identification, assessment, and treatment* (pp. 525–526). Hoboken, NJ: Wiley.

Mathews, L. L., & Gerrity, D. A. (2002). Therapists' use of boundaries in sexual abuse groups: An exploratory study. *Journal for Specialists in Group Work, 27*, 78–91.

McFarlane, A. C. (1996). Traumatic stress in childhood and adolescence: Recent developments and current controversies. In B. van der Kolk, A. C. McFarlane,

& L. Weisaeth (Eds.), *Traumatic stress: The effects of overwhelming experience on mind, body and society* (pp. 331–358). New York, NY: Guilford Press.

McKay, M., Hibbert, R., Hoagwood, K., Rodriguez, J., Murray, L., Legerski, J., & Fernandez, D. (2004). Integrating evidence-based engagement interventions into "real world" child mental health settings. *Journal of Brief Treatment and Crisis Intervention*, *4*, 177–186.

Messman-Moore, T. L., Walsh, K. L., & DiLillo, D. (2010). Emotion dysregulation and risky sexual behavior in revictimization. *Child Abuse and Neglect, 34*, 967–976.

Murray, L. K., Nguyen, A., & Cohen, J.A. (2014). Child sexual abuse. *Child Adolescent Psychiatric Clinic of North America, 23*, 321–337.

Murphy, R. A. Sink, H. E., Ake, G. S., III, Carmody, K. A., Amaya-Jackson, L. M., & Briggs, E. C. (2014). Predictors of treatment completion in a sample of youth who have experienced physical or sexual trauma. *Journal of Interpersonal Violence, 29*, 3–19.

National Immigrant Justice Center. (2014). *Unaccompanied immigrant children: A policy brief from Heartland Alliances National Immigrant Justice Center. Winter*. Retrieved from https://immigrantjustice.org/sites/immigrantjustice.org/files/NIJC%20Policy%20 Brief%20-%20Unaccompanied%20Immigrant%20Children%20FINAL%20 Winter%202014.pdf

Noll, J. G., Horowitz, L. A., Bonanno, G. A., Tricket, P. K., & Putman, F. W. (2003). Revictimization and self-harm in females who experienced childhood sexual abuse: Results from a prospective study. *Journal of Interpersonal Violence, 18*, 1452–1471.

Noll, J. G., Trickett, P. K., & Putnam, F. W. (2003). A prospective investigation of the impact of childhood sexual abuse on the development of sexuality. *Journal of Consulting and Clinical Psychology, 71*, 575–586.

O'Callaghan, P., McMullen, J., Shannon, C., Rafferty, H., & Black, A. (2013). A randomized controlled trial of trauma-focused cognitive behavioral therapy for sexually exploited, war-affected Congolese girls. *Journal of the American Academy of Child and Adolescent Psychiatry, 52*(4), 359–69.

Offermann, B. J. (1998) *SMART Model Treatment Guide*, Center for Child and Family Traumatic Stress at Kennedy Krieger Institute, Baltimore, MD.

Offermann, B. J., Belcher, H. M. E., Johnson, E., & Johnson-Brooks, S. T. (2008). Get SMART: Effective treatment for sexually abused children with problematic sexual behavior. *Journal of Child and Adolescent Trauma, 1*, 179–191.

Osofsky, J. D., Putnam, F., & Lederman, C., (2008). Vicarious traumatization and compassion fatigue: How to maintain emotional health when working with trauma. *Juvenile and Family Court Journal, 59*, 91–101.

Pisaruk, H. I., Shawchuck, C. R., & Hoier, T. S. (1992). Behavioral characteristics of child victims of sexual abuse: A comparison study. *Journal of Clinical Child Psychology, 21*, 16–17.

Putnam, F. W. (2003). Ten-year research update review: Child sexual abuse. *Journal of American Academy Child and Adolescent Psychiatry, 42*, 269–279.

Putman, S. E. (2009). The monsters in my head: Posttraumatic stress disorder and the child survivor of child sexual abuse. *Journal of Counseling and Development, 87*, 80–89.

Pynoos, R., & Steinberg, A. (2013) UCLA PTSD Reaction Index for DSM-5.

Saunders, B. E., Berliner, L., & Hanson, R. F. (Eds.). (2004). *Child physical and sexual abuse: Guidelines for treatment* (Revised Report: April 26, 2004). Charleston, SC: National Crime Victims Research and Treatment Center.

Shechtman, Z., & Mor, M. (2010). Groups for children and adolescents with trauma-related symptoms: Outcomes and processes. *International Journal of Group Psychotherapy, 60,* 221–244.

Silverman, W. K., Ortiz, C. D., Viswesvaran C., Burns, B. J., Kolko, D. J., Putnam, F. W., & Amaya-Jackson L. (2008). Evidence-based psychosocial treatments for children and adolescents exposed to traumatic events. *Journal of Clinical Child and Adolescent Psychiatry, 37,* 156–183.

Simon, V. A., Feiring, C., & Kobielski McElroy, S. (2010). Making meaning of traumatic events: Youths' strategies for processing childhood sexual abuse are associated with psychosocial adjustment. *Child Maltreatment, 15*(3), 229–241.

Smith, A. P., & Kelly, A. B. (2008). An exploratory study of group therapy for sexually abused adolescents and nonoffending guardians. *Journal of Child Sexual Abuse, 17,* 101–116.

Smith, L., Vardaman, S., & Snow, M. (2009). *The national report on domestic minor sex trafficking: America's prostituted children.* Arlington, VA., Shared Hope International.

Snell-Johns, J., Mendez, J. L., & Smith, B. H. (2004). Evidence-based solutions for overcoming access barriers, decreasing attrition, and promoting change with underserved families. *Journal of Family Psychology, 18,* 19–35.

Tavkar, P., & Hansen, D. J. (2011). Interventions for families victimized by child sexual abuse: Clinical issues and approaches for child advocacy center-based services. *Aggression and Violent Behavior, 16*(3), 188–199.

Tourigny, M., & Hébert, M. (2007). Comparison of open versus closed group Interventions for sexually abused adolescent girls. *Violence and Victims, 22,* 334–349.

Tourigny, M., Hébert, M., Daigneault, I., & Simoneau, A. C. (2005). Efficacy of a group therapy for sexually abused adolescent girls. *Journal of Child Sexual Abuse, 14*(4), 71–93.

Trickett, P. K., & Putnam, F. W. (1993). The impact of sexual abuse on female development towards a developmental, psychobiological integration. *Psychological Science, 4,* 81–87.

Trotzer, J. (2006). The counselor and the group: Integrating theory, training, and practice, (4th ed., pp. 93–129). New York, NY: Routledge Taylor & Francis Group

Trowell, J., Kolvin, T., Weeramanthri, H., Sadowski, M., Berelowitz, D., Glasser, D., & Leitch, I. (2002). Psychotherapy for sexually abused girls: Psychopathological outcome findings and patterns of change. *British Journal of Psychiatry, 180,* 234–247.

US Department of Health and Human Services. (2007). *Mental health: Culture, race, and ethnicity—A supplement to mental health: A report of the Surgeon General.* Rockville, MD: US Department of Health and Human Services, Public Health Service, Office of the Surgeon General.

UUS Department of Health and Human Services, Administration for Children and Families, Administration on Children, Youth, and Families, Children's Bureau. (2012). *Child Maltreatment 2012.* Rockville, MD: US Department of Health and Human Services.

Valle, L. A., & Silovsky, J. F. (2002). Attributions and adjustment following child sexual and physical abuse. *Child Maltreatment, 7,* 9–25.

Walsh, K., DiLillo, D., & Scalora, M. J. (2011). The cumulative impact of sexual revictimization on emotion regulation difficulties: An examination of female inmates. *Violence against Women, 17*(8), 1103–1118.

Wanlass, J., Moreno, K., & Thomson, H. (2006). Group therapy for abused and neglected youth: Therapeutic and child advocacy challenges. *Journal for Specialists in Group Work, 31,* 311–326.

Wilcox, D. T., Richards, F., & O'Keefe, Z. C. (2004). Resilience and risk factors associated with experiencing childhood sexual abuse. *Child Abuse Review, 13,* 338–352.

Young, L. (1992). Sexual abuse and the problem of embodiment. *Child Abuse and Neglect, 16,* 89–100.

Zajac, K., Ralston, M. E., & Smith, D. W. (2015). Maternal support following child sexual abuse: Associations with children's adjustment post-disclosure and at 9-month follow-up. *Child Abuse and Neglect, 44,* 66–75.

Part Four

The Community

Chapter Twenty

Group Work With Urban African American Parents in Their Neighborhood Schools

Geoffrey L. Greif and Darnell Morris-Compton

This chapter describes a parenting support group approach used in four different Baltimore city public schools in neighborhoods that have historically been underserved. Dominated by housing projects and young families, the areas are frequently described as some of the worst in Baltimore in terms of crime rate and poverty. One of the neighborhoods was the scene of rioting in 2015 following the death of Freddie Gray, a resident of the neighborhood who died of the result of injuries sustained while in the care of the police. Three of the four groups have been held in schools that are composed of a student population that is more than 95% African American. The fourth school has a combination of African American, White, Latino, and Asian students. This chapter will focus primarily on working with African American families, describing the group format and the parenting issues that members have brought to the group over the past 20 years. Discussion of how these issues are handled is included.

The percentage of African Americans living below poverty in 2013 was 27.2%, remaining as the highest among all ethnic and racial groups in the United States (DeNavas-Walt & Proctor, 2013). Poverty, in part, stems from the legacy of racism in the United States, and it can be associated with the many problems faced by those African Americans living in the inner city, including drugs, homelessness, crime, stress, problems with mental and physical well-bring, and being incarcerated (Utsey & Constantine, 2008).

The school systems, often underfunded in major cities due to a shrinking or static tax base, can be ill equipped to meet the educational, much less the emotional, needs of children. Parents and parent figures are also affected by these problems, as well as by the high unemployment rate. Their own resources are sorely depleted. A feeling of powerlessness, a traditional target of social work practice (Cedeno, Elias, Kelly, & Chu, 2010), abounds. A cycle is maintained in which parents with diminished resources are raising children in great need. Traditional attempts to assist minority clients often fall short because of a lack of understanding of the culture (Boyd-Franklin, 2006; Hattery & Smith, 2012), a lack of resources, and a failure to focus on strengths and a family's resilience (Hollingsworth, 2013).

In the face of overwhelming problems and needs (Kelly, Maynigo, Wesley, & Durham, 2013), low-income African American families have historically received few or no services (US Department of Health and Human Services, 2012). Group work, based on the concept of mutual aid (Shulman, 2016), provides a forum for parents to join together and help each other. The parenting suggestions emanating from the group will be consistent with the neighborhood's and culture's style of parenting. Group work also has the potential to reduce the isolation so often felt by these parents while providing education and support (Steinberg, 2014). The benefits of groups also include experiences of universality, the instillation of hope, and the feeling of greater strength in numbers. Rehearsal of new parenting behaviors can be attempted, and parents may gain insight into their own approaches to the children they are raising (Shulman, 2016). A parenting group can also help parents deal with any personal problems they may be experiencing like depression, which can affect their ability to parent and their child's well-being (McLeod, Wood, & Weisz, 2006; Yap & Jorm, 2015). In fact, studies have shown parenting groups have been effective at decreasing child conduct problems (Fabiano, Schatz, Aloe, Chacko, & Chronis-Tuscano, 2015), increasing parental satisfaction and competence (Kjøbli, Hukkelberg, & Ogden, 2013), and improving interactions between the parent and child (McGilloway et al., 2012).

The social worker as a partner in the school setting is a well-established role, whether functioning as an employee or as a consultant. As social workers lead parenting groups, they provide both intervention and prevention (see, e.g., Alameda-Lawson, Lawson, & Lawson, 2010), which is clearly part of the social work function. Social workers focus on the strengths of children and parents they serve and tap into their resiliency. They also effect change in the school system by advocating for families, teachers, and staff and being aware of when services are needed.

Not much has been written, though, about group work specifically with African American parents. Literature on work with the African American family in general has suggested the importance of relationship building, focusing on strengths, keeping interventions concrete, and gathering information about who is considered part of the family (Boyd-Franklin, 2006; Hall, 2007; Hines, 2011).

The notion of family, particularly for a White worker, often needs to be reconsidered to include more than individuals related by blood (Nelson, 2013). In addition, race cannot be ignored, whether the worker is of the same race or a different race (Boyd-Franklin, 2006; Teasley, Archuleta, & Miller, 2014). The worker must show his or her skills, concern, and ability to offer meaningful help during the group meetings.

PRACTICE PRINCIPLES

This group is called "Help! My Kids Are Driving Me Crazy!" The title was selected to convey with humor what parents frequently experience while raising their children. A more straightforward title might have been more off-putting. The group has been held in several public elementary schools in Baltimore. The attendees are usually mothers and occasionally grandmothers, great-grandmothers, and fathers. It is a 60-minute drop-in group set up to provide mutual aid (see Shulman, 2016), with parents encouraged to help each other. In addition, it functions as a socioeducational group. As Radin (1985) states, such groups can be educative in format, place the worker on a more equal footing with the clients, and build on nonpathological assumptions. Philosophically, the group is driven by the notion that parenting is a developmental process and that each new stage of a child's growth may pose difficulty for both the child and the parent. The group can help ease that transition by providing support and education about normal stages of development. These parents are also buffeted by the stresses inherent in their environment and by larger social institutions, like Child Protective Services, the Housing Authority, and the Department of Social Services. Although these institutions are designed to assist families, they are often perceived as unresponsive and/or intrusive. Thus, the group also deals with issues impinging on the family from the outside.

Although long-term supportive work is the major purpose of the group, some parents attend only one or two sessions. For this reason, each group should be a learning and supportive experience in itself. Some sessions address a specific topic that is planned in advance, whereas others have an open format. The members are encouraged to share concerns about their children and are asked to keep confidential information they hear from other members. Members are informed by the leaders that instances of child maltreatment will be reported to Child Protective Services.

The leader's level of participation is an important component, particularly when working with a client population from a different racial and economic background. Too much input too early in the group process might be construed as controlling. Yet it is also standard practice for a leader to be active at the beginning of a group in order to establish group structure and allay normal anxiety. There was a beginning period at the first school when the members and worker sized each other up. An African American co-leader from the parent body, a key person in the success of that particular group, was more active at the beginning. With the parents (the first author is White, and the second author is African American), once the worker was accepted by the group, it was important to be active, as he had been incorporated into the group as a parent and as a person with expertise. The danger of taking a peripheral role during the middle phase of group work, a role often suggested in the literature on group therapy, is that the leader is perceived as withholding or rejecting. The standard approach was modified. Once the leader was accepted, an active role was assumed and parent issues were both discussed by the leader and turned back on the group. At the most recent group, the leader asked for feedback from the group about his level of activity and what the group was seeking from the leader. It became possible to be active during all phases with the group's permission. The leader also met occasionally outside of the group for consultation with parents who did not feel comfortable using the group to discuss their issues. Although this approach theoretically might have undermined the work of the group, given the drop-in nature of the group, it was seen as accommodating the needs of the parents.

The groups, which have been conducted for different lengths of time since they started in 1990, were set up to meet weekly or monthly (depending on the school). The parents and leader agreed to meet for a certain period of time, and then stop and determine if they wished to continue. This held the parents and worker to a joint commitment and, depending on the culture of the school, proved effective most of the time. The most recent group included MSW students who were completing field education at the elementary school. They were able to follow up with parents and children when issues were raised in the group in a more thorough way than an outside consultant could.

COMMON THEMES

A number of issues have surfaced at various schools during the years the groups have been in existence. These tend to center on the following themes: disciplining the difficult child; dealing with the noncustodial parent who visits occasionally (usually the father and sometimes the mother if a grandmother was attending the group); parents' feeling undermined by their children's grandparents; being triangulated between a child and Child Protective Services; keeping children safe in the neighborhood; enhancing self-esteem; dealing with stress; and giving a child what he or she wants when there is little money.

Disciplining the Difficult Child

Perhaps foremost in concern among the parents is unhappiness with the behavior of their children. It is this problem that initially drives parents to attend these groups. Complaints range from the mundane to the extraordinary, from normal developmental concerns to examples of extreme behaviors and exposure to highly traumatic events.

Parents raise routine concerns about children who will not sit still during dinner, who do not finish their homework, who balk at doing chores, and who ignore or talk back to them. They raise more troublesome complaints about teenagers feeling unsafe in schools and getting into fights, dropping out of school, and of running the streets until late at night. Occasionally, striking concerns are brought up. One parent worried about how to talk to her 5-year-old daughter who had seen a dead body in a dumpster (see case example later). She also wanted assistance in dealing with the same daughter who was sexually abused by a 7-year-old neighborhood boy. The question of how to handle the parent of the boy after the boy was reported to the police was also raised. One great-grandmother did not know what to do about her great-grandson, who, at the age of 10, often stayed out all night without her knowing his whereabouts.

Underlying these concerns and, in some cases, instigating them is a sense some parents have of feeling overwhelmed by their environment. As cited, poverty, unsafe neighborhoods, inadequate resources, and, sometimes, their own history of school failure and having been inadequately parented combine to drain the parents of the ability to cope. Their own needs are so great that marshalling strength to contend with the environmental pressures on their children is nearly impossible.

Dealing With the Noncustodial Parent Who Visits Occasionally

Many parents (usually mothers) are raising children alone. As such, their lives often remain entwined with those of the father or fathers of their children, particularly if the father shows an interest in his offspring. Visits pose a problem for two reasons: Some fathers say they will visit and do not. When they do visit, they often have more control over the children than the mother.

As with many separations and divorces, the logistics of contact between the noncustodial parent and the child can be problematic. Even in the best of situations, visitation schedules get miscommunicated and last-minute cancellations wreak havoc on plans. In these families, where some children have been the product of brief relationships, commitments are more tenuous. Thus, promises to visit end up being hollow, leaving the custodial parent to deal with the upset child whose father did not stop by to take the child for the outing he had promised.

Group members also raise the problem of having less control over the child than the father seems to have. Mothers complain that their attempts to discipline fall short, whereas all the father has to do is "raise his voice," "stamp his foot," or "shout once" and the children fall into line. The seeming power of the father poses a triple threat to the mother: It makes her feel incompetent; it reinforces the importance of men over women in her community; and it angers her, as she is the one who usually spends the most time with the child.

One mother in a group complained. "I am there for the loving. I am there for the boo-boos. Yet he can walk in and do his thing and waltz out again."

Occasionally, it is the grandmother raising a grandchild who discusses this issue. In these situations, the grandmother may complain about her own child's lack of concern and sporadic involvement or that when her child does visit, she or he spoils the grandchild.

Parents Feeling Undermined by Their Parents

Many group members live with their parents due to financial constraints and a lack of available child care. These situations lead easily to disagreements over how to parent. Group members sometimes feel undercut by their parents, who invoke certain rules because it is their home. The members, having few options about where to live, are caught between succumbing to their parents' suggestions about childrearing and wishing to follow their own parenting guidelines.

Being Caught Between a Child and Child Protective Services

Parents of older children often feel challenged in their attempts to discipline their child when the child threatens to call 911 or Child Protective Services if the parent is on the verge of physically punishing the child. At times this may be appropriate from the child's perspective. As indicated by the parents, though, it is a threat the child raises for even minor acts of discipline. For the parents, this tips the balance of power in the home and is an example of how outside institutions may intrude on their family. For some parents, it reminds them how life has changed from the time when they were young and parents were in charge of their children.

Keeping Children Safe in the Neighborhood

One of the larger problems in these neighborhoods is the safety of the streets. Members often lament that they were able to play outside until nighttime when they were young, whereas their own children cannot. Yet keeping the children inside in a small apartment or house, especially on a hot evening, poses other problems and adds to the general level of stress in the home. This discussion often results in parents complaining about being unable to control older children who are running the streets. When older children are brought up, and because the groups are held in elementary schools, we reframe the discussion in terms of the family system and how such behavior might affect the elementary school child.

Enhancing Self-Esteem

Some parents have been exposed to other parent education programs in the schools. Chief among these programs' goals is the enhancement of personal self-esteem. A few group members (who often emerge as internal leaders) are able to use what they have learned in these programs and relate their feelings as parents to their feelings about themselves as people. This can then become a group topic and lead to a discussion about how making oneself feel better about oneself as a person will lead to becoming a better parent.

Self-esteem can also be built through one's children. A recent group ended with the leader asking each parent to say something positive about their child or something they took pride in with their child. This ending exercise is meant to have parents leave on a positive note and avoid the sense that sometimes permeates parenting groups that children were out of control and unlovable.

Parents smiled and gave examples ranging from the wonderful art that was hanging outside the child's classroom to the great job a child was doing in keeping his room clean. One father, a recent widower, said his children did not do anything well. A mother in the group who knew the father and his children reminded him that his daughter ran and gave him a big hug the day before when he picked her up after school. The leader helped the father acknowledge this by framing the daughter as someone who showed affection well and gave good hugs. It also meant that the father was a lovable parent, an attempt to get him to view himself differently. This was one example of getting the father to accept a compliment about his child and, indirectly, about himself. The leader must always look for such opportunities to enhance self-esteem.

Dealing With Stress

Parents are constantly bombarded by the chaos in their neighborhoods. They complain that they are stressed out and unable to meet the continuing needs of their children. An ongoing theme is the request for information about how to deal with this stress. In some cases, helping the parent deal with anxiety by helping her identify when she is most anxious will also help reduce anxiety in her interactions with her child (Wood, McLeod, Sigman, Hwang, & Chu, 2003).

Giving a Child What He or She Wants When There Is Little Money

Parents on limited incomes are often scraping the bottom of the barrel by the end of the month to make ends meet. Giving a child even a small bonus for good behavior or a good school performance can be a financial stretch. Finding enjoyable family activities like a visit to a fast food restaurant or a movie may be out of a parent's range. As a result, chances to celebrate in a way that is meaningful for a child are few. This makes the parent feel incompetent as a provider and nurturer.

RECOMMENDED WAYS OF WORKING

The approaches used with these group members must be consistent with their culture and cognizant of their inherent strengths. Suggestions for interventions that are outside their resources will not be successful or accepted and may well be experienced as destructive.

Broadly, and consistent with the educative part of the group, giving instructions about child development is a primary stage in helping parents to discipline more effectively. Parents of very young children often interpret rambunctious behavior as disobedience, rather than normal exuberance, and get into battles with their children. For example, the 18-month-old who looks at the parent and then throws food on the floor is not trying to anger the parent. Messy rooms are not meant to be disrespectful but rather could be a reflection of the child's feelings about himself or herself or a lack of interest in cleanliness. Often child development information comes from the group members themselves, and not from the leaders, which helps foster self-esteem in the parents and makes learning feel less like a formal classroom. For some members, depending on their acceptance or rejection of authority in the form of the leader, this may make the information more palatable. It also gives a sense of competence and altruism to the provider of the information.

More serious discipline issues are usually handled in two ways. First, the group provides specific suggestions. If these seem inappropriate, as sometimes occur, or if the group is put off by the difficulty of the issue, the leaders step in and will guide a discussion. If an assessment of the parent has not been made in advance (e.g., this is the parent's first meeting), a few questions about the context of the problem (e.g., who is in the family and who is affected by the problem) sometimes clarify the picture. As suggested previously in relation to dealing with stress, looking at the pattern of behavior, when it occurs, is one way to help a parent understand the context of when it occurs. Family system strengths are often the focus of the conversation. Group members may also be asked: "What has worked for you in the past?" and "When are you most proud of your child?" Ideas from structural family therapy (Nichols, 2012) are often applied. In addition, rituals are prescribed that are intended to enhance enduring family patterns and build closeness (Mackey & Greif, 1994). For example, encouraging parents to read to their children every night, have a special pizza night once a week, or have a "choose a TV show" night introduces structure to families that often live in chaos. Although these rituals do not deal specifically with the discipline problem, they build family strength and set the stage for solving the problem. Concepts underpinning short-term therapy are also applied (Nickerson, 1995), with an eye toward providing a different view of the problem. The role of the leader tends to become more central the more serious the problem. Yet the group, when it is working well, provides support around these intractable problems that can touch a reserve of strength in the parent.

Inadvertently, the timing of some disciplinary interventions may be fortuitous. Something that failed once may work again a year later. The parent who comes occasionally, gets a little information from the group, and does not come back is reminded of that information when he or she sees a sign advertising the group, even if the parent chooses not to return. Over the course of many years of working in the same school, the mere presence of the group, even for one-time attendees, becomes a reminder of suggestions for change.

Dealing with the noncustodial parent, particularly a man, requires an acknowledgment of the differential status men hold in the community, where women so frequently are in the majority. Although airing thoughts and feelings can be helpful, unless a context and a limit for group discussion are set, members tend to spiral off into diatribes about men that are ultimately unproductive. Helping to set the context can include leading discussions about the role of men and fathers in the parents' lives when they were younger and focusing on the current precarious position that men, particularly men of color, occupy in many communities.

Group members often believe that the visiting father should be treated harshly, perhaps reflecting the members' own feelings of anger and helplessness. Ideally, the group can be helped to reach the conclusion that, with most fathers, involvement is a positive experience for the child when it is regulated. If the father visits and undermines the authority of the mother, both parents should be encouraged to work together on setting rules for the child. Often this does not work, though, and the influence of the outside father becomes something that the custodial parent and her children have to learn to live with. In that case, the mother is assisted to view the father's involvement in a way that does not get her so upset. This can include discussing what other behaviors surround the visit that the mother can better understand and change. For example, the mother who yells at the father the minute he walks in the door will be asked to anticipate his visit with a different reaction. The purpose is to handle the visit in a way that makes her feel more in control and that can benefit her children.

At the most recent group, a mixed-race one with one father in the room, talking about how men and women are socialized by society to fulfill certain roles has been helpful to group members in understanding the demands on both parents and to move the topic to a level outside of the individual. The emphasis was on the expectations for providing and for nurturing the family and how those expectations shape parental engagement. With issues of gender, care is taken to include the messages that mothers/women/daughters receive from society, too.

In dealing with intrusive grandparents, we return to the tenets of structural family therapy. Boundary issues are emphasized at the same time that group members are asked to explore any unresolved problems they may have with their own parents that affect how they themselves parent. The advantage of the group is that grandmothers caring for grandchildren are also present, giving an intergenerational perspective to the discussion. Sometimes, when a mother or grandmother sees the conflict from another perspective, change can occur.

When group members believe that their attempts to parent are being impeded by a child's threat to call Child Protective Services, we empathize with them by saying, "It must be hard to be unable to parent the way you want to." The underlying interventions must speak to two themes: helping the members find a way of parenting that will work for them (i.e., increasing their sense of competence) and acknowledging the presence of other institutions in their lives. The first theme is approached by turning the question back to the group of what solutions they have found for the particular problem. Then the discussion can turn to other ways in which the members feel that outsiders are interfering, including referring to the group leader as a potential outsider. This sometimes opens up issues about being referred by the school principal to the parenting group and the members' reactions to that referral.

When safety concerns keep children cooped up in their homes, suggestions about alternative modes of entertainment in Baltimore are usually given by other group members. The discussion then evolves into how life has changed since the members were young. To broaden the topic, members can be asked to discuss how they can recapture part of their past that they enjoyed and pass that on to their children. These discussions usually occur simultaneously with parents exchanging ideas about how to improve their position on public housing lists so that they can move to a safer neighborhood sooner. Thus, practical suggestions for moving away are mixed with concrete suggestions for coping.

Self-esteem is built within the group process. By supporting the parents' adaptive attempts to parent and by parents helping other group members, self-esteem does increase. Breaking down parenting into small steps helps the parents gain a sense of control. Just as social workers have often used partializing to help clients address a myriad of problems, group members are asked to look at parenting as a series of small actions. If the group provides helpful suggestions that are put into action when the parent gets home, the members often feel better.

Stress is handled the same way. Parents are encouraged to find a small thing they can accomplish that will make their lives more pleasurable. Stress often seems to loom over these parents as a mountain that they can never scale. Suggesting to parents that they have the right to have time for themselves, by asking a trusted neighbor to watch their children one day in exchange for their watching the neighbor's children the next, and stating that they should be allowed to take a shower or go to the bathroom without interruption provides solace to some parents.

Stress is also handled by helping the parent feel more competent, an issue related to self-esteem.

> The parent (referenced earlier) whose young daughter was sexually abused by a neighbor's child and had also observed a dead body in a trash dumpster adjacent to their high-rise development described the child as being significantly traumatized by one event and then retraumatized by the second event. The mother wanted assistance in dealing with the child's nightmares and increasingly uncontrollable behavior.
>
> Borrowing from structural family theory, we tried to place the mother in charge of the situation by increasing her feeling of competence. The belief was that if the mother felt more competent, the child would feel less upset. (The child was also in occasional individual treatment related to the sexual trauma.)

We asked the mother to read to her child at bedtime. If she was able to find books about children coping successfully, so much the better. We also asked her to involve her daughter in other activities where the mother was clearly the expert, like cooking and game playing. The hope was that such activities would enhance the role of the mother, reenforce a hierarchy where the parent was in charge, and show the child that the mother was competent. The intervention succeeded in reducing the child's nightmares but was less successful with the discipline problem.

Other suggestions for stress-related issues sometimes emerge from the parents' own language rather than our developing an intervention. A parent in a recent group wanted help with her 5-year-old who was acting out. The parent went into a lengthy description of all the child's misdeeds. The mother then talked about her sense of self having a "good mommy" and a "bad mommy" who could respond to her child. We asked her how to bring out the "good mommy" more often. Then we turned to the group and asked the other members to describe their "good" and "bad" sides and when they felt most capable of bringing out their "good" sides. With this approach we were using a common strengths–based, solution-focused approach (see, e.g., Nichols, 2013) that asks the group to look for answers. Tuning into what works helps parents to feel more positively about their situation and to see the group as a place to find answers that are transferable to home.

Finally, we try to help parents discuss money management. Groups whose members receive government assistance often have low attendance when checks arrive at the beginning of the month because parents are making purchases. By the end of the month, little money is left. Parents who can learn to use money more effectively are not bereft the final week of the month when the child wants change to buy a candy bar. Sound money management by the parent also shows the child that the parent will be consistent in meeting the child's needs, a message that all children need to hear and one that reenforces the parent's competence.

Some parents are unreachable through the group. They may be what have been called "help-rejecting complainers." These are people who come to the group and turn back every suggestion, saying "I tried that and it does not work." Others may be in the group because of pressure from a teacher or the principal and be, essentially, involuntary participants in what is billed as a voluntary drop-in group. The task here is to directly address this involuntary participation, empathize with it, and ask what they would like to have happen in the group that would make their attendance worthwhile for them.

EVALUATION AND CONCLUSION

It must be noted that despite the examples given of successful group interventions, some problems presented by the group members are unsolvable in the group context. They push the limits of social work practice because of the extreme nature of the situation and the lack of resources available to families. Some members with intractable problems drop out of the group, perhaps believing that another attempt to help them has failed. Unfortunately, when that happens, the net result is to reinforce their sense of helplessness.

The success of the drop-in group is judged by the answers to three questions: (1) Do parents return? (2) Do the parents who attend even one session appear to get something out of it? This is often a subjective assessment because paper-and-pencil tests sometimes scare off potential attendees. At the end of each group, the leaders ask if the group has been helpful. Parents often say they feel better at the end of the group because they have had a chance to vent, have received some ideas about parenting, and have learned that they are not alone in their struggles. The parents' self-report at subsequent sessions is another key gauge. If they are returning with stories of success in parenting, even minor success, the group is working for them; and (3) does the principal think it is working?

Many parents return, depending in part on the culture of the school. In three of the four schools, the group has been successful with returning parents; in the fourth school, where attendance is low, the parent–school liaison reports that the parents still request the group, even though they do not always attend. For some principals, the mere presence of the group is greeted warmly because it serves as a statement that the school is trying to meet parents' needs. Some principals may overinflate the impact of the group to maintain its presence in their school. As long as the group is constructive, the principals of all four schools are happy to sponsor it, though the level of support (a quiet room, coffee, signs in the school announcing the group) tends to vary from one school to the next.

Empowering disadvantaged parents through group work can be a key element in any plan to improve the situations of at-risk children. By assisting those who want help and building on their strengths, greater parenting competence may develop throughout the community. Although urban families face many challenges, they often present with strength and resiliency. It is these components that must be drawn upon to assist them in raising their children and making schools a better educational environment for all families.

RESOURCES

Because I Love You
P.O. Box 2062
Winnetka, CA 91396-2062
818-884-8242
http://www.bily.org/

Child and Family WebGuide
Tufts University
105 College Ave.
Medford, MA 02155
http://www.cfw.tufts.edu/

Home and School Institute
1500 Massachusetts Ave., NW
Suite 42
Washington, DC 20002
202-466-3633
http://www.megaskillshsi.org

International Association for Social Work with Groups, Inc.
101 West 23rd Street
Suite 108
New York, NY 10011
718-316-0299
http://iaswg.org/

KidsHealth
The Nemours Foundation
1600 Rockland Road
Wilmington, DE 19803
302-651-4000
http://kidshealth.org/

National Black Child Development Institute
1313 L. Street, NW
Suite 110
Washington, DC 20005
202-387-1281
http://www.nbcdi.org

National Council of La Raza
1126 16th Street, NW
Suite 600
Washington, DC 20036
202-785-1670
http://www.Nclr.org

REFERENCES

Alameda-Lawson, T., Lawson, M. A., & Lawson, H. A. (2010). Social workers' roles in facilitating the collective involvement of low-income, culturally diverse parents in an elementary school. *Children and Schools, 32*(3), 172–182.

Boyd-Franklin, N. (2006). *Black families in therapy: Understanding the African American experience* (2nd ed.). New York, NY: Guilford Press.

Cedeno, L. A., Elias, M. J., Kelly, S., & Chu, B. C. (2010). School violence, adjustment, and the influence of hope on low-income, African American youth. *American Journal of Orthopsychiatry, 80*(2), 213–226. doi:10.1111/j.1939-0025.2010.01025.x

DeNavas-Walt, C., & Proctor, B. D. (2013). *Income and poverty in the United States: 2013.* (Current Population Reports, P60-249). Washington, DC: US Government Printing Office.

Fabiano, G., Schatz, N., Aloe, A., Chacko, A., & Chronis-Tuscano, A. (2015). A systematic review of meta-analyses of psychosocial treatment for attention-deficit/hyperactivity disorder. *Clinical Child and Family Psychology Review, 18*(1), 77–97.

Hall, J. (2007). *African American behavior in the social environment: New perspectives.* New York, NY: Haworth Press.

Hattery, A. J., & Smith, E. (2012). *African American families today: Myths and realities.* Lanham, MD: Rowman & Littlefield.

Hines, P. M. (2011). The life cycle of African American families living in poverty. In M. McGoldrick, B. A. Carter, & N. A. Garcia Preto (Eds.), *The expanded family life cycle: Individual, family, and social perspectives* (4nd ed., pp. 89–102). Boston, MA: Pearson Allyn & Bacon.

Hollingsworth, L. D. (2013). Resilience in Black families. In D. S. Becvar (Ed.), *Handbook of family resilience* (pp. 229–243). New York, NY: Springer.

Kelly, S., Maynigo, P., Wesley, K., & Durham, J. (2013). African American communities and family systems: Relevance and challenges. *Couple and Family Psychology: Research and Practice, 2*(4), 264–277.

Kjøbli, J., Hukkelberg, S., & Ogden, T. (2013). A randomized trial of group parent training: Reducing child conduct problems in real-world settings. *Behavior Research and Theory, 51*(3), *113–121.*

Mackey, J., & Greif, G. L. (1994). Using rituals to help parents in the school setting: Lessons from family therapy. *Social Work in Education, 16,* 171–178.

McGilloway, S., Mhaille, G. N., Bywater, T., Furlong, M., Leckey, Y., Kelly, P., . . . Donnelly, M. (2012). A parenting intervention for childhood behavioral problems: A randomized controlled trial in disadvantaged community-based settings. *Journal of Consulting and Clinical Psychology, 80,* 116–127. doi:10.1037/a0026304

Nelson, M. K. (2013). Fictive kin, families we choose, and voluntary kin: What does the discourse tell us? *Journal of Family Theory and Review, 5,* 259–281.

Nichols, M. (2013). *The essentials of family therapy* (6th ed.). Boston, MA: Pearson/Allyn and Bacon.

Radin, N. (1985). Socioeducation groups. In M. Sundel, P. Glasser, & R. Vintner (Eds.), *Individual change through small groups* (2nd ed., pp. 101–116). New York, NY: Free Press.

Shulman, L. (2016). *The skills of helping individuals, families, groups, and communities* (8th ed.). Belmont, CA: Thomson-Brooks/Cole.

Steinberg, D. M. (2014). *A mutual-aid model for social work with groups* (3rd ed.). New York, NY: Routledge.

Teasley, M. L., Archuleta, A., & Miller, C. (2014). Perceived levels of cultural competence for school social workers: A follow-up study. *Journal of Social Work Education, 50,* 694–711. doi:10.1080/10437797.2014.947903

US Department of Health and Human Services. (2012). *Action plan to reduce racial and ethnic health disparities*. Retrieved from http://minorityhealth.hhs.gov/npa/files/Plans/HHS/HHS_Plan_complete.pdf

Utsey, S. O., & Constantine, M. G. (2008). Mediating and moderating effects of racism-related stress on the relation between poverty-related risk factors and subjective well-being in a community sample of African Americans. *Journal of Loss and Trauma, 13,* 186–204.

Wood, J. J., McLeod, B. D., Sigman, M., Hwang, W-C., & Chu, B. C. (2003). Parenting and childhood anxiety: Theory, empirical findings, and future directions. *Journal of Child Psychology and Psychiatry, 44,* 134–151.

Yap, M. B. H., & Jorm, A. F. (2015). Parental factors associated with childhood anxiety, depression, and internalizing problems: A systematic review and meta-analysis. *Journal of Affective Disorders, 175,* 424–440.

Chapter Twenty-One

Group Work With Children and Adolescents in Response to Community Violence and/or Trauma

Alison Salloum

For many children and adolescents, community violence is pervasive throughout the neighborhoods in which they live. Exposure to community violence (ECV) is a major public health problem, and many children and adolescents are exposed to a range of traumatic events. In a national representative sample in the United States of 3,614 youth aged 12 to 17 years, 37.8% reported witnessing violence (approximately 9.6 million based on 2005 US Census estimates), with community violence (as opposed to familial or domestic) being the most commonly identified. The most frequently mentioned type of community violence was witnessing someone being beaten and requiring medical attention (28.4%) and witnessing someone threaten someone else with a knife, gun, or other weapon (19%) (Zinzow et al., 2009).

The National Child Traumatic Stress Network defines community violence as "exposure to intentional acts of interpersonal violence committed in public areas by individuals who are not intimately related to the victim. Common types of community violence that affect youth include individual and group conflicts (e.g., bullying, fights among gangs and other groups, shootings in public areas such as schools and communities, civil wars in foreign countries or 'war-like' conditions in U.S. cities, spontaneous or terrorist attacks, etc.)" (National Child Traumatic Stress Network, n.d.). Some scholars have taken a more narrow definition of community violence such that specific types of violence are excluded. For example, Kennedy and Ceballo (2014) state that ECV is generally defined as "instances of interpersonal harm or threats of harm within one's neighborhood or community, and excludes related constructs such as domestic violence, physical maltreatment, sexual abuse, peer bullying, and media and video game violence" (Kennedy & Ceballo, 2014, p. 69). Although there have been inconsistencies in definitions, researchers are calling for a more multidimensional approach to studying ECV that takes into account type, severity, physical proximity, relational proximity (familiarity with victims), and chronicity (Kennedy & Ceballo, 2014).

Exposure to community violence has been associated with a range of biological, social, emotional, and cognitive problems (Margolin & Gordis, 2000). Research has found strong associations between ECV and aggression (Busby, Lambert, & Ialongo, 2013), antisocial behavior (Bacchini, Miranda, & Affuso, 2011), internalizing and externalizing problems (Dinizulu et al., 2014), anxiety (Cooley-Quille, Boyd, Frantz, & Walsh, 2001), posttraumatic stress, depression (Fowler, Tompsett, Braciszewski, Jacques-Tiura, & Baltes, 2009; Zinzow et al., 2009), academic problems (Epstein-Ngo, Maurizi, Bregman, & Ceballo, 2013), somatic symptoms (Hart, Hodgkinson, Belcher, Hyman, & Cooley-Strickland, 2013), sleep problems (Kliewer & Lepore, 2014), suicidal ideation (Lambert, Copeland-Linder, & Ialongo, 2008), and substance abuse (Wright, Fagan, & Pinchevsky, 2013).

RISK AND PROTECTIVE FACTORS

Although community violence affects all racial and ethnic groups, those living in poverty in both urban and rural areas are at greatest risk. In fact, a recent report suggested that persons living in poverty had double the risk of violent victimization as persons from high-income households; victimization rates were high regardless of living in urban or rural areas (Harrell, Langton, Berzofsky, Couzens, & Smiley-McDonald, 2014). Considerable research has focused on low-income African American children who live in neighborhoods characterized by high poverty, crime, and violence as these children are often faced with numerous and ongoing traumatic events (Hill, Levermore, Twaite, & Jones, 1996). For decades, Black males, due to numerous factors, including economic and sociocultural disparities, have had the highest rate of being victims of homicide. From 2002 to 2011, data indicated that the homicide rate for Black males during young adulthood (20 to 23 years old) was almost nine times higher than for White males (Smith & Cooper, 2013).

Findings have been inconsistent related to gender as a moderator of ECV and its consequences, perhaps due to methodological issues. Some studies suggest that males are more likely to experience ECV than females (Menard & Huizinga, 2001), whereas other studies have found no differences in ECV based on gender (Lambert, Nylund-Gibson, Copeland-Linder, & Ialongo, 2010). There is some evidence to suggest that the type of community violence (e.g., hearing about, witnessing, or direct victimization; strangers versus individuals known to the child; sexual or physical victimization) may lead to differential outcomes for boys and girls (Javdani, Abdul-Adil, Suarez, Nichols, & Farmer, 2014; Kaminer, Hardy, Heath, Mosdell, & Bawa, 2013). However, the relationship between gender and ECV is more complex due to a multitude of other variables (e.g., age, cumulative exposure to violence; coping abilities), which can lead to differential outcomes (Mendelson, Turner, & Tandon, 2010; Turner, Finkelhor, & Ormrod, 2006).

Many children and youth exposed to community violence may have also experienced maltreatment (Cecil, Viding, Barker, Guiney, & McCrory, 2014; Hunt, Martens, & Belcher, 2011), family conflict (Holtzman & Roberts, 2012), or other traumatic events. These additional negative events may amplify the child's difficulties and/or contribute to additional challenges such as depression and/or anxiety. Research suggests that cumulative traumatic events in more than one context predicted higher subsequent posttraumatic stress (Dubow et al., 2012). In addition to assessing type of ECV, cumulative exposure, and gender, the relationship and closeness of the youth to the victim may influence the outcomes. For example, Lambert, Boyd, Cammack, and Ialongo (2012) found differential associations between aggression and depression and witnessing community violence by gender and type of relationship (e.g., stranger, close friend, family member). When the victim was known to the child, more serious consequences followed.

Although more research is needed to understand these interactions and influences of different intervening variables on outcomes, assessments and interventions need to be tailored to address the uniqueness of the experiences of the youth exposed to community violence, including cumulative and ongoing exposure, and experiencing multiple traumatic events that may occur in different contexts (e.g., community, home, and/or at school).

For some youth, protective factors may not be enough to shield them from negative outcomes because the effects of community violence may overwhelm the protective factors (Dinizulu et al., 2014; Luthar, Cicchetti, & Becker, 2000; Salzinger, Rosario, Feldman, & Ng-Mak, 2008). Nonetheless, research has found that positive coping strategies (Epstein-Ngo et al., 2013); a strong parent–child relationship (Dinizulu et al., 2014); family support, positive peers, neighborhood support (Jain, Buka, Subramanian, & Molnar, 2012); healthy family functioning such as problem solving, communication, clear roles, affective responsiveness and involvement, and behavioral control (Margolin & Gordis, 2000); involvement in structured neighborhood-based activities (Francois, Overstreet & Cunningham, 2012; Jain et al., 2012); and high self-efficacy and low impulsivity (McMahon et al., 2013) may help to moderate the relationship between ECV and psychological well-being. Although intervention strategies are needed to promote protective factors at the individual, family, school, neighborhood, and community level, major and sustained efforts to intervene on all levels are needed to address the core problem of violence, which is endemic in disadvantaged communities (Salzinger, Feldman, Rosario, & Ng-Mak, 2011).

COMMUNITY VIOLENCE AND DISASTERS

Researchers have started to examine the interactive effects of ECV and disasters on child and adolescent well-being. Self-Brown, Lai, Thompson, McGill, and Kelley (2013) found that youth who were exposed to community violence and to Hurricane Katrina were at increased risk for posttraumatic stress disorder (PTSD) trajectories compared to those youth who had not experienced community violence. In a study with children who experienced Hurricane Katrina and community violence, the effects of the approach of another hurricane (Gustav) were examined. Salloum, Carter, Burch, Garfinkel, and Overstreet (2011) found that for children with high or low levels of prior disaster exposure from Hurricane Katrina and ECV, there was a positive association between exposure to Hurricane Gustav and posttraumatic stress symptoms.

However, among children who reported high or low levels of exposure to both a prior disaster other than Hurricane Katrina and ECV, there was no association between Hurricane Gustav and distress. It may be that another disaster (and one with lesser impact) did not affect the subjects' already high levels of distress, and that the previous low levels of ECV and disaster exposure protected the child from perceiving Gustav as threatening or distressing. Group work interventions that occur after disasters may need to assess for prior and current ECV and include interventions that take into account how community violence and/or disaster-related stress may contribute to group members' overall well-being.

PRACTICE PRINCIPLES

The first guiding principle, using DEC[1], sets the stage for the remaining five. Interventions must be developmentally specific, conducted using an ecological perspective, and tailored with participants' culture in mind (DEC: Salloum, 2015; Salloum, Garfield, Irwin, Anderson, & Francois, 2009). Group work facilitators will need to adjust group activities to meet the developmental needs of the participants. Facilitators must be keenly aware of the environmental context within which participants live and take into potential risk or protective factors. It may be necessary to intervene and advocate on multiple levels with, for example, family members, the school, and legal and social service systems. It also is important that facilitators understand the cultural practices and beliefs of the participants, especially related to mourning rituals, beliefs about dying and the afterlife, and so on. The remaining five principles are discussed below.

Psychoeducation

Information about common trauma and grief responses at various developmental stages after being exposed to community violence and/or trauma can be very helpful to participants and those close to them, especially caregivers. Normalizing and validating experiences and reactions can be quite beneficial in helping members cope with prior and continuing exposure to community violence.

Assessment

It may be very difficult for a person, particularly a child, exposed to community violence to convey what he or she is experiencing. Furthermore, it would be would be quite time consuming to assess each prospective group member's unique reactions, given the range of possible responses. Therefore, it is recommended that prior to beginning the group, the facilitator assess potential members' functioning using a structured trauma-grief-strengths-focused assessment. The section on evaluation in this chapter provides some standardized measures that may be helpful. The assessment can provide information about the level of intervention that may be needed, including the type of group (i.e., psychoeducational or support), additional support through individual and/or family counseling, and a psychiatric assessment for suicidality or medication.

Safety

Conducting a safety assessment and addressing safety skills to help group members cope with prior ECV and/or future violence and trauma is essential. When conducting a safety assessment, it may be helpful to assess the physical safety of the child or adolescent and her or his caregiver(s) as well as perceived safety in the different locations such as home, school, work, and neighborhood. Group members can be asked to identify individuals and places or areas that are safe and/or feel safe, and individuals or places that may be considered a threat or potentially unsafe. Children and adolescents need to have—or create—a place where they can feel a sense of safety. In addition, they need to have at least one safe person, someone with whom they can share their feelings and whom they know will be consistently loving and supportive.

Outreach and Accessibility

Outreach may be needed to let families know that group work services will be available. Avoidance is a common symptom of posttraumatic stress disorder. Even if a child, an adolescent, or a caregiver sees a flier indicating that group services are available, he or she may avoid inquiring about them as a way of denying reminders about the traumatic event(s). Therefore, it may take active outreach to engage participants, such as having a respected community member, teacher, or someone familiar with the child or adolescent and her or his family to explain the potential benefits of group participation. The group facilitator should be persistent in reaching out to potential participants, meeting with them and their caregivers in advance to establish initial rapport and trust.

Group interventions need to be provided in locations that are easily accessible and familiar such as neighborhood community centers, churches, or schools. For children and adolescents, school-based settings provide an optimal location. When two evidence-based interventions were provided to children post Hurricane Katrina, participation was significantly higher for children who participated at school as compared to children who were offered outpatient treatment (Jaycox et al., 2010). When interventions are provided in settings such as schools or after-school programs, facilitators will need to work out arrangements with the setting that promote the work of the group but remain consistent with the agency's operation.

Self-Care for Professionals

Due to consistently being exposed to group members' stories about exposure, workers may experience secondary traumatic stress or compassion fatigue, which may result in emotional and behavioral reactions similar to posttraumatic stress symptoms (Figley, 1995; Nelson-Gardell & Harris, 2003) or vicarious traumatization. Vicarious traumatization occurs when one experiences cognitive changes in beliefs related to trust, safety, power, independence, esteem, and intimacy (McCann & Pearlman, 1990). To counter these negative outcomes, workers need to practice positive self-care activities routinely.

Just as we stress the importance to clients to have multiple methods for coping that can be used in different contexts, the same is true for group work facilitators working with individuals exposed to community violence. Self-care practices include physical self-care (e.g., exercise, eating healthy), emotional self-care (e.g., identifying and expressing feelings to caring others), spiritual self-care (e.g., meditating, praying, or worshiping with others), and workplace self-care (e.g., attending training on secondary trauma, creating a workplace culture that recognizes the potential stress of working with individuals exposed to community violence, and workplace policies that promote self-care and that are trauma informed).

COMMON THEMES

The themes and methods (discussed in the next section) that are addressed in the intervention *GTI for children* can be grouped within three overlapping areas: (1) resilience and safety, (2) restorative retelling, and (3) reconnecting (Herman, 1997; Rynearson, 2001; Salloum, 2015). For more on the use of restorative retelling techniques with adults see Rynearson, 2001.

Resilience and Safety

Overcoming ECV requires strong coping skills, social support, and a positive psychological outlook. It goes without saying that everyone should be able to live in a safe environment without ongoing exposure to violence. Unfortunately, this is not possible for many children, adolescents, and their families. Group participation has the potential to provide members with the means to address past, current, and future ECV. Themes related to resilience and safety are related to protective factors such as seeking out positive peer relationships and fostering neighborhood support. Other themes include identifying a safe place and safe individuals, developing the ability to regulate emotions, including the capacity to calm and soothe oneself, and creating feelings of hopefulness, self-efficacy, and spirituality.

Healthy family functioning also is an essential component of managing ECV. Therefore, participants' families may need assistance with problem solving, communication, clarifying roles, affective responsiveness, behavioral control, and involvement in neighborhood-based activities that promote cohesion and a sense of community. Family intervention may need to be offered in conjunction with groups for children and adolescents to promote healthier functioning.

Restorative Retelling

Group interventions should include a process for helping children and adolescents develop a coherent narrative about what happened and what they experienced. This narrative is created in a way that attaches meaning to what occurred and that allows members to tell their story without experiencing overwhelming distress or maladaptive cognitions. Group members are often left to fend for themselves, since their family members are also struggling with ECV and may avoid discussion about or reminders of the trauma.

In a group, the mutual support and reassurance that come from "being in the same boat" reduce isolation and can counter members' reluctance to recount their experiences and blunt the manifestations of PTSD, including reexperiencing, avoidance, negative cognitions and mood, and increased arousal.

Reconnecting

Groups provide a place for members to experience understanding and support, which facilitates connecting with others in similar straits. Feeling and being connected to supportive others can help with both resilience and safety and restorative retelling.

RECOMMENDED WAYS OF WORKING

For each of the three themes previously identified—resilience and safety, restorative retelling, and reconnecting—a variety of group work strategies can be utilized.

Resilience and Safety

Conducting a safety assessment is recommended, and this can be done as easily as asking group members to list the places where they feel safe and then list the people with whom they feel safe. It is often helpful to spend some time before the assessment discussing what it means to feel safe. A helpful activity for children and adolescents is to have them draw (or describe) their neighborhood and then have them indicate safe places and not so safe places. If the child or adolescent does not have a safe place, she or he can be asked to imagine or draw a place that would feel safe. Also, when children and adolescents continue to live in violent environments, it may be helpful to explore places where they may feel "moments of safety" such as when they are hugging a parent or caring person or in their classroom.

Promoting and building coping capacities are other important tasks that can be accomplished through group work. One method for doing this is to teach and promote relaxation exercises. Individuals of all ages can learn deep breathing exercises that can be used in any setting. The following example is illustrative of how the group leader can assist participants in identifying a safe place. The group was provided at school for children who lost a loved one due to homicide and/or who had witnessed community violence. All of the children who participated were experiencing at least moderate symptoms of posttraumatic stress and were between the ages of 7 and 12. A social worker and a master's-level social work intern facilitated the group, which lasted for an hour every week for 11 weeks.

One of the leaders asked the children, "What does it mean to feel safe?" Gerald said, "It means not having to watch your back." Ron stated, "Man, you better always watch your back." The children, including Gerald, all agreed. The co-leader responded, "Yes, if you live in an area where it is not safe, you may have to be alert and aware of danger or potentially not safe situations, but I wonder, have you ever felt safe?" Ron said, "Yea, I feel safe when I am in my home and only my family is around." Gerald said, "I feel safe when I am playing basketball." Melissa added that she felt safe when she was in her room, and other members stated that they felt safe when they were with their mother or grandmother.

The co-leader praised the children for identifying these people or places and stated, "Okay, so you feel safe with specific family members, in your home, and, for some of you when you are playing. What is it about these people or places do you think makes you feel safe?" Gerald, always quick to answer first, stated, "When I am playing ball, I am not worried that something bad will happen." The co-leader affirmed, "Okay, so then, in that place, you believe nothing bad will happen." Ron asked Gerald, "Do you always feel that way?" and Gerald explained that where he plays is across the street from the police station and it is "like a protected area."

Melissa stated, "It feels peaceful in my room," and Angela, who said she felt safe with her grandmother, added, "I know she will always have my back, no matter what." One of the group workers said, "It sounds like these people and places make you feel safe because you feel nothing bad will happen, protected, peaceful, and that you are cared for and supported, right?" Ron smiled and said, "Hey, I think what you said is what it means to feel safe." With the leaders' assistance, the group continued to identify places and people that made them feel safe.

Restorative Retelling

There are many methods for helping group members create a coherent and re-storative narrative. The approach used in *GTI for children* utilizes two strategies that have been found to be helpful. First, the trauma/loss narrative is divided into four segments that help members tell the story in order and highlight the most distressing part. The segments are before it happened, when it happened, after it happened, and the worst moment. The process used with each of the four segments is known as DDWW. Members first draw (D) a picture of before, when, after, and the worst moment (older children and adolescents may be asked to describe the segments). After the drawing, the leader engages in discussion (D) by challenging members to think about what occurred in a more restorative manner. For example, the facilitator might ask, "So tell us more about what you did that was helpful to others?" In cases where a member has lost a loved one, the leader can ask what she or he would want for the member now.

After the discussion, members write (W) the story (the facilitator can write it for the youngest members). Often members will incorporate the more restorative elements of their narrative into the written version. Finally, the group members and facilitators bear witness (W) to each child's story. The example that follows is based upon the same group discussed previously. In this excerpt, the leader effectively utilizes the DDWW strategy. This process helped group members to develop their trauma narrative and to begin to expand it and revise it in ways that were more helpful and promoted healing and resilience.

Gerald drew a picture of his uncle, who was like a brother to him, lying on the ground with his mother standing over the uncle crying. While the other children were drawing the picture of when it happened, the facilitator asked Gerald, "So tell me about your drawing." Gerald said in a low voice, "This is my brother. He was shot and my mom was crying." The facilitator followed up with three ques-tions: "Where were you when this happened? What do you remember thinking or feeling? What was your relationship like with your brother?" Gerald then wrote a story about this picture and from the discussion that followed was able to add that he did not witness his uncle being shot to death but that he saw his uncle when he was dead lying on the pavement. He wrote that he remembered his mother screaming so loud, but he felt numb "like he could not move."

After all of the members completed their drawings, they shared them and their accompanying story with the group. Gerald went first, sharing the information he had disclosed to the leader. When he finished, Melissa quickly said, "I am sorry that happened. I know when I saw that man shot, I felt like I could not move either." The facilitator observed that there are many reactions that people might have when they experience a traumatic event. Other members then shared their story and discovered common experiences. At the end, the facilitator asked members what it was like to create and share their story in the group. Ron said, "It felt okay. I really liked talking about my brother and all the things we used to do together." Gerald said, "Yea, like it was the first time I have really said how important my brother, really my uncle, was to me. I know he wants me to live my dreams and be somebody."

Reconnecting

Although reconnecting is listed last, it actually begins immediately. One of the first group activities should be discussing who in the group member's life provides support and comfort, and to name the type of support and comfort that individual provides. For example, facilitators may ask members questions such as Who hugs you? Who makes you feel good about yourself? Who would you cry in front of and feel okay? Who makes you laugh? Who cooks your favorite foods for you? Who teaches you things you enjoy? Who do you like spending time with? Who can you talk to about what happened? It is also important to help group members get involved in activities that provide positive socialization, opportunities to build confidence and competencies, and physical exercise.

Group facilitators will need to promote cohesion and help members to feel connected with one another. Due to their exposure to community violence, members may have learned not to trust anyone and to keep to themselves. The experience of connectedness that results from members recognizing their common experiences begins to counter their sense of isolation and aloneness. Group facilitators also may need to work with members' immediate environment to help create opportunities for members to get involved in community activities. This final excerpt is drawn from the same group described previously.

In one session, group members were asked to identify one or two supportive people in their lives, and Ron identified his mother as supportive but stated, "Since my brother died, I don't trust anyone." He reported he had also stopped playing basketball at school and did not want to go anywhere where there were large crowds. Prior to his brother dying, he was close with his teammates and coach but had withdrawn from them. During the course of the group, Ron and Gerald had become friendly. In another meeting when Gerald talk about playing basketball in the neighborhood in a safe area, Ron said, "I wish I had some place like that." The facilitator suggested that maybe they could both talk with their mothers about arranging a time to play basketball together at Gerald's park. Gerald liked this idea, and said, "Yea, how about we have the group at the basketball court next week." Everyone laughed. Melissa said, "Well, you can play with Ron so that he can get ready to play on the team again."

When the facilitator met with Ron and his mother during a family session, the facilitator explored ways to get Ron back playing basketball. Mom and Ron reported that he had actually played the previous week with Gerald at his court. Ron talked about how that felt for him, and he indicated it felt "good" and "safe." At the end of the group intervention, Ron had signed up for this basketball team again and was no longer scared to be in crowds.

EVALUATION

There are five main categories of assessment that may be helpful for monitoring and evaluating group interventions for children and adolescents: (1) trauma/loss exposure; (2) broadband measures; (3) targeted measures of PTSD, and depression and grief; (4) strengths and resilience; and (5) session review. There are many standardized measures that may be used, but below are a few suggestions.

In addition to the standardized measures for assessment and outcomes, it is recommended that clinicians track over time group processes that are essential for members' coping with community violence, such as group cohesion, communication, active participation, and progress toward individual goals. Tracking these group work processes after each session (which may entail keeping a written record on a progress note) can help clinicians know when changes in the group process may be needed. An example of questions to ask after each session to track group processes can be found in *Group Work With Adolescents After Violent Death* (Salloum, 2004).

Trauma Exposure

Trauma measures should be administered prior to the group work and then periodically, to ascertain if exposure has occurred during group work.

• Children's Report of Exposure to Violence (CREV; Cooley, Turner, & Beidel, 1995) is a 29-item self-report of children's lifetime exposure to community violence. Children indicate, using a 5-point Likert scale (0 = no, never to 4 = every day), the frequency of exposure to community violence via media, hearsay, witnessing, and being a victim of violence.

• The Survey of Exposure to Community Violence (SECV; Richters & Saltzman, 1990) consists of 52 items assessed on a 9-point Likert scale (0 = never to 8 = almost every day), including exposure related to being victimized (14 items), witnessing violence (21 items), and hearing about violence (17 items). Although this measure was originally used with school-age children (age 6 to

10 years), it has been used with children up to age 15 (Kliewer et al., 2004; Overstreet & Braun, 2000; Taylor & Kliewer, 2006).

• Traumatic Events Screening Inventory for Children (TESI-C) is a 15-item clinician-administered assessment of past and current exposure to different types of potentially traumatic events (Ford & Rogers 1997). A modified version for younger children (age 0 to 6 years) has been developed, and both child and parent versions are available (Ippen et al. 2002). The TESI-C is available for free at the US Department of Veterans Affairs (http://www.ptsd.va.gov/professional/assessment/child/tesi.asp).

Broadband Measures

• Child Behavior Checklist (Achenbach, 2009) provides broad and specific information based on internalizing and externalizing symptoms and competencies for children and adolescents of all ages. There are several versions of this measure that are available by age, child report, parent report, and teacher report as well as multicultural options. This measure can be used to evaluate changes, but it is longer than other more specific instruments. Therefore, if time does not allow for this measure to be administered before and after the intervention, clinicians may choose to use this measure at baseline only in order to have a broad understanding of some of the issues that the child may be experiencing as well as areas of strengths (see http://www.aseba.org/).

• Strengths and Difficulties Questionnaire is a brief behavioral questionnaire for children ages 3 to 16 years that assesses emotional, hyperactivity/inattention, conduct, and peer relationship problems and prosocial behavior. There are child, adolescent, and parent versions of this measure. The measure is copyrighted but may be downloaded and used free of charge (see http://www.sdqinfo.com/a0.html).

Targeted Measures of Posttraumatic Stress Disorder, Depression, and Grief

• UCLA PTSD Reaction Index for Children and Adolescents DSM-5 (Martin, Revington, & Seedat, 2013) is a self-report instrument for trauma exposure and *DSM-5* PTSD symptoms. It may be used with children ages 7 to 18 years. The instrument may be administered verbally by a clinician, or the child/adolescent may complete it independently. There may be a fee for use. More information can be obtained by emailing hfinley@mednet.ucla.edu.

• Child PTSD Symptom Scale (Foa, Johnson, Feeny, & Treadwell, 2001) assesses for PTSD symptoms and functioning and is appropriate to use with children ages 8 to 18 years. The instrument may be administered verbally by a clinician, or the child/adolescent may complete it independently. Versions in English and Spanish are available and it is free of charge, but it must be requested from Dr. Foa.

- Mood and Feelings Questionnaire assesses for symptoms of depression (Angold et al., 1995). There is a short version and a long version for children, parents, and adults. The response format consists of three Likert responses that are very easy for children to understand: not at all, sometimes, and most of the time. The measure is free of charge and may be used for research purposes as long at the authors are cited (please see http://devepi.duhs.duke.edu/MFQ.html).

- The Persistent Complex Bereavement Disorder (PCBD) Checklist (Layne, Kaplow, & Pynoos, 2014) is designed to assess content domains corresponding to *DSM-5* proposed persistent complex bereavement disorder symptom criteria (e.g., separation, reactive, existential/identity distress, and circumstance over the death distress) for children ages 8 to 18 years. The PCBD Checklist replaces the (now-retired) early prototype measure, the UCLA Extended Grief Inventory (Layne, Savjak, Saltzman, & Pynoos, 2001). Copyright and licensing of the PCBD Checklist are currently being managed by Katherine Fibiger, JD, LLM; kfibiger@research.ucla.edu (phone: 310-794-0205). Email inquiries to Katherine Fibiger and copy Dr. Layne at CMLayne@mednet.ucla.edu.

Strengths and Resilience

- Posttraumatic Growth Inventory for Children–Revised (Kilmer et al., 2009) includes 10 items using a 4-point Likert scale assessing for posttraumatic growth outcomes such as new possibilities, relating to others, personal strength, appreciation of life, and spiritual change. For more information, please see the article by Kilmer et al. (2009).

- The Child and Youth Resilience Measure (Liebenberg, Ungar, & Van de Vijver, 2012) includes different measures of resilience for children (ages 5 to 9 years), youth (ages 10 to 23 years), adults (ages 24 years and older), or persons most knowledgeable about the child, and there is also a shorter version (12 items as opposed to 28 items) being developed for children and adolescents (Liebenberg, Ungar, & LeBlanc, 2013). This measure is available at no cost but has to be requested at http://resilienceresearch.org/.

CONCLUSION

Far too many children, adolescents, and their families, especially those living in poverty, are exposed to community violence. Group work interventions that are easily accessible, tailored to the developmental needs of the members, culturally relevant, and that respond to all levels within the environmental context can help mitigate or even prevent the potential lasting effects of ECV. Due to the long-lasting and negative effects of ECV, facilitators must use the best available practices and provide evidence-based assessments and group work interventions to help children, adolescents, and families.

RESOURCES

There are several Web sites that are listed in the evaluation section that may be helpful to find other resources. Two additional national Web sites that may be helpful are as follows:

- National Center for PTSD (http://www.ptsd.va.gov/public/types/violence/effects-community-violence-children.asp). This Web site has information about community violence, PTSD, and a host of other information about trauma for use by the public and professionals.
- National Child Traumatic Stress Network (http://nctsnet.org/). This Web site has a measures section with information about other assessment measures that may be helpful as well as resources about community violence. There are also psychoeducational handouts for parents and school personnel about the effect of violence, and many of these handouts are available in English and Spanish.

REFERENCES

Achenbach, T. M. (2009). *The Achenbach System of Empirically Based Assessment (ASEBA): Development, findings, theory, and applications.* Burlington: University of Vermont Research Center for Children, Youth, & Families.

Angold, A., Costello, E. J., Messer, S. C., Pickles, A., Winder, F., & Silver, D. (1995). The development of a short questionnaire for use in epidemiological studies of depression in children and adolescents. *International Journal of Methods in Psychiatric Research, 5,* 237–249.

Bacchini, D., Miranda, M. C., & Affuso, G. (2011). Effects of parental monitoring and exposure to community violence on antisocial behavior and anxiety/depression among adolescents. *Journal of Interpersonal Violence, 26*(2), 269–292.

Busby, D. R., Lambert, S. F., & Ialongo, N. S. (2013). Psychological symptoms linking exposure to community violence and academic functioning in African American adolescents. *Journal of Youth and Adolescence, 42*(2), 250–262.

Cecil, C. A. M., Viding, E., Barker, E. D., Guiney, J., & McCrory, E. J. (2014). Double disadvantage: The influence of childhood maltreatment and community violence exposure on adolescent mental health. *Journal of Child Psychology and Psychiatry, 55*(7), 839–848.

Cooley, M., Turner, S., & Beidel, D. (1995). Assessing community violence: The children's report of exposure to violence. *Journal of the American Academy of Child and Adolescent Psychiatry, 34*(2), 201–208.

Cooley-Quille, M., Boyd, R. C., Frantz, E., & Walsh, J. (2001). Emotional and behavioral impact of exposure to community violence in inner-city adolescents. *Journal of Clinical Child Psycholology, 30*(2), 199–206. doi:10.1207/s15374424jccp3002_7

Dinizulu, S. M., Grant, K. E., Bryant, F. B., Boustani, M. M., Tyler, D., & McIntosh, J. M. (2014). Parent–adolescent relationship quality and nondisclosure as mediators of the association between exposure to community violence and psychological distress. *Child and Youth Care Forum, 43*(1), 41–61.

Dubow, E., Boxer, P., Huesmann, L., Landau, S., Dvir, S., Shikaki, K., & Ginges, J. (2012). Cumulative effects of exposure to violence on posttraumatic stress in Palestinian and Israeli youth. *Journal of Clinical Child and Adolescent Psychology, 41*(6), 837–844.

Epstein-Ngo, Q., Maurizi, L. K., Bregman, A., & Ceballo, R. (2013). In response to community violence: Coping strategies and involuntary stress responses among Latino adolescents. *Cultural Diversity and Ethnic Minority Psychology, 19*(1), 38–49.

Figley, C. R. (1995). *Compassion fatigue.* New York, NY: Brunner/Mazel

Foa, E. B., Johnson, K. M., Feeny, N. C., & Treadwell, K. R. (2001). The child PTSD symptom scale: A preliminary examination of its psychometric properties. *Journal of Clinical Child Psycholology, 30*(3), 376–384. doi:10.1207/s15374424jccp3003_9

Ford, J. D., & Rogers, K. (1997). Traumatic events screening inventory (TESI). Hanover, NH: US Department of Veteran's Affairs, National Center for PTSD

Fowler, P. J., Tompsett, C. J., Braciszewski, J. M., Jacques-Tiura, A. J., & Baltes, B. B. (2009). Community violence: A meta-analysis on the effect of exposure and mental health outcomes of children and adolescents. *Developmental Psychopathology, 21*(1), 227–259. doi:10.1017/s0954579409000145

Francois, S., Overstreet, S., & Cunningham, M. (2012). Where we live: The unexpected influence of urban neighborhoods on the academic performance of African American adolescents. *Youth and Society, 44,* 307–328.

Harrell, E., Langton, L., Berzofsky, M., Couzens, L., & Smiley-McDonald, H. (2014). *Household poverty and nonfatal violent victimization, 2008-2012.* (Ncj 248384). Washington, DC: Bureau of Justice Statistics. Retrieved from http://www.bjs.gov/index.cfm?ty=pbdetail&iid=5137

Hart, S. L., Hodgkinson, S. C., Belcher, H. M. E., Hyman, C., & Cooley-Strickland, M. (2013). Somatic symptoms, peer and school stress, and family and community violence exposure among urban elementary school children. *Journal of Behavioral Medicine, 36*(5), 454–465.

Herman, J. L. (1997). *Trauma and recovery.* New York, NY: Basic Books.

Hill, H. M., Levermore, M., Twaite, J., & Jones, L. P. (1996). Exposure to community violence and social support as predictors of anxiety and social and emotional behavior among African American children. *Journal of Child and Family Studies, 5*(4), 399–414.

Holtzman, R. J., & Roberts, M. C. (2012). The role of family conflict in the relation between exposure to community violence and depressive symptoms. *Journal of Community Psychology, 40*(2), 264–275.

Hunt, K. L., Martens, P. M., & Belcher, H. M. E. (2011). Risky business: Trauma exposure and rate of posttraumatic stress disorder in African American children and adolescents. *Journal of Traumatic Stress, 24*(3), 365–369.

Ippen, C. G., Ford, J., Racusin, R., Acker, M., Bosquet, M., Rogers, K., . . . Edwards, J. (2002). *Traumatic events screening inventory—parent report revised (TESI-PRR).* Hanover, NH: US Department of Veteran's Affairs, National Center for PTSD.

Jain, S., Buka, S. L., Subramanian, S. V., & Molnar, B. E. (2012). Protective factors for youth exposed to violence: Role of developmental assets in building emotional resilience. *Youth Violence and Juvenile Justice, 10,* 107–129. doi:10.1177/1541204011424735

Javdani, S., Abdul-Adil, J., Suarez, L., Nichols, S. R., & Farmer, A. D. (2014). Gender differences in the effects of community violence on mental health outcomes in a sample of low-income youth receiving psychiatric care. *American Journal of Community Psychology, 53*(3–4), 235–248.

Jaycox, L. H., Cohen, J. A., Mannarino, A. P., Walker, D. W., Langley, A. K., Gegenheimer, K. L., . . . Schonlau, M. (2010). Children's mental health care following Hurricane Katrina: A field trial of trauma-focused psychotherapies. *Journal of Traumatic Stress, 23*(2), 223–231. doi:10.1002/jts.20518

Kaminer, D., Hardy, A., Heath, K., Mosdell, J., & Bawa, U. (2013). *Gender patterns in the contribution of different types of violence to posttraumatic stress symptoms among South African urban youth.*

Kennedy, T. M., & Ceballo, R. (2014). Who, what, when, and where? Toward a dimensional conceptualization of community violence exposure. *Review of General Psychology, 18*(2), 69–81.

Kilmer, R. P., Gil-Rivas, V., Tedeschi, R. G., Cann, A., Calhoun, L. G., Buchanan, T., & Taku, K. (2009). Use of the revised Posttraumatic Growth Inventory for Children. *Journal of Traumatic Stress, 22*(3), 248–253. doi:10.1002/jts.20410

Kliewer, W., Cunningham, J. N., Diehl, R., Parrish, K. A., Walker, J. M., Atiyeh, C., . . . Mejia, R. (2004). Violence exposure and adjustment in inner-city youth: Child and caregiver emotion regulation skill, caregiver-child relationship quality, and neighborhood cohesion as protective factor. *Journal of Clinical Child and Adolescent Psycholology, 33*(3), 477–487. doi:10.1207/s15374424jccp3303_5

Kliewer, W., & Lepore, S. J. (2014). Exposure to violence, social cognitive processing, and sleep problems in urban adolescents. *Journal of Youth and Adolescence, 44*(2), 507–517.

Lambert, S. F., Boyd, R. C., Cammack, N. L., & Ialongo, N. S. (2012). Relationship proximity to victims of witnessed community violence: Associations with adolescent internalizing and externalizing behaviors. *American Journal of Orthopsychiatry, 82*(1), 1–9.

Lambert, S. F., Copeland-Linder, N., & Ialongo, N. S. (2008). Longitudinal associations between community violence exposure and suicidality. *Journal of Adolescent Health, 43*(4), 380–386. doi:10.1016/j.jadohealth.2008.02.015

Lambert, S. F., Nylund-Gibson, K., Copeland-Linder, N., & Ialongo, N. S. (2010). Patterns of community violence exposure during adolescence. *American Journal of Community Psychology, 46*(3/4), 289–302. doi:10.1007/s10464-010-9344-7

Layne, C. M., Kaplow, J. B., & Pynoos, R. S. (2014). *Test administration manual for the Persistent Complex Bereavement Disorder Checklist-Youth Version.* Los Angeles: University of California, Los Angeles Office of Intellectual Property.

Layne, C. M., Savjak, N., Saltzman, W. R., & Pynoos, R. S. (2001). *Extended grief inventory.* Unpublished psychological test, University of California, Los Angeles.

Liebenberg, L., Ungar, M., & LeBlanc, J. C. (2013). The CYRM-12: A brief measure of resilience. *Canadian Journal of Public Health, 104*(2), e131–e135.

Liebenberg, L., Ungar, M., & Van de Vijver, F. (2012). Validation of the Child and Youth Resilience Measure-28 (CYRM-28) among Canadian youth. *Research of Social Work Practice*, *22*(2), 219–226.

Luthar, S. S., Cicchetti, D., & Becker, B. (2000). The construct of resilience: A critical evaluation and guidelines for future work. *Child Development*, *71*(3), 543–562.

Margolin, G., & Gordis, E. B. (2000). The effects of family and community violence on children. *Annual Review of Psychology*, *51*, 445–479.

Martin, L., Revington, N., & Seedat, S. (2013). The 39-item Child Exposure to Community Violence (CECV) Scale: Exploratory factor analysis and relationship to PTSD symptomatology in trauma-exposed children and adolescents. *International Journal of Behavioral Medicine*, *20*(4), 599–608.

McCann, L., & Pearlman, L. A. (1990). Vicarious traumatization: A framework for understanding the psychological effects of working with victims. *Journal of Traumatic Stress*, *3*(1), 131–149.

McMahon, S. D., Todd, N. R., Martinez, A., Coker, C., Sheu, C-F., Washburn, J., & Shah, S. (2013). Aggressive and prosocial behavior: Community violence, cognitive, and behavioral predictors among urban African American youth. *American Journal of Community Psychology*, *51*(3–4), 407–421.

Menard, S., & Huizinga, D. (2001). Repeat victimization in a high-risk neighborhood sample of adolescents. *Youth and Society*, *32*, 447–472. doi:10.1177/0044118X01032004003

Mendelson, T., Turner, A. K., & Tandon, S. D. (2010). Violence exposure and depressive symptoms among adolescents and young adults disconnected from school and work. *Journal of Community Psychology*, *38*(5), 607–621.

National Child Traumatic Stress Network. (n.d.) *Community violence.* Retrieved from http://www.nctsn.org/trauma-types/community-violence

Nelson-Gardell, D., & Harris, D. (2003). Childhood abuse history, secondary traumatic stress, and child welfare workers. *Child Welfare*, *82*(1), 5–26.

Overstreet, S., & Braun, S. (2000). Exposure to community violence and post-traumatic stress symptoms: mediating factors. *American Journal of Orthopsychiatry*, *70*(2), 263–271.

Richters, J. E., & Saltzman, W. (1990). *Survey of exposure to community violence: Self-report version.* Rockville, MD: National Institute of Mental Health.

Rynearson, R. (2001). *Retelling violent death.* Philadelphia, PA: Brunner-Routledge.

Salloum, A. (2004). *Group work with adolescents after violent death: A manual for practitioners.* Philadelphia, PA: Brunner-Routledge.

Salloum, A. (2015). *Grief and trauma in children: An evidence-based treatment manual.* New York, NY: Routledge.

Salloum, A., Carter, P., Burch, B., Garfinkel, A., & Overstreet, S. (2011). Impact of exposure to community violence, Hurricane Katrina, and Hurricane Gustav on post-traumatic stress and depressive symptoms among school age children. *Anxiety Stress Coping*, *24*(1), 27–42. doi:10.1080/10615801003703193

Salloum, A., Garfield, L., Irwin, A., Anderson, A., & Francois, A. (2009) Grief and trauma group therapy with children after Hurricane Katrina. *Social Work with Groups*, *32*(1–2), 67–79. doi:10.1080/01609510802290958

Salzinger, S., Feldman, R. S., Rosario, M., & Ng-Mak, D. S. (2011). Role of parent and peer relationships and individual characteristics in middle school children's behavioral outcomes in the face of community violence. *Journal of Research on Adolescence, 21*(2), 395–407. doi:10.1111/j.1532-7795.2010.00677.x

Salzinger, S., Rosario, M., Feldman, R. S., & Ng-Mak, D. S. (2008). Aggressive behavior in response to violence exposure: Is it adaptive for middle-school children? *Journal of Community Psychology, 36*(8), 1008–1025. doi:10.1002/jcop.20275

Self-Brown, S., Lai, B. S., Thompson, J. E., McGill, T., & Kelley, M. L. (2013). Posttraumatic stress disorder symptom trajectories in Hurricane Katrina affected youth. *Journal of Affective Disorders, 147*(1–3), 198–204.

Smith, E. L., & Cooper, A. (2013). *Homicide in the U.S. known to law enforcement, 2011.* (NJC 243035). Washington, DC: US Department of Justice, Bureau of Justice Statistics. Retrieved from http://www.bjs.gov/content/pub/pdf/hus11.pdf

Taylor, K. W., & Kliewer, W. (2006). Violence exposure and early adolescent alcohol use: An exploratory study of family risk and protective factors. *Journal of Child and Family Studies, 15*, 207–221.

Turner, H. A., Finkelhor, D., & Ormrod, R. (2006). The effect of lifetime victimization on the mental health of children and adolescents. *Social Science Medicine, 62*(1), 13–27. doi:10.1016/j.socscimed.2005.05.030

Wright, E. M., Fagan, A. A., & Pinchevsky, G. M. (2013). The effects of exposure to violence and victimization across life domains on adolescent substance use. *Child Abuse and Neglect, 37*(11), 899–909.

Zinzow, H. M., Ruggiero, K. J., Resnick, H., Hanson, R., Smith, D., Saunders, B., & Kilpatrick, D. (2009). Prevalence and mental health correlates of witnessed parental and community violence in a national sample of adolescents. *Journal of Child Psychology and Psychiatry, 50*(4), 441–450. doi:10.1111/j.1469-7610.2008.02004.x

Chapter Twenty-Two

Group Work With Gay Men

Steven Ball and Benjamin Lipton

Social group work for people with same-sex orientations developed and continues to evolve in response to a history of mental health services that started from a predominantly pathological stance that regarded homosexuals as mentally ill to an affirmative model that assists these people in asserting their equal, healthy, and ethical place in society (Abelove; 1993; Gonsiorek, 1985; Isay, 1996, Ritter & Terndrup, 2002). Because many of the psychosocial issues facing all gay men and women are the result of adapting to an environment that still denies them full recognition and acceptance, groups serving these population can provide a healing antidote to a lifelong history of second-class citizenship. The developmental process of growing up in a world still debating their intrinsic self-worth on political, social, and religious stages across the world creates a stigmatized identity for all gay people. Even four decades after the Stonewall Riot signaled gay liberation and ever-increasing numbers of gay men and women began living openly, gay affirmative psychotherapy regards homophobia—antihomosexual attitudes and behaviors (O'Hanlan et al., 1997)—rather than homosexuality, as the major pathological variable affecting the mental health of this population (Margolies, Becker, & Jackson-Brewer, 1987; Meyer, 1995). As a result, it is essential that workers understand the overriding psychosocial factors arising from homophobia that inform individual responses to particular environmental stressors and life issues. Societal and internalized homophobia; stigmatization; coming out; familial, work, and social relationships; and ego-dystonic sexual orientation continue to inform the process of all group work with gay men and lesbians, regardless of the specific commonalities around which these groups may be organized. Although the psychosocial needs and experiences of gay men are as diverse as those of any other minority group, this chapter will provide essential clinical information about the aforementioned issues that can inform practice with more specific subgroups of the population in a variety of social service settings. Because certain issues that gay men face in society today are similar to what gay women encounter, some of what follows in this chapter can be directly applicable to group work with lesbians as well. However, despite the reality that over the years these populations have been continually grouped together in the clinical and sociological literature (Gibson, Alexander, & Meem, 2014), there are many, significant areas of divergence in working with these populations. Importantly, lesbians face the double stigmatization of being women as well as oriented toward the same gender, and this creates its own complex of concerns, among which is sociocultural invisibility. Mindful of the misguided propensity to lump gay men and lesbians together when considering their psychosocial needs, we want to be clear that this chapter is not intended to follow in that wrong direction. Nonetheless, there may be resonant areas of overlap that can assist a social worker who is interested in providing group work to lesbian populations.

REVIEW OF THE LITERATURE

Any overview of the social service and mental health literature on gay men must be understood within the rapidly changing social context of the past four decades (Abelove, 1993; Adamczyk & Pitt, 2009; Duberman, 1991; Krogstad, 2013; Miller, 2006; Signorile, 1997; Stein & Cohen, 1986). The response of social workers to those with a same-sex orientation reflects the historical progression from pathology to ambivalence across all mental health professions. Prior to 1973, when the American Psychiatric Association officially declassified homosexuality as pathological, gay men were considered mentally ill or perverse because of their sexual object choice. Although a small but dedicated group of influential practitioners to this day remain committed to labeling homosexuality an illness (Cohen, 2007; Nicolosi, 1991), growing numbers of gay and lesbian mental health practitioners, including many social workers (Deyton & Lear, 1988; Getzel, 1998), have united with an increasingly vocal and organized gay community in leading the way toward dismantling homophobic myths and creating a psychosocial model for healthy homosexuality. By openly challenging traditional models of pathology and exposing their lack of empirical support (Friedman & Downey, 1993), these men (and women) have paved the way toward developing an alternative, affirmative practice base for working with gay and lesbian clients.

Practitioners began developing a significant body of literature on the theory and practice of gay affirmative counseling and psychotherapy prior to the onset of AIDS in the early 1980s (Bell & Weinberg, 1978; Cass, 1979; Coleman, 1982; Gonsiorek, 1977). During this same period, psychotherapy groups for gay men primarily came out of the private practices and agency work of increasing numbers of openly gay mental health practitioners who were responding to the long-suppressed needs of their clients. Reviews of the literature on group psychotherapy with this population in the 1980s by Conlin and Smith (1985) and by Schwartz and Hartstein (1986) revealed that there were few articles of their kind that specifically address the role of group work in fostering psychosexual maturation in gay men rather than focusing on a particular psychosocial stressor affecting this population. Their articles documented the ongoing need of designing groups for gay men whose purpose is to foster disclosure of sexual orientation and sexuality, provide opportunities for emotional intimacy, and confront both external stigmatization and internalized homophobia. Outside of personal Web sites and gay service organizations, there still exists a paucity of new research and documentation on general group work with gay men.

How can we account for the gap in the literature over the past decades? We believe there are at least four related reasons. First, many social workers conventionally think of first contacts as individual, often relegating group treatment to a secondary or auxiliary position in treatment. Initial developments in gay affirmative psychotherapy seem to reflect this pattern. Second, at the historical moment when mental health agencies were beginning to sanction the use of affirmative models for group work with gay men, the biopsychosocial crisis of AIDS necessitated an immediate shift in treatment to this population (Caputo, 1985; de la Vega, 1990; Nichols, 1986; Shernoff, 1991). As clients and workers began to view the ongoing external and internal stressors of being self-identified as a gay man through the lens of the human immunodeficiency virus (HIV), the literature on practice with gay men focused on AIDS-related issues of immediate concern and provided a new context in which to understand gay identity development (Burnham, Cadwell, & Forstein, 1994; Isay, 1989; Odets, 1994). Third, self-help has always been a necessary and essential part of the gay experience in a heterosexist, homophobic environment and consistently filled the gap in social services long before mainstream professionals formally responded by incorporating services into their organizations and documenting their work with contributions to the literature (Eller & King, 1990). The most powerful example of this process was the rapid and comprehensive organization of the gay community in response to AIDS when their needs were not addressed by social service agencies. And lastly, as acceptance and integration of gay people have rapidly grown in the mind of the general culture over the last decade, a focus on the concerns of same-sex couples and families and transgendered rights seems to have moved into the forefront of social concerns (McCarthy, 2015).

Although much remains to be written about groups for same-sex couples and their specific coupling and family concerns, the literature on HIV-related group work provides an invaluable resource not only for understanding HIV issues but also for understanding deeper conflicts about being gay that will inform the process of working with any group of gay men (Tunnell, 1994). Regardless of the particular focus of any group, whether or not related to HIV, what is most crucial is the opportunity to build social supports and interpersonal connections. *Homosocialization*, defined as building relationships with other gay men, is essential to the healthy integration of a gay identity and the discovery of positive role models (Isay, 1989). In their discussions of their work with gay populations, Hetrick and Martin (1987), Conlin and Smith (1985), and Schwartz and Hartstein (1986) all suggest that commonly shared issues arising from stigmatization such as social, cognitive, and emotional isolation—the negative outcomes of stigmatization—can best be coped with by creating opportunities for socialization with peers. Despite increasing visibility of gay people and debates in public law and social policy, recent research continues to uphold these earlier findings (Frable, Platt, & Hoey, 1998; Frable, Wortman, & Joseph, 1997; Greene, 1996; Igreja, Zuroff, Koestner, & Saltaris, 2000; Lambda Legal Defense and Education Fund, 1999; Meyer, 1995). Because gay men are one of the few minorities still denied the opportunity to developmentally identify with others like themselves because of both the absence of identifying factors and the oppression of a homonegative environment, group work with this population takes on ever-increasing importance in the lives of its members.

PRACTICE PRINCIPLES

Based on the pervasive impact of stigmatization and homonegativity on gay male development, as well as the need for homosocialization to mitigate the influence of these factors, the following practice principles and procedures should guide a social worker in beginning group work with the population.

Level of Worker Activity Inside and Outside of the Group

The worker's role in any group for gay men extends far beyond facilitating the group process. When developing a group for gay men, the need for outreach and psychoeducation can be guaranteed. Those most in need of a gay men's group may be the hardest to reach, as they remain unaffiliated with the gay community or unacknowledged within it, as is the case with adolescents and was the case for HIV-negative men as well as gay men living with chronic illnesses other than HIV (Ball, 1998; Lipton, 1998, 2004; Odets, 1994). Outreach to the larger, nonspecifically gay environment, away from traditional resources for membership such as community centers, bars, and social clubs, may provide new awareness not only to those isolated men who could benefit from a gay group but also to the nongay community at large about issues confronting gay men.

Although a secondary gain of outreach efforts may be public education about the realities of gay life, an essential task of a social worker leading a gay men's group is to educate the staff of his or her social service agency about gay men. In-service training in addition to formal and informal individual interactions will increase understanding about gay men and their particular issues as well as the potential for referrals. The combined acknowledgment of the community at large and a specific agency positively influences the functioning of a gay men's group, as potential members see the group as an acceptable and accepted source of support and a safe place to explore their concerns.

When the group process moves from the stage of pregroup formation to the beginning phase of group work, the social worker's role as an educator continues. Not only must the worker lend a vision and contribute data to the group as it begins to take shape, but throughout the life of the group he or she must continue to provide resources, conceptual frameworks, interpersonal modeling, and general education to counter the cognitive and experiential deficits that result from growing up in an environment void of healthy and varied gay role models and gay affirmative information. Implicit in a social worker's vision of the group must be the awareness that a gay person's stigmatization stems from a society—and a gay community—that often dictate a rigid repertoire of physical and social expressions that may impair healthy psychosocial development.

The Group as a Basic Resource

Although the leader is initially responsible for guiding the development of group norms and modeling adaptive interpersonal relating, the goal of these interventions is to help group members see themselves as a source of support for each other and to develop a sense of belonging. Gay men often enter groups with a legacy of isolation. Historically, societal groups have been sources of persecution for this population that reinforce a feeling of powerlessness rather than resources for affiliation and validation. When the group recognizes and employs their communal resources for support, group members can begin to counteract their collective history of disenfranchisement. Groups offer an opportunity to clarify emotional priorities and increase their capacity for building cohesive interpersonal networks. To this end, the social worker must consistently introduce, model, and reinforce group norms that invite the group to join with the leader as a basic resource for answers, empathy, and conflict resolution.

Boundaries and Confidentiality

A powerful effect of homophobia and stigmatization has been the internalization by many in the gay community of a narrow sense of identity organized around sex rather than sexual orientation. This reality makes group contracting around the issues of interacting both within and outside of the group of paramount importance in developing an environment of safety and trust. Often group members initially alternate between expressions of excitement and pleasure resulting from identification among members, and fear that the group will become yet another sexualized experience and lose its credibility as a safe space for exploring feelings. To foster and preserve a safe environment, the role of sex within the group process must be addressed from the outset. Although setting limits for socialization may include members abstaining from having sex with each other, it is particularly important in a group where sexual identity is an essential commonality to help members explore how sexual involvement between them would affect the ability of the group to function successfully. A social worker's initial interventions must reflect and normalize sexualized interactions such as flirting among members while helping the group to identify the role of these interactions in potentially defending against emotional intimacy. Modeling an affirming and curious stance toward the role of sexuality in initiating relationships in the group empowers members to begin to question what modes of socializing will best fit their needs and help them to realize their treatment goals.

Because gay men have historically had to respond to rather than determine the social norms, boundaries, and limits established by a heterosexual culture, social workers must recognize the interplay between the opportunity for self-determination and the fear of acquiescing to the restrictive norms of a dominant culture. It is the authors' experience that even in large cities that offer some sense of anonymity within the gay community, members may share some past or present social connection to other members. As a result, restricting socialization to the group may, on the one hand, not meet the needs of isolated gay men who would benefit from outside social support and, on the other hand, fail to mesh with the social reality of men already socialized within the gay community. Although the group may recognize the need for guidelines on sexual interactions among members, efforts to restrict outside socialization, a common limit in traditional group therapy, need to be explored, contracted, and recontracted throughout the group process.

All of the principles discussed here must be founded on a firm commitment to the guiding group work principle of confidentiality. The leader must actively address the place of confidentiality in the group process and in outside contacts in order to establish a feeling of safety, particularly for those who have yet to speak openly about their sexual orientation. An ongoing exploration of this principle may provide a powerful opening to discussions of stigmatization and shame.

COMMON THEMES

Although the themes discussed in this section will assume varying degrees of priority in groups organized around any number of commonalities, including coming out, substance abuse, sexual abuse, parenting, couples, marriage, bereavement, HIV concerns, aging, and socialization, they may also serve as the target issues around which groups for gay men are developed.

Homophobia

The socialization of every gay man still involves exposure to homophobia. The literature refers to the subsequent internalization of the social animosity that a gay man experiences (Hetrick & Martin, 1987) as *internalized homophobia* and widely supports the view that the external and internal impacts of the resulting stigmatization must be addressed in treatment (Hetrick & Martin, 1987; Isay,

1989; Margolies et al., 1987; Silverstein, 1991; Tunnel, 2003). Homophobia frequently manifests itself alongside heterosexism, the culturally conditioned bias that heterosexuality is superior to other sexual orientations (Gonsiorek, 1985; Sears & Williams, 1997).

Homophobia manifests itself in a variety of ways, blatant and subtle, internal and external, within the gay community and in society at large. It is essential to understand, first, that recognizing homophobia is not equal to eradicating it and, second, that one's same-sex orientation does not preclude homophobic beliefs and behaviors. Within the group process, homophobia may present as fear of disclosure in general; fear of disclosing one's sexual orientation; fear of commitment to the group; discomfort with more open group members or leaders; generalized rejection of heterosexuality; and denial of social differences between gay and heterosexual men. Although some of these manifestations may on the surface seem far from homophobic, exploration of feelings will most often unearth negative attitudes and beliefs about what it means to be a gay man.

Stigmatization and Shame

As previously noted, stigmatization is the inevitable result of developing within a homophobic environment. Stigma is the precursor to shame in the psychosocial development of every gay man (Cadwell, 1992; Cain, 1991; Cornett, 1993). As members begin to share life histories, whether anecdotally in support groups or more formally in psychotherapy groups, common themes of rejection, isolation, violence, and abuse will often surface. This retelling of the impact of stigmatization will frequently find its complement in the current group process. Isensee (1991) and Cornett (1993) carefully outline the process by which shame interferes with interpersonal relating and fosters the development of a false self. Because the legacy of shame leads gay men to embrace negative stereotypes about their potential for developing lasting and important relationships, members may initiate a self-fulfilling prophecy that often results in treating one another in the same hostile/rejecting ways in which they fear being treated themselves.

Coming Out

As a gay man begins to integrate his sexuality, the impact of homophobia and stigmatization on gay male development necessitates a process that the literature defines as coming out—an ongoing developmental process of gay identity formation organized around accepting and revealing one's sexual orientation. Of seminal importance to the coming-out literature have been Coleman's (1982) five-stage model, which describes a developmental process from before coming out to integration, and Cass's (1979) six-stage model, which leads from identity confusion to identity synthesis as the gay man works to synthesize his sexuality with his self-concept. For a review of the coming-out literature that also provides insight into the impact of HIV on gay male development, see Linde (1994) and Martin and Hunter (2001).

To understand the impact of any life crisis or stressor around which a group for gay men has been formulated, it is necessary to recognize the impact of coming out on each of the group members and on the group process as a whole (Cass, 1979). As stereotypes and dormant issues of homophobia, self-definition, and self-acceptance are activated by the diverse psychosocial issues and stages of members, a group organized around any task can offer a powerful experience on the coming-out continuum for those just beginning the process, as well as for those more openly identified as gay. Initial movements toward coming out are often limited to sexual experimentation and sexualized socialization in bars, dance clubs, parties, and through the digital space. There are few opportunities to attend to the powerful emotions that generate and are generated by the coming-out experience. Whether beginning to come out or already identified as gay, gay men often arrive at a group with a lack of knowledge related to the diversity of gay lifestyles, range of social outlets, and ways of relating to others like themselves. A gay men's group can serve not only as an emotional anchor to explore turbulent feelings about self and others in regard to a specific common issue; it can also be a window on the diversity of the gay experience as one begins to identify more openly as a gay man and/or to expand one's understanding of what it means to be gay.

HIV

Even as HIV has retreated from the headlines and prominence in sociocultureal consciousness, HIV still remains a consistent and often hidden stressor in the daily lives of all gay men, regardless of their HIV status (Burnham et al., 1994; see also Chapter 3). Living with HIV is not only a long-term health issue; it is a mental health issue that may further exacerbate existing stressors related to family, friends, relationships, life choices, and a sense of the future. Agencies may organize groups for gay men presenting with any number of HIV-related issues: adjustment to new HIV conversion, serodiscordant coupling, risk reduction and prevention, or comorbid substance use and abuse (Tunnel, 1994: Gardner & Kosten, 2008).

Regardless of the particular task around which a social worker organizes a group for gay men, and regardless of whether the group task is itself specific to HIV, this concern will undoubtedly appear as a theme in the group process. Gay men of all ages, particularly younger men unaware of the history and reality of AIDS, need to make sense of their identity in a world where HIV remains a powerful stigma (Kershaw, 2008; Lee, 2014). In this era, uncertainty remains a powerful challenge for both HIV-positive and HIV-negative gay men. For HIV-negative men, the threat of infection is often looming. Such anxiety may manifest itself in hypervigilance—a preoccupation with any signs of illness at the expense of more productive and fulfilling activities of daily living. Additionally, decision-making anxiety around whether or not to take PrEP (pre-exposure prophylaxis) in order to radically reduce the risk of HIV transmission is a new choice that evokes powerful reactions among sexually active gay men (Centers for Disease Control and Prevention [CDC], 2015). For HIV-positive men, the anxiety regarding prognosis and treatment may manifest as depression and a radical reevaluation of life goals. For men who have lived through the worst of AIDS, anxiety may also manifest itself unconsciously as survivor guilt, a complex process through which one maladaptively manages overwhelming feelings of loss and abandonment by acting out a variety of more or less overtly self-destructive behaviors (Odets, 1994).

As gay men struggle with survivor guilt, internalized homophobia, and the realities that they are still the population most at risk for contracting HIV (with Black and Latino men having the highest rates of infection; CDC, 2015), they may play out conflicting feelings in unsafe sexual practices or feelings of fear in abstinence. Additionally, challenges to HIV medication adherence can become entangled in psychological struggles that both predate and relate to one's status as HIV positive. The same adherence issues might also be affecting those who have elected to take PrEP. These issues require support and exploration toward empowering men to care for themselves most effectively. In an environment in which the link between sex and survival has been turned upside down for well over three decades, groups for gay men may offer invaluable forums for normalizing fears, clarifying values, disseminating information, and building a community of concern to mitigate against overwhelming feelings of confusion and isolation that might otherwise lead to self-destructive behavior. To this end, social workers must be willing to take on a psychoeducational role on the issues of protected sex, drug use, and the latest information on HIV. Workers must not only respond to requests for information and discussion but also initiate them. When necessary, they must be prepared to make empathic, attuned interventions to clarify and address maladaptive defense structures of members and foster effective problem-solving skills.

Family Issues

As in group work with any population, the group process recapitulates for each gay member the family dynamics that he brings to the group (Yalom, 1985). For gay men who have most often grown up hiding their true selves from their families of origin, this aspect of the group process can prove either particularly traumatizing or extremely empowering. Even in families that appear to function well and attend to the psychosocial needs of all members, apparent attunement can mask underlying, unintentional emotional neglect. As the family fails even to consider the possibility that a son, brother, or father may be gay, the gay member remains silenced by shame, guilt, and secretiveness. If the group process recreates this experience for its members by failing to reach for and affirm self-disclosure and self-reflection about being gay, then the group will perpetuate emotional trauma. If, on the other hand, members are made aware of the dynamic of familial recapitulation in the group process and helped to use it to create new scripts of acceptance and affirmation, then the group can be an important place for developing and consolidating feelings of empowerment (Cornett, 1993; Isay, 1996).

For many gay men, particularly those who came of age in the period preceding public debate about the place of gay men within social structures, their definition of *family* has been expanded to include families of choice in addition to families of biological origin. Families of choice often develop during the initial stages of the coming-out process, as gay men have had to look outside of their families for acceptance and affirmation, as well as for affiliation with other gay men. Interdependent groups of gay men develop out of this search and provide each other with the physical and emotional caring that heterosexuals can usually expect from their families of origin. For some gay men, families of choice may even replace their families of origin as the primary reservoirs of emotional security. When working with gay men, it is essential to value and respect the place of these families within the lives of group members and to assess the roles that a member may play within his family of choice. Often these roles coincide with earlier roles played out in a member's family of origin and provide helpful information toward understanding the interpersonal dynamics that a member may bring to the group. With older gay men, social workers must also be alert to the devastating impact of multiple losses and continual grieving on this system of psychosocial support since the beginning of the AIDS epidemic.

Gender Roles

Popular gay culture seems to have evolved, at least in part, in reaction to the collective childhood trauma of gender role nonconformity (Friedman, 1988). Literature on gay male development (Isay, 1989; Schwartz & Hartstein, 1986) suggests that such trauma may begin with a prehomosexual boy's relationship with his father. Emotional distance and unavailability of fathers often develop out of the father's conscious or unconscious homophobia and contribute to poor relations between these men and their gay children. Early negative relationships with fathers then are reinforced as developing gay men continue to interact with heterosexual males in larger social circles. Teased and ostracized for not taking part in traditionally masculine social and sexual pursuits, gay adolescents and younger men often develop feelings of shame and insecurity for failing to fit into heterosexual definitions of masculinity. In keeping with theories of oppressed populations, gay men may defend against these feelings by identifying with the same stereotypical images of traditional masculinity that oppress them.

Unfortunately, identification with traditional masculine gender roles creates significant problems with building intimacy, trust, and a willingness to depend on other men.

Because many gay men come to groups with scarred self-images and difficulty relating openly to other men, an important task of any social worker will be to foster interdependence and group cohesion by exploring and normalizing an expansive, inclusive definition of masculinity unimpaired by traditional limitations. The group leader can use basic, supportive social work skills to help members identify their feelings and learn to hear each other in increasingly empathic ways. The particular tasks of any group for gay men may allow members to peel away layers of maladaptive, rigid identifications in search of more fluid, emotionally responsive, true selves.

Relationships and Intimacy

Men who choose membership in a gay men's group desire relationships with other gay men. Often men may want to use the group either to get help in finding a romantic partner or to explore difficulties in their already existing partnerships. Although the impulse to fall in love and partner exists for heterosexual as well as gay men, a social worker must be sensitive to the particular difficulties confronting single and coupled group members. Despite the right to marry for more and more same-sex couples in the majority of the United States, there still exists a powerful homophobic subculture that works actively to exclude gay men from the legal, religious, financial, and social structures that affirm and sanctify heterosexual coupling. Nevertheless, surveys of gay men demonstrate that more than half of them are involved in ongoing partnerships (Peplau, 1991).

To provide help in this area of psychosocial development, social workers must come to understand the ways in which both societal oppression and the characteristics of same-sex relationships impact on gay male couples and on gay men looking for a partner (Greenan & Tunnel, 2002). For example, in contrast to the accepted heterosexual model of monogamy, many male couples in durable, committed relationships—including marriage—distinguish between emotional and sexual fidelity (Johnson & Keren, 1996). As members of a culture steeped in heterosexual norms, social workers must reflect carefully on their heterosexist biases and strive not to assign pathology or dysfunction to gay couples. A group leader must transfer these challenges to group members as well, reinforcing hope by presenting the group as a model for the potential in each member to build intimate relationships. At the same time, the social worker must identify the negative impact of internalized homophobia, heterosexist assumptions, and misleading stereotypes on the process of building intimacy in the group and help the group to reflect on how each of these affects external partnerships or efforts to establish them.

Ethnocultural Diversity

Contrary to prevalent stereotypes, racial, cultural, and ethnic diversity impact on the development and functioning of individual gay men (Fukuyama & Ferguson, 2000; Greene, 1996). Just as the White, middle-class male does not represent all of American society, so a social worker also must recognize that the most easily identifiable gay men do not represent the population in all of its complexity. Because the majority of the literature on gay men is based on samples of White, middle-class men, neither the theory nor research that has resulted is necessarily relevant to all subgroups of the gay population. The marginalized place of ethnic and racial minorities within the literature on gay men parallels the social realities of minority populations not only within society at large but also within the gay community. Being gay does not preclude one from experiencing or fomenting ethnocultural prejudice. It is imperative for a group leader to recognize the additional stigmas of discrimination based on race, gender, age, or ethnicity that many men must carry.

Social workers must help group members to articulate and validate their particular ethnocultural experiences and conflicts in relation to their sexual orientation. For example, African American gay men may experience identity conflicts as they search for a healthy place amid two problematic environments: their homophobic African American heritage, on one hand, and the racist White gay culture, on the other (Adams & Kimmel, 1997; Crisp, 1998; Martinez & Sullivan, 2000). Furthermore, men of color may have a difficult time coming out as they juggle the forces of ethnic communities that have strong ties to religious beliefs and stereotypic male gender roles. In recognition of the dissonance for some men between their privately and publicly expressed sexual orientation as well as their lack of identification with sociocultural concepts of what it is to be "gay," the term MSM (men who have sex with men) is now used to describe this subgroup (Wyatt, 2014). Carballo-Dieguez (1989), Colon (2001), Diaz (1997), Pares-Avila (1994), Rodriguez (1996), and Chan (1989) explore similar difficulties that arise from the interplay of race, ethnicity, and sexual orientation for Latino and Asian American gay men. A group leader can help clients develop effective coping strategies for traversing seemingly exclusive cultures and provide a safe place for ventilating painful feelings of alienation from one or both groups.

In addition to ethnocultural factors, age affects one's identity as a gay man. Since AIDS began to take its toll on the lives of gay men, the concept of longevity has undergone radical redefinition for subsequent generations. After the deaths of thousands of gay men from AIDS, men in their 40s and 50s are joining those in their 60s, 70s, and 80s in the developmental tasks of survivorship as they continue to work through issues of loss and strive for regeneration (Rofes, 1996). As they tackle these difficult tasks, gay men who are middle-aged and older must develop an identity outside of a mainstream gay culture that continues to laud youth and pays little regard to its older members or to the realities of aging

(Adams & Kimmel, 1997; Behney, 1994; Herdt, Beeler, & Rawls, 1997; Kooden & Flowers, 2000; Rosenfeld, 1999). It is ironic that so many younger members in groups for gay men lament the scarcity of role models, while the culture in which these men are trying to find a place continues to marginalize older gay men. These men, the first generation to have had the possibility of living as openly gay for most of their adult lives, are invaluable and overlooked resources for the younger generation.

RECOMMENDED WAYS OF WORKING

The authors' clinical and anecdotal experiences reveal that many gay men continue to mistrust mental health providers, particularly in nongay settings. Such mistrust underscores the marginalized place of gay men within the mental health system, the need for outreach to the gay community, and the ways in which misattuned social work agencies and workers might reinforce injurious feelings of difference, isolation, and invisibility among gay people. To this end, the following section will provide information on effective ways of addressing the needs of this population through group work.

Pregroup Interview

The pregroup interview, an essential procedure for composing all groups, is particularly charged for gay men. It must initiate a process of attunement. For an individual whose identity and way of relating to his environment rest on anticipated rejection, the pregroup interview must set a tone of acceptance as the social worker actively normalizes a gay identity. As social workers attend to the psychosocial assessment of a prospective group member, including a determination of his developmental stage in the coming-out process, the worker must demonstrate real knowledge and awareness of gay issues and the gay community. At the same time, the worker who is less informed about these subjects must acknowledge his ignorance and demonstrate a willingness to learn more about them from sources *outside* of the group so as not to reinforce or repeat negative experiences of members requiring them to confront homophobic misinformation from the group leader (Kus, 1990). Clients must be informed about the diversity of membership and told that the group will not focus on labels or definitions, but instead on their own needs regarding their concerns about being gay and how it may relate to the specific focus of the group.

Member Selection

Groups for gay men must affirm inclusion. As a social worker evaluates an interviewee's appropriateness for group membership, he or she must guard vigilantly against recapitulating a lifelong process of rejection and exclusion from social group participation. Excluding gay men from groups designed specifically for them may not only perpetuate feelings of isolation but may actually leave the client isolated from specific gay services, particularly in geographic areas where there are few alternative resources for this population. Because many agencies do not offer a wide variety of group services to gay men, social workers may find themselves leading groups that must address myriad divergent needs. As a result, the major criteria for membership should be an expressed desire to be a group member and a willingness to commit to the group process. For groups that do not require specific inclusion criteria, only those who are unable to acknowledge consciously that they are attracted primarily to other men to satisfy their sexual and affectional needs, or who are actively psychotic or antisocial in personality, should be excluded (Getzel, 1998). The question of whether to include bisexual clients in groups for gay men often depends on the specific focus and setting of the group. If the group is a more general therapy group, then including bisexual men may prove very helpful in fostering acceptance of diversity and recognition of the complexity of sexual identity. Similarly, in a coming-out group, one could include bisexual men because they share issues with gay men regarding accepting their desire for members of the same sex. In fact, many men who later identify as gay prefer to label themselves bisexual when they first begin to integrate their same-sex object choice (Isay, 1989). If, however, group cohesion is organized around a particular issue or theme not focused on identity formation, then including bisexual men may prove counterproductive to the group task. In an HIV-negative men's group, for example, including bisexual men may create scapegoating and divert the group's process away from the established group focus. At the same time, the limitations of agency provisions and geographic realities may require the group leader to adjust inclusion criteria for the needs of a bisexual client.

Self-Disclosure and Modeling

The social worker's disclosure of his or her own sexual orientation is essential to creating an affirmative environment in which clients can explore their sexuality. Cornett (1993) and Frommer (1994) suggest that clients enter treatment with an inherently nonneutral, heterosexist assumption of a social worker's orientation. As a result, they believe a gay social worker should disclose this information when asked by the client and after a careful exploration to determine its meaning for the client in treatment. They contend that gay leaders provide invaluable opportunities for positive gay role models in a world where too few exist (Isay, 1996). Failure to self-disclose as a gay leader at the beginning of the group experience forsakes an invaluable opportunity to model an affirmative stance toward homosexuality in the service of establishing a trusting environment and building cohesion. Conlin and Smith (1985) believe that gay social workers leading groups for gay men should be in the late stage of their coming-out process. Such leaders may be more able to tolerate the often powerful and ambivalent feelings of those members who remain at earlier stages in the process and reflect to the group more subtle manifestations of homophobia in the group process.

The issue of self-disclosure for heterosexual social workers leading groups for gay men has not been adequately addressed in the literature. Gay affirmative theory seems to be moving toward asserting the value of gay clients receiving treatment from gay practitioners (Ball, 1998; Isay, 1989). However, the reality of human resources within social service agencies requires that heterosexual social workers also provide services to gay clients. The question of self-disclosure remains for heterosexual leaders, but the dynamics are significantly different. Particularly in short-term, problem-focused, and support groups, persistent focusing on the group leader who does not disclose may well sidetrack or derail the necessary tasks of the group and permit the development of maladaptive defenses against group affiliation and intimacy. In any group, a heterosexual social worker must have become a social anthropologist prior to beginning work with the group. He or she must not only identify his or her own homo-negative attitudes, beliefs, and behaviors but also develop a firm understanding of and belief in the complexity of gay culture and life experiences.

Although self-disclosure is important, how one handles disclosure is as important as the act of disclosing itself. The tension between offering a supportive, positive environment for self-exploration, on the one hand, and impinging on a client's ability to verbalize any and all feelings of shame and self-doubt, on the other, must inform the social worker's process of disclosing his or her sexual orientation to group members. The social worker who does not remain keenly aware of his or her own internalized homophobia may shut the door on more helpful explorations of shame and guilt and the healthy desire of members to identify with the gay group leader as a positive role model or a heterosexual leader as a genuinely informed and nurturing influence.

> A heterosexual female social worker experienced in group work with gay men was assigned to lead a coming-out group in the absence of openly gay staff at the university counseling service where she worked. After the second group session, the group fell into several weeks of very little activity despite the worker's skilled efforts to elicit participation. Long periods of silence were followed by occasional bickering and apologies between members. After 5 weeks, two members had dropped out of the group and those remaining began to express feelings of hopelessness. The worker's supervisor stated that these dynamics were not unusual in the beginning stages of group work and focused on processing the worker's anxiety about her difference from group members. Nonetheless, after reviewing the group process of the preceding weeks, the social worker suggested to the group in the

next session that their disappointment and difficulty in moving forward were related not only to her gender difference but also to her perceived sexual orientation as heterosexual.

The group immediately responded. Several members finally expressed feelings of mistrust, anger, and disappointment that the leader was not a gay man. The social worker validated their concerns and managed to redirect the group's anger away from each other and toward her. Her ability to remain supportive and empathic during this period in the group process helped move the group to a new level of openness, understanding, and cohesion.

After many weeks, group members expressed idealized feelings toward the social worker and expressed surprise that they could experience her as particularly nurturing. One client joked, "You must be a lesbian." The group immediately picked up on this theme and demanded an answer, which the leader agreed to provide after the group explored their thoughts and fantasies on the subject. When the social worker acknowledged her heterosexuality, the members were able to explore more fully both their heterophobia and their homophobia within a safe environment.

Group Prospectus

A social worker, and sometimes an agency or another sponsoring organization, must decide whether a group should be open or closed and short or long term, based on the group's task and setting. To hasten acceptance within a non-gay-identified agency that has not previously had a gay-related group, a worker should structure the group to imitate the prevailing model for group work in the agency in order to integrate and normalize the group within the agency culture. These efforts not only elicit acceptance by staff and administration but also suggest to gay clients that the agency provides a safe place to discuss and explore their sexual orientation.

> An openly gay social worker in a continuing day treatment program recognized the need for a gay men's group after several clients confided feeling isolated and unable to express themselves openly in groups, the primary treatment modality at the agency. The worker confronted agency homophobia by educating the staff about the needs of gay and lesbian clients and documenting clients' concerns. The executive director ultimately overrode the worker's immediate supervisor and sanctioned the group.
>
> Initially, the group was composed of clients who had been attending the treatment program for some time. The group process seemed to parallel longstanding institutional beliefs that the group did not belong in the treatment program. Members projected powerful feelings of internalized homophobia onto each other and prevented group cohesion by verbally

attacking each for coming out to community members outside of the group. One member stated, "I didn't come to this place to work on my sexual orientation or identity stuff. I came here to deal with my psychiatric problems."

As some of the more hostile, intensely homophobic clients left the group, new clients who had entered treatment after the gay group had already been integrated into the agency began contributing more to the process. Members developed greater social relatedness as they began to see themselves not only as part of an affirming gay subgroup, but also as people integrated and accepted by the rehabilitative community.

Whether gay, lesbian, bisexual, transgendered, or heterosexual, a social worker leading groups for gay men must be gay affirmative; cognizant of the powerful impact of homophobia on oneself and on one's clients and willing to address the issue directly; sensitive to the diverse experiences of gay and bisexual men; vigilant against subscribing to destructive stereotypes; and open to exploring all sexual identities without permitting personal ideology to contaminate professional explorations. In the authors' experience, coming out professionally not only enhances one's self-esteem and professional identity but also may be a primary step toward helping an agency respond to the emotional needs of its gay, lesbian, transgender, and bisexual clients and staff. Hiring motivated, openly gay social workers may increase interest in and attention to the particular needs of gay men while providing essential role models for an all too often silenced, shamed, and ignored population. Armed with awareness, acceptance, and a genuine desire to be helpful, social workers working with gay men can create precious spaces in which these individuals can work toward developing self-esteem, integrating their sexuality, and building emotionally intimate relationships with their peers.

EVALUATION APPROACHES

Outcome measures for clients in gay men's groups remain anecdotal. To date, no instruments directly addressing the outcomes of work with this population in groups have been developed for public use, although instruments for addressing individual problems such as low self-esteem or homophobia could certainly be incorporated into an outcome study of group work with gay men. As in most group work, eliciting outcome information is an essential component of termination. Statements about improved psychosocial functioning seem to be the best barometer for determining the effectiveness of the group. Desire for continued affiliation with other gay men, a sense of belonging both within the gay community and within the larger social environment, improved social and intimate relationships, and diminished homophobic statements and behaviors all would testify to positive outcomes. As men in these groups learn to celebrate their everyday heroism and hard-earned strengths in living as openly gay, it is hoped that they will carry their resilience outside of their groups, use it to expand on previous roles, and adopt a more affirmative sense of themselves.

RESOURCES

For the most part, mental health services for this population are provided at the local and regional levels. To locate these services in a particular region, we suggest consulting the Gay Yellow Pages (gayyellowpages.com), which can be found online or in libraries, in addition to utilizing search engines to locate local resources via key words.

American Civil Liberties Union
Lesbian and Gay Rights Project
125 Broad Street
New York, NY 10004
212-944-9800
http://www.aclu.org

The ACLU provides legal services aimed at advancing the rights of gay men and lesbians and educating the public about discrimination.
Gay Asian Pacific Support Network (GAPSN)
PO Box 461104
Los Angeles, CA 90046
http://www.gapsn.org

GAPSN is a source of support and information for gay, lesbian, bisexual, and transgender people of Asian/Pacific Islander descent.
Gay and Lesbian Alliance Against Defamation (GLAAD)
104 West 29th Street, 4th Floor
New York, NY 10011
212-629-3332
http://www.glaad.org

GLAAD promotes visibility of the gay and lesbian community and organizes grassroots responses to homophobia in the media.
Gay, Lesbian and Straight Education Network (GLSEN)
90 Broad Street
New York, NY 10004
212-727-0135
http://www.glsen.org

GLSEN is a national alliance with regional offices and local chapters that advocates for the dignity and respect of all students regardless of sexual orientation.
Gay Men of African Descent (GMAD)
44 Court Street, Suite 1000
Brooklyn, NY 11201
718-222-6300
http://www.gmad.org

The mission of GMAD is to empower gay men of African descent through education, advocacy, health and wellness, prevention, and social support.
The Hetrick Martin Institute
2 Astor Place
New York, NY 10003
212-674-2400
http://www.hmi.org

The Hetrick Martin Institute provides comprehensive social services, high school education, and referrals for gay and lesbian adolescents.
Lambda Legal Defense and Education Fund
120 Wall Street, Suite 1500
New York, NY 10005
http://www.lambdalegal.org

Lambda is an organization of gay men and lesbians providing political advocacy and legal services to gay men and lesbians.
Llego
PO Box 444483
Washington, DC 20026
202-544-0092
http://www.llego.org

Llego is a national organization whose mission is to effectively address issues of concern to lesbian, gay, bisexual, and transgender Latinas/Latinos at local, state, regional, national, and international levels.
Parents and Friends of Lesbians and Gays (P-FLAG)
1726 M. Street, NW, Suite 400
Washington, DC 20036
202-467-8180
http://www.pflag.org

With chapters throughout the country, P-FLAG is an invaluable resource for gay people, families, and friends, particularly those struggling with coming out.

Pride Institute Hotline
800-54-PRIDE
612-934-7554 (within Minnesota)
http://www.pride-institute.com

The Pride Institute provides residential chemical dependency programs as well as referral to local resources.
Senior Action in a Gay Environment (SAGE)
208 West 13th Street
New York, NY 10011
212-741-2247
http://www.sageusa.org

SAGE provides services and socializing for older gay men and lesbians. The New York office may provide referrals to services throughout the nation.

REFERENCES

Abelove, H. (1993). Freud, male homosexuality and the Americans. In H. Abelove, M. A. Barale, & D. M. Halperin (Eds.), *The lesbian and gay studies reader* (pp. 381–393). New York, NY: Routledge Press.

Adams, C. L., & Kimmel, D. C. (1997). Exploring the lives of older African American gay men. In B. Greene (Ed.), *Ethnic and cultural diversity among lesbians and gay men: Psychological perspectives on lesbian and gay issues* (Vol. 3, pp. 132–151). Thousand Oaks, CA: Sage.

Adamczyk, A., & Pitt, C. (2009). Shaping attitudes about homosexuality: The role of religion and cultural context. *Social Science Research, 38*(2), 338–351.

Ball, S. (Ed.). (1998). *The HIV-negative gay man.* New York, NY: Harrington Park Press.

Behney, R. (1994). The aging network's response to gay and lesbian issues. *Outword, Winter,* pp. 2–5.

Bell, A. P., & Weinberg, M. S. (1978). *Homosexualities: A study of diversity among men and women.* New York, NY: Simon & Schuster.

Burnham, R. A., Cadwell, S. A., & Forstein, M. (Eds.). (1994). *Therapists on the front line: Psychotherapy with gay men in the age of AIDS.* Washington, DC: American Psychiatric Press.

Cadwell, S. (1992). Twice removed: The stigma suffered by gay men with AIDS. *Smith Studies in Social Work, 61*(3), 236–246.

Cain, R. (1991). Stigma management and gay identity development. *Social Work, 36*(1), 67–73.

Caputo, L. (1985). Dual diagnosis: AIDS and addiction. *Social Work, 30*(4), 361–363.

Carballo-Dieguez, A. (1989). Hispanic culture, gay male culture, and AIDS: Counseling implications. *Journal of Counseling and Development, 68*(1), 26–30.

Cass, V. (1979). Homosexual identity formation: A theoretical model. *Journal of Homosexuality, 4*, 219–235.

Centers for Disease Control and Prevention. (2015). *Gay and bisexual men's health.* http://www.cdc.gov/msmhealth/

Chan, C. (1989). Issues of identity development among Asian-American lesbians and gay men. *Journal of Counseling and Development, 68*(1), 16–20.

Cohen, R. (2007). *Coming out straight.* Winchester, VA: Oakhill Press.

Coleman, E. (1982). The developmental stages of the coming out process. In J. C. Gonsiorek (Ed.), *Homosexuality and psychotherapy: A practitioner's handbook of affirmative models* (pp. 31–43). New York, NY: Haworth Press.

Colon, E. (2001). An ethnographic study of six Latino men. *Journal of Gay and Lesbian Social Services, 12*(3–4), 77–92.

Conlin, D., & Smith, J. (1985). Group psychotherapy for gay men. In J. Gonsiorek (Ed.), *A guide to psychotherapy with gay and lesbian clients* (pp. 105–112). New York, NY: Harrington Park Press.

Cornett, C. (Ed.). (1993). *Affirmative dynamic psychotherapy with gay men.* Northvale, NJ: Jason Aronson.

Crisp, D. (1998). African American gay men: Developmental issues, choices and self concept. *Family Therapy, 25*(3), 161–168.

De la Vega, E. (1990). Considerations for reaching the Latino population with sexuality and HIV/AIDS information and education. *SIECUS Report, 18*(3), 1–8.

Deyton, B., & Lear, W. (1988). A brief history of the gay/lesbian health movement in the U.S.A. In M. Shernoff & W. Scott (Eds.), *The sourcebook of lesbian/gay healthcare* (2nd ed., pp. 15–19). Washington, DC: National Lesbian/Gay Health Foundation.

Diaz, R. (1997). Latino gay men and psycho-cultural barriers to HIV prevention. In M. Levine & P. Nardi (Eds.), *Changing times: Gay men and lesbians encounter HIV/AIDS* (pp. 221–244). Chicago, IL: University of Chicago Press.

Eller, M., & King, D. (1990). Self help groups for gays, lesbians and their loved ones. In R. Kus (Ed.), *Keys to caring* (pp. 330–339). Boston, MA: Alyson Publications.

Frable, D. E. S., Platt, L., & Hoey, S. (1998). Concealable stigma and positive self perceptions: Feeling better around similar others. *Journal of Personality and Social Psychology, 24*(4), 909–922.

Frable, D. E. S., Wortman, C., & Joseph, J. (1997). Predicting self-esteem, wellbeing, and distress in a cohort of gay men: The importance of cultural stigma, personal visibility, community networks, and positive identity. *Journal of Personality, 65*(3), 599–624.

Friedman, R. C., & Downey, J. (1993). Psychoanalysis, psychobiology and homosexuality. *Journal of the American Psychoanalytic Association, 41*(4), 1159–1198.

Frommer, M. S. (1994). Homosexuality and psychoanalysis: Technical considerations revisited. *Psychoanalytic Dialogues, 4, 215–233.*

Fukuyama, M. A., & Ferguson, A. D. (2000). Lesbian, gay and bisexual people of color: Understanding cultural complexity and managing multiple oppressions. In R. Perez & K. DeBord (Eds.), *Handbook of counseling and psychotherapy with lesbian, bay and bisexual clients* (pp. 81–105). Washington, DC: American Psychological Association.

Gardner, T., & Kosten, T. (2008). International Implications of HIV and substance younger gay men and HIV abuse. *American Journal of Drug and Alcohol Abuse*, *34*(1), 1–3.

Getzel, G. (1998). Group work with gay men and lesbians. In G. Mallon (Ed.), *Foundations of social work practice with gay men and lesbian women* (pp. 131–144). New York, NY: Haworth Press.

Gibson, M., & Alexander, J., & Meem, D. (2014). *Finding out: An introduction to LGBT studies*. Thousand Oaks, CA: Sage.

Gonsiorek, J. (1977). Psychological adjustment and homosexuality. (MS No. 1478). *JSAS Catalog of Selected Documents in Psychology*, *7*, 45.

Gonsiorek, J. (1985). *A guide to psychotherapy with gay and lesbian clients*. New York, NY: Harrington Park Press.

Greenan, D., & Tunnel, G. (2002). *Couples therapy with gay men*. New York, NY: Guilford Press.

Greene, B. (1996). Lesbian and gay men of color: The legacy of ethnosexual mythologies in heterosexim and homophobia. In E. D. Rothblum & L. A. Bond (Eds.), *Preventing heterosexism and homophobia: Primary prevention of psychopathology* (Vol. 17, 59–70). Thousand Oaks, CA: Sage.

Herdt, G., Beeler, J., & Rawls, T. W. (1997). Life course diversity among old lesbians and gay men: A study in Chicago. *Journal of Gay, Lesbian and Bisexual Identity*, *2*(3/4), 231–246.

Igreja, I., Zuroff, D., Koestner, R., & Saltaris, C. (2000). Social motives, social support and distress in gay men differing in HIV Status. *Journal of Research in Personality*, *34*(3), 287–304.

Isay, R. (1989). *Being homosexual: Gay men and their development*. New York, NY: Farrar, Straus & Giroux.

Isay, R. (1996). *Becoming gay: The journey to self-acceptance*. New York, NY: Pantheon Books.

Isensee, R. (1991). *Growing up gay in a dysfunctional family*. New York, NY: Prentice Hall Press.

Johnson, T. W., & Keren, M. S. (1996). Creating and maintaining boundaries in male couples. In J. Laird & R. Green (Eds.), *Lesbians and gays in couples and families: A handbook for therapists* (pp. 231–239). San Francisco, CA: Jossey-Bass.

Kershaw, S. (2008, January 2). New HIV cases drop but rise in young gay men. *The New York Times*. Retrieved from http://www.nytimes.com/2008/01/02/nyregion/02hiv.html?_r=0

Kooden, H., & Flowers, C. (2000). *Golden men: The power of gay midlife*. New York, NY: Avon Books.

Krogstad, J. M. (2013, January 27). Survey of LGBT Americans. *Pew Research Center*. Retrieved from http://www.pewresearch.org/fact-tank/2015/01/27/what-lgbt-americans-think-of-same-sex-marriage/

Kus, R. (1990). *Keys to caring*. Boston, MA: Alyson Publications.

Lambda Legal Defense and Education Fund. (1999). *State-by-state sodomy law update*. New York, NY: Author.

Lee, S. (2014, September 25). National survey of gay men reveals deep HIV stigma. *LGBT Weekly*. Retrieved from http://lgbtweekly.com/2014/09/25/

national-survey-of-gay-men-reveals-deep-hiv-stigma-new-speakouthiv-campaign-aims-to-get-gay-men-talking-video/

Linde, R. (1994). Impact of AIDS on adult gay male development: Implications for psychotherapy. In R. A. Burnham, S. A. Cadwell, & M. Forstein (Eds.), *Therapists on the front line: Psychotherapy with gay men in the age of AIDS* (pp. 453–471). Washington, DC: American Psychiatric Press.

Lipton, B. (2004). *Gay men living with chronic illnesses and disabilities: From crisis to crossroads.* New York, NY: Harrington Park Press.

Margolies, L., Becker, M., & Jackson-Brewer (1987). Internalized homophobia: Identifying and treating the oppressor within. In Boston Lesbian Psychologies Collective, *Lesbian psychologies: Explorations and challenges* (pp. 229–241). Chicago: University of Illinois.

Martin, J., & Hunter, S. (2001). *Lesbian, gay, bisexual and transgender issues in social work: A comprehensive bibliography with annotations.* Alexandria, VA: Council on Social Work Education.

Martinez, D. G., & Sullivan, S. C. (2000). African American gay men and lesbians: Examining the complexity of gay identity development. In L. A. Letha (Ed.), *Human behavior in the social environment from an African American perspective* (pp. 243–264). Athens: University of Georgia Press.

McCarthy, J. (2015, January 22). Satisfaction with acceptance of gay people plateaus at 53%. *Gallup.* http://www.gallup.com/poll/181235/

Meyer, I. H. (1995). Minority stress and mental health in gay men. *Journal of Health and Social Behavior, 36*(March), 38–56.

Miller, N. (2006). *Out of the past: Gay and lesbian history form 1899 to present.* New York, NY: Alyson Books

Nichols, S. E. (1986). Psychotherapy and AIDS. In T. S. Stein & C. J. Cohen (Eds.), *Contemporary perspectives on psychotherapy with lesbians and gay men* (pp. 209–239). New York, NY: Plenum Press.

Nicolosi, J. (1991). *The reparative therapy of male homosexuality: A new clinical approach.* Northvale, NJ: Jason Aronson.

Odets, W. (1994). Survivor guilt in seronegative gay men. In R. A. Burnham, S. A. Cadwell, & M. Forstein (Eds.), *Therapists on the front line: Psychotherapy with gay men in the age of AIDS* (pp. 473–491). Washington, DC: American Psychiatric Press.

O'Hanlan, K., Cabaj, R. B., Schatz, B., Lock, J., & Nemrow, P. (1997). A review of the medical consequences of homophobia with suggestions for resolution. *Journal of the Gay and Lesbian Medical Association, 1*(1), 25–40.

Pares-Avila, J. (1994). Issues in the psychosocial care of Latino gay men with HIV infection. In R. Burnham, S. Cadwell & M. Forstein (Eds.), *Therapists on the front line: Psychotherapy with gay men in the age of AIDS* (pp. 339–362). Washington, DC: American Psychiatric Press.

Peplau, L. (1991). Lesbian and gay relationships. In J. Gonsiorek & J. Weinrich (Eds.), *Homosexuality: Research implications for public policy* (pp. 177–196). Newbury Park, CA: Sage.

Ritter, K., & Terndrup, A. (2002). *Handbook of affirmative psychotherapy with lesbians and gay men.* New York, NY: Guilford Press.

Rodriguez, R. (1996). Clinical issues in identity development in gay Latino men. In C. Alexander (Ed.), *Gay and lesbian mental health: A sourcebook for practitioners* (pp. 127–157). New York, NY: Haworth Park Press.

Rofes, E. (1996). *Reviving the tribe: Regenerating gay men's sexuality and culture in the ongoing epidemic.* New York, NY: Harrington Park Press.

Rosenfeld, D. (1999). Identity work among the homosexual elderly. *Journal of Aging Studies, 13*(2), 121.

Schwartz, R., & Hartstein, N. (1986). Group psychotherapy with gay men. In T. Stein & C. Cohen (Eds.), *Contemporary perspectives on psychotherapy with lesbians and gay men* (pp. 157–177). New York, NY: Plenum Press.

Sears, J. T., & Williams, W. L. (Eds.) (1997). *Overcoming heterosexism and homophobia: Strategies that work.* New York, NY: Columbia University Press.

Shernoff, M. (1991). Eight years of working with people with HIV: The impact upon a therapist. In C. Silverstein (Ed.), *Gays, lesbians, and their therapists* (pp. 227–239). New York, NY: W. W. Norton.

Signorile, M. (1997). *The Signorile report on gay men: Sex, drugs, muscles and the passages of life.* New York, NY: Harper Collins.

Silverstein, C. (Ed.). (1991). *Gays, lesbians, and their therapists.* New York, NY: W. W. Norton.

Stein, T. S., & Cohen, C. J. (Eds.). (1986). *Psychotherapy with lesbians and gay men.* New York, NY: Plenum Press.

Tunnel, G. (1994). Special issues in group psychotherapy for gay men with AIDS. In R. A. Burnham, Jr., S. A. Cadwell, & M. Forstein (Eds.), *Therapists on the front line: Psychotherapy with gay men in the age of AIDS* (pp. 453–471). Washington, DC: American Psychiatric Press.

Tunnel, G. (2003, Jan/Feb). Social change in working with gay and lesbian clients. *Family Therapy Magazine 2*(1)(January/February), 32–33.

Wyatt, J. (2014). *LGBT coming out and men of color.* Retrieved from http://www.academia.edu/8066371/LGBT_Coming_Out_and_People_Of_Color

Yalom, I. (1985). *The theory and practice of group psychotherapy* (3rd ed.). New York, NY: Basic Books.

Chapter Twenty-Three

Group Work With Fathers
Who Are Incarcerated

Geoffrey L. Greif

Almost two thirds of federal and slightly more than half of state inmates are parents of children 18 years and under , with the vast majority of these parents being fathers (Glaze & Maruschak, 2010). More than 1.7 million children age 18 years and under have a parent in prison (Office of the Deputy Attorney General, 2013). Many of these parents, including the fathers, were highly involved with their children prior to incarceration. Geller (2013) reported that over 60% of imprisoned fathers with children 5 years old and younger lived with their children prior to incarceration.

This chapter describes common themes that emerged during more than 4 years of leading short-term groups for incarcerated fathers and offers suggestions for how to respond to those themes in a group setting (see also, Greif, 2014, for a version of this chapter). The groups were held at a federal facility in Baltimore, where fathers were either awaiting trial or awaiting placement in a federal facility after being convicted. Working with fathers in groups has the advantage of normalizing their parenting experiences, enhancing their ability to listen to others as they wait while others speak, and gaining a better perspective on their parenting role and how it can be fulfilled while behind bars. Hearing from other men in a similar situation and who have a similar background has proven to be a powerful antidote to the common feeling that no one understands or appreciates what they are facing from behind bars. In addition, and from a social justice perspective, the presence of such groups in a prison sends an important message to prison administrators and staff about the needs of fathers to have contact with their children.

FATHERING WHILE INCARCERATED

It is incumbent on the social worker to acknowledge that parenting roles as well as fathering roles can be conceptualized in multiple ways. Not only does the social worker hold conscious and unconscious ideas about how fathers *should* be relating to their children and other family members based on the social worker's own experiences and training, but fathers hold expectations for themselves that vary greatly from one father to the next, even if they were raised in the same neighborhood. These expectations differ by race and culture, by the generation in which they grew up, by religion, by their idiosyncratic family history and the messages they received from their elders, and by their own experiences both inside and outside of prison. While society sends messages about parental financial responsibilities, the roles of provider and nurturer, the nature of masculinity and femininity, and how couples share child care and employment responsibilities, messages are also communicated within the family and the peer group about these issues. These messages may be in conflict with each other and with what social workers typically believe are good parenting practices. Thus, a social worker in this setting must widen the lens of what is an appropriate intervention and acknowledge that what may work for one father with his child in his unique situation may be inappropriate for the next father.

Fathers come into the group with diverse views about what good parenting entails. Some believe a father's primary role is to provide while mothers nurture. Some recognize that their time with and attention to the child are paramount. Some believe they should be a tough disciplinarian while others describe themselves as a "softie" when compared with the mother. A few admit to having no idea how to father because they never had a father or a father figure in their life.

Although the fathers hold diverse views about their own parenting behavior, they tend to share expectations for their children. Educational achievement, staying out of trouble in school, and "making it" within society are universally acclaimed when children's accomplishments are described by group members.

Differences do appear about visitation. Some fathers expect their children to visit them, and others think it would be upsetting for children to see them in the prison environment and with a glass wall between them.

Although recent research has shown that fathers with a history of incarceration are not harsher disciplinarians than those without a history (Mustaine & Tewksbury, 2015), sometimes, as observed in the group, a father's self-concept as a man and parent includes being in control of his children. For example, behavior that is adaptive on the street or in prison (taking charge; not showing emotion; not appearing vulnerable) carries with it the expectation that children will obey. Yet such expectations may not be realistic with a 1-year-old who is throwing food on the floor. Such expectations also may not be realistic for the father who thinks his child should come to the telephone when he calls from prison, even though his 3-year-old is watching a television show that is, in the moment, more important than he is. If the father already has a tenuous feeling of competence as a parent, his inability to "control" his children will further erode it.

General concepts about good parenting are taught in the group (e.g., don't be upset if your 3-year-old son doesn't want to talk on the phone), but such advice is offered with an awareness that nothing works for everyone and that each father's situation is different. In a group where the age range can be 35 years between members, where some fathers grew up in a two-parent home and others on the street or in foster homes, where some fathers have multiple mothers involved in raising their children and others have one, parenting suggestions are offered with multiple caveats as to the applicability to anyone in the room. If we do not offer these caveats, the members are quick to remind us of differences between each other.

What the Research Says

Although parenting experiences vary greatly, studies show that risks do exist for these men's children. According to Geller and Walker's (2014) analysis of data from the Fragile Families and Child Wellbeing Study, having an incarcerated father puts a child at increased risk for economic and residential insecurity. In addition, sons of incarcerated fathers are at particular risk for manifesting behavioral problems. Sons also are at greater risk for displaying aggressive behaviors, according to Wildeman (2010). Although such a chicken-and-egg effect seems evident, and tends to blame the parents, any research must be viewed carefully. For example, Johnson and Easterling (2012) note that some children had behavior problems and displayed aggressive behavior *prior* to parental incarceration. Further clouding definitive statements about the impact of a father's incarceration on his children is the difficulty in comparing children whose parents are incarcerated for short versus lengthy periods of time and at different ages and with varying family and residential situations.

For the father wishing to be actively engaged, factors in the community may prevent their involvement with the family. They may be incarcerated, particularly federal prisoners, far from home. The mothers may be blocking contact or the children may be unwilling to stay in touch, as one study based on interviews with 185 incarcerated fathers found (Swanson, Lee, Sansone, & Tatum, 2013).

Despite these challenges, incarcerated fathers often want to stay involved with their children and improve their parenting abilities (Greif, 2013; Harrison, 1997; Mendez, 2000; Muth & Walker, 2013). Unfortunately, even though fathers comprise the larger segment of the incarcerated parenting population, limited programs exist to help them with their parenting when compared with the availability of programs for mothers (Craig, 2009; Loper & Tuerk, 2006).

Research suggests that fathering programs, like mothering programs (e.g., Loper & Tuerk, 2011), can be helpful to parent–child relationships (e.g., McCrudden, Braiden, Sloan, McCormack, & Treacy, 2014; see also, the Resources section at the end of this chapter for information about fathering programs). But this area of research, like that quantifying the impact of a father's incarceration on his children, is difficult to study. Defining the extent of a father's involvement from prison, allowing for his potentially having children by different mothers, and then studying outcomes of interventions, such as a fathering group, is a daunting task. The involvement of the father in the family when not incarcerated has been correlated with less maternal stress (Harmon & Perry, 2011), more adaptive behavior and cognitive skills in children (Black, Dubowitz, & Starr, 1999), and, as suggested by Geller and Franklin (2014), greater residential and financial security. Putting together the benefits of father involvement and the benefits shown by parenting programs, it can be suggested that improving fathering behavior from prison should continue to be a target of social work intervention.

GROUP SETTING AND CONTEXT

The author (as a volunteer) has co-led a 4-week 75-minute group with a caseworker from a detention facility and, more recently, another social worker for more than 4 years (Greif, 2013, 2014). The group was initiated at the request of a federal judge who believed fathering services, along with GED classes and Alcoholics Anonymous groups, should be offered at the facility where no such services existed. Over 450 detainees have attended the group as of this writing, with the typical group consisting of 12 men.

When the group was first offered, 100 detainees responded to a flyer distributed by the caseworker about the new group. Given the strong initial interest and constraints on the author's and caseworker's time, a 4-week group was proposed that would allow the leaders to reach more fathers before they left the facility (the typical stay is about 1 year).

Federal detainees are incarcerated for a variety of reasons. These include drug trafficking, drug-gang membership, armed robbery, assault, murder, money laundering, and forgery. These detainees usually range in age from their early 20s to late 40s. Their children range in age from newborns to early 30s. The majority of detainees attending the groups have been African American, although a few have been Caucasian, Latino, Asian, Caribbean, and African. Some who attend are married to, or in a long-term partnership with, the mother of all their children. Others have children by different mothers and have varying degrees of contact with the mothers and their children.

In this facility, visits between detainees and family members occur with a glass wall between them. The facility was originally designed as a maximum security prison so no large meeting rooms or cafeterias exist where large-scale visits can occur. Only fathers who complete the 4-week group are allowed to have a one-time, 1-hour visit with physical contact that occurs in small rooms usually reserved for lawyer–client meetings. The opportunity for physical contact, which might be a father's first time holding his child, was initiated 6 months after the group began and was not in the original plan for the group. Although this is an improvement over the former policy of no contact visits, and was a concession made by the facility's administration, it is inadequate when the needs of fathers and children having greater contact are considered. Furthermore, it compels fathers to have to attend a parenting group they may not want to attend. Now, understandably, it is the prime reason the fathers want to enroll in the group.

PRACTICE PRINCIPLES

Unlike other parenting groups that offer specific curricula (e.g., Loper & Tuerk, 2011), the 4-week group provides opportunities to have guided discussions about experiences with parenting around general topics. After each week's theme is introduced and each father responds to it, discussion ensues on the issue. In the first week, the fathers describe their parenting situations and what they hope to get from the group. In the second week, the fathers are shown a copy of a genogram within which are embedded other potential influences on their parenting. These include spirituality, tough love, masculinity, money, the street, race, and culture. The leaders give the message that the fathers may have been raised with certain values and views about parenting and they need to decide what they want to preserve from their upbringing that is positive and what they want to discard.

The third week focuses on the members' relationship with the mother or mothers of their children. The final week focuses on how to make the most of their 1-hour contact visit and any specific concerns they have about their children. There is also a brief graduation ceremony during which each father receives a Certificate of Completion of the class. Some fathers present these Certificates to the judge hearing their case with the hope that participation in the program will help mitigate their sentence.

As noted, and as a practice principle, the group leaders do not lecture at length about specific parenting techniques. The leaders' position is that the fathers are the experts on their children and know them much better than the leaders do. Great respect is paid to the members (they are referred to as "sir") and to the differences that exist between members and between the leaders and the members. The leaders' position, with the exception of brief opening remarks at the beginning of each session, is to respond globally about a father's role when offering suggestions about parenting following a group discussion. The only universal theme, which the leaders state at the beginning of the group, is the belief that fathers should remain involved with their children no matter how long they are incarcerated and no matter how far they live from their children. If children are not interested in contact, we encourage the fathers to write or send drawings or poems to them and that fathers should try and stay in touch, even if there is little or no response. This is based on the premise that when the child grows up, the child may realize that the father tried to stay in touch and did not drop out of contact.

As it is a group, members are encouraged to interact with each other and to ask for and be willing to consider advice from other group members. The members, many of whom had unsuccessful school experiences, remark at the conclusion of the group that they enjoyed hearing from other fathers about parenting approaches and appreciated that the group did not have a lecture-based classroom format. Their chance to engage in the dialectical, the debating of ideas, was one of the high points for them.

Two family therapy theories, family systems theory, developed by Murray Bowen, and structural family therapy, developed by Salvador Minuchin (see, for example, Nichols, 2014), are utilized for thematic discussions. For example, the second group session begins with group members being asked to consider how their upbringing affects how they raise their children. The use of the genogram as an illustration is based on Bowen's theory. In the third group session, fathers are asked to discuss their relationship with the mother(s) of their children. A triangle is drawn to show how parents may communicate with each other through their children and how clear lines of communication and boundaries are needed.

The group atmosphere varies greatly from one 4-week group to the next. Older group members often help bring a gravitas to the discussions. Their experiences with adult children, as well as, at times, a history of prior incarceration and separation from their children, can help guide younger members about how to adapt to separation from their children. Group discussions can raise strong emotions related to feelings of loss in some fathers. A few have cried in the group. Fathers who report they were the primary caregivers for their children are particularly vulnerable to feeling they have lost the most by being incarcerated.

The fathers' own upbringings also vary greatly. Many grew up in emotionally and economically impoverished homes with absent parents, sometimes due to addiction. Some came of age in the "street" and raised themselves with the help of a gang. Others hail from two-parent families who were economically stable with emotionally present parents. These differences underline the need for the group leader to avoid making assumptions about group members and to look for broader themes that are relevant to the diverse population being served in any 4-week group program. The leader should also remember that prisoners are a vulnerable and often underserved population. Like any vulnerable population, their situation is inherently disempowering and the leader should be attuned to advocating on their behalf as a detainee and as a father.

COMMON THEMES AND RECOMMENDED WAYS OF WORKING

The themes offered here are typical of what a father may be experiencing while detained. They provide a guide as to what may be brought up in other fathering groups. By knowing what common themes may arise, the group leader can be better prepared to respond in the group and to offer potential programmatic changes to better serve the group within the prison structure.

The Difficulties Associated With Parenting While Incarcerated

This broad theme encompasses a number of subthemes, some of which are listed separately next. To understand the difficulties in parenting, it is important to remember that father involvement generally takes three forms that may vary from one child to the next, depending on with whom the child is residing:

1. The highly involved father who was living in the home prior to incarceration and may even have been the primary parent. Some of the fathers describe taking their children to school every day, helping them with homework, and coaching sports.
2. The somewhat involved father who may be living in the home but is not overly involved in childrearing, as well as the father who lives elsewhere but is still a fairly consistent presence. Fathers who have more than one child by different mothers and are trying to parent them all are often in this group.
3. The peripheral or uninvolved father who has occasional or minimal contact with his children. He may want more closeness and cannot achieve it, or he may feel staying close causes too much disruption for the child's mother, the child, or for himself.

The relationship the father has with his child(ren) influences the difficulties he encounters. Clearly, a highly involved father may feel more comfortable speaking to a child over the telephone and parenting him or her (both through praise and discipline) than a father with a peripheral relationship. On the other hand, fathers who have not been active in their child's life are unclear what role they can play as a parent from prison. They acknowledge that the mother or a grandparent has been a more central figure in childrearing. Feelings of incompetence around how to parent are common for this group of fathers, especially if they feel they did not have a father figure in their own life. Such feelings of uncertainty about the father's relationship with his children may continue on release, as revealed during interviews with fathers in transitional housing (Kelly-Trombley, Bartels, & Wieling, 2014).

Layered on top of feelings of incompetence are feelings of guilt. Fathers who were raised without a father figure often promise themselves they will be more available to their children than their father was to them. Then, when they become incarcerated, they cannot fulfill that promise.

Many fathers lament not having much control over the raising of their children because they are in prison. If they had prior involvement with their children, not only has their involvement been diminished by a lack of hands-on contact, they are no longer as knowledgeable about their child's daily life. Their information is filtered through the mother or other caregivers. They may be called on to discipline by telephone about an event they are learning about second or third hand. For example, a mother may want the father to speak to the child about the child's poor behavior in school that the mother has learned about from the principal. The father would need to have a good relationship with the child in order to have a fruitful conversation. Even with a good relationship, the father has to guard against always being cast as the disciplinarian, a role society and family cultures often thrust upon him. When parenting is characterized by a tenuous relationship with the child and the mother and weakened by feelings of guilt, being an effective parent can be difficult.

To make matters harder, if the father tries to assert himself, the child and the caregiver can hang up the telephone if they do not like the direction the conversation is going. An older child and a mother can also collude in not telling the father something. If the father has been sentenced to prison for many years, his position is weakened further.

Specific parenting difficulties that have been voiced in the group include: Will my child listen to me if I am in prison and will not be home for 2–5 years? Do I let my child make the same mistakes I made, or should I give him advice from prison about where I went wrong? Should I tell my child that I am her father and she should ignore the man living with her mother? When I have children by different mothers, how can I equalize their treatment if my relationships with the mothers are not the same?

Interventions

As with all interventions in a group, it is important to let the group members respond to parenting difficulties first. If a leader is too active and offers too many suggestions, it can shut down the group from generating suggestions. As Shulman (2012) has written, altruism is one of the benefits of group treatment. If the leader is too active, it can stop other members from helping each other and experiencing altruism. After listening to others, if needed, the group leaders will offer suggestions they have heard from fathers in previous groups as well as those they generate themselves.

For example, one approach to helping fathers with their physical separation is found in the framework of ambiguous loss, a concept developed by Pauline Boss (2006, 2010). Such a framework can provide an umbrella under which to consider more specific interventions. Ambiguous loss refers to a loss that is un-resolved; for example, the kidnapped child may be emotionally present in the lives of the family but physically absent. It is not a complete loss because the body of the child has not been found, so the hope of recovery alive remains, sometimes for years. Whereas with a complete loss, mourning can occur; with an ambiguous loss, grieving is thwarted. Incarcerated fathers are in a similar half-there, half-not-there situation. They may be emotionally present in the family but physically absent; that is, their "presence" is ambiguous. They are "there" but not there, making it difficult for some family members to react to them and for them to act as a full member of a family.

In a recent group, a 35-year-old man with two sons, one 15 years old and one 16 years old was asked by his sons how long he was "going to be gone." The father was not sure how many years of incarceration he was facing but by giving a time frame, he was agreeing to the term "gone" as a way of framing his situation. It was suggested to him that he not used the term "gone" because he was still going to be present for them emotionally, regardless of where he was incarcerated.

The suggestion is often given that the feelings of ambiguous loss fathers experience when incarcerated are normal and expected. They, in turn, may have experienced an ambiguous loss with their own parents if, for example, their father had experienced addiction. In such a case, he would be physically present but emotionally absent. Fathers are encouraged to recognize that imprisonment is a form of ambiguous loss similar to other losses they may have experienced and they should still try to remain connected to their children.

Pursuing educational advancement (e.g., a GED or other classes) while in prison can also set the stage for building a new relationship with the children. Fathers are encouraged to tell their children that they have participated in a fathering group and that they want to talk about what they are learning in the group. Such suggestions do not respond to the idiosyncratic problems the fathers raise in the group but provide a global intervention about how to frame their situations, that one can experience loss and still be engaged.

Children Do Not Know Why Their Father Is in Prison or for How Long

A common concern for fathers, especially with younger children, is what to tell them about why they are in prison and what the length of their incarceration will be if convicted. Some fathers have not told their children that they are in prison and have said they are in school or away on business. The older the children, the more likely it is the father has told them about their situation because it is difficult to conceal this information from children with access to a computer who can google their father's name or who have the wherewithal to figure out what is going on. Fathers have stated that it is better to be honest with children and deal with it because they will find out eventually, either from the Internet or from other family members. Furthermore, if fathers get out in front of the information, they can shape the narrative and establish more open lines of communication.

The question is often raised about the proper age to tell a child about the father's incarceration. Is it good parenting to tell a child his father sold drugs in a gang and, if so, at what age should the child be told? There may be consensus that a 3-year-old does not need to hear where his father is and what he has done but what about a 5-year-old?

Interventions

The leaders are clear to not take a position about when and how this issue should be addressed because fathers' situations vary greatly. Rather, the message is given that this is something that all fathers should be considering. The discussion can be broadened to one concerning secrecy. For example, even the group leaders have done things they would not want shared with their children. When is it appropriate for a father to tell a child he has acted in a way he might be ashamed of, even if he was never caught doing it or it was not illegal? Although this does not tell the father what to do, it helps build group cohesion and reframe secrecy.

Fathers Do Not Know How to Respond to Teenage Daughters

A number of fathers have a difficult time interacting with teenage daughters when the girls are emotionally expressive. This may come from a lack of developmental knowledge about young females or a general feeling of discomfort with the expression of emotions. It might also be that the father has been socialized to believe sons are his responsibility and daughters are the mothers' responsibility, so he is not willing to engage with his daughter. Complicating the father's interactions with his daughter may be the fact that the daughter is consciously or unconsciously colluding with the mother and expressing what the mother is unable to express to the father herself. If the father and mother have a strained relationship, the daughter becomes the stand-in for the mother and the father interacts with his daughter as if he were interacting with her mother.

Interventions

If fathers feel their value to their daughters is minimal, they may not want to deal with issues their daughters raise. The goal here is to help fathers recognize their value to their daughters. The fathers are asked to consider that they are a model for what their daughters should look for in other men. Fathers are encouraged to reach out to daughters when they are emotionally expressive, even though their first instinct is to withdraw. When talking with daughters, as well as sons, they are coached that they do not need to respond perfectly to everything that is said. They are encouraged to listen actively and seek out the expression of feelings, rather than try to shut them off. Fathers are also coached to anticipate some of their daughters' feelings so they can have a nondefensive response ready.

Fathers Are Upset About Being Unable to Attend Specific Events

When fathers miss significant events in their children's lives (e.g., birthdays, graduations, sporting events), it can be highly upsetting and add to their sense of being disconnected from their family. One father in his 40s told the group he had been at his son's high school graduation but was unable to attend his daughter's because of his incarceration. He felt he was disappointing her and was, of course, also disappointing himself.

Interventions

Although the pain of incarceration and missing out on key events in children's lives is inevitable, other ways of participating may be possible. For example, members suggested to this father that he could write his daughter a letter and send a photograph of himself which she could carry in her pocket at graduation so he could be "present." If he had access to a telephone at the time of the ceremony, he could call in to a cell phone and hear her name being called. These suggestions provide a reframe for what presence and absence mean, a recurring theme for these fathers, as cited in previous examples. Although the father is physically absent, he can still be psychologically present.

Fathers' Value Is Only Financial

The fathers describe "doing stuff" (implying illegal activity) to get money to provide for their family. As mentioned earlier, the pressure to provide financially is related to the way that men are socialized. Many fathers lose this part of their identity when they are incarcerated and wonder what value they still have in the family or will have when they are released.

Interventions

Often group members will encourage fathers who raise this theme to think about their value as a father in a broader way. The conversation can then center on how children want attention from their father and time with them, not just money. This may require the fathers to think about what they wanted from their own father when they were growing up as well as what they would like from their father in adulthood. This has heightened relevance after fathers talk about their early upbringing and what they learned from their families, the topic of the second session. With the genogram, fathers are asked to consider how their upbringing affects how they are raising their children. When they reflect on the attention and love, not just the money, they sought from their father, it helps them understand that their own role may extend beyond that of financial provider.

Fathers Worry Their Children Will Turn Out Like Them

A concern of some fathers is that their children, especially their sons, will follow their footsteps into crime. Many, when giving their personal history in the second session, report they began criminal activities when they were in their early teens. Some also see their children struggling in school, which brings up their own academic struggles. As their children reach the age at which the father had problems, the fathers' concerns increase. Fathers sometimes become hypervigilant about their child's behaviors and may overreact in an attempt to protect him or her.

Interventions

All parents wonder to what extent they should intervene in a child's life. Knowing how much concern to hold about a child is a difficult balance to strike because overreaction by a parent can backfire, but some dangers are inherent in many of their child's living situations. With incarcerated fathers, their role is weakened because of their absence and they are often unsure what to do. One strategy is to encourage the father to be open about his concerns with his children. He can also be encouraged to reinforce good behavior in the child as a way of shaping the positives and downplaying the negatives.

Interacting With the Mother

A number of subthemes emerge in relation to the relationships the fathers have with the mother(s) of their children. Fathers who had a rocky or inconsistent relationship with the mother, but felt they were on equal footing with her before detention, now find themselves relying heavily on her for access to the children. She can facilitate phone calls and visitation with the father in prison or block those activities. The power differential often shifts.

Fathers are keenly aware of the precarious position they are in if they have a tenuous relationship with the mother. When interacting with her either by telephone or during visitation, they may hide any negative feelings they have toward her in order to have an anchor to their children and the outside world. They may subjugate their own wishes for the purpose of pleasing her and keeping the lines of communication open. A few fathers fear they will lose all contact with their children and that the mother will make no attempt to help with the father–child relationship.

Some fathers are also dealing with multiple mothers who may not get along with each other. This requires additional balancing of relationships. In some cases, particularly for the younger fathers in the group, their own mother may be serving as an intermediary and may bring the children for visitation or have holiday events at her house and invite the father's children.

Interventions

When fathers hear from other group members about their struggles with the mother(s) of their children, it helps to significantly reduce the feeling that they are the only one in this situation. Their frustrations and fears about being cut out of their children's lives get normalized.

Fathers will often coach each other to accept what can and cannot be changed about their situation and that "being a man" may mean acting in ways that do not feel comfortable if they want to see their children. The leaders might suggest that it is impossible to raise children by different mothers the same way—that some perceptions of favoritism of one over the other are inevitable. If difficulties arise with the mother, fathers are coached to guide the conversation away from past conflicts in the relationships and focus on the present rather than replaying old scripts. Complimenting the mother for her caregiving is also encouraged. The goal is to get the fathers to recognize when dysfunctional cycles of conversation are emerging and to try to divert them to a more productive form of communication.

Linked to this, some fathers believe their children are being actively turned against them when mothers refuse to bring them for visits or do not compel them to speak on the telephone. Fathers sometimes learn from their children that negative things are said about them when the children are with other family members. Given the criminal history of the fathers, critical remarks about a father and or a mother's curtailing his involvement are not always unreasonable measures to take.

The leaders are aware that some fathers may be a negative influence on their children and should have little if any contact with them despite the fathers' wishes. In these cases, discussion in the group may center on parents taking a longer view of childrearing and the father positioning himself for a future relationship when a child is older and may be more capable of a more multidimensional view of the father and his behavior. With time, the father may be able to prove to others that he has changed. In the interim, if he is being blocked from contact, he can communicate through letters that he could mail or hold on to if he thinks they will not be read. If they are written and not sent, this would leave a record of positive thoughts about his child that he could share in the future.

Fathers Feel Support From the Mother and Children

Some themes that emerge in the group are positive ones, of course. Fathers describe wonderful relationships with their wife/girlfriend and their children. They are convinced that they will be waiting for them upon their release. The fathers get frequent communication from the mother and are consulted about the children's upbringing. When asked to talk about their situation and raise any problems they are experiencing, they reassure the group and the leaders that no issues exist. Grandmothers and other family members are often noted as playing important roles also.

Challenge to the Group Leaders' Competence

Occasionally, group members will wonder about the leaders' knowledge about the fathers' lifestyle. This is a direct challenge as to whether the group leaders (all of whom are male and are fathers) can be helpful to them. Group leaders may be asked if they have been in prison or have a relative in prison. Recently, as one father was talking about the number of women with whom he had fathered children, he looked at one of the leaders and said about him that he probably had married his high school sweetheart and had not been with a lot of women. This was interpreted by one leader as "You don't understand me." Another leader saw it as the father complimenting the leader's professional and personal success.

Depending upon the situation, the leaders may respond directly to the question and provide information relevant to their own experiences. But underlying the challenge, and also needing to be addressed, is the father's wondering whether the group leader will be able to help him. Why should a father invest in the group or listen to feedback from a leader if the father believes a leader will have nothing to offer? "I guess you are wondering if I will be able to help you, if I have any relevant knowledge," is one way to respond. The leader cannot guarantee that he can help, but he can promise to give feedback and try to build a group atmosphere where others can provide feedback to the member. In saying this, the leader is giving power to the group process through mutual aid.

EVALUATION

Attempts to evaluate the effectiveness of this 4-week fathering group need to be considered within the context of the setting. These are fathers *awaiting* trial. As they have not been tried yet, they may wish to present a highly positive face to the group, both in terms of their own parenting abilities and in terms of what they will report they learned in the group. Furthermore, their caseworker is a co-leader. He has the ability to advocate for them in terms of exceptions to the visitation policy and is the conduit to other services in the prison (yoga, GED classes, Narcotics Anonymous, etc.). Finally, the fathers receive a contact visit at the end of the group and a certificate of completion. They may believe if they give negative feedback to the group leaders, even if given anonymously, that their visitation and certificate will be jeopardized in some way.

With these caveats, the majority of the fathers report that by the end of the group they have a greater appreciation for their fathering role and that they will make greater attempts to stay in touch with their children if they are convicted. Specifically, some say they have changed their mind about telling their children where they are and are going to reveal that they are in prison. Others report that learning they are not the only one with parenting issues and that some level of disobedience in children is normal have helped them accept themselves and feel more confident as a parent. Some groups appear much more productive than others; groups with older men seem to engage in more meaningful conversation. A rough estimate would be that 20% of the fathers get a great deal from the group, 60% get something from the group, and 20% evince no immediate gain. It is impossible to gauge the long-term effect of the group experience.

CONCLUSION

As the country that has the highest incarceration rate in the developed world (Freudenberg, Daniels, Crum, Perkins, & Richie, 2008), the United States clearly needs fathering programs (Modecki & Wilson, 2009). The task that leaders face is to make such groups meaningful to the fathers. It is hoped that by understanding the themes that may emerge in these groups, this will help prepare them to accomplish that task. Allowing guided discussion, rather than instituting a manualized approach, gives the fathers a voice and a place to explore issues that are relevant to them. Talking to each other about parenting insures that the fathers have the chance to help each other, one of the benefits of a positive group experience.

The group provides a setting where fathers' feelings can be explored and hope given to combat the losses that are often associated with incarceration. Many fathers gauge their self-worth based on feedback from their children. Building or rebuilding a connection with a child has the potential for buoying the father's mood and offering a sense of purpose while in prison. Ultimately, and hopefully, this may make him a better parent.

RESOURCES

InsideOut is one program promoted by the Fatherhood Initiative that has a manualized, Christian-based approach for incarcerated fathers. See:
FatherSOURCE™ Resource Center
c/o National Fatherhood Initiative
20410 Observation Dr., Suite 107
Germantown, MD 20876

Phone: 240-912-1263
Fax: 301-948-6776
E-mail: fathersource@fatherhood.org

Various states offer Fatherhood Initiatives. See, for example, Alabama's:
Alabama Department of Child Abuse & Neglect Prevention
Fatherhood Initiatives
Children's Trust Fund
100 North Union Street
Montgomery, AL 36104
Phone: 334-242-5710
Fax: 334-242-5711

Also, for other examples of fathering programs from the Health and Human Service Web site, aspe.hhs.gov/hsp/08/mfs-ip/Innovative/rb.shtml, see the following:

Centerforce, California	Curriculum: Back to the Family (offered in fathers-only and joint formats)	• Relationship education • Family case management • Family skills mentoring/coaching
Child and Family Services of New Hampshire	Curricula: Fathers Connecting with Children, Long Distance Dads (offered to fathers only)	• Relationship education • Family reentry planning • Video visiting
Indiana Department of Correction	Curriculum: 24/7 Dad (offered to fathers only)	• Relationship education
Lutheran Social Services of South Dakota	Curriculum: Long Distance Dads (offered to fathers only)	• Relationship education • Family case management • Domestic violence education • Video diaries
Maryland Department of Human Resources	Curriculum: InsideOut Dad (offered to fathers only)	• Relationship education • Domestic violence education • Support groups • Case management • Employment assistance

REFERENCES

Black, M. M., Dubowitz, H., & Starr, R. H. (1999). African American fathers in low income, urban families: Development, behavior, and home environment of their 3-year-old children. *Child Development, 70*, 967–978.

Boss, P. (2006). *Loss, trauma, and resilience: Therapeutic work with ambiguous loss.* New York, NY: Norton.

Boss, P. (2010). The trauma and complicated grief of ambiguous loss. *Pastoral Psychology, 59*, 137–145.

Craig, S. (2009). A historical review of mother and child programs for incarcerated women. *Prison Journal, 89*, 35S–53S.

Freudenberg, N., Daniels, J., Crum, M., Perkins, T., & Richie, B. E. (2008). Coming home from jail: The social and health consequences of community reentry for women, male adolescents, and their families and communities. *American Journal of Public Health, 98*, 191–202.

Geller, A. (2013). Paternal incarceration and father-child contact in fragile families. *Journal of Marriage and Family, 75*, 1288–1303.

Geller, A., & Franklin, A. W. (2014). Parental incarceration and the housing security of urban mothers. *Journal of Marriage and Family, 76*, 411–427.

Glaze, L. E., & Maruschak, L M. (2010). *Parents in prison and their minor children* (NCJ 222984). Washington, DC: US Department of Justice. Retrieved from http://bjs.ojp.usdoj.gov/index.cfm?ty=pbdetail&iid=823

Greif, G. L. (2013). Fathers in a pretrial detention facility—lessons learned. *Corrections Today, 75*, 60–63, 67.

Greif, G. L. (2014). The voices of fathers in prison: Implications for family practice. *Journal of Family Social Work, 17*, 68–80

Harmon, D. K., & Perry, A. R. (2011). Fathers' unaccounted contributions: Paternal involvement and maternal stress. *Families in Society, 47*, 176–182.

Harrison, K. (1997) Parental training for incarcerated fathers: Effects on attitudes, self-esteem, and children's self-perception. *Journal of Social Psychology, 137*, 588–593.

Johnson, E. L., & Easterling, B. (2012). Understanding unique effects of paternal incarceration on children: Challenges, progress, and recommendations. *Journal of Marriage and Family, 74*, 342–356.

Kelly-Trombley, H. M., Bartels, D., & Wieling, E. (2014). "She's my baby": How recently incarcerated fathers experience their relationship with their daughters. *Fathering, 12*, 94–114.

Loper, A. B., & Tuerk, E. H. (2006). Parenting programs for incarcerated parents: Current research and future directions. *Criminal Justice Policy Review, 17*, 407–427.

Loper, A. B., & Tuerk, E. H. (2011). Improving the emotional adjustment and communication patterns of incarcerated mothers: Effectiveness of a prison parenting intervention. *Journal of Child and Family Studies, 20*, 89–101.

McCrudden, E., Braiden, H. J., Sloan, D., McCormack, P., & Treacy, A. (2014). Stealing the smile from my child's face: A preliminary evaluation of the "Being a dad" programme in a Northern Ireland prison. *Child Care in Practice, 20*, 301–312.

Mendez, G. A. (2000). Incarcerated African American men and their children: A case study. *Annals of the American Academy of Political and Social Science, 569,* 86–101.

Modecki, K. L., & Wilson, M. N. (2009). Associations between individual and family level characteristics and parenting practices in incarcerated African American fathers. *Journal of Child and Family Studies, 18,* 530–540.

Mustaine, E. E., & Tewksbury, R. (2015). Fathers' methods of child discipline: Does incarceration lead to harsh and physical punishment? A research note. *American Journal of Criminal Justice, 40,* 89–99.

Muth, W., & Walker, G. (2013). Looking up: Temporal horizons of a father in prison. *Fathering, 11,* 292–305.

Nichols, M. P. (2014). *The essentials of family therapy,* 6th ed. Boston, MA: Allyn & Bacon.

Office of the Deputy Attorney General. (2013). *Giving a boost to kids of incarcerated parents.*Washington, DC: US Department of Justice. Retrieved from http://www.justice.gov/opa/blog/giving-boost-kids-incarcerated-parents

Shulman, L. (2012). *The skills of helping individuals, families, groups, and communities,* 7th ed. Belmont, CA: Brooks/Cole.

Swanson, C., Lee, C-B., Sansone, F., & Tatum, K. (2013). Incarcerated fathers and their children: Perceptions of barriers to their relationships. *Prison Journal, 93,* 453–474.

Wildeman, C. (2010). Paternal incarceration and children's physically aggressive behaviors: Evidence from the Fragile Families and Child Wellbeing Study. *Social Forces, 89,* 295–310.

Chapter Twenty-Four

Group Work With Homeless Parents

Carolyn Knight

The fastest growing population of homeless individuals is parents, typically single mothers, and children (Dotson, 2011). The "feminization of homelessness" (Richards, Garland, Bumphus, & Thompson, 2010) is a significant and continuously evolving social problem. The theoretical and empirical literature is just now beginning to catch up to this changing face of homelessness (Zlotnick, Tam, & Bradley, 2010). Research into the causes of homelessness and prevention and intervention strategies have, until relatively recently, focused on single men (Arangua, Andersen, & Gelberg, 2005).

Shelters, day programs, and transitional housing services have historically catered to the needs of homeless men, providing such services as GED programs, substance abuse and mental health treatment, and job search assistance. Homeless parents and their children often require a different array of services, owing to the different factors that contribute to their homeless status (Wilson, 2005). While scant, there is evidence that group participation, in which members have a chance to address their current situation, as well as the underlying challenges they face, not only provides parents with much-needed support and validation but also empowers and promotes independence, resilience, and self-sufficiency (Berzoff, 2013; Speirs, Johnson, & Jirojwong, 2013).

REVIEW OF THE LITERATURE

Scope of the Problem

Definitions of homelessness vary widely. One of the most widely disseminated definitions, and the one that will be used in this chapter, is as follows: "not having customary and regular access to a conventional housing" (Rossi, 1989, p. 24). Implicit in Rossi's definition is the critical role that economics plays in explaining why individuals become homeless. Lack of income is an especially significant determinant of homelessness among parents with children.

Thirty years ago, women accounted for less than 3% of homeless individuals. By 2003, this proportion had climbed to almost one third, and more recent research suggests this number is continuing to rise, even as the overall rate of homelessness among the general population has decreased (Richards, Garland, Bumphus, & Thompson, 2010). Coincidental to the increase in the number of homeless women is the significant upsurge in the number of homeless children (Lee, Tyler, & Wright, 2010). Recent estimates suggest that of the approximately 3.5 million individuals who are homeless at any one time, 39% are children (National Association to End Homelessness, 2014; National Coalition for the Homeless, 2014). Furthermore, the size of homeless families grew from an average of 3.05 to 3.10 over the last 3 years. The racial makeup of homeless families has remained relatively steady over time with a disproportionate number of these individuals self-identifying as Black, African American, Afro-Caribbean, or Latina (Lee, Tyler, & Wright, 2010; National Coalition for the Homeless, 2014).

In the vast majority of cases, homeless families are headed by a single parent, typically a mother. But a significant proportion is headed by a single man or even two parents. The circumstances that contribute to families' homeless status differ in significant ways from those of single homeless men (Caton et. al., 2005).

According to studies done in 2012, the last year for which such data were available, the majority of homeless individuals, regardless of status, resided in emergency shelters or transitional housing; yet almost 40% resided in cars, abandoned buildings, on the streets, or other places not fit for human habitation (National Association to End Homelessness, 2014; National Coalition for the Homeless, 2014). Research suggests that homeless families stay in shelters for brief periods of time, relative to other groups of homeless individuals, and tend not to return (Culhane, Metraux, Park, Schretzman, & Valente, 2007). Additional research suggests that a smaller subpopulation of homeless families experience more extended periods of homelessness and have high rates of recidivism. In these instances, adult members tend to have significant preexisting and coexisting challenges, including mental illness, substance abuse, medical problems, past and present trauma, criminal backgrounds, and developmental disabilities (Jahiel & Babor, 2005).

In January 2012, the last year for which statistics are available, states reported an inventory of over 700,000 beds available for homeless individuals and families, with one half designated for individuals and the remaining one half available to families (National Association to End Homelessness, 2014). This finding is at odds with the increased number of families experiencing homelessness and the decrease in the number of individuals facing this challenge, as noted (Speirs et al., 2013).

Characteristics of Homeless Parents and Children

A limitation of most of the research on homeless families is its focus on mothers and children, rather than two-parent or father-headed households (Dykeman,

2011). It does appear that the primary factor that contributes to homelessness among families is economic. This is a multidimensional variable consisting of lack of affordable housing; insufficient, no, or loss of income; unexpected financial misfortune; mismanagement of finances; and in the case of women, particularly, insufficient or nonexistent child support (Arangua et. al., 2006; Hertlein & Killmer, 2004). Homeless families, like their individual counterparts, almost always come from impoverished circumstances (Jahiel & Babor, 2005; Lee, Tyler, & Wright, 2010).

When compared to homeless individuals, parents with children have lower rates of substance abuse and mental illness. Both groups, particularly women, report high rates of intimate partner violence and trauma in childhood, such as sexual and physical abuse (Lewinson, Thomas, & White, 2014). Both groups report high rates of placement in out-of-home care as children (Zlotnick et. al., 2010). This last finding is related to another factor that contributes to homelessness among families and that is the lack of viable support systems. Homeless parents and children are likely to stay in multiple locations and either leave voluntarily because of unsafe, dangerous conditions, or are asked to leave due to overcrowding or "wearing out their welcome" (Zlotnik et. al., 2010).

Homeless parents with children report high levels of depression, anxiety, and diminished feelings of self-efficacy and positive esteem (DeForge, Belcher, O'Rourke, & Lindsey, 2008). Unlike their single, childless counterparts, whose affective reactions tend to be chronic and predate their homeless status, homeless parents' affective responses seem to be more the *result* of their situation or are greatly exacerbated by it (Dykeman, 2011). Homeless parents who have custody of their children are less likely to experience co-occurring problems with mental illness and substance abuse than parents who have lost custody of their children, though both groups typically have experienced past trauma, as noted (Teruya et al., 2010; Zlotnick, Tam, & Bradley, 2007). A characteristic that appears to pervade all categories of homeless individuals and families is stigmatization, and this may be particularly true of parents, who struggle with feelings of guilt and failure associated with being unable to provide adequately for their children (Cosgrove & Flynn, 2005; Lee, Tyler, & Wright, 2010).

Resiliency and Homeless Families

Increasing attention is being focused on homeless individuals' strengths. This is in keeping with resilience theory, which has a solid theoretical and empirical foundation and has been applied to a wide range of individuals and adverse situations (Greene, Galambos, & Lee, 2003). Investigators have examined the ways in which homeless parents with children successfully cope with this stressor (Haber & Toro, 2004; Lee, Tyler, & Wright, 2010). A particularly useful way of looking at the adaptive capacities of homeless families is through the lens of "overcoming," which is comprised of three aspects: recognizing that a situation, event, or problem exists and is undesirable; demonstrating a readiness to confront, change, and surmount the situation, event, or problem; and believing that changing the adverse event, situation, or problem will improve one's future existence (Brush, Kirk, Gultekin, & Baiardi, 2011).

Researchers have identified three coping mechanisms that help homeless individuals and families overcome their situation (Lee, Tyler, & Wright, 2010). The first is the ability to aggressively and persistently seek out and access whatever resources may be available such as soup kitchens, free medical care, clothing and food banks, job training, and housing assistance. Second, homeless individuals look for ways to earn money, often in an underground economy of jobs that pay cash, until more stable employment becomes available. Finally, establishing connections with other homeless individuals not only has the advantage of providing much-needed support and understanding; it also provides a network through which individuals can identify and access resources.

In the case of homeless parents with children, yet another potent adaptive capacity is the desire to protect children and the accompanying sense of urgency that motivates them to eliminate their homeless status as quickly as possible (Brush, Kirk, Gultekin, & Baiardi, 2011). This last point is consistent with the concept of overcoming since it suggests that homeless parents can view their status not simply as a traumatic event of which they are victims but also as an opportunity to make things better for themselves and their children (Huey, Fthenos, & Hryniewicz, 2013; Tischler, Edwards, & Vostanis, 2009).

Group Work With Homeless Parents

Group work is a modality that lends itself especially well to working with homeless parents (Plasse, 2001; Speirs et al., 2013). Group work is a natural vehicle through which resilience and overcoming can be enhanced (Coker, Meyer, Smith, & Price, 2010; Gitterman & Knight, 2015). Members' shared experiences provide validation and lessen feelings of isolation (Fraenkel, Hameline, & Shannon, 2009). Feelings of mastery and self-efficacy are enhanced as members learn and grow from one another's experiences and insights (Berzoff, 2013; Washington, Moxley, & Garriott, 2009). When homeless parents work in partnership with shelter providers and others to develop groups that are responsive to their unique needs, this further enhances feelings of mastery and empowerment and reduces stigma because parents are treated as "experts in their own lives" (Cosgrove & Flynn, 2005; Fraenkel et al., 2009).

Groups for homeless parents can take on an advocacy and social justice component, and this further enhances feelings of esteem (Berzoff, 2013; Coker et. al., 2010; Speirs et. al., 2013). In fact, groups for homeless parents appear to be most helpful when they address both the personal/background issues that contribute to their current status *and* assist members in finding their own voice and cultivate their adaptive capacities. Members are helped to see that their current situation is a *state* not a *trait*. Fraenkel and his colleagues call this externalization—distinguishing the problem from the person—and label the process as "putting homelessness in its place" (2009, p. 332).

PRACTICE PRINCIPLES

Working with homeless parents can be especially challenging, given the complex nature of their problems and the paucity of resources available to them. The practice principles identified next reflect these challenges as well as underscore the need for the group worker to maintain a focus on empowerment.

The first principle, remaining flexible, is necessitated by the nature of services available to homeless parents as well as the crisis-oriented nature of their lives. In both residential and day programs, clients cycle in and out. Residential shelters typically have time limits on clients' stays; in both practice contexts, homeless parents' circumstances often change quickly. Thus, the group worker must anticipate that members attending one week may be gone the next. Each session may be a first session for some, if not all, members. The first session also may be the only session for some members. Issues discussed one week may not emerge in the next, owing to the different needs of members in attendance and a changing sense of urgency. There are certain themes that regularly surface (discussed later). But it is critical that the worker be responsive to the concerns that are raised by members in each session. Although the group leader may wish to initiate the group session with some idea of where he or she would like to go in the session, this must be balanced against a basic precept of clinical practice, which is to "start where the client—in this case the group—is."

A related principle, and one that also is basic to clinical work, is the need to remain nonjudgmental. This would seem to be self-evident, but the actions and decisions of homeless parents can be frustrating to the practitioner, whose life and choices are likely to be very different. A complex array of factors contributes to parents' homeless status. But one cannot ignore the possibility that parents themselves bear at least some responsibility for their status. If the group worker is going to approach the group from an empowerment perspective, she or he must be able to help members learn from their mistakes in a way that isn't accusatory or that reflects a blaming-the-victim mentality. This requires that the group worker be acutely aware of personal biases and values so that these do not get in the way of how she or he works within the group (Fraenkel et al., 2009).

The following example illustrates the importance of maintaining a neutral stance and the corresponding need for the group worker to be self-aware.[1] Members in this session were mostly new to the shelter, so a good bit of time was spent sharing their stories and experiences, particularly those related to how they ended up homeless. A common lament among the members—all women—was the lack of support, financial and otherwise, from their babies' fathers. Monique, 25 years old, echoed members' anger and then eagerly disclosed that she was pregnant with her fourth child. None of the fathers of her other three children were in her life, owing to incarceration and/or drug addiction. The father of her unborn child was a drug dealer awaiting trial on charges of distributing heroin.

Although members provided Monique with support and understanding, the author found herself feeling frustrated at Monica's naïveté and wondering how she could be so happy with the prospect of having yet another child. The author also found herself being puzzled by the other members' support of and happiness for Monique. The author was immediately aware of her reactions, and even as she writes this here, is embarrassed by them. *However*, she is human, as is every other group leader. Although we may understand how homeless parents got into their situation, we also may question their choices and decisions, based upon our—rather than their—frame of reference.

The challenge is to be in the world of "is" (our clients' world) not in the world of "should" (the world as we think it should be for them). This is often a difficult balance to maintain. If homeless parents are to overcome their situation, they must be able to see the role they played in their current status, learning what not to do in the future. If this learning is accompanied by blame and accusation, this undermines self-efficacy and empowerment (Cosgrove & Flynn, 2005).

Another principle is the need to attend to manifestations of transference. These may play out in a variety of ways. Many homeless parents have had numerous experiences with "helpers" who were perceived as not helpful. Members of the author's group often talk about "getting the run around" from agency staff, being treated with disrespect and disregard, and being given incorrect and inaccurate information. Furthermore, as is true in the author's case, the group leader may differ in significant ways (for example, race, class, and age) from the members, leading to questions about the leader's ability to understand and be helpful. Most obviously, it is unlikely that the professional will have experienced homelessness or the poverty and disadvantaged conditions that often accompany this. Finally, group members may have experienced exploitation, abuse, and neglect at the hands of those who should have protected and nurtured them as children.

Each of these differences can lead the members to approach the group worker with a mixture of mistrust, resentment, and bitterness. The leader may represent to members those who have hurt, ignored, and disappointed them. Thus, group workers must expect that they will need to directly address members' concerns about them, helping them see the connection between their reactions and their past experiences. To accomplish this, leaders must remain self-aware and understand that members' reactions are not about them, even as they are directed at them.

Transference also may be manifested in members' relationships with one another. For example, Jerry had been living at the shelter for several weeks with his two daughters. He was reluctant to share too much about his past and how he ended up in the shelter, but he did reveal that his wife had passed away from cancer several months ago, and he had then lost his job and home, and had no relatives to whom he could turn. He was the only father living at the shelter; thus, he was the only man in the group. In one particular session, the female members were talking about having been abused by their boyfriends, expressing both anger and pain. This led to disclosures of childhood sexual abuse. Jerry remained silent throughout this discussion and appeared uncomfortable. When he attempted to join the discussion, the female members ignored him or expressed the belief that he couldn't understand because "he was one of them." The author intervened at this point, observing that the women in the group appeared angry at Jerry, and that he seemed to represent to them all the men who had hurt, exploited, and disappointed them. Members were able to see this and proceeded to ask Jerry what it was he wanted to share. Ironically, Jerry revealed his own sexual abuse as a child at the hands of several of his mother's boyfriends.

A final principle is to identify and build upon members' strengths. This sounds straightforward, but as Fraenkel and his colleagues note, "[p]roblems have a way of 'flooding the field' of experience, dominating persons' attention and identity" (2009, p. 332). Group members *and* leaders are likely to devote their attention to dysfunction and pathology, rather than to strengths, resilience, and overcoming. Techniques borrowed from solution-focused and narrative perspectives can be especially useful in focusing attention on positive ways that members have coped in the past and the present (deShazer, 1991; Fraenkel, 2006; Knight, 2006; Styron, Janoff-Bulman, & Davidson, 2000). Skills include treating homeless parents as experts in their own lives, inquiring about exceptions—that is, about times when things were going better for group members—and asking how members are coping, given the stress they are under. The members' current situation is framed as a transient state that provides them with the opportunity to start over, learn from their mistakes, and move on. One noteworthy point is that when the group leader adopts this strengths-oriented perspective, she or he also will have an easier time being in the world of "is." In a previous example, the author acknowledged the judgmentalism she experienced as she listened to Monique talk about her unborn baby. When she treated Monica as the expert in her life, it became easier to understand her happiness: her baby represented hope for the future and gave Monique's life meaning and purpose.

The following exchange demonstrates how members' can turn their attention to their strengths, even as they struggle with their current challenges. This session consisted of seven members, a married couple, Janae and Samuel, and five single mothers, Sheila, Teresa, Loretta, Beverly, and Towanda. Much of the session was influenced by Samuel's anger and bitterness at his circumstances and his guilt for not being able to provide for his family.

> *Samuel:* A man is supposed to take care of hisself and his wife and children. I can't hardly look my boy in the eye because I ain't doing what a man is supposed to do.
>
> *Janae:* (*crying*)
>
> *Samuel:* See—I can't even take care of my wife. She got mental problems, and she be all stressed out about me not working and us being on the street.
>
> *Sheila:* Samuel, I wish I had a man like you in my life. I don't have nobody; my babies' daddies ain't around; one of them won't even claim him as his own. You be a good man, Samuel, and things will turn around for you.
>
> *Beverly:* You so right, Sheila. Janae be a lucky woman. You know, I try not to think about how bad things are. I thank God that I am here in the shelter. I think it is a blessing, and I am looking at it as a time for me to get my shit together, to put the past behind me and look forward.
>
> *Author:* So, Beverly is suggesting that this can be a time for you all to make positive changes in your lives, changes that keep you from being in this situation again.*All members nod their heads.*
>
> *Samuel:* It's hard to think this way. It just feels so f—ing bad, you know? But I guess I should be glad we have a roof over our heads, to have time to figure out what we going to do next.
>
> *Author:* Right . . . you can think about how you've dealt with tough times in the past, and put those things to use now.

This example typifies what the author has encountered: There is usually at least one member, often several, who are able to identify and express the resilience that all members possess. This is the essence of mutual aid—members pointing out and affirming each other's strengths.

COMMON THEMES

Anger emerges as a recurring dynamic in groups for homeless parents and has several sources and targets. Members may express anger at the shelter or day program, citing all the rules and regulations, claiming that they are being "treated like children." Members in the authors' groups often refer to their experience as being in a sort of "jail," with curfews, set times for dinner, prohibitions on what they can do, say, and wear. Parents feel undermined in their ability to parent as they see fit, since they see themselves as being "parented" by the agency (Hertlein & Killmer, 2004).

In many instances, the agency setting is an easy target. Shelters and day programs *do* have restrictions, and they *do* diminish members' feelings of self-efficacy; yet these are necessary for the smooth operation of the facility. Underlying this anger, however, is an array of other issues. These include members' disappointment in those they thought they could trust but who ultimately didn't help in their time of need and/or exploited them financially, emotionally, and physically, thus contributing to their homeless status. Anger at "the system" and the lack of resources and the difficulties associated with obtaining them is another source of anger.

Most noteworthy is the anger that members feel toward themselves for their homeless status and for what they see as "letting their children down." In many situations such anger may be understandable, as in the case of Tijuana and James. They were renting a townhome in a nice neighborhood, and James was working full-time for a construction company. When the work slowed, James was let go and had been unable to find work. During and even after his employment ended, both Tijuana and James spent carelessly on, as they put it, "stuff we didn't need but that made us feel good." They acknowledged that buying things they couldn't afford allowed them to avoid the realities associated with James's unemployment. Ultimately, they lost their home because they couldn't pay their rent or utilities, and they had run up almost $10,000 in credit card debt.

If Tijuana and James were to get back on their feet again and achieve stability, they had to accept responsibility for their actions. This, however, is different from being angry at oneself. In a situation such as this, the worker can help members see how they contributed to their current homeless status but take the position of "what can be learned from this, so that you don't make the same mistake again." Anger at oneself is counterproductive; taking responsibility for one's mistakes, on the other hand, promotes adopting new ways of acting.

There may be other instances when members' anger at themselves is unwarranted and reflects a chronic pattern of self-defeating and negative thinking. Shakira disclosed to members that her husband was a "changed man" upon his release from prison. Where he had once been loving and supportive and steadily employed, he became withdrawn, unemployed and unwilling to seek employment, and increasingly abusive toward her, both verbally and physically. She ended up in the shelter when he left her with her three children, taking what little money they had with him. She had nowhere to go, as she had grown up in a series of foster homes, none of which provided a lasting bond or connection. In group, Shakira claimed that her husband wanted her to have more children, but on the advice of her doctor, she had her tubes tied, since a future pregnancy could be life-threatening for her. Crying, she said, "If only I had done what my husband wanted and respected him, I wouldn't be in the shelter and he wouldn't have left me." Shakira also reported being a survivor of significant physical and sexual abuse at the hands of her biological and foster parents. Thus, her feelings of guilt and responsibility were chronic and deeply held. Members challenged her, telling her that she wasn't responsible for her husband's leaving and questioned why she would want to be with a man who hurt and exploited her. Her response was telling: "I love him. He's all I have. It's all I know."

Shakira's comment leads to a second theme, which is members' disclosures of a traumatic past and the pain, hurt, and humiliation that accompany this. Like Shakira, homeless parents with histories of past trauma typically hold themselves responsible for this, believing themselves to be "bad," "unlovable," and unworthy. These core beliefs become more or less ingrained and define how the individual views self and others and create a self-defeating and self-reinforcing cycle (Jenkins, Meyer, & Blissett, 2013; Knight, 2009). Members assume they aren't worth anything; therefore, they don't expect anything for themselves and then receive precisely what they expect: nothing. In the case of homeless parents, such negative belief systems have profound consequences. Most notably, they have difficulty advocating for themselves, making it hard for them to successfully navigate the network of resources that they must utilize. They also are likely to approach their current situation from a defeatist perspective, adopting the attitude of "Why should I bother? I know I'll fail."

Childhood trauma leaves homeless parents with a host of problems, including depression, low self-esteem, and addiction (for a more detailed discussion, see Chapter 15, in this volume). Many homeless parents also struggle with more current challenges that may directly or indirectly contribute to their homelessness such as intimate partner violence, incarceration, and drug abuse. Thus, as they are attempting to address their current homeless situation, they also are plagued by past and present challenges. Understandably, then, members may present themselves as overwhelmed and unable to address their current homeless situation constructively. This underscores how important it is to operate from a strengths perspective but also explains how challenging this can be.

Yet another theme that surfaces is the stigma associated with being homeless. To some extent, this may reflect the internalized core beliefs discussed previously. Yet popular stereotypes associated with homelessness, and cultural and racial biases serve to reinforce homeless parents' already negative self-definitions (Bullock & Lott, 2001; Cosgrove & Flynn, 2005). Members are likely to report numerous experiences with both laypersons and professionals in which they have been degraded, humiliated, and embarrassed. Unfortunately, shelter and day program personnel are not immune from engaging in this behavior and reinforcing negative stereotypes (Coker et al., 2010; Cormack, 2009).

Marietta's experiences are typical. She and her three young children arrived at the shelter after having been evicted from their apartment for nonpayment of rent. The authorities literally threw her belongings on the street; Marietta pleaded with them to give her time to obtain assistance in moving and storing these items, but she was told, "This is what happens to deadbeat mothers with too many children." Neighbors stole everything of value, while she stood by and cried. Marietta and her children spent the first couple of nights in her car; twice she was told to move by the police, who said her car was in a no-parking zone. In neither instance did law enforcement personnel inquire about the children in the car or the family's status or well-being. Finally, Marietta went to a shelter in the city that served women and children. Exhausted, hungry, and with just the clothing on their backs, the family requested help from an intake counselor. According to Marietta, the counselor gave her a look of disgust, stating, "We don't want no smelly people in here. When are you people going to take better care of yourselves and your children?"

As Marietta disclosed this to the group, other members began to share their own experiences with being treated, as one member said, as "nobodies, nothings." A fellow member astutely observed, "They [nonhomeless individuals] don't want to think they could be us. They like to pretend that we don't exist because then they don't have to do nothing to help." The benefit of group participation is that members help one another resist identifying with the stereotypes that surround their status as homeless persons.

RECOMMENDED WAYS OF WORKING

Underlying all of the group workers' efforts should be a focus on empowerment and self-advocacy. Given the negative thinking and the economic and social barriers that homeless parents encounter, the group should become a place where their strength and resilience are both recognized and nurtured. The mutual aid that defines group work practice with any client population is the critical first step toward empowering members (Gitterman & Knight, 2015). A first set of practice behaviors, then, involves fostering mutual aid. The worker assists members in talking and listening to one another, points out the underlying commonalities of experience that lessen isolation and provide validation, and encourages members to support one another.

This seems straightforward, but the group worker faces several challenges. First, one member's sense of urgency may be so great that the leader devotes all of her or his attention to that individual. Such actions are misguided, since they deny others the opportunity to provide insight, assistance, and support to the individual member. They also deny the individual the opportunity to experience acceptance from others in the same boat. These opportunities are the essence of mutual aid and empowerment.

Second, because membership can change from session to session, members may have a hard time seeing their commonalities and may be reluctant to disclose personal information with one another. In residential settings, members may know something about other residents, but typically this knowledge is superficial. In both nonresidential and residential settings, group members may worry about confidentiality. Yet, given their urgency to share their stories, they usually are willing to reveal personal information. They may need the assistance of the leader to help them risk opening up to one another. In the author's groups, the importance of confidentiality is emphasized in each session; this applies both to the members and her. As a result, the group has become facetiously known as the "Vegas" group—what happens in the group stays in the group.

Finally, members are likely to be overwhelmed, discouraged, and frightened by their situation. Therefore, their desire—and need—to talk about their difficulties and challenges may override their ability to recognize their strengths. The leader will need to balance encouraging members to support one another in their time of need—which is in and of itself empowering to all—and encouraging them to see their strengths and promote resilience. The following brief exchange reflects this balance. Six members were in attendance, two of whom were new to the shelter (Melba and Norma); the four other members had been in the shelter for 2 months and had been regular attendees (Juanita, Salome, Jeffery, and Lynn). Given the four members' familiarity, group discussion quickly focused on the chronic difficulties members faced and their fears about their ability to get themselves out of the current predicament.

> *Juanita:* There ain't nobody for me to turn to. NOBODY! I'm raising my two grandchildren because my daughter be a junkie and whore. And then I have my own three young children. Their daddies be no good sons-of-bitches. My father is in jail, my mother is a drunk. What am I going to do?!
> *Silence. Salome starts to cry.*
> *Author:* It seems like Juanita's comments have triggered something for Salome. They hit a little too close to home?
> *Salome:* It's so lonely. I'm so lonely. I've been on my own since I was 15, after my stepfather starting molesting me and my mom beat me for it. I don't have no one. It's just me and my babies.
> *Author:* And it seems so overwhelming to you (looking at Salome) and I suspect to others as well? Yet, you know what strikes me is that, even with all you have on your plates, you just keep pushing through. I know it's tough, but you haven't given up.
> *Jeffrey:* It's my kids. I gotta keep going for them.
> *Members nodded in agreement.*
> *Author:* So, let's take a minute and talk about how you keep going. What you're doing to get your lives back on track.

A spirited discussion then ensued in which all members participated. With assistance from the author and from each other, members were able to identify coping strategies they were using or could use, based upon suggestions they provided to one another.

Another significant strategy involves acknowledging the past and its effects in the present—particularly on members' ability to address their homelessness constructively —but maintaining a focus on getting back on their feet. Members' pasts may be filled with trauma, pain, and a host of disappointments and losses, as discussed. These experiences leave homeless parents with self-defeating core beliefs about themselves and others, as well as unresolved feelings and reactions. The issue is not whether members need a place to delve in depth into these issues—they do. The issue is whether the shelter or agency group is the place to do it—it isn't. Membership shifts frequently, which impedes the development of the intimacy necessary to disclose honestly and work though past and present trauma. Furthermore, the more members focus on the past, the less able they are to address their current homelessness and work proactively to correct this. The group leader can affirm members' pasts, using the commonality of experience to deepen members' connections, which provides validation and assurance. But she or he needs to do this in a way that assists members in understanding how the past may be getting in the way of their ability to manage their lives in the present.

In the following excerpt, the seven members in attendance had all been coming to the group for at least a month. Therefore, a level of intimacy had developed between them that allowed them to engage in more sensitive disclosures. In this particular session, four of the seven members disclosed histories of sexual abuse as children (Jeffrey, Salome, Miriam, and Mae). This experience and these members' resulting pain, loss, and anger dominated the discussion. The other three members (Paula, Walter, and Angela) were silent but attentive, offering their sympathy and support.

Miriam (crying): I have felt dirty and ashamed my whole life. When my brothers (the perpetrators) were messing with me, I just took it, and took the candy they gave me to keep me quiet. I didn't tell nobody. It was my fault.
Several members start crying.

Mae: I hear you, girl. Ain't right what these shits did to us. They make us feel like it be our fault.

Jeffrey: I always felt like I invited it. I gave off some vibes that I wanted it.

Author: What Mae, Miriam, and Jeffrey are talking about is so common when people are abused as children. They feel like it's *their* fault, not the fault of those who hurt them and didn't protect them. The other sad reality is that those feelings of guilt and shame follow you into adulthood, so that you have a hard time knowing how to make good choices.

> *Angela:* Thank God nobody touched me, but I have those feel-
> ings . . . being beaten up by the man who's supposed to
> love you makes you feel small and worthless.
>
> *Author:* Right, so whether it was something that happened in
> childhood, or something more recent, it's hard to deal
> with the homelessness when you got all this other stuff
> churning around inside.
>
> *Mae:* Ain't that the truth! It sure is nice to know that we ain't
> alone. It helps a lot. Makes it easier to do what needs to
> be done to get the hell out of this place.

It is clear that some members needed to talk about past trauma. Yet to focus
too much on the past not only can exclude others who don't have such a history, but it also undermines members' abilities to deal with the challenges in
the present.

Yet another intervention tool is to encourage members—individually and
collectively—to advocate for themselves. The most obvious and direct way to
empower members is to provide them with opportunities to become their own
advocates. Members can support one another in this regard, offering advice and
relevant information. The group worker also can provide information, including
how to go about being an effective advocate, as the following example illustrates.
The nine members of this group were relatively long-term residents of the shelter
and knew one another well. Most were regular members of the group. Members
were complaining about the shelter and its policies and regulations when the following exchange occurred.

> *Leanora:* We're like f—ing prisoners in here. They tell us when to eat,
> sleep, dress, clean. Might as well be in jail.
> *Members nodded their heads in agreement and expressed anger.*
>
> *Pamela:* My boy, he come home from school and be hungry, but they
> don't have nothing for him to eat that he like. They tell me I need
> to buy him some food, but I ain't got the money! If I had the
> money, we wouldn't be here!
>
> *Angela:* You be so right. My boy—he be 16 and he be hungry all the time!
> *Members laugh.*
>
> *Angela:* They don't have nothing he like. He ain't no 3-year-old, he be a
> growing boy.
>
> *Author:* So it sounds like a number of you would like to see different
> sorts of after-school snacks for the older children. I wonder, has
> anyone said anything to Ms.— (shelter manager).
> *Members shake their heads.*

Leanora: Aw, it won't make no difference. They don't give us the time of
day. Like I say, we be like prisoners.
Members voice their agreement.

Author: I understand you feel like you don't have a say in things, and for
some things, that's probably true, but maybe if you all said something about the need for different snacks, Ms.— would make a
change. It sure makes sense to me. It could be that the shelter
is more used to little kids, and so they haven't quite figured out
how to respond to the needs of the older kids.
Members were silent, looking to one another.

Author: I know it might seem like a long shot, but maybe it's worth a try.
How about if we talk about how you all could approach Ms.— in
a way that she can hear what you have to say?

Although members were initially reluctant to consider taking action, assuming they
wouldn't be heard, ultimately they came up with a strategy to request a change in
snacks. The manager was very receptive and even somewhat apologetic that she
hadn't thought about the older children. It is important for the author to note that her
initial idea was to go to the manager herself with the members' complaints. Luckily,
she realized that members should do this themselves, that this would enhance feelings of mastery. Of course, there was always the risk that members could have been
shut down. But it is better to err on the side of encouraging self and collective advocacy than it is to allow members to vent, without taking any action at all. This was a
turning point in the life of this group. From this point forward, it gained a reputation
as a place where members could openly talk about their concerns and gain strength
from one another, which significantly increased its appeal to other shelter residents.

Another strategy that is critical when working with homeless parents in shelters is to address out-of-group issues in the group. Living in a shelter is stressful, often demeaning, and restrictive. Residents already overwhelmed with their
homeless status may have a difficult time adjusting to shelter life and its rules
and regulations. Living in close quarters is likely to lead to conflicts and disagreements. Inevitably, these will spill over into the group. It is important for
the leader to address these issues when they surface. Unless they are dealt with
directly, they will undermine the ability of the group to engage in mutual aid.
Furthermore, as the disagreements are openly aired and addressed, all members
learn valuable lessons about how to negotiate, compromise, and resolve conflict,
even when the solution is to agree to disagree.

A final intervention strategy is to address directly members' concerns about
the leader, and, when needed, the mandatory nature of their attendance in the
group. In many settings, homeless parents are required to attend group as a condition of their receiving shelter and its attendant services. This is true of the

shelter at which the author volunteers. The irony is not lost on the author that while the group fosters empowerment, it is mandated for its members. This is a reality that many group leaders face when they work with homeless parents. As discussed earlier, members already may approach the leader with suspicion and hostility, which are manifestations both of transference and of the cultural differences that typically exist between leader and members. It is naïve to assume that if the leader ignores members' reactions to her or him, they will disappear. In fact, the longer the group worker goes without addressing the "authority theme" (Shulman 2012), the more intrusive and disruptive a force it becomes.

Because membership in the author's groups changes almost weekly, she routinely addresses members' questions about her, acknowledging the differences between the members and her and conveying to them that *they* are the experts, not her. She invites members to tell their stories, to tell her what it has been like for them. She also is careful to make sure that the group session is responsive to members' concerns, not a reflection of what *she* thinks that they need to talk about.

This does not mean that the group worker cannot work with an agenda or predetermined curriculum for the group. In fact, a number of groups for homeless individuals, including parents, rely upon manuals (Coker et al., 2010; Cosgrove & Flynn, 2005). A predetermined curriculum can be suggestive to the leader of the sorts of topics that may surface in the group and can be an invaluable guide, particularly for group workers new to working with homeless parents. However, if the leader adheres too rigidly to the manual, she or he increases—rather than diminishes—members' mistrust and resistance. This also undermines empowerment of members. It also may not be feasible or practical, given the changing nature of the membership.

EVALUATION

An obvious indicator of the success of the group would be members leaving the shelter or agency and securing stable, safe housing. Yet, as repeatedly noted in this chapter, there is a complex set of factors that contribute to homelessness among parents. Thus, it is unlikely that group participation alone can end members' homeless status. There are, however, five potential indicators of the group's effectiveness:

- Mandated participants become voluntary members.
- Members take a more active role in securing resources to end their homeless status.
- Members report heightened feelings of empowerment and self-efficacy.
- Members demonstrate the ability to advocate for themselves.
- Members recognize how their actions, choices, and decisions contributed to their homeless status.

RESOURCES

National Alliance to End Homelessness. http://www.endhomelessness.org/

National Coalition for the Homeless. http://www.homeless.org

REFERENCES

Arangua, L., Andersen, R., & Gelberg, L. (2005). The health circumstances of homeless women in the United States. *International Journal of Mental Health, 34,* 62–92.

Berzoff, J. (2013). Group therapy with homeless women. *Smith College Studies in Social Work, 83,* 233–248.

Bullock, H., & Lott, B. (2001). Building a research and advocacy agenda on issue of economic justice. *Analysis of Social Issues and Public Policy, 1,* 147–162.

Brush, B., Kirk, K., Gultekin, L., & Baiardi, J. (2011). Overcoming: A concept analysis. *Nursing Forum, 46,* 160–168.

Caton, C., Dominguez, B., Schanzer, B., Hasin, D, Shrout, P., Felix, A., . . . Hsu, E. (2005). Risk factors for long-term homelessness: Findings from a longitudinal study of first-time homeless single adults. *American Journal of Public Health, 95,* 1753–1759.

Coker, A., Meyer, D., Smith, R., & Price, A. (2010). Using social justice group work with young mothers who experience homelessness. *Journal for Specialists in Group Work, 35,* 220–229.

Cormack, J. (2009). Counseling marginalized young people: A qualitative analysis of young homeless people's views of counseling. *Counseling and Psychotherapy Research, 9,* 71–77.

Cosgrove, L., & Flynn, C. (2005). Marginalized mothers: Parenting without a home. *Analyses of Social Issues and Public Policy, 5,* 127–143.

Culhane, D., Metraux, S., Park, J., Schretzman, M., & Valente, J. (2007). Testing a typology of family homelessness based on patterns of public shelter utilization in four U.S. jurisdictions: Implications for policy and program planning. *Housing Policy Debate, 18,* 1–21.

DeForge, B., Belcher, J., O'Rourke, M., & Lindsey, M. (2008). Personal resources and homelessness in early life: Predictors of depression in consumers of homeless multiservice centers. *Journal of Loss and Trauma, 13,* 222–242.

deShazer, S. (1991). *Putting differences to work.* New York, NY: Newton.

Dotson, H. M. (2011). Homeless women, parents, and children: A triangulation approach analyzing factors influencing homelessness and child separation. *Journal of Poverty, 15*(3), 241–258

Dykeman, B. (2011). Intervention strategies with the homeless population. *Journal of Instructional Psychology, 38,* 32–39.

Fraenkel, P. (2006). Engaging families as experts: Collaborative family program development. *Family Process, 45,* 237–257.

Fraenkel, P., Hameline, T., & Shannon, M. (2009). Narrative and collaborative practices in work with families that are homeless. *Journal of Marital and Family Therapy, 35,* 325–342.

Gitterman, A., & Knight, C. (2015). Resilience and adversarial growth: Promoting client empowerment through group work. *Journal of Social Work Education*, forthcoming.

Greene, R., Galambos, C., & Lee, Y. (2003). Resilience theory: Theoretical and professional conceptualizations. *Journal of Human Behavior and the Social Environment*, *8*, 75–91.

Haber, M., & Toro, P. (2004). Homelessness among families, children, and adolescents: An ecological-developmental perspective. *Clinical Child and Family Psychology Review*, *7*, 123–164.

Hertlein, K., & Killmer, J. (2004). Toward differentiated decision-making: Family systems theory with the homeless clinical population. *American Journal of Family Therapy*, *32*, 255–270.

Huey, L., Fthenos, G., & Hryniewicz, D. (2013). "If something happened, I will leave it, let it go, and move on": Resiliency and victimized homeless women's attitudes toward mental health counseling. *Journal of Interpersonal Violence*, *28*, 295–319.

Jahiel, R., & Babor, T. F. (2011). Toward a typology of homeless families: conceptual and methodological issues. *Characteristics and dynamics of homeless families with children: Final report to the Office of the Assistant Secretary for Planning and Evaluation, Office of Human Services Policy, US Department of Health and Human Services.*

Jenkins, P. E., Meyer, C., & Blissett, J. M. (2013). Childhood abuse and eating psychopathology: The mediating role of core beliefs. *Journal of Aggression, Maltreatment and Trauma*, *22*, 248–261.

Knight, C. (2009). *Introduction to working with adult survivors of childhood trauma: Strategies and techniques for helping professionals*. Belmont, CA: Thomson/Brooks-Cole.

Knight, C. (2006). Integrating solution-focused principles and techniques into clinical practice and supervision. *Clinical Supervisor*, *23*, 153–173.

Lee, B., Tyler, K., & Wright, J. (2010). The new homelessness revisited. *Annual Review of Sociology*, *36*, 501–521.

Lewinson, T., Thomas, M., & White, S. (2014). Traumatic transitions: Homeless women's narratives of abuse, loss, and fear. *Affilia: Journal of Women and Social Work*, *29*, 192–205.

National Alliance to End Homelessness. (2014). *The state of homelessness in America*. Retrieved from http://www.endhomelessness.org/library/entry/the-state-of-homelessness-2014

National Coalition of the homeless. (2016) http://www.coalitionforthehomeless.org/the-catastrophe-of-homelessness/

Plasse, B. (2003). A stress reduction and self-care group for homeless and addicted women: Meditation, relaxation, and cognitive methods. *Social Work with Groups*, *24*, 117–133.

Richards, T., Garland, T., Bumphus, V., & Thompson, R. (2010). Personal and political?: Exploring the feminization of the American homeless population. *Journal of Poverty*, *14*, 97–115.

Rossi, P. (1989). *Down and out in America: The origins of homelessness*. Chicago, IL: University of Chicago Press.

Shulman, L. (2012). *The skills of helping individuals, families, groups, and communities* (7th ed.). Belmont, CA: Brooks/Cole Cengage Learning.

Speirs, V., Johnson, M., & Jirojwong, S. (2013). A systematic review of interventions for homeless women. *Journal of Clinical Nursing, 22*, 1080–1093.

Styron, T., Janoff-Bulman, R., & Davidson, L. (2000). "Please ask me how I am:" Experiences of family homelessness in the context of single mothers' lives. *Journal of Social Distress and the Homeless, 9*, 143–165.

Teruya, C., Longshore, D., Andersen, R., Arangua, L., Nyamathi, A., Leake, B., & Gelberg, L. (2010). Health and health care disparities among homeless women. *Women and Health, 50*, 719–736.

Tischler, V., Edwards, V., & Vostanis, P. (2009). Working therapeutically with mothers who experience the trauma of homelessness: An opportunity for growth. *Counselling and Psychotherapy Research, 9*, 42–46.

Washington, O., Moxley, D., & Garriott, L. (2009). The telling my story quilting workshop: Group work with older African-American women transitioning out of homelessness. *Journal of Psychosocial Nursing and Mental Health Services, 47*, 42–52.

Wilson, M. (2005). Health-promoting behaviors of sheltered homeless women. *Family and Community Health, 28*, 51–63.

Zlotnick, C., Tam, T., & Bradley, K. (2007). Impact of adulthood trauma on homeless mothers. *Community Mental Health Journal, 43*, 13–32.

Zlotnick, C., Tam, T., & Bradley, K. (2010). Long-term and chronic homelessness in homeless women and children. *Social Work in Public Health, 25*, 470–485.

NOTE

1 All case material comes from the author's work as a group leader in a 90-day residential shelter for homeless families. Unless the parents are working or have another appointment, they are required to attend the weekly group, the purpose of which is to provide mutual support and assistance.

Chapter Twenty-Five

Group Work in Context: Organizational and Community Factors

Elizabeth A. Mulroy

Group work, as seen from an organizational perspective, is a method of practice set in larger systems of organizations and communities. Most formalized groups, such as those for students at risk of dropping out of school, incarcerated mothers, people with mental illness, children of divorce, disabled soldiers wounded in conflicts abroad, or people with HIV/AIDS, operate under the auspices of some type of organization or institutional structure. As a method of social work practice, group work is conducted within social programs that operate in, and are supported by, formal and informal organizations. Each program has specific goals, objectives, and outcomes. The success of a specific group depends in part on the viability of the overall social program; that program is itself dependent on the capacity of the sponsoring organization to operate *efficiently, effectively*, and *equitably*. To support its many programs, an organization needs to maintain financial stability, demonstrate program effectiveness through responsiveness to at-risk clients, and demonstrate a commitment to social justice.

However, many social agencies are struggling to meet the aforementioned criteria. Whether they are public or nonprofit child welfare agencies, nonprofit or for-profit medical facilities, Veterans Affairs, refugee acculturation associations, or YMCAs for example, they have increasingly functioned with severely reduced financial resources. It is not surprising that such public and nonprofit agencies have experienced rapidly changing "turbulent institutional environments" (Hasenfeld, 1992, 2010) that, in turn, contribute to internal program uncertainties (Netting & O'Connor, 2003).

Environmental turbulence caused by a range of economic downturns and upticks, national social policy tensions, global military conflicts, rise of social media, and a myriad of environmental factors spawned various forms of collective responses (Mulroy & Austin, 2004). When successful, these became models of practice in which agencies worked together either voluntarily or involuntarily to implement a particular program. Community problem solving

brought neighbors, client interest groups, developers, funders, community or-
ganizers, advocates, and government officials together to listen, learn, and ultimately find solutions. Participants were drawn from diverse fields, including
medicine, law, planning, social policy, education, and social work, necessitat-
ing complicated cross-sector and multisector working relationships. Common
ground was achieved through *facilitative leadership*, a method that gives local
citizens "respect and value . . . we see how deeply committed parties working across boundaries of class, ethnicity, value commitments, and territorial
identities can transform thoroughly suspicious and contested relationships into
ones enabling mutual learning, growth, and actually useful practical outcomes"
(Forester, 2013, p. xiii).

The purpose of this chapter is to examine some principles of organizations
so that the beginning social worker can understand and appreciate the organizational context of group work in social work, and the effects of its community context on program implementation, service delivery, and, ultimately, social
change.

THE ORGANIZATIONAL CONTEXT

A human service organization has a *transformative* purpose to help clients or consumers fulfill their unmet needs and improve their situations. Hasenfeld (1992)
suggests that this transformative quality means human service organizations
engage in "moral work" (p. 5), a powerful concept that adds to the complexity
of operating human service organizations and measuring their outcomes. A first
step in understanding organizations that exist to serve human needs is to know
sector differences. *Public sector* agencies are governmental agencies that were established and continue to operate through legislative mandate. Some examples
include federal, state, and county child welfare departments; family assistance
agencies (formerly called public welfare); health; or education. Funding comes
from legislative appropriations. *Nonprofit sector* organizations are nongovern-
mental, tax exempt, and run by voluntary boards of directors. They are not profit
generating, and they exist to fulfill a particular mission, social purpose, or public
benefit. Nonprofit organizations receive funding from a variety of sources, such
as charitable contributions, government grants and contracts, fees for service,
and fundraising endeavors.

There is great diversity in types of nonprofit, socially oriented organizations.
They may be large or small; highly structured, traditional bureaucracies or informal, nontraditional, alternative organizations; employ professional staffs or
use only volunteers; have no geographic affiliation or be closely affiliated with
and accountable to one neighborhood or community. Some examples include
large, well-established child and family agencies, residential treatment facilities,

YMCAs and YWCAs, settlement houses, crisis centers, shelters for the homeless, or relatively new community development organizations.

In contrast, organizations in the *for-profit sector* are commercial and form the backbone of the market economy (Netting & O'Connor, 2003). Their purpose is to make money, and they pay taxes. Although traditionally not social service providers, large multinational private firms such as Lockheed Martin, Andersen Consulting, and Electronic Data Systems have moved into human services delivery as a result of privatization. Some examples include for-profit residential treatment facilities, hospitals, or employment development agencies with job training programs.

Privatization and Competition

Human service organizations, irrespective of sector, have been affected by privatization—the contracting out of public services to nonprofit and for-profit organizations. Privatization has been operating for years in many public spheres, such as public works in which cities contract with private firms to pick up trash or plow snow; school districts that contract with private bus companies to transport students to and from public schools; transportation, in which counties contract with private construction companies to build or repair roads and highways; or social service departments that contract with private consulting firms to set up management information systems.

The implications of this development for nonprofit organizations and for social work became profound in the 1980s with the convergence of privatization in health and human services *and* deep cuts in federal spending for domestic social programs designed to help the poor. By the end of the 1980s, government contracts had replaced charitable contributions as the major source of funding for many large, established, nonprofit human service organizations such as child and family agencies, as well as for the vast majority of nonprofits that are small, community-based organizations (Perlmutter, 1984; Rathgeb Smith, 2010; Salamon, 1999). By the end of the 1990s, privatization—and the increased competition it generated—had accelerated the commercialization of health and mental health care and shifted social work administrators in public agencies into roles of contract managers (Austin, 2000; Austin, Brody, & Packard, 2009). Increased dependence on these fluctuating public grants and contracts weakened the financial base of small, community-based nonprofit organizations with social justice goals (Fabricant & Fisher, 2002; Gibelman & Demone, 2002). Some large nonprofits maximized opportunities in this environment and managed to grow and thrive. Privatization also enabled the for-profit sector to emerge as a major competitor in the provision of human services (Frumkin & Andre-Clarke, 2000).

With these politically turbulent environmental forces as a backdrop, we turn the discussion to the five stages of organizational development.

Organizational Life Stages

Human service organizations adapt in response to the environmental changes just described, and their ability to do this successfully is influenced by their life cycle stage of organizational development. This section will concentrate on the nonprofit sector because of its prominence in human service delivery, and because public agencies and private for-profit firms have different characteristics, roles, and functions. Very large, complex nonprofits; very small, grassroots organizations; and nontraditional organizations with unique circumstances such as non-Western cultures may find the following typology less helpful. It is a model for the majority of nonprofits.

Simon (2001), after conducting a thorough review of the organizational development literature, posits that organizations go through a journey of five life stages:

Stage One: Imagine and Inspire. This is the "I want to do a dream" stage, the inspirational beginning characterized by the enthusiasm and energy of a charismatic, entrepreneurial leader.

Stage Two: Found and Frame. In the start-up phase, the organization gets its official nonprofit tax status and becomes incorporated, formally establishing the organization. Some staff members may resist moving from an informal, participatory approach to decision making to a more formal arrangement.

Stage Three: Ground and Grow. This stage focuses on establishing procedures, growing the "business," and working through the challenges, opportunities, and choices that present themselves.

Stage Four: Produce and Sustain. Productivity is at its peak as workers are effective and procedures become routine. This has its benefits because systems are needed to keep the organization moving forward. Some employees, however, may feel their creativity and opportunities for growth have slowed down.

Stage Five: Review and Renew. In this stage, managers of mature nonprofits engage in continuous surveillance of the organization's external environment (Mulroy, 2004) so that timely reviews and strategic decisions are made for renewal. It is argued that stressful conditions generate possibilities for new patterns of action to form. Thoughtful organizational self-assessment in Stage Five helps revisit the mission, vision, products, services, and structure to make major or minor changes as indicated. It may mean cycling back to earlier stages. For example, if changes to the basic mission and philosophy are needed, then the organization revisits Stage Two. If modifications in services or structure are necessary, then it revisits Stage Four.

Organizations generally move forward in a predictable path, but several factors influence where the organization is in its life cycle: its age, its size, growth rate of its field or domain, social environment, and characteristics of its primary leader (Simon, 2001, p. 9). Younger organizations with few staffers and a small budget, for example, are in the early stages of the life cycle. Those involved in a growth industry such as residential treatment facilities may move through the early life cycle stages quickly. Welfare-to-work programs mandated by the Personal Responsibility and Work Opportunity Reconciliation Act of 1996 created market pressures for both nonprofit and for-profit organizations, and many nonprofits rushed through the life cycle stages to capture these new federal funding streams.

Achieving success in each stage helps the nonprofit grow and thrive. In reality, boundaries between the five stages may blur, so that movement from one stage to another is not obvious. But problems can be expected to emerge in every stage, and a nonprofit organization can *decline and dissolve* in any one of them. The organization can become destabilized through the departure of a charismatic, highly respected founding executive director, loss of program funding, or staff turnover. This model does not predict an endpoint for organizational life. "At some point the organization chooses to remain status quo, stagnate, regenerate, or dissolve" (Simon, 2001, p. 10). The extent of environmental turbulence suggests the need for continuous surveillance, review of impacts, and renewal of agency functions to keep the organization responsive and moving forward.

To do this well, managers must oversee a number of internal functions that exist in every life cycle stage. These include the following:

1. *Governance*—legal decision-making structure of a board of directors, agency policies, and procedures
2. *Staff leadership*—executive director's role
3. *Financing*—resource development and financial management of multiple grants, contracts, donations, endowments, and fundraising
4. *Administrative systems*—equipment, office space, accounting, support staff, and technology needed to accomplish the mission
5. *Products and services*—design and delivery of services, activities, and products needed to accomplish the mission
6. *Staffing*—size, composition, and pattern of relationships among staff; pay schedules; and use of volunteers
7. *Marketing*—how the organization portrays itself to the public and to consumers

In sum, we can see the complexity of organizational life and the importance of managing both internal and external factors that affect a nonprofit's well-being so it can be a healthy organization.

Social Programs

Programs are the heart of organizations because it is through programs that social policies passed by federal and state legislative bodies actually get implemented. In effect, social policies are translated into action at the local community level through programs with services that reach intended beneficiaries. Human service programs are concerned with (1) personal development of individuals and families through direct services such as education, training, counseling, therapy, or casework; and (2) social development in communities and with special populations through policy and advocacy, community organizing, planning, interorganizational collaboration, and network formation. The intended outcome of social programs, regardless of the methods used, is to enhance the well-being of clients or consumers, be they individuals, families, organizations, communities, or special populations (Lewis, Lewis, Packard, & Souflee, 2001).

The effectiveness of health and human service programs has long been a concern of policy makers and funders. To address this concern, Kettner, Moroney, and Martin (1996, 2008) recommend that, before any new program is developed, social workers systematically take stock of the strengths and weaknesses of their organization's existing programs. Their eight-step effectiveness-based programming guide is outlined next. Primarily designed as a problem assessment tool, it is adapted here to include strengths and assets in the analysis (for further discussion, see Mulroy, 2008).

1. *Define the organization's programs.* Learn how the organization defines and organizes its programs. Are they separated by type of client, by geographical region, by type of service provided, or by resources required?

2. *Problem/issue analysis.* How well is the issue understood? What is the condition the program seeks to address? Ideally, it should be grounded in a thorough review of research in terms of the type, size, and scope of the issue as it pertains to a target population, as well as historical precedents, community and policy factors, and theories of change on which the intervention is based.

3. *Needs and assets assessment.* How well is the need understood—as defined by experts, and as defined by those experiencing the need? What resources (assets) already exist in the community to address the need?

4. *Selecting a strategy and selecting objectives.* Based on data from the foregoing analysis, a program hypothesis is developed. A hypothesis is a statement about what outcomes are expected if a person with the problems or issues outlined earlier receives the services about to be designed (Kettner et al., 1996, p. 20; 2010). This becomes the framework for the development of precisely stated goals, objectives, and activities. Examine existing programs to see how they accomplished this step.

5. *Program design.* This important phase allows a social worker or a team of people to creatively assemble services (such as groups) or a combination of

services and activities (groups, individual therapy, casework, community activities) that appear to have the best chance of achieving program objectives. This is a critical step in the planning and management of programs because it is based on a carefully thought-out assessment of the needs of a particular at-risk population *relative to* the needs and resources of the agency and the community.

6. *Management information systems.* To what extent did existing programs use agency resources such as the computer network to design and implement a database for their specific programs? A client data system is essential to produce data and information about the progress of clients throughout each episode of service, which helps determine service effectiveness at termination. When linked to other data sets, it facilitates communication and coordinates services among several persons working with a client, while assisting management with its need to measure service effectiveness agency-wide.

7. *Budgeting.* Service delivery costs the agency money, so a social program needs to budget projected costs. An eight-session group could be less expensive to operate than an alternative service, such as one-on-one casework, and therefore more cost-effective. Social workers will want to use available data at an agency to calculate costs for items such as units of service (one group session for 2 hours), achievement of a measurable outcome (for a group), or achievement of a program objective.

8. *Program evaluation.* In the final analysis, the funders of a social program will want to know how successful the program was in meeting its objectives. Those who render direct services and those who manage the program need to provide evidence of how well the intervention helped achieve program outcomes. Assess the evaluation methods used by existing programs in the agency, and draw lessons learned from their experiences. The point is this: Methods exist to evaluate an individual group; use them, but know that the group is not run in isolation. The group is also evaluated in the context of a social program, and the social program is evaluated in the larger context of the organization's mission and purpose.

Programs usually comprise a number of *services* designed to meet the needs of a population at risk. These services may be concrete, such as emergency financial assistance for rent and utilities for very poor families in public housing, or a transportation system that helps them get food at the food bank, or clothing and furniture at the Salvation Army thrift store. Or they may be less concrete, such as classes in financial literacy, job readiness training, volunteer training, crisis counseling, or leadership development. All of these services work together at various levels of need to keep families at risk of homelessness from being evicted from public housing. We will now turn to community issues because it is from the community that an agency and its social workers draw their clients.

THE COMMUNITY CONTEXT

Because a purpose of group work is to serve clients and the community, knowing the demographics of a community will help guide social workers in deciding who needs to be served by agency programs, what types of services and methods are most appropriate, and whether the agency mission statement is congruent with rapidly changing community conditions and needs. A community analysis can provide social workers with much needed data and should be conducted before a new program or group is created. The following general framework can be used as a beginning point for a community analysis. I call this the *Reconnaissance* phase:

1. Use most recent census data to identify community characteristics of a geographically bounded area.
2. Identify a target at-risk population and its demographic characteristics within this area.
3. Determine resident needs and assets, and existing institutional resources available to meet those needs.
4. Identify leaders within the at-risk population if appropriate.
5. Identify community structure, including presence of potential institutional partners and competitors inside the bounded area and outside of it (adapted from Netting, Kettner, & McMurtry, 2004).

Knowledge of the local area is important. In very poor communities, residents often have more than one at-risk condition, as discussed in the six parts of this book. In a study of homelessness prevention in public housing, the households in the study sample identified as being at risk of homelessness typically had family members with multiple at-risk conditions at the same time—including health issues, adjusting to change, violence (as victims or perpetrators), substance abuse, or problems with institutions such as schools, the workplace, and the justice system (Mulroy & Lauber, 2002, 2004). Some of their most salient shared conditions included being very poor, living in unsafe housing conditions, and in unsafe neighborhood environments.

The extent to which the group worker is able to address these multiple layers of at-risk conditions in one group may depend on the agency's community-based orientation, a commitment to serve the very poor as reflected in the organization's mission statement, and the worker's own cultural competence to respond appropriately. For example, the resident population living in the housing project described earlier was drawn from diverse immigrant groups. At least 19 different languages were spoken. Increased diversity and multiculturalism are central factors in many communities today and are predicted to become more important throughout the next decade.

Keeping close to the pulse of a community—whether defined as the public housing project, a particular neighborhood, or a whole city—opens up opportunities for group workers to serve the public interest. One example can be found in immigration and refugee movement into cities and towns across America, to be considered next.

Immigrants and Refugees as At-Risk Populations

The international movement of displaced persons who are political refugees or immigrant workers—both legal and illegal—is arguably one of the greatest social challenges facing the world, and it will be felt locally because it will alter the realities of diversity in our communities, organizations, and in civic life. Social workers on the front lines—particularly those skilled in group work, case management, community building, program development, and agency management—will be at the center of institutional and community problem solving and will change in the decades to come. The following examples will help to illustrate some of the emerging trends and challenges.

For school social workers, for example, these issues may arise:

1. How do we gain access to disparate groups in order to mediate disagreements among students, or between teachers, administrators, parents, and students from many different languages, cultures, and religions?
2. How do we work collaboratively and inclusively with all parties, including every immigrant and refugee group represented in the school district, to develop assimilation and language programs from kindergarten through twelfth grade?
3. What social work roles and responsibilities should we assume as grassroots partners with Community Development Corporations as they increasingly expand their missions beyond affordable housing to include both comprehensive community transformation and academic improvement among neighborhood students? (see Naimark, 2012)

Other organizational and institutional settings provide different challenges and needs.

1. To what extent should workers in employment assistance programs be transferred or reassigned to accommodate space for the diversity of new employees? Social workers in an employee assistance program of a large nonprofit or for-profit organization may be asked to help solve misunderstandings and resentments that appear to be getting in the way of productivity and worker retention in its increasingly multicultural and multiethnic workforce.

2. What should a medical social worker in the hospital emergency department do when he or she observes there is not enough trained multilingual staff, that improved communication is needed between the rapidly increasing number of immigrant and refugee patients and the medical staff? The worker must define the unmet need and create the program with the cooperation and input from the at-risk populations, then appear before numerous decision-making groups inside the hospital to reframe the issues and offer concrete options that justify the increased costs in cost-cutting times.

3. Using a larger unit of analysis, how have cities responded to the challenges of ethnic diversity? City officials in places experiencing "sudden ethnic diversification" such as Lewiston, Maine (Blais, 2003), sought out nonprofit organizations with whom to collaborate in order to develop creative public–private partnerships capable of doing more together than each could do alone. City mayors looked to both nonprofit and public agencies to develop support groups that helped refugees in the following ways: find affordable housing, health care, job training, and jobs; identify business startups and other for-profit programs— resources typically located in many different types of organizations, public, nonprofit, and for-profit. From the local government perspective, fresh ways of thinking and acting to resolve civic matters are needed on a community-wide basis, and these new approaches are being developed through coalitions and partnerships of which social workers skilled in developing groups are playing a key part.

In sum, communities with an influx of immigrant and refugee populations seek leadership and guidance in devising programs and services to assimilate newcomer populations. The social work profession's skills, values, and knowledge base prepare practitioners to respond to these opportunities and challenges.

CONCLUSION

This chapter introduced the reader to theoretical frameworks, assessment models, and life stages of programs, organizations, and communities that concern group work with populations at risk. The chapter began by identifying recent large-scale trends in the social environment that call for a shifting role for social work practitioners generally and groups work practitioners specifically. The chapter took a deep dive into an analysis of for-profit, nonprofit, and public sector organizational types. It then discussed the current and future benefits of creating and participating in new variations of organizational structure and community purpose through public–private partnerships, coalitions, and interorganizational collaborations. The chapter concludes by identifying successful social change approaches for group work practitioners that include collective responses (Mulroy & Austin, 2004: Naimark, 2012) and facilitative leadership (Forester, 2013).

RESOURCES

Alliance for Justice
11 Dupont Circle NW, 2nd Floor
Washington, DC 20036
http://www.afj.org

Association for Community
Organization and Social Administration
http://www.acosa.org

Center for Community Change
1000 Wisconsin Ave.
Washington, DC 20007
202-342-0519
http://www.communitychange.org

National Community Building Network
8718 Mary Lee Lane
Annandale, VA 22003
703-425-6296
http://www.ncbn.org

REFERENCES

Austin, D. (2000). Social work and social welfare administration: A historical perspective. In R. Patti (Ed.), *The handbook of social welfare management* (pp. 27–54). Thousand Oaks, CA: Sage.

Austin, M., Brody, R., & Packard, T. (2009). *Managing the challenges in human service organizations*. Thousand Oaks, CA: Sage.

Blais, P. (2003). The shock of the new: Lewiston, Maine, learns how to treat Somali immigrants like anyone else in town. *Planning, February*, 14–17.

Fabricant, M., & Fisher, R. (2002). *Settlement houses under siege*. New York, NY: Columbia University Press.

Forester, J. (2013). *Planning in the face of conflict: The surprising possibilities of facilitative leadership*. Washington, DC: Planners Press.

Frumkin, P., & Andre-Clarke, A. (2000). When missions, markets, and politics collide: Values and strategy in the nonprofit human services. *Nonprofit and Voluntary Sector Quarterly, 29*(1), 141–163.

Gibelman, M., & Demone, H., Jr. (2002). The commercialization of health and human services: National phenomenon or cause for concern? *Families in Society, 83,* 387–397.

Hasenfeld, Y. (1992). *Human services as complex organizations.* Newbury Park, CA: Sage.

Hasenfeld, Y. (2010). *Human services as complex organizations* (2nd ed.). Thousand Oaks, CA: Sage.

Kettner, P., Moroney, R., & Martin, L. (1996). *Designing and managing programs.* Thousand Oaks, CA: Sage.

Kettner, P., Moroney, R., & Martin, L. (2008). *Designing and managing programs* (3rd ed.). Thousand Oaks, CA: Sage.

Lewis, J., Lewis, M., Packard, T., & Souflee, F. (2001). *Management of human service programs* (3rd ed.). Belmont, CA: Brooks/Cole.

Mulroy, E. (2004). Theoretical approaches to the social environment for management and community practice: An organization-in-environment approach. *Administration in Social Work, 28,* 77–96.

Mulroy, E., & Lauber, H. (2002). Community building in hard times: A post-welfare view from the streets. *Journal of Community Practice, 10*(1), 1–16.

Mulroy, E., & Lauber, H. (2004). An approach to user-friendly evaluation and community interventions for families at risk of homelessness. *Social Work, 49,* 573–586.

Naimark, S. (2012). How two CDCs added school reform to their agenda. *Shelterforce, Fall*(171), 40–44.

Netting, E., Kettner, P., & McMurtry, S. (2004). *Social work macro practice* (3rd ed.). Boston, MA: Allyn & Bacon.

Netting, E., & O'Connor, M. K. (2003). *Organization practice: A social worker's guide to understanding human services.* Boston, MA: Allyn & Bacon.

Perlmutter, F. (1984). *Human services at risk.* Lexington, MA: Lexington Books.

Rathgeb Smith, S. (2010). The political economy of contracting and competition. In Y. Hasenfeld (Ed.), *Human services as complex organizations* (2nd ed., pp. 139–160) Thousand Oaks, CA: Sage.

Salamon, L. (1999). *America's nonprofit sector: A primer.* New York, NY: Foundation Center.

Simon, J. S. (2001). *The five life stages of nonprofit organizations.* St. Paul, MN: Amherst Wilder Foundation.

Part Five

Evaluating Practice and Practice Skills

Using Evidence-Based Practice and Intervention Research With Treatment Groups for Populations at Risk

Edna Comer and Andrea Meier

Nearly two decades ago, the social work profession joined with other health and human service systems in the call for the incorporation of systematically collected data and research evidence into clinical practice, which is commonly referred to as evidence-based practice (EBP). This phenomenon is driven by the need for greater attention to practice research and a mechanism for the dissemination of findings (Satterfield, Spring, Browson, Mullen, Newhouse, Walker, & Whitlock, 2009). The National Association of Social Workers Code of Ethics (1996) addresses social workers' obligation to maintain and promote high standards of practice and to monitor and evaluate policies in the implementation of programs and practice interventions. Achievement of this goal requires the application of conscientious, explicit, and judicious use of the best available evidence in making decisions about the care of the clients so that the treatments offered would have high odds of success (Fraser, 2003; Sackett, Richardson, Gray, Haynes, & Richardson, 1996). For example, the Standards for Social Work practice with clients with substance abuse disorders states that "by developing and applying evidence-informed approaches that incorporate established interventions and evolving techniques based on emerging research findings, social workers can markedly improve treatment services for clients and their families" (p. 6).

Significant progress has been made toward the adaptation of EBP as part of the standards for social work practice (Macgowan, 2008; Mathiesen & Hohman, 2013; Parrish & Rubin, 2012). Numerous publications describe the process and content of EBP (Bretton & Macgowan, 2009; Gambrill, 2006; Howard, Himle, Jenson, & Vaughn, 2009; Ngo, Langley, Nadeem, Escudero, & Stein, 2008; Pollio; 2006; Rosen & Proctor, 2003). Entire texts are devoted to the conceptualization, development, and implementation of EBP (Fraser, Richman, Galinsky, & Day, 2009; Macgowan, 2008; O'Hare, 2015; Rosen & Proctor, 2003). The Council on Social Work Education, the sole accrediting agency for social work education, has specified that knowledge of and practice skills for EBP are competencies that graduating students from MSW programs must have to practice professional social work (Council on Social Work Education, 2006). Current trends in social work education support teaching students the values and skills they need to critically appraise and apply practice-relevant scientific evidence over the course of their professional careers (Howard, Mathiesen, & Hohman, 2011; McMillen & Pollio, 2003; Mullen, Bellamy, Bledsoe, & Francois, 2007). Collaborative efforts between social work researchers and educators and human services organizations have been undertaken to implement changes in social work education through curriculum changes that reflect the paradigm shift toward evidence-based professional practice. One example is the Connecticut Transformation Initative coordinated by Wheeler Clinic, a private nonprofit behavioral health agency, which administers the project *Current Trends in Family Intervention: Evidence-Based and Promising Practice Models of In-home Treatment in Connecticut* (Cannata & Hoge, 2012). This state-funded project focuses on building a workforce skilled in providing home-based services through coordinated curriculum development, faculty training, university-based coursework, experiential learning through internships, and recruitment of graduating students.

In light of the growing interest in research relevant to social work practice and the expanding body of knowledge available to guide practice, this chapter is intended to help social workers, particularly those who conduct groups, in their efforts toward the use of research evidence in practice situations. General principles of EBP and some strategies for evaluating the quality of research evidence for treatment of individuals and groups are discussed. The authors describe the application of EBP principles in social work with groups and some means for carrying out this process within agency settings. The authors speculate about methodological reasons for the paucity of outcome research in social work with groups. They propose the use of intervention research (IR) as an alternative research methodology and discuss how social workers can use it to guide them in systematically modifying groups they are currently running or in developing innovative new ones. Information is presented on where social workers can obtain information about EBP principles and procedures and sources of research evidence related to their work with groups.

GENERAL PRINCIPLES OF EVIDENCE-BASED PRACTICE

At the core of the EBP approach is that there is evidence to support the conclusion that an intervention has a reasonable probability of effectiveness (Macgowan, 2008; O'Hare, 2015). As purposeful actions toward influencing positive change, interventions may work at the individual, family, group, organizations, or community level (Fraser et al., 2009). A common goal of social work is to serve populations at risk—peoples with particular physical and psychological conditions, often stigmatized or discriminated against by society or social institutions, or by challenges that arise from their stage of life or personal life situations (Greif & Ephross, 2011). Practice with these populations should include interventions that are unique to their needs and have demonstrated helpfulness in treatment outcomes. An intervention is considered evidence based when it "has been evaluated using scientific methods, and the cumulative findings from evaluations that demonstrate that the intervention is effective in producing a desired outcome" (Fraser et al., 2009, p. 11).

There are two major components of EBP. First, practitioners make systematic use of clinically relevant research to select accurate and precise diagnostic tests, identify prognostic markers, and assess the potential effectiveness and safety of different kinds of treatments (Sackett et al., 1996). Properly used, this type of information may support or invalidate previously accepted diagnostic tests and treatments, spurring practitioners to modify or replace them with new ones that are more powerful, accurate, and safer. Practitioners can acquire this knowledge by reading professional journals, attending conference presentations about specific populations, and by generating evidence through their own observations and research (Pollio, 2002; Wike, Bledsoe, Bellamy, & Grady, 2013).

The second component of EBP is that practitioners are expected to draw from multiple sources for information to inform their treatment decisions. That is, they should not use the "cookbook" approach, relying on only one source of evidence (e.g., clinical trials). Instead, practitioners are called on to think ecologically, taking into account findings about population characteristics and reports about the social environments in which their clients live (Bilsker & Golsner, 2000; Council on Social Work Education, 2008). They should try to integrate relevant research evidence, social science theory, and theory-based interventions with "practice wisdom" (Fraser, 2003; Sackett et al., 1996). Their diagnoses and treatment decisions should take into account clients' predicaments, rights, and preferences (NASW, 1996; Sackett et al., 1996). Practitioners are expected to discuss with their clients the range of treatment options and their associated risks and benefits, to the extent that they are known. Practitioners and clients work together to decide whether and how available evidence applies to their specific circumstances (Fraser, 2003; Sackett et al., 1996).

EVALUATING RESEARCH EVIDENCE

"What is the best evidence available for me to use in making my treatment decisions with the clients? This is the key questions underlying all discussions of EBP. Figure 26.1 lists the three main categories of research evidence: observational, systematic, and preprocessed. Within each category, evidence ranges from weak

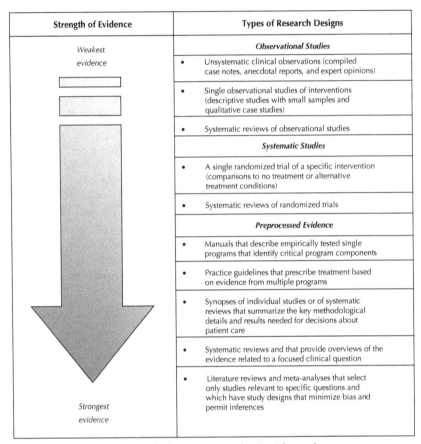

Strength of Evidence	Types of Research Designs
Weakest *evidence*	***Observational Studies***
	• Unsystematic clinical observations (compiled case notes, anecdotal reports, and expert opinions)
	• Single observational studies of interventions (descriptive studies with small samples and qualitative case studies)
	• Systematic reviews of observational studies
	Systematic Studies
	• A single randomized trial of a specific intervention (comparisons to no treatment or alternative treatment conditions)
	• Systematic reviews of randomized trials
	Preprocessed Evidence
	• Manuals that describe empirically tested single programs that identify critical program components
	• Practice guidelines that prescribe treatment based on evidence from multiple programs
	• Synopses of individual studies or of systematic reviews that summarize the key methodological details and results needed for decisions about patient care
	• Systematic reviews and that provide overviews of the evidence related to a focused clinical question
Strongest *evidence*	• Literature reviews and meta-analyses that select only studies relevant to specific questions and which have study designs that minimize bias and permit inferences

Figure 26.1 Types of research designs: strength of evidence for treatment decisions.

to strong in the practitioners' confidence in generalizing such findings to a larger population, or to specific clients.

Observational Studies

It should be clear from Figure 26.1 that social workers have a wide variety of sources of evidence. The most common sources are unsystematic clinical observations, in which researchers simply observe the natural course of events and record the results without trying to influence them (Fraser et al., 2009; Guyatt et al., 2000; Macgowan, 2008). For social workers, this type of evidence includes their compiled case notes, ancillary reports from colleagues and clients, expert opinions, qualitative case studies, and other descriptive studies that have used small samples.

Systematic Studies

In systematic research designs, investigators exert more control over the study variables, using sampling and treatment procedures that enable them to compare samples of participants who had a treatment with participants who did not (Guyatt et al., 2000). Researchers who are able to use these study designs can draw some conclusions about causal relationships between interventions and outcomes. The gold standard of systematic intervention research designs is the randomized clinical trial (RCT) that uses experimental designs (Fraser et al., 2009). Here, participants are randomly assigned to a treatment or control group. When it is impossible to use the direct comparisons of an RCT, quasi-experimental research designs can approximate experimental controls by comparing the group that received a particular treatment to a similar sample of participants who were not exposed to the treatment.

Preprocessed Evidence

New resources are being developed to increase the efficiency of the clinical evidence–seeking process. New journals and database services are now made available that include "preprocessed" evidence (Chorpita, Becker, & Daleiden, 2007; Gibbs & Gambrill, 2003; Guyatt et al., 2000). These reports vary in the level of detail they contain to support practitioners' assessments of the strength of the evidence. The particular usefulness to social workers of each type of information source is summarized next:

- Evidence-based treatment manuals, practice guidelines, and textbook summaries of particular practice areas are designed to support systems of care, to help practitioners identify the tradeoff between treatment costs and benefits, and to guide them in their decisions through the treatment cycle (Galinsky, Terzian, & Fraser, 2006; Henggeler & Schoenwald, 2002).
- Research synopses of individual studies and summaries provide information on key methodological details and results that practitioners need to apply research evidence to treatment decisions of individual patients (Chorpita, Daleiden, & Weisz, 2005; Jobli, Gardner, Hodgson, & Essex, 2015).
- Systematic summaries of research evidence vary in their comprehensiveness and scope, but all include assessments of the methodological rigor of the studies contained in their reviews (Lee, 2015).
- Compilations of primary studies of specific issues are being compiled that include only those with study designs that minimize bias, enabling readers to have confidence in their clinical inference reviews (Jobili, Gradner, Hodgson, & Essex 2015; Lee, 2015).

When they apply research evidence to their treatment decisions, social workers should be mindful of the strengths and limitations of each of these types of evidence (Guyatt et al., 2000). When evidence was not systematically collected, there can be no certainty that it was effective. The apparent benefits of a treatment may be due to other factors: changes in the local environment where the intervention took place, placebo effects, or client's and practitioner's expectations. Experts' opinions may be biased if they have not systematically considered the full range of options and possible outcomes. Observational studies may have larger samples and use treatment and nontreatment control groups, but apparent intervention effects may actually be due to differences in the characteristics of participants in each of the groups. Intervention effectiveness from observational studies is stronger when the effect size of a single group is very large, or when a systematic review of similar interventions shows comparable outcomes. Although evidence from clinical trials is considered the strongest evidence of intervention effectiveness, it, too, has its limitations. Recommendations based on those studies reflect the characteristics of the "average client." Social workers who are able to find evidence based on RCTs should keep in mind that those findings are not always applicable to their individual client's particular circumstances.

Most descriptions of EBP principles reflect their historical roots in the medical profession, where EBP has been more fully articulated (Sackett et al., 1996; Scatterfield, et al., 2009). In the medical context, evidence is used to characterize an individual patient's "clinical status" and guide the selection of treatments and the monitoring of patient progress. In this context, it is possible to use a very high standard of evidence. That is because more laboratories and randomized controlled trials have been done for medical treatments. Research on social interventions rarely achieves this level of rigor, because it is generally impossible to control most of the conditions of the research. This means that social workers must use the best-quality evidence available to them, recognize its limitations, and be conservative in their expectations about its applicability to particular clients or groups.

APPLYING EVIDENCE-BASED PRACTICE PRINCIPLES TO GROUP WORK

Group workers have many opportunities to incorporate research evidence to answer clinical questions that arise as they go through the phases of assessment, treatment planning, and intervention monitoring. Each question requires different kinds of evidence, and, as always, social workers have to adapt their decision-making strategies to the uncertainties inherent in each evidence type (Fouche & Lunt, 2009; Galinsky et al., 2006; Gambrill, 2000; Macgowan, 2008).

How Are Clients' Needs and Strengths Assessed?

Group workers use assessments for two purposes. They need to identify clients with the characteristics that would make them appropriate for a particular group. They must know how to formulate a client-centered answerable question that is relevant to the health and behavioral status of the individual or target population (Council for Training in Evidence-Based Behavioral Practice, 2008; Gibbs & Gambrill, 2003; Macgowan, 2008). This process is described as being tantamount to a well-defined treatment goal. Having done that, they must determine the stage of development or severity of each individual's problems in order to match them to groups composed of members with similar conditions. They begin to collect data and use that evidence from the moment they meet their clients. They draw on client intake information, biopsychosocial assessments, and, possibly, standardized psychological tests (Gambrill, 2006). The accuracy and soundness of this information depend on the reliability and validity of the instruments used to collect data, the client's willingness to disclose truthful information, and on the social worker's skill in doing assessments and integrating information.

Social workers will not always be familiar with the types of problems their clients present. When social workers are uncertain about aspects of presenting problems, they should consult with more experienced colleagues and refer to research for studies describing problem etiology (Gambrill, 2006). The worker can seek out reviews and practice guidelines describing alternative treatments for the client's identified problem and the range of probable outcomes for each type of treatment (Macgowan, 2008). Even experienced workers who specialize in a particular kind of clinical problem should check the research literature periodically to see if any progress has been made in their specialty areas.

After reviewing all the evidence, the social worker must decide whether or not any intervention is necessary. If an intervention seems advisable, his or her next question should be "What intervention or interventions can I use to solve it?" The social worker would then review the treatment alternatives. At this stage, the social worker must also take into account what services are available through the agency and within the community. Although a client may have characteristics that make him or her appropriate for group treatment, research evidence may suggest that individual counseling or psychotropic medication may also be effective. Or a combination of a group and other kinds of individual treatments may be helpful. The information will help the social worker determine the best available treatment (e.g., group, group and some other treatment, or some other treatment rather than a group) for the client.

What evidence could a social worker use to determine whether participation in a treatment group could help remedy the client's problem? Group interventions are most often used to aid clients who are socially isolated, have difficulty with interpersonal relationships, and/or desire to develop their human potential

(Toseland & Rivas, 2012). Groups are contraindicated when clients are intensely private, have problems that would be difficult for them to disclose to others, or behave in ways that other members might find intolerable.

In some settings, clients are court-mandated into specialized treatment groups, such as addiction treatment or anger management. These clients do not have a choice about being in a group, but they can make choices about whether and how they will take advantage of the group experience. A major goal of the social workers is to help these clients understand how they might be helped through the group process (Chovanec, 2009). They can also help clients understand that by cooperating in the group they may be able to reduce the time they stay under court supervision (Toseland & Rivas, 2012). There is evidence that some types of treatment groups can be effective for some involuntary or mandated populations such as cognitive-behavioral groups for multifamily juvenile first offenders (Quinn, Van Dyke, & Kurth, 2002) and psychotherapy groups for incarcerated offenders (Morgan, 2002). By drawing appropriately on this research, social workers can instill hope in their clients for their ultimate success, while sustaining their own optimism about successful outcomes they can achieve when working with challenging groups.

What Are the Desired Outcomes of Treatment?

After determining that the client is appropriate for group treatment, the social worker and client discuss what the client wants from treatment and how a group treatment could help achieve those goals. In general, the goal of treatment is to reduce the risk of harm or increase the number of protective factors—the resources and strategies the client can draw on to manage her or his problem condition most effectively. The client may have multiple concerns, but the social worker needs to clarify which ones can be addressed through group treatment.

Few clinical trials have been conducted to investigate the effectiveness of group treatments. Our knowledge of outcomes is founded primarily on consistent findings of many observational studies (Macgowan, 2008; Marziali, 2008; Pollio, Brower, & Galinsky, 2000). Overall, these findings indicate that treatment groups can alleviate clients' feelings of isolation, restore hope, and, in some cases, empower them (Yalom & Leszcz, 2005). Groups can provide members with accurate information about areas of concern and ways to cope more effectively (Toseland & Rivas, 2012). Members may learn about cognitive self-management and practice new behaviors that improve their communication and social skills. They can develop greater awareness of their psychological processes and insight into their motivations.

What Are the Risks of Each Treatment Alternative?

According to EBP principles, practitioners must help clients understand the possible risks associated with each type of suggested intervention, including costs, the likelihood of no improvement, and possible adverse effects. One reason that treatment groups are such a common type of service is that administrators and program funders view them as economical compared to individual treatments (Crosby & Sabein, 1995), but this advantage must be compared to the relative convenience, effectiveness, and costs of medication or individual therapy.

Systematic studies of group intervention are scarce, making it difficult to judge in advance the likelihood of no improvements or other adverse effects (Macgowan, 2008). Group leaders try to establish guidelines that will assure the safety and well-being of each group member, but members are still at risk of experiencing unpleasant situations such as breach of confidentiality, or that other members may not respond to them in constructive ways (Corey, Corey, & Corey, 2010). For example, a member may be scapegoated or struggle to fit into the group (Toseland & Rivas, 2012). Observational studies suggest that some groups do not improve member psychosocial functioning but, instead, promote conformity and dependency. If a group has a few dominant or very talkative members, the group may focus on their needs and neglect those of more passive members (Yalom & Leszcz, 2005).

Is the Intervention Available to the Client?

Having reached agreement that a group experience is appropriate, the worker and client must then decide which type of group would most likely meet the client's needs and preferences. Their decisions regarding the choice of a group will be based on the client's reasons for joining the group. For example, the client might desire education regarding a particular topic, support in coping with a life situation, to focus on emotional growth or stability, or opportunities for socialization. To make it likelier that the client will receive the full group intervention, the social worker must help the client find a group with the appropriate objectives, and that is held at a convenient location and time. And as much as possible assist the client to deal with challenges (e.g., transportation, child care, etc.) that might prevent him or her from getting to the meetings.

Was the Group Conducted as Planned?

To judge the effectiveness of a group treatment, we must first know whether it was carried off as planned. Researchers refer to this concern as "intervention fidelity." By systematically collecting data from each session (Macgowan, 2008; Meier, 1999; Meier, Galinsky, & Rounds, 1995; Toseland & Rivas, 2012), social workers answer a variety of questions about intervention fidelity. What proportion of members attended all the sessions? To what extent and in what ways did members participate in discussions? Were the topics that were supposed to be covered actually discussed? How many members participated in group activities? Group leaders and supervisors, in consultation with group members, can use this information to decide whether and how the group's content or activities should be modified.

In group treatments, the group simultaneously provides the means for providing a service and the setting in which that service takes place (Vinter, 1985). To do this, the group must be viable as a social entity. Groups that function well usually achieve cohesion. Cohesion is not a stage in itself, but the result of all the forces acting on members that motivate them to remain in the group (Toseland & Rivas, 2012). As groups progress toward cohesiveness over time, members shift psychologically from seeing themselves only as individuals to identifying with the group.

Of the group leader's many functions, one of the most important is to help the group achieve cohesion. To do this, the leader must plan and manage the group so that discussions and activities are aligned with the group's developmental processes (Toseland & Rivas, 2012). As members get to know and trust one another, they become better able to satisfy their individual needs for affiliation and to help each other in achieving their group's goals. They learn to communicate effectively, interact in constructive ways, and take on roles that are essential to reaching optimum treatment outcomes.

If group cohesion is so important in group treatment, what member behaviors should social workers watch for to determine whether their groups are becoming more cohesive? Group leaders should be familiar with the research describing these behaviors (Marziali, 2015). For example, members openly express their satisfaction with the group. They become more willing to invest in and take responsibility for what happens in the group. They take more risks in their self-revelations. Members become more tolerant of individual differences and are better able to resolve conflict using consensus.

Group leaders select activities that they believe will encourage members to engage in these behaviors (Comer & Hirayama, 2008). In keeping with EBP principles, the group leader would also systematically monitor the group's development, documenting his or her observations of each session to determine whether those strategies helped the group to achieve its goals (Toseland & Rivas, 2012). What leaders do in any session of their groups will vary according to the type of the group, its stage of development, and their leadership styles and skill levels (Toseland & Rivas, 2012). Agencies should collect evidence about their social workers' leadership styles so that leaders will be appropriately matched to the type of group (Toseland & Rivas, 2012).

One variant in group formats calls for two co-leaders. From the EBP perspective, the presence of two leaders means that the group benefits from having a second expert. Co-led groups can offer greater flexibility in meeting members' needs, since leaders can decide whether they would be most effective by sharing the primary leader's role or trading off observer and primary leader roles (Toseland & Rivas, 2012). The co-leader's documented observations could offer additional evidence about intervention fidelity and group functioning.

How Did the Client Respond to the Group?

Treatment groups are opportunities for individual members to learn new information, acquire cognitive self-management and social skills, and receive and give support. Assuming that their assignment to the group was appropriate to begin with, the benefits individual members receive from their groups will be related to how regularly they attend and how actively they participate in discussions and activities. Depending on the context of the service, information about individual members' participation in and reactions to their groups can be compiled from group progress/process notes, group member's verbal feedback and completion of questionnaires, and in their individual case records.

How Will Intervention Outcomes Be Assessed?

In group treatments, social workers should assess process *and* behavioral change outcomes. In process evaluations of groups, we ask, "To what extent and in what ways was the group satisfying to group members?" Here, social workers need to distinguish the sources of member satisfaction (the attractiveness to the group, symptom relief, or some combination of both). In keeping with EBP, group workers may want to collaborate with members to help in developing group self-monitoring procedures, including inventing their own measurement instruments and data collection methods. Or members could be consulted about the best ways to administer standardized measures. Members' reactions to being asked to complete particular instruments may help group workers interpret data collected using them. Group leaders need to document members' comments and incorporate this feedback when planning for future sessions and in assessing the manner in which the group influenced data collecting and analysis.

For a group to be viable, the group leader must be reasonably satisfied with the experience, too. In their session report forms, group leaders should document the challenges they faced as well as successes they achieved (Comer, 1999). After their groups are over, leaders can compare their own perceptions of how well the group worked to members' feedback on evaluation surveys. This evidence can be used as the basis for discussions in supervision or other occasions when leaders need to reflect on their practice.

Individual-Level Behavioral Outcomes

We measure individual outcomes when we want to discover whether an intervention had the desired effect on individual group members. Measures used to assess clients before starting the group (baseline) can be readministered just after the group ends to discover whether there were measurable changes in desired behaviors, and the degree and direction of those changes. If social workers want to know how well changes are sustained over time, they can also administer the measure again at prespecified dates.

Most readers should be familiar with these observational approaches to measuring individual client outcomes. They are variants of the single-subject research design commonly taught in social work programs (Bloom, Fischer, & Orme, 2006; Gambrill, 2006; Yegidis, Weinbach, & Meyers, 2011). Although very useful for understanding what happened in a specific group, findings based on this kind of evidence would be considered relatively weak. Due to the small sample size, these findings could not be considered representative of the population, and the group would have to have a very large effect in order to be detectable using statistical analyses.

By examining their agency's best practices, social workers can approximate a larger scale outcome study of their group intervention (Epstein, 2001). This entails reviewing the records of all the clients who participated in past groups and comparing the characteristics and outcomes of the clients who completed a specific kind of group with those who did not receive any group treatment, or with those who did not complete the treatment. Other useful analyses would be to identify the types of clients who have completed their groups and then go on to complete other treatment or service plan goals.

Group-Level Outcomes

When we want to know the overall effectiveness of a group intervention for all members, we can compile and average the differences between pre- and post-group scores of the measures administered to each group member. Here again, however, even if statistically significant changes have occurred, small sample sizes make it unlikely that they would be detected.

Social workers can overcome the problem of small sample size inherent in group treatment outcome studies by using wait-list control designs. This methodology is appropriate when it is impossible to randomly assign members to treatment and nontreatment groups (Rice, 2001). For groups routinely offered in an agency, social workers can take advantage of delays between the time that group members are recruited and when a group starts. In this approach, clients are assessed three times: at intake (Time A), just before the group begins (Time B), and at the end of the group (Time C). The amount and direction of change between Time A and Time B (no-treatment period) is compared to the amount and direction of change between Times B and C. This method enables practitioners to compare individual client outcomes when clients have not received any treatment to the outcomes after they have. Doing wait-list control studies by accumulating data on groups that are routinely offered in an agency results in stronger evidence because findings are based on larger samples.

Thus far, we have devoted the discussion to descriptions of how EBP principles apply to treatment groups. Yet it is important to acknowledge social work with task groups within organizations and social action groups. In these contexts, the desired outcomes of a group could be the team's completion of assigned tasks, or changes in organizations, communities, or policies (Fraser et al., 2009; Hulse-Killacky, Killacky, & Donigian, 2000; Toseland & Rivas, 2012). Although the application of EBP principles to task groups is beyond the scope of this chapter, social workers in macropractice settings should also be alert to the ways they could use evidence systematically. They can apply EBP principles by drawing on administrative data (Meier & Usher, 1998) and research in social psychology on social organizations (Seekins, Mathews, & Fawcett, 1984). This evidence can be helpful when deciding how to form teams and committees, facilitate team decisions, monitor team progress toward the achievement of their tasks, or assess the impact of their collective efforts within organizations, and communities, or on policy making.

THE INTERVENTION RESEARCH PARADIGM AND EVIDENCE-BASED PRACTICE

Prevailing trends in social work education are moving toward a paradigm that will help future social workers think critically about the application of practice-relevant scientific evidence in practice situations (Howard, McMillen, & Pollio, 2003; Mullen, Bellamy, Bledsoe, & Francois, 2007). Yet as they begin working toward becoming evidence based, they may still encounter barriers instead of facilitative conditions and gaps in the available information. In the authors' experiences, MSW students are becoming familiar with the concept of evidence-based practice. However, they have not fully achieved this task and still need help in developing and enhancing skills needed to use evidence competently (Hepworth, Rooney, Rooney, Strom-Gottfried, & Larsen, 2010; Peterson, Phillips, Bacon, & Machunda, 2011). Moreover, once on the job, they are unlikely to get experience collecting data systematically or using research evidence.

At present, social workers who are interested in applying EBP principles will find few reports of systematic research or treatment guidelines that apply directly to the kinds of work they do. Group workers, in particular, will have difficulty obtaining systematic evidence on the efficacy of small-group interventions. Most articles in social group work journals are devoted to descriptions of group programming and group dynamics. Outcome studies are relatively rare. Fewer still use experimental or quasi-experimental designs. Experimental research studies need standardized protocols. Because of the nature of the group's developmental processes, it is difficult to maintain such high levels of control. Few studies achieve the statistical power needed to detect treatment effects, in part because researchers have problems obtaining and retaining large enough samples.

Given the scarcity of clinical trials on group interventions and the difficulty in conducting them, what can group workers do to systematically develop evidence to demonstrate the feasibility and value of their groups? One alternative is to employ a research methodology that better accommodates the realities of social work with groups in practice situations. The intervention research (IR) paradigm offers such an alternative. Rothman and Thomas developed the IR paradigm to provide an integrated perspective for understanding, developing, and examining the feasibility and effectiveness of innovative human service interventions (Fraser et al., 2009; Rothman & Thomas, 1994). Because IR methodologies take the uncontrollability of practice settings into account, this paradigm is more practical for testing innovative interventions than the social science research paradigm (Rothman & Thomas, 1994; Soydan, 2010). A recent publication, *Intervention Research* by Fraser, Richman, Galinsky, and Day (2009), builds on Rothman and Thomas's work by integrating their own perspective and experiences in developing a school-based intervention. It details the *Making Choices* program, an intervention guided by principles of IR and is a specific example of its application in social work.

The conventional social science paradigm ascribes the greatest value to evidence from "black box" experimental studies that allow researchers to say with some confidence that changes in behavior are associated with participation in the intervention and not some other factor. They pay less attention to the intervention's specific mechanisms that may have caused those changes. The IR Paradigm is founded on the principles of industrial research and development. In this context, interventions are seen as "social inventions" that must be systematically pilot-tested and modified until they work as planned under specified conditions. Here, an intervention's reliability and validity are primarily defined in terms of its feasibility under practice conditions (Thomas, 1985). In social work intervention research, social workers systematically test various aspects of their interventions using small-scale studies. Such pilot studies require relatively few resources. Early studies are conducted with abbreviated or simulated versions of the intervention and trial runs of data collection instruments. This design and development process (D&D) allows researcher/practitioners to determine whether their interventions are feasible and promising enough to be worth investing in full-scale field trials (Table 26.1).

In EBP, social workers are not expected to be researchers but rather to draw upon research syntheses in making their treatment decisions (Fraser, 2003). In developmental intervention research, social workers are integral members of research teams. As in EBP, the IR approach embodies a collaborative approach. Practitioners and researchers work as a team, with group members providing vital feedback at many points in the intervention's development. Practitioners may take the lead in identifying problems about their groups that need study. Alternatively, researchers, from within or outside the agency, identify problems through their surveys of the literature and ask practitioners to collaborate in developing new groups. Researchers often (but not necessarily) take the lead in reviewing the research literature and bringing information (or the lack thereof) about population and community characteristics, assessment methods, treatment alternatives, and monitoring strategies back for the team's consideration. People who are members of the intervention's target population may be asked to participate in the focus groups or other simulations to obtain their perspectives

Table 26.1 Intervention Research (IR) Design and Development Activities for Group Interventions

Project Design and Development Stage	Activities	
	Refining an Existing Group	*Inventing a New Group*
Stage 1: Identify the problem	Identify the aspects of the current group that are problematic.	Select the problem to remedy. Identify a range of possible strategies for achieving desired outcomes. Is a group a plausible intervention?
Stage 2: Characterize the problem	Conduct literature reviews and analyze administrative data. • *To what extent and in what ways have the characteristics of the client population changed since the group was first offered?* Determine whether there has been new research to indicate that: • *the content or structure of the group should be modified, or* • *there are better ways to evaluate the group's effectiveness.*	Conduct literature reviews to see what researchers have done to determine the prevalence and severity of the problem, its causes, and its etiology. Consult with professional experts and other people who have lived with the problem to determine whether there are other perspectives not found in the research literature. Identify criteria for an appropriate and effective intervention.
	Integrate new information into the intervention design.	
Stage 3: Specify the elements of the intervention	Identify the changes to be made in the scope and sequence of the existing group's discussions and activities.	Decide on the scope and sequence of discussion content and the activities of the new group.
	Modify or design new materials and activity plans.	Design materials and activity plans.
	Conduct feasibility studies of pilot version of the group.	
Stage 4: Pilot testing	Modify or develop procedures for training and supervising group leaders.	
	Modify or develop procedures for monitoring group processes to insure intervention fidelity.	
	Select or develop evaluation instruments and satisfaction surveys.	
	Analyze pilot-study data to identify the intervention's strengths and flaws.	
	Modify group designs based on these findings to insure that the intervention is as accessible and satisfying as possible for participants.	
	If the pilot study indicates that the intervention is feasible, conduct further small-scale studies to insure that all elements of the intervention can be implemented reliably under real-life conditions.	

(continued)

Table 26.1 Continued

Project Design and Development Stage	Activities	
	Refining an Existing Group	Inventing a New Group
Stage 5: Experimental field testing	Conduct full-scale, experimental, or quasi-experimental field tests of the interventions.	
Stage 6: Dissemination of information about the project	Present preliminary findings from early studies at conferences and in publications.	
	Make available manuals and other materials developed along the way to other researchers and practitioners so they can use them to learn how to implement the intervention.	
	Present and publish on findings from the full-scale field tests.	

about whether and how the group works. Researchers and practitioners collaborate in developing the programming of the group's content, selecting activities, and developing ways to monitor group leader behavior and group development. Once the group is under way, practitioners and group members give feedback periodically on how the intervention design works. If it is not going well, researchers and practitioners work together to modify it to make positive outcomes more likely.

   In design and development research on groups, group members are asked frequently for feedback that may, on occasion, prompt the research team to make "midstream" alterations in the group protocol in order to keep the group viable (Comer, 2004; Meier, 1999). Practitioners/researchers are trained to view such modifications not as failures, but as opportunities to extend the understanding about interventions to new populations or conditions (Comer, 2004). At the end of the group, members are assessed to see if their participation in the group helped them achieve their desired outcomes. In addition, members and practitioners are surveyed to find out how satisfied they were with the group experience, and to allow them to offer suggestions about how to improve it. Practitioners and group members' suggestions are incorporated into each successive pilot study, thereby insuring the intervention's acceptability, appropriateness, and validity.

RESEARCH ON GROUP INTERVENTIONS USING DEVELOPMENTAL INTERVENTION RESEARCH METHODOLOGIES

There have been few published reports of studies that explicitly incorporated D&D strategies to develop innovative group interventions (Comer, 2004). The studies that have been done used D&D procedures to invent groups for varied purposes using face-to-face and technology-mediated communication channels. Face-to-face groups have been developed for people coping with chronic pain and sickle cell disease (Subramanian, 1991) and psychoeducational groups for HIV-affected people (Pomeroy, Rubin, & Walker, 1995). Telephone support groups have been developed for people with AIDS (Rounds et al., 1995), family caregivers of people with AIDS (Meier et al., 1995), and dementia caregivers (Lee, 2015). Meier has developed professionally facilitated, Internet-mediated support groups for social workers suffering from job stress (Meier, 2000b) and spouses of survivors of colon cancer (Meier, 2003).

In these studies, researchers used the early stages of pilot testing to investigate the appropriateness of specific elements of their research and intervention designs, such as recruitment (Meier, 2000a, 2003); data collection methods (Meier, 1999, 2003; Rounds et al., 1995); participants' comfort levels with the telecommunications technology used to conduct the interventions (Meier, 1999, 2003; Rounds et al., 1995); group discussion formats (Comer, 1999; Meier, 1999, 2003; Pomeroy et al., 1995; Subramanian, 1991); group development issues (Comer, 2004; Comer, Meier, & Galinsky, 1999,2004; Meier, 1999, 2003); and participant satisfaction (Meier, 2003; Meier et al., 1995, 1999; Rounds et al., 1995). All these researchers used findings from their preliminary studies to improve their research designs and data collection techniques, and to clarify and extend intervention models.

DESIGNING AND DEVELOPING GROUP INTERVENTION MODELS

Practitioner/researchers can use the D&D procedures prescribed by the IR paradigm as a map to guide them in refining existing groups or developing new ones. But the map is not the territory. As with any journey, travelers may have to make unexpected detours not shown on the map before they arrive at their destinations. The stages shown in Table 26.1 are as if they were discrete and linear, but they are often cyclical and iterative. Practitioner/researchers should expect to make many modifications in their plans for their groups before completing any study. Practitioner/researchers often discover along the way that components in their interventions or their research designs need to be changed. In Meier's early studies of facilitated Internet support groups, for example, she discovered repeatedly that using the Internet as her only communication channel to recruit members was neither effective nor efficient (Meier, 1999, 2003). These findings led her to conclude that, in future studies, she should investigate whether the combination of face-to face and online recruitment strategies will work better. In Comer's (1999) study of a face-to-face cognitive-behavioral group intervention for African Americans with sickle cell anemia and depression, she discovered that group members felt the self-management

tasks (recording and maintaining journals about their activities) were too burdensome. Because group leader observations and interim measures of members'
depression levels showed positive trends, members were allowed to stop doing
some of these tasks.

Whether the goal is to improve an existing group or develop a new one, re-
searcher/practitioners who use the IR design and developmental procedures go
through similar steps. The greatest difference in procedures for these two types
of studies will arise during the early stages of problem identification and definition that precede the actual design or redesign of the intervention model. Table
26.1 summarizes the different starting points of their associated activities and
(in stages 4 through 6 at the bottom of the table) shows where the tasks for both
types of projects converge.

Modifying an Existing Group

Much of the preliminary work of modifying a group involves fieldwork within
the agency. If a group has been offered as a service for a long time, researcher/
practitioners should consult coworkers and supervisors and agency records to
reconstruct the group's history to answer the following questions: "When was
the group first offered?" "Whom was it intended to serve?" "What changes have
occurred that prompted the decision to modify the group?" The research team
uses the information to clearly define the problem. Has it become more difficulty
to recruit and retain participants? If group leaders are reporting problems, what
kinds of difficulties are they encountering? Are group members reporting low
levels of satisfaction? Are group members not achieving their desired therapeutic
outcomes? Answering these questions may illuminate several, interrelated problems that will impel changes in the intervention design.

For example, problems may arise from group composition. A group may stop
working well if it was initiated to serve one type of client but was later opened
to clients with other needs. In constructing the developmental history of the
group, the research team needs to examine client records to see whether recent
groups were still composed of members from the original target group. If not, the
practitioner/researcher team may suggest reviewing treatment alternatives for the
original target population. Alternatively, they may decide that their intervention
research studies should focus on developing a group adapted to greater diversity
among members.

As group members and group leaders change, so does group structure. Before
attempting to modify an existing group, practitioner/researchers must have a
clear understanding about how group leaders are running their groups. The research team reviews whatever documentation about the group is available and
consults with the leaders. Group leaders are asked to describe the scope and sequence of the discussions and planned activities, their clinical rationales, and

how the selection and sequencing of activities are related to group developmental processes. The team also needs to know what group leaders think works well—or badly—and their recommendations for changes. If several group leaders are running the same kind of group, the team may also decide to examine the evidence to see how similar or different the groups are in content and dynamics. Similarly, the team may review whatever data are available about member satisfaction. Afterward, the team may decide to tap members' reactions to the group by conducting surveys or focus groups.

Practitioner/researchers must also discover what kinds of data have been collected on the group itself, and whether they have been collected systematically. For example, they need to find out whether and how intervention fidelity has been monitored. Are reports on each session required as well as notes in individual client records? If so, what aspects of the session are documented? When and how is this information reviewed? If group leaders or the agency do these kinds of reviews, how are these findings used in ongoing decisions about how the group should be run?

The practitioner/researcher team goes through a similar process to discover whether the client behaviors that the group is supposed to change are systematically assessed. If they have, when and how are these assessments administered? If standardized instruments have been used, are they reliable? Were they normed on the group's target population? Are they valid for use with this particular group, in that items on the instruments tap into the group's content?

Besides learning about the group intervention as it is currently used, the research team gathers the information they will need to help them decide how to modify it. As with EBP, they delve into the current research to update their understanding of the characteristics of the group's target population, the root causes and prevalence of the specific problem, the range of interventions available, and the expected outcomes. To focus this part of the search, practitioner/researchers may also decide to consult with experts in the field.

When they review local census and agency services data, the researcher/practitioner team may find that the community's racial or ethnic composition or its economic health has changed since the group was first offered. Alternatively, recent research on particular health and mental health conditions may suggest new causes of those problems or new opportunities for intervention. Updated information about client and problem characteristics may lead practitioner/researchers to recommend changes in group discussion content or activities. It may turn out that research indicates that a group intervention is no longer considered the most appropriate intervention for a given condition, or that combination therapy regimens, such as groups and antidepressant medications, offer the most benefits. If there are no standardized baseline and outcome measures being used, or the ones that are do not appear to be reliable and valid, the literature review should include a search for better measures.

Developing a New Group

In the previous scenario, the agency had already identified a problem and offered a group intervention to remedy it. Practitioner/researchers were prompted to modify the group because it was not working well in some way. In this second scenario, researcher/practitioners start from scratch, with the realization that there is a problem to be remedied. They must do preliminary investigations to determine its prevalence and severity in the community. Next, they must decide that the problem is significant enough to warrant investing the time and resources needed to develop and implement a new service. Finally, they must decide, based on research, problem prevalence and root causes, agency resources, and client preferences, that a group is the most appropriate intervention.

Designing and Developing the Group Intervention Model

In D&D Stages 1 and 2, practitioner/researchers use EBP strategies to decide on the group format and the information to be conveyed in their groups. In Stage 3, they begin to focus concretely on what group members and group leaders will discuss and do in each session of their groups, coordinating them with the parallel psychosocial group development processes. Group workers will be relying largely on their practice wisdom in this aspect of intervention design. Although experience tells us that the group is the vehicle for individual change through the support and challenge group members give each other, there is very little evidence available to help social workers understand how these processes and dynamics influence the group's outcomes (Macgowan, 2008). Thus, group workers can make important contributions to our understanding of these relationships by systematically collecting evidence and reporting on their experiences with their groups in intervention research studies.

In Stage 3, existing program content is modified or new elements are created. For example, handouts used in sessions may be modified or new ones developed; videos, games, or other activities are selected; and group leaders are trained to use them. Once all these elements are in place, the members are recruited for the initial pilot group. Because many aspects of the group are still untested, such pilots are often shortened versions of the full-scale version. These pilots are opportunities to get participant reactions to the discussion content, activities, and written materials, and data collection instruments. At this stage, practitioners and researchers are interested in getting a tentative answer to the feasibility question, "Can this group be conducted as planned?"

In Stage 4, practitioners/researchers draw on their experiences implementing the group to identify the group's strengths and flaws. If recruiting was not as successful as anticipated, service marketing and recruiting procedures may have to be changed or intensified. Group leaders may discover other things they need to know to be effective facilitators. If they are receiving supervision, they may also learn that a different kind of supervisory support will be needed. Feedback from participants may reveal that they would like a different type, number, or range of activities. Staff and researcher discussions on all these different issues can lead to decisions about what procedures should be modified, with the aim of making the group accessible to participants and the experience as satisfying as possible. If the intervention protocol was changed in response to member feedback, the data collection instruments used to assess outcomes may no longer tap into the group content, and new ones will need to be selected for the next pilot study (Meier, 1999).

Given all the ways that the intervention research plans can go awry, practitioner/researcher teams need to plan for multiple pilot tests of their groups to discover the most workable combination of elements for the research design and the intervention. Practitioner/researchers take advantage of opportunities to pilot different aspects of the group. They can try things out in the groups they run themselves, or collaborate with group workers whom they supervise. Sometimes they can find small amounts of funding to conduct small studies. With each succeeding pilot, the evidence about what works accumulates.

In Stage 4, practitioner/researchers draw on their experiences implementing the group to identify the group's strengths and flaws. If recruiting was not as successful as anticipated, service marketing and recruiting procedures may have to be changed or intensified. Group leaders may discover other things they need to know to be effective facilitators. If they are receiving supervision, they may also learn that a different kind of supervisory support will be needed. Feedback from participants may reveal that they would like a different type, number, or range of activities. Staff and researcher discussions on all these different issues can lead to decisions about what procedures should be modified, with the aim of making the group accessible to participants and the experience as satisfying as possible. If the intervention protocol was changed in response to member feedback, the data collection instruments used to assess outcomes may no longer tap into the group content, and new ones will need to be selected for the next pilot study (Meier, 1999).

Given all the ways that the intervention research plans can go awry, practitioner/researcher teams need to plan for multiple pilot tests of their groups to discover the most workable combination of elements for the research design and the intervention. Practitioner/researchers take advantage of opportunities to pilot different aspects of the group. They can try things out in the groups they run themselves or collaborate with group workers whom they supervise. Sometimes they can find small amounts of funding to conduct small studies. With each succeeding pilot, the evidence about what works accumulates.

Stage 5 calls for practitioner/researchers to conduct full-scale, quasi-experimental evaluations of intervention effectiveness. They only proceed to this stage after multiple pilot studies confirm that the intervention is feasible under practice conditions. Obviously, field testing for IR with groups can only be done if the funding and institutional resources for implementing a larger study are available.

In Stage 6, practitioner/researchers disseminate what they are learning about their interventions. In Table 26.1, dissemination is shown as the last step. Typically, researchers present findings from outcome studies of their projects at conference presentations and scholarly publications when the full-scale field testing has been completed. Researchers following the IR paradigm will also present and publish articles on preliminary findings from early studies. They also make available manuals and other training materials developed along the way, which other practitioners can use to learn how to implement the intervention.

RESOURCES

Evidence-based practice and IR both call for social workers to go beyond their daily work routines, to learn more about their clients and interventions and how to improve their practice. Practically speaking, social workers face barriers that may deter them from even beginning. Heavy workloads are common. Many may not have the skills (Gambrill, 1999) or the practical experience (Kirk & Penka, 1992) to do either. Where can social workers acquire the knowledge they need to understand EBP and IR processes? How can they be efficient in their information searches? How can they get help to do IR with their groups? In this final section, we describe how to find help in understanding the principles of EBP, IR design, and development processes as they apply to group work.

Much of the early debate on EBP has taken place within the medical profession. Currently, social work researchers have also begun to express their views on the value and the applicability of EBP principles in social work (Fraser, 2003; Gambrill, 1999; Gibbs & Gambrill, 2002; Pollio, 2002). As with all innovations, the response has been mixed. One of the strongest critiques has been in response to EBP's emphasis on the value of evidence from clinically controlled trials to identify best practices. Social worker critics have argued that this standard of evidence is inappropriate for social work, particularly for group work, where it is rarely available. Moreover, the uncontrollability of practice settings makes it difficult to replicate experimentally validated interventions.

In this chapter we have advocated for more realistic ways for social workers to incorporate research evidence in their decisions regarding the use of groups, and for systematically modifying or inventing groups. Online databases make the search for information about research evidence for social work practice more available through their computers. Social workers who do not have adequate access to the Internet or the skills to use online databases themselves should contact the libraries in their communities to see what resources and help they can offer. The impetus for EBP is leading to investments in the information infrastructure, such as the ongoing professional training and development of knowledge bases needed to support it. All of these developments will make it progressively easier for social workers to know about and take advantage of the evidence that exists when making treatment decisions. It will also support their efforts to conduct research on their groups.

Training to Assess Research Evidence and Use Practice Guidelines

Social workers seeking to learn how to assess research evidence can find lots of help online. For example, the Center for Health Evidence (http://www.cche. net/) and the Netting the Evidence (http://www.shef. ac.uk/shar/ir/netting/ first.html) Web sites provide instructions and tools for appraising research evidence. The National Institutes of Health are funding a network of Evidence-Based Practice Centers to review and summarize research for a variety of medical problems, including mental health and substance abuse (http://www.ahcpr. gov/clinic/epcix.htm).

Online Resources for Health and Mental Health Research Evidence

All social workers with Internet access can now delve into numerous health and behavioral sciences research databases. One of the most fully developed is the PubMed Web site (http://www.ncbi.nlm.nih.gov/PubMed/), a service of the National Institutes of Health's National Library of Medicine. This database provides access to over 19 million MEDLINE citations dating back to the mid-1960s and additional life science journals, and links to other Web sites where users can download full-text versions of many articles listed in the database. SCOPUS covers more than 40 million records in life, health, and physical sciences, and over 5,000 in social science and humanities (http://info. scopus.com/)

Social workers who have graduated in the past 10 years will also be familiar with other social work–specific computerized or online databases, such as Family and Society Studies Worldwide, PsychInfo, Social Work Abstracts, Social Services Abstracts, and Sociological Abstract. The Cochrane Collaborative offers practitioners free online access to a database (C2SPECTR) of publications containing over 10,000 randomized and possibly randomized trials in education, social work and welfare, and criminal justice. It includes a methodology for conducting systematic reviews of research on psychosocial interventions (see The Campbell Collaboration, http://www.campbellcollaboration.org/). It supports users and reviewers by including useful information about study methods, outcomes, and the rigor of the research designs. These databases are usually not available over the Internet to users who are unaffiliated with a university or college, but they are likely to be available through university libraries. Some of these databases include downloadable full-text versions of the publications. By reviewing the abstracts, users can select and receive many of these articles electronically. University libraries may also be able to offer social workers access to the Health and Psychosocial Instruments database, which provides information on measurement instruments, including questionnaires, interview schedules, checklists, index measures, coding schemes/manuals, rating scales, projective techniques, vignettes/scenarios, and tests, developed for use in the fields of health, psychosocial sciences, and organizational behavior.

Computerized databases make it easy to identify many potentially relevant articles. The challenge is to determine the key research studies that address important questions and use the most rigorous research designs. In PubMed and the other databases mentioned earlier, it is possible to limit the scope of the search results by specifying the topic of interest and "reviews" as the publication type. This search strategy will select only review articles on the specified topic. Although some of the databases may not be fully developed, they do provide knowledge that might be useful to social workers interested in group interventions. Reviewers might not be able to draw conclusions about the efficacy of all group interventions they could find published studies using clinical trials. In most studies, sample sizes were small, or the quality of design and reporting was inadequate. Although these conditions might not be as helpful for group workers who want to be "EBP compliant," these sources provide examples of how to conceptualize, develop, and implement IR projects and guidelines so they can create evidence about their interventions.

Collaborative Relationships With Researchers

Collaboration is strongly valued in EBP and the IR paradigm. Many practitioners know how to design a group intervention, but they may feel less confident about their ability to conduct research on their interventions or analyze data. By developing collaborative relationships with colleges and universities, practitioners can gain access to needed expertise and resources that university faculty and students can provide. Such partnerships between the faculty and practitioners can benefit both groups. The faculty member might wish to collaborate with the practitioner in applying for research grants to develop group interventions or study group outcomes. For social workers, this would also provide opportunities to strengthen their EBP skills. They could get expert advice about what information to look for and how to do efficient literature searches. Social workers would be exposed to role models who could demonstrate and coach them in how to assess research evidence and apply it to the design of future projects and interventions. If these collaborative efforts result in research projects, social workers on research teams could also get experience in selecting appropriate measures and analyzing data.

Collaborative Relationships With Schools of Social Work

In agencies where social work students have field placements, students can be asked to participate in these collaborative research arrangements. Students who chose to join the team would have opportunities to learn about intervention design and development in the context of group work. For example, if the agency decides to modify a group, students could be asked to compile the information about the group's developmental history within the agency, or data on changes in community, population, and client characteristics. Students could help practitioners update their knowledge by identifying alternative interventions and new assessment tools. In the process, students would get to practice their skills with online research databases. Because design and development work with group interventions usually extends over several years, these projects could provide an opportunity for a number of students to gain knowledge and training in IR research methodologies on a single project. Meanwhile, the agency would also benefit from the accumulation of data from a larger sample that would enable them to conduct rigorous analyses of their group's outcomes.

CONCLUSION

All scientific work is incomplete—whether it be observational or experimental. All scientific work is liable to be upset or modified by advancing knowledge. This does not confer upon us the freedom to ignore the knowledge we already have or to postpone the action that it appears to demand at a given time (Hill, 1965, p. 300).

This chapter discusses the importance of EBP in social work practice and some of the advances made toward its adaptation to the social work practice standards. It provides basic elements of EBP and ways of discerning the quality of research evidence. Guidelines are suggested for the application of EBP in practice situations. Evidence-based social work with groups is seen as being most helpful to people in group treatment. Emphasis is placed on intervention research as an alternate research methodology that is uniquely suited to the development or modification of treatment strategies in practice situations. Gaps in our knowledge about what makes social work group interventions work make using EBP and IR with groups challenging. We have much to learn about who benefits the most from what groups and under what conditions. Clearly, filling those gaps using intervention research methodologies will be time consuming and energy intensive. Yet social workers' efforts to incorporate evidence in their treatment decisions and in conducting developmental research on groups are also intrinsically valuable. When they seek out the best available evidence to back their clinical judgments, or develop pilot studies on their groups, they are mining the knowledge bases that can help them better understand the people and communities they serve and the range of possible treatments they can offer. Moreover, it is judicious to use our best practice techniques to make a difference in the lives of the peoples we serve.

REFERENCES

Bloom, M., Fischer, J., & Orme, J. (2006). *Evaluating practice* (5th ed.). Boston, MA: Allyn & Bacon.

Bretton, E., & Macgowan (2009). A critical review of adolescent substance abuse group treatments. *Journal of Evidence-based Social Work, 6*(3), 217–243.

Cannata, E., & Hoge, M. (2012). Higher education reform on evidence-based practices: The Connecticut Transformation Initiative, *Report on Emotional & Behavioral Disorders in Youth, 12*(1), 18–23.

Chorpita, B., Daleiden, E., & Weisz, J. (2005). Identifying and selecting the common elements of evidence-based interventions: A distillation and matching model. *Mental Health Services Research, 7*(1), 5–20.

Chorpita, B., Becker, K., & Daleiden, E. (2007). Understanding the common elements of evidence-based practice: Misconceptions and clinical examples. *Journal of American Academy of Child and Adolescent Psychiatry, 46*(5), 647–652.

Chovanec, M. (2009). Involuntary clients. In A. Gitterman & R. Salmon (Eds.), *Encyclopedia of social work with groups* (pp.284–286). New York, NY: Routledge.

Comer, E. (2004). Integrating the health and mental health needs of the chronically ill: A group for individuals with depression and sickle cell disease. *Social Work and Health Care, 38*(4), 57–76.

Comer, E., & Hirayama, K. (2008). Activity use and selection. In A. Gitterman & R. Salmon (Eds.), *Encyclopedia of social work with groups* (pp. 62–64). New York, NY: Routledge.

Comer, E., Meier, A., & Galinsky, M. J. (2001, October). *Studying innovations in group work practice: Applications of the intervention research paradigm.* Paper presented at the American Association for the Advancement of Social Work with Groups, 21st Annual Symposium, Denver, CO.

Comer, E., Meier, A., & Galinsky, M. J. (2004). Development of innovative group work practice using the Intervention Research Paradigm: Two cases. *Social Work, 49*(2), 250–260.

Comer, E. E. (1999). *Effects of a cognitive behavioral group intervention on the reduction of depressive symptoms in individuals with sickle cell disease.* Unpublished doctoral dissertation, University of North Carolina, Chapel Hill, NC.

Corey, M., Corey, G., & Corey, C. (2010). *Groups: Process and practice* (8th ed.). Belmont, CA: Thomson Higher Education.

Crosby, G., & Sabein, J. E. (1995). Developing and marketing time-limited groups. *Psychiatric Services, 47*(1), 7–8.

Council for Training in Evidence-Based Behavioral Practice. (2008). Definition and competencies for evidence-based behavioral practice (EBBP). Retrieved from http://www.ebbp.org/documents/EBBP_competencies.pdf

Council on Social Work Education. (2008). *Educational policy and accreditation standards.* Alexandria, VA: Council on Social Work Education.

Epstein, I. (2001). Using available clinical information in practice-based research: Mining for silver while dreaming for gold. *Social Work in Health Care, 33*(3/4), 15–32.

Fouche, C., & Lunt, N. (2009). Using groups to advance social work practice-based research social work with groups. *Social Work with Groups, 32*, 47–63. doi:10.1080/01609510802314659

Fraser, M. (2003). Intervention research in social work: A basis for evidence-based practice and practice guidelines. In A. Rosen & E. K. Proctor (Eds.), *Developing practice guidelines of social work interventions: Issues, methods and research agenda* (pp. 17–36). New York, NY: Columbia University Press.

Fraser, M., Richman, J., Galinsky, M., & Day, S. (2009). *Intervention research.* New York, NY: Oxford University Press.

Galinsky, M., Terzian, M., & Fraser, M. (2006). The art of group work practice using manualized curricula. *Social Work Practice with Groups, 29*(1), 11–26.

Gambrill, E. (1999). Evidence-based practice: An alternative to authority-based practice. *Families in Society, 89*(4), 341–350.

Gambrill, E. (2000). The role of critical thinking in evidence-based social work. In P. Allen-Meares & C. Garvin (Eds.), *The handbook of social work direct practice* (pp. 43–63). Thousand Oaks, CA: Sage.

Gambrill, E. (2006). *Social work practice: A critical thinker's guide* (2nd ed.). New York, NY: Oxford University Press.

Gibbs, L., & Gambrill, E. (2002). Evidence-based practice: Counterarguments to objections. *Research on Social Work Practice, 12*(3), 452–476.

Gibbs, L., & Gambrill, E. (2003). *Evidence-based practice for the helping professions.* Pacific Grove, CA: Thompson Learning.

Greif, G., & Ephross, P. (2011). *Group work with populations at risk* (3rd ed.). New York, NY: Oxford University Press.

Guyatt, G. H., Haynes, B., Jaescheke, R. Z., Cook, D. J., Green, L., Nayolor, C. D., . . . Richardson, W. S. (2000). EBM: Principles of applying users' guides to patient care. *Centre for Health Evidence.* Retrieved from http://www.cche.net/userguide/applying.asp

Henggeler, S., & Schoenwald, S. (2002). Treatment manuals: Necessary, but far from sufficient. *Clinical Psychology: Science and Practice, 9*(4), 419–420.

Hepworth, D., Rooney, G., Rooney, G., Strom-Gottfried, K., & Larsen, J. (2010). *Direct social work practice* (8th ed.). Belmont, CA: Brooks/Cole.

Hill, A. B. (1965). The environment and disease: Association or causation? *Proceedings of the Royal Society of Medicine, 58*, 295–300.

Howard, M., Himle, J., Jenson, J., & Vaughn, M. (2009). Revisioning social work clinical education: Recent developments in relation to evidence-based practice. *Journal of Evidence-Based Social Work, 6*, 256–273. doi:10:1080/15433710802686963

Howard, M., McMillen, C., & Pollio, E. E. (2003). Teaching evidence-based practice: Toward a new paradigm for social work education. *Research in Social Work Practice, 13*(2), 234–259.

Hulse-Killacky, D., Killacky, J., & Donigian, J. (2000). *Making task groups work in your world.* Upper Saddle River, NJ: Merrill Prentice Hall.

Jobli, E., Gardner, S., Hodgson, A., & Essex, A. (2015). The review of new evidence five years later: SAMHSA's national registry of evidence-based programs and practices. *Evaluation and Program Planning, 48*, 117–123.

Kirk, S., & Penka, C. E. (1992). Research utilization and MSW education: A decade of progress? In A. J. Grasso & I. Epstein (Eds.), *Research utilization in the social services* (pp. 497–421). New York, NY: Haworth Press.

Lee, E. (2015). Do technology-based support groups reduce care burden among dementia caregivers? A review. *Journal of Evidence-informed Social Work, 1*, 1–4. doi:10.1080/15433714.2014.930362

Macgowan, M. (2008). *A guide to evidence-based group work.* New York, NY: Oxford University Press.

Marziali E. (2008). Developing evidence for an internet-based psychotherapeutic group intervention. *Journal of Evidence-based Social Work, 3*(3/4), 149–165. doi:10.1300/J394v03n03_11

Mathiesen, S., & Hohman, M. (2013). Revalidation of an evidence-based practice scale for social work. *Journal of Social Work Education, 49*, 451–460. doi:10:1080/10437797.2013.796793

Meier, A. (1999). *A multi-method evaluation of a computer-mediated, stress management support group for social workers: Feasibility, process, and effectiveness.* Unpublished doctoral dissertation, University of North Carolina, Chapel Hill.

Meier, A. (2000a). Offering social support via the Internet: A case study of an online support group for social workers. *Journal of Technology in Human Services, 17*(2/3), 237–266.

Meier, A. (2000b). Offering social support via the Internet: A case study of an online support group for social workers. In J. Finn & G. Holden (Eds.), *Human services online: A new arena for service delivery* (pp. 237–266). New York, NY: Haworth Press.

Meier, A. (2003). *Colon cancer caregivers' online support group project: Research feasibility, and intervention feasibility and outcomes* (Final report). Chapel Hill: University of North Carolina, Lineberger Comprehensive Cancer Center.

Meier, A., Galinsky, M. J., & Rounds, K. (1995). Telephone support groups for caregivers of persons with AIDS. In M. J. Galinsky & J. H. Schopler (Eds.), *Support groups: Current perspectives on theory and practice* (pp. 99–108). Binghamton, NY: Haworth Press.

Meier, A., & Usher, C. L. (1998). New approaches to program evaluation. In R. L. Edwards & J. A. Yankey (Eds.), *Skills for effective nonprofit organizations* (pp. 371–405). Washington, DC: NASW Press.

Morgan, R. D. (2002). Group psychotherapy with incarcerated offenders: A research synthesis. *Group Dynamics, 6*(3), 203–218.

Mullen, E. J., Bellamy, S. E., Bledsoe, S., & Francois, J. J. (2007). Teaching evidence-based practice. *Research on Social Work Practice, 17*, 574–582.

National Association of Social Workers. (1996). *Code of ethics.* Washington, DC: National Association of Social Workers.

Ngo, V., Langley, A., Nadeem, E., Escudero, P., & Stein, B. (2008). Providing evidence-based practice to ethnically diverse youths: Examples from the cognitive behavioral intervention for trauma in school programs. *Journal of the American Academy of Child and Adolescent Psychiatry, 47*(8), 858–862.

O'Hare, T. (2015). *Evidence-based practices for social workers* (2nd ed.). Chicago, IL: Lyceum Books.

Parrish, D., & Rubin, A. (2012). Social workers' orientations toward the evidence-based practice process: A comparison with psychologists and licensed marriage and family therapists. *Social Work, 57*(3), 201–210. doi:10.1093/sw/sws016

Peterson, S., Phillips, A., Bacon, S., & Machunda, Z. (2011). Teaching evidence-based practice at the BSW level: An effective capstone project. *Journal of Social Work Education, 47*, 509–524. doi:10.5175/JSWE.2011.200900129

Pollio, D. E. (2002). The evidence-based social worker. *Social Work with Groups, 25*(4), 57–70.

Pollio, D. E. (2006). The art of evidence-based practice. *Research on social work, 16*(2), 224–232.

Pollio, D. E., Brower, A. M., & Galinsky, M. J. (2000). Change in groups. In P. Allen Meares & C. Garvin (Eds.), *The handbook of social work direct practice* (pp. 281–300). Thousand Oaks, CA: Sage.

Pomeroy, E. C., Rubin, A., & Walker, R. J. (1995). Effectiveness of a psychoeducational and task-centered group intervention for family members of people with AIDS. *Social Work Research, 19*(3), 142–151.

Quinn, W. H., Van Dyke, D. J., & Kurth, S. T. (2002). A brief multiple family group model for juvenile first offenders. In C. R. Figley (Ed.), *Brief treatments for the traumatized: A project of the Green Cross Foundation* (pp. 226–251). Westport, CT: Greenwood Press.

Rice, A. H. (2001). Evaluating brief structured group treatment of depression. *Research on Social Work Practice, 11*(1), 53–78.

Rosen, A., & Proctor, E. (2003). *Developing practice guidelines for social work intervention.* New York, NY: Columbia Press.

Rothman, J., & Thomas, E. J. (1994). *Intervention research: Design and development for human service.* New York, NY: Haworth Press.

Rounds, K., Galinsky, M. J., & Despard, J. R. (1995). Evaluation of telephone support groups for persons with HIV disease. *Research on Social Work Practice, 5*(4), 442–459.

Sackett, D. L., Richardson, W. M. C., Gray, J. A. M., Haynes, R. B., & Richardson, W. S. (1996). Evidence-based medicine: What it is and what it isn't. *British Medical Journal, 312*, 71–72.

Satterfield, J., Spring, B., Brownson, R., Mullen, E., Newhouse, R., Walter, B., & Whitlock, E. (2009). Toward a transdisciplinary model of evidence-based practice. *Milbank Quarterly, 87*(2), 368–390. doi:10.1111/j.1468-0009.2009.00561

Seekins, T., Mathews, R. M., & Fawcett, S. B. (1984). Enhancing leadership skills for community self-help organizations through behavioral instruction. *Journal of Community Psychology, 12*, 155–163.

Soydan, H. (2010). Intervention research in social work. *Research on Social Work Practice, 20*(5), 457–458. doi:10.1177/1049731510361480

Subramanian, K. (1991). Structured group work for the management of chronic pain: An experimental investigation. *Research on Social Work Practice, 1*(1), 32–45.

Thomas, E. J. (1985). The validity of design and development and related concepts in developmental research. *Social Work Research and Abstracts, 21*(2), 50–55.

Toseland, R. W., & Rivas, R. F. (2012). *An introduction to group work practice* (7th ed.). Boston, MA: Allyn and Bacon.

Vinter, R. (1985). Essential components of social group work practice. In M. Sundel, P. Glasser, R. Sarri, & R. Vinter (Eds.), *Individual change through small groups* (2nd ed., pp. 11–34). New York, NY: The Free Press.

Wike, T., Bledsoe, S., Bellamy, J., & Grady, M. (2013). Examining inclusion of evidence-based practice on social work training program websites. *Journal of Social Work Education, 49*, 439–450. doi:10:1080/10437797.2013.796791

Yalom, I. D., & Leszcz, M. (2005). *The theory and practice of group psychotherapy* (5th ed.). New York, NY: Basic Books.

Yegidis, B., Weinbach, R., & Meyers, L. (2011). *Research methods for social workers* (7th ed.). Boston, MA: Pearson Education.

Index

trauma (*Cont.*)
  exposure, 401–2
  of homeless parents, 460, 463–64
  of immigrants and refugees, 204
  smartphones as instruments of, 248–49
  symptoms of, 322
  trauma-informed perspective,
    321–22, 353–54
  trauma-sensitive orientation, 275
  triggers, 223, 234
Trauma Symptom Checklist for
  Children, 364
Traumatic Events Screening Inventory for
  Children (TESI-C), 402
treatment
  for cancer, 50, 51, 56, 58–59
  court-mandated, 492
  for CSA, 350, 353, 354–55, 365
  culture and, 185
  effectiveness of, 492
  for gay men, 411
  goals, 491–92
  for hate crimes victims, 296
  for HIV/AIDS, 83, 91
  for immigrant family
    caregivers, 184–85
  for mental illness, 75
  for older adults, 164, 165
  outcomes, 487, 492, 494–96
  risks of alternative, 492–93
  for sex trafficking survivors, 315
  for sexual abuse, adult survivors of
    childhood, 271, 274–75
  strategies, 509
  for substance use disorders, 129
  for veterans, 224, 225, 236–37
trust, 105–6, 276, 277, 318–19, 329, 330
"two client paradigm," 9–11

UCR. *See* Uniform Crime Reporting
uncertainty, 91, 106
Uniform Crime Reporting (UCR), 293,
  294, 295*f,* 296
urban African American parents, 375
  activities, 381
  common themes of, 378–81

  disciplining difficult children,
    378–79, 381–82
  evaluation of, 385–86
  family and, 382
  grandparents, 379–80, 383
  income of, 381
  isolation of, 376
  leaders of, 377–78
  money management for, 385
  mutual aid and, 376
  noncustodial parents, 379–80, 383
  practice principles for, 377–78
  recommended ways of working
    with, 381–82
  resources for, 386–87
  safety of children in neighborhood,
    380, 384
  self-esteem of, 380–81, 384
  stress and, 381, 384–85
  success with, 386
use practice guidelines, 507

VA. *See* Department of Veterans Affairs
vaccines, 85
validation, 5, 277
VA National Suicide Hotline, 238
verbal communication, 30
veterans
  adrenaline of, 224
  anger of, 233, 235
  anxiety of, 223, 234
  arousal and alertness of, 233–34
  battle mind, 222–23
  children of, 225
  civilians and, 233
  common themes of, 231–35
  confidentiality for, 230
  coping skills of, 228, 235
  deployments of, 228, 231–32
  depression of, 226, 236
  economic issues of, 232
  embarrassment of, 235
  emotions of, 227
  environment of, 235
  evaluation of, 236
  family of, 224–25, 227, 231–32